IT Essentials: PC Hardware and Software Lab Manual

Fifth Edition

Cisco Networking Academy

CISCO

Cisco Press
800 East 96th Street
Indianapolis, Indiana 46240

IT Essentials: PC Hardware and Software Lab Manual, Fifth Edition
Cisco Networking Academy

Copyright© 2013 Cisco Systems, Inc.

Published by:
Cisco Press
800 East 96th Street
Indianapolis, IN 46240 USA

Printed in the United States of America

Third Printing July 2014

ISBN-13: 978-1-58713-310-7

ISBN-10: 1-58713-310-5

Warning and Disclaimer

This book is designed to provide information about PC Hardware and Software. Every effort has been made to make this book as complete and as accurate as possible, but no warranty or fitness is implied.

The information is provided on an "as is" basis. The authors, Cisco Press, and Cisco Systems, Inc. shall have neither liability nor responsibility to any person or entity with respect to any loss or damages arising from the information contained in this book or from the use of the discs or programs that may accompany it.

The opinions expressed in this book belong to the author and are not necessarily those of Cisco Systems, Inc.

Trademark Acknowledgments

All terms mentioned in this book that are known to be trademarks or service marks have been appropriately capitalized. Cisco Press or Cisco Systems, Inc., cannot attest to the accuracy of this information. Use of a term in this book should not be regarded as affecting the validity of any trademark or service mark.

This book is part of the Cisco Networking Academy® series from Cisco Press. The products in this series support and complement the Cisco Networking Academy curriculum. If you are using this book outside the Networking Academy, then you are not preparing with a Cisco trained and authorized Networking Academy provider.

For more information on the Cisco Networking Academy or to locate a Networking Academy, please visit www.cisco.com/edu.

CISCO.

Feedback Information

At Cisco Press, our goal is to create in-depth technical books of the highest quality and value. Each book is crafted with care and precision, undergoing rigorous development that involves the unique expertise of members from the professional technical community.

Readers' feedback is a natural continuation of this process. If you have any comments regarding how we could improve the quality of this book, or otherwise alter it to better suit your needs, you can contact us through email at feedback@ciscopress.com. Please make sure to include the book title and ISBN in your message.

We greatly appreciate your assistance.

Publisher	**Paul Boger**
Associate Publisher	**Dave Dusthimer**
Business Operations Manager, Cisco Press	**Jan Cornelssen**
Executive Editor	**Mary Beth Ray**
Managing Editor	**Sandra Schroeder**
Project Editor	**Mandie Frank**
Proofreader	**Sarah Kearns**
Editorial Assistant	**Vanessa Evans**
Cover Designer	**Mark Shirar**
Compositor	**TnT Design, Inc.**

ı|ı.ı|ı.
CISCO™

Americas Headquarters
Cisco Systems, Inc.
San Jose, CA

Asia Pacific Headquarters
Cisco Systems (USA) Pte. Ltd.
Singapore

Europe Headquarters
Cisco Systems International BV
Amsterdam, The Netherlands

Cisco has more than 200 offices worldwide. Addresses, phone numbers, and fax numbers are listed on the Cisco Website at **www.cisco.com/go/offices**.

CCDE, CCENT, Cisco Eos, Cisco HealthPresence, the Cisco logo, Cisco Lumin, Cisco Nexus, Cisco StadiumVision, Cisco TelePresence, Cisco WebEx, DCE, and Welcome to the Human Network are trademarks; Changing the Way We Work, Live, Play, and Learn and Cisco Store are service marks; and Access Registrar, Aironet, AsyncOS, Bringing the Meeting To You, Catalyst, CCDA, CCDP, CCIE, CCIP, CCNA, CCNP, CCSP, CCVP, Cisco, the Cisco Certified Internetwork Expert logo, Cisco IOS, Cisco Press, Cisco Systems, Cisco Systems Capital, the Cisco Systems logo, Cisco Unity, Collaboration Without Limitation, EtherFast, EtherSwitch, Event Center, Fast Step, Follow Me Browsing, FormShare, GigaDrive, HomeLink, Internet Quotient, IOS, iPhone, iQuick Study, IronPort, the IronPort logo, LightStream, Linksys, MediaTone, MeetingPlace, MeetingPlace Chime Sound, MGX, Networkers, Networking Academy, Network Registrar, PCNow, PIX, PowerPanels, ProConnect, ScriptShare, SenderBase, SMARTnet, Spectrum Expert, StackWise, The Fastest Way to Increase Your Internet Quotient, TransPath, WebEx, and the WebEx logo are registered trademarks of Cisco Systems, Inc. and/or its affiliates in the United States and certain other countries.

All other trademarks mentioned in this document or website are the property of their respective owners. The use of the word partner does not imply a partnership relationship between Cisco and any other company. (0812R)

Contents

About This Lab Manual

IT Essentials: PC Hardware and Software Lab Manual is a supplemental book that helps the students in the Cisco®
Networking Academy course prepare to take the CompTIA® A+ 220-801 and 220-802 exams.

All the hands-on labs and worksheets from the course are printed within this book—including Windows 7, Windows Vista,
and Windows XP variations covered in the CompTIA exam objectives. Practicing and performing these tasks will rein-
force the concepts and help you become a successful PC technician.

Command Syntax Conventions

The conventions used to present command syntax in this book are the same conventions used in the IOS Command
Reference. The Command Reference describes these conventions as follows:

- **Boldface** indicates commands and keywords that are entered literally as shown. In actual configuration
  examples and output (not general command syntax), boldface indicates commands that are manually input
  by the user (such as a **show** command).

- *Italic* indicates arguments for which you supply actual values.

- Vertical bars (|) separate alternative, mutually exclusive elements.

- Square brackets ([ ]) indicate an optional element.

- Braces ({ }) indicate a required choice.

- Braces within brackets ([{ }]) indicate a required choice within an optional element.

Chapter 0: IT Essentials Introduction

0.2.2.2 Worksheet - Job Opportunities

In this worksheet, you will use the Internet, magazines, or a local newspaper to gather information for jobs in the computer service and repair field. Be prepared to discuss your research in class.

1. Research three computer-related jobs. For each job, write the company name and the job title in the column on the left. Write the job details that are most important to you, as well as the job qualifications in the column on the right. An example has been provided for you.

Company Name and Job Title	Details and Qualifications
Gentronics Flexible Solutions/ Field Service Representative	Company offers continuing education. Work with hardware and software. Work directly with customers. Local travel. • A+ certification preferred • 1-year installation or repair experience of computer hardware and software required • Requires a valid driver's license • Must have reliable personal transportation • Mileage reimbursement • Ability to lift and carry up to 50 lbs

2. Based on your research, which job would you prefer and why? Be prepared to discuss your answer in class.

Chapter 1: Introduction to the Personal Computer

1.1.1.4 Worksheet - Ohm's Law

In this worksheet, you will answer questions based on electricity and Ohm's Law. Show all steps when solving problems.

Note: The amounts used in these problems may not be realistic.

1. What are the four basic units of electricity? Provide the variable name and symbol, and unit name and symbol.

2. Write the equation for Ohm's Law.

3. Re-arrange the Ohm's Law equation to solve the following:

    I =   R =

4. Power is equal to voltage times current. Add the missing information in each of the following power equations.

    P = V   P = R   P = V²

5. The yellow wire connected to a power supply carries 12V. If the power supply provides 60W of power to the yellow wire, how much current is passing through the yellow wire?

6. There are 3.3V passing through an orange power supply cable, and there are 0.025 ohms of resistance in the orange wire. How much power is supplied to the orange wire by the power supply?

7. A wire from the power supply is carrying 120W of power and 24A of current. Which color(s) of cable is the wire?

1.2.1.11 Worksheet - Research Computer Components

In this worksheet, you will use the Internet, a newspaper, or a local store to gather information about the components you will need to complete your customer's computer. Information is provided for the components that your customer already has. Use these specifications to make sure that the components you research are compatible with the components your customer already owns. Be prepared to discuss your selections.

1. List three components that must have the same compatible form factor.

2. List three components that must conform to the same socket type.

3. List two components that must utilize the same front side bus speed.

4. List three considerations when you choose memory.

5. What component must be compatible with every other component of the computer?

6. Your customer already owns the **case** described in the table below.

Brand and Model Number	Features	Cost
Cooler Master HAF-932	EATX Mid Tower ATX, Micro-ATX compatible form factor 7 external 5.25" drive bays 2 external 3.5" drive bays 5 internal 3.5" drive bays 7 expansion slots USB3.0, firewire, eSata	

7. Your customer already owns the **motherboard** described in the table below.

Brand and Model Number	Features	Cost
GIGABYTE Z77X-UD3H	LGA 1155 DDR3 2666/1600/1333/1066 3 x PCI express x 16 3 x PCI express x 1 1 x PCI 2 x SATA 6.0 Gb/s interfaces 4 x SATA 3.0 Gb/s interfaces 1.5V RAM voltage 1066/800/533 MHz front side bus 4 memory slots Dual channel memory supported ATA100 connector RAID 0/1/5/10 6 USB 3.0/2.0 ports ATX form factor	

8. Your customer already owns the **hard disk drive** described in the table below.

Brand and Model Number	Features	Cost
Seagate ST2000DM001	2 TB 7200 RPM 64 MB cache SATA 3.0Gb/s interface	

9. Search the Internet, a newspaper, or a local store to research a **power supply** compatible with the components that your customer owns. Enter the specifications in the table below.

Brand and Model Number	Features	Cost

10. Search the Internet, a newspaper, or a local store to research a **CPU** compatible with the components that your customer owns. Enter the specifications in the table below.

Brand and Model Number	Features	Cost

11. Search the Internet, a newspaper, or a local store to research a **cooling device** compatible with the components that your customer owns. Enter the specifications in the table below.

Brand and Model Number	Features	Cost

12. Search the Internet, a newspaper, or a local store to research **RAM** compatible with the components that your customer owns. Enter the specifications in the table below.

Brand and Model Number	Features	Cost

13. Search the Internet, a newspaper, or a local store to research a **video adapter card** compatible with the components that your customer owns. Enter the specifications in the table below.

Brand and Model Number	Features	Cost

1.3.1.6 Worksheet - Build a Specialized Computer System

In this worksheet, you will use the Internet, a newspaper, or a local store to gather information about building a specialized computer system that supports hardware and software that allows a user to perform tasks that an off-the-shelf system cannot perform. Be prepared to discuss your selections.

For this worksheet, assume the customer's system will be compatible with the parts you order.

1. The customer runs an audio and video editing workstation to record music, create music CDs, CD labels, and to create home movies. The customer wishes to upgrade the components listed in the table.

Brand and Model Number	Features	Cost
Audio card		
Video card		
Hard drive		
Dual monitors		

Provide reasons for the components purchased. How will they support the customer's needs?

2. The customer runs computer-aided design (CAD) or computer-aided manufacturing (CAM) software and wishes to upgrade the components listed in the table.

Brand and Model Number	Features	Cost
CPU		
Video card		
RAM		

Provide reasons for the components purchased. How will they support the customer's needs?

3. The customer uses virtualization technologies to run several different operating systems to test software compatibility. The customer wishes to upgrade the components listed in the table.

Brand and Model Number	Features	Cost
RAM		
CPU		

Provide reasons for the components purchased. How will they support the customer's needs?

4. The customer wishes to upgrade a home theater personal computer with the components listed in the table.

Brand and Model Number	Features	Cost
Case		
Power supply		
Surround sound audio		
TV tuner and cable cards		

Provide reasons for the components purchased. How will they support the customer's needs?

5. The customer wishes to upgrade a gaming computer with the components listed in the table.

Brand and Model Number	Features	Cost
CPU		
Video card		
Sound card		
Cooling system		
RAM		
Hard drive		

Provide reasons for the components purchased. How will they support the customer's needs?

Chapter 2: Lab Procedures and Tool Use

2.2.2.3 Worksheet - Diagnostic Software

In this worksheet, you will use the Internet, a newspaper, or a local store to gather information about a hard drive diagnostic program. Be prepared to discuss the diagnostic software you researched.

1. Based on your research, list at least two different hard drive manufacturers.

2. Based on your research, choose a hard drive manufacturer. Does this manufacturer offer hard drive diagnostic software to go with their products? If so, list the name and the features of the diagnostic software.

     Manufacturer:

     Software Name:

     File Name:

     File Size:

     Version:

     Publish Date:

     Description:

3. Why do manufacturers offer hard drive diagnostic software? What are the potential benefits of doing so to the manufacturer and/or customer?

2.2.4.4 Lab - Using a Multimeter and a Power Supply Tester

Introduction

In this lab, you will learn how to use and handle a multimeter and a power supply tester.

Recommended Equipment

- A digital multimeter - a Fluke 110 series or similar
- The multimeter manual
- A battery
- A power supply tester
- A manual for the tester
- A power supply

Note: The multimeter is a sensitive piece of electronic test equipment. Do not drop it or handle it carelessly. Be careful not to accidentally nick or cut the red or black wire leads, called probes. Because it is possible to check high voltages, extra care should be taken to avoid electrical shock.

Part 1: Multimeter

Step 1: Set up the multimeter

a. Insert the red and black leads into the proper jacks on the meter. The black probe should go in the COM jack and the red probe should go in the + (plus) jack.

b. Turn on the multimeter (consult the manual if there is no ON/OFF switch).

What is the model of the multimeter?

What action must be taken to turn the meter on?

Step 2: Explore the different multimeter measurements

a. Switch or turn to different measurements. For example, the multimeter can be adjusted to measure Ohms.

How many different switch positions does the multimeter have?

What are they?

b. Switch or turn the multimeter to the voltage measurement.

What is the symbol shown for this?

Step 3: Measure the voltage of a battery

Place the battery on the table. Touch the tip of the red (positive) probe on the positive side of a battery. Touch the tip of the black (negative) probe on the other end of the battery.

What is shown on the display?

If the multimeter does not display a number close to the battery voltage, check the multimeter setting to ensure it is set to measure voltage, or replace the battery with a known good battery. If the number is a negative number, reverse the probes.

Name one thing that you should not do when using a multimeter.

Name one important function of a multimeter.

Disconnect the multimeter from the battery. Switch the multimeter to OFF. Part 1 of the lab is complete. Have your instructor verify your work.

Why is a digital multimeter an important piece of equipment for a technician? Explain your answer.

Part 2: Power Supply Tester

Complete only the steps for the connectors supported by the power supply tester that you are using.

Step 1: Check the testing ports for the power supply tester

Many power supply testers have connector ports to test the following power supply connectors:

- 20-pin/24-pin motherboard connector
- 4-pin Molex connector
- 6-pin PCI-E connector
- P4 +12V connector
- P8 +12V EPS connector
- 4-pin Berg connector
- 5-pin SATA connector

Which connectors does the power supply tester you are using have?

Complete the following steps for the connectors supported by the power supply tester that you are using.

Step 2: Test the power supply motherboard connector

a. Set the power supply switch (if available) to the OFF (or 0) position.

b. Plug the 20-pin or 24-pin motherboard connector into the tester.

c. Plug the power supply into an AC outlet.

d. Set the power supply switch (if available) to the ON (or 1) position.

If the power supply is working, LEDs will illuminate and you might hear a beep. If the LED lights do not illuminate, it is possible the power supply might be damaged or the motherboard connector has failed. In this instance, you must check all connections, ensure the power supply switch (if available) is set to ON (or 1), and try again. If the LEDs still do not illuminate, consult your instructor.

Possible LED lights include +5 V, -5 V, +12 V, +5 VSB, PG, -12 V, or +3.3 V.

Which LED lights are illuminated?

Step 3: Test the power supply Molex connector

Plug the 4-pin Molex connector into the tester. The LED illuminates on +12 V and +5 V. (If the power output fails, the LEDs will not illuminate.)

Which LED lights are illuminated?

Step 4: Test the 6-pin PCI-E connector

Plug the 6-pin PCI-E connector into the tester. The LED will illuminate on +12 V. (If the power output fails, the LED will not illuminate.)

Does the LED light illuminate?

Step 5: Test the 5-pin SATA connector

Plug the 5-pin SATA connector into the tester. The LED will illuminate on +12 V, +5 V, and +3.3 V. (If the power output fails, the LEDs will not illuminate.)

Which LED lights are illuminated?

Step 6: Test the 4-pin Berg connector

Plug the 4-pin Berg connector into the tester. The LED will illuminate on +12 V and +5 V. (If the power output fails, the LEDs will not illuminate.)

Which LED lights are illuminated?

Step 7: Test the P4/P8 connectors

a. Plug the P4 +12 V connector into the tester. The LED will illuminate on +12 V. (If the power output fails, the LEDs will not illuminate.)

b. Plug the P8 +12 V connector into the tester. The LED will illuminate on +12 V. (If the power output fails, the LEDs will not illuminate.)

c. Which LED lights are illuminated?

Switch the power supply to OFF (or 0) if available. Disconnect the power supply from the AC outlet. Disconnect the power supply from the power supply tester. The lab is complete. Have your instructor verify your work.

Why is a power supply tester an important piece of equipment for a technician? Explain your answer.

2.2.4.5 Lab - Testing UTP Cables Using a Loopback Plug and a Cable Meter

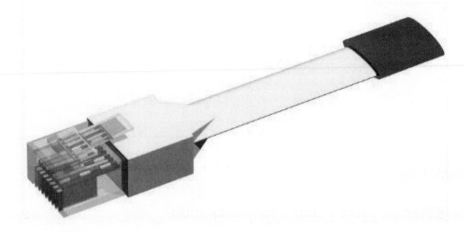

Loopback Plug

Coupler

Introduction

In this lab, you will use a loopback plug and a cable meter to test an Ethernet cable.

Recommended Equipment

- A LAN hub or switch
- Loopback plug and coupler
- A known good Ethernet cable
- A Fluke series 620 LAN CableMeter
- A manual for the cable meter
- Good Category 5 straight-through cables of different colors
- Good Category 5 crossover cables (T568A on one end and T568B on the other end)
- Category 5 straight-through cables of different colors and different lengths with open connections in the middle, or one or more conductors shorted at one end
- Category 5 straight-through cable with a split pair or a mis-wire

    Wire maps can be very helpful in troubleshooting cabling problems with UTP cable. A wire map shows which wire pairs connect to what pin on the plug or socket.

Part 1: Loopback Plug

Step 1: Test an Ethernet cable using a loopback plug

    a. Plug the loopback plug into one end of the coupler.

    b. Plug one end of the Ethernet cable into the other end of the coupler.

    c. Power on the hub or switch.

    d. Plug the other end of the Ethernet cable into a port on the hub or switch.

After plugging the cable into the port, does a link light appear on the port?

If a link light does not appear, the problem is with the hub or switch. If the port displays a link light, then the cable has passed the continuity test.

Part 1 of the lab is complete. Ask your instructor to verify your work.

Part 2: Cable meter

Testing UTP Cables

Step 1: Set up the cable meter

On the cable meter, select the WIRE MAP function.

Ensure that the following settings (if available) are set properly.

Tester Option	Desired Setting - UTP
CABLE:	UTP
WIRING:	10BASE-T OR EIA/TIA 4PR
CATEGORY:	CATEGORY 5
WIRE SIZE:	AWG 24
CALIBRATE TO CABLE?	NO
BEEPING:	ON or OFF

Once the meter is set up, exit the setup mode.

Step 2: Test cabling procedure

When testing with a Fluke LAN CableMeter, use the following procedure:

a. Place one end of the cable into the RJ-45 jack labeled UTP/FTP on the tester.

b. Place the other end of the cable into the RJ-45 female coupler (labeled LAN Use).

c.   Insert the cable identifier (labeled Net Tool) into the other side of the coupler. The coupler and the cable identifier are accessories that come with many cable meters.

Coupler and Cable Identifier

Step 3: Use the Wire Map function

The wire map function and a cable identifier can be used to determine the wiring of both the near and far end of the cable. One set of numbers displayed on the LCD screen is the near end, and the other set is the far end.

a.   Perform a wire map test on each of the cables provided.

Fill in the following table based on the testing results for each Category 5 cable. For each cable, write down the identifying number of the cable and the cable color. Also write down whether the cable is straight-through or crossover, the tester screen test results, and a description of the problem.

Cable No.	Cable Color	Straight-Through or Crossover	Displayed Test Results (Note: Refer to the meter manual for detailed description of test results for the wire map test.)	Problem/Description
			Top: Bot:	
			Top: Bot:	
			Top: Bot:	
			Top: Bot:	
			Top: Bot:	

Step 4: Use the Length function

Using the tester LENGTH function, perform a basic cable test on the same cables used previously. Fill in the additional information for each cable.

Cable No.	Cable Length	Tester Test Results (Pass/Fail)

2.2.4.7 Lab - Computer Disassembly

In this lab, you will disassemble a computer using safe lab procedures and the proper tools. Use extreme care and follow all safety procedures. Familiarize yourself with the tools you will be using in this lab.

NOTE: If you cannot locate or remove the correct component, ask your instructor for help.

Recommended Tools

Safety glasses or goggles	Part retriever (or tweezers or needle-nose pliers)
Antistatic wrist strap	Thermal compound
Antistatic mat	Electronics cleaning solution
Flat head screwdrivers	Can of compressed air
Phillips head screwdrivers	Cable ties
Torx screwdrivers	Parts organizer
Hex driver	Computer with hard drive installed
Wire cutters	Plastic tub for storing computer parts
Plastic	Antistatic bags for electronic parts

Step 1

Turn off and disconnect the power to your computer.

Step 2

Locate all of the screws that secure the side panels to the back of the computer. Use the proper size and type of screwdriver to remove the side panel screws. Do not remove the screws that secure the power supply to the case. Put all of these screws in one place, such as a cup or a compartment in a parts organizer. Label the cup or compartment with a piece of masking tape on which you have written "side panel screws." Remove the side panels from the case.

NOTE: Some manufacturers do not use screws to fasten components inside of the computer case. Some may use plastic or metal clips that fasten components to the computer chassis. Be careful to remove only screws that are holding components in place, and not the screws that hold components together.

What type of screwdriver did you use to remove the screws?

How many screws secured the side panels?

Step 3

Put on an antistatic wrist strap. One end of the conductor should be connected to the wrist strap. Clip the other end of the conductor to an unpainted, metal part of the case.

If you have an antistatic mat, place it on the work surface and put the computer case on top of it. Ground the antistatic mat to an unpainted, metal part of the case.

Step 4

Locate the hard drive. Carefully disconnect the power and data cable from the back of the hard drive.

Which type of data cable did you disconnect?

Step 5

Locate all of the screws that hold the hard drive in place. Use the proper size and type of screwdriver to remove the hard drive screws. Put all of these screws in one place and label them.

What type of screws secured the hard drive to the case?

How many screws secured the hard drive to the case?

Is the hard drive connected to a mounting bracket? If so, what type of screws secure the hard drive to the mounting bracket?

CAUTION: Do NOT remove the screws for the hard drive enclosure.

Step 6

Gently remove the hard drive from the case. Look for a jumper reference chart on the hard drive. If there is a jumper installed on the hard drive, use the jumper reference chart to see if the hard drive is set for a Master, Slave, or Cable Select (CS) drive. Place the hard drive in an antistatic bag.

Step 7

Locate the floppy disk drive. Carefully disconnect the power and data cable.

Step 8

Locate and remove all of the screws that secure the floppy drive to the case. Put all of these screws in one place and label them.

Place the floppy drive in an antistatic bag.

How many screws secured the floppy drive to the case?

Step 9

Locate the optical drive (CD-ROM, DVD, etc). Carefully disconnect the power and data cable from the optical drive. Remove the audio cable from the optical drive.

What kind of data cable did you disconnect?

Is there a jumper on the optical drive? What is the jumper setting?

Step 10

Locate and remove all of the screws that secure the optical drive to the case. Put all of these screws in one place and label them. Place the optical drive in an antistatic bag.

How many screws secured the optical drive to the case?

Step 11

Locate the power supply. Find the power connection(s) to the motherboard.

Gently remove the power connection(s) from the motherboard. How many pins are there in the motherboard connector?

Does the power supply provide power to a CPU fan or case fan? If so, disconnect the power cable.

Does the power supply provide auxiliary power to the video card? If so, disconnect the power cable.

Step 12

Locate and remove all of the screws that secure the power supply to the case. Put all of these screws in one place and label them.

How many screws secure the power supply to the case?

Carefully remove the power supply from the case. Place the power supply with the other computer components.

Step 13

Locate any adapter cards that are installed in the computer, such as a video, NIC, or modem adapter.

Locate and remove the screw that secures the adapter card to the case. Put the adapter card screws in one place and label them.

Carefully remove the adapter card from the slot. Be sure to hold the adapter card by the mounting bracket or by the edges. Place the adapter card in an antistatic bag. Repeat this process for all of the adapter cards.

List the adapter cards and the slot types below.

Adapter Card   Slot Type

_____   _____

_____   _____

_____   _____

Step 14

Locate the memory modules on the motherboard.

What type of memory modules are installed on the motherboard?

How many memory modules are installed on the motherboard?

Remove the memory modules from the motherboard. Be sure to release any locking tabs that may be securing the memory module. Hold the memory module by the edges and gently lift out of the slot. Put the memory modules in an antistatic bag.

Step 15

Remove all data cables from the motherboard. Make sure to note the connection location of any cable you disconnect.

What types of cables were disconnected?

You have completed this lab. The computer case should contain the motherboard, the CPU, and any cooling devices. Do not remove any additional components from case.

Chapter 3: Computer Assembly

3.1.1.3 Lab - Install the Power Supply

Introduction

In this lab, you will install a power supply in a computer case.

Recommended Equipment

- Power supply with a compatible form factor to the computer case
- Computer case
- Tool kit
- Power supply screws

Step 1

Remove the screws from the side panels.

Remove the side panels from the computer case.

Step 2

Align the screw holes in the power supply with the screw holes in the case.

Secure the power supply to the case with the power supply screws.

Step 3

If the power supply has a voltage selection switch, set this switch to match the voltage in your area.

What is the voltage in your area?

How many screws secure the power supply in the case?

What is the total wattage of the power supply?

This lab is complete. Please have the instructor verify your work.

3.1.2.4 Lab - Install the Motherboard

Introduction

In this lab, you will install a CPU, a heat sink/fan assembly, and a RAM module on the motherboard. You will then install the motherboard in the computer case.

Recommended Equipment

- Computer case with power supply installed
- Motherboard
- CPU
- Heat sink/fan assembly
- Thermal compound
- RAM module(s)
- Motherboard standoffs and screws
- Antistatic wrist strap and antistatic mat
- Tool kit
- Motherboard manual

Step 1

Place the motherboard, the CPU, the heat sink/fan assembly, and the RAM module on the antistatic mat.

Step 2

Put on your antistatic wrist strap and attach the grounding cable to the antistatic mat.

Locate Pin 1 on the CPU. Locate Pin 1 on the socket.

NOTE: The CPU may be damaged if it is installed incorrectly.

Align Pin 1 on the CPU with Pin 1 on the socket.

Place the CPU into the CPU socket.

Close the CPU load plate and secure it in place by closing the load lever and moving it under the load lever retention tab.

Step 3

Apply a small amount of thermal compound to the CPU and spread it evenly.

NOTE: Thermal compound is only necessary when not included on the heat sink. Follow all instructions provided by the manufacturer for specific application details.

Step 4

Align the heat sink/fan assembly retainers with the holes on the motherboard around the CPU socket.

Place the heat sink/fan assembly onto the CPU and the retainers through the holes on the motherboard.

Tighten the heat sink/fan assembly retainers to secure it.

Plug the fan connector into the motherboard. Refer to the motherboard manual to determine which set of fan header pins to use.

Step 5

Locate the RAM slots on the motherboard.

In what type of slot(s) will the RAM module(s) be installed?

How many notches are found on the bottom edge of the RAM module?

Align the notch(es) on the bottom edge of the RAM module to the notches in the slot.

Press down until the side tabs secure the RAM module.

Ensure that none of the RAM module contacts are visible. Reseat the RAM module if necessary.

Check the latches to verify that the RAM module is secure.

Install any additional RAM modules using the same procedures.

Step 6

Install the motherboard standoffs.

Align the connectors on the back of the motherboard with the openings in the back of the computer case.

Place the motherboard into the case and align the holes for the screws and the stand-offs. You may need to adjust the motherboard to line up the holes for the screws.

Attach the motherboard to the case using the appropriate screws.

This lab is complete. Please have the instructor verify your work.

3.1.3.4 Lab - Install the Drives

Introduction

In this lab, you will install the hard disk drive, the optical drive, and the floppy drive.

Recommended Equipment

- Computer case with power supply and motherboard installed
- Antistatic wrist strap and antistatic mat
- Tool kit
- Hard disk drive
- Hard disk drive screws
- Floppy drive
- Floppy drive screws
- Optical drive
- Optical drive screws
- Motherboard manual

Step 1

Align the hard disk drive with the 3.5-inch drive bay.

Slide the hard disk drive into the bay from the inside of the case until the screw holes line up with the holes in the 3.5-inch drive bay.

Secure the hard disk drive to the case using the proper screws.

Step 2

Note: Remove the 5.25-inch cover from one of the 5.25-inch external drive bays if necessary.

Align the optical drive with the 5.25-inch drive bay.

Insert the optical drive into the drive bay from the front of the case until the screw holes line up with the holes in the 5.25-inch drive bay and the front of the optical drive is flush with the front of the case.

Secure the optical drive to the case using the proper screws.

Step 3

Note: Remove the 3.5-inch cover from one of the 3.5-inch external drive bays if necessary.

Align the floppy drive with the 3.5-inch drive bay.

Insert the floppy drive into the drive bay from the front of the case until the screw holes line up with the holes in the 3.5-inch drive bay and the front of the floppy drive is flush with the front of the case.

Secure the floppy drive to the case using the proper screws.

This lab is complete. Please have the instructor verify your work.

3.1.4.5 Lab - Install Adapter Cards

Introduction

In this lab, you will install a NIC, a wireless NIC, and a video adapter card.

Recommended Equipment

- Computer with power supply, motherboard, and drives installed
- NIC
- Wireless NIC
- Video adapter card
- Adapter card screws
- Antistatic wrist strap and antistatic mat
- Tool kit
- Motherboard manual

Step 1

What type of expansion slot is compatible with the NIC?

Locate a compatible expansion slot for the NIC on the motherboard.

Remove the slot cover from the back of the case, if necessary.

Align the NIC to the expansion slot.

Press down gently on the NIC until the card is fully seated.

Secure the NIC by attaching the PC mounting bracket to the case with a screw.

Step 2

What type of expansion slot is compatible with the wireless NIC?

Locate a compatible expansion slot for the wireless NIC on the motherboard.

Remove the slot cover from the back of the case, if necessary.

Align the wireless NIC to the expansion slot.

Press down gently on the wireless NIC until the card is fully seated.

Secure the wireless NIC by attaching the PC mounting bracket to the case with a screw.

Step 3

What type of expansion slot is compatible with the video adapter card?

Locate a compatible expansion slot for the video adapter card on the motherboard.

Remove the slot cover from the back of the case, if necessary.

Align the video adapter card to the expansion slot.

Press down gently on the video adapter card until the card is fully seated.

Secure the video adapter card by attaching the PC mounting bracket to the case with a screw.

This lab is complete. Please have the instructor verify your work.

3.1.5.3 Lab - Install Internal Cables

Introduction

In this lab, install the internal power and data cables in the computer.

Recommended Equipment

- Computer with power supply, motherboard, drives, and adapter cards installed
- Hard disk drive data cable
- Optical drive data cable
- Floppy drive data cable
- Antistatic wrist strap and antistatic mat
- Tool kit
- Motherboard manual

Step 1

Align the motherboard power supply connector to the socket on the motherboard.

Gently press down on the connector until the clip clicks into place.

Step 2

NOTE: This step is necessary only if your computer has an auxiliary power connector.

Align the auxiliary power connector to the auxiliary power socket on the motherboard.

Gently press down on the connector until the clip clicks into place.

Step 3

Plug a power connector into the hard disk drive, optical drive, and floppy drive. Ensure that the floppy drive power connector is inserted right side up.

Step 4

NOTE: This step is necessary only if your computer has a fan power connector.

Connect the fan power connector into the appropriate fan header on the motherboard.

Step 5

NOTE: Pin 1 on a PATA cable must align with Pin 1 on the motherboard connector and the hard disk drive connector.

Align and plug the hard disk drive data cable into the motherboard connector.

Align and plug the other end of the hard disk drive data cable into the hard disk drive connector.

Step 6

NOTE: SATA cables are keyed to ensure correct orientation with the motherboard connector and the hard disk drive connector.

Align and plug the hard disk drive data cable into the motherboard connector.

Align and plug the other end of the hard disk drive data cable into the hard disk drive connector.

Step 7

NOTE: Pin 1 on a PATA cable must align with Pin 1 on the motherboard connector and the optical drive connector.

Align and plug the optical drive data cable into the motherboard connector.

Align and plug the other end of the optical drive data cable into the optical drive connector.

Step 8

NOTE: Pin 1 on a floppy drive cable must align with Pin 1 on the motherboard connector and the floppy drive connector.

Align and plug the floppy drive data cable into the motherboard connector.

Align and plug the other end of the floppy drive data cable into the floppy drive connector.

This lab is complete. Please have the instructor verify your work.

3.1.5.5 Lab - Install Front Panel Cables

Introduction

In this lab, install the front panel cables in the computer.

Recommended Equipment

- Computer with power supply, motherboard, drives, and adapter cards installed
- Computer front panel
- Antistatic wrist strap and antistatic mat
- Tool kit
- Motherboard manual

Step 1

Each switch and LED on the front panel must be connected to the appropriate pins on the motherboard.

Pin name may be printed on one side of each pin and along the motherboard.

Step 2

Gently press down on the Reset switch connector until the clip clicks into place.

Step 3

Gently press down on the Power switch connector until the clip clicks into place.

Step 4

Gently press down on the Power LED connector until the clip clicks into place.

Step 5

Gently press down on the HDD LED connector until the clip clicks into place.

Step 6

Gently press down on the speaker connector until the clip clicks into place.

Step 7

If your case also has front USB and front audio jacks, gently press down on the connector until the clip clicks into place.

Step 8

NOTE: If any LED or switch does not work when the computer is first started, remove the pin for that item and turn it around and plug it back in.

3.1.5.8 Lab - Complete the Computer Assembly

Introduction

In this lab, you will install the side panels and the external cables on the computer.

Recommended Equipment

- Computer with power supply, motherboard, drives, and adapter cards installed, and internal cables connected
- Monitor cable (DVI or VGA)
- Keyboard
- Mouse
- USB cable for the USB hub
- USB cable for the USB printer
- Network cable
- Wireless antenna
- Power cable
- Tool kit
- Motherboard manual

Step 1

Attach the side panels to the computer case.

Secure the side panels to the computer using the panel screws.

Step 2

Attach the monitor cable to the video port.

Secure the cable by tightening the screws on the connector.

Step 3

Plug the keyboard cable into the USB or PS/2 keyboard port.

Step 4

Plug the mouse cable into the USB or PS/2 mouse port.

Step 5

Plug the hub USB cable into any USB port.

Step 6

Plug the printer USB cable into a USB port in the hub.

Step 7

Plug the Ethernet cable into the Ethernet port.

Step 8

Connect the wireless antenna to the antenna connector.

Step 9

Plug the power cable into the power socket of the power supply.

This lab is complete. Please have the instructor verify your work.

3.2.2.5 Lab - Boot the Computer

Introduction

In this lab, you will boot the computer for the first time, explore the BIOS setup program, and change the boot order sequence.

Recommended Equipment

- Assembled computer without an operating system installed
- Motherboard manual

Step 1

Plug the power supply cable into an AC wall outlet.

Turn on the computer.

NOTE: If the computer beeps more than once, or if the power does not come on, notify your instructor.

Step 2

During POST, press the BIOS setup key or key combination.

The BIOS setup program screen will appear.

What is the key or combination of keys used to enter the BIOS setup program?

Who manufactures the BIOS for your computer?

What is the BIOS version?

Step 3

List the main menu options and describe what is monitored in each menu?

Step 4

Navigate through each screen to find the security settings.

What security settings and feature are available?

Step 5

Navigate through each screen to find the CPU settings.

What is the CPU speed?

What other information is listed for the CPU?

Step 6

Navigate through each screen to find the RAM settings.

What is the RAM speed?

What other information is listed for the RAM?

Step 7

Navigate through each screen to find the hard drive settings.

What information is listed for the hard drive?

Step 8

Navigate through each screen to find the boot order sequence.

What is the first boot device in the boot order sequence?

How many additional devices can be assigned in the boot order sequence?

Step 9

Ensure that the first boot order device is the optical drive.

Ensure that the second boot order device is the hard disk drive.

Why would you change the first boot device to the optical drive?

What happens when the computer boots and the optical drive does not contain bootable media?

Step 10

Navigate through each screen to find the power management setup screen, or ACPI screen.

What power management settings are available?

Step 11

Navigate through each screen to find the PnP settings.

What PnP settings are available?

Step 12

Navigate through each screen to find the splash screen settings.

What splash screen settings are available?

Step 13

Save the new BIOS settings and exit the BIOS setup program.

Step 14

The computer will restart.

An operating system can be installed at this time.

This lab is complete. Please have the instructor verify your work.

3.3.1.6 Lab - BIOS File Search

Introduction

In this lab, you will identify the current BIOS version, and then search for BIOS update files.

Recommended Equipment

- Computer running Windows XP Professional
- Internet access

Step 1

Boot your computer.

During POST, BIOS information is displayed on the screen for a short period of time.

```
AMIBIOS(C)2001 American Megatrends, Inc.
BIOS Date: 08/14/03 19:41:02  Ver: 08.00.02

Press DEL to run Setup
Checking NVRAM..

1024MB OK
Auto-Detecting Pri Master..IDE Hard Disk
Auto-Detecting Pri Slave...Not Detected
Auto-Detecting Sec Master..CDROM
Auto-Detecting Sec Slave...Not Detected
```

Do not log on to Windows.

What key or combination of keys is used to run Setup on your computer?

Restart your computer and enter Setup.

Step 2

The "BIOS Setup Utility" screen appears.

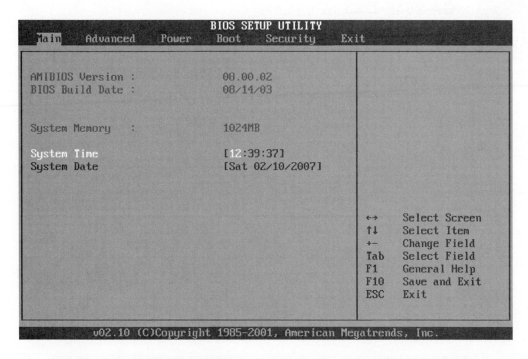

Who is the manufacturer of the BIOS?

Which BIOS version is installed in your computer?

○ Enlarge View

GA-965P-DS3 (rev. 1.3)
Intel P965+ ICH8 chipset

1. Supports Intel® Core™2 Extreme Quad-Core / Core™2 Duo processor
2. Supports Dual channel DDR2 800 memory
3. Features PCI-E graphics interface
4. Features SATA 3Gb/s interface with RAID function (2 ports with RAID function supported by GIGABYTE SATA2)
5. Intel High Definition 8 Channels Audio
6. Optimized Gigabit LAN connection
7. Industry's leading all solid capacitor motherboard design

○ Related link

- Overview
- Specification
- Accessories
- BIOS
- Driver
- Manual
- FAQ
- Utility
- CPU Support List
- Memory Support List
- Comparison Sheet
- Awards
- Where To Buy

○ BIOS

Download	Version	Date	Description
Download from ...	F10	2007/01/12	1. Enhance FSB frequency flexibility
Download from ...	F9	2006/12/27	1. Update CPU ID 2. FSB 1333 MHz support for rev 3.3 only
Download from ...	F8	2006/12/19	1. Update CPU ID

CAUTION: Do not update your BIOS.

What is the current BIOS version available for the motherboard?

What features, if any, have been added to the new BIOS version?

What changes, if any, have been made to the new BIOS version to fix problems?

What are the instructions to update the new BIOS version?

3.3.3.2 Worksheet - Upgrade Hardware

In this worksheet, you will use the Internet, a newspaper, or a local store to gather information about hardware components. Your customer's computer currently has 1 module of 2 GB of RAM, a 500 GB hard disk drive, and a PCIe video adapter card with 256 MB of RAM. Your customer wants to be able to play advanced video games.

1. Shop around, and in the table below, list the brand, model number, features, and cost for two different 4 GB modules of DDR3-1600 (PC3-12800).

Brand and Model Number	Features	Cost

2. Based on your research, which RAM would you select? Be prepared to discuss your decisions regarding the RAM you select.

3. Shop around, and in the table below, list the brand, model number, features, and cost for two different 2 TB 7200 rpm SATA 3 hard disk drives.

Brand and Model Number	Features	Cost

4. Based on your research, which hard disk drive would you select? Be prepared to discuss your decisions regarding the hard disk drive you select.

5. Shop around, and in the table below, list the brand, model number, features, and cost for two different PCIe video adapter cards with 1 GB RAM.

Brand and Model Number	Features	Cost

6. Based on your research, which video adapter card would you select? Be prepared to discuss your decisions regarding the video adapter card you select.

Chapter 4: Overview of Preventive Maintenance

There are no labs in this chapter.

Chapter 5: Operating Systems

5.1.2.3 Worksheet - Search NOC Certifications and Jobs

In this worksheet, you will use the Internet, a newspaper, or magazines to gather information about network operating system certifications and jobs that require these certifications.

1. Use the Internet to research three different network operating system certifications. Based on your research, complete the table below.

	Network Operating System(s) Covered	Certification(s) Title	Courses/Training Required for Certification

2. Use the Internet, a newspaper, or a magazine to find at least two network jobs available in your area. Describe the network jobs and the required certifications needed for the position.

3. Which job would you prefer? List reasons for your selection.

5.1.4.4 Lab - Data Migration in Windows 7

Introduction

In this lab, you will use Windows 7.

Recommended Equipment

The following equipment is required for this exercise:

- A computer with Windows 7 Professional
- A USB flash drive

Step 1

Logon to the computer and create a folder on the desktop called "For Transferring".

Next, use Notepad to create a file, add the following text: "From older PC", and save the file in the folder called "For Transferring". Name the file "Data".

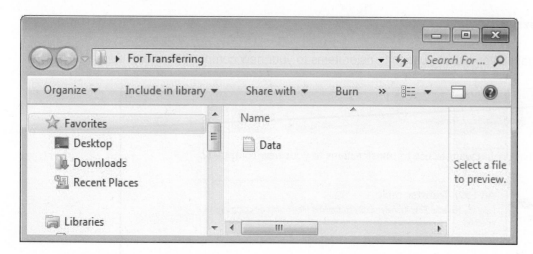

Create a folder called "Transfer data files" in the USB flash drive.

Step 2

Click **Start > All Programs > Accessories > System Tools > Windows Easy Transfer**.

The "Windows Easy Transfer" window opens.

Click **Next**.

The "What do you want to use to transfer items to your new computer?" screen appears.

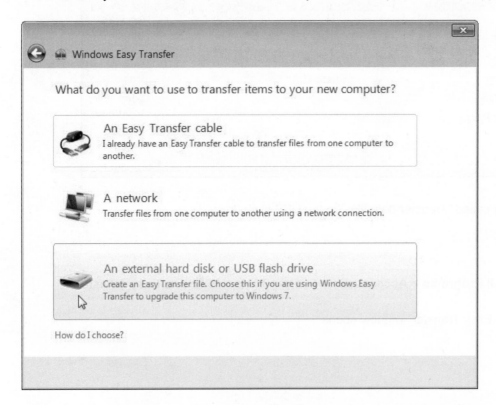

Select **An external hard drive or USB flash drive**.

The "Which computer are you using now?" screen appears.

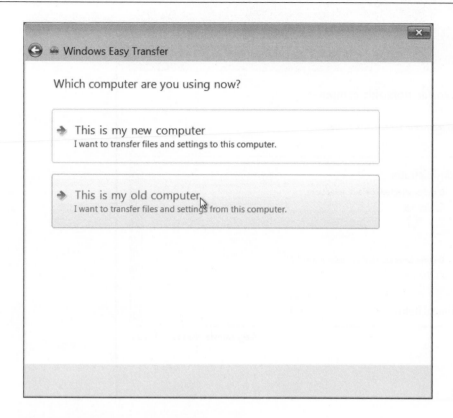

Select **This is my old computer**.

The "Checking what can be transferred…" screen appears.

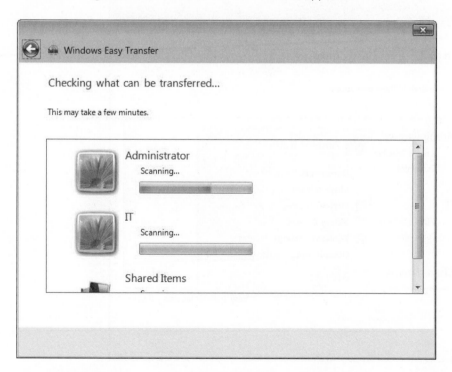

The "Choose what to transfer from this computer" screen appears.

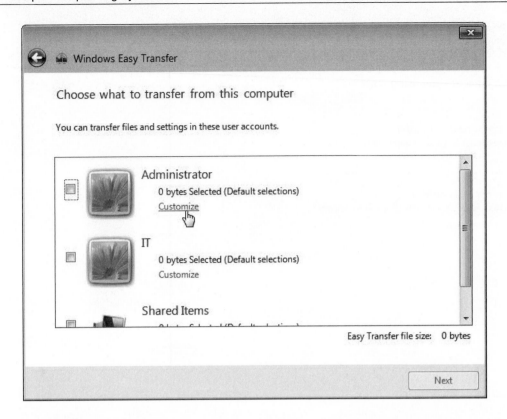

Uncheck the box next to each account, and then click **Customize** for the account you are logged in under.

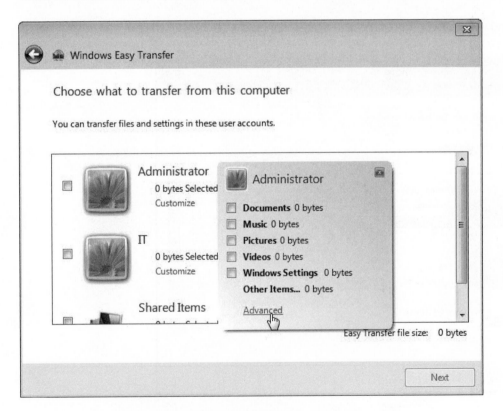

When the customize window opens for the account, click **Advanced**.

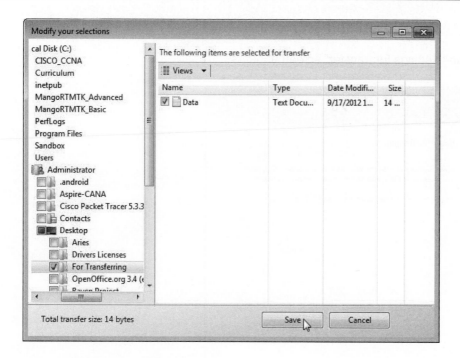

Locate the "For Transferring" folder.

This will be the location where files are transferred from.

Select the **Data** file and click **Save**.

The "Choose what to transfer from this computer" screen appears.

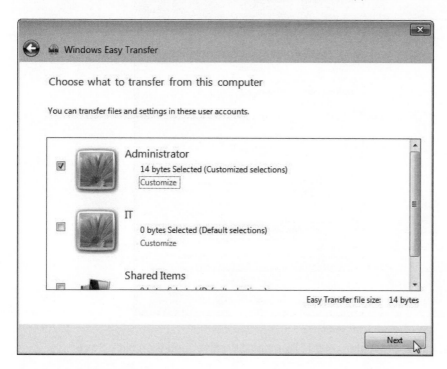

What is the size of the file being transferred?

Click **Next**.

The "Save your files and settings for transfer" screen appears.

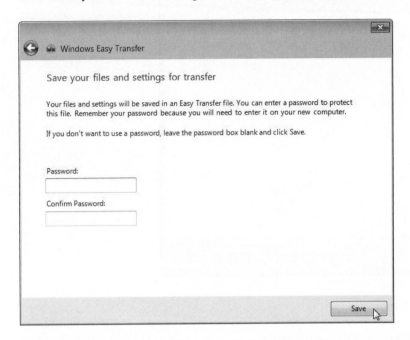

Since you are simply transferring the files back to the same computer, a password is not required.

Click **Save**.

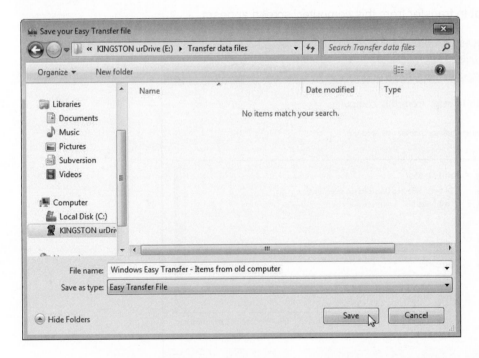

On the USB flash drive, locate the folder called "Transfer data files" and then click **Save**.

The "These files and settings have been saved for your transfer" screen appears.

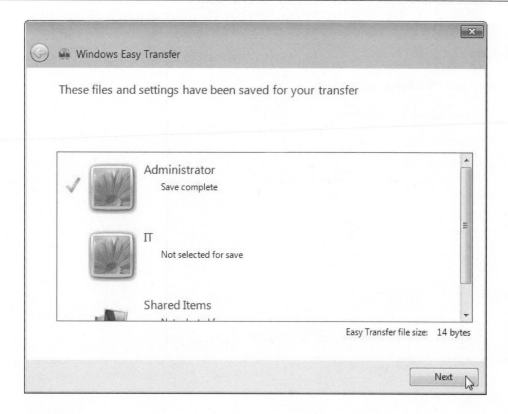

Click **Next**.

The "Your transfer file is complete" screen appears.

Click **Next**.

The "Windows Easy Transfer is complete on this computer." screen appears.

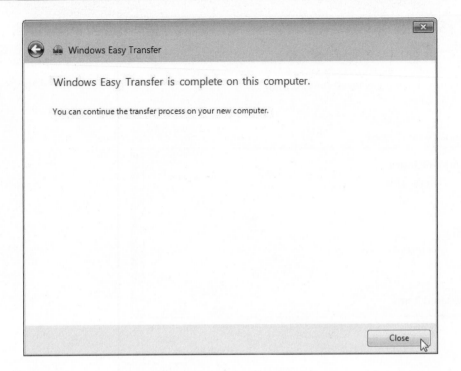

Click **Close**.

Step 3

Locate and delete the "For Transferring" folder that is located on the desktop.

Empty the Recycle Bin.

Step 4

Click **Start > All Programs > Accessories > System Tools > Windows Easy Transfer**.

The "Welcome to Windows Easy Transfer" screen opens.

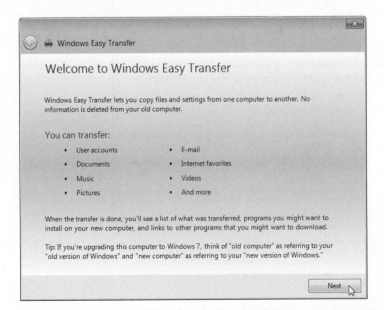

Click **Next**.

The "What do you want to use to transfer items to your new computer?" screen appears.

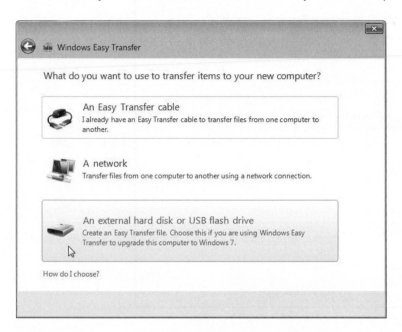

Select **An external hard disk or USB flash drive**.

The "Which computer are you using now?" screen appears.

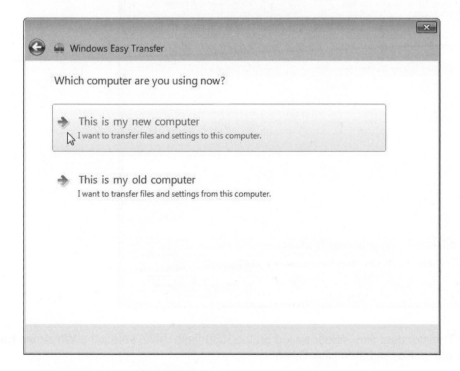

Select **This is my new computer**.

The "Has Windows Easy Transfer already saved your files from your old computer to an external hard disk or USB flash drive?" screen appears.

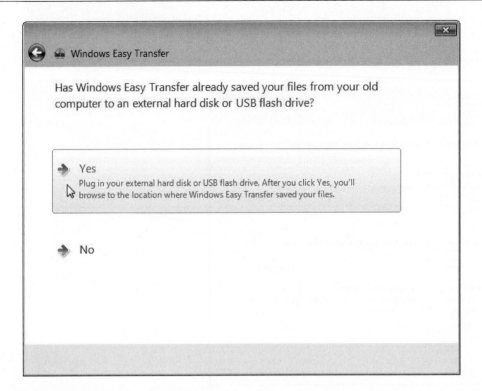

Click **Yes**.

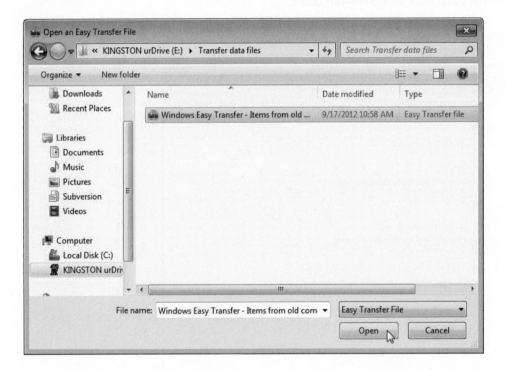

Locate and open the "Transfer data files" folder saved on the USB flash drive, select the **Windows Easy Transfer – Item from old ...** file, and then click **Open**.

The "Choose what to transfer to this computer" screen appears.

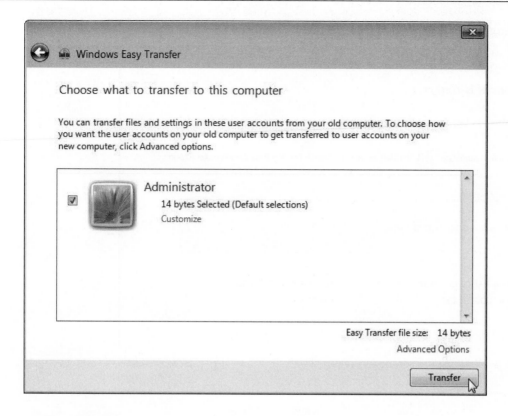

Click **Transfer**.

The "Transfer items to this computer" screen appears.

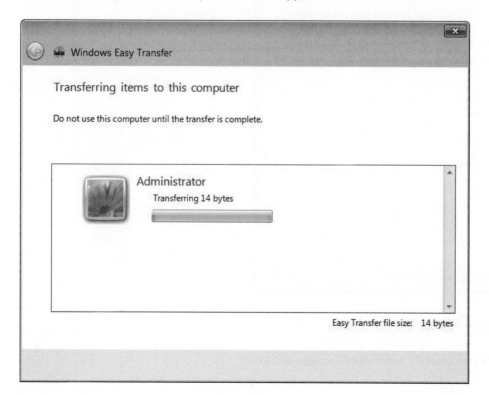

The "Your transfer is complete" screen appears.

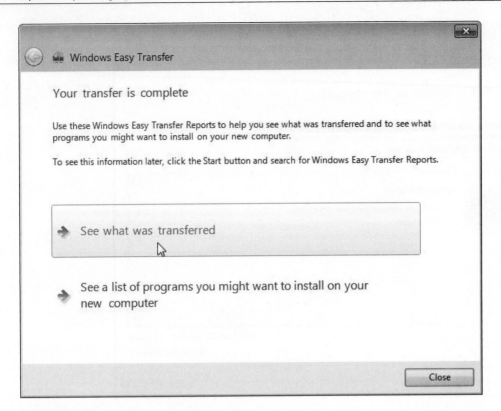

Click **See what was transferred**.

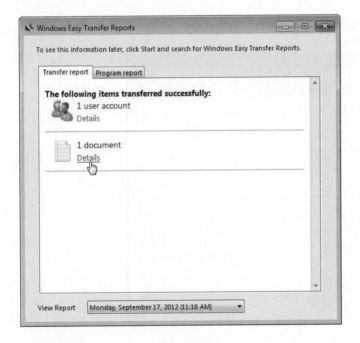

Click **Details** below 1 document.

The "Documents successfully transferred" screen appears.

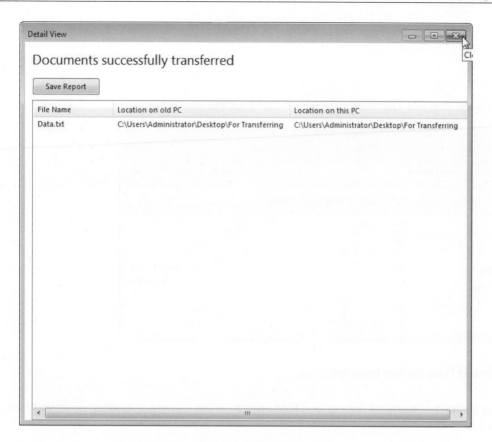

What do you notice about the location of the new Data file?

Close the "Detail View" window and the "Windows Easy Transfer Reports" window.

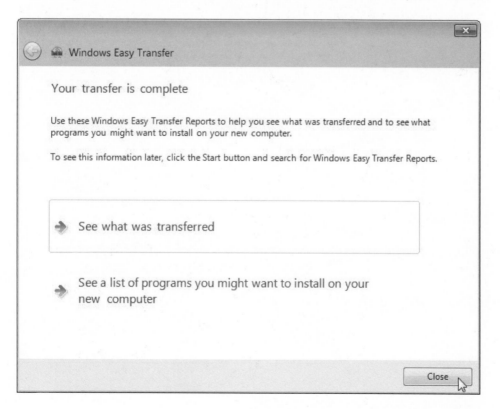

When the "Window Easy Transfer" window appears, click **Close**.

Step 5

Navigate to and open the "For Transferring" folder located on the desktop.

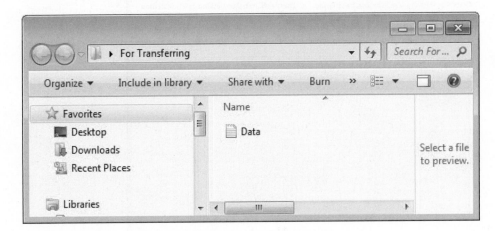

Notice the folder and Data file has been restored.

If advised by the instructor, delete all folders and files create on the computer desktop and USB flash drive during this lab.

5.1.4.5 Lab - Data Migration in Windows Vista

Introduction

In this lab, you will use Windows Vista.

Recommended Equipment

The following equipment is required for this exercise:

- A computer with Windows Vista Business
- A USB flash drive

Step 1

Logon to the computer and create a folder on the desktop called "For Transferring".

Next, use Notepad to create a file, add the following text: "From older PC", and save the file in the folder called "For Transferring". Name the file "Data".

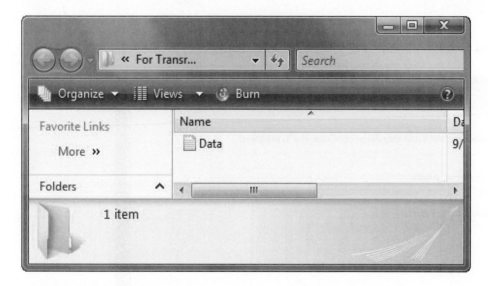

Create a folder called "Transfer data files" in the USB flash drive.

Step 2

Click **Start > All Programs > Accessories > System Tools > Windows Easy Transfer > Continue**.

The "Windows Easy Transfer" window opens.

Click **Next**.

The "Do you want to start a new transfer or continue one in progress?" screen appears.

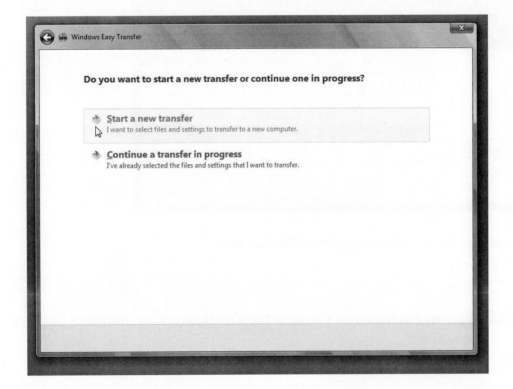

Select **Start a new transfer**.

The "Which computer are you using now?" screen appears.

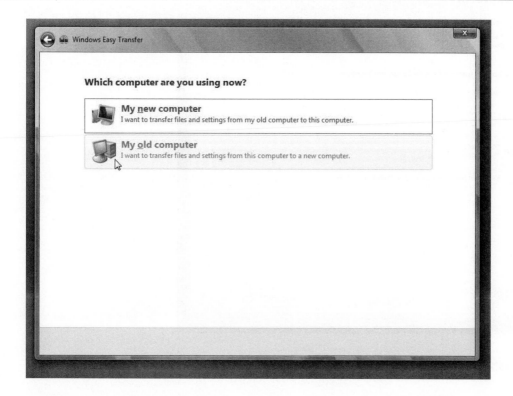

Click **My old computer**.

The "Choose how to transfer files and settings to your new computer" screen appears.

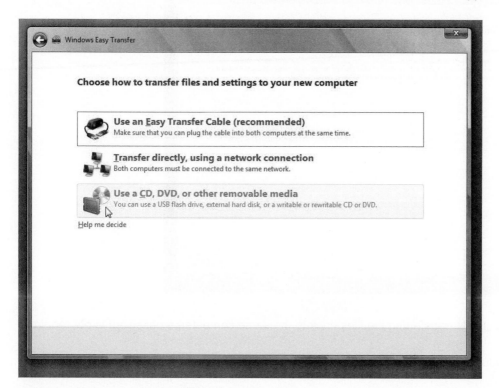

Click **Use a CD, DVD, or other removable media**.

The "Choose how to transfer files and program settings" screen appears.

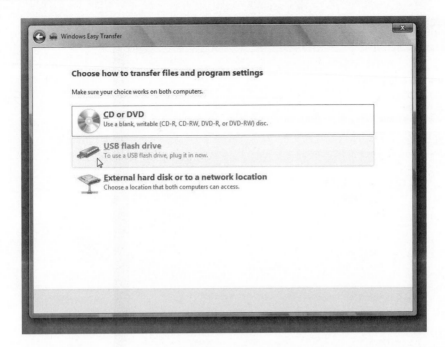

Click **USB flash drive**.

The "Plug in an empty USB flash drive" screen appears.

Since you are simply transferring the files back to the same computer, a password is not required.

Note: Since you will only transfer a small amount of data, the USB does not have to be empty.

Click **Next**.

The "What do you want to transfer to your new computer?" screen appears.

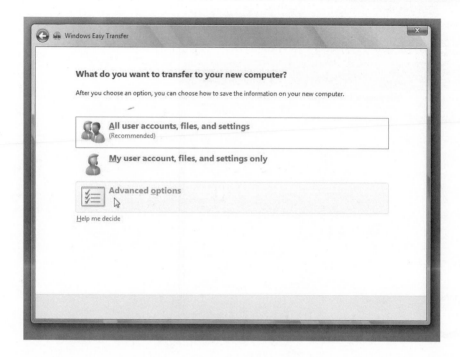

Click Advanced options.

The "Select user accounts, files, and settings to transfer" screen appears.

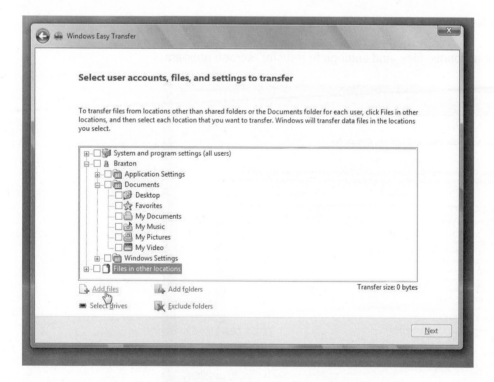

Remove the check mark from each box shown in the window.

Click **Add files**.

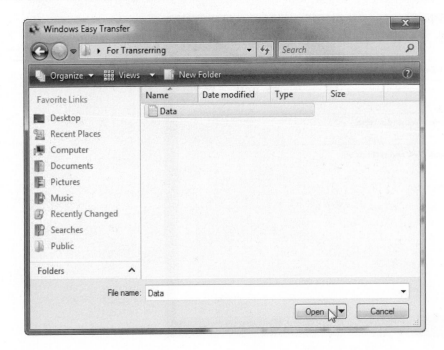

Locate the "For Transferring" folder.

This will be the location where files are transferred from.

Select the **Data** file and click **Open**.

The "Select user accounts, files, and settings to transfer" screen appears.

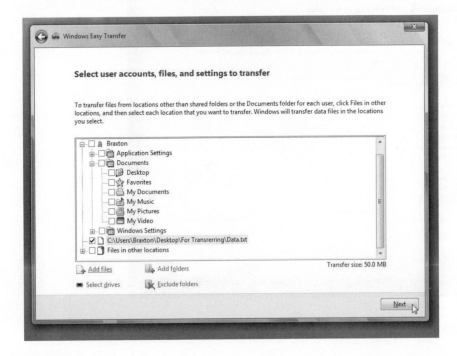

Click **Next**.

The "You're ready to transfer files and settings to your new computer" screen appears.

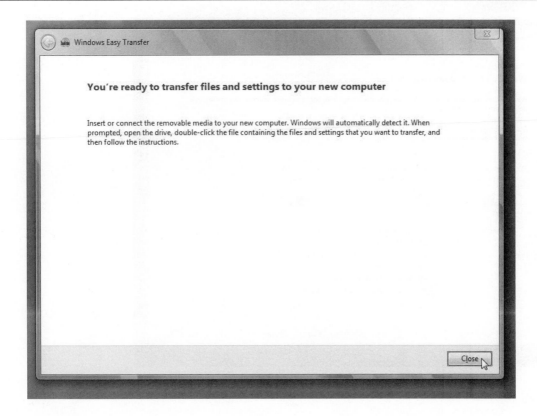

Click **Close**.

Step 3

Locate and delete the Data file located in the "For Transferring" folder that is located on the desktop.

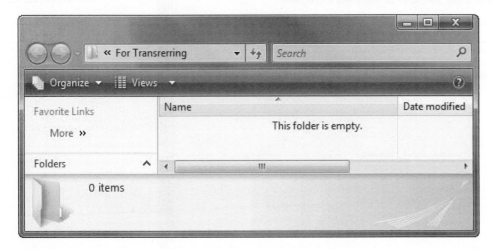

Empty the Recycle Bin.

Step 4

Click **Start > All Programs > Accessories > System Tools > Windows Easy Transfer > Continue**.

The "Welcome to Windows Easy Transfer" screen opens.

Click **Next**.

The "Do you want to start a new transfer or continue one in progress?" screen appears.

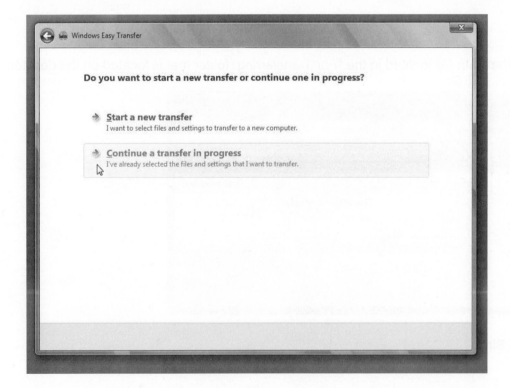

Select **Continue a transfer in progress**.

The "Are your computers connected to a network?" screen appears.

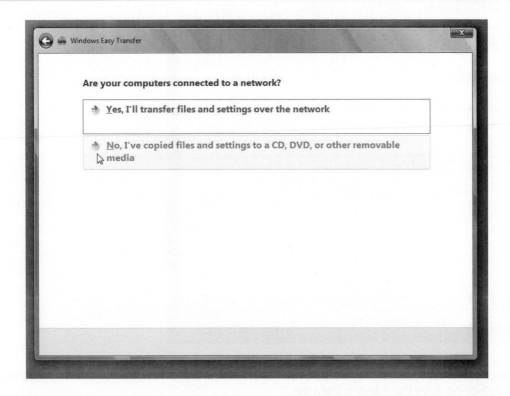

Select **No, I've copied files and settings to a CD, DVD, or other removable media**.

The "Where did you save the files and settings you want to transfer?" screen appears.

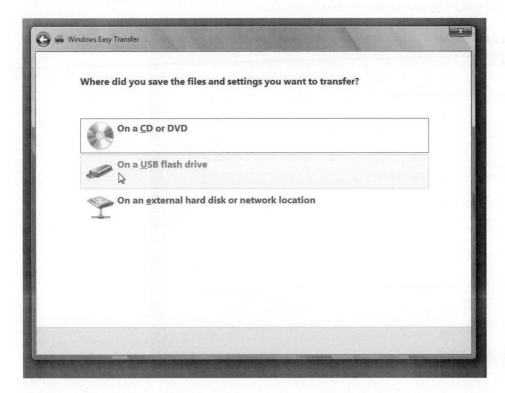

Click **On a USB flash drive**.

The "Plug in the flash drive" screen appears.

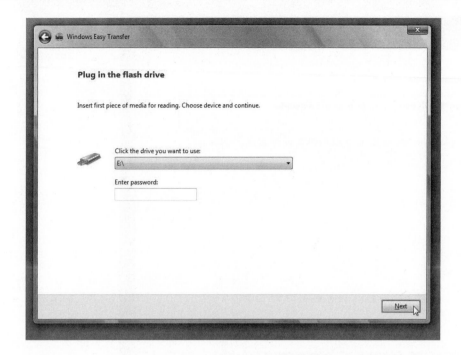

The USB flash drive will be automatically detected; if there is more than one USB flash drive plugged into the computer, select the drive that has the Data file.

Click **Next**.

The "Review selected files and settings" screen appears.

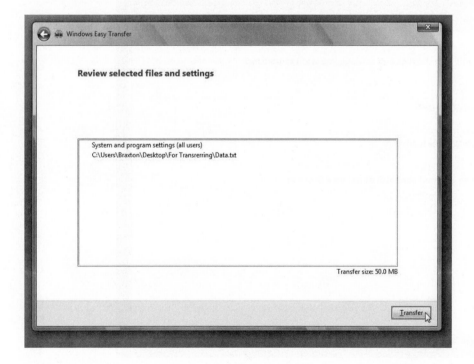

Click **Transfer**.

The "The transfer is complete" screen appears.

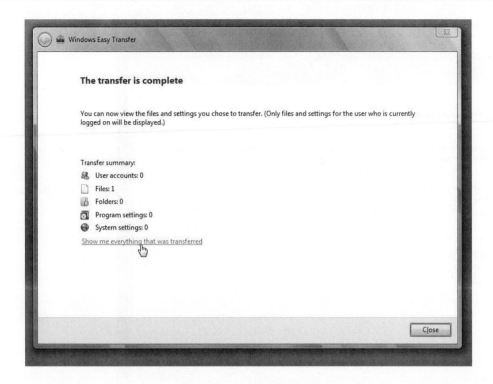

Click **Show me everything that was transferred**.

The "Windows Easy Transfer Report" window appears.

What do you notice about the location of the new Data file?

Click **OK**.

Close the "Detail View" window and the "Windows Easy Transfer Reports" window.

When the "Window Easy Transfer" window appears, click **Close**.

Step 5

Navigate to and open the "For Transferring" folder located on the desktop.

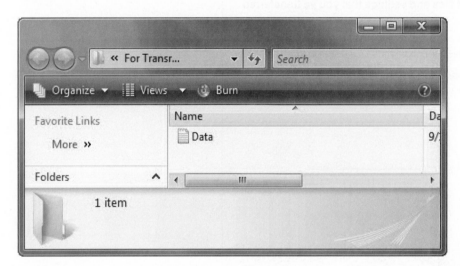

Notice the folder and "Data" file have been restored.

If advised by the instructor, delete all folders and files created on the computer desktop and USB flash drive during this lab.

5.1.4.6 Lab - Data Migration in Windows XP

Introduction

In this lab, you will use Windows XP.

Recommended Equipment

The following equipment is required for this exercise:

  - A computer with Windows XP Professional
  - A USB flash drive

Step 1

Logon to the computer and create a folder on the desktop called "For Transferring".

Next, use Notepad to create a file, add the following text: "From older PC", and save the file in the folder called "For Transferring". Name the file "Data".

Create a folder called "Transfer data files" in the USB flash drive.

Step 2

Click **Start > All Programs > Accessories > System Tools > Files and Settings Transfer Wizard**.

The "Files and Settings Transfer Wizard" window opens.

Click **Next**.

The "Which computer is this?" screen appears.

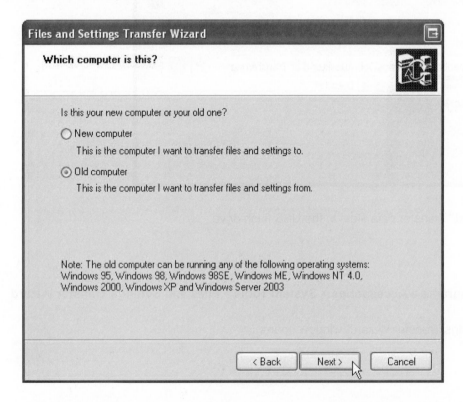

Select **Old computer**, then click **Next**.

The "Please wait…" screen appears.

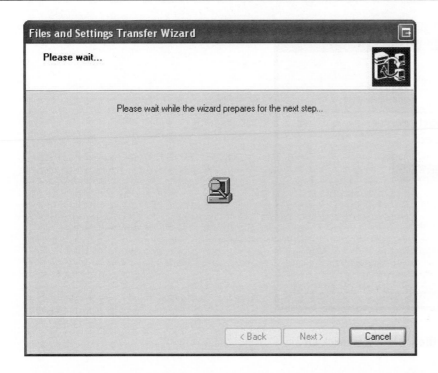

The "Select a transfer method." screen appears.

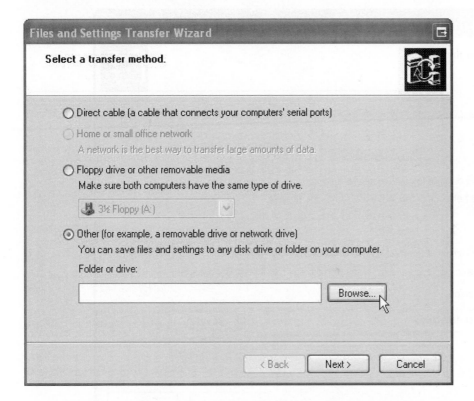

Select **Other (for example, a removable drive or network drive)**.

Click **Browse** and then locate the "Transfer data files" folder.

This will be the location where files are transferred to.

Select the **Transfer data files** folder and click **OK**.

The "Select a transfer method." screen appears.

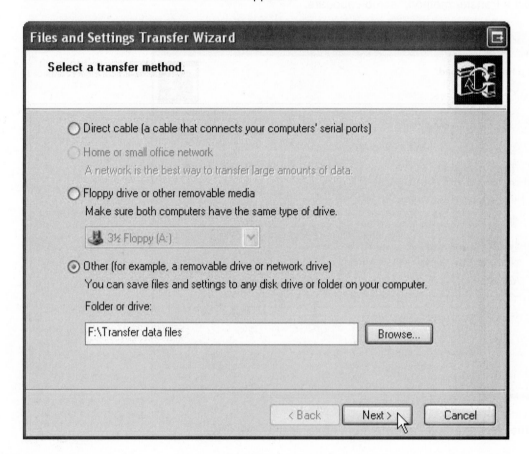

Click **Next**.

The "What do you want to transfer." screen appears.

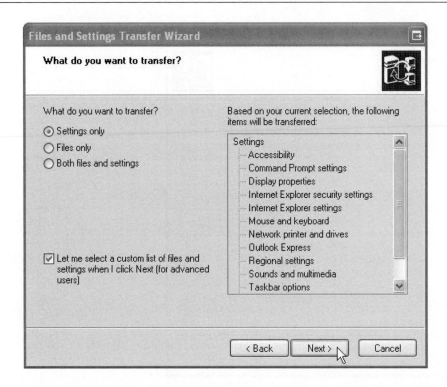

Select **Settings only**, place a check mark in the box **Let me select a custom list of files and setting when I click Next (for advanced users)**, and then click **Next**.

The "Select custom files and settings." screen appears.

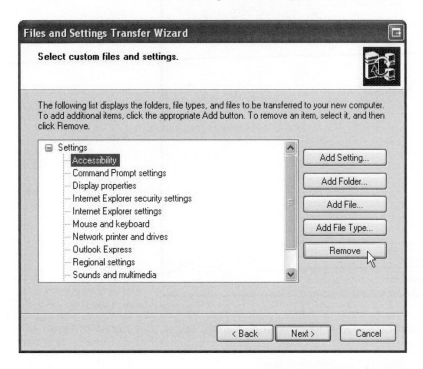

Select each item below Settings and then click **Remove**. Do this until there are no items in the list.

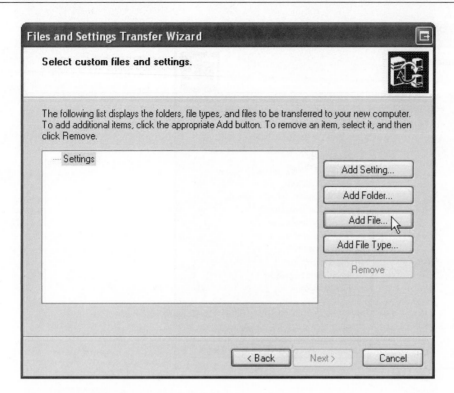

Click **Add File**.

Locate and select the **Data** file you saved in the "For Transferring" folder, and then click **Open**.

The "Select custom files and settings." screen appears.

Click **Next**.

The "Collection in progress…" screen appears.

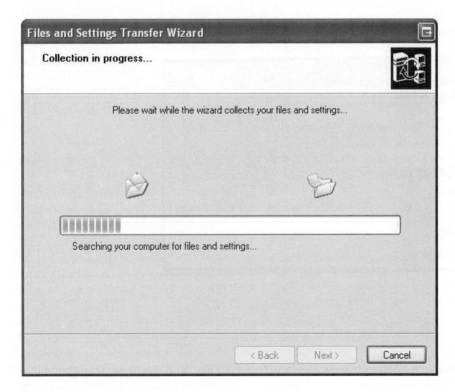

Click **Next**.

The "Completing the Collection Phase" screen appears.

Click **Finish**.

Step 3

Open the "For Transferring" folder located on the desktop and delete the file called "Data".

Empty the Recycle Bin.

Step 4

Click **Start > All Programs > Accessories > System Tools > Files and Settings Transfer Wizard**.

When the "Files and Settings Transfer Wizard" opens, click **Next**.

The "Which computer is this?" screen opens.

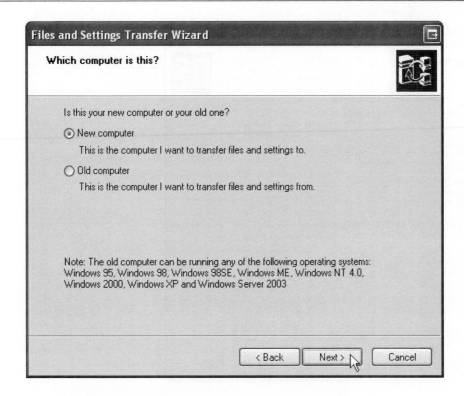

Select **New computer**, and then click **Next**.

The "Do you have a Windows XP CD?" screen opens.

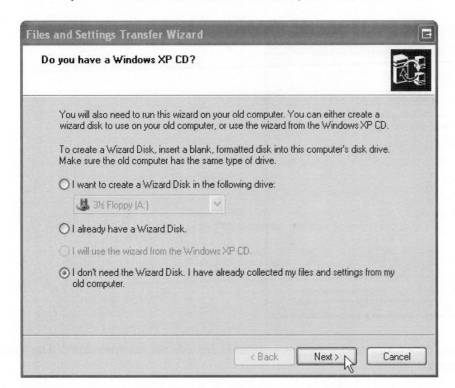

Select **I don't need the Wizard Disk. I have already collected my files and settings from my older computer** and then click **Next**.

The "Where are the files and settings?" screen appears.

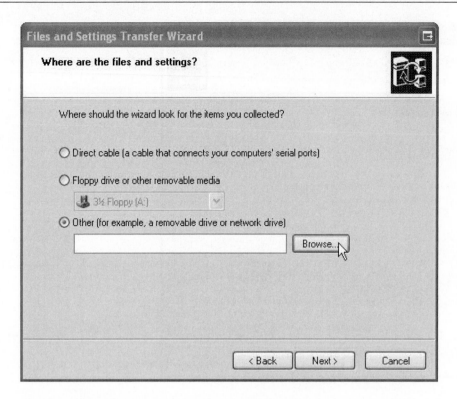

Select **Other (for example, a removable drive or network drive)**.

Click **Browse** and locate the "Transfer data files" folder on the USB flash drive.

Select the **Transfer data files** folder. Notice there is another folder with the extension **UNC**. The files that were transferred are located there.

Click **OK**.

The "Where are the files and setting?" screen appears.

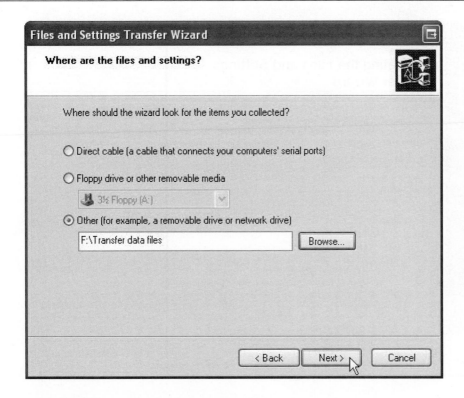

Click **Next**.

The "Transfer in progress..." screen appears.

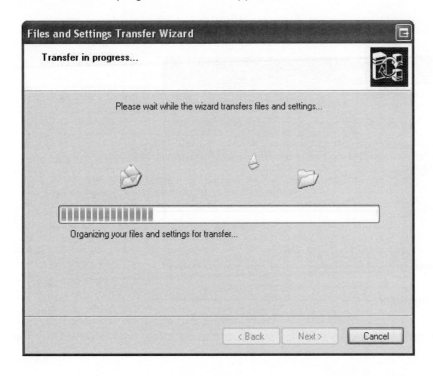

The "Completing the Files and Settings Transfer Wizard" screen appears.

Click **Finish**.

Step 5

Navigate to and open the "For Transferring" folder located on the desktop.

Notice the Data file has been restored.

If advised by the instructor, delete all folders and files create on the computer desktop and USB flash drive during this lab.

5.2.1.3 Worksheet - Answer NTFS and FAT32 Questions

Hard disk drives can be formatted using different file systems. NTFS and FAT32 are file systems used by the Windows operating system and provide different file system features.

Answer the following questions about the NTFS and FAT32 file systems.

1. What is the default cluster size setting when formatting a Windows NTFS partition on a hard disk drive larger than 2 GB?

2. What is the command used to change a FAT32 partition to an NTFS partition?

3. What is the Master File Table (MFT) and what does it contain?

4. What is NTFS journaling?

5. How does journaling help an operating system recover from system failures?

6. Why is an NTFS partition more secure than FAT32?

5.2.1.5 Lab - Install Windows 7

Introduction

In this lab, you will install the Windows 7 operating system.

Recommended Equipment

The following equipment is required for this exercise:

- A computer with a blank hard disk drive.
- Windows 7 installation DVD or USB flash drive.

Step 1

Insert the Windows 7 installation DVD into the DVD-ROM drive or plug the USB flash drive into a USB port.

When the system starts up, watch for the message "Press any key to boot from CD or DVD.".

If the message appears, press any key on the keyboard to boot the system from the DVD. If the press any key message does not appear, the computer automatically starts loading files from the DVD.

The computer starts loading files from the DVD or USB flash drive.

Step 2

The "Windows 7 boot" screen appears.

Step 3

The "Install Windows" window opens. Press **Next** unless you need to change the default settings.

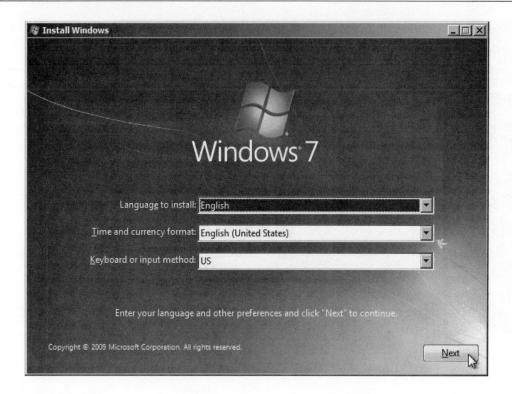

Step 4

Press **Install now** to continue.

Step 5

The Collecting information section of the installation begins.

The "Setup is starting…" screen appears.

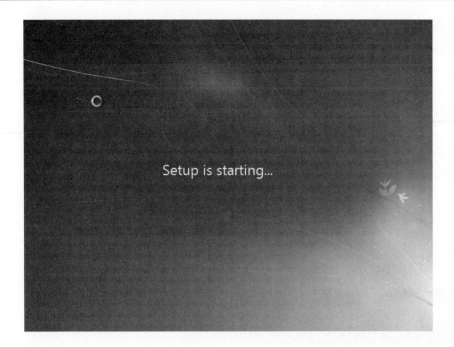

Next the "Please read the license terms" screen appears. Read and confirm that you accept the license by selecting the box "I accept the license terms". Click **Next**.

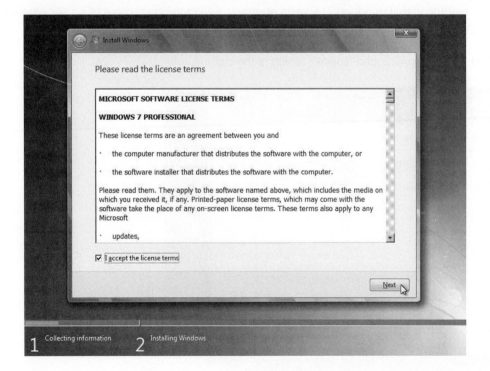

Step 6

The "Which type of installation do you want?" screen appears. Click **Custom (advanced)**.

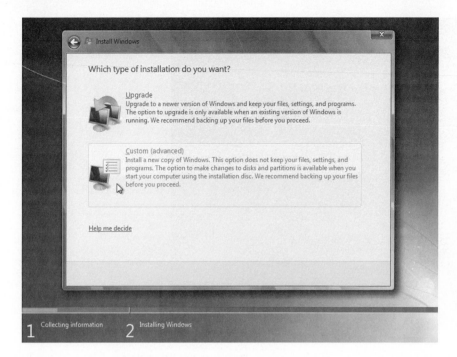

Step 7

The "Where do you want to install Windows?" screen appears. Select the hard drive or partition on which Windows 7 will be installed.

Click **Next** to select "Disk 0 Unallocated Space", which is the default setting.

The Collecting information section of the installation ends.

Step 8

The Installing Windows section begins.

The "Installing Windows…" screen appears. Windows 7 Setup may take up to 50 minutes to configure your computer.

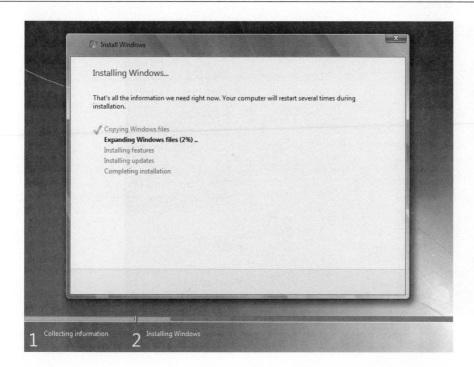

Step 9

The "Windows needs to restart to continue" screen appears. Your computer will automatically restart or you can click **Restart now**.

If you get the message "Press any key to boot from CD or DVD.", **do not press any key** and Windows will boot from the hard disk to continue the installation.

Step 10

The "Setup is updating registry settings" message appears.

Step 11

The "Setup is starting services" message appears.

Step 12

The "Installing Windows…" screen appears again. Windows may reboot a few more times. This may take several minutes.

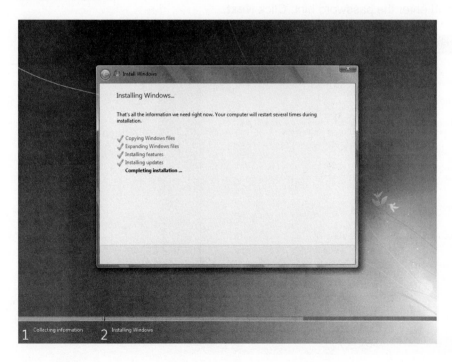

The Installing Windows section of the installation is completed.

Step 13

The "Set Up Windows" section begins.

Type the user name and computer name provided by your instructor. Click **Next**.

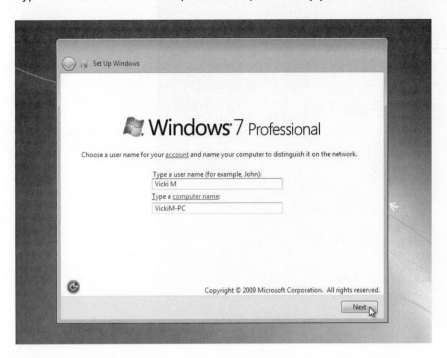

Step 14

The "Set a password for your account" screen appears. Type the password provided by your instructor. Retype the password and enter the password hint. Click **Next**.

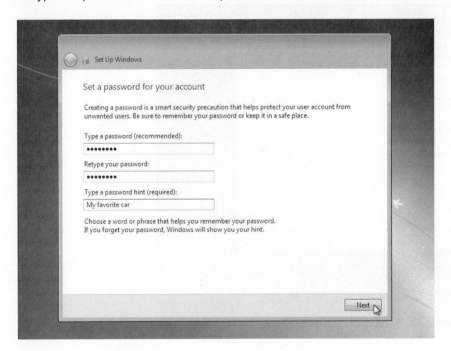

Step 15

The "Type your Windows product key" screen appears. On this page, type your product key as it appears on your Windows 7 DVD case. Click **Next**.

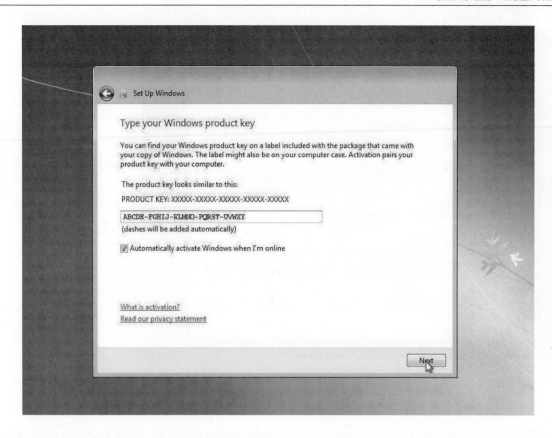

Note: If you entered your product key, Setup will not ask you the following:

"Do you want to enter your product key now?" screen appears. If you were instructed not to enter a product key, click **No**.

Step 16

On the "Help protect your computer and improve Windows automatically" screen, click **Use recommended settings**.

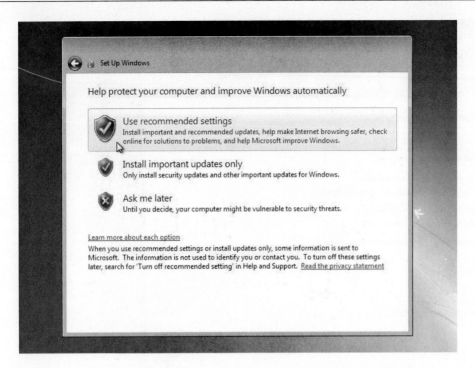

Step 17

On the "Review your time and date settings" screen, configure the computer clock to match your local date, time, and time zone. Click **Next**.

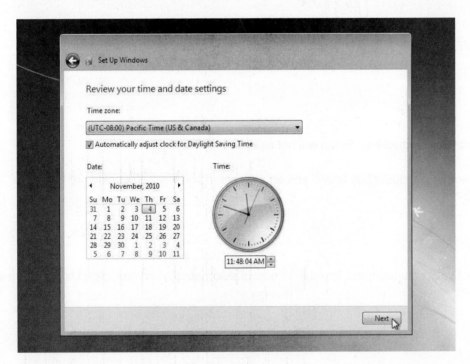

Step 18

The "Select your computer's current location" screen appears. Select the option provided by your instructor.

Note: This screen will not show up if the installation did not correctly install drivers for the network card.

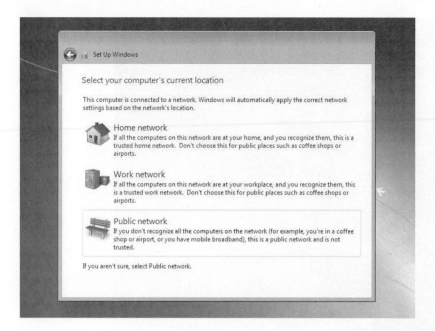

Step 19

The "Windows is finalizing your settings" screen appears.

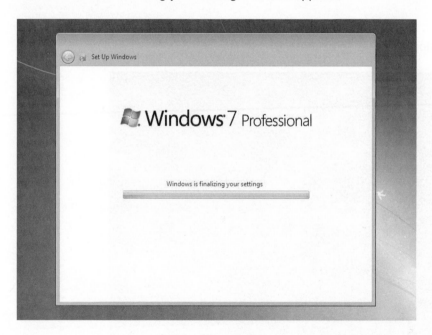

The "Set Up Windows" section is completed.

Step 20

The "Welcome" message appears.

Step 21

The "Preparing your desktop…" message appears.

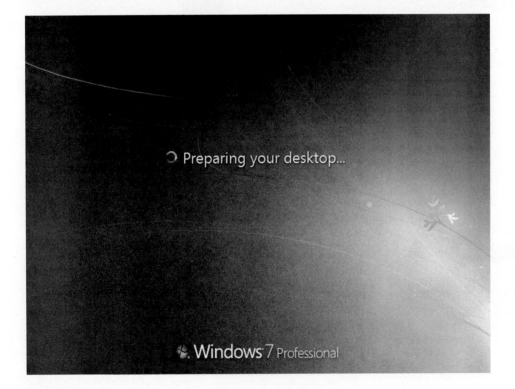

Step 22

You are logged in to Windows 7 for the first time.

5.2.1.6 Lab - Install Windows Vista

Introduction

In this lab, you will install the Windows Vista operating system.

Recommended Equipment

The following equipment is required for this exercise:

- A computer with a blank hard disk drive.

- Windows Vista installation DVD or USB flash drive.

Step 1

Insert the Windows Vista installation DVD into the DVD-ROM drive or plug the USB flash drive into a USB port.

When the system starts up, watch for the message "Press any key to boot from CD or DVD.".

If the message appears, press any key on the keyboard to boot the system from the DVD. If the press any key message does not appear, the computer automatically starts loading files from the DVD.

The computer starts loading files from the DVD or USB flash drive.

Step 2

The Windows Vista boot screen appears.

Step 3

The "Install Windows" window opens. Press **Next** unless you need to change the default settings.

Step 4

Press **Install now** to continue.

Step 5

The Collecting information section of the installation begins.

The "Type your product key for activation" screen appears. On this page, type your product key as it appears on your Windows Vista DVD case. Click **Next**.

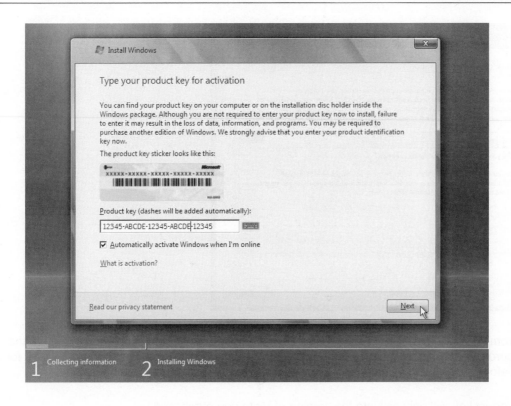

Note: If you entered your product key, Setup will determine the Vista product edition to install and will not display the next two screens.

Because you have left the product key field blank, the "Do you want to enter your product key now?" window appears. If you were instructed not to enter a product key, click **No**.

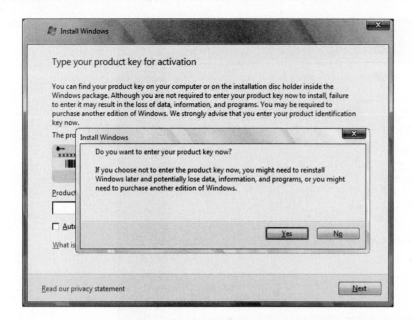

Setup now prompts you to select the Vista version you purchased. In general, you should choose the version you purchased, but note that you can install any Vista version listed and experiment with it for a limited time before product activation requires you to activate the version you purchased.

Note: Your product key will only activate the version of Vista you purchased.

Select the Windows Vista version that will be installed, check the item title "I have selected the edition of Windows that I purchased," and then click **Next**.

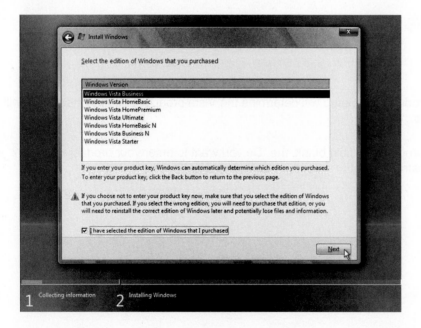

Step 6

The "Please read the license terms" screen appears. Read and confirm that you accept the license by selecting the box "I accept the license terms". Click **Next**.

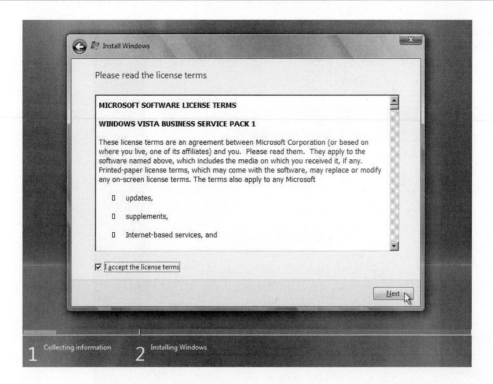

Step 7

The "Which type of installation do you want?" screen appears. Click **Custom (advanced)**.

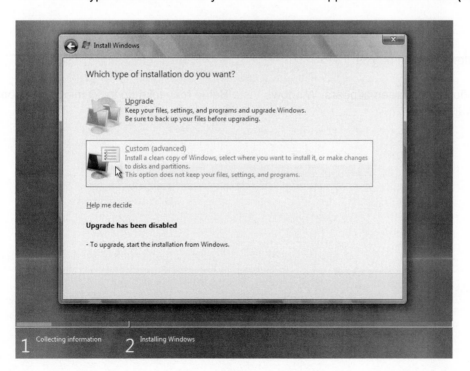

Step 8

The "Where do you want to install Windows?" screen appears. Select the hard drive or partition on which Windows Vista will be installed.

Click **Next** to select "Disk 0 Unallocated Space", which is the default setting.

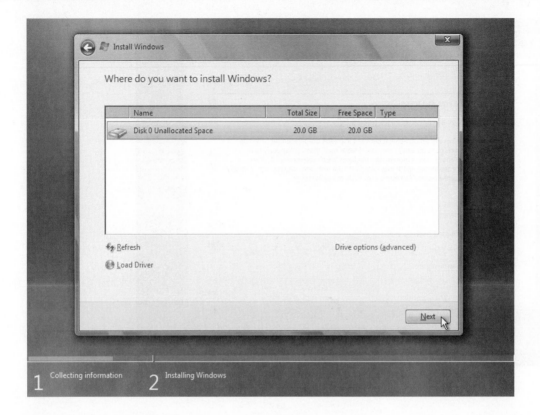

The Collecting information section of the installation ends.

Step 9

The Installing Windows section begins.

The "Installing Windows …" screen appears. Windows Vista Setup may take up to 50 minutes to configure your computer.

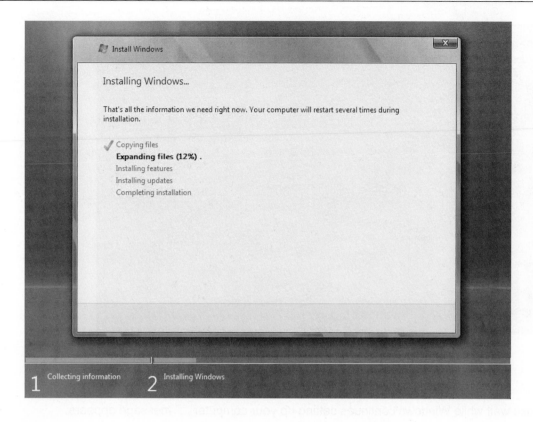

Step 10

The "Windows needs to restart to continue" screen appears. Your computer will automatically restart or you can click **Restart now**.

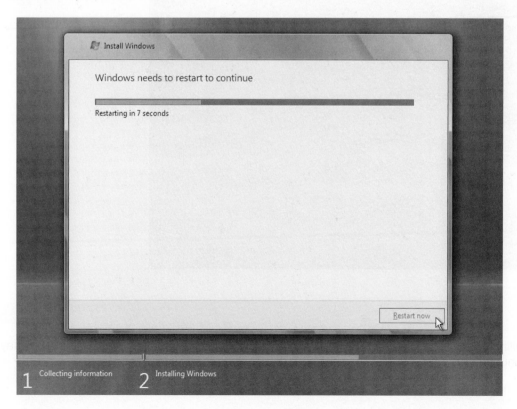

If you get the message "Press any key to boot from CD or DVD.", **do not press any key** and Windows will boot from the hard disk to continue the installation.

Step 11

The "Please wait while Windows continues setting up your computer ..." message appears.

Step 12

The "Installing Windows ..." screen appears again. Windows may reboot a few more times. This may take several minutes.

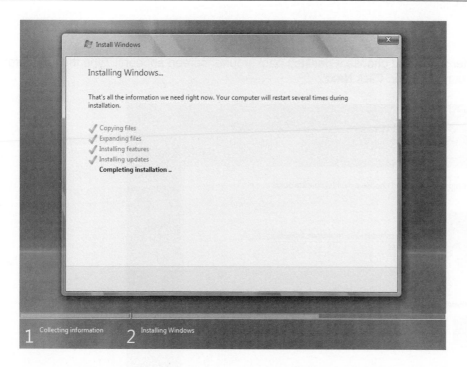

The Installing Windows section of the installation is completed.

Step 13

The "Set Up Windows" section begins.

The "Choose a user name and picture" screen appears. Type the name provided by your instructor. Type the Administrator password provided by your instructor. When you type in a password, two new fields will appear. Retype the password and the password hint. Click **Next**.

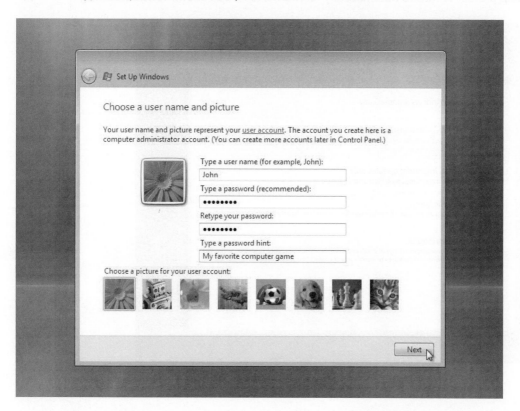

Step 14

The "Type a computer name and choose a desktop background" screen appears. Type the computer name provided by your instructor. Click **Next**.

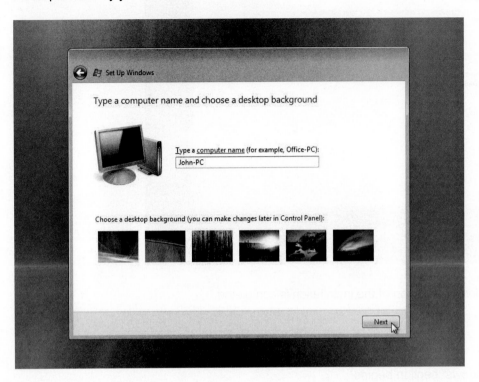

Step 15

On the "Help protect Windows automatically" screen, click **Use recommended setting**.

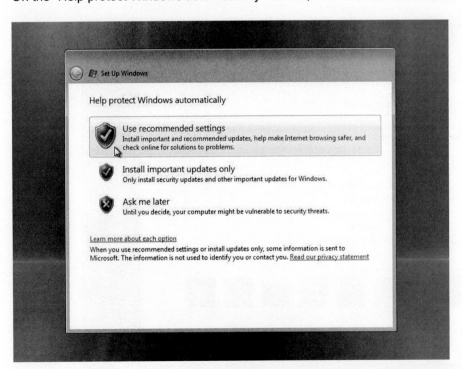

Step 16

On the "Review your time and date settings" screen, configure the computer clock to match your local date, time, and time zone. Click **Next**.

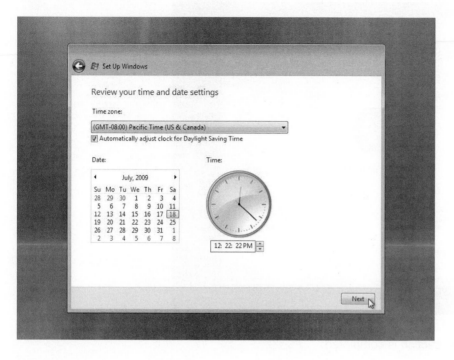

Step 17

The "Select your computer's current location" screen appears. Select the option provided by your instructor.

Note: This screen will not show up if the installation did not correctly install drivers for the network card.

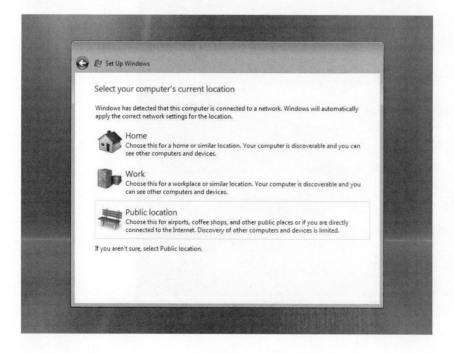

Step 18

On the "Thank you" screen, click **Start**.

The "Set Up Windows" section is completed.

Step 19

The "Please wait while Windows checks your computer's performance" message appears.

Step 20

Windows Vista boots for the first time.

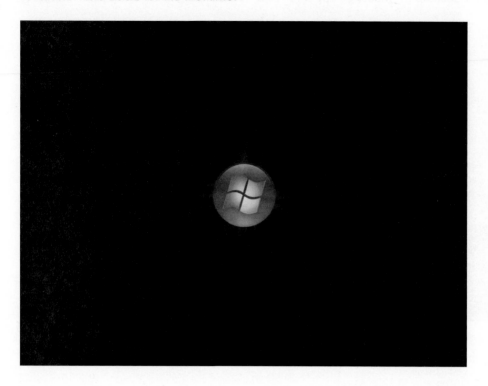

Step 21

The login window appears. Enter the password that you used during the install process and click the **blue arrow** to login.

Step 22

The "Preparing your desktop …" message appears. Your account profile is created and configured.

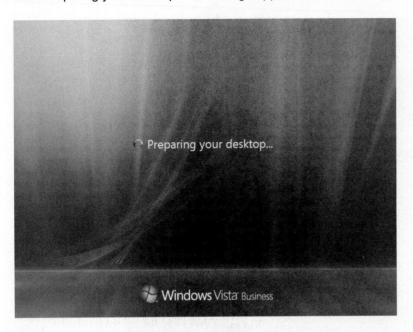

Step 23

The "Welcome" screen appears. Windows Vista is now installed.

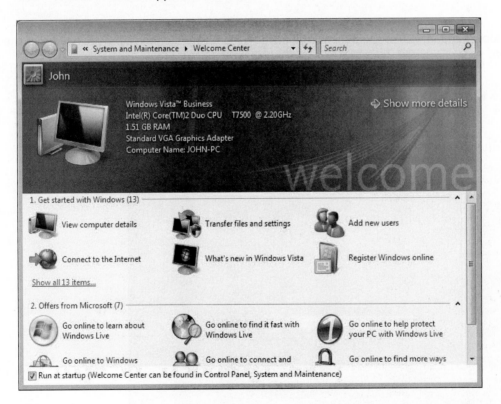

5.2.1.7 Lab - Install Windows XP

Introduction

In this lab, you will install the Windows XP Professional operating system.

Recommended Equipment

The following equipment is required for this exercise:

- A computer with a blank hard disk drive.
- Windows XP Professional installation CD.

Step 1

Insert the Windows XP installation CD into the CD-ROM drive.

When the system starts up, watch for the message "Press any key to boot from CD".

If the message appears, press any key on the keyboard to boot the system from the CD. The system will now begin inspecting the hardware configuration. If the message does not appear, the hard drive is empty and the system will now begin inspecting the hardware configuration.

Step 2

The "Windows XP Professional Setup" window opens. During this part of setup, the mouse will not work, so you must use the keyboard. On the "Welcome to Setup" screen, press **Enter** to continue.

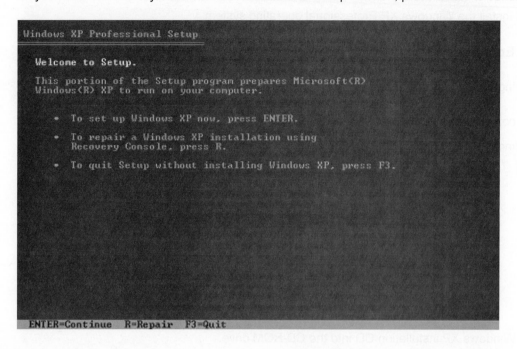

Step 3

The "Windows XP Licensing Agreement" window opens. Press the **Page Down** key to scroll to the bottom of the license agreement. Press the **F8** key to agree to the license.

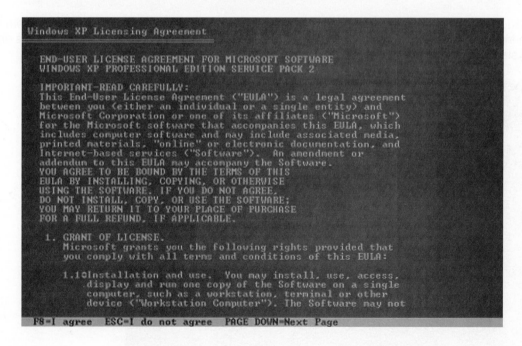

Step 4

Select the hard drive or partition on which Windows XP will be installed.

Press **Enter** to select "Unpartitioned space", which is the default setting.

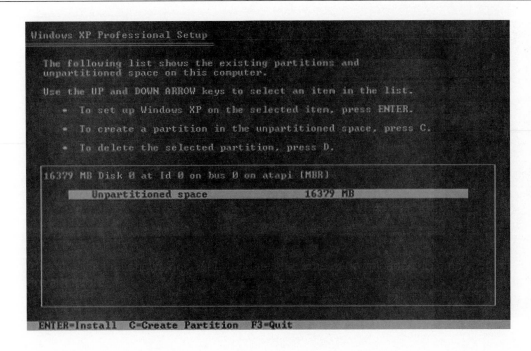

Step 5

Press **Enter** again to select "Format the partition using the NTFS file system", which is the default setting.

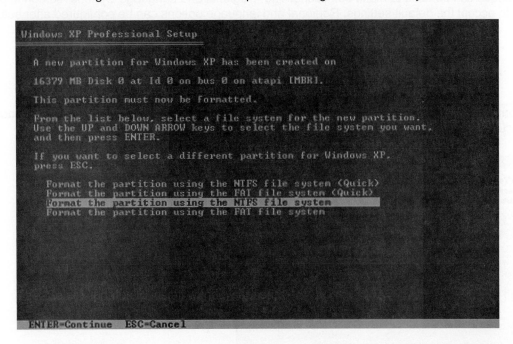

Windows XP Professional Setup erases the hard disk drive, formats the hard disk drive, and copies the setup files from the installation CD to the hard disk drive. This process should take between 20 and 30 minutes to complete.

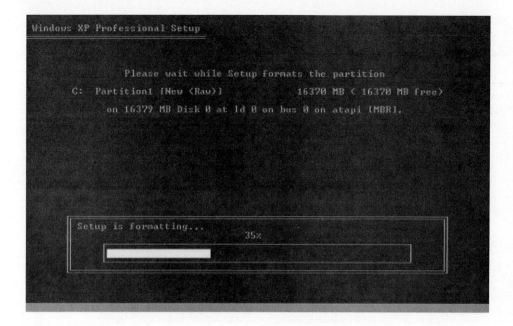

Step 6

After the formatting process, Windows XP restarts and continues with the installation process. At this point, the mouse can be used to make selections. The "Regional and Language Options" screen appears. Click **Next** to accept the default settings. Regional and language options can be configured after setup is complete.

The "Personalize Your Software" screen appears. Type the name and the organization name provided by your instructor. Click **Next**.

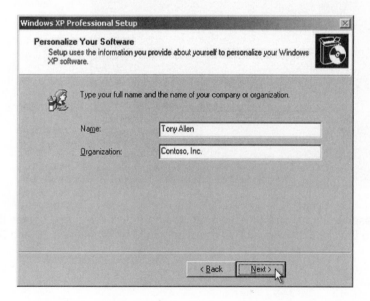

Step 7

The "Your Product Key" screen appears. On this page, type your product key as it appears on your Windows XP CD case. Click **Next**.

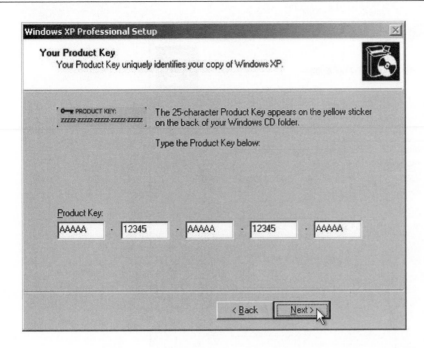

On the "Computer Name and Administrator Password" screen, type the computer name provided by your instructor. Type the Administrator password provided by your instructor. Retype it in the Confirm password section. Click **Next**.

Step 8

On the "Date and Time Settings" screen, configure the computer clock to match your local date, time, and time zone. Click **Next**.

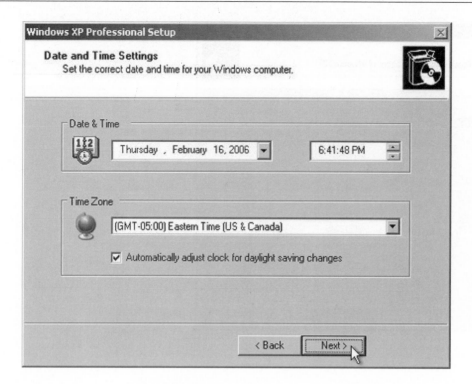

Step 9

On the "Networking Settings" screen, click **Next** to accept "Typical settings". "Custom settings" can be configured after setup is complete.

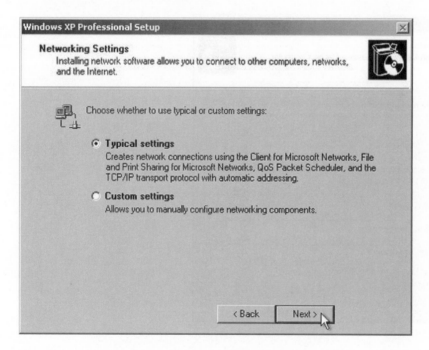

Step 10

On the "Workgroup or Computer Domain" screen, accept the default settings and click **Next**.

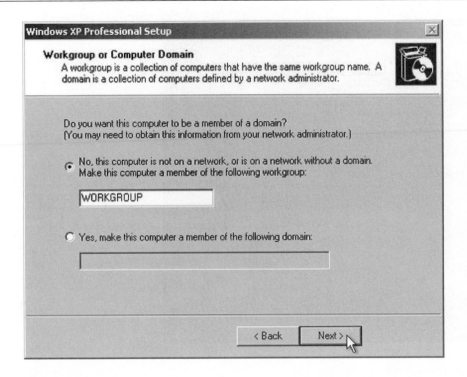

Step 11

Windows XP Professional Setup may take about 25 minutes to configure your computer. Your computer will automatically restart when the setup program is complete. When the "Display Settings" window opens, click **OK**.

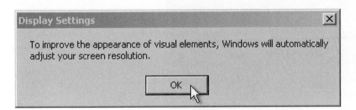

Step 12

When the "Monitor Settings" window opens, click **OK**.

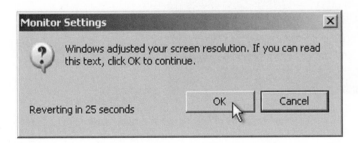

Step 13

The final phase of Windows XP Professional Setup begins. On the "Welcome to Microsoft Windows" screen, click **Next**.

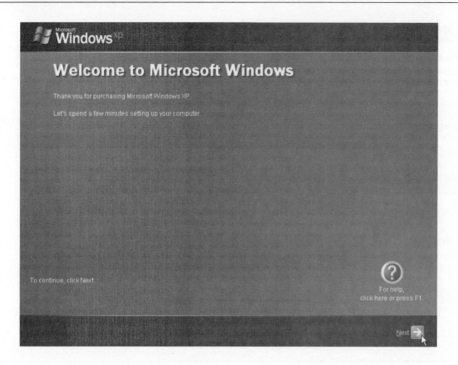

Step 14

On the "Help protect your PC" screen, select "Help protect my PC by turning on Automatic Updates now". Click **Next**.

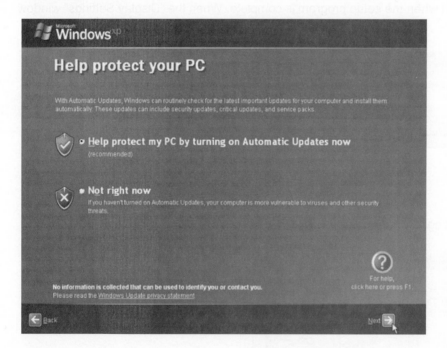

Step 15

Windows XP will now check to make sure that you are connected to the Internet. If you are already connected to the Internet, select the choice that represents your network connection. If you are unsure of the connection type, accept the default selection, and click **Next**.

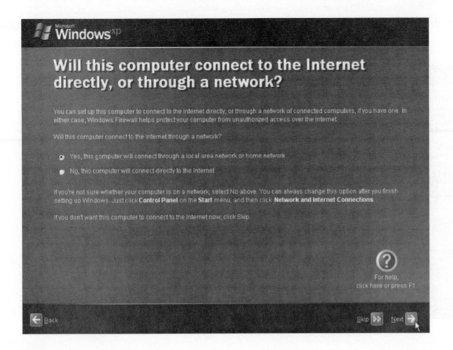

Step 16

If you use dial-up Internet access, or if Windows XP Professional Setup cannot connect to the Internet, you can connect to the Internet after setup is complete. Click **Skip** to continue.

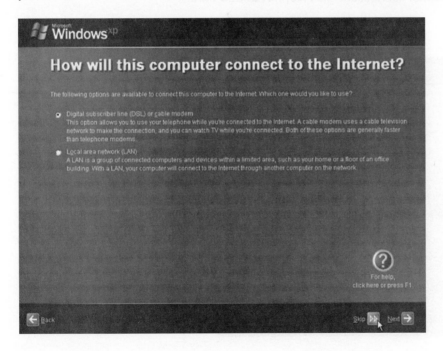

Step 17

Windows XP Professional Setup displays the "Ready to activate Windows?" screen.

If you are already connected to the Internet, click **Yes**, and then click **Next**.

If you are not yet connected to the Internet, click **No**, and then click **Next**.

After setup is complete, Windows XP setup program will remind you to activate and register your copy of Windows XP.

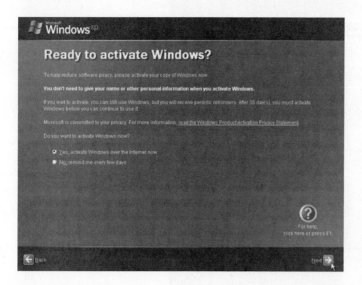

Step 18

If you have an Internet connection, click **Yes, I'd like to register with Microsoft now**.

If you do not have an Internet connection, click **No, not at this time**.

Click **Next**.

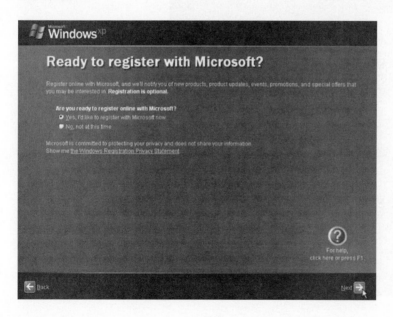

Step 19

On the "Collecting Registration Information" screen, fill in the fields using the information provided by your instructor and click **Next**.

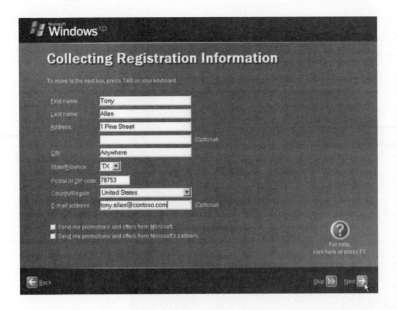

Step 20

On the "Who will use this computer?" screen, enter the information provided by your instructor. Click **Next**.

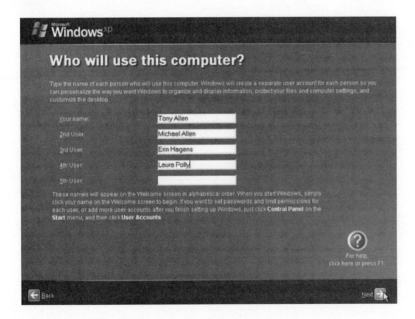

Step 21

On the "Thank you!" screen, click **Finish** to complete the installation.

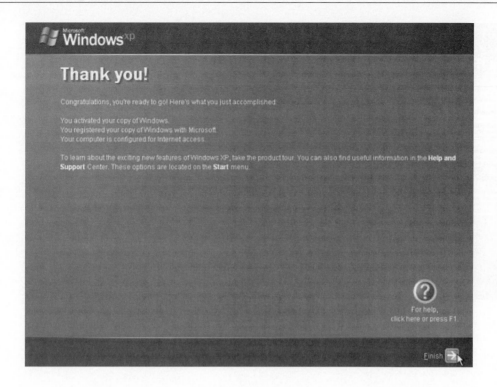

5.2.1.9 Lab - Check for Updates in Windows 7

Introduction

In this lab, you will configure the operating system so you can select which updates are installed and then change the settings so updates are downloaded and installed automatically.

Recommended Equipment

The following equipment is required for this exercise:

   • A computer with a new installation of Windows 7

Step 1

Boot the computer. Navigate to the "Control Panel" window by clicking **Start > Control Panel > System > Windows Update > Change settings**.

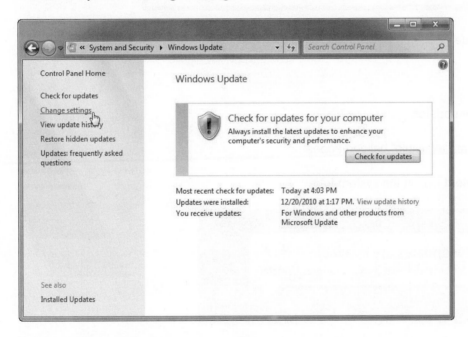

In the Important updates drop-down menu, select **Check for updates but let me choose whether to download and install them**.

Click **OK > Continue**.

Step 2

Windows checks for updates.

The "New updates are available" balloon appears.

Double-click the **shield** icon in the system tray.

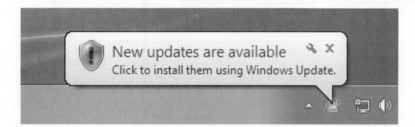

Click the link that shows how many updates have been downloaded. Example: **16 important updates are available**.

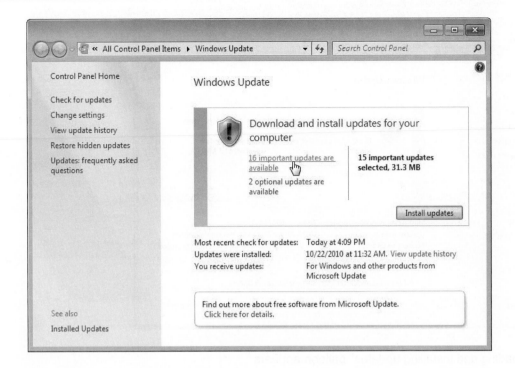

The "Select updates to install" window appears.

Before selecting which updates will be installed, ask the instructor for permission to install the updates.

Place a check mark next to the important and optional updates to be installed, and then click **OK**.

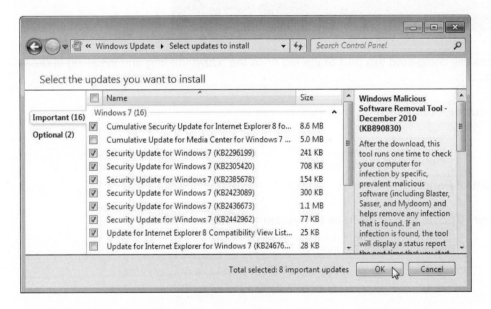

When the "Windows Update" window appears, click **Install updates**.

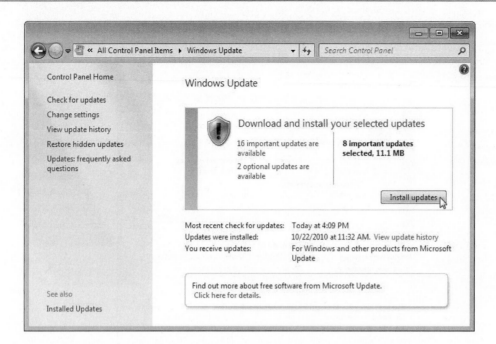

The "Downloading and installing updates" balloon appears.

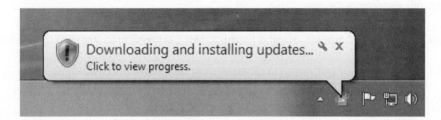

You have successfully completed this part of the lab once the "Downloading and installing updates" balloon appears.

Reboot the computer.

Step 3

Click **Start > Control Panel**.

Click the **Windows Update** icon or navigate to **System > Windows Update**.

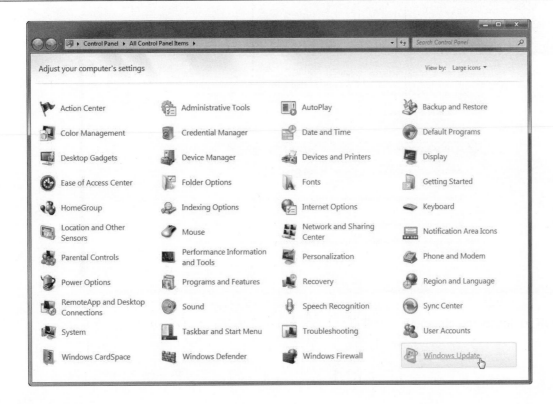

Step 4

The "Windows Update" dialog box appears.

Click **Change settings**.

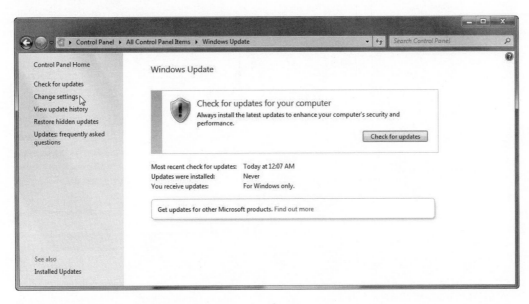

The "Choose how Windows can install updates" dialog box appears.

Select **Install updates automatically (recommended)** from the drop-down menu.

Click **OK** to accept the change.

5.2.1.10 Lab - Check for Updates in Windows Vista

Introduction

In this lab, you will configure the operating system so you can select which updates are installed and then change the settings so updates are downloaded and installed automatically.

Recommended Equipment

The following equipment is required for this exercise:

- A computer with a new installation of Windows Vista

Step 1

Boot the computer. Navigate to the "Control Panel" window by clicking **Start > Control Panel >** double-click **Windows Update > Change settings**.

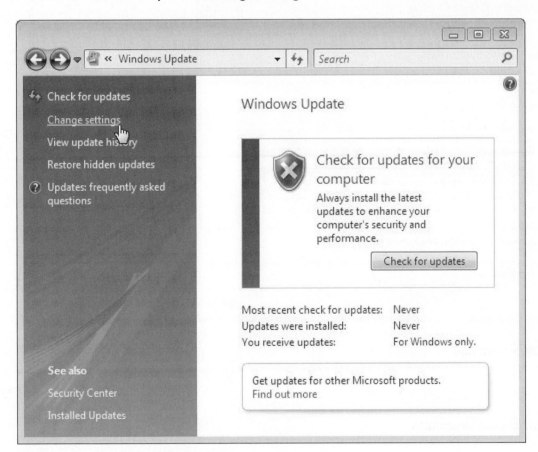

Note: The newest Windows Vista Update program has a different user interface. Both the original and new user interface are shown here.

Select the **Download updates but let me choose whether to install them** radio button.

"Original Windows Vista Update" program

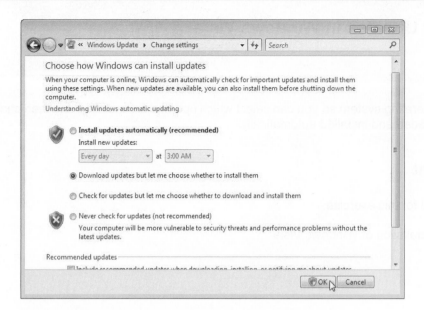

"New Windows Vista Update" program

Click **OK > Continue**.

Step 2

Windows checks for updates.

The "New updates are available" balloon appears.

Double-click the **shield** icon in the system tray.

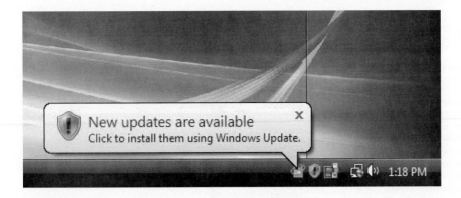

Click the link that shows how many updates have been downloaded. Example: **50 important updates are available**.

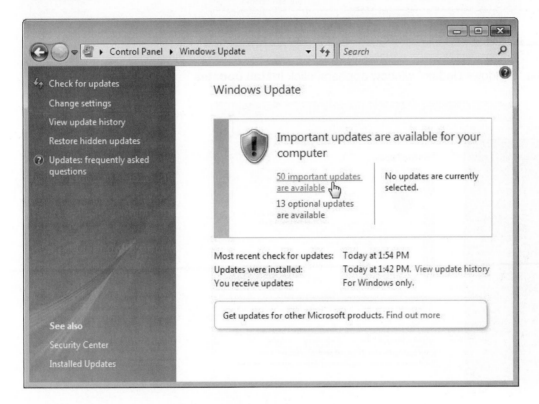

The "Select updates to install" window appears.

Before selecting which updates will be installed, ask the instructor for permission to install the updates.

Place a check mark next to the important and optional updates to be installed, and then click **OK**.

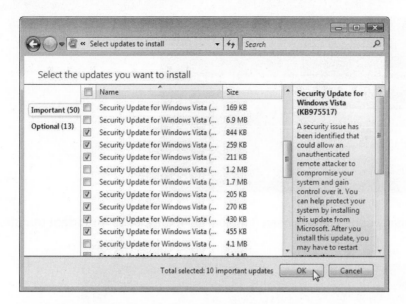

When the "Windows Update" window appears, click **Install updates**.

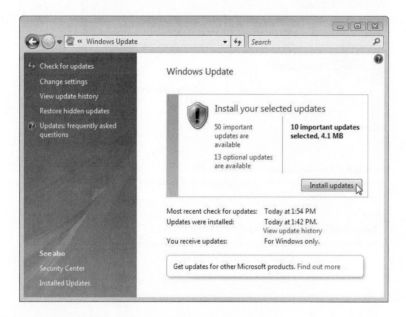

The "Installing updates" balloon appears.

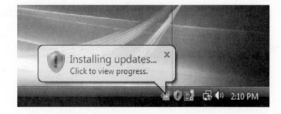

You have successfully completed this part of the lab once the "Installing updates" balloon appears.

Reboot the computer.

Step 3

Click **Start > Control Panel**.

Double-click the **Windows Updates** icon.

Step 4

The "Windows Updates" dialog box appears.

Click **Change settings**.

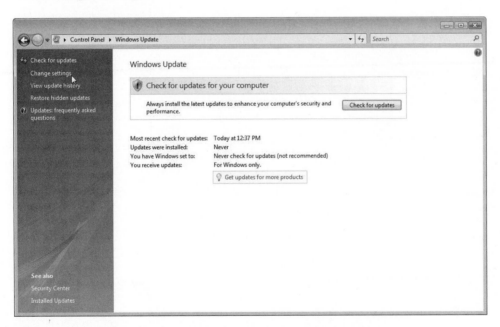

The "Choose how Windows can install updates" dialog box appears.

Select the **Install updates automatic (recommended)** radio button.

Click **OK** to accept the change.

Click **Continue** if asked for permission and close the dialog box.

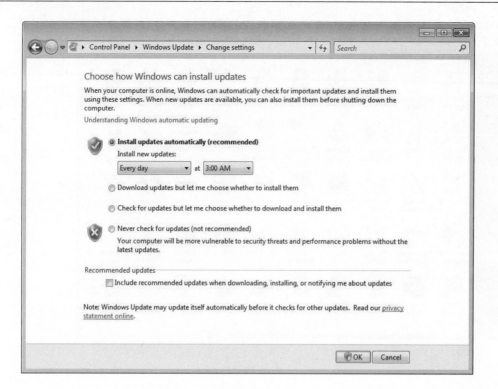

5.2.1.11 Lab - Check for Updates in Windows XP

Introduction

In this lab, you will configure the operating system so you can select which updates are installed and then change the settings so updates are downloaded and installed automatically.

Recommended Equipment

The following equipment is required for this exercise:

• A computer with a new installation of Windows XP Professional

Step 1

Boot the computer. Navigate to the "Control Panel" window by clicking **Start > Control Panel**.

Right-click **My Computer**, and then choose **Properties**.

Click the **Automatic Updates** tab.

Select the **Download updates for me, but let me choose when to install them** radio button.

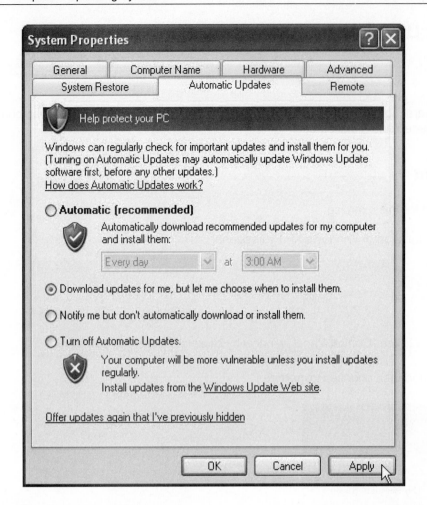

Click **Apply**, and then click **OK**.

Step 2

Windows checks for updates.

The "Updates are ready for your computer" balloon appears.

Double-click the **shield** icon in the system tray.

Select **Custom Install (Advanced)**, and then click **Next**.

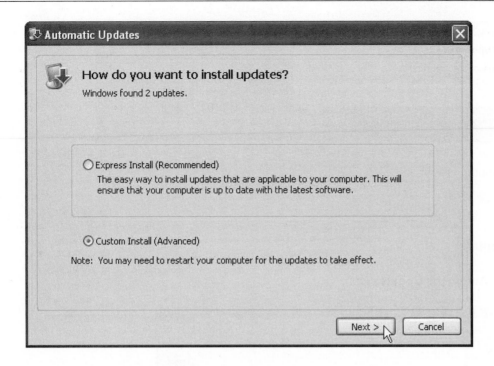

The "Choose updates to install" window appears.

Before selecting which updates will be installed, ask the instructor for permission to install the updates.

Click **Install**.

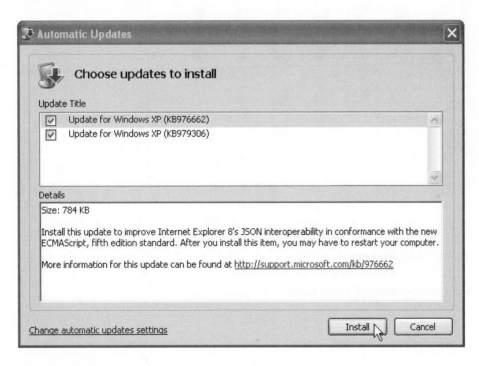

The "Installing updates" balloon appears.

Reboot the computer if required.

Step 3

Click **Start > Control Panel**.

Double-click the **Automatic Updates** icon.

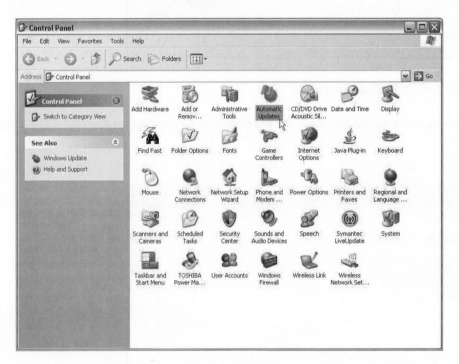

Step 4

The "Automatic Updates" dialog box opens.

Select the **Automatic (recommended)** radio button.

Click **OK** to accept the change and close the dialog box.

5.2.2.3 Lab - Advanced Installation of Windows 7

Introduction

In this lab, you will install a Windows 7 operating system by using an answer file for automation. You will customize partition settings and create an Administrator account and User accounts.

Recommended Equipment

The following equipment is required for this exercise:

- A computer with a new installation of Windows 7
- Windows Automated Installation Kit (Windows AIK) installation media
- Windows 7 installation media
- A blank, formatted floppy disk or a USB flash drive

Step 1

Ask the instructor for the following required information for the answer file:

Regional and language settings _____

Windows 7 product key _____

Partition sizes: Primary _____ Logical 1 _____ Logical 2 _____

Administrator account: User name _____

Password _____

User account: User name _____

Password _____

Computer name _____

Registered organization _____

Registered owner _____

Time zone _____

Step 2

Log on to the computer as Administrator.

Installation from a DVD-ROM: Insert the Windows Automated Installation Kit (AIK) DVD.

When the "AutoPlay" window opens, click **Run StartCD.exe**.

Click **Yes** if prompted by User Account Control.

The "Welcome to Windows Automated Installation Kit" window opens, click **Windows AIK Setup**.

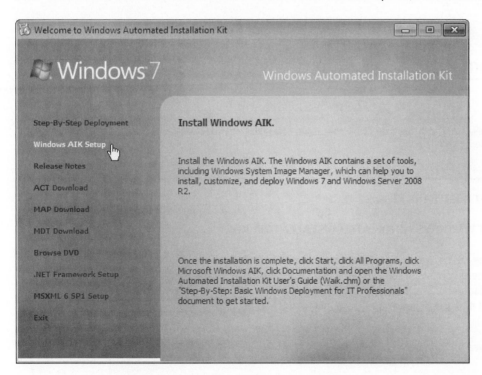

When the "Setup Wizard" opens, click **Next**.

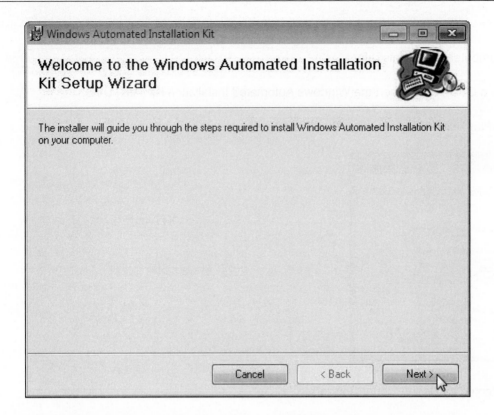

Select **I Agree** to license terms and then click **Next**.

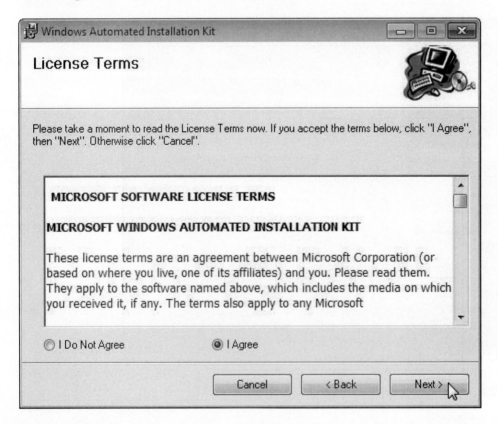

For the "Select Installation Folder" window, keep the default settings and click **Next**.

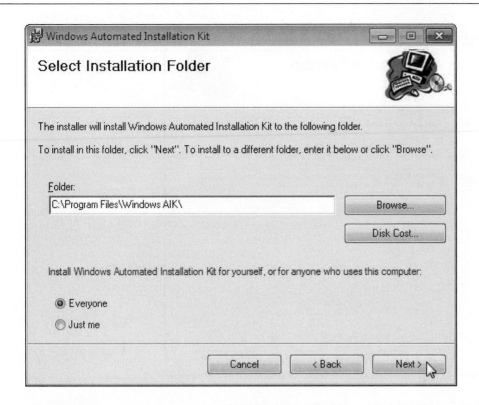

Click **Next** to confirm and start the installation.

A window opens displaying the file installation progress.

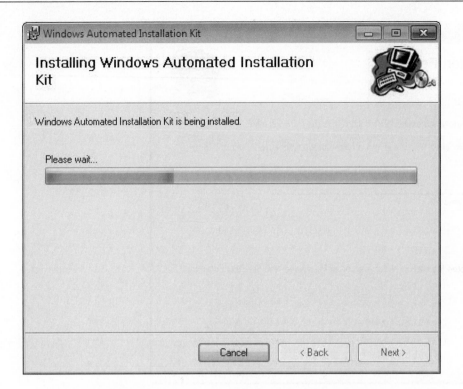

When the "Installation Complete" screen appears, click **Close**.

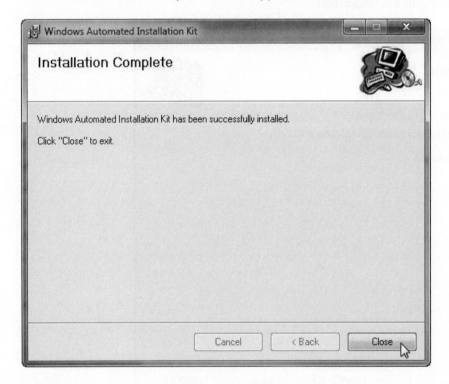

Click **Exit**.

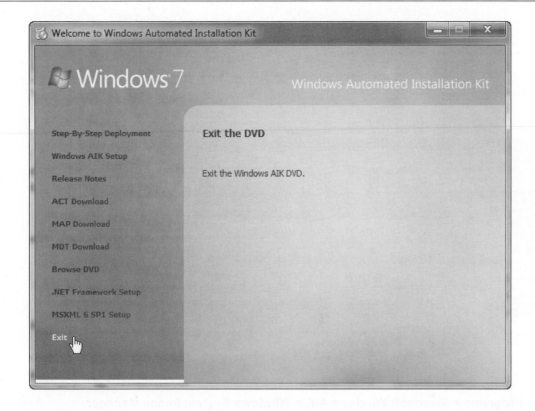

Step 3

Create a folder called **Windows_7_Installation** at the root of C:.

Example: **C:\Windows_7_Installation**.

Insert the Windows 7 media in the appropriate drive.

Close the Windows 7 media Install Windows window if it opens.

Navigate to **D:\sources** and copy **install.wim** and **install_Windows 7 PROFESSIONAL.clg** from the Windows 7 installation media to **C:\Windows_7_Installation**.

Note: The install.wim file is 1.94GB and may take several minutes to copy.

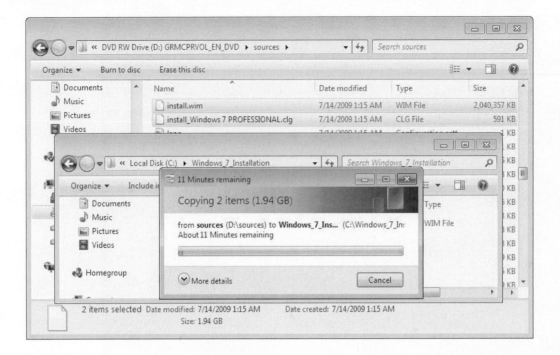

Step 4

Start > All Programs > Microsoft Windows AIK > Windows System Image Manager.

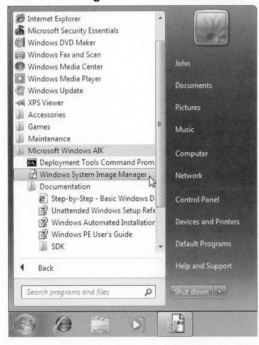

Step 5

The "Windows System Image Manager" window opens.

Right-click **Select a Windows image or catalog file > Select Windows Image**.

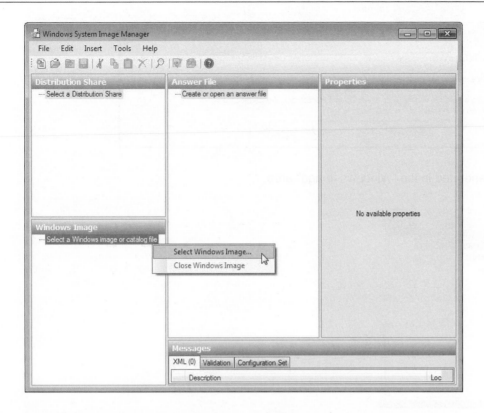

Browse to **C:\Windows_7_Installation > install.wim > Open**.

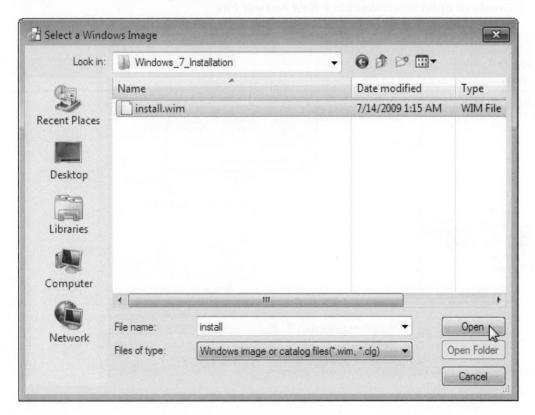

Click **Yes**. Click **Yes** if prompted by User Account Control.

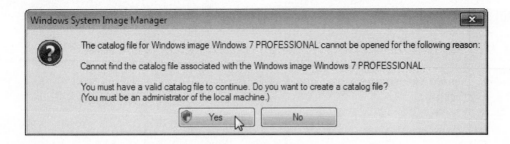

A catalog file is generated in the "Windows Image" area.

Right-click **Create or open an answer file > New Answer File**.

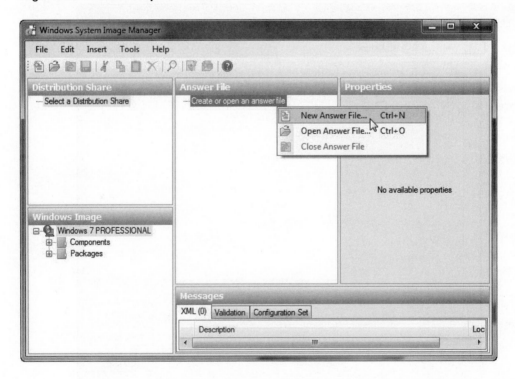

A new answer file is created in the "Answer File" area.

To name the file, select the root node **Untitled**.

Click **File > Save Answer File >** name the file **autounattend**. Make sure the **Windows_7_Installation** folder is selected and then click **Save**.

Note: It is important to name the file **autounattend**, as Windows 7 will only search for that file name when performing an unattended installation.

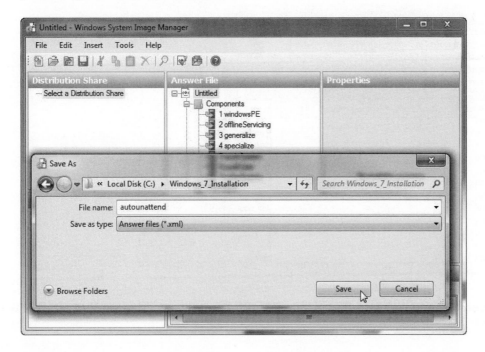

Step 6

In the "Windows Image" area, expand **Components**.

Note: The name of the components will have a prefix and suffix attached, for example: **x86_Microsoft-Windows-International-Core-WinPE_6.1.7600.16385_neutral**. The prefix is **x86** and the suffix is **6.1.7600.16385_neutral**. For simplicity, the prefix and suffix will be left out in the lab instructions.

Right-click **Microsoft-Windows-International-Core-WinPE > Add Settings to Pass 1 windowsPE**.

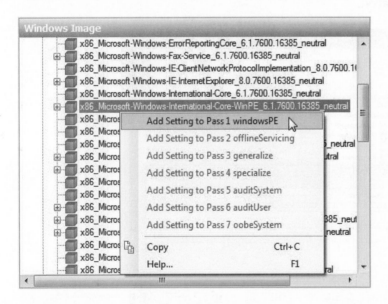

Notice that **Microsoft-Windows-International-Core-WinPE** has been added to the "Answer File" and "Properties" areas.

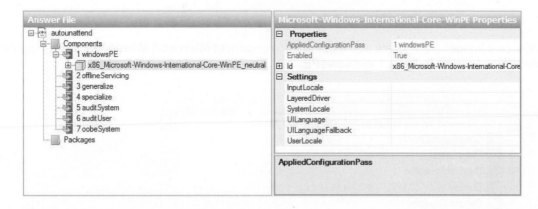

Select **Microsoft-Windows-International-Core-WinPE** in the **Answer File** area. In the **Microsoft-Windows-International-Core-WinPE Properties** area, type the language settings, provided by your instructor, in the following locations: InputLocale, SystemLocale, UILanguage, UILanguageFallback, and UserLocale. For example: **en-us**.

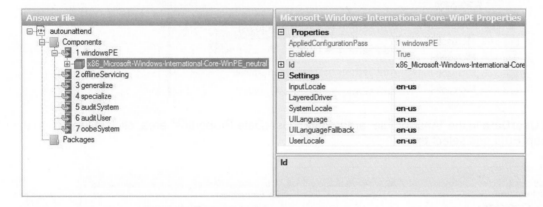

Note: Place the curser next to a setting in the "Properties" area and press the **F1** key to view the Windows Help file for the setting. Supported regional and language settings are also located here: http://msdn.microsoft.com/en-ca/library/ms533052(VS.85).aspx

In the "Answer File" area, expand **Microsoft-Windows-International-Core-WinPE >** select **SetupUILanguage**. In the "SetupUILanguage Properties" area, type the language settings provided by your instructor in the UILanguage location. For example: **en-us**.

Confirm **OnError** is selected for **WillShowUI**.

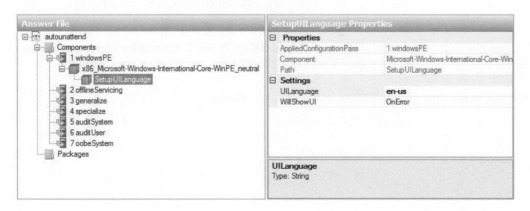

Step 7

In the "Windows Image" area, locate and expand the component **Microsoft-Windows-Setup >** right-click **UserData > Add Setting to Pass 1 windowsPE**.

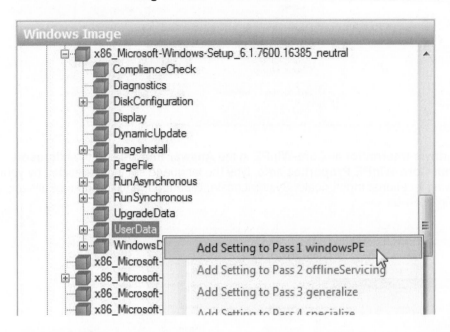

Select **UserData** in the "Answer File" area. In the "UserData Properties" area, click in the box to the right of **AcceptEula** and select **true**.

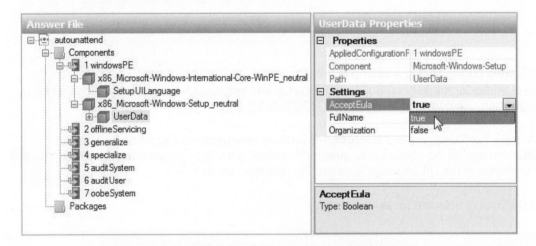

In the "Answer File" area, expand **UserData > ProductKey**. In the "ProductKey Properties" area, click in the box to the right of **Key** and enter the Windows 7 product key provided by the instructor.

Click in the box to the right of the **WillShowUI** and select **Never**.

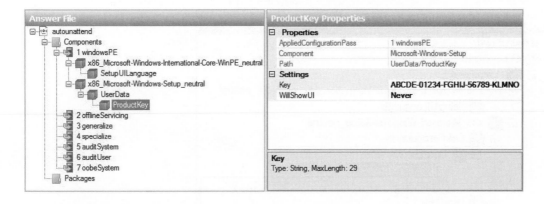

Step 8

In the "Windows Image" area, locate and expand component **Microsoft-Windows-Setup\ DiskConfiguration** > right-click **Disk** > **Add Setting to Pass 1 windowsPE**.

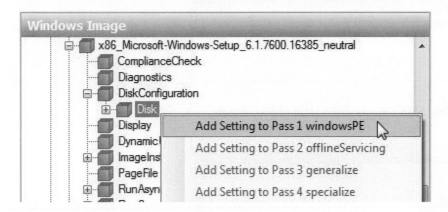

Select **Disk** in the "Answer File" area. In the "Disk Properties" area, click in the box to the right of **DiskID** and type the number **0**. Set **WillWipeDisk** to **true**.

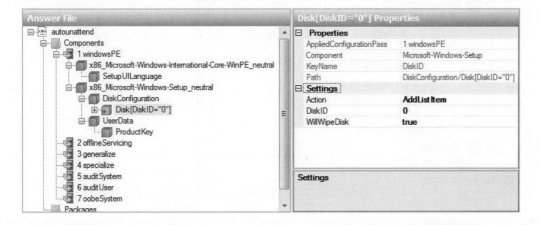

In the "Answer File" area, expand **Disk[DiskID="0"]** > right-click **CreatePartitions** > **Insert New Create-Partition**.

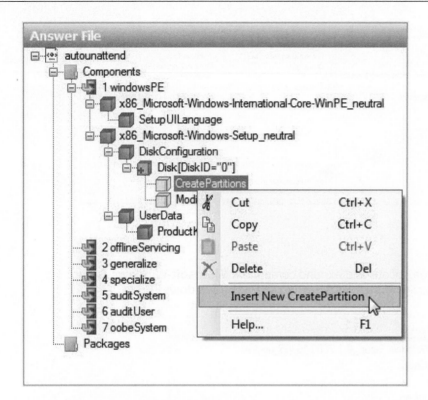

Add four more **CreatePartition** objects, for a total of five objects.

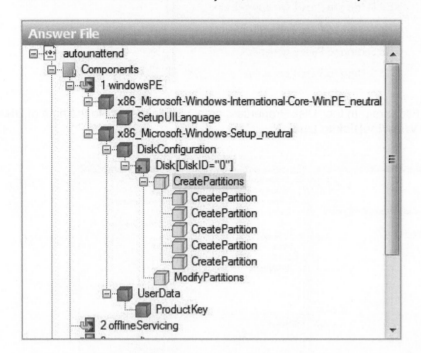

Select the top **CreatePartition** in the "Answer File" area. In the "CreatePartition Properties" area, set the following values: Extend = **false**, Order = **1**, Size = **100**, and Type = **Primary**.

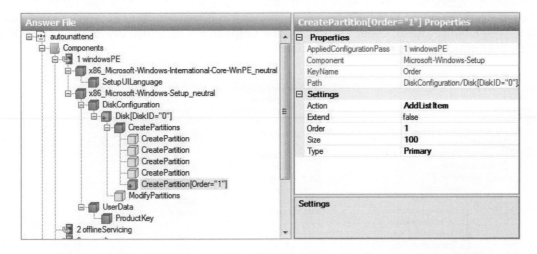

Notice that the newly configured partition moves to the bottom of the five **CreatePartition** objects.

Select the top **CreatePartition** in the "Answer File" area. In the "CreatePartition Properties" area, set the following values: Extend = **false**, Order = **2**, and Type = **Primary**. For Size, use the primary partition size provided by the instructor. For example: Size = **16000**.

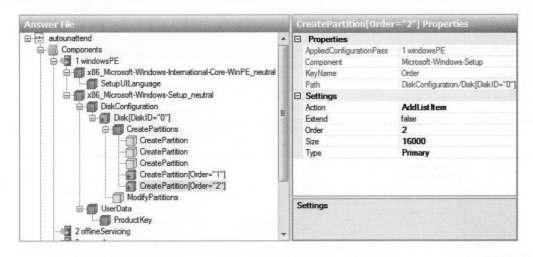

Select the top **CreatePartition** in the "Answer File" area. In the "CreatePartition Properties" area, set the following values: Extend = **True**, Order = **3**, and Type = **Extended**.

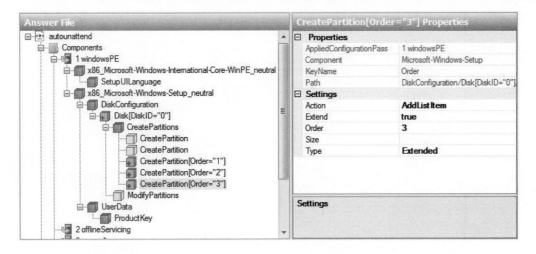

Select the top **CreatePartition** in the "Answer File" area. In the "CreatePartition Properties" area, set the following values: Extend = **false**, Order = **4**, and Type = **Logical**. For Size, use the logical 1 partition size provided by the instructor. For example: Size = **5000**.

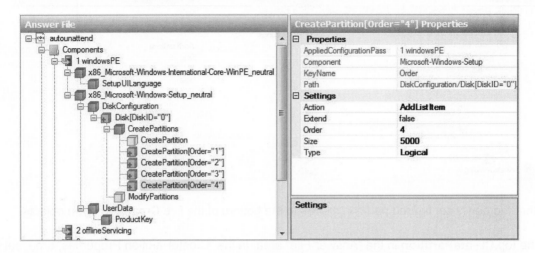

Select the top **CreatePartition** in the "Answer File" area. In the "CreatePartition Properties" area, set the following values: Extend = **false**, Order = **5**, and Type = **Logical**. For Size, use the logical 2 partition size provided by the instructor. For example: Size = **5000**.

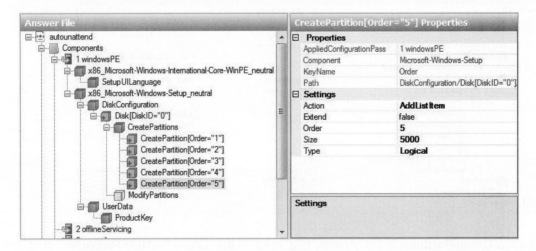

In the "Answer File" area, right-click **ModifyPartitions > Insert New ModifyPartition**.

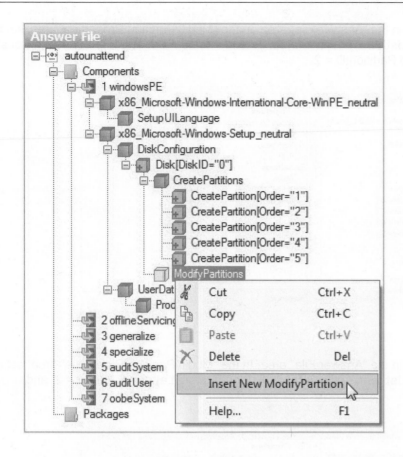

Add three more **ModifyPartition** objects, for a total of four objects.

Select the top **ModifyPartition** in the "Answer File" area. In the "ModifyPartition Properties" area, set the following values: Action = **AddListItem**, Active = **true**, Extend = **false**, Format = **NTFS**, Label = **System Reserved**, Letter = leave this blank, Order = **1**, PartitionID = **1**, and TypeID = **0x27**.

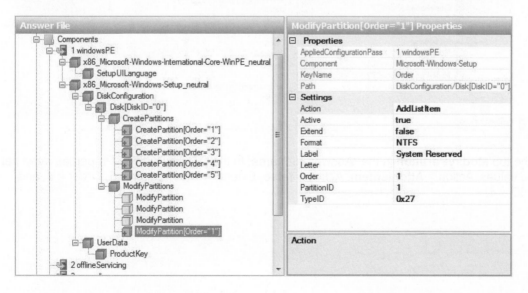

Select the top **ModifyPartition** in the "Answer File" area. In the "ModifyPartition Properties" area, set the following values: Action = **AddListItem**, Active = **false**, Extend = **false**, Format = **NTFS**, Label = **Local Disk**, Letter = **C**, Order = **2**, and PartitionID = **2**.

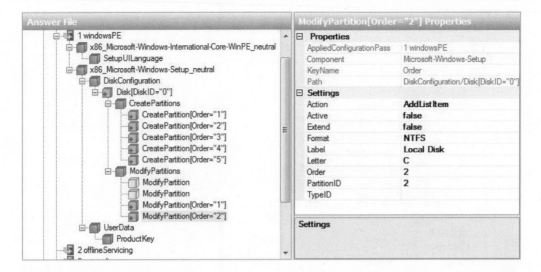

Select the top **ModifyPartition** in the "Answer File" area. In the "ModifyPartition Properties" area, set the following values: Action = **AddListItem**, Active = **false**, Extend = **false**, Letter = **E**, Order = **3**, and PartitionID = **3**.

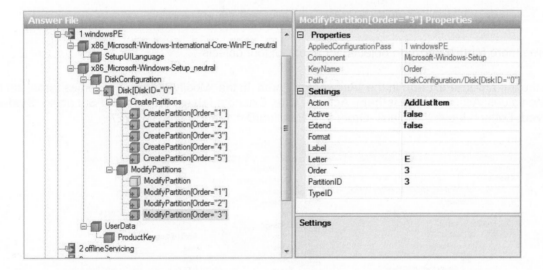

Select the top **ModifyPartition** in the "Answer File" area. In the "ModifyPartition Properties" area set the following values: Action = **AddListItem**, Active = **false**, Extend = **false**, Letter = **F**, Order = **4**, and PartitionID = **4**.

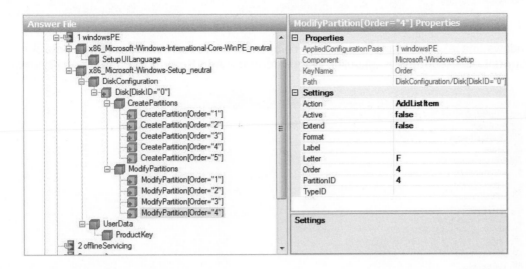

In the "Windows Image" area, locate and expand component **Microsoft-Windows-Setup\DiskConfigu-ration\ImageInstall\OSImage\InstallTo >** right-click **InstallTo > Add Setting to Pass 1 windowsPE**.

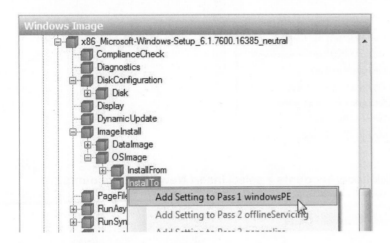

Select **InstallTo** in the "Answer File" area. In the "InstallTo Properties" area, set the following values: DiskID = **0** and PartitionID = **2**.

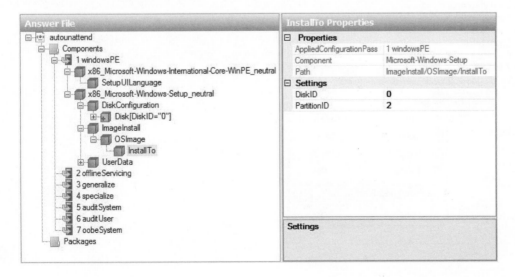

Step 9

In the "Windows Image" area, locate and expand component **Microsoft-Windows-Shell-Setup\ UserAccounts\LocalAccounts >** right-click **LocalAccount > Add Setting to Pass 7 oobeSystem**.

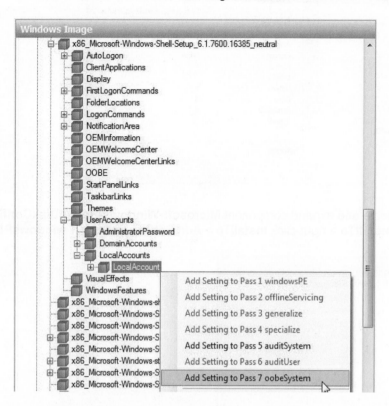

In the "Answer File" area, right-click **LocalAccounts >** select **Insert New LocalAccounts**.

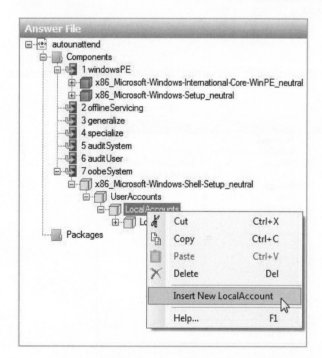

You should now have two **LocalAccounts** objects.

Set up an Administrators account.

Select the top **LocalAccount** in the "Answer File" area. In the "LocalAccount Properties" area, type the **DisplayName** and the **Name** provided by your instructor. Example: **Vicki** and **Vicki M**.

Type **Administrators** as the name of the Group.

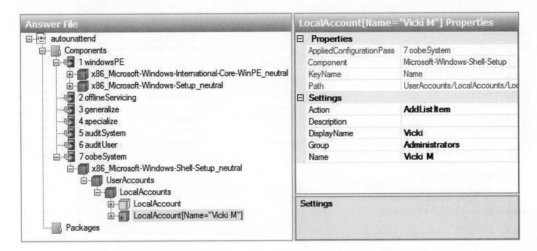

Expand **LocalAccount[Name="Vicki M"] > Password**. In the "Password Properties" area, type the **password** provided by your instructor in the Value setting. Example: **Pa$$w0rd**.

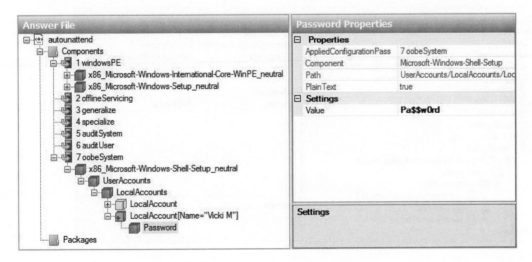

Set up a User account.

Select the top **LocalAccount** in the "Answer File" area. In the "LocalAccount Properties" area, type the **DisplayName** and the **Name** provided by your instructor. Example: **John** and **John M**.

Type **Users** as the name of the Group.

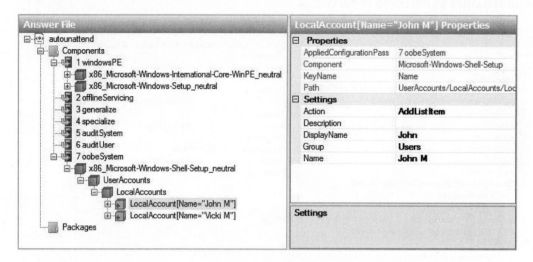

Expand **LocalAccount[Name="John M"] > Password**. In the "Password Properties" area, type the **password** provided by your instructor in the Value setting. Example: **Pa$$w0rd**.

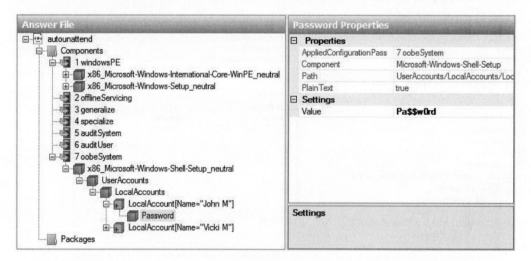

Step 10

In the "Windows Image" area, locate **Microsoft-Windows-Shell-Setup >** and right-click **Themes > Add Setting to Pass 4 specialize**.

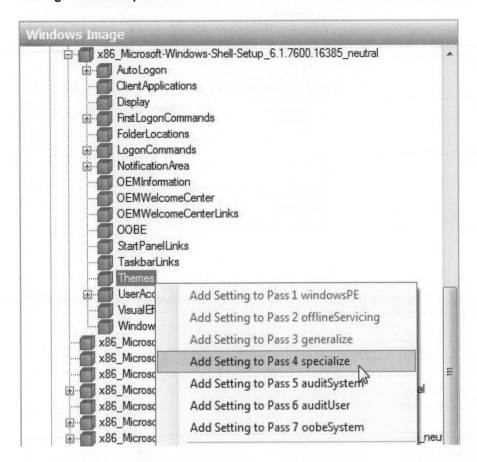

Select **Microsoft-Windows-Shell-Setup** in the "Answer File" area below **component 4 specialize**. In the "Microsoft-Windows-Shell-Setup Properties" area, type the ComputerName, RegisteredOrganization, and RegisteredOwner provided by your instructor. Example: **Computer1**, **Cisco**, and **Vicki**.

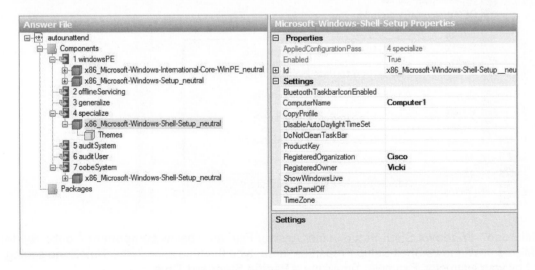

Expand **Microsoft-Windows-Shell-Setup** in **component 4 specialize** of the "Answer File" area. Locate and select **Themes**. In the "Themes Properties" area, set the following value: DefaultThemesOff = **false**.

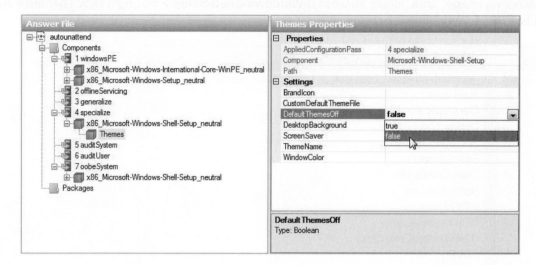

Step 11

In the "Windows Image" area, locate and expand component **Microsoft-Windows-Shell-Setup** > right-click **OOBE > Add Setting to Pass 7 oobeSystem**.

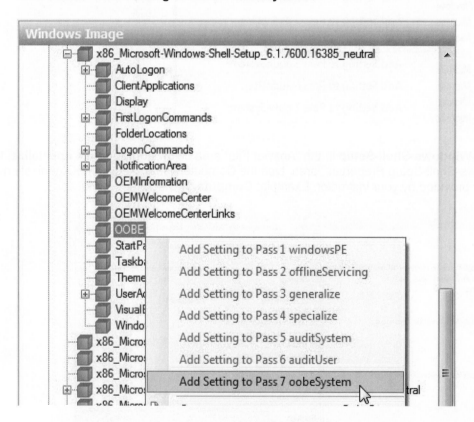

Select **Microsoft-Windows-Shell-Setup** in the "Answer File" area below **component 7 oobe System**. In the "Microsoft-Windows-Shell-Setup Properties" area, type the time zone in the **TimeZone** setting, provided by your instructor. Example: TimeZone = **Pacific Standard Time**.

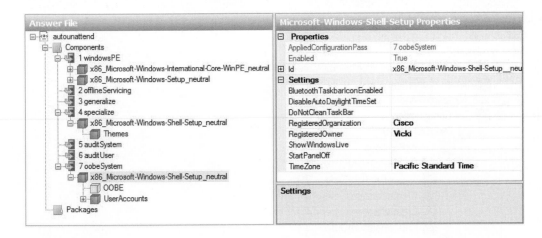

Select **OOBE** in the "Answer File" area. In the "OOBE Properties" area, set the following value: Network-Location = **Work** and ProtectYourPC = **3**. This will disable automatically installed updates.

Note: Normally you would set ProtectYourPC to 1, automatically install updates. But to reduce the installation time for this lab, we will set the value to 3.

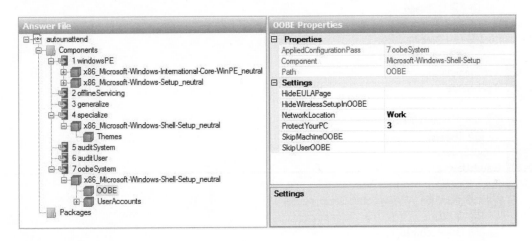

Step 12

Before validating the answer file, expand all components in the **autounattend** file to make sure everything is properly added.

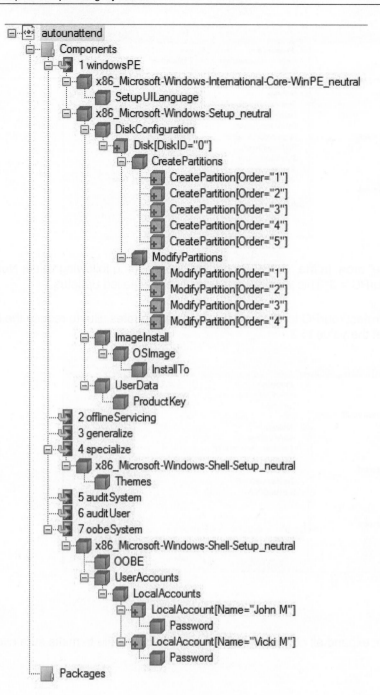

If anything is missing, go back over the lab and add the missing components or settings.

Click **Tools > Validate Answer File**.

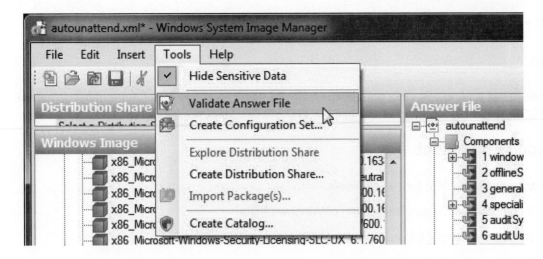

Select the **Validation** tab in the "Messages" area.

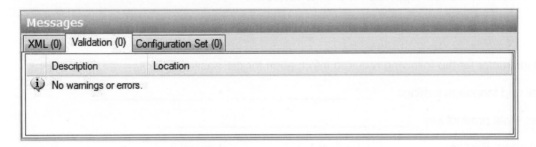

If you see any error or warning messages, ask your instructor for assistance in correcting them before proceeding with the lab.

If there are no error or warning messages, click **File > Save Answer File**.

Step 13

Copy the **autounattend.xml** file from **C:\Windows_7_Installation** to the root of the floppy disk or USB flash drive.

Insert the floppy disk in the floppy drive or connect the USB flash drive to a USB port.

Insert the Windows 7 media in the appropriate drive.

Restart the computer.

Step 14

When the **Press Any Key to Boot from CD or DVD** message appears, press any key on the keyboard.

The installation of Windows 7 will proceed in a completely unattended fashion, and finally you will be presented with the logon screen.
Note: The system will flash on and off several times, restart several times, and other times only a black or blue screen will appear with nothing else shown during the installation.
Logon to the computer using the administrator name and password used in the **autounattend** file.
What was the name of the file used to automate the installation located on the floppy disk or USB flash drive?

How do you think automating the installation will help the IT Department if they have to repeat the procedure on 100 computers?

5.2.2.4 Lab - Advanced Installation of Windows Vista

Introduction

In this lab, you will install a Windows Vista operating system by using an answer file for automation. You will customize partition settings and create an Administrator account and User accounts.

Recommended Equipment

The following equipment is required for this exercise:

- A computer with a new installation of Windows Vista
- Windows Automated Installation Kit (AIK) installation media
- Windows Vista installation media
- A blank, formatted floppy disk or a USB flash drive

Step 1

Ask the instructor for the following required information for the answer file:

Regional and language settings _____

Windows Vista product key _____

Partition sizes: Primary _____ Logical 1 _____ Logical 2 _____

Administrator account: User name _____

Password _____

User account: User name _____

Password _____

Computer name _____

Registered organization _____

Registered owner _____

Time zone _____

Step 2

Log on to the computer as Administrator.

Insert the Windows Automated Installation Kit (AIK) DVD in the DVD-ROM drive.

When the "AutoPlay" window opens, click **Run StartCD.exe**.

The "Welcome to Windows Automated Installation Kit" window opens.

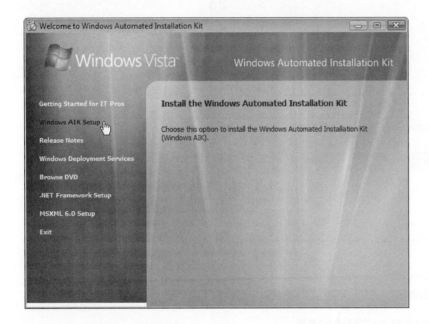

Click **Windows AIK Setup**.

When the "Setup Wizard" opens, click **Next**.

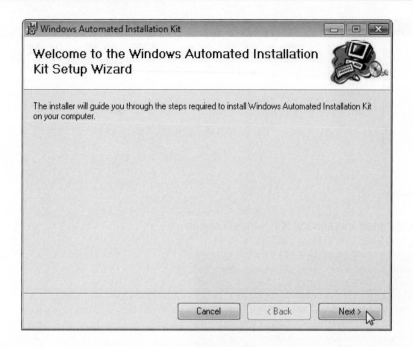

Select **I Agree** to license terms and then click **Next**.

For the "Select Installation Folder" screen, keep the default settings and click **Next**.

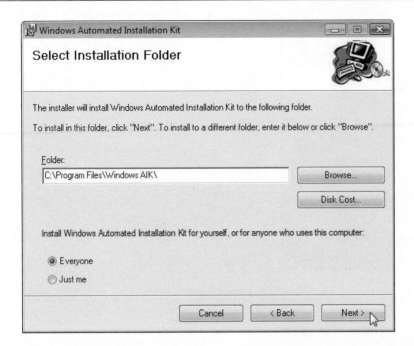

Click **Next** to confirm and start the installation.

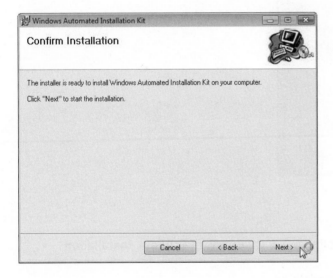

When the "Installation Complete" screen appears, click **Close**.

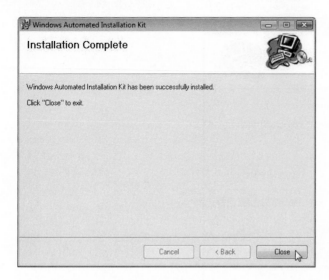

Click **Exit**.

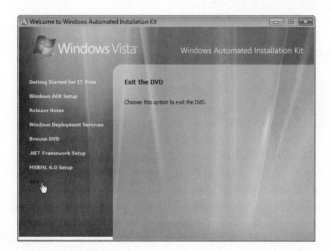

Step 3

Create a folder called **Vista_Installation** at the root of C:. Example: **C:\Vista_Installation**.

Insert the Windows Vista media in the appropriate drive.

Close the "Install Windows" window if it opens.

Navigate and copy **install.wim** from the Windows Vista installation media to C:\Vista_Installation.

Note: The install.wim file is 2.6GB and may take several minutes to copy.

Step 4

Start > All Programs > Microsoft Windows AIK > Windows System Image Manager.

Step 5

The "Windows System Image Manager" window opens.

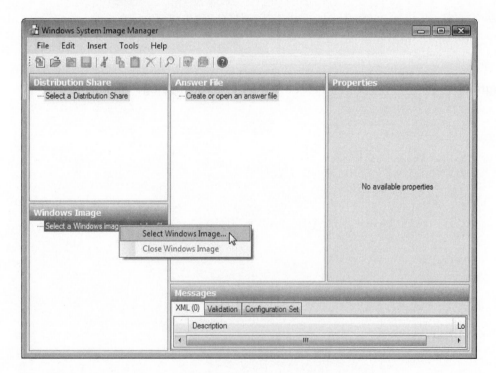

Right-click **Select a windows image > Select Windows Image**.

Browse to **C:\Vista_Installation > install.wim > Open**.

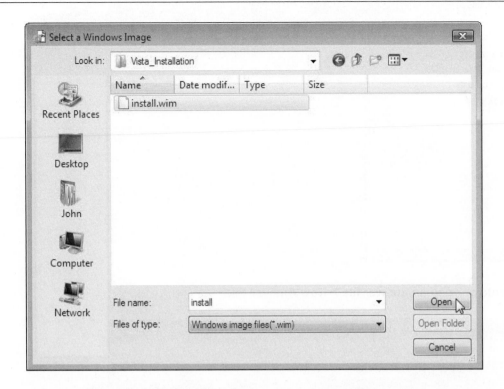

Select **Windows Vista BUSINESS > OK**.

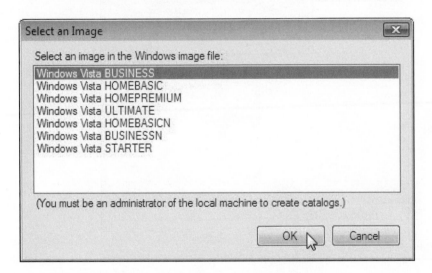

Click **Yes > Continue**. This may take several minutes.

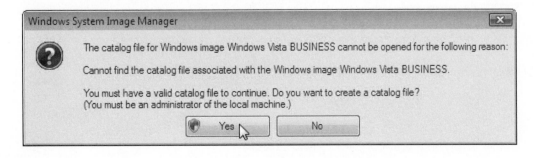

A catalog file is generated in the "Windows Image" area.

Right-click **Create or open an answer file > New Answer File**.

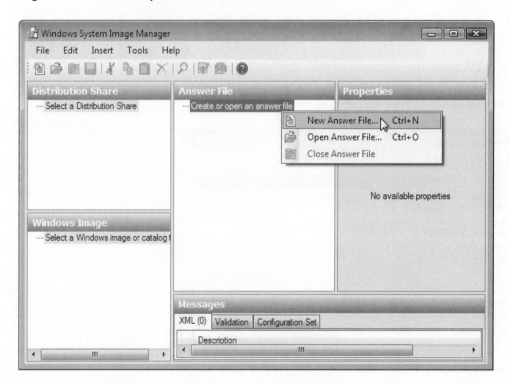

A new answer file is created in the "Answer File" area.

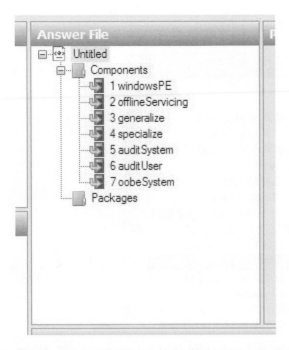

To name the file, select the root node **Untitled**.

Click **File > Save Answer File >** name the file **autounattend**. Make sure the **Vista_Installation** folder is selected and then click **Save**.

Note: It is important to name the file **autounattend** as Vista will only search for that file name when performing an unattended installation.

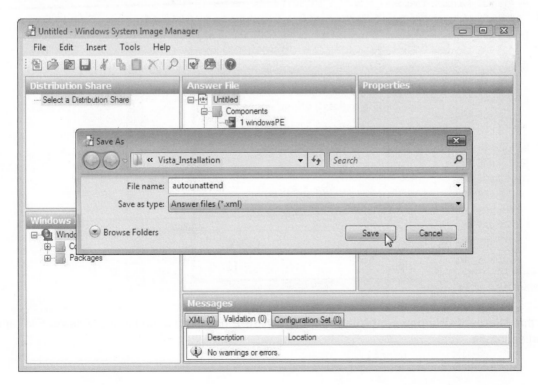

Step 6

In the "Windows Image" area, expand **Components**.

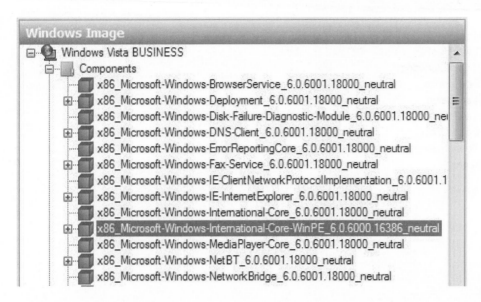

Note: The name of the components will have a prefix and suffix attached, for example: **x86_Microsoft-Windows-International-Core-WinPE_6.0.6000.16386_neutral**. The prefix is **x86** and the suffix is **6.0.6000.16386_neutral**. For simplicity, the prefix and suffix will be left out in the lab instructions.

Right-click **Microsoft-Windows-International-Core-WinPE > Add Settings to Pass 1 windowsPE**.

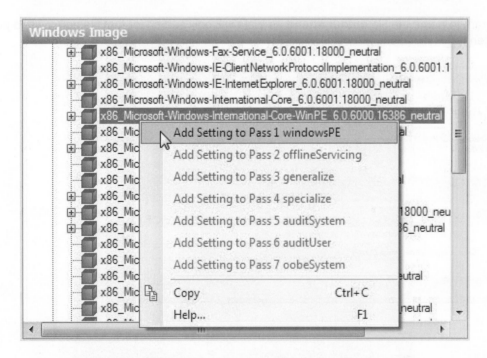

Notice that **Microsoft-Windows-International-Core-WinPE** has been added to the "Answer File" and "Properties" areas.

Select **Microsoft-Windows-International-Core-WinPE** in the "Answer File" area. In the "Microsoft-Windows-International-Core-WinPE Properties" area, type the language settings provided by your instructor in the following locations: InputLocale, SystemLocale, UILanguage, UILanguageFallback, and UserLocale. For example: **en-us**.

Note: Place the curser next to a setting in the "Properties" area and press the **F1** key to view the Windows Help file for the setting. Supported regional and language settings are located here: http://technet.microsoft.com/en-us/library/cc722435(WS.10).aspx.

In the "Answer File" area, expand **Microsoft-Windows-International-Core-WinPE >** select **SetupUILanguage**. In the "SetupUILanguage Properties" area, type the language settings provided by your instructor in the UILanguage location. For example: **en-us**.

Confirm **OnError** is selected for **WillShowUI**.

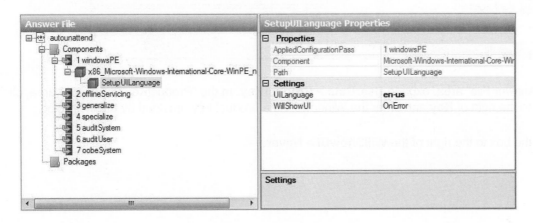

Step 7

In the "Windows Image" area, locate and expand the component **Microsoft-Windows-Setup >** right-click **UserData > Add Setting to Pass 1 windowsPE**.

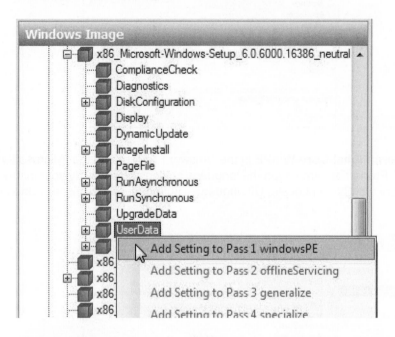

Select **UserData** in the "Answer File" area. In the "UserData Properties" area, click in the box to the right of **AcceptEula > true**.

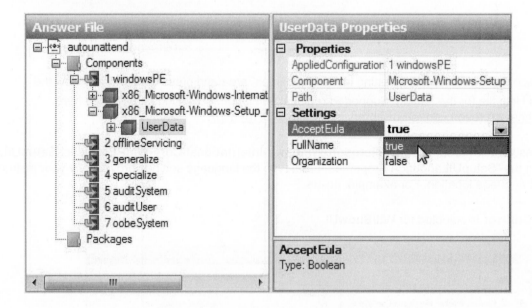

In the "Answer File" area, expand **UserData > ProductKey**. In the "ProductKey Properties" area, click in the box to the right of **Key** and enter the Windows Vista product key provided by the instructor.

Click in the box to the right of the **WillShowUI > Never**.

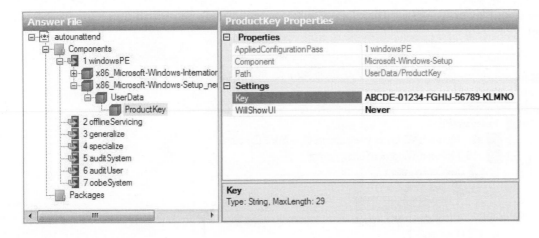

Step 8

In the "Windows Image" area, locate and expand component **Microsoft-Windows-Setup\ DiskConfiguration >** right-click **Disk > Add Setting to Pass 1 windowsPE**.

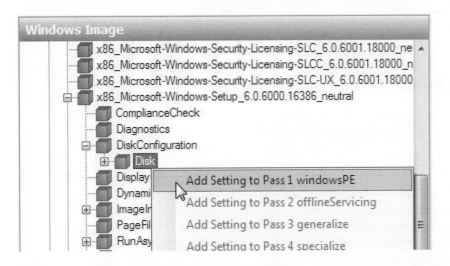

Select **Disk** in the "Answer File" area. In the "Disk Properties" area, click in the box to the right of **DiskID** and type the number **0**. Set **WillWipeDisk** to **true**.

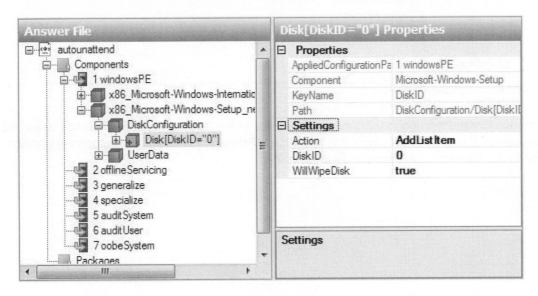

In the "Answer File" area, expand **Disk[DiskID="0"] >** right-click **CreatePartitions > Insert New Create-Partition**.

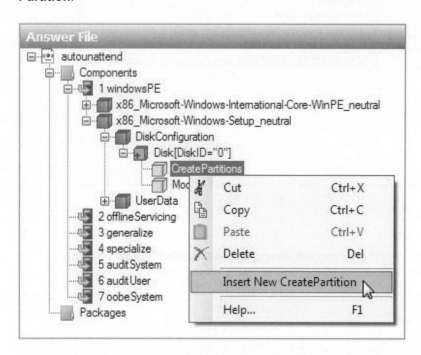

Add three more **CreatePartition** objects, for a total of four objects.

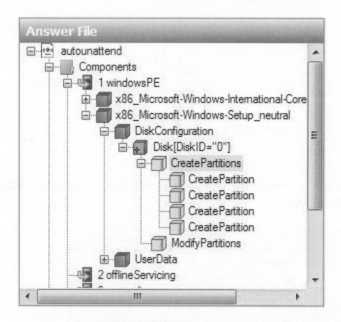

Select the top **CreatePartition** in the "Answer File" area. In the "CreatePartition Properties" area, set the following values: Extend = **false**, Order = **1**, and Type = **Primary**. For Size, use the primary partition size provided by the instructor. For example: Size = **15000**.

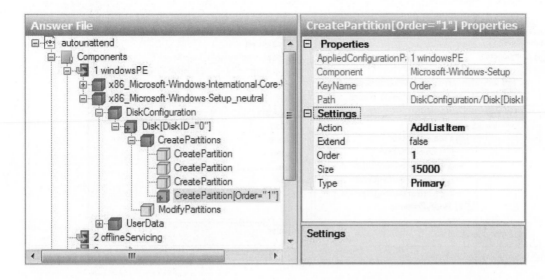

Notice that the newly configured partition moves to the bottom of the four **CreatePartition** objects.

Select the top **CreatePartition** in the "Answer File" area. In the "CreatePartition Properties" area, set the following values: Extend = **True**, Order = **2**, and Type = **Extended**.

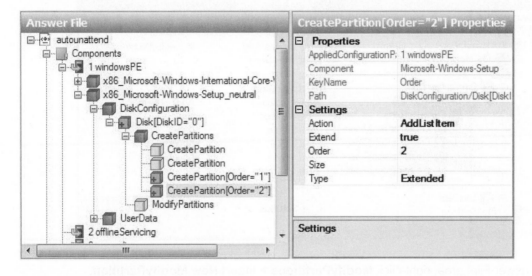

Select the top **CreatePartition** in the "Answer File" area. In the "CreatePartition Properties" area, set the following values: Extend = **false**, Order = **3**, and Type = **Logical**. For Size, use the logical 1 partition size provided by the instructor. For example: Size = **5000**.

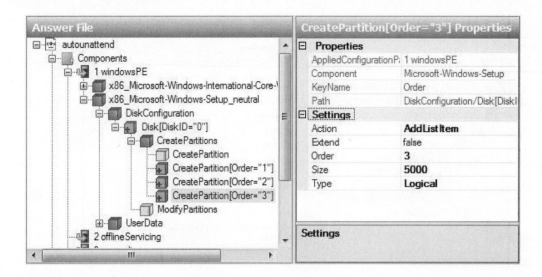

Select the top **CreatePartition** in the "Answer File" area. In the "CreatePartition Properties" area, set the following values: Extend = **false**, Order = **4**, and Type = **Logical**. For Size, use the logical 2 partition size provided by the instructor. For example: Size = **5000**.

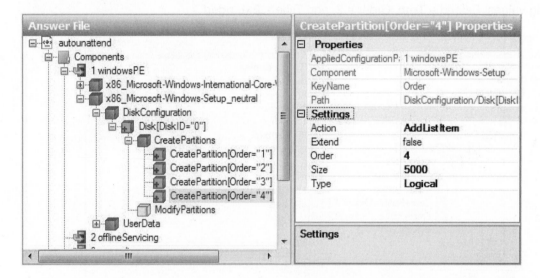

In the "Answer File" area, right-click **ModifyPartitions > Insert New ModifyPartition**.

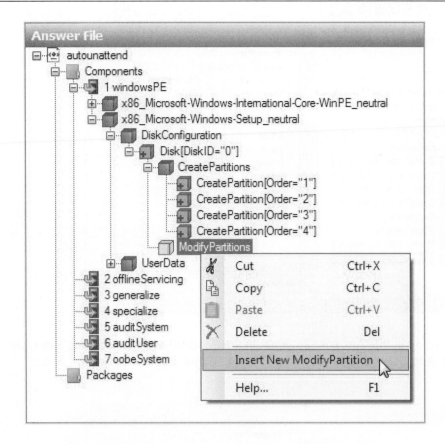

Add two more **ModifyPartition** objects, for a total of three objects.

Select the top **ModifyPartition** in the "Answer File" area. In the "ModifyPartition Properties" area, set the following values: Action = **AddListItem**, Active = **true**, Extend = **false**, Format = **NTFS**, Label = **Vista_Business**, Letter = **C**, Order = **1**, and PartitionID = **1**.

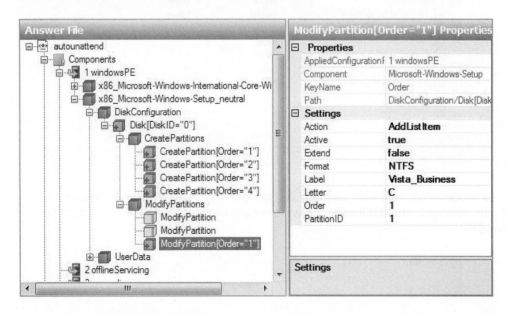

Select the top **ModifyPartition** in the "Answer File" area. In the "ModifyPartition Properties" area, set the following values: Action = **AddListItem**, Active = **false**, Extend = **false**, Letter = **E**, Order = **2**, and PartitionID = **2**.

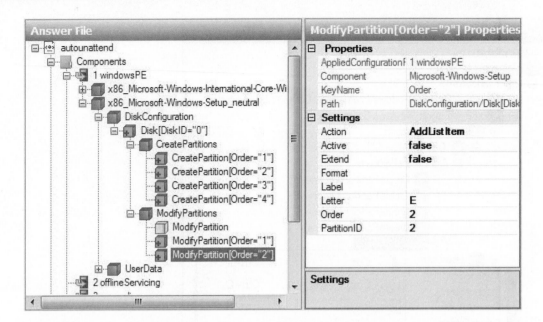

Select the top **ModifyPartition** in the "Answer File" area. In the "ModifyPartition Properties" area, set the following values: Action = **AddListItem**, Active = **false**, Extend = **false**, Letter = **F**, Order = **3**, and PartitionID = **3**.

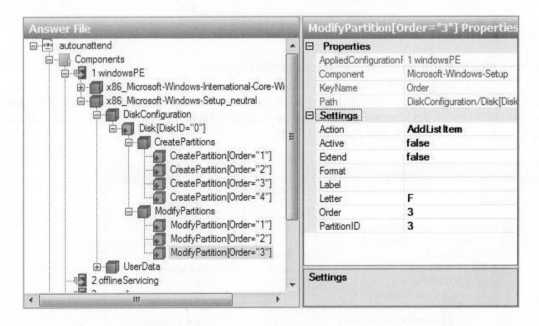

In the "Windows Image" area, locate and expand component **Microsoft-Windows-Setup\ DiskConfiguration\ImageInstall\OSImage\InstallTo** > right-click **InstallTo** > **Add Setting to Pass 1 windowsPE**.

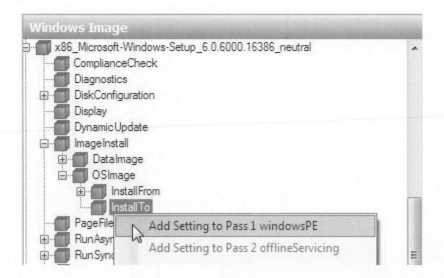

Select **InstallTo** in the "Answer File" area. In the "InstallTo Properties" area, set the following values: DiskID = **0** and PartitionID = **1**.

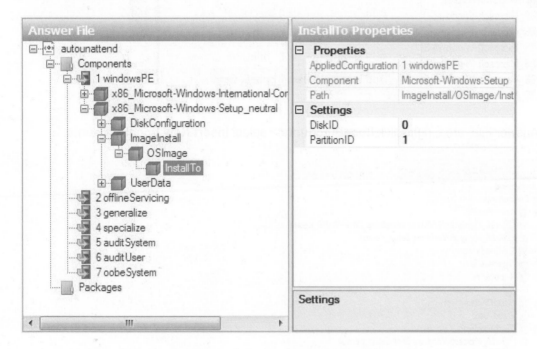

Step 9

In the "Windows Image" area, locate and expand component **Microsoft-Windows-Shell-Setup\ UserAccounts\LocalAccounts >** right-click **LocalAccount > Add Setting to Pass 7 oobeSystem**.

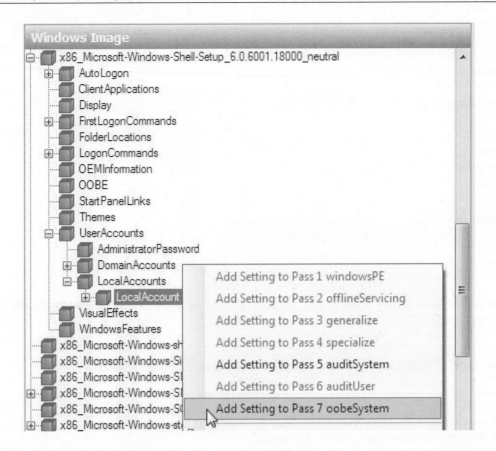

In the "Answer File" area, right-click **LocalAccounts >** select **Insert New LocalAccounts**.

You should now have two **LocalAccounts** objects.

Setup an Administrators account.

Select the top **LocalAccount** in the "Answer File" area. In the "LocalAccount Properties" area, type the **DisplayName** and the **Name** provided by your instructor. Example: **John** and **John M**.

Type **Administrators** for the Group.

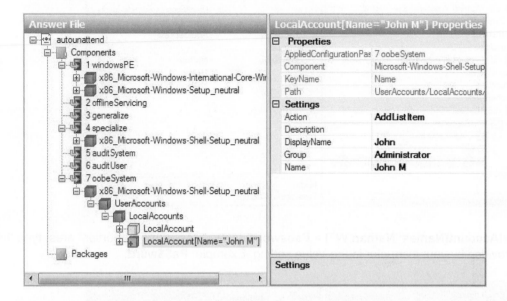

Expand **LocalAccount[Name="John M"] > Password**. In the "Password Properties" area, type the **password** provided by your instructor in the Value setting. Example: **Pa$$w0rd**.

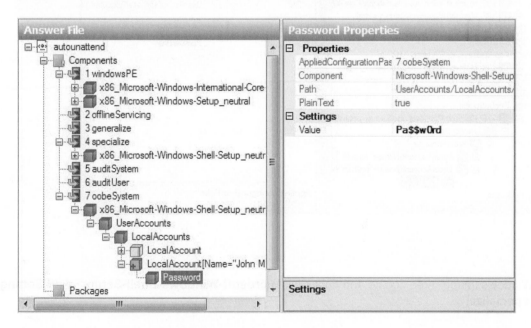

Set up a User account.

Select the top **LocalAccount** in the "Answer File" area. In the "LocalAccount Properties" area, type the **DisplayName** and the **Name** provided by your instructor. Example: **Nathan** and **Nathan W**.

Type **Users** for the Group.

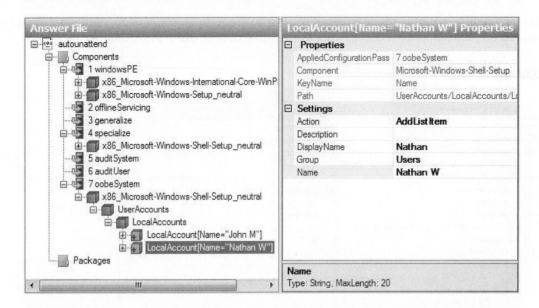

Expand **LocalAccount[Name="Nathan W"] > Password**. In the "Password Properties" area, type the **password** provided by your instructor in the Value setting. Example: **Pa$$w0rd**.

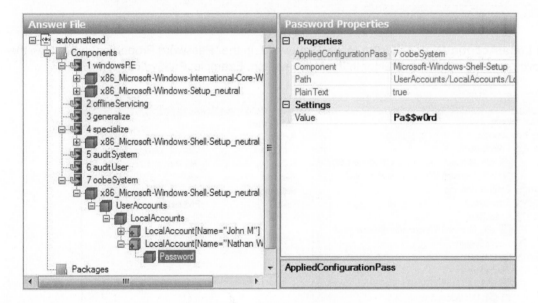

Step 10

In the "Windows Image" area, locate and right-click **Microsoft-Windows-Shell-Setup > Add Setting to Pass 4 specialize**.

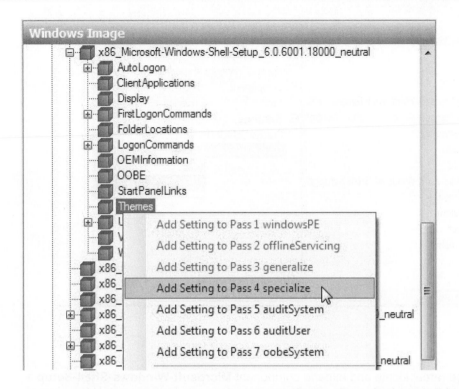

Select **Microsoft-Windows-Shell-Setup** in the "Answer File" area below **component 4 specialize**. In the "Microsoft-Windows-Shell-Setup Properties" area, type the ComputerName, RegisteredOrganization, and RegisteredOwner provided by your instructor. Example: **Computer1, Cisco**, and **John**.

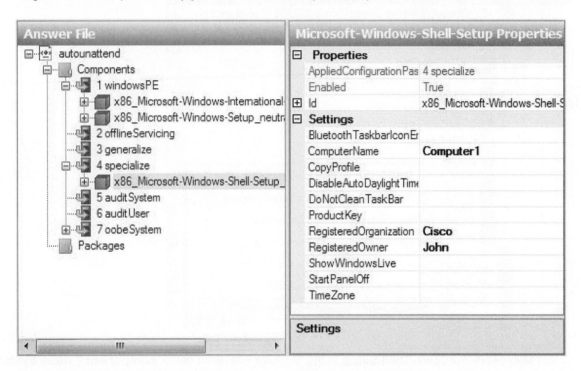

Expand **Microsoft-Windows-Shell-Setup** in **component 4 specialize** of the "Answer File" area. Locate and select **Themes**. In the "Themes Properties" area, set the following value: DefaultThemesOff = **false**.

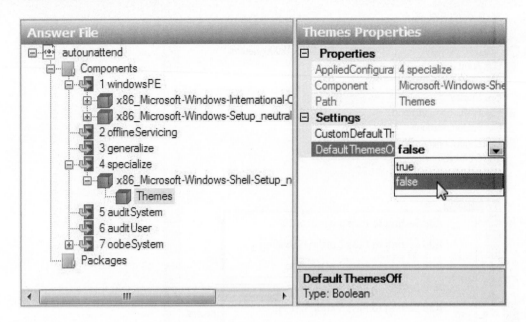

Step 11

In the "Windows Image" area, locate and expand component **Microsoft-Windows-Shell-Setup >** right-click **OOBE > Add Setting to Pass 7 oobeSystem**.

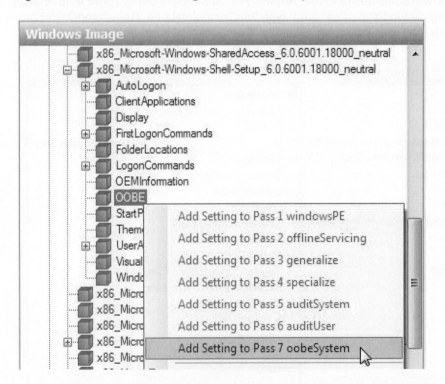

Select **Microsoft-Windows-Shell-Setup** in the "Answer File" area below **component 7 oobe System**. In the "Microsoft-Windows-Shell-Setup Properties" area, type the time zone in the **TimeZone** setting, provided by your instructor. Example: TimeZone = **Pacific Standard Time**.

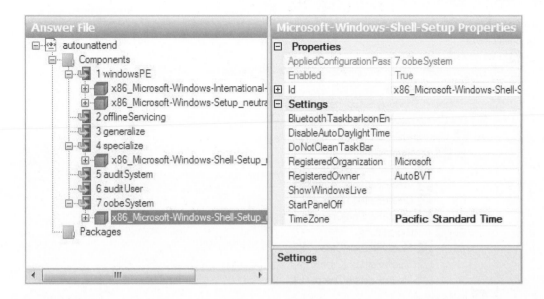

Select **OOBE** in the "Answer File" area. In the "OOBE Properties" area, set the following value: NetworkLocation = **Work** and ProtectYourPC = **3**. This will disable automatically installed updates.

Note: Normally you would set ProtectYourPC to 1, automatically install updates. But to reduce the installation time for this lab, we will set the value to 3.

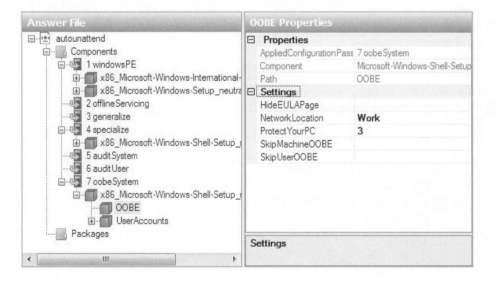

Step 12

Before validating the answer file, expand all components in the **autounattend** file to make sure everything is properly added.

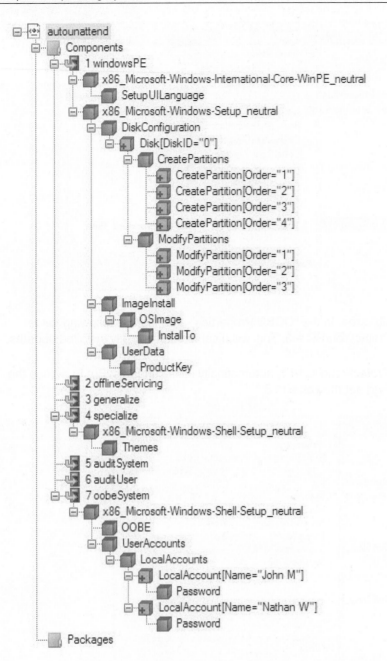

If anything is missing, go back over the lab and add the missing components or settings.

Click **Tools > Validate Answer File**.

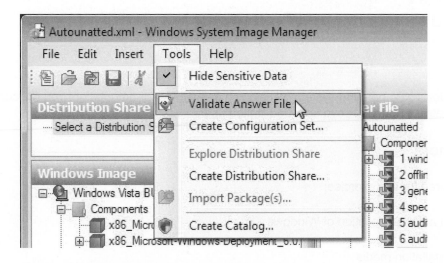

Select the **Validation** tab in the "Messages" area.

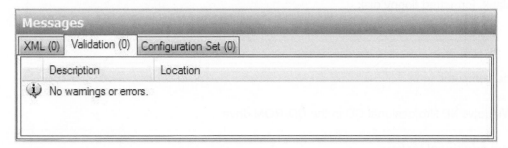

If you see any error or warning messages, ask your instructor for assistance in correcting them before proceeding with the lab.

If there are no error or warning messages, click **File > Save Answer File**.

Step 13

Copy the autounattend.xml file from **C:\Vista_Installation** to the root of the floppy disk or USB flash drive.

Insert the floppy disk in the floppy drive or connect the USB flash drive to a USB port.

Insert the Windows Vista media in the appropriate drive.

Restart the computer.

Step 14

When the **Press Any Key to Boot from CD or DVD** message appears, press any key on the keyboard.

The installation of Windows Vista will proceed in a completely unattended fashion, then Vista will run a performance check, and finally you will be presented with the logon screen.

Note: The system will flash on and off several times, restart several times, and other times only a black or blue screen will appear with nothing else shown during the installation.

Logon to the computer using the administrator name and password used in the **autounattend** file.

What was the name of the file used to automate the installation located on the floppy disk or USB flash drive?

How do you think automating the installation will help the IT Department if they have to repeat the procedure on 100 computers?

5.2.2.5 Lab - Advanced Installation of Windows XP

Introduction

In this lab, you will install a Windows XP operating system by using an answer file for automation. You will customize partition settings and create an administrative user and limited user.

Recommended Equipment

The following equipment is required for this exercise:

- A computer with a new installation of Windows XP

- Windows XP installation media

- A blank, formatted floppy disk

Step 1

Log on to the computer.

Insert the Windows XP Professional CD in the CD-ROM drive.

Click **Perform additional tasks**.

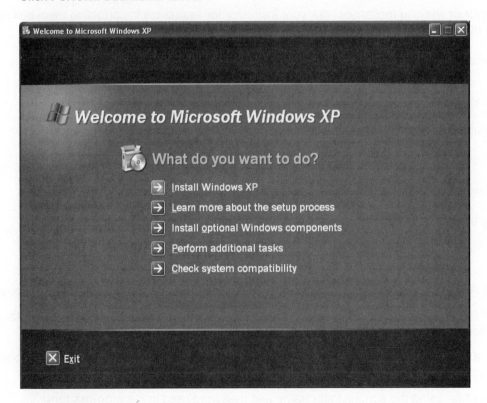

Step 2

Click **Browse this CD**.

Double-click the **Support** folder.

Double-click the **Tools** folder.

Double-click **Deploy.CAB**.

Highlight all of the files by clicking **Edit > Select All**.

Right-click **setupmgr.exe** and then click **Extract**.

Click **Make New Folder** to create a folder on the C: drive.

Name the folder "Deploy".

Click **Extract** to extract the files from the CD to C:\Deploy.

Browse to C:\Deploy.

Step 3

Double-click **setupmgr.exe**.

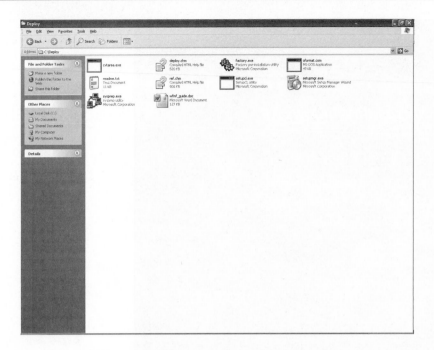

Step 4

The "Setup Manager" window opens.

Click **Next**.

The **Create new** button should be checked by default.

Click **Next**.

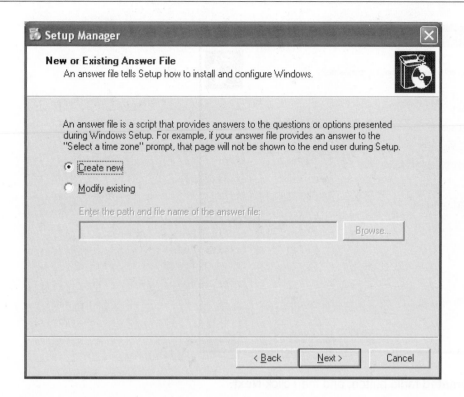

Select the **Unattended setup** radio button.

Note that a CD-based answer file name must be Winnt.sif.

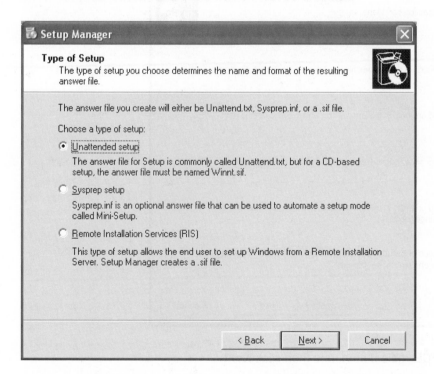

Select the **Windows XP Professional** radio button, and then click **Next**.

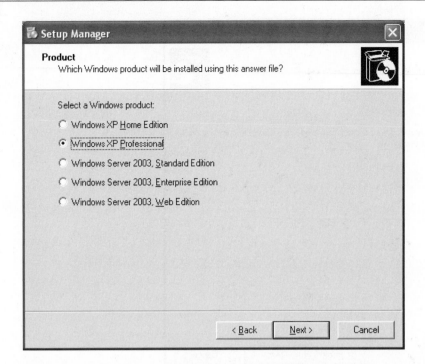

Select the **Fully automated** radio button, and then click **Next**.

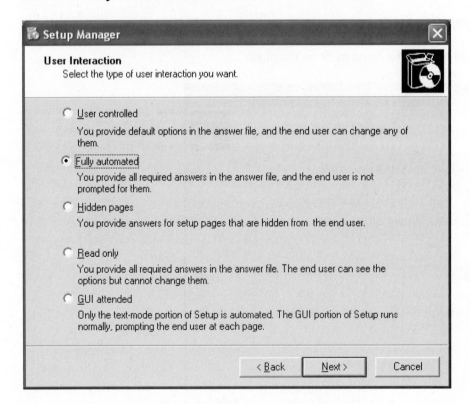

Select the **Set up from a CD** radio button, and then click **Next**.

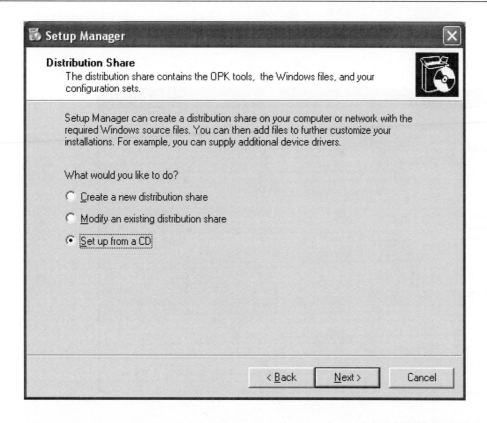

Click the **I accept the terms of the License Agreement** checkbox, and then click **Next**.

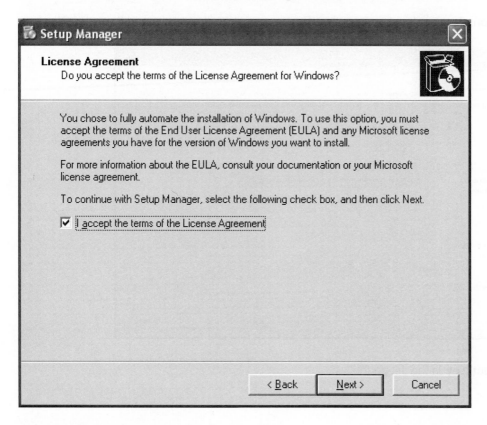

Click **Name and Organization** in the list on the left.

Type the name and the organization name provided by your instructor.

Click **Next**.

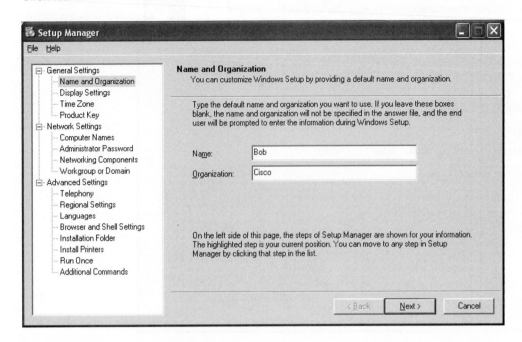

Click **Time Zone** in the list on the left.

Click the time zone for your location from the "Time zone:" drop-down box, and then click **Next**.

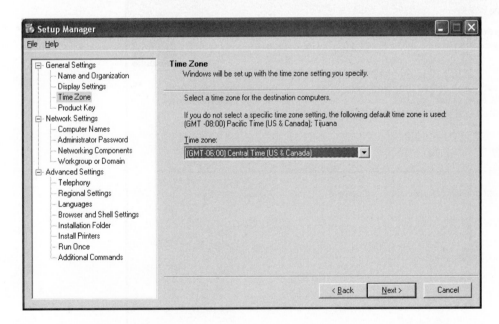

Highlight **Product Key** in the list on the left.

Type the Windows XP Professional product key supplied by your instructor in the "Product Key:" fields.

Click **Next**.

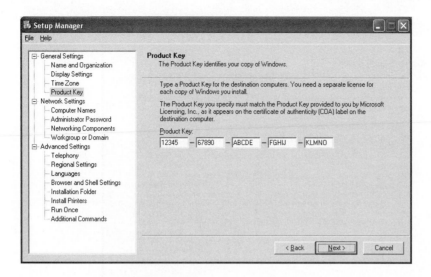

Click **Computer Names** in the list on the left.

Type the computer name provided by your instructor in the "Computer name:" field, and then click **Add**.

The computer name will then display in the "Computers to be installed:" field.

Click **Next**.

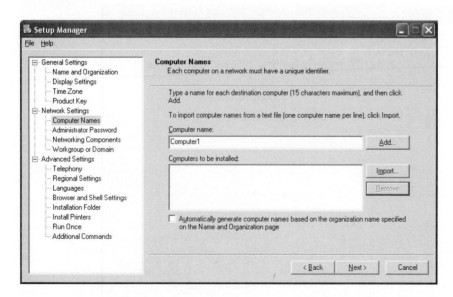

Click **Administrative Password** in the list on the left.

Type your first initial of your first name and your complete last name in the "Password:" and "Confirm password:" fields (for example, jsmith).

Click **Next**.

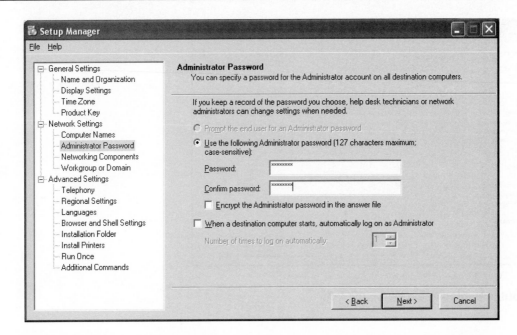

Click **Workgroup or Domain** in the list on the left.

Select the **Workgroup** radio button.

Type the Workgroup name **LabGroup1** in the "Workgroup:" field, and then click **Next**.

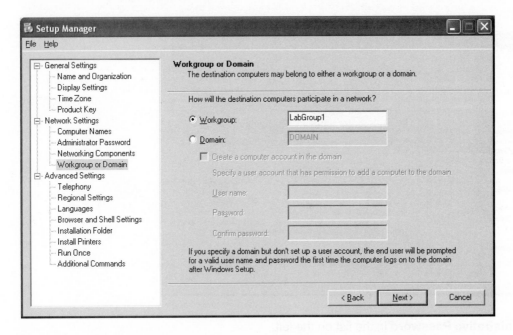

Click **Additional Commands** in the list on the left, and then click **Finish**.

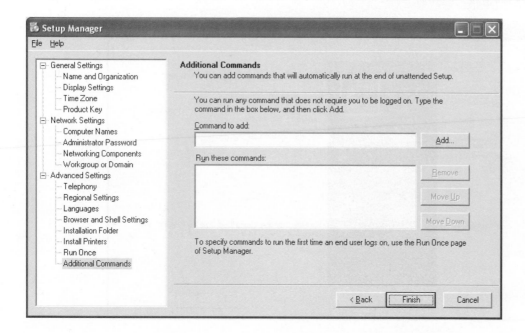

Type "C:\Deploy\unattend.txt" in the "Path and file name:" field if it is not already displayed.

Click **OK**.

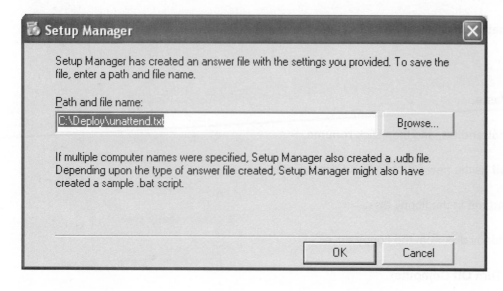

Click **File > Exit**.

Step 5

Browse to "C:\Deploy".

Right-click **unattend.txt**, and then click **copy**.

Browse to "A:\".

Click **File > Paste**.

Right-click **unattend.txt**, and then click **rename**.

Type **Winnt.sif** as the new file name, and press **Enter**.

Copy **unattend.bat** to the floppy disk.

Remove the floppy disk from the floppy drive.

Click **Start > Turn Off Computer**.

Click **Restart**.

Step 6

When the "Press Any Key to Boot from CD" message appears, press any key on the keyboard. Insert the floppy disk. The system will inspect the hardware configuration.

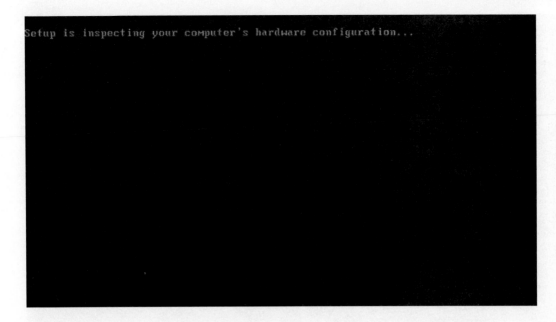

The "Windows Setup" screen appears while the program loads the necessary files.

Step 7

The "Welcome to Setup" screen appears. Press **Enter**.

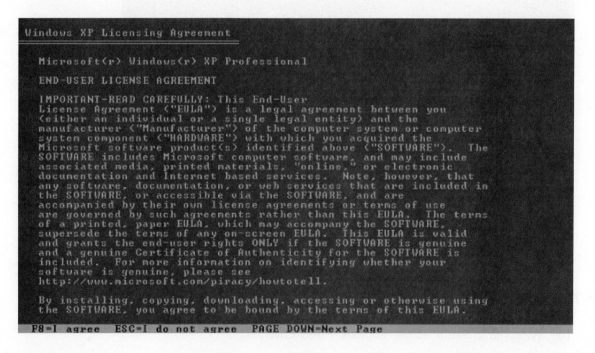

```
Windows XP Professional Setup

  Welcome to Setup.

  This portion of the Setup program prepares Microsoft(R)
  Windows(R) XP to run on your computer.

      •  To set up Windows XP now, press ENTER.

      •  To repair a Windows XP installation using
         Recovery Console, press R.

      •  To quit Setup without installing Windows XP, press F3.




  ENTER=Continue    R=Repair    F3=Quit
```

The "Windows XP Licensing Agreement" screen appears.

Press **F8**.

```
Windows XP Licensing Agreement

  Microsoft(r) Windows(r) XP Professional

  END-USER LICENSE AGREEMENT

  IMPORTANT-READ CAREFULLY: This End-User
  License Agreement ("EULA") is a legal agreement between you
  (either an individual or a single legal entity) and the
  manufacturer ("Manufacturer") of the computer system or computer
  system component ("HARDWARE") with which you acquired the
  Microsoft software product(s) identified above ("SOFTWARE").  The
  SOFTWARE includes Microsoft computer software, and may include
  associated media, printed materials, "online," or electronic
  documentation and Internet based services.  Note, however, that
  any software, documentation, or web services that are included in
  the SOFTWARE, or accessible via the SOFTWARE, and are
  accompanied by their own license agreements or terms of use
  are governed by such agreements rather than this EULA.  The terms
  of a printed, paper EULA, which may accompany the SOFTWARE,
  supersede the terms of any on-screen EULA.  This EULA is valid
  and grants the end-user rights ONLY if the SOFTWARE is genuine
  and a genuine Certificate of Authenticity for the SOFTWARE is
  included.  For more information on identifying whether your
  software is genuine, please see
  http://www.microsoft.com/piracy/howtotell.

  By installing, copying, downloading, accessing or otherwise using
  the SOFTWARE, you agree to be bound by the terms of this EULA.

  F8=I agree   ESC=I do not agree   PAGE DOWN=Next Page
```

Windows XP Professional Setup will search to determine if another operating system already exists on the hard drive.

Press **ESC**.

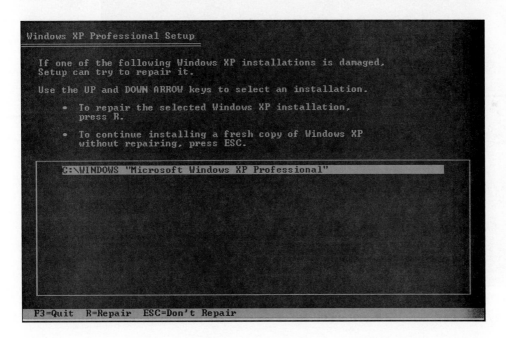

Press the **D** key.

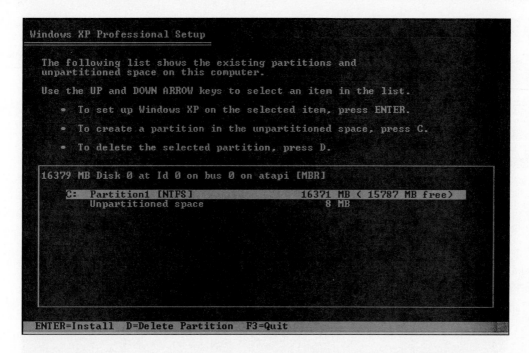

Press **Enter**.

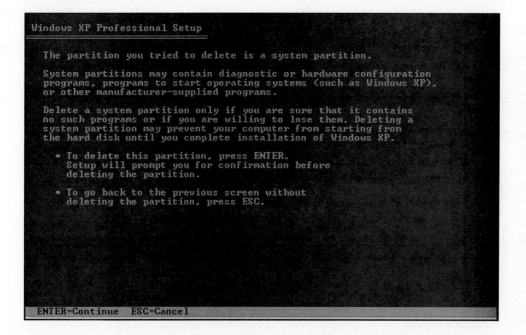

Press the **L** key.

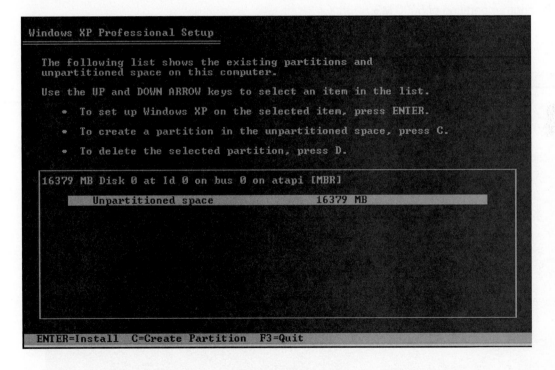

```
Windows XP Professional Setup

    You asked Setup to delete the partition

        C:  Partition1 [NTFS]                       16371 MB ( 15787 MB free)

    on 16379 MB Disk 0 at Id 0 on bus 0 on atapi [MBR].


        •   To delete this partition, press L.
            CAUTION: All data on this partition will be lost.

        •   To return to the previous screen without
            deleting the partition, press ESC.












    L=Delete   ESC=Cancel
```

Press the **C** key.

```
Windows XP Professional Setup

    The following list shows the existing partitions and
    unpartitioned space on this computer.

    Use the UP and DOWN ARROW keys to select an item in the list.

        •   To set up Windows XP on the selected item, press ENTER.

        •   To create a partition in the unpartitioned space, press C.

        •   To delete the selected partition, press D.

    16379 MB Disk 0 at Id 0 on bus 0 on atapi [MBR]
            Unpartitioned space             16379 MB








    ENTER=Install   C=Create Partition   F3=Quit
```

Type **5000** in the "Create partition of size <in MB>:" field.

Press the **Enter** key.

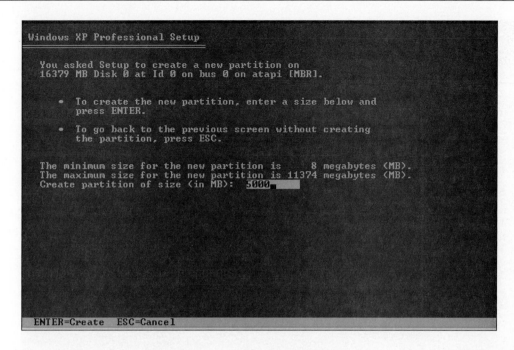

Press the **down arrow** key to select "Unpartitioned space".

Press the **C** key.

Create another partition of 5000 MB.

Repeat this process one more time. You will have three partitions of 5000 MB each.

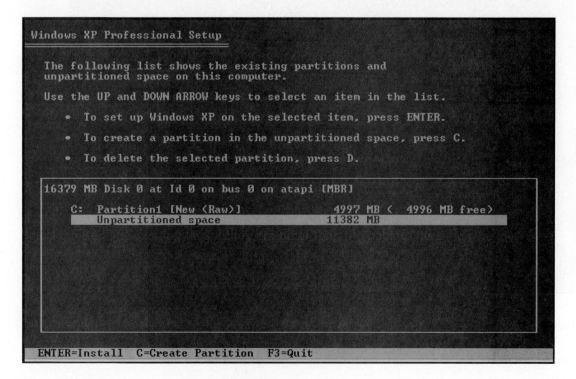

Select **C: Partition1** and press the **Enter** key.

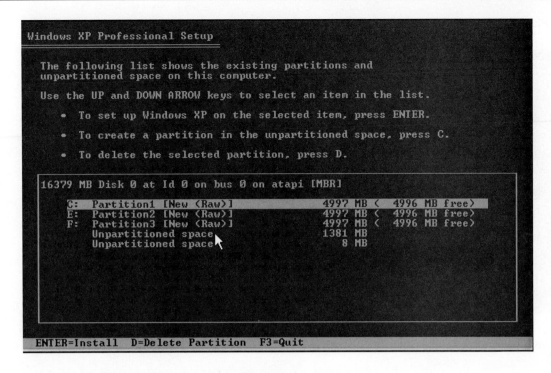

Select "Format the partition using the NTFS file system".

Do not select ""Format the partition using the NTFS file system <Quick>".

Press the **Enter** key.

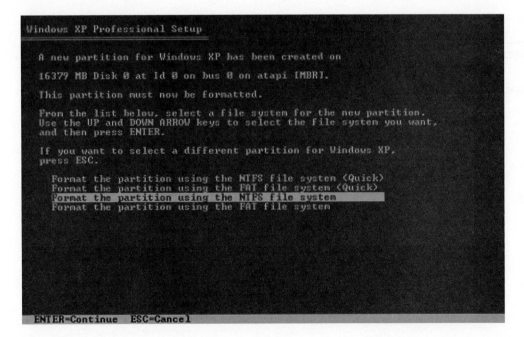

The "Please wait while Setup formats the partition" screen appears.

The system will restart automatically.

After the system restarts, the message "Press Any Key to Boot from CD" appears.

Do not press any keys.

The installation should continue without prompting you for any settings.

The system will restart automatically.

After the system restarts, the message "Press Any Key to Boot from CD" appears.

Do not press any keys.

Step 8

The "Welcome to Microsoft Windows" screen appears.

Click **Next**.

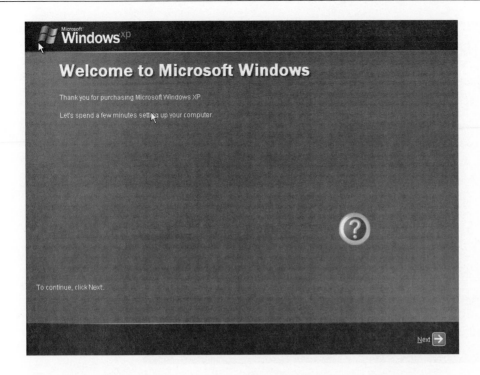

Select the **Help protect my PC by turning on Automatic Updates now** radio button.

Click **Next**.

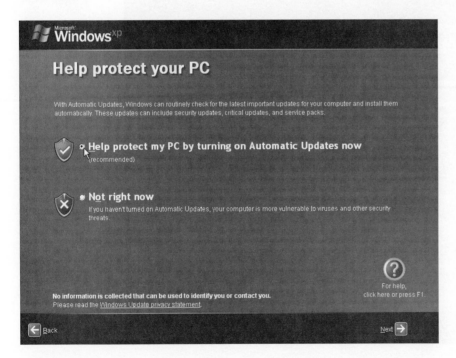

Select the **Yes, this computer will connect through the local area network or home network** radio button.

Click **Next**.

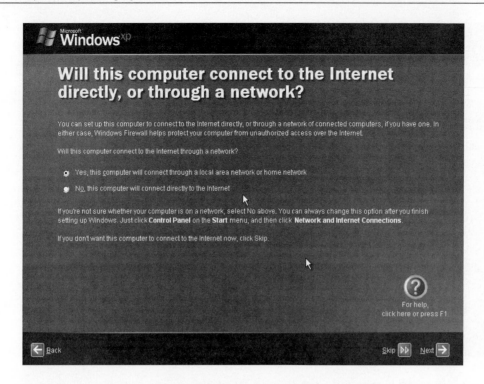

Select the **No, not at this time** radio button, and then click **Next**.

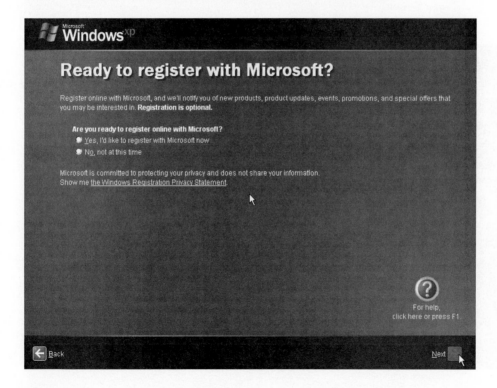

Type the name provided by your instructor in the "Your name:" field.

Click **Next**.

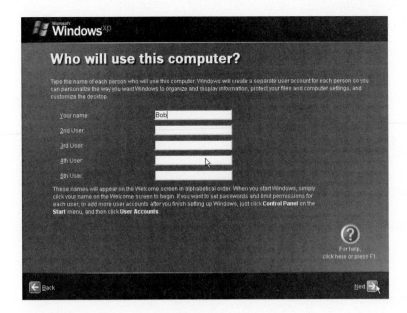

The "Thank you!" screen appears.

Click **Finish**.

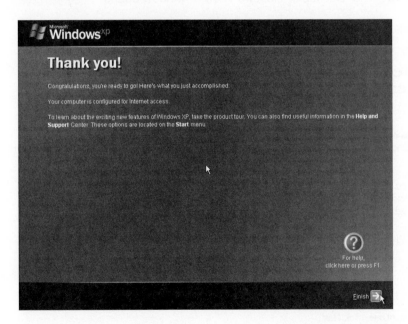

What was the name of the file used to automate the installation located on the floppy disk?

How do you think automating the installation will help the IT Department if they have to repeat the procedure on 100 computers?

5.2.3.4 Lab - Registry Backup and Recovery in Windows XP

Introduction

In this lab, you will back up a computer registry. You will also perform a recovery of a computer registry. The registry is also called System State data.

Recommended Equipment

The following equipment is required for this exercise:

- A computer system running Windows XP is required for this exercise.

Step 1

Log on to the computer as yourself.

Click **Start > Run**.

Type **ntbackup** and then click **OK**. The "Backup or Restore Wizard" window opens.

Click **Advanced Mode**.

Step 2

The "Backup Utility" window opens.

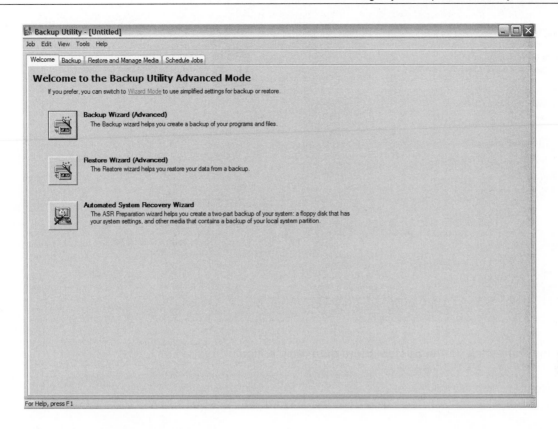

Click **Backup Wizard (Advanced)**.

Step 3

The "Welcome to the Backup Wizard" window opens.

Click **Next**.

Step 4

The "What to Back Up" screen appears.

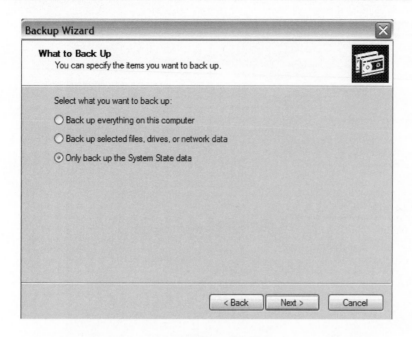

Click the **Only back up the System State data** radio button.

Click **Next**.

Step 5

The "Backup Type, Destination, and Name" screen appears.

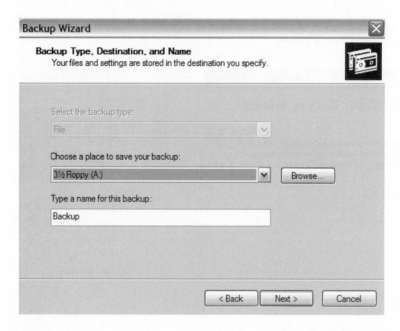

Click **Browse**.

If you are asked to insert a disk into the floppy disk drive, click **Cancel**.

Step 6

The "Save As" dialog box open.

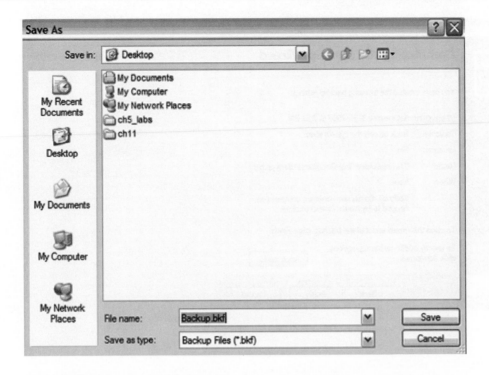

Click the **My Documents** icon on the left side of the "Save As" dialog box.

Click **Save**.

Step 7

The "Backup Type, Destination, and Name" screen re-appears.

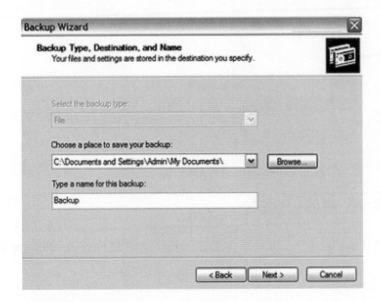

Click **Next**.

Step 8

The "Completing the Backup Wizard" screen appears.

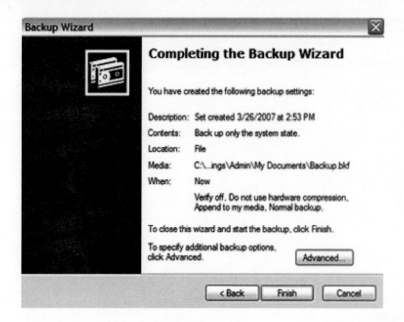

Click **Advanced**.

Step 9

The "Type of Backup" screen appears.

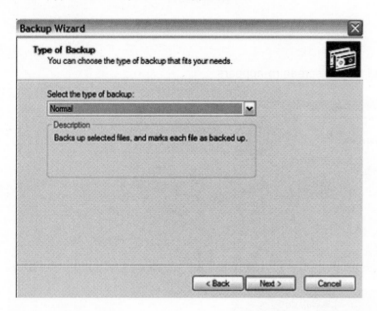

The default backup type is "Normal". If available, make sure that "Backup Migrated Remote Storage Data" is not checked.

Click **Next**.

Step 10

The "How to Back Up" screen appears.

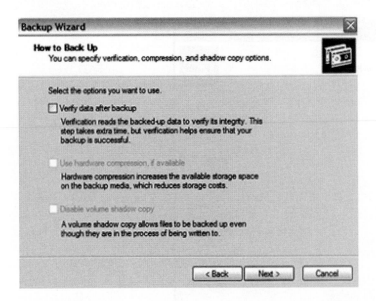

Click the **Verify data after backup** check box, and then click **Next**.

Step 11

The "Backup Options" screen appears.

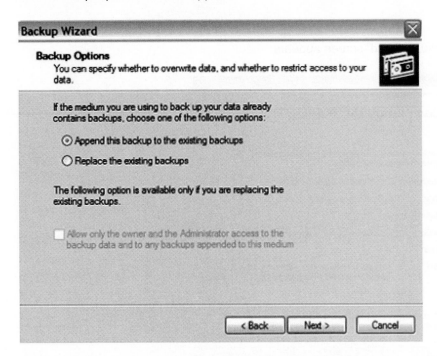

Select **Replace the existing backups**, and then click **Next**.

Step 12

The "When to Back Up" screen appears.

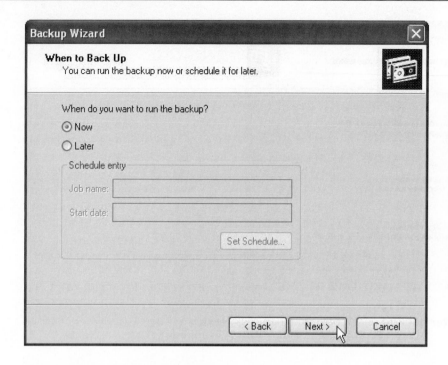

Select **Now** and then click **Next**.

Step 13

The "Completing the Backup Wizard" screen appears.

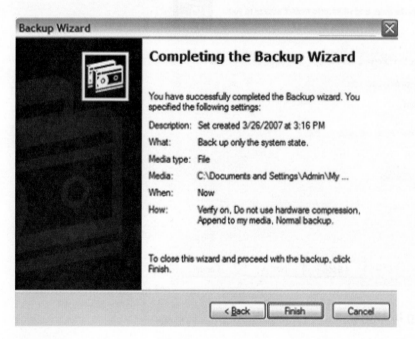

Click **Finish**.

Step 14

The "Backup Progress" window opens.

The "Backup Progress" window indicates that the backup is complete.

Click **Report**.

Step 15

The "Notepad" application window opens containing the report.

Close Notepad.

In the Backup Progress dialog box, click **Close**.

Close the Backup Utility.

Step 16

Click **Start > Run…**.

Type **regedit** in the "open:" field.

The "Registry Editor" window opens.

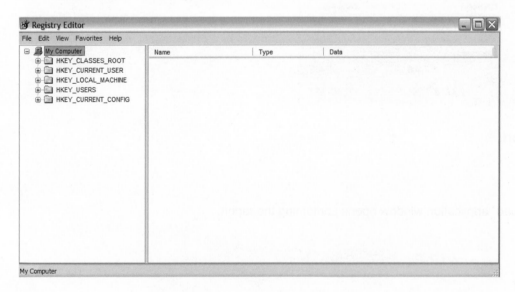

Expand the **HKEY_CURRENT_USER** Registry Key.

Expand the **Control Panel** Registry Key.

Expand the **PowerCfg** Registry Key.

Right-click the **Screen Saver.Stars** Registry Key.

Click **Delete**.

Click **File > Exit** in the Registry Editor window.

Step 17

Browse to the "My Documents" folder and locate the "backup.bkf" file.

Double-click the backup file to bring up the Backup Utility Wizard.

Click **Next**.

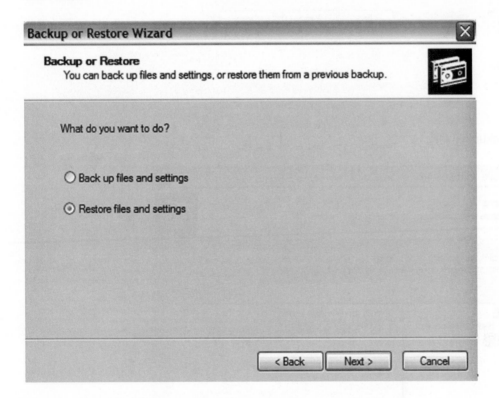

Click the **Restore files and settings** radio button and then click **Next**.

Step 18

The "What to Restore" screen appears.

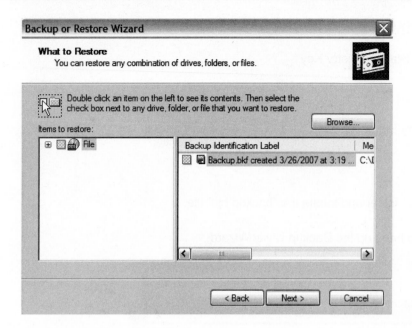

Expand the file.

Step 19

Expand the backup.bkf file.

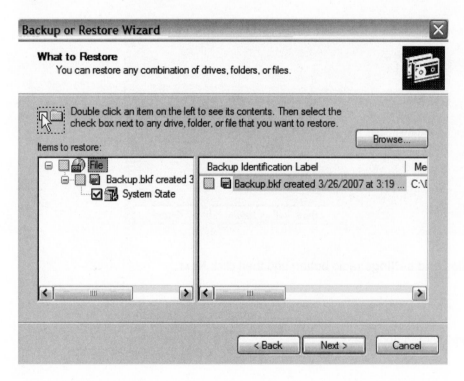

Click the **System State** check box.

Click **Next**.

Step 20

The "Completing the Backup or Restore Wizard" screen appears.

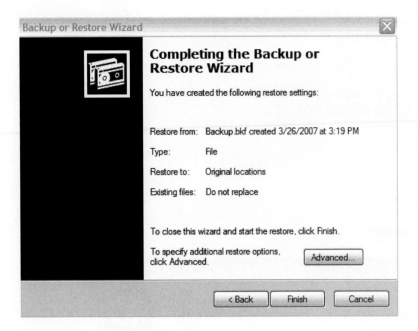

Click **Advanced**.

Step 21

The "Where to Restore" screen appears.

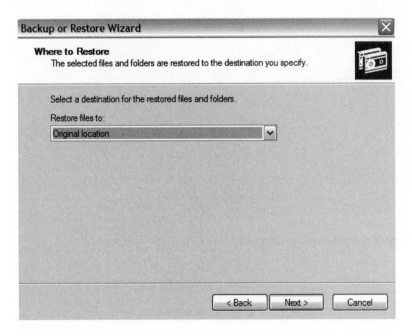

The default restoration location is "Original location".

Click **Next**.

Step 22

The "Restoring System State will always overwrite current System State unless restoring to an alternate location." Warning window appears.

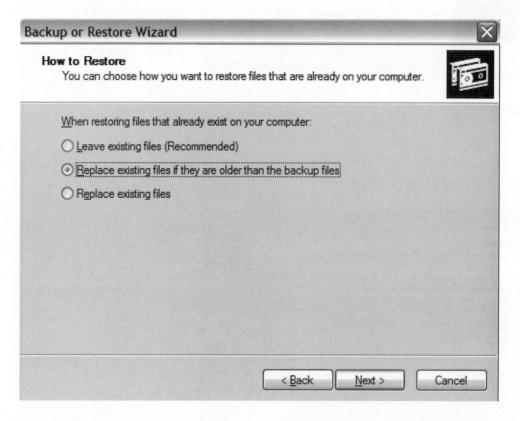

Click **OK**.

Step 23

The "How to Restore" screen appears.

Select the **Replace existing files if they are older than the backup files** radio button.

Click **Next**.

Step 24

The "Advanced Restore Options" screen appears.

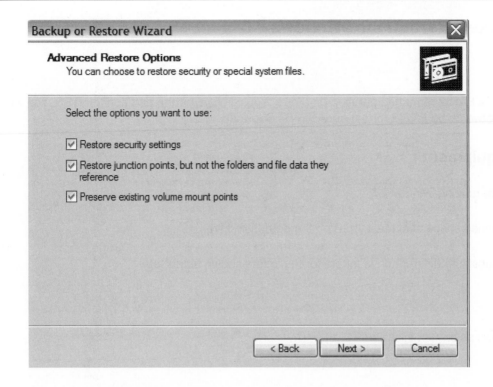

Be sure that all three check boxes are selected, and then click **Next**.

Click **Finish**.

The system recovery begins by copying the files back to the computer.

When prompted to restart the computer, click **Yes**. The computer will restart.

Step 25

Click **Start > Run…**.

Type **regedit** in the "open:" field.

Click **OK**.

You should see the "Screen Saver.Stars" Registry key in the Registry Editor application window.

Click **File > Exit**.

How does backing up the system state files save time?

5.2.4.3 Lab - Create a Partition in Windows 7

Introduction

In this lab, you will create a FAT32 formatted partition on a disk. You will convert the partition to NTFS. You will identify the differences between the FAT32 format and the NTFS format.

Recommended Equipment

- Computer running Windows 7

- Unpartitioned space of at least 1 GB on the hard disk drive

Note: You may need to substitute different drive letters for the letters shown in this lab.

Step 1

Log on to Windows as an Administrator.

Click **Start**.

Right-click **Computer > Manage**.

Step 2

The "Computer Management" window appears.

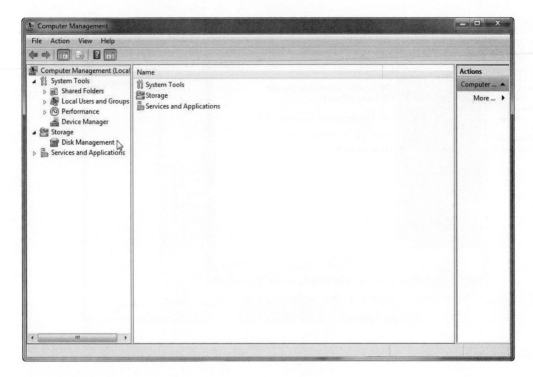

Click **Disk Management** on the left side of the screen.

Right-click the green-outlined block of **Free Space**.

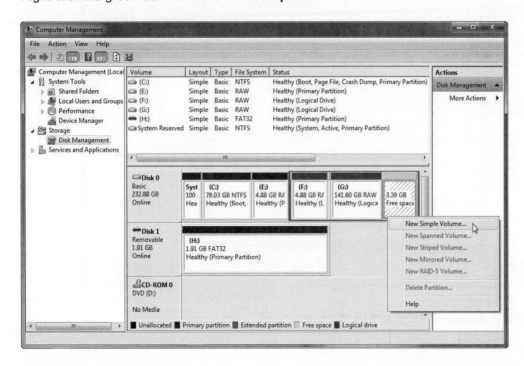

Click **New Simple Volume**.

Step 3

The "New Simple Volume Wizard" window appears.

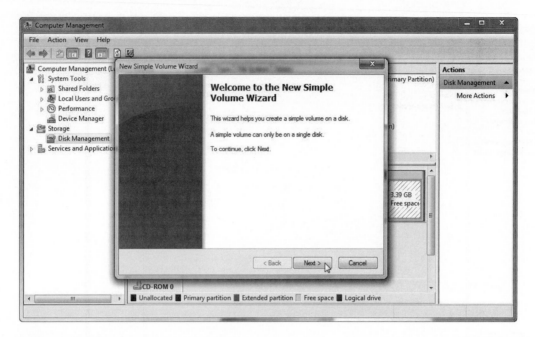

Click **Next**.

The "Specify Volume Size" screen appears.

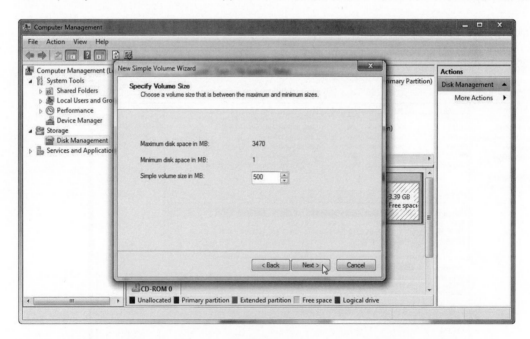

Type **500** in the **Simple volume size in MB**: field.

Click **Next**.

The "Assign Drive Letter or Path" screen appears.

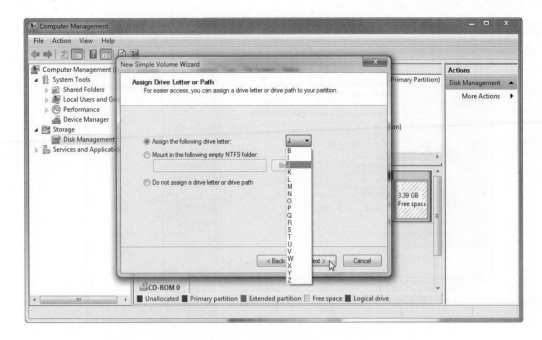

Click the **Assign the following drive letter:** radio button.

Select **J** from the drop-down menu.

Click **Next**.

The "Format Partition" screen appears.

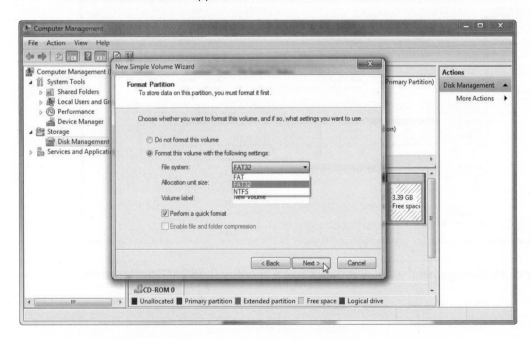

Click the **Format this volume with the following settings:** radio button.

Select **FAT32** from the File system drop-down menu.

Click **Next**.

The "Completing the New Simple Volume Wizard" screen appears.

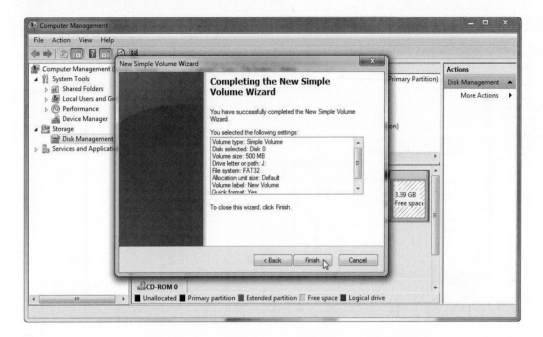

Click **Finish**.

Step 4

The "Computer Management" window re-appears while the new volume is formatted.

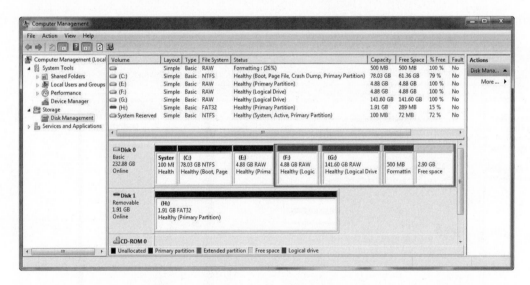

The "Computer Management" window shows the new **Healthy (Logical Drive)** volume.

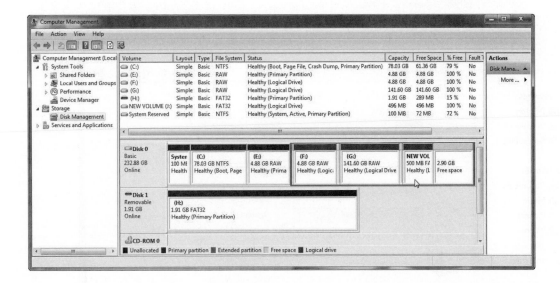

Step 5

Open **Computer**.

Click the **NEW VOLUME (J:)** drive.

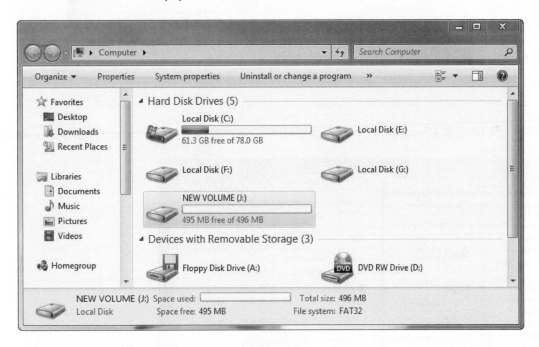

The **Details** area on the bottom of the **Computer** window displays information about the J: drive.

What is the File System?

How much Free Space is shown?

Right-click the **NEW VOLUME (J:)** drive.

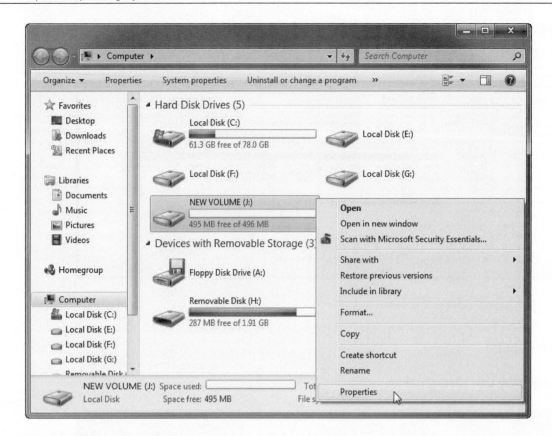

Click **Properties**.

Step 6

The "NEW VOLUME (J:) Properties" window appears.

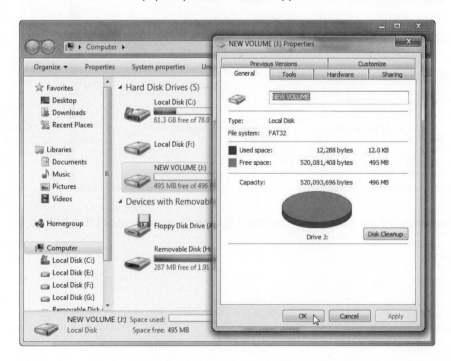

What is the File System of the J: drive?

List the tabs found in the **NEW VOLUME (J:) Properties** window.

Click **OK**.

Double-click the **NEW VOLUME (J:)** drive.

Step 7

Right-click anywhere in the white space of the window.

Click **New > Text Document**.

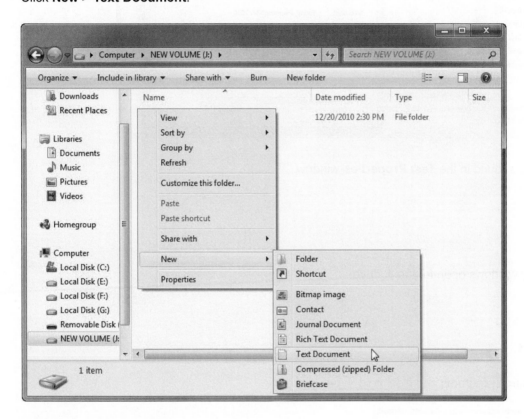

Type **Test** and press **Enter**.

Step 8

Right-click the **Test** document in the window and choose **Properties**.

The "Test Properties" window appears.

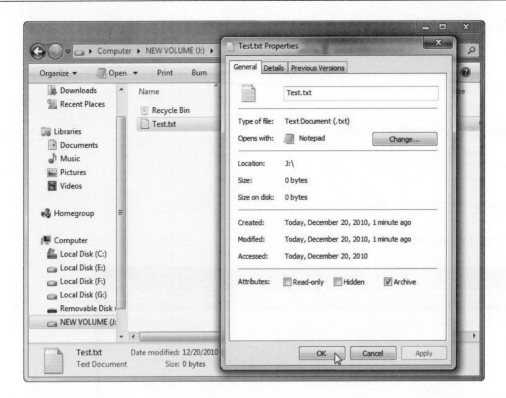

List the tabs found in the **Test Properties** window.

Click **OK**.

Close any windows open for the J: drive.

Step 9

Click **Start**.

In the "Search programs and files" field, type **cmd**.

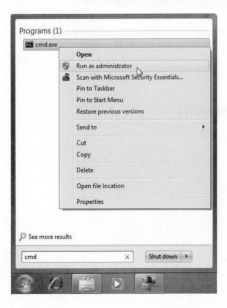

When the cmd program appears, right-click **cmd > Run as administrator**.

Click **Yes** if prompted by User Account Control.

Step 10

The "Administrator: C:\Windows\System32\cmd.exe" window appears.

The **convert** command changes the file system of a volume without losing data.

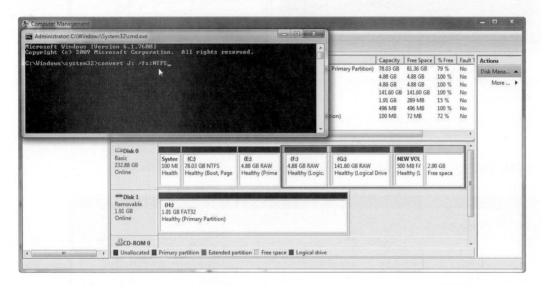

Type **convert J: /fs:NTFS >** press the **Enter** key.

You will be prompted to enter the current volume label for drive J:. Type **NEW VOLUME** and press the **Enter** key.

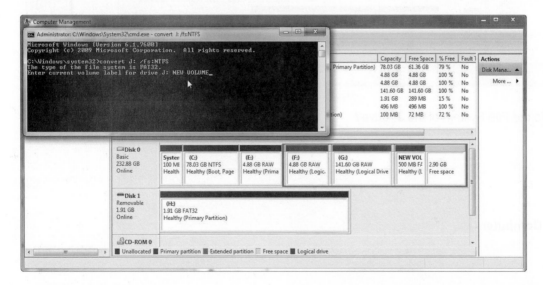

After the drive is converted, type **exit** in the "Administrator: C:\Windows\System32\cmd.exe" window, and then press **Enter**.

Step 11

The "C:\WINDOWS\System32\cmd.exe" window closes.

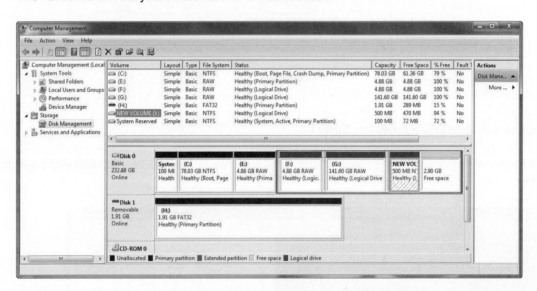

What is the File System of the **J:** drive?

Step 12

Open **Computer**.

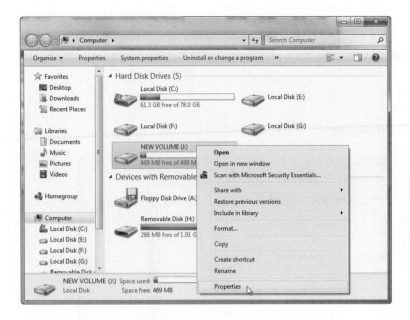

Right-click **NEW VOLUME (J:) > Properties**.

Step 13

The "NEW VOLUME (J:) Properties" window appears.

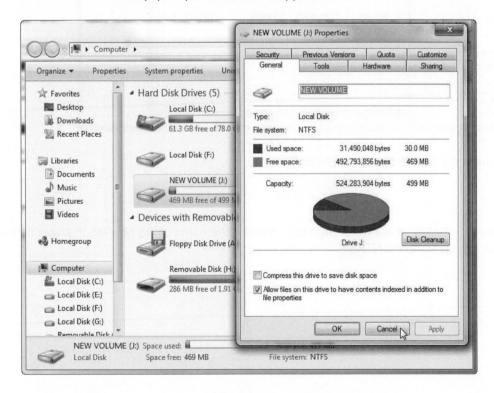

What are the tabs in the **NEW VOLUME (J:) Properties** window?

When the volume was FAT32, there were six tabs. What are the names of the new tabs that were added after the volume was converted to NTFS?

Click **Cancel**. Double-click the **NEW VOLUME (J:)** drive.

Step 14

Right-click the **Test** document **> Properties**.

What are the tabs in the **Test Properties** window?

When the volume was FAT32, there were three tabs. What is the name of the new tab that was added after the volume was converted to NTFS?

Click **OK**.

5.2.4.4 Lab - Create a Partition in Windows Vista

Introduction

In this lab, you will create a FAT32 formatted partition on a disk. You will convert the partition to NTFS. You will identify the differences between the FAT32 format and the NTFS format.

Recommended Equipment

- Computer running Windows Vista

- Unpartitioned space of at least 1 GB on the hard disk drive

Step 1

Log on to Windows as an Administrator.

Click **Start**.

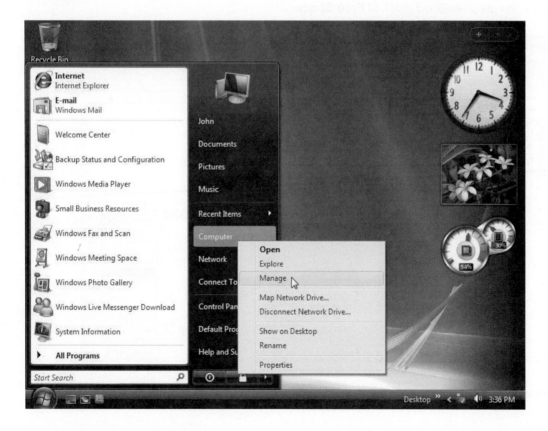

Right-click **Computer > Manage**.

Step 2

The "Computer Management" window appears.

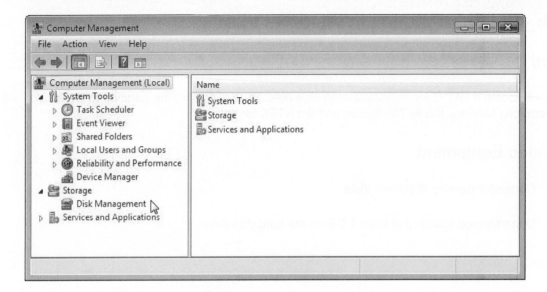

Click **Disk Management** on the left side of the screen.

Right-click the green-outlined block of **Free Space**.

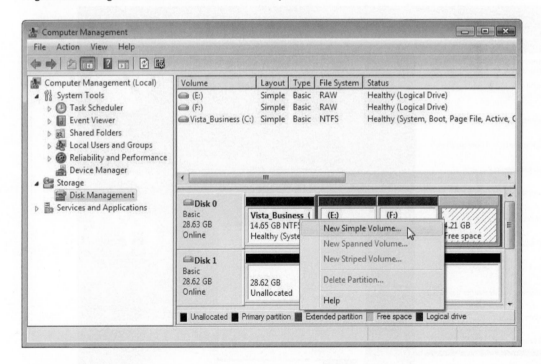

Click **New Simple Volume**.

Step 3

The "New Simple Volume Wizard" window appears.

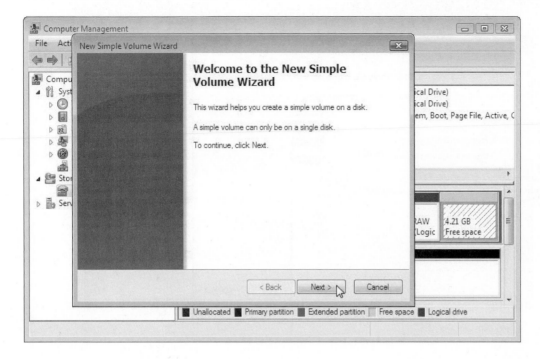

Click **Next**.

The "Specify Volume Size" screen appears.

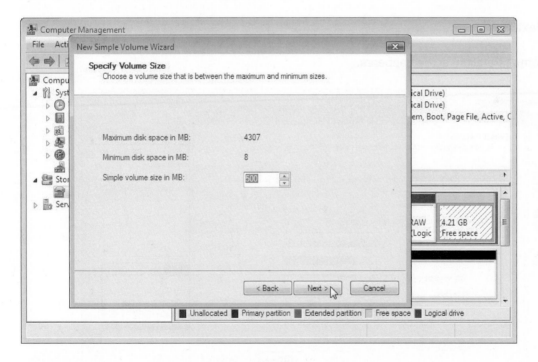

Type **500** in the **Simple volume size in MB**: field.

Click **Next**.

The "Assign Drive Letter or Path" screen appears.

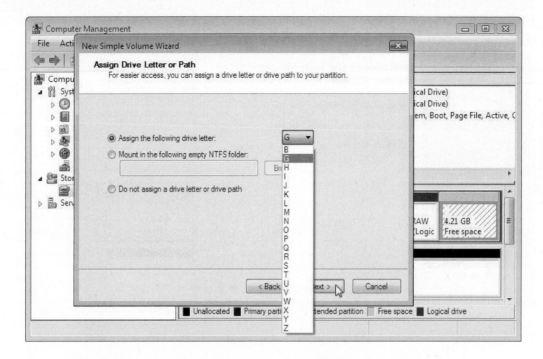

Click the **Assign the following drive letter:** radio button.

Select **G** from the drop-down menu.

Click **Next**.

The "Format Partition" screen appears.

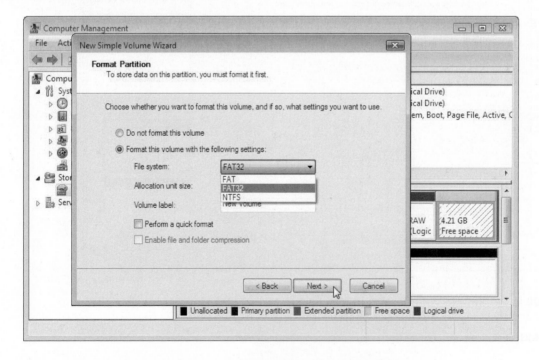

Click the **Format this volume with the following settings:** radio button.

Select **FAT32** from the File system drop-down menu and then click **Next**.

The "Completing the New Simple Volume Wizard" screen appears.

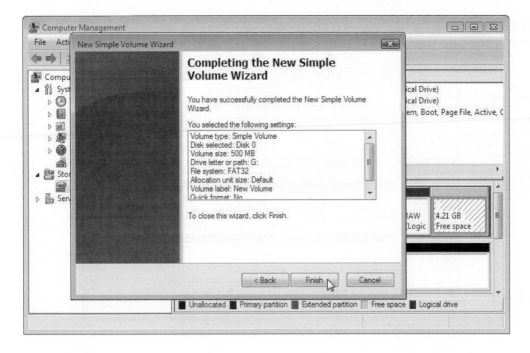

Click **Finish**.

Step 4

The "Computer Management" window re-appears while the new volume is formatted.

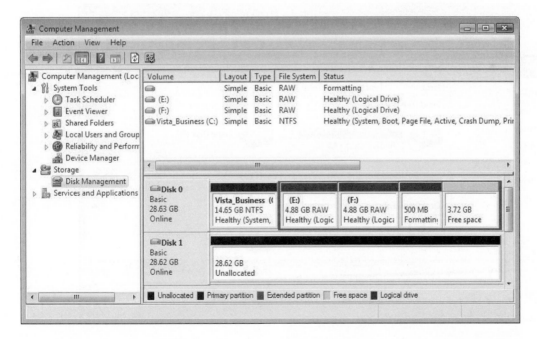

The "Computer Management" window shows the new **Healthy (Logical Drive)** volume.

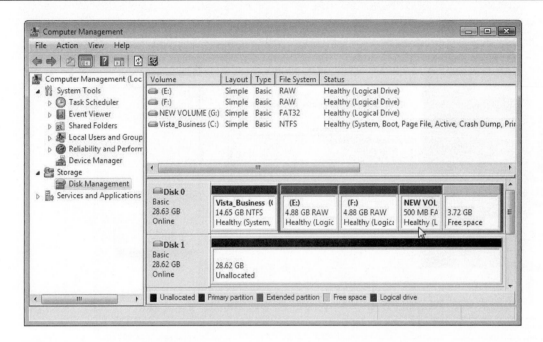

Step 5

Click **Start > Computer**.

Click the **NEW VOLUME (G:)** drive.

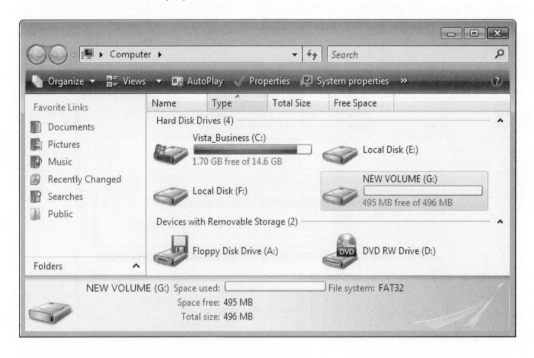

The **Details** area on the bottom of the **Computer** window displays information about the G: drive.

What is the File System?

How much Free Space is shown?

Right-click the **NEW VOLUME (G:)** drive.

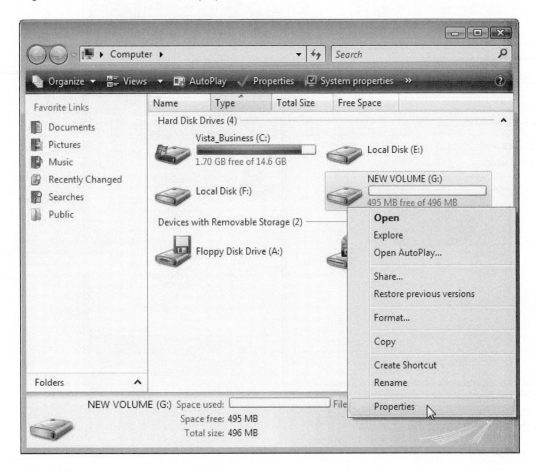

Click **Properties**.

Step 6

The **NEW VOLUME (G:) Properties** window appears.

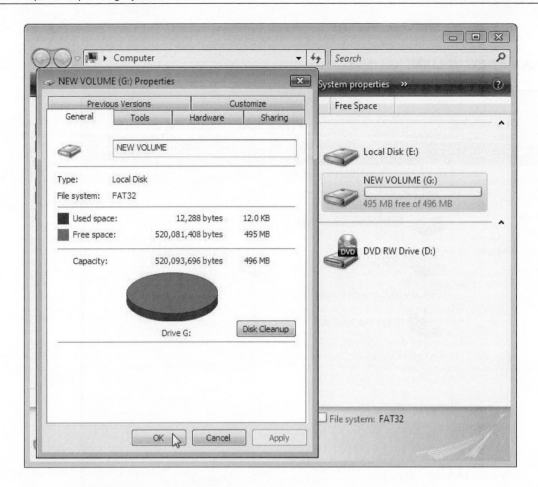

What is the File System of the G: drive?

List the tabs found in the **NEW VOLUME (G:) Properties** window.

Click **OK**.

Double-click the **NEW VOLUME (G:)** drive.

Step 7

Right-click anywhere in the white space of the window.

Click **New > Text Document**.

Type **Test** and press **Enter**.

Step 8

Right-click the **Test** document in the window and choose **Properties**.

The **"Test Properties"** window appears.

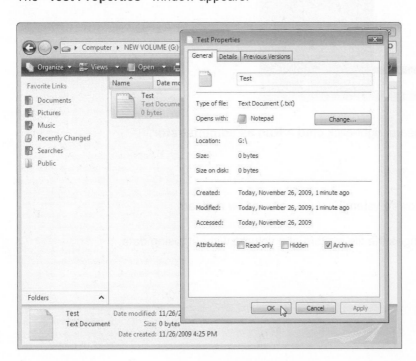

List the tabs found in the **Test Properties** window.

Click **OK**.

Close any windows open for the G: drive.

Step 9

Click **Start**.

In the **Start Search** field, type **cmd**.

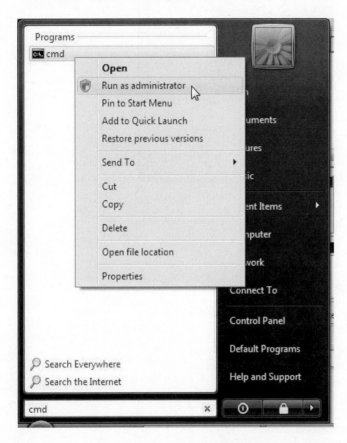

When the cmd program appears, right-click **cmd > Run as administrator**.

Step 10

The "Administrator: C:\Windows\System32\cmd.exe" window appears.

The **convert** command changes the file system of a volume without losing data.

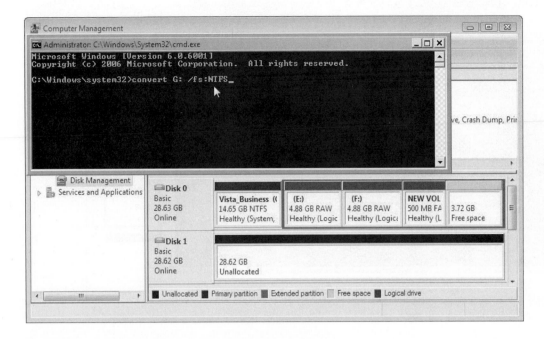

Type **convert G: /fs:NTFS >** press the **Enter** key.

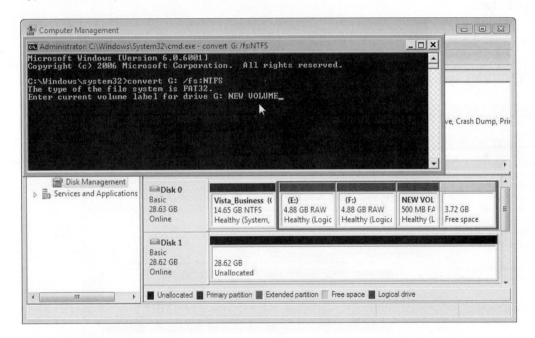

You will be prompted to enter the current volume label for drive G:. Type **NEW VOLUME** and then press the **Enter** key.

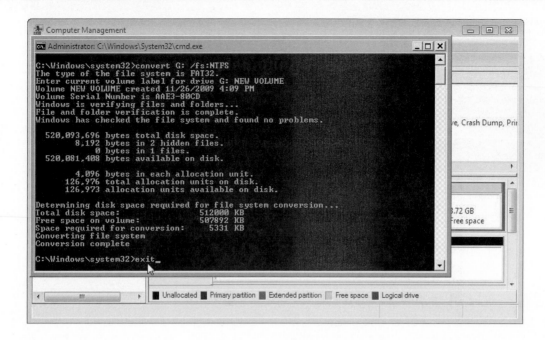

After the drive is converted, type **exit** in the "Administrator: C:\Windows\System32\cmd.exe" window, and then press **Enter**.

Step 11

The "C:\WINDOWS\System32\cmd.exe" window closes.

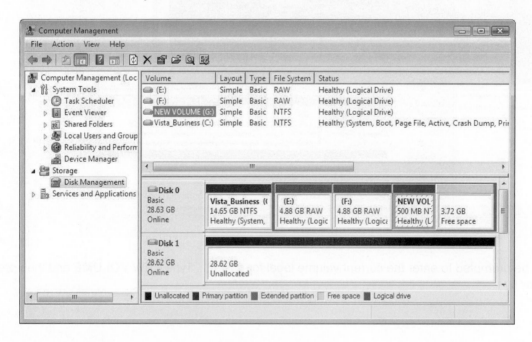

What is the File System of the **G:** drive?

Step 12

Open **Computer**.

Right-click **NEW VOLUME (G:) > Properties**.

Step 13

The "NEW VOLUME (G:) Properties" window appears.

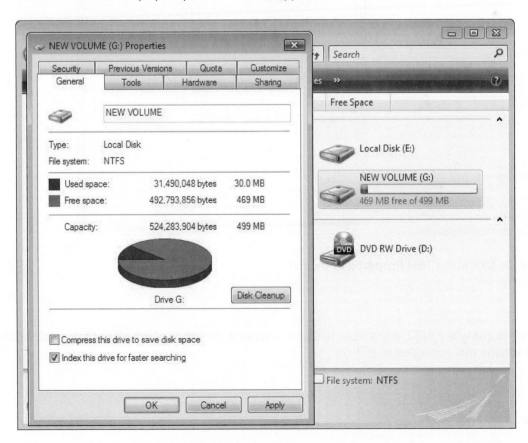

What are the tabs in the **NEW VOLUME (G:) Properties** window?

When the volume was FAT32, there were six tabs. What are the names of the new tabs that were added after the volume was converted to NTFS?

Click **Cancel**.

Double-click the **NEW VOLUME (G:)** drive.

Step 14

Right-click the **Test** document > **Properties**.

What are the tabs in the **Test Properties** window?

When the volume was FAT32, there were three tabs. What is the name of the new tab that was added after the volume was converted to NTFS?

Click **OK**.

5.2.4.5 Lab - Create a Partition in Windows XP

Introduction

In this lab, you will create a FAT32 formatted partition on a disk. You will convert the partition to NTFS. You will identify the differences between the FAT32 format and the NTFS format.

Recommended Equipment

- Computer running Windows XP

- Unpartitioned space of at least 1 GB on the hard disk drive

Step 1

Log on to Windows as an administrator.

Click **Start** > right-click **My Computer** > **Manage**.

Step 2

The "Computer Management" window appears.

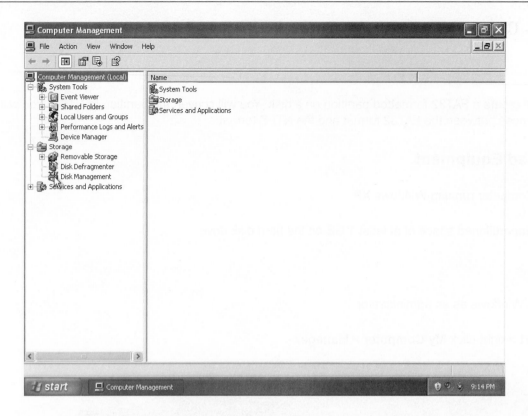

Click **Disk Management** on the left side of the screen.

Right-click the green-outlined block of **Free Space**.

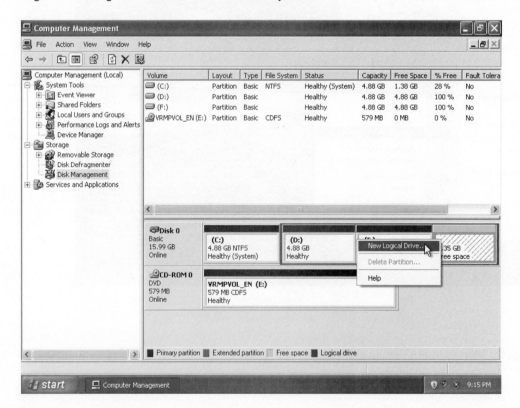

Click **New Logical Drive**.

Step 3

The "New Partition Wizard" window appears.

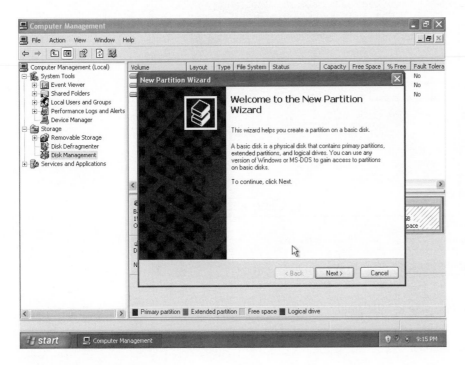

Click **Next**.

The "Select Partition Type" screen appears.

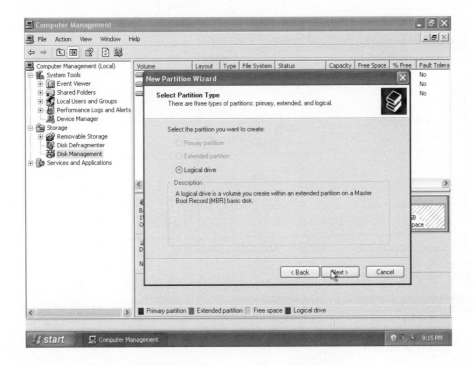

Click the **Logical drive** radio button, and then click **Next**.

The "Select Partition Size" screen appears.

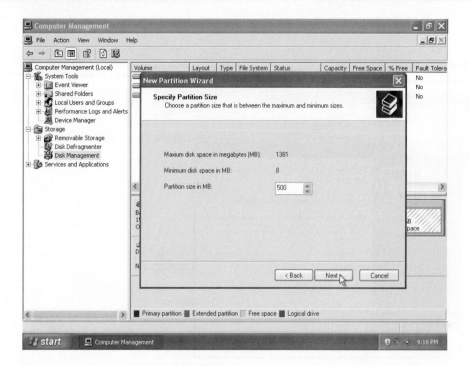

Type **500** in the "Partition size in MB:" field.

Click **Next**.

The "Assign Drive Letter or Path" screen appears.

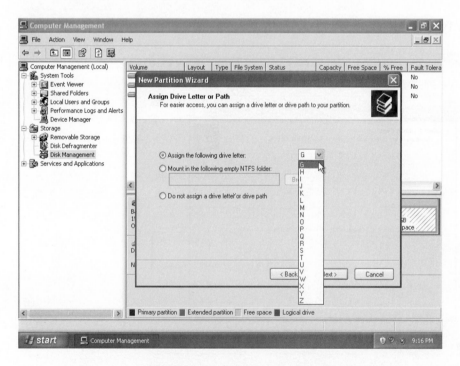

Click the **Assign the following drive letter:** radio button.

Select **G** from the drop-down menu and then click **Next**.

The "Format Partition" screen appears.

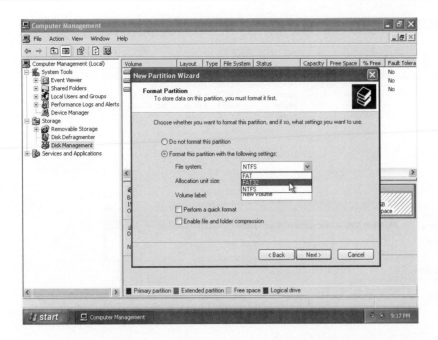

Click the **Format this partition with the following settings:** radio button.

Click **Next**.

The "Completing the New Partition Wizard" screen appears.

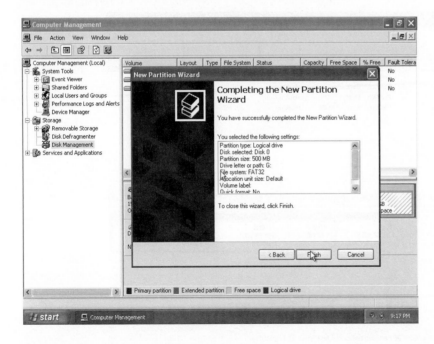

Click **Finish**.

Step 4

The "Computer Management" window re-appears while the new volume is formatted.

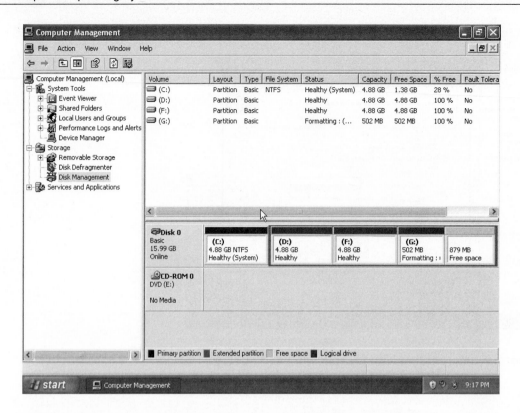

The "Computer Management" window shows the new "Healthy" volume.

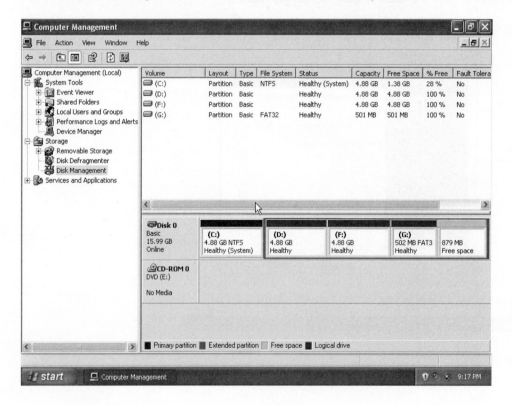

Step 5

Open **My Computer**.

Click the new partition you just created. For example: **Local Disk (G:)** drive.

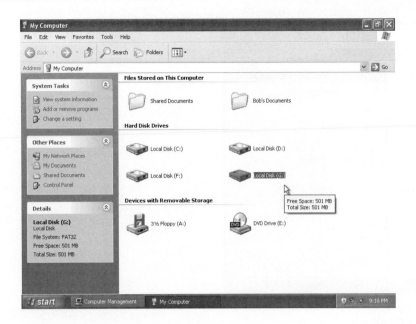

The "Details" area on the left of the "My Computer" window displays information about the G: drive.

What is the File System?

How much Free Space is shown?

Right-click the new partition: **Local Disk (G:)** drive.

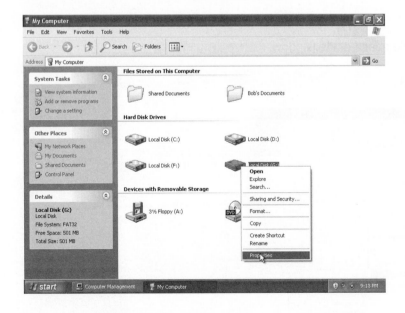

Choose **Properties**.

Step 6

The "Local Disk (G:) Properties" window appears.

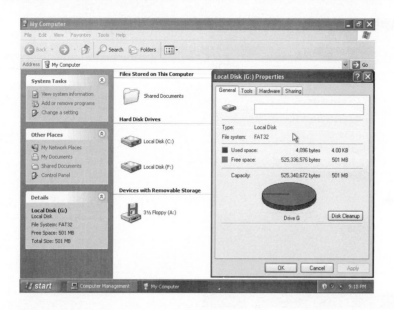

What is the File System of the G: drive?

List the tabs found in the "Local Disk (G:) Properties" window.

Click **OK**.

Double-click the new partition: **Local Disk (G:)** drive.

Step 7

Right-click anywhere in the white space of the window.

Choose **New > Text Document**.

Type **Test** and press **Enter**.

Step 8

Right-click the **Test** document in the window and choose **Properties**.

The "Test Properties" window appears.

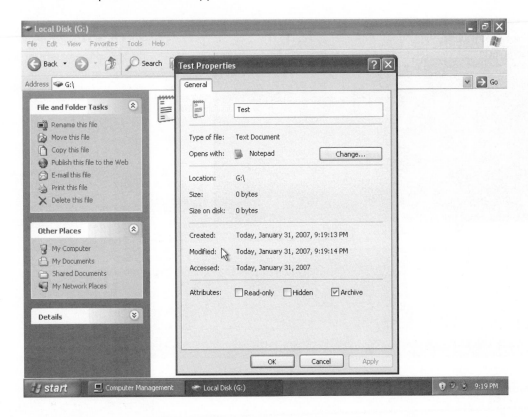

What is the name of the tab in the "Test Properties" window?

Click **OK**.

Step 9

Choose **Start > Run**.

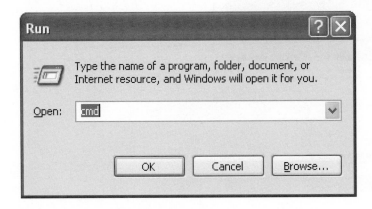

In the "Open:" field, type **cmd**, and then click **OK**.

Step 10

The "C:\WINDOWS\system32\cmd.exe" window appears.

The **convert** command changes the file system of a volume without losing data.

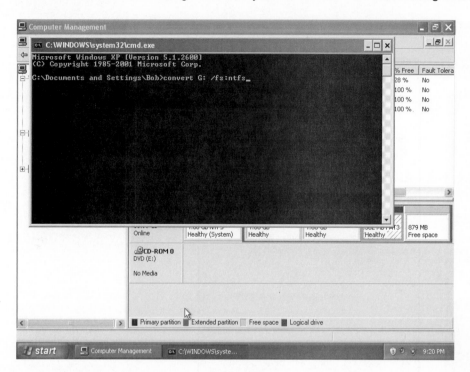

Type **convert G: /fs:NTFS**.

Press the **Enter** key.

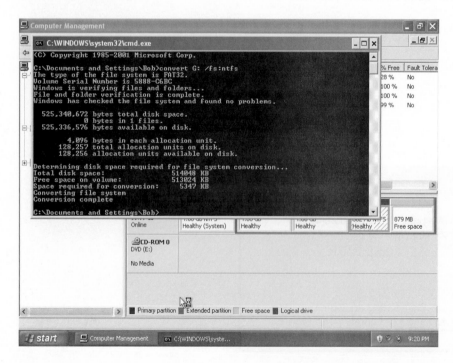

Type **exit**, and then press **Enter**.

Step 11

The "C:\WINDOWS\System32\cmd.exe" window closes.

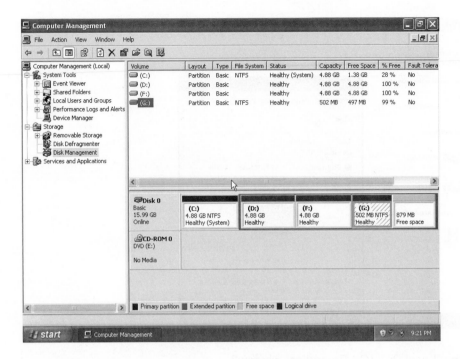

What is the File System of the **G:** drive?

Step 12

Open **My Computer**.

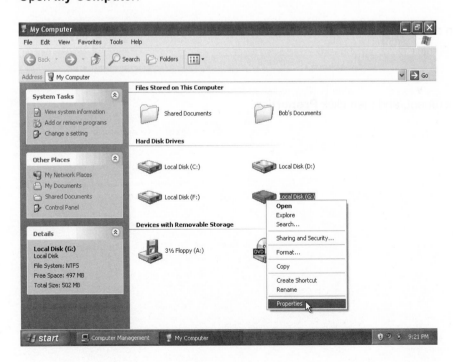

Right-click the **G:** drive, and then click **Properties**.

Step 13

The "Local Disk (G:) Properties" window appears.

What are the tabs in the "Local Disk (G:) Properties" window?

When the volume was FAT32, there were four tabs. What is the name of the new tab that was added after the volume was converted to NTFS?

Click **Cancel**, and then double-click the G: drive.

Step 14

Right-click the **Test** document, and then click **Properties**.

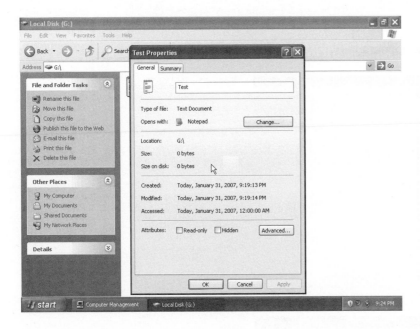

What are the tabs in the "Test Properties" window?

When the volume was FAT32, there was one tab. What is the name of the new tab that was added after the volume was converted to NTFS?

Click **OK**.

Step 15

Choose **Tools > Folder Options**.

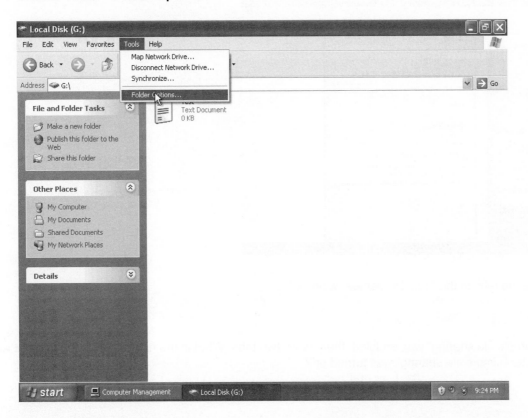

Step 16

The "Folder Options" window appears.

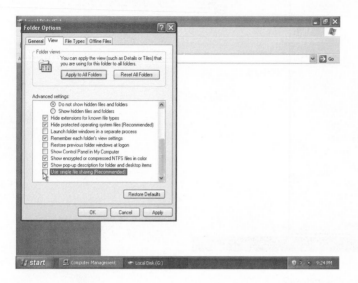

Click the **View** tab.

Scroll to the bottom of the "Advanced settings:" area, and then uncheck **Use simple file sharing (Recommended)**.

Click **OK**.

Step 17

The "Folder Options" window closes.

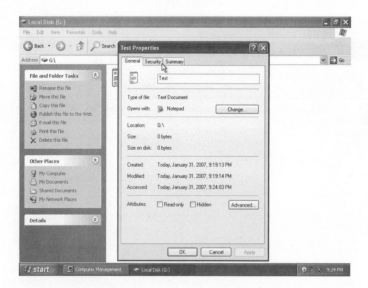

What are the tabs in the "Test Properties" window?

When "simple file sharing" was enabled, there were two tabs. What is the name of the new tab that was added after "simple file sharing" was turned off?

Step 18

Right-click the **G:** drive, and then choose **Properties**.

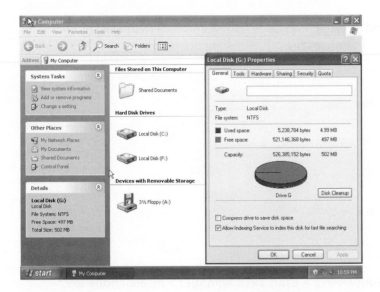

What are the tabs in the "Local Disk (G:) Properties" window?

When "simple file sharing" was enabled, there were five tabs. What is the name of the new tab that was added after "simple file sharing" was turned off?

5.3.1.5 Lab - Task Manager (Managing Processes) in Windows 7

Introduction

In this lab, you will explore Task Manager and manage processes from within Task Manager.

Recommended Equipment

The following equipment is required for this exercise:

   • A computer running Windows 7

Step 1

Log on to Windows as an administrator.

Open a browser and a folder.

Click on the desktop and press **Ctrl-Alt-Delete > Start Task Manager > Applications** tab.

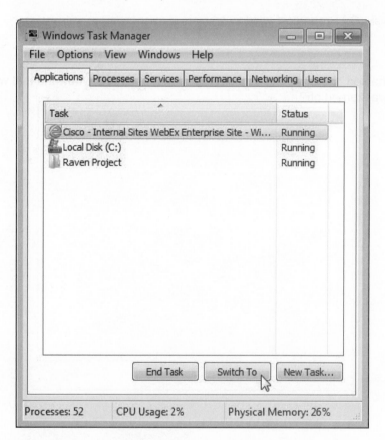

Select the open browser and then click **Switch To**.

What happened to the browser?

Bring Task Manager to the front of the desktop.

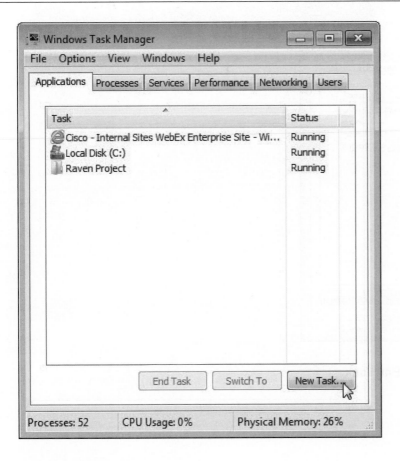

Click **New Task**.

The "Create New Task" window opens.

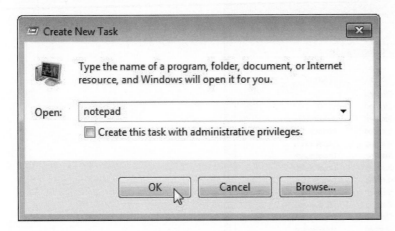

In the Open field, type **Notepad** and then click **OK**.

What happens?

Navigate back to Windows Task Manager.

Select **Notepad** and then click **End Task**.

What happens?

Step 2

Click the **Services** tab.

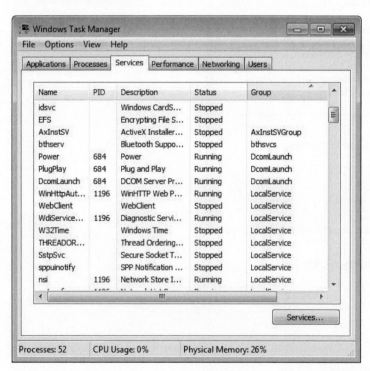

What is the Status of all services?

Step 3

Click the **Performance** tab.

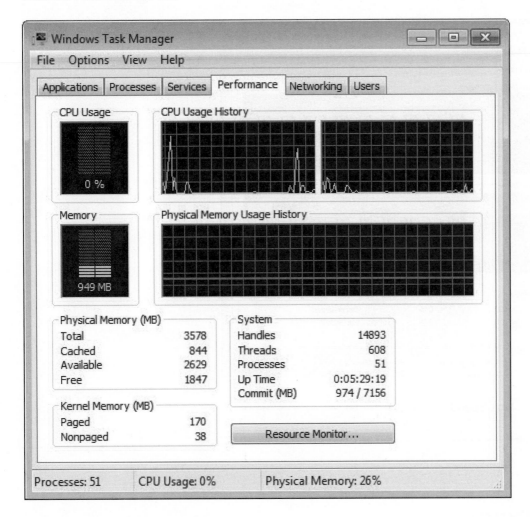

How many Threads are running?

How many Processes are running?

What is the Total Physical Memory (MB)?

What is the Available Physical Memory (MB)?

How much Physical Memory (MB) is being used by the system?

Step 4

Click the **Networking** tab.

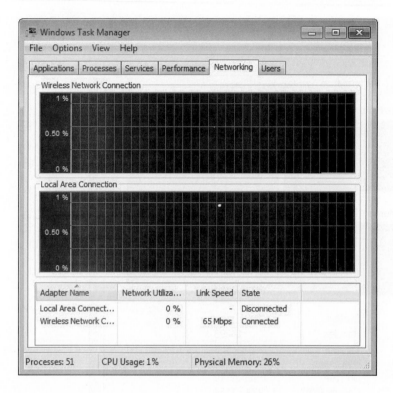

What is the Link Speed?

Step 5

Click the **Users** tab.

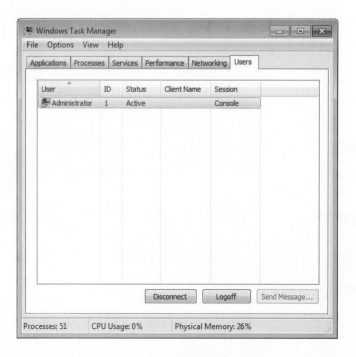

List all users and their Status.

What actions can you perform on the user from this window?

Step 6

Click the **Processes** tab.

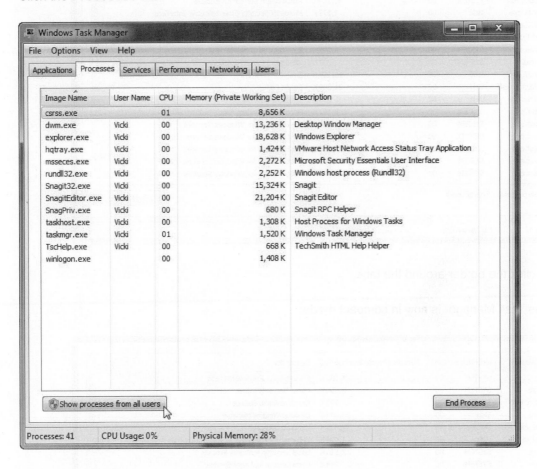

Click **Show processes from all users**.

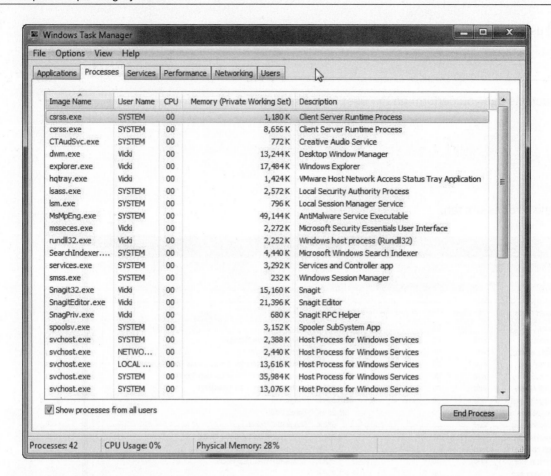

Double-click the border around the tabs.

Windows Task Manager is now in compact mode.

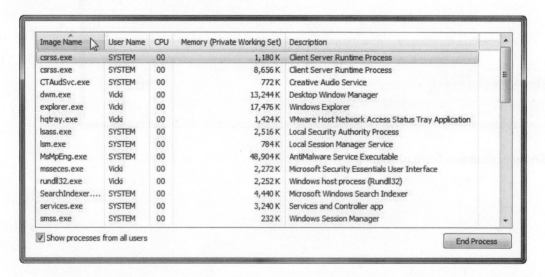

Click **Image Name**.

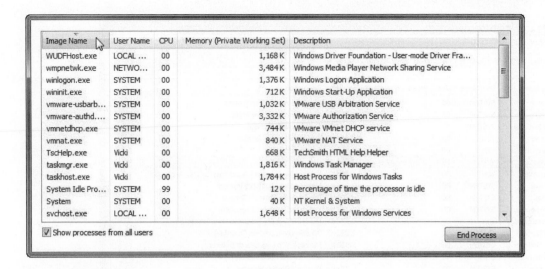

Click **Image Name** again.

What effect does this have on the columns?

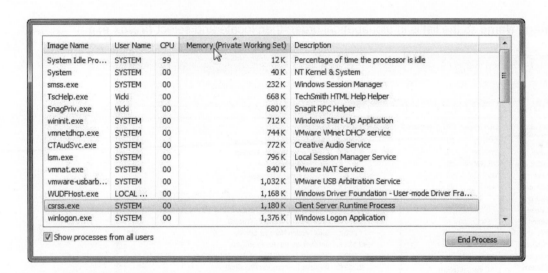

Click **Memory (Private Working Set)**.

What effect does this have on the columns?

Double-click the outside border again to return to tabs mode.

Step 7

Open a browser.

Note: Firefox is used in this lab. However, any browser will work. Just substitute your browser name whenever you see the word Firefox.

Return to the **Windows Task Manager**.

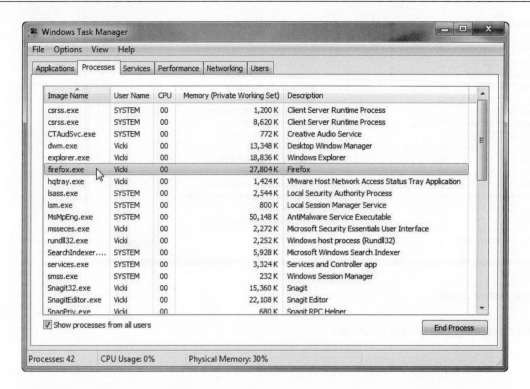

Click **Image Name** so the list is in alphabetical order; then locate and select **firefox.exe**.

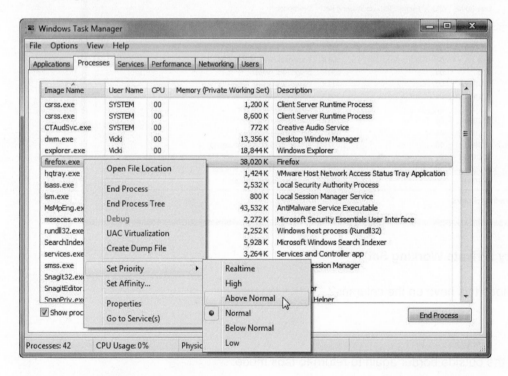

Right-click **firefox.exe > Set Priority**.

What is the default priority for the browser?

Set the priority to **Above Normal**.

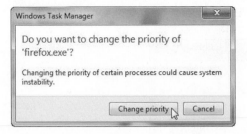

Click **Change priority** to the Windows Task Manager warning message.

Step 8

Click **View > Select Columns**.

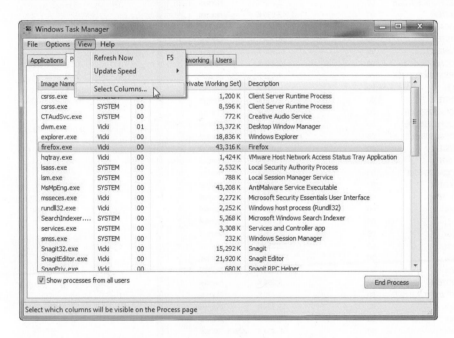

The "Select Process Page Columns" window appears.

Place a check mark next to **Base Priority** > click **OK**.

Expand the width of the "Windows Task Manager" so the "Base Priority" column is visible.

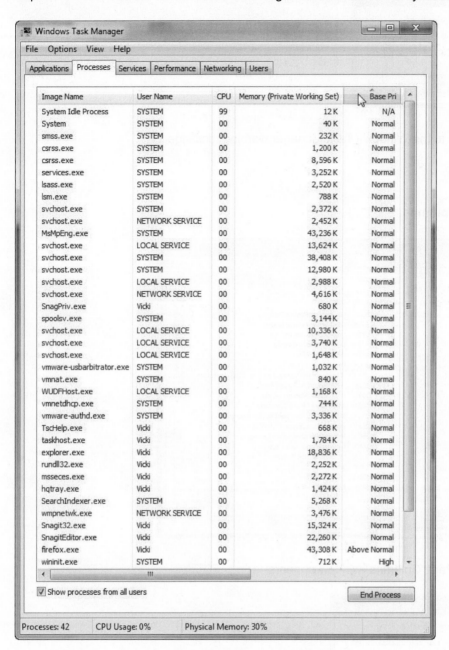

Click **Base Pri**.

Which image name has a base priority of N/A?

List the image name that has a base priority of Above Normal.

Step 9

Reset Firefox.exe base priority to normal. Right-click **firefox.exe > Set Priority > Normal > Change priority**.

Click **View > Select Columns >** uncheck **Base Priority > OK**.

Close Firefox.

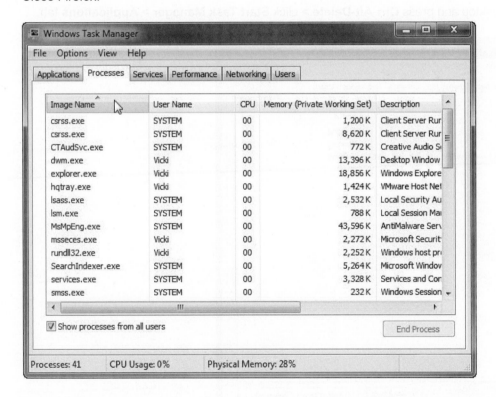

Is Firefox listed as a process?

Close all open windows.

5.3.1.6 Lab - Task Manager (Managing Processes) in Windows Vista

Introduction

In this lab, you will explore Task Manager and manage processes from within Task Manager.

Recommended Equipment

The following equipment is required for this exercise:

   • A computer running Windows Vista

Step 1

Log on to Windows as an administrator.

Open a browser and a folder.

Click on the desktop and press **Ctrl-Alt-Delete > ** click **Start Task Manager > Applications** tab.

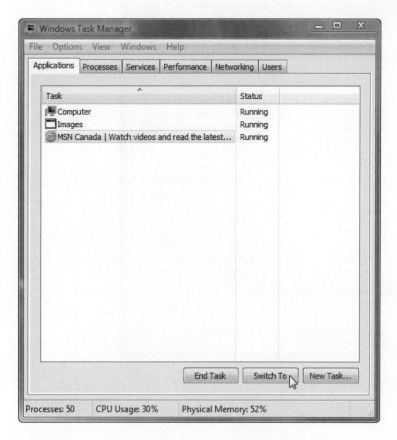

Select the open browser and then click **Switch To**.

What happened to the browser?

Bring Task Manager to the front of the desktop.

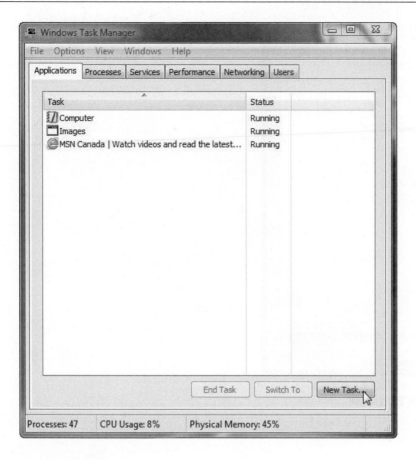

Click **New Task**.

The "Create New Task" window opens.

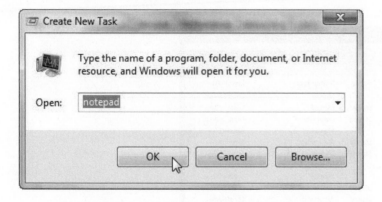

In the Open field, type **Notepad** and then click **OK**.

What happens?

Navigate back to Windows Task Manager.

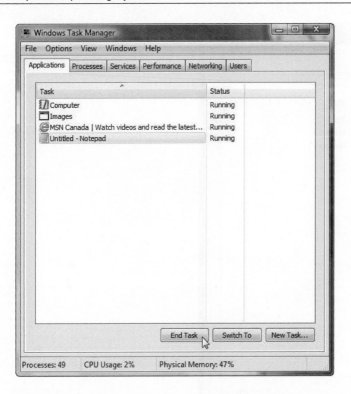

Select **Notepad** and then click **End Task**.

What happens?

Step 2

Click the **Services** tab.

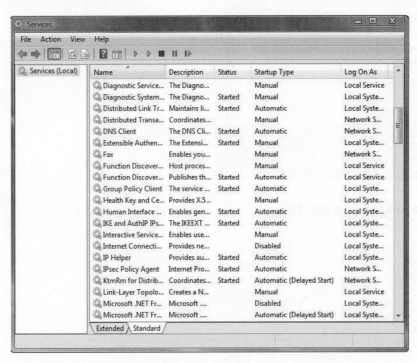

What Startup Types are listed?

Step 3

Click the **Performance** tab.

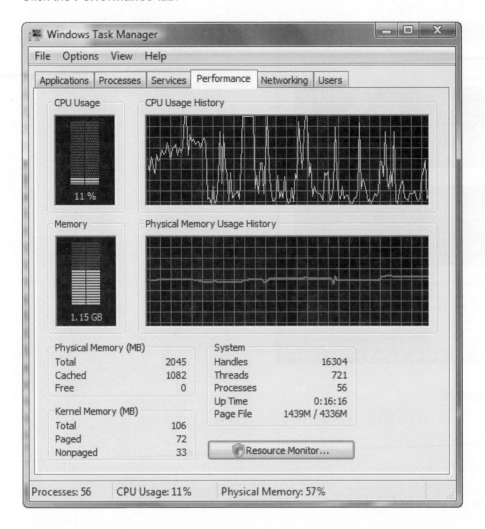

How many Threads are running?

How many Processes are running?

What is the Total Physical Memory (MB)?

What is the Available Physical Memory (MB)?

How much Physical Memory (MB) is being used by the system?

Step 4

Click the **Networking** tab.

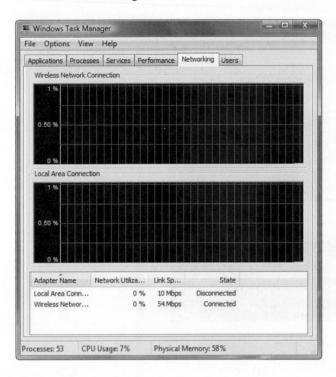

What is the Link Speed?

Step 5

Click the **Users** tab.

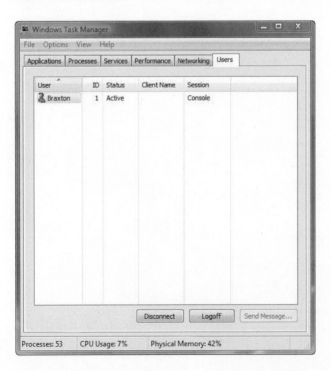

List all users and their Status.

What actions can you perform on the user from this window?

Step 6

Click the **Processes** tab.

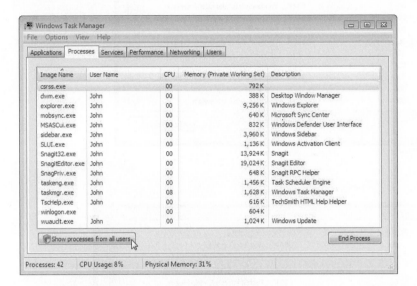

Click **Show processes from all users**.

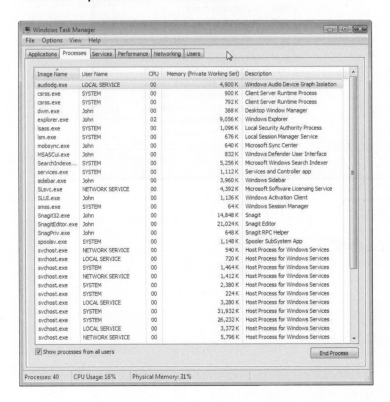

Double-click the border around the tabs.

Windows Task Manager is now in compact mode.

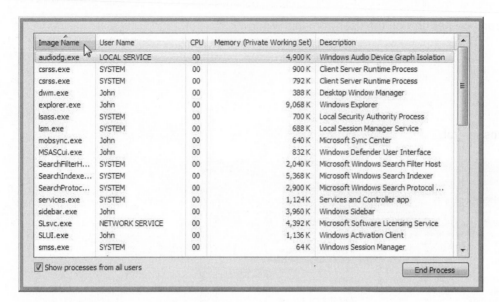

Click **Image Name**.

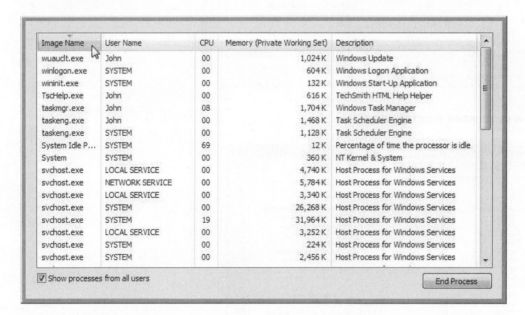

Click **Image Name** again.

What effect does this have on the columns?

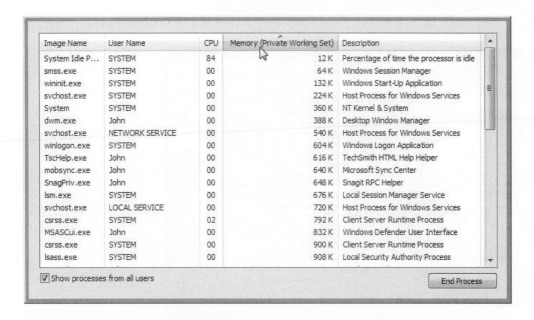

Click **Memory (Private Working Set)**.

What effect does this have on the columns?

Double-click the outside border again to return to tabs mode.

Step 7

Open a browser.

Note: Firefox is used in this lab. However, any browser will work. Just substitute your browser name whenever you see the word **Firefox**.

Return to the "Windows Task Manager".

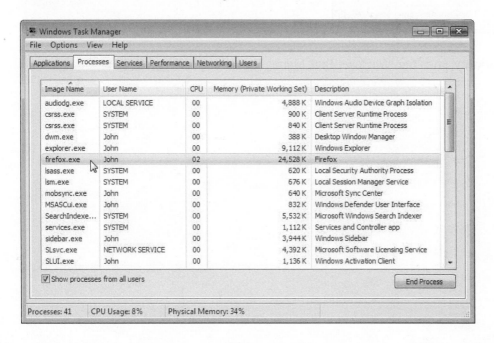

Click **Image Name** so the list is in alphabetical order; then locate and select **firefox.exe**.

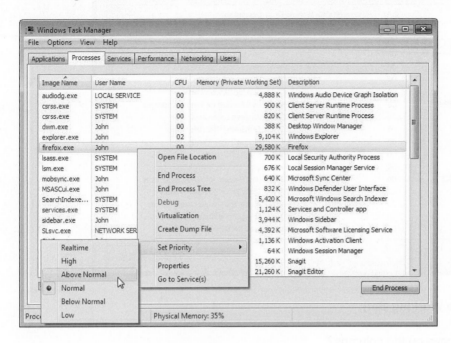

Right-click **firefox.exe > Set Priority**.

What is the default priority for the browser?

Set the priority to **Above Normal**.

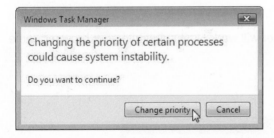

Click **Change priority** when the "Windows Task Manager" warning message opens.

Step 8

Expand the width of the "Windows Task Manager" window.

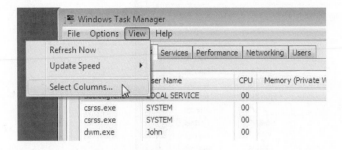

Click **View > Select Columns**.

Place a check mark next to **Base Priority >** click **OK**.

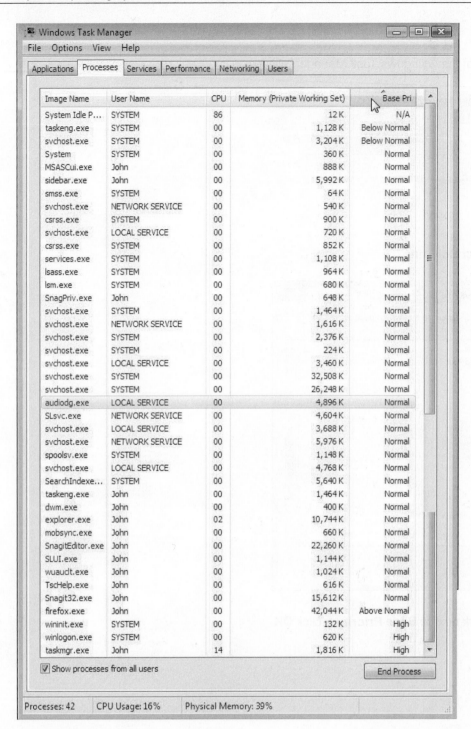

Click **Base Pri**.

Which image name has a base priority of N/A?

List one image name that has a base priority of Above Normal.

Step 9

Reset Firefox.exe base priority to **Normal > Change priority**.

Click **View > Select Columns > uncheck Base Priority > OK**.

Close Firefox.

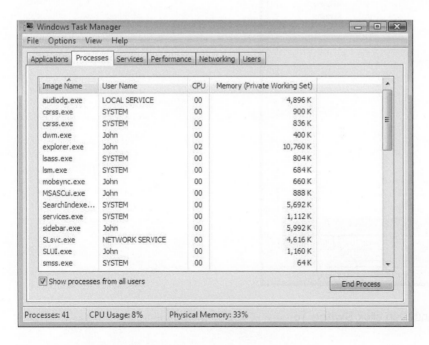

Is Firefox listed as a process?

5.3.1.7 Lab - Task Manager (Managing Processes) in Windows XP

Introduction

In this lab, you will explore Task Manager and manage processes from within Task Manager.

Recommended Equipment

The following equipment is required for this exercise:

  • A computer running Windows XP Professional

Step 1

Log on to Windows as an administrator.

Open a browser and a folder.

Click on the desktop and press **Ctrl-Alt-Delete**.

Click the **Applications** tab.

Select the open browser and then click **Switch To**.

What happened to the browser?

What happened to Windows Task Manager?

Open Task Manager, press **Ctrl-Alt-Delete**.

Click the **Applications** tab.

Click **New Task**.

The "Create New Task" window opens.

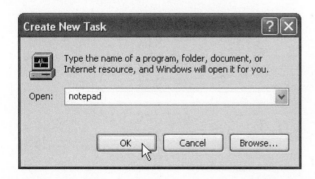

In the Open field, type **notepad** and then click **OK**.

What happens?

Navigate back to Windows Task Manager.

Select **Notepad** and then click **End Task**.

What happens?

Step 2

Click the **Performance** tab.

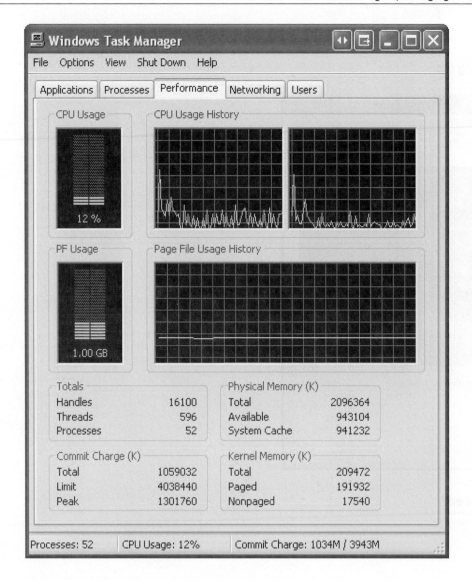

How many Threads are running?

How many Processes are running?

What is the Total Physical Memory (K)?

What is the Available Physical Memory (K)?

How much Physical Memory (K) is being used by the system?

Step 3

Click the **Networking** tab.

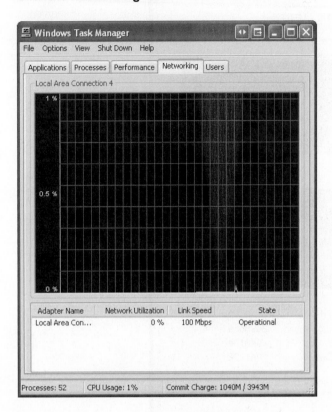

What is the Link Speed?

Step 4

Click the **Users** tab.

List all users and their Status.

What actions can you perform on the user?

Step 5

Click the **Processes** tab.

Double-click the border around the tabs.

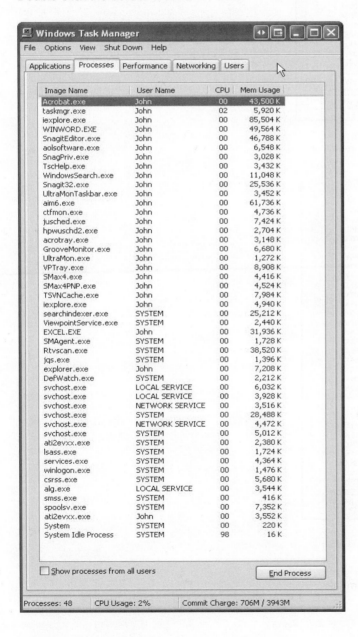

Windows Task Manager is now in compact mode.

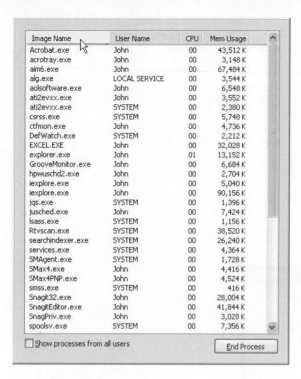

Click **Image Name**.

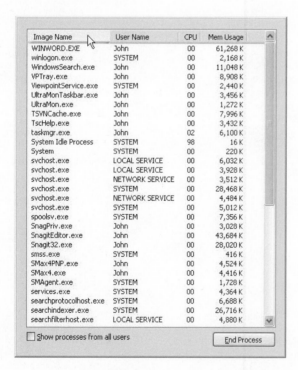

Click **Image Name** again.

What effect does this have on the columns?

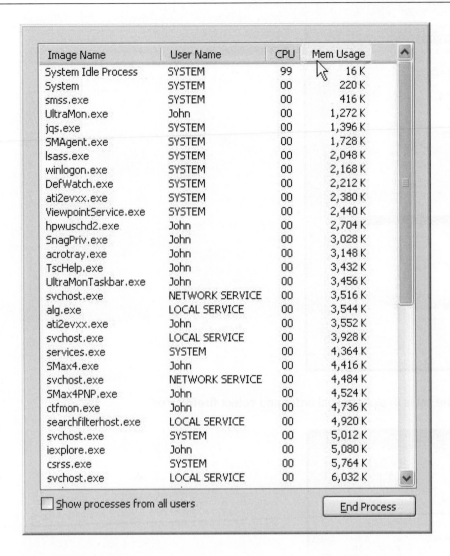

Image Name	User Name	CPU	Mem Usage
System Idle Process	SYSTEM	99	16 K
System	SYSTEM	00	220 K
smss.exe	SYSTEM	00	416 K
UltraMon.exe	John	00	1,272 K
jqs.exe	SYSTEM	00	1,396 K
SMAgent.exe	SYSTEM	00	1,728 K
lsass.exe	SYSTEM	00	2,048 K
winlogon.exe	SYSTEM	00	2,168 K
DefWatch.exe	SYSTEM	00	2,212 K
ati2evxx.exe	SYSTEM	00	2,380 K
ViewpointService.exe	SYSTEM	00	2,440 K
hpwuschd2.exe	John	00	2,704 K
SnagPriv.exe	John	00	3,028 K
acrotray.exe	John	00	3,148 K
TscHelp.exe	John	00	3,432 K
UltraMonTaskbar.exe	John	00	3,456 K
svchost.exe	NETWORK SERVICE	00	3,516 K
alg.exe	LOCAL SERVICE	00	3,544 K
ati2evxx.exe	John	00	3,552 K
svchost.exe	LOCAL SERVICE	00	3,928 K
services.exe	SYSTEM	00	4,364 K
SMax4.exe	John	00	4,416 K
svchost.exe	NETWORK SERVICE	00	4,484 K
SMax4PNP.exe	John	00	4,524 K
ctfmon.exe	John	00	4,736 K
searchfilterhost.exe	LOCAL SERVICE	00	4,920 K
svchost.exe	SYSTEM	00	5,012 K
iexplore.exe	John	00	5,080 K
csrss.exe	SYSTEM	00	5,764 K
svchost.exe	LOCAL SERVICE	00	6,032 K

☐ Show processes from all users   [End Process]

Click **Mem Usage**.

What effect does this have on the columns?

Double-click the outside border again for tabs mode.

Step 6

Open a browser.

Note: Firefox is used in this lab. However, any browser will work. Just substitute your browser name whenever you see the word Firefox.

Return to the Windows Task Manager.

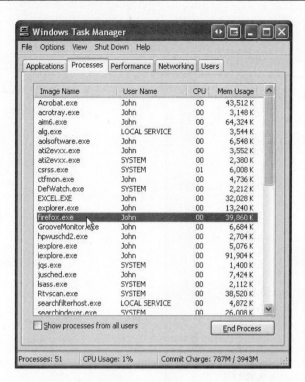

Click **Image Name** so the list is in alphabetical order and select **firefox.exe**.

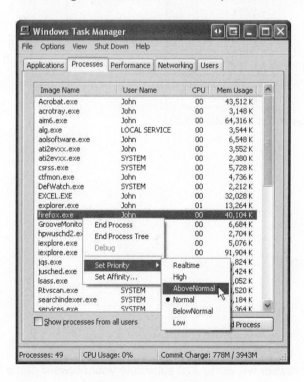

Right-click **firefox.exe > Set Priority**.

What is the default priority for the browser?

Set the priority to **Above Normal**.

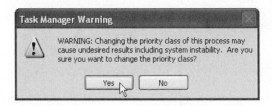

Click **Yes** in the Task Manager Warning window.

Step 7

Expand the width of the **Windows Task Manager** window.

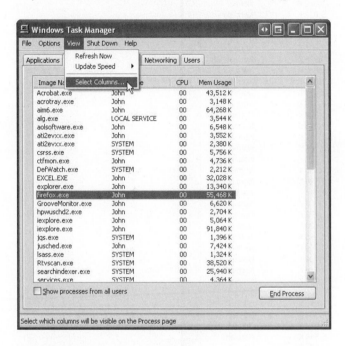

Click **View > Select Columns**.

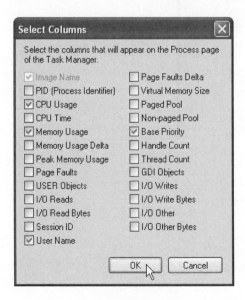

Place a check mark next to **Base Priority** and click **OK**.

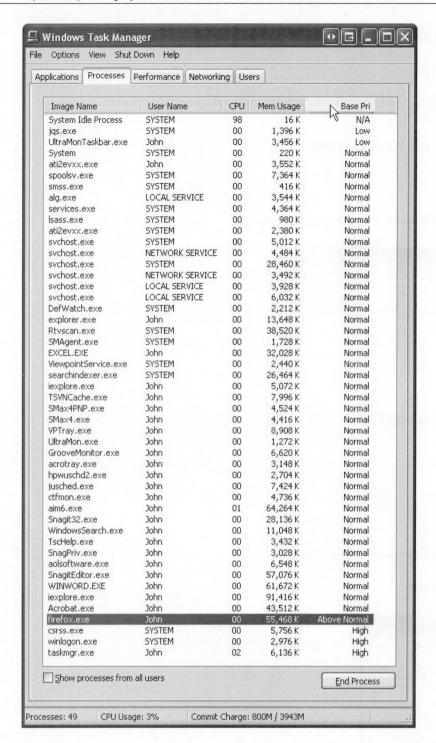

Click **Base Pri**.

Which image name has a base priority of N/A?

List one image name that has a base priority of Above Normal.

Step 8

Reset Firefox.exe base priority to **Normal > Yes**.

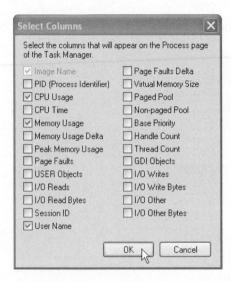

Click **View > Select Columns >** uncheck **Base Priority > OK**.

Close Firefox.

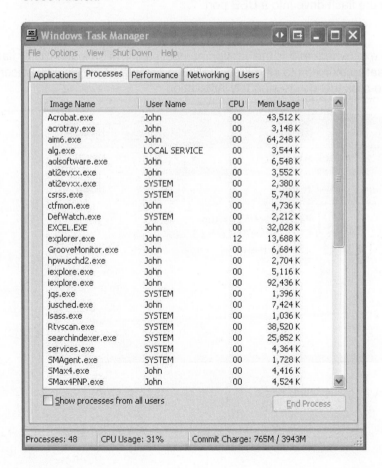

Is Firefox listed as a process?

5.3.1.11 Lab - Install Third-Party Software in Windows 7

Introduction

In this lab, you will install and remove a third-party software application supplied by your instructor. You will install the Packet Tracer Windows application.

Recommended Equipment

The following equipment is required for this exercise:

- A computer system that is using Windows 7
- A flash drive or CD with the latest Packet Tracer Windows install package

Step 1

Log on to the computer with the Administrator account.

Use Windows Explorer to navigate to the Packet Tracer folder.
If installing from a CD, place the CD into the CD drive.
Navigate to D:\Packet Tracer.

If installing from a flash drive, place the flash drive into a USB port.
Navigate to E:\Packet Tracer.

Locate the PacketTracer###_setup.exe (where ### is the version number) application in the CD or flash drive. Click the **PacketTracer533_setup.exe** icon to start the installation process of the Packet Tracer application. You may need to double-click the icon to start the installation.

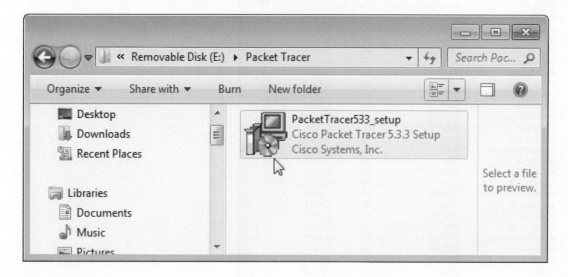

If the "User Account Control" window appears, click **Yes**.

Step 2

The "Setup – Cisco Packet Tracer 5.3.3" window opens.

Click **Next**.

The "License Agreement" screen appears.

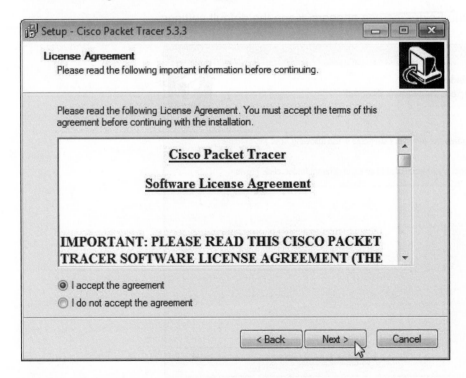

Select **I accept the agreement** and then click **Next**.

The "Select Destination Location" screen appears. Keep the default settings.

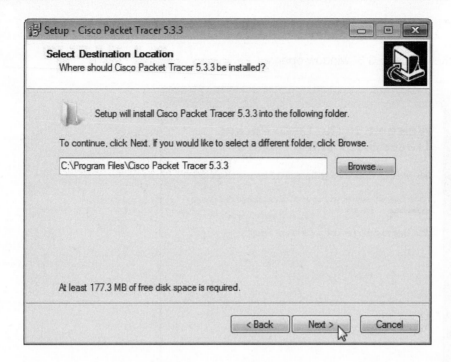

What is the default location for Packet Tracer?

Click **Next**.

The "Select Start Menu Folder" screen appears. Keep the default settings.

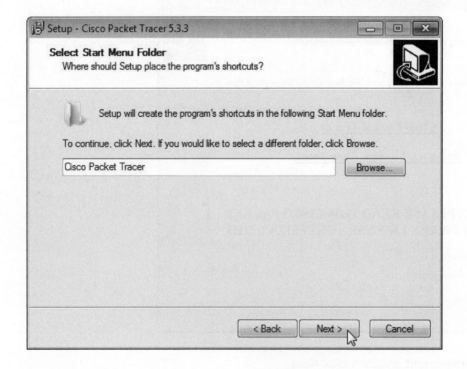

Click **Next**.

The "Select Additional Tasks" screen appears. Keep the default settings.

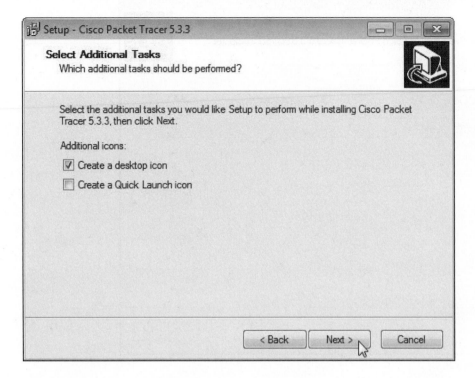

Click **Next**.

The "Ready to Install" screen appears.

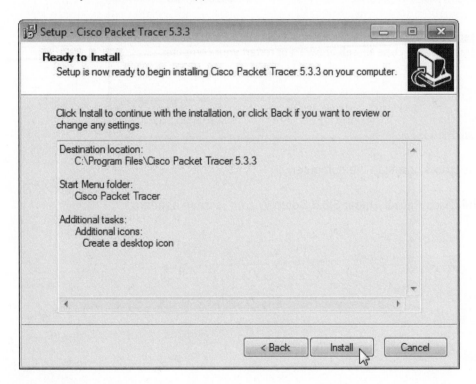

Click **Install**.

The "Installing" progress screen appears.

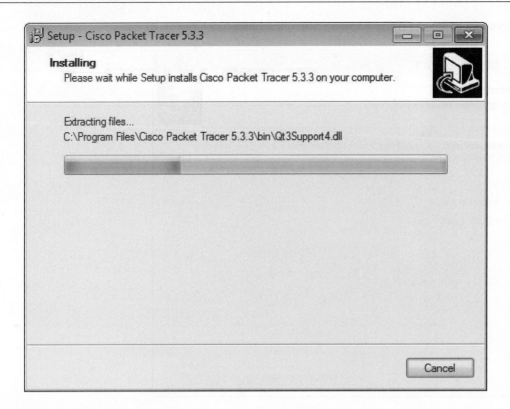

If an information screen appears, click **OK**.

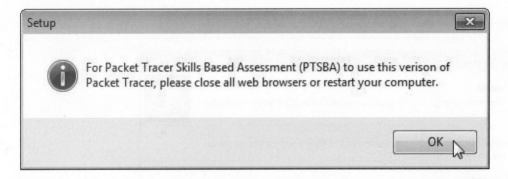

Do not close any programs or restart the computer.

The "Completing the Cisco Packet Tracer 5.3.3 Setup Wizard" screen appears.

Click **Finish**.

The "You are running Packet Tracer for the first time" screen appears.

Click **OK**.

If Windows Security Alert appears, click **Unblock**.

Packet Tracer starts.

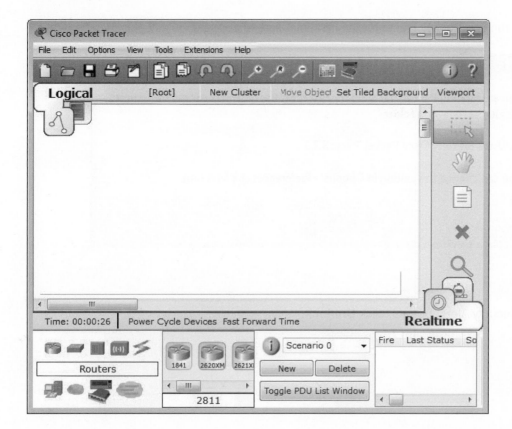

Close all open windows.

Step 3

Log on to the computer with the Administrator account.

To uninstall a program, choose **Start > Control Panel > Programs and Features**. Click **Cisco Packet Tracer** in the list.

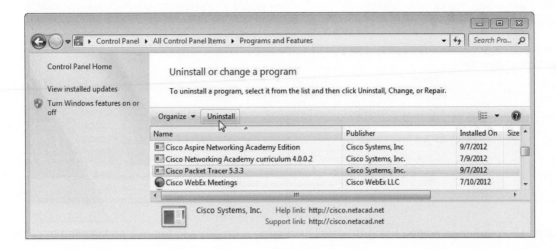

Click **Uninstall**.

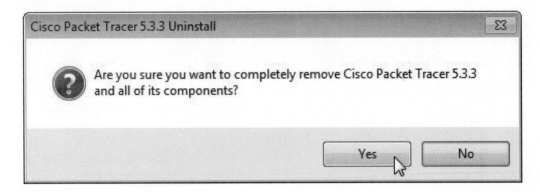

Click **Yes** to confirm the removal.

When the successfully removed screen appears, click **OK**.

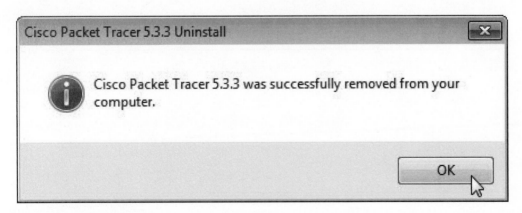

After the application removal process, the Programs and Features window no longer shows Cisco Packet Tracer in the list.

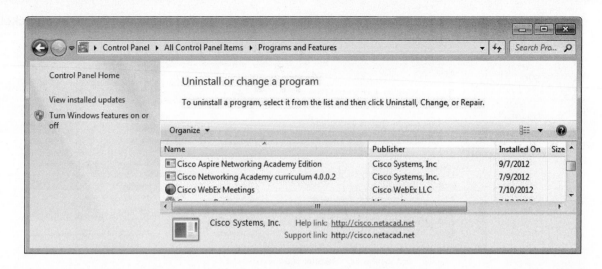

Why does Microsoft recommend using Uninstall or change a program to remove an installed application?

5.3.1.12 Lab - Install Third-Party Software in Windows Vista

Introduction

In this lab, you will install and remove a third-party software application supplied by your instructor. You will install the Packet Tracer Windows application.

Recommended Equipment

The following equipment is required for this exercise:

- A computer system that is using Windows Vista
- A flash drive or CD with the latest Packet Tracer Windows install package

Step 1

Log on to the computer with the Administrator account.

Use Windows Explorer to navigate to the Packet Tracer folder.

If installing from a CD, place the CD into the CD drive and navigate to Packet Tracer.

If installing from a flash drive, place the flash drive into a USB port and navigate to Packet Tracer.

Locate the PacketTracer###_setup.exe (where ### is the version number) application in the CD or flash drive. Double-click the **PacketTracer533_setup.exe** icon to start the installation process of the Packet Tracer application.

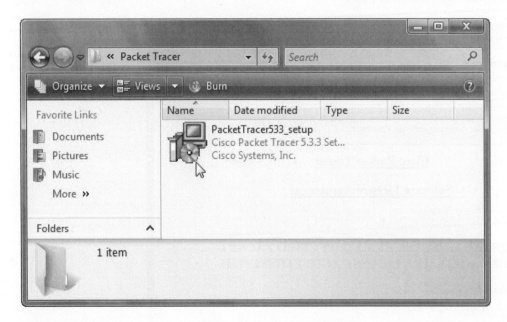

If the "User Account Control" window appears, click **Allow**.

Step 2

The "Setup – Cisco Packet Tracer 5.3.3" window opens.

Click **Next**.

The "License Agreement" screen appears.

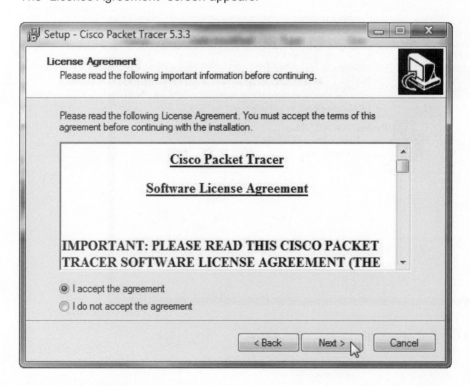

Select **I accept the agreement** and then click **Next**.

The "Select Destination Location" screen appears. Keep the default settings.

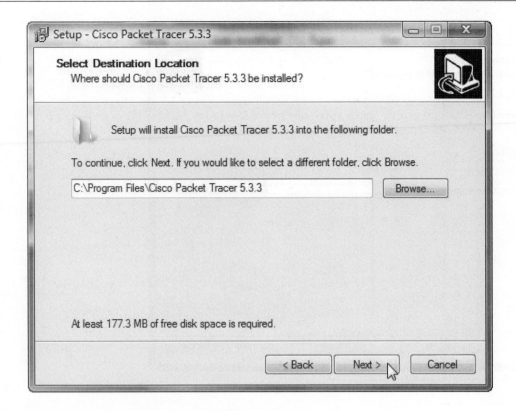

What is the default location for Packet Tracer?

Click **Next**.

The "Select Start Menu Folder" screen appears. Keep the default settings.

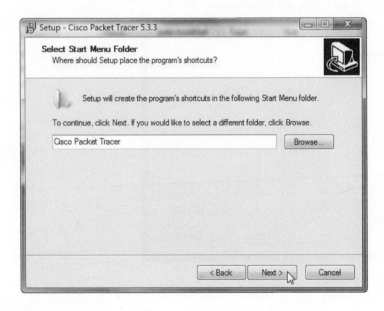

Click **Next**.

The "Select Additional Tasks" screen appears. Keep the default settings.

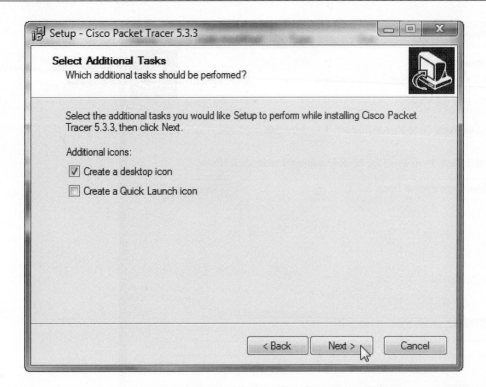

Click **Next**.

The "Ready to Install" screen appears.

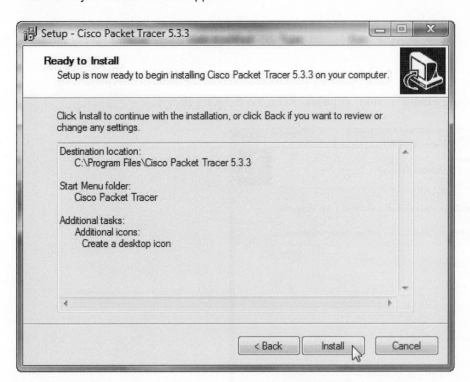

Click **Install**.

The "Installing" progress screen appears.

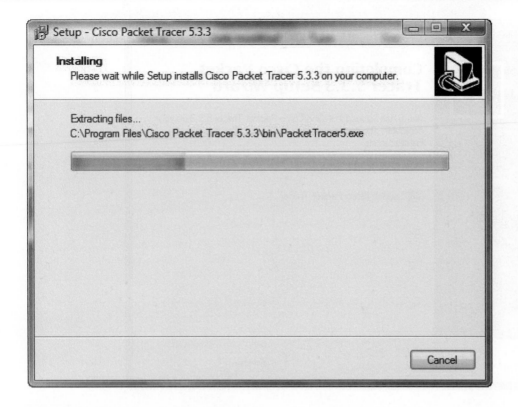

If an information screen appears, click **OK**.

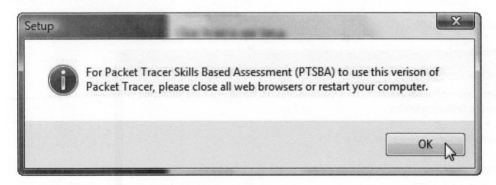

Do not close any programs or restart the computer.

The "Completing the Cisco Packet Tracer 5.3.3 Setup Wizard" screen appears.

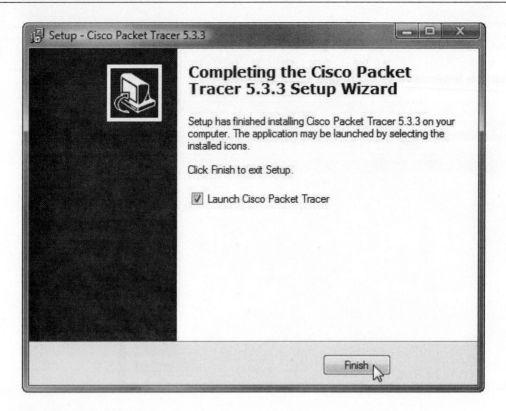

Click **Finish**.

The "You are running Packet Tracer for the first time" screen appears.

Click **OK**.

If Windows Security Alert appears, click **Unblock**.

Packet Tracer starts.

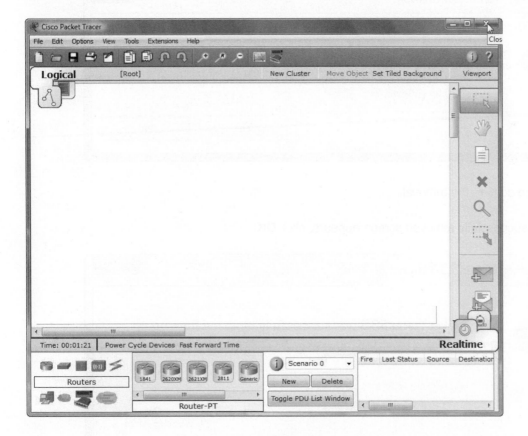

Close all open windows and restart the computer.

Step 3

Log on to the computer with the Administrator account.

To uninstall a program, choose **Start > Control Panel > Programs and Features**. Click **Cisco Packet Tracer** in the list.

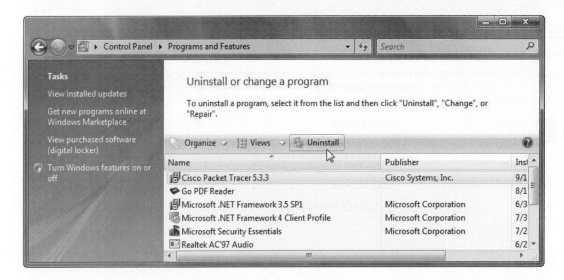

Click **Uninstall > Continue**.

Click **Yes** to confirm the removal.

When the successfully removed screen appears, click **OK**.

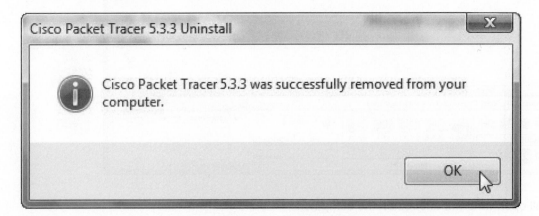

After the application removal process, the Programs and Features window no longer shows Cisco Packet Tracer in the list.

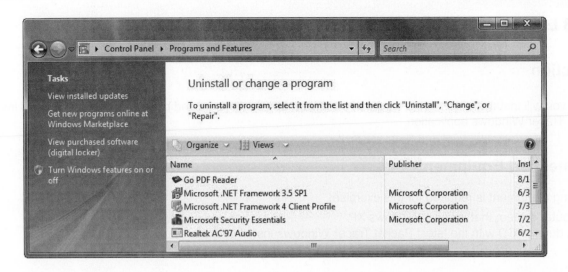

Why does Microsoft recommend using Uninstall or change a program to remove an installed application?

5.3.1.13 Lab - Install Third-Party Software in Windows XP

Introduction

In this lab, you will install and remove a third-party software application supplied by your instructor. You will install the Packet Tracer Windows application.

Recommended Equipment

The following equipment is required for this exercise:
- A computer system that is using Windows XP
- A flash drive or CD with the latest Packet Tracer Windows install package

Step 1

Log on to the computer with the Administrator account.

Use Windows Explorer to navigate to the Packet Tracer folder.
If installing from a CD, place the CD into the CD drive and navigate to Packet Tracer.

If installing from a flash drive, place the flash drive into a USB port and navigate to Packet Tracer.

Locate the PacketTracer###_setup.exe (where ### is the version number) application in the CD or flash drive. Double-click the **PacketTracer533_setup.exe** icon to start the installation process of the Packet Tracer application.

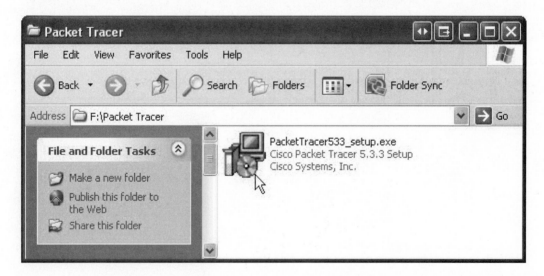

Step 2

The "Setup – Cisco Packet Tracer 5.3.3" window opens.

Click **Next**.

The "License Agreement" screen appears.

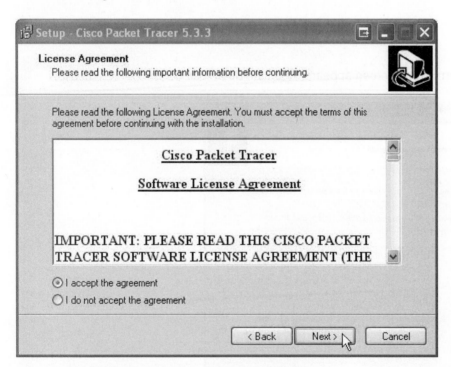

Select **I accept the agreement** and then click **Next**.
The "Select Destination Location" screen appears. Keep the default settings.

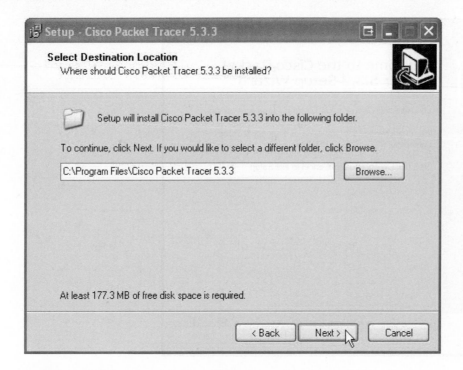

What is the default location for Packet Tracer?

Click **Next**.

The "Select Start Menu Folder" screen appears. Keep the default settings.

Click **Next**.

The "Select Additional Tasks" screen appears. Keep the default settings.

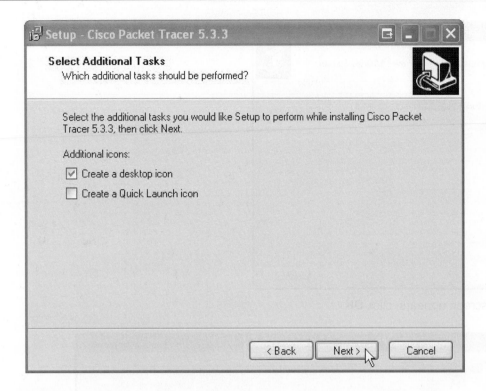

Click **Next**.

The "Ready to Install" screen appears.

Click **Install**.

The "Installing" progress screen appears.

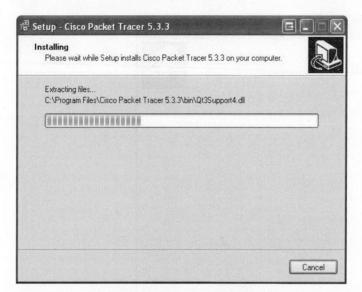

If an information screen appears, click **OK**.

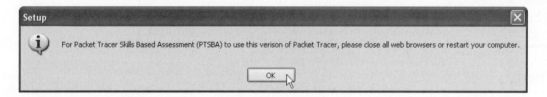

Do not close any programs or restart the computer.

The "Completing the Cisco Packet Tracer 5.3.3 Setup Wizard" screen appears.

Click **Finish**.

Packet Tracer starts.

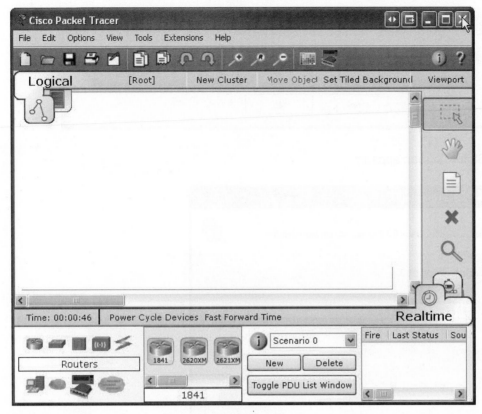

Close all open windows and restart the computer.

Step 3

Log on to the computer with the Administrator account.

To uninstall a program, choose **Start > Control Panel > Add or Remove Programs**. Click **Cisco Packet Tracer** in the list. Click **Remove**.

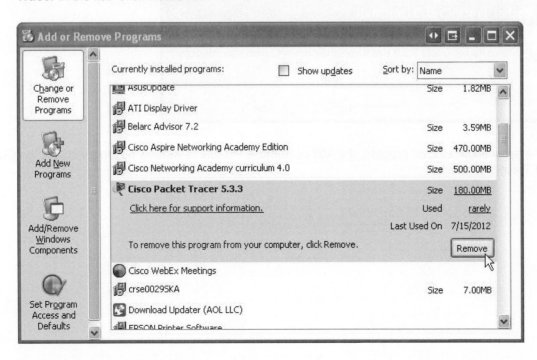

Click **Yes** to confirm the removal.

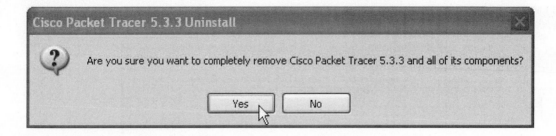

The "Uninstall Status" screen appears.

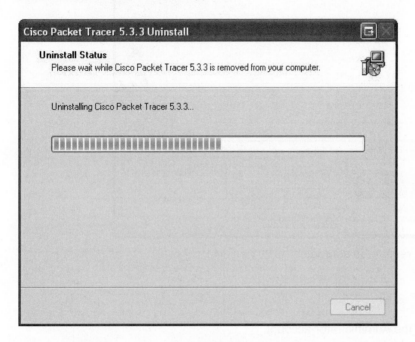

When the successfully removed window opens, click **OK**.

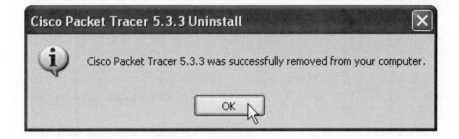

After the application removal process, the Add or Remove Programs window no longer shows the Cisco Packet Tracer in the list.

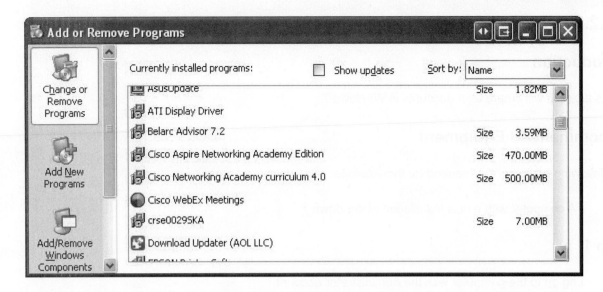

Why does Microsoft recommend using Add/Remove Programs to remove an installed application?

5.3.2.3 Lab - Create User Accounts in Windows 7

Introduction

In this lab, you will create user accounts in Windows 7.

Recommended Equipment

The following equipment is required for this exercise:

   • A computer with a new installation of Windows 7

Step 1

Log on to the computer with the Administrator account.

Navigate to the "Control Panel" window by clicking **Start > Control Panel**.

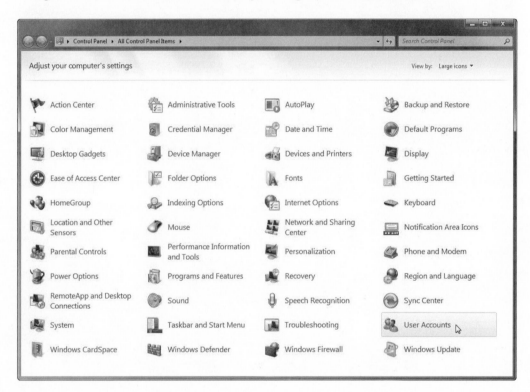

Double-click the **User Accounts** icon.

Step 2

The "User Accounts" window appears.

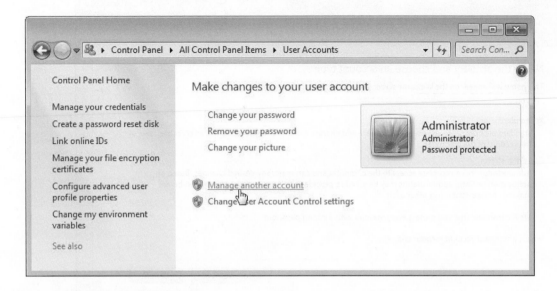

Click **Manage another account**.

The "Manage Accounts" window appears.

Click **Create a new account**.

Step 3

The "Create New Account" window appears.

What can a user do with a limited account?

What limitations does this type of an account have?

Type the name provided by your instructor in the "Name the account and choose an account type" field and select **Standard user** as the account type.

Click **Create Account**.

Step 4

Click the user account you just created.

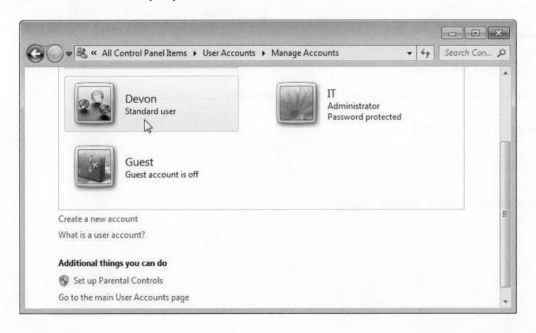

The "Make changes to Devon's account?" screen appears.

What information is listed for the new account?

Click **Create a password**.

Type in the password provided by the instructor and then click **Create password**.

Step 5

The "Make changes to Devon's account?" screen appears.

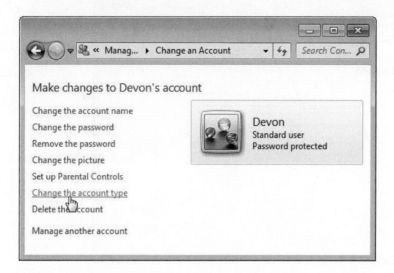

What information is listed for the new account?

Click **Change the account type**.

Step 6

The "Change Account Type" window appears.

Select **Administrator** as the account type.

What can a user do with an administrator account?

Click **Change Account Type**.

Step 7

The "Make changes to Devon's account?" screen appears.

Click **Delete the account**.

The "Do you want to keep Devon's files?" screen appears.

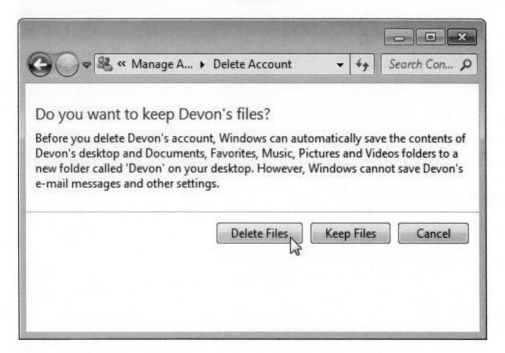

Click **Delete files**.

The "Are you sure you want to delete Devon's account?" screen appears.

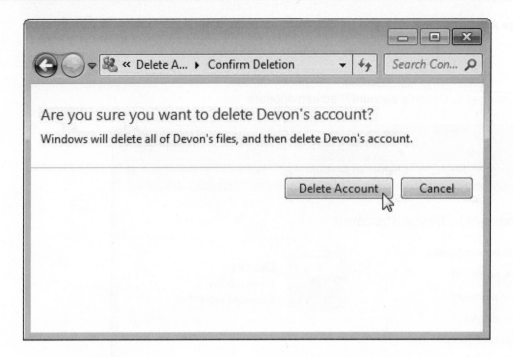

Click **Delete Account**.

Notice the account is no longer listed.

Close all opened windows.

5.3.2.4 Lab - Create User Accounts in Windows Vista

Introduction

In this lab, you will create user accounts in Windows Vista.

Recommended Equipment

The following equipment is required for this exercise:

- A computer with a new installation of Windows Vista

Step 1

Log on to the computer with the Administrator account.

Navigate to the "Control Panel" window by clicking **Start > Control Panel**.

Double-click the **User Accounts** icon.

Step 2

The "User Accounts" window appears.

Click **Manage another account > Continue** if asked for permission.

The "Manage Accounts" window appears.

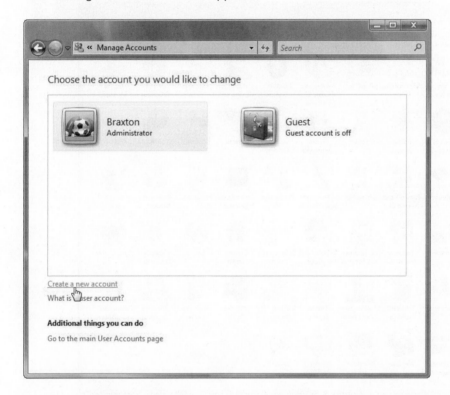

Click **Create a new account**.

Step 3

The "Create New Account" window appears.

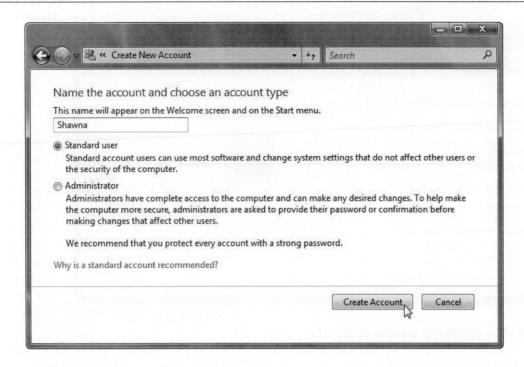

What can a user do with a limited account?

What limitations does this type of an account have?

Type the name provided by your instructor in the "Name the account and choose an account type" field and select **Standard user** as the account type.

Click **Create Account**.

Step 4

Click the user account you just created.

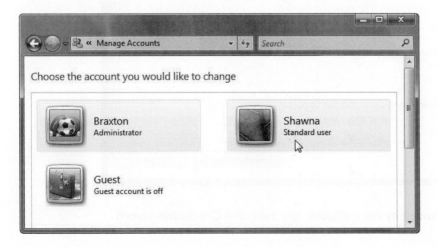

The "Make changes to Shawna's account?" screen appears.

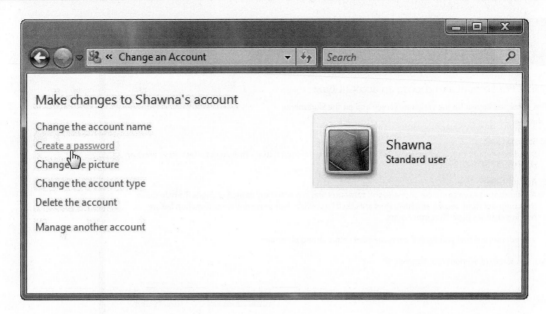

What information is listed for the new account?

Click **Create a password**.

Type in the password provided by the instructor and then click **Create password**.

Step 5

The "Make changes to Shawna's account?" screen appears.

What information is listed for the new account?

Click **Change the account type**.

Step 6

The "Change Account Type" window appears.

Select Administrator as the account type.

What can a user do with an administrator account?

Click **Change Account Type**.

Step 7

The "Make changes to Shawna's account?" screen appears.

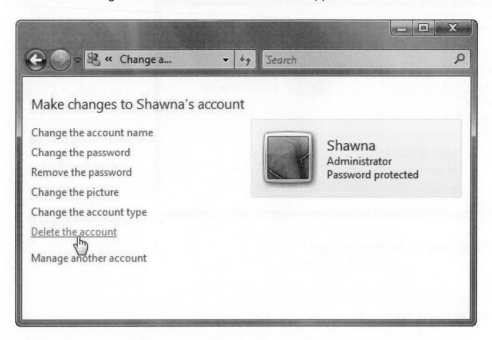

Click **Delete the account**.

The "Do you want to keep Shawna's files?" screen appears.

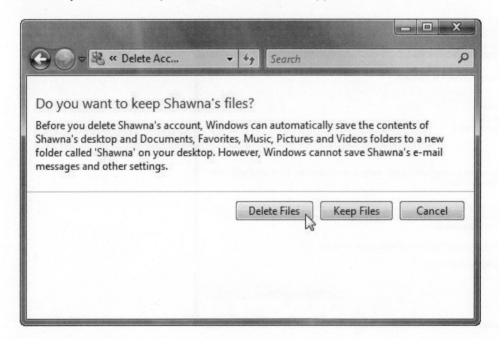

Click **Delete files**.

The "Are you sure you want to delete Shawna's account?" screen appears.

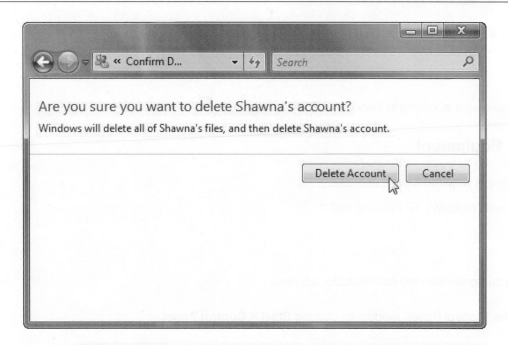

Click **Delete Account**.

Notice the account is no longer listed.

Close all opened windows.

5.3.2.5 Lab - Create User Accounts in Windows XP

Introduction

In this lab, you will create user accounts in Windows XP Professional.

Recommended Equipment

The following equipment is required for this exercise:

   • A computer with Windows XP Professional

Step 1

Log on to the computer with the Administrator account.

Navigate to the "Control Panel" window by clicking **Start > Control Panel**.

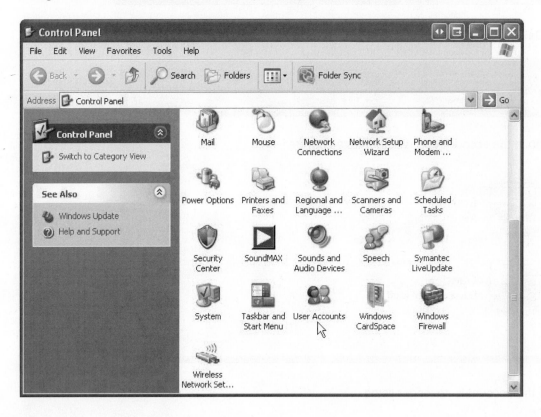

Double-click the **User Accounts** icon.

Step 2

The "User Accounts" window appears.

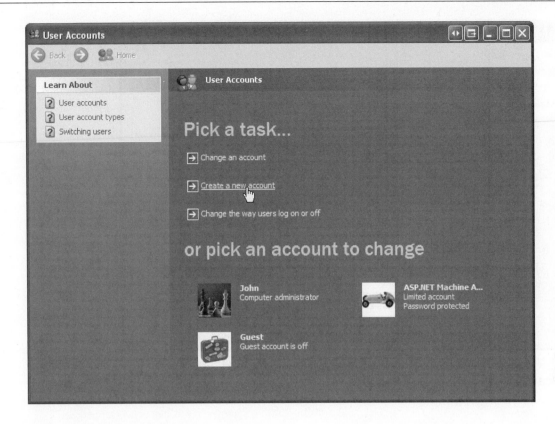

Click **Create a new account**.

Step 3

The "Name the new account" screen appears.

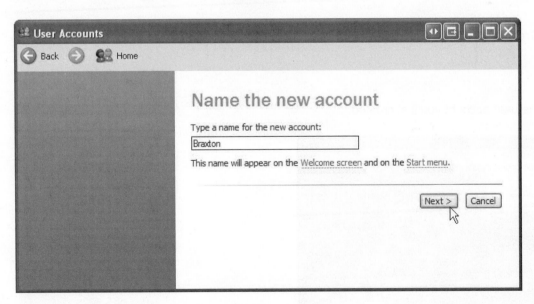

Type the name provided by your instructor in the "Type a name for the new account:" field and then click **Next**.

The "Pick an account type" screen appears.

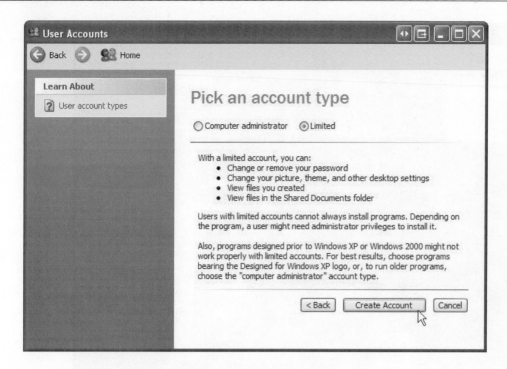

What can a user do with a limited account?

What limitations does this type of an account have?

Click **Create Account**.

Step 4

Click the user account you just created.

The "What do you want to change about Braxton's account?" screen appears.

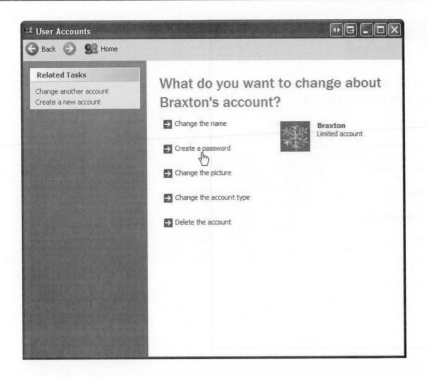

What information is listed for the new account?

Click **Create a password**.

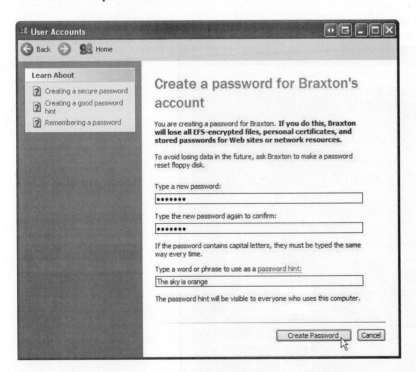

Type in the password provided by the instructor and then click **Create Password**.

Step 5

The "What do you want to change about Braxton's account?" screen appears.

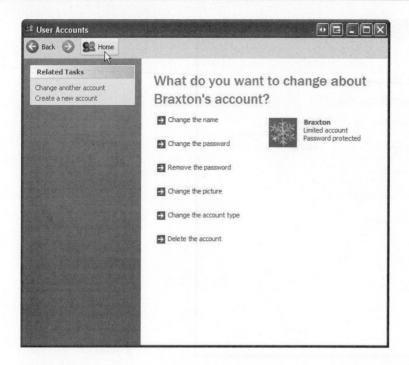

What information is listed for the new account?

Click **Home**.

The "User Accounts" screen appears.

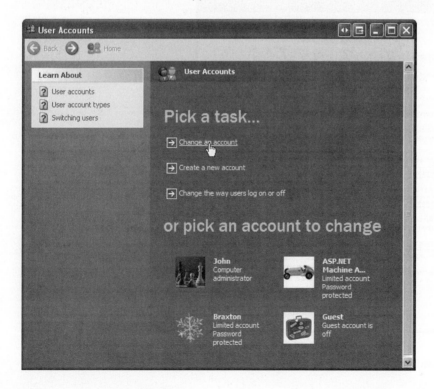

Click **Change an account**.

The "What do you want to change about Braxton's account?" screen appears.

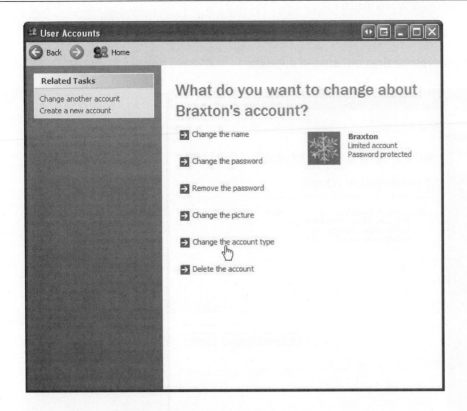

Click **Change the account type**.

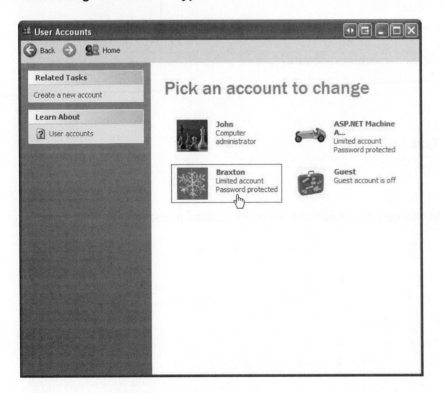

Click the account you created.

Step 6

The "Pick a new account type for Braxton" screen appears.

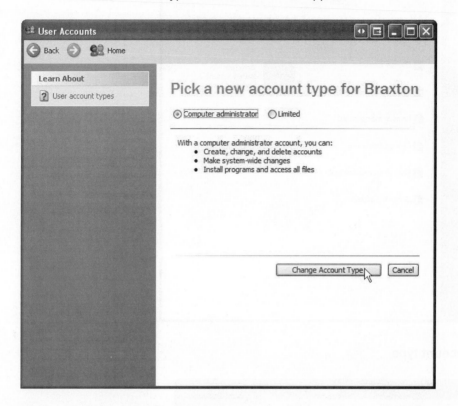

What can a user do with an administration account?

Click **Change Account Type**.

Step 7

The "What do you want to change about Braxton's account?" screen appears.

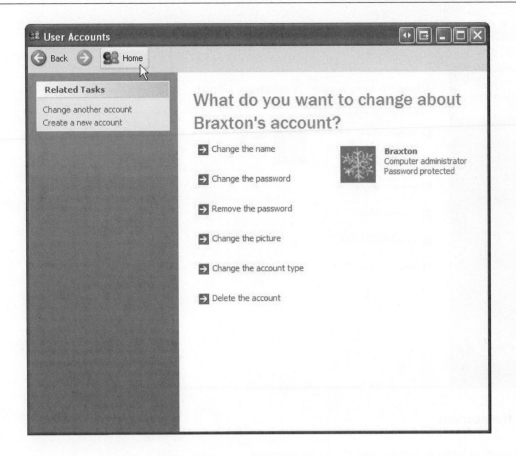

What information is listed for the new account?

Click **Home** and click the account you created.

Step 8

The "What do you want to change about Braxton's account?" screen appears.

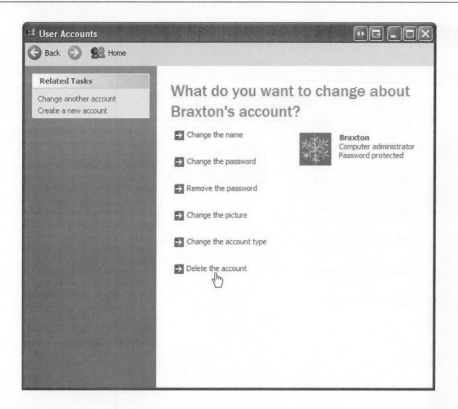

Click **Delete the account**.

The "Do you want to keep Braxton's files?" screen appears.

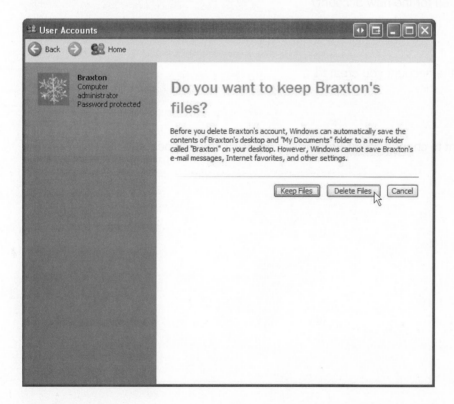

Click **Delete files**.

The "Are you sure you want to delete Braxton's account?" screen appears.

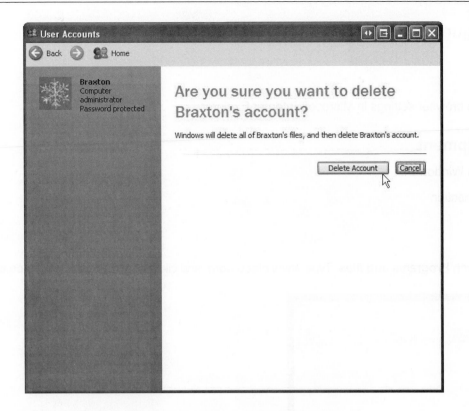

Click **Delete Account**.

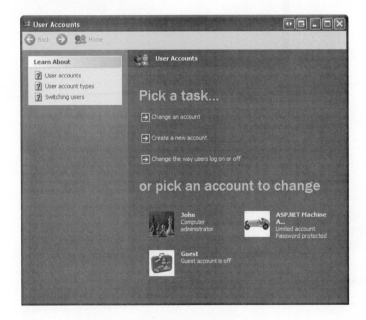

Notice the account is no longer listed.

Close all open windows.

5.3.2.7 Lab - Configure Browser Settings in Windows 7

Introduction

In this lab, you will configure browser settings in Microsoft Internet Explorer.

Recommended Equipment

- A computer with Windows 7
- An Internet connection

Step 1

Choose **Start > Search Programs and files**. Type **www.cisco.com**, and click the link **http://www.cisco.com**.

Which browser was used to open the web page?

If you did not answer "Internet Explorer", make Internet Explorer your default browser.

Choose **Start > All Programs > Internet Explorer**.

Choose **Tools > Internet Options**, and then click the **Programs** tab.

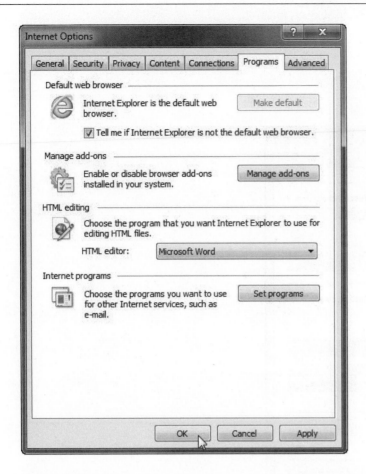

Select **Tell me if Internet Explorer is not the default web browser.** and then click **OK**.

Close the browser.

Choose **Start > All Programs > Internet Explorer**.

Click **Yes** to make Internet Explorer the default browser.

Click **Help > About Internet Explorer**.

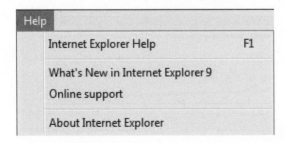

Which version of Internet Explorer is installed on your computer?

Step 2

Choose **Tools > Internet Options**.

The "Internet Options" window opens.

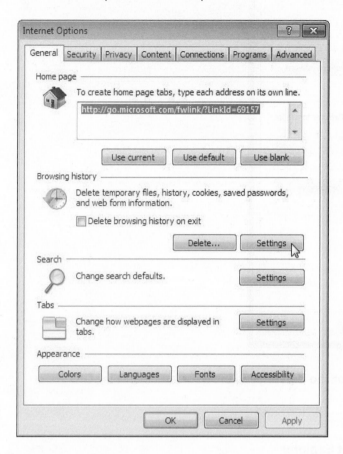

Click the **Settings** button in the "Browsing history" section.

The "Temporary Internet Files and History Settings" window opens.

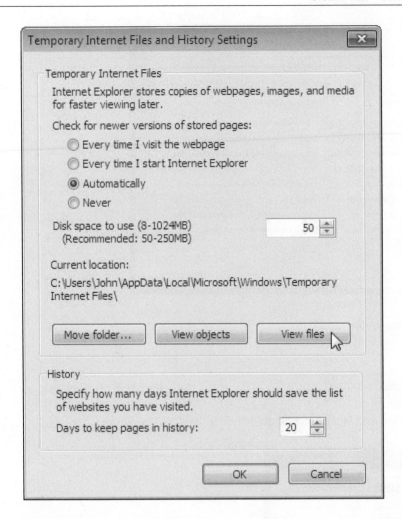

Which setting is configured to "Check for newer versions of stored pages"?

How many days is "History" set to store visited websites?

Click the **View files** button.

The "Temporary Internet Files" window opens.

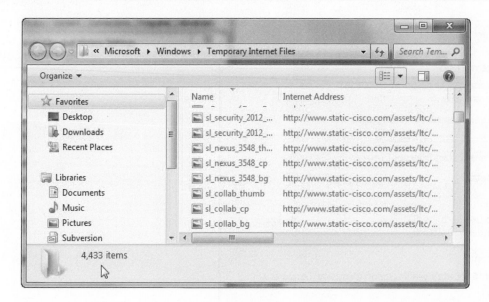

How many temporary Internet files were listed?

Close the "Temporary Internet Files" window.

Close the "Temporary Internet Files and History Settings" window

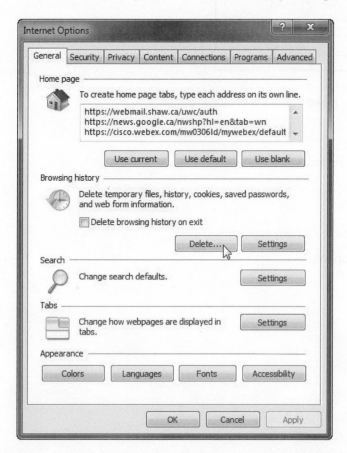

Click the **Delete** button in the "Browsing history" section.

The "Delete Browsing History" window opens.

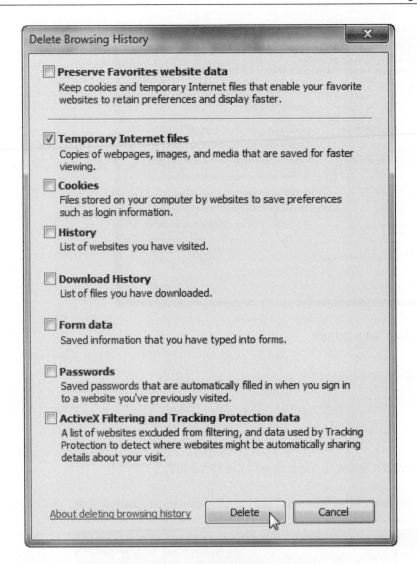

Which options are there for deleting browsing history?

Remove all selected options except for **Temporary Internet files**.

Click **Delete**.

When completed, you will see this message in the browser.

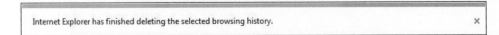

Click the **Settings** button, and then click the **View files** button.

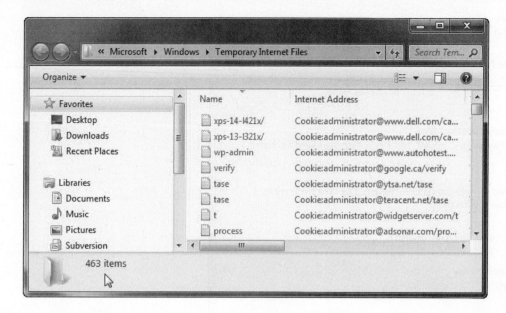

How many temporary Internet files were listed?

Close all opened windows.

Step 3

Open up Internet Explorer and visit a few web-sites all with the same tab.

Click the **down** arrow at the right end of the "address" field to view previously visited sites.

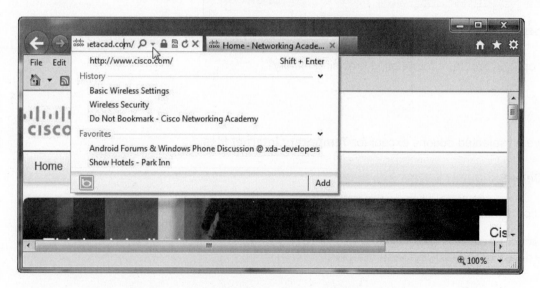

How many sites are listed in the drop-down box for "History"?

To clear the browser history, choose **Tools > Internet Options > Delete**.

Remove all selected options except for **History**.

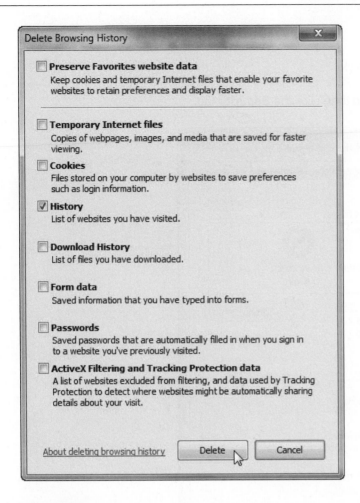

Click **Delete**.

Close all open windows except for Internet Explorer.

When completed, click the **down** arrow at the right end of the "address" field to view previously visited sites.

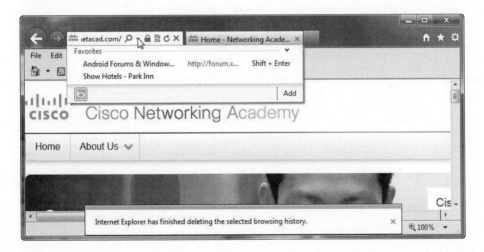

How many sites are now found in the drop-down box for "History"?

Step 4

Use this path to change Security settings:

Choose **Tools > Internet Options**, and then click the **Security** tab.

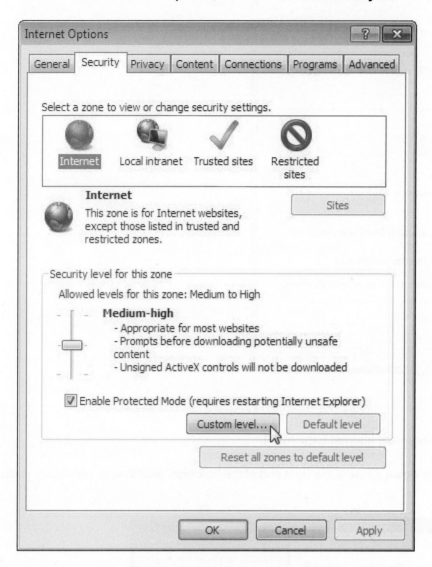

Click on each of the four zones and describe what they are used for.

Internet:

Local intranet:

Trusted sites:

Restricted sites:

Click the **Custom level** button.

The "Security Settings – Internet Zone" window opens.

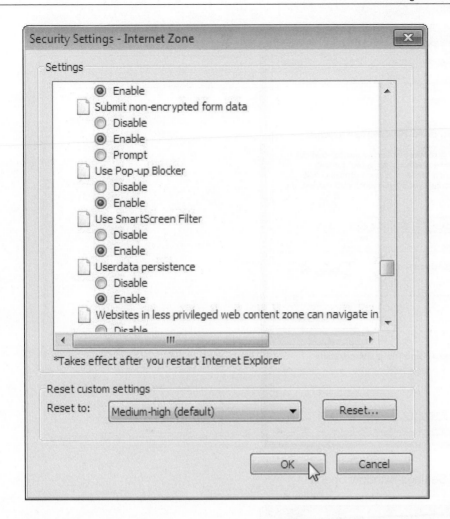

Here is where you select the options in the list that you wish to change for a zone.

Click **OK**.

Step 5

Click the **Privacy** tab **> Advanced**.

The "Advanced Privacy Settings" window opens.

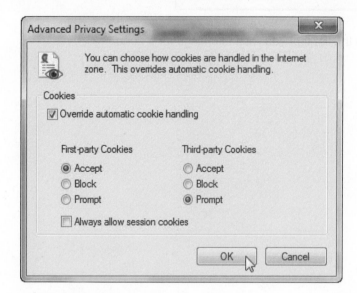

Set the following settings:

Override automatic cookie handling box has a check mark.

First-party Cookies is set to **Accept**.

Third-party Cookies is set to **Prompt**.

Click **OK** and close all opened windows.

5.3.2.8 Lab - Configure Browser Settings in Windows Vista

Introduction

In this lab, you will configure browser settings in Microsoft Internet Explorer.

Recommended Equipment

- A computer with Windows Vista
- An Internet connection

Step 1

Choose **Start > Start Search**. Type **www.cisco.com**, and click **Search the Internet**.

Which browser was used to open the web page?

If you did not answer "Internet Explorer", make Internet Explorer your default browser.

Choose **Start > All Programs > Internet Explorer**.

Choose **Tools > Internet Options**, and then click the **Programs** tab.

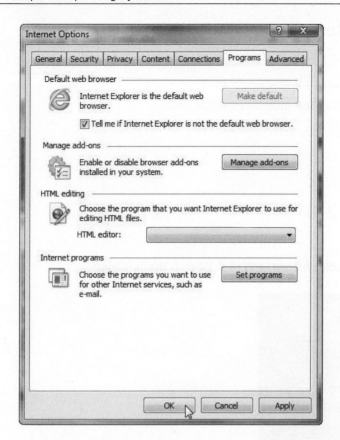

Select **Tell me if Internet Explorer is not the default web browser.** and then click **OK**.

Close the browser.

Choose **Start > All Programs > Internet Explorer**.

Click **Yes** to make Internet Explorer the default browser.

Click **Help > About Internet Explorer**.

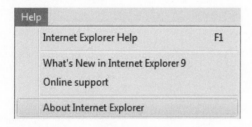

Which version of Internet Explorer is installed on your computer?

Step 2

Choose **Tools > Internet Options**.

The "Internet Options" window opens.

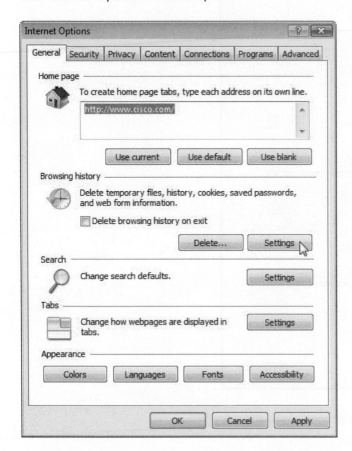

Click the **Settings** button in the "Browsing history" section.

The "Temporary Internet Files and History Settings" window opens.

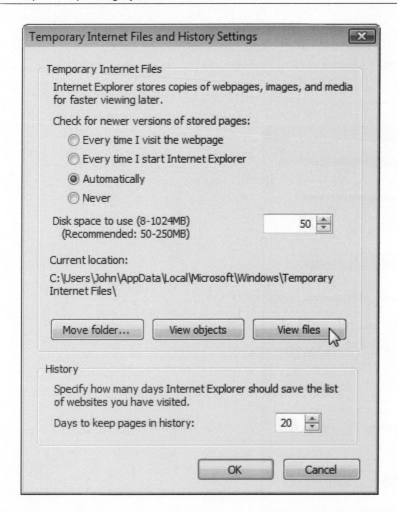

Which setting is configured to "Check for newer versions of stored pages"?

How many days is "History" set to store visited websites?

Click the **View files** button.

The "Temporary Internet Files" window opens.

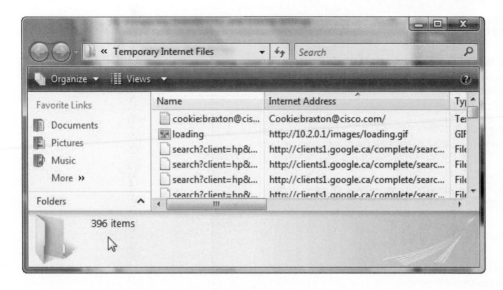

How many temporary Internet files were listed?

Close the "Temporary Internet Files" window.

Close the "Temporary Internet Files and History Settings" window

Click the **Delete** button in the "Browsing history" section.

The "Delete Browsing History" window opens.

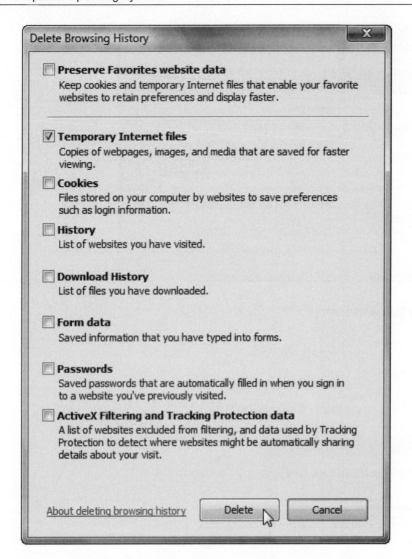

Which options are there for deleting browsing history?

Remove all selected options except for **Temporary Internet files**.

Click **Delete**.

When completed, you will see this message in the browser.

Click the **Settings** button, and then click the **View files** button.

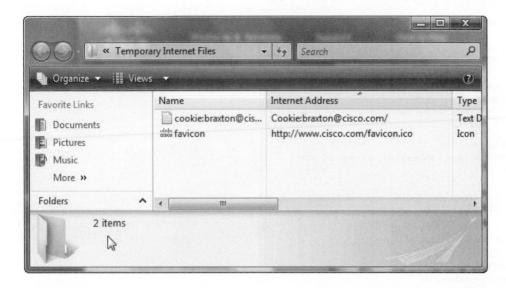

How many temporary Internet files were listed?

Close all opened windows.

Step 3

Open up Internet Explorer and visit a few web-sites all with the same tab.

Click the **down** arrow at the right end of the "address" field to view previously visited sites.

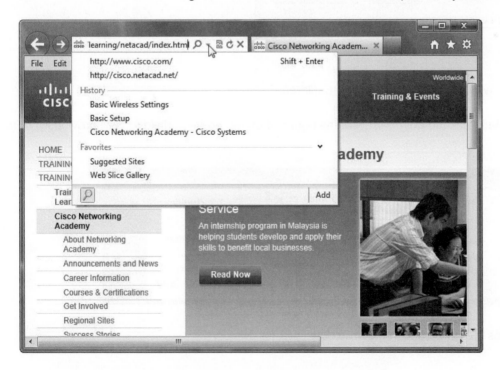

How many sites are listed in the drop-down box for "History"?

To clear the browser history, choose **Tools > Internet Options > Delete**.

Remove all selected options except for **History**.

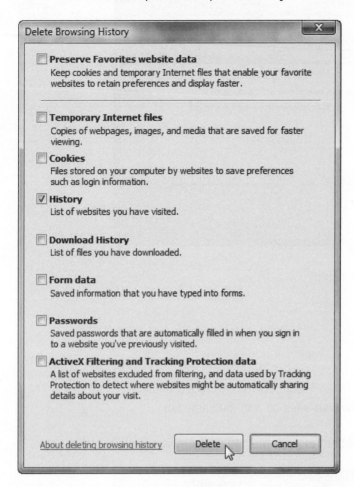

Click **Delete**.

Close all open windows except for Internet Explorer.

When completed, click the **down** arrow at the right end of the "address" field to view previously visited sites.

How many sites are now found in the drop-down box for "History"?

Step 4

Click **Tools > Internet Options**, and then click the **Security** tab.

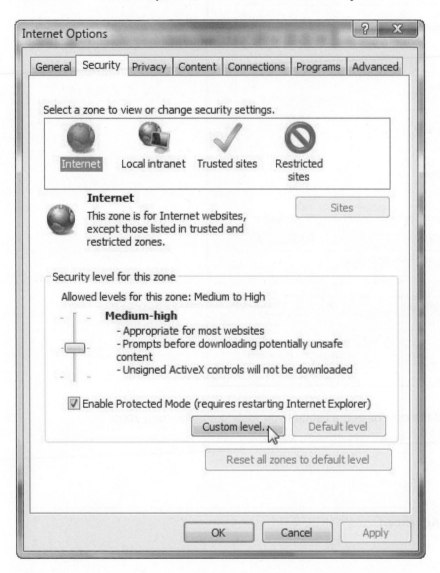

Click on each of the four zones and describe what they are used for.

Internet:

Local intranet:

Trusted sites:

Restricted sites:

Click the **Custom level** button.

The "Security Settings – Internet Zone" window opens.

Here is where you select the options in the list that you wish to change for a zone.

Click **OK**.

Step 5

Click the **Privacy** tab > **Advanced**.

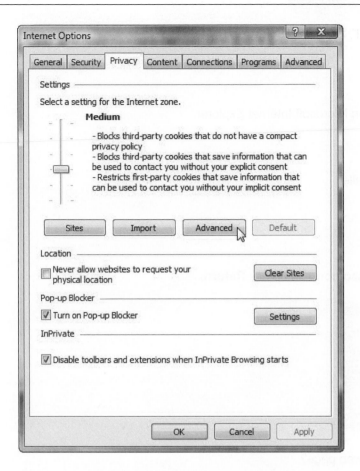

The "Advanced Privacy Settings" window opens.

Set the following settings:

Override automatic cookie handling box has a check mark.

First-party Cookies is set to **Accept**.

Third-party Cookies is set to **Prompt**.

Click **OK**.

5.3.2.9 Lab - Configure Browser Settings in Windows XP

Introduction

In this lab, you will configure browser settings in Microsoft Internet Explorer.

Recommended Equipment

- A computer with Windows XP installed
- An Internet connection

Step 1

Choose **Start > Run…**. Type **www.cisco.com**, and press **Return**.

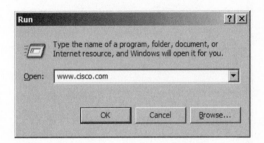

Which browser was used to open the web page?

If you did not answer "Internet Explorer", make Internet Explorer your default browser.

Choose **Start > All Programs > Internet Explorer**.

Choose **Tools > Internet Options**, and then click the **Programs** tab.

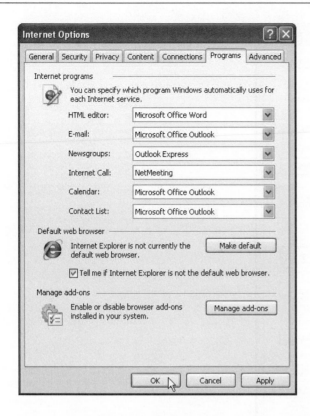

Select **Tell me if Internet Explorer is not the default web browser.** and then click **OK**.

Close the browser.

Choose **Start > All Programs > Internet Explorer**.

Click **Yes** to make Internet Explorer the default browser.

Click **Help > About Internet Explorer**.

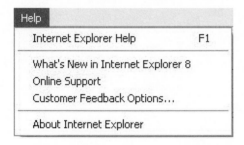

Which version of Internet Explorer is installed on your computer?

Step 2

Choose **Tools > Internet Options**.

The "Internet Options" window opens.

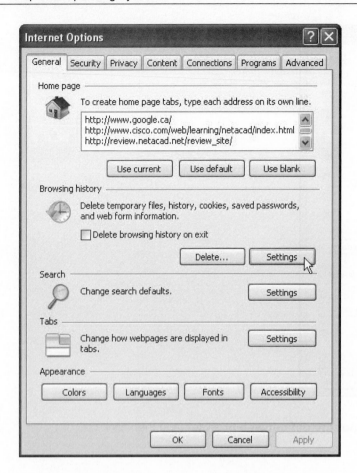

Click the **Settings** button in the "Browsing history" section.

The "Temporary Internet Files and History Settings" window opens.

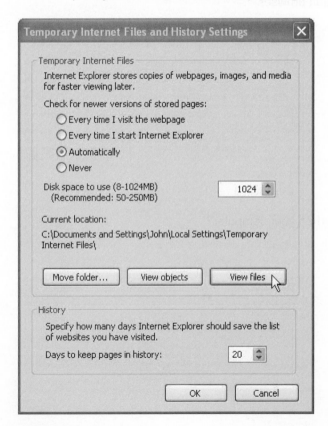

Which setting is configured to "Check for newer versions of stored pages"?

How many days is "History" set to store visited websites?

Click the **View files** button.

The "Temporary Internet Files" window opens.

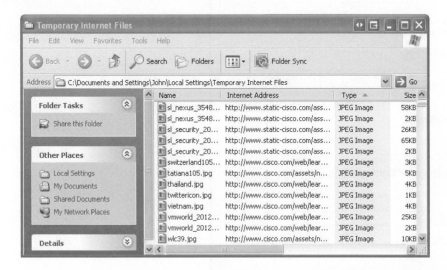

Estimate how many temporary Internet files were listed? Do not include cookies.

Close the "Temporary Internet Files" window.

Close the "Temporary Internet Files and History Settings" window.

Click the **Delete** button in the "Browsing history" section.

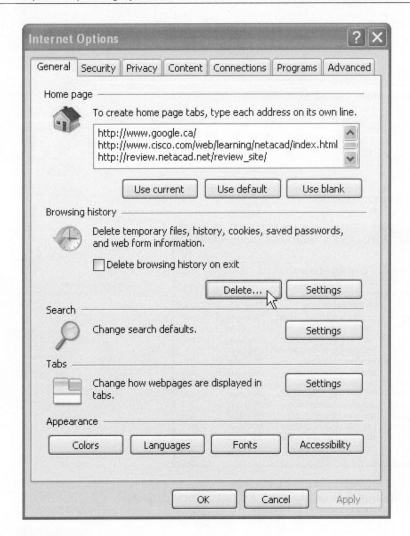

The "Delete Browsing History" window opens.

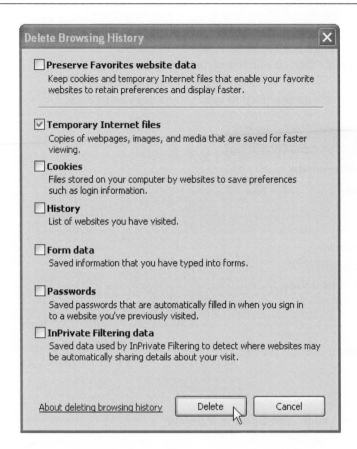

Which options are there for deleting browsing history?

Remove all selected options except for **Temporary Internet files**.

Click **Delete**.

The "Delete Browsing History" window opens.

When completed, click the **Settings** button, and then click the **View files** button.

How many temporary Internet files were listed?

Close all opened windows.

Step 3

Open up Internet Explorer and visit four web-sites all with the same tab.

Click the **down** arrow at the right end of the "address" field to view previously visited sites.

How many sites are listed in the drop-down box for "History"?

To clear the browser history, choose **Tools > Internet Options > Delete**.

Remove all selected options except for **History**.

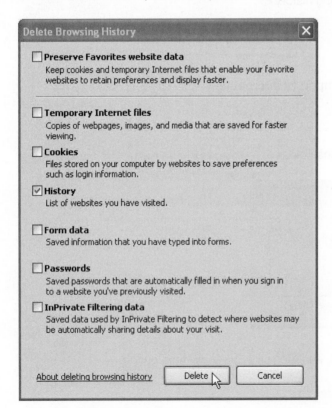

Click **Delete**.

The "Delete Browsing History" window opens.

When completed, click the **down** arrow at the right end of the "address" field to view previously visited sites.

How many sites are now found in the drop-down box for "History"?

Step 4

Click the **Security** tab.

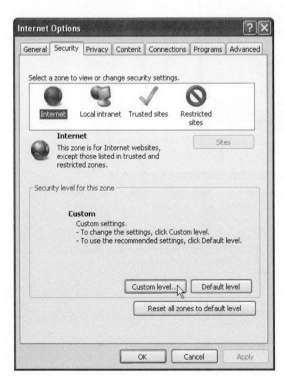

Click on each of the four zones and describe what they are used for.

Internet:

Local intranet:

Trusted sites:

Restricted sites:

Click the **Custom level** button.

The "Security Settings – Internet Zone" window opens.

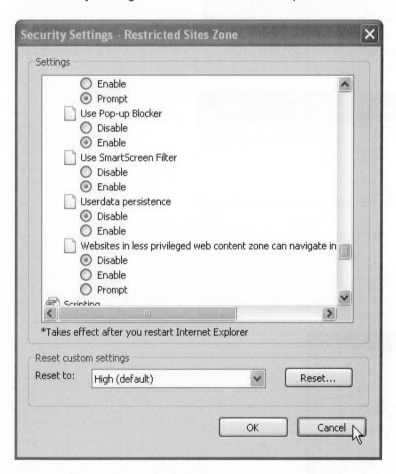

Here is where you select the options in the list that you wish to change for a zone.

Click **Cancel**.

Step 5

Click the **Privacy** tab **> Advanced**.

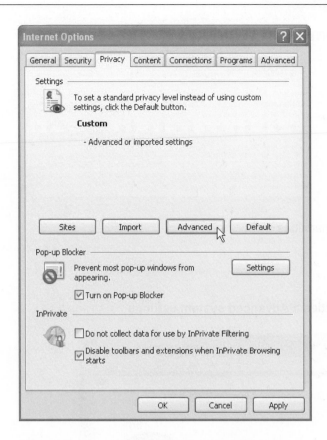

The "Advanced Privacy Settings" window opens.

Set the following settings:

Override automatic cookie handling box has a check mark.

First-party Cookies is set to **Accept**.

Third-party Cookies is set to **Prompt**.

Click **OK**.

5.3.2.16 Lab - Managing Virtual Memory in Windows 7

Introduction

In this lab, you will customize Virtual Memory settings.

Recommended Equipment

- A computer with Windows 7 installed

- The hard drive must have two or more partitions

Step 1

Click Start > right-click **Computer** > **Properties** > **Advanced system settings**.

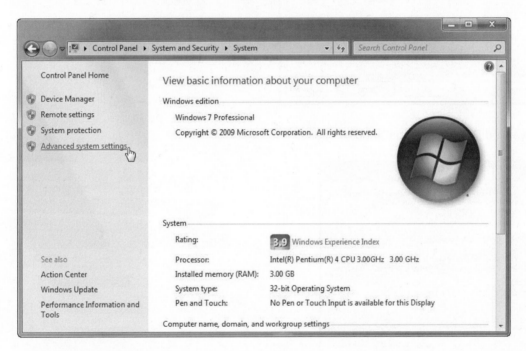

The "System Properties" window opens.

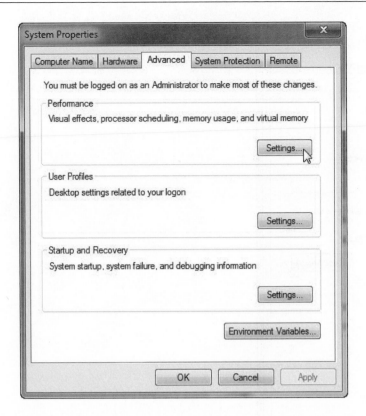

Select the **Advanced** tab and then click **Settings** in the "Performance" area.

Step 2

The "Performance Options" window opens.

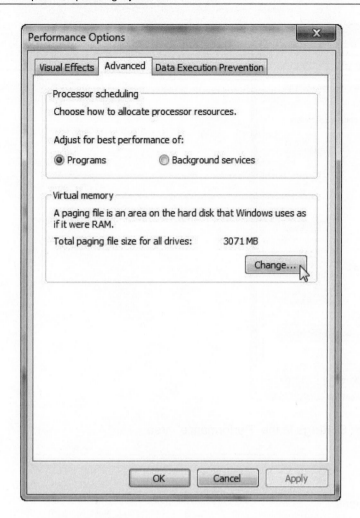

Click the **Advanced** tab.

What is the current size of the Virtual Memory (paging file)?

Click **Change** in the "Virtual Memory" area.

The "Virtual Memory" window opens.

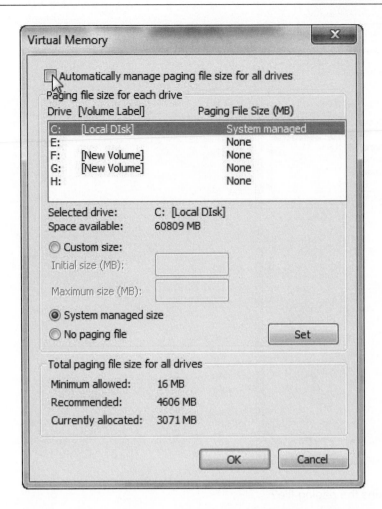

Remove the check mark from **Automatically manage paging file size for all drives**.

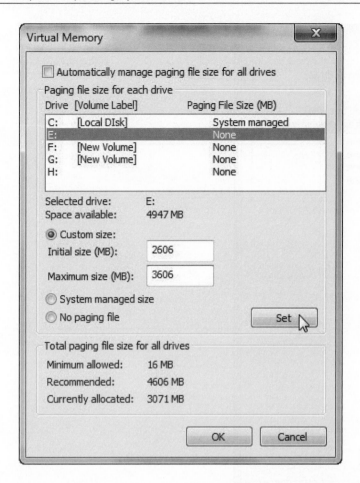

What Drive or [Volume Label] contains the paging file?

Choose the **E:** drive.

Select the **Custom size:** radio button.

Look at the "Recommended" size in the "Total paging file size for all drives" section of the "Virtual Memory" window.

Type in a number smaller than the recommended file size in the **Initial size (MB):** field.

Type in a number that is larger than the Initial size but smaller than the recommended file size in the **Maximum size (MB):** field.

Click **Set**.

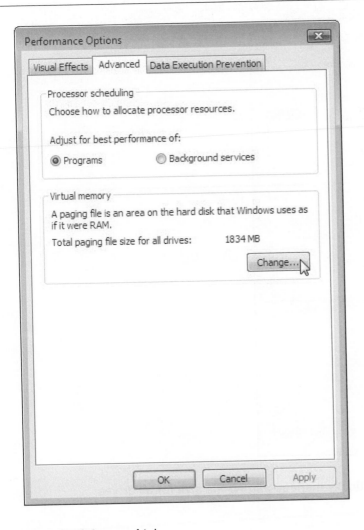

Click the **Advanced** tab.

What is the current size of the Virtual Memory (paging file)?

Click **Change** in the "Virtual Memory" area.

The "Virtual Memory" window opens.

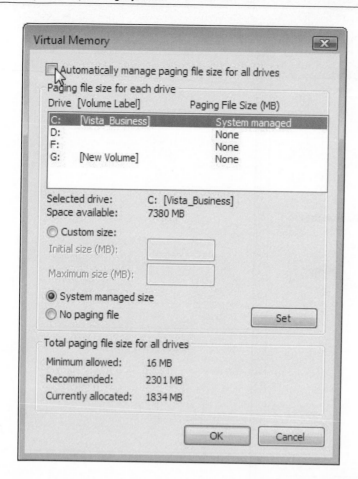

Remove the check mark from **Automatically manage paging file size for all drives**.

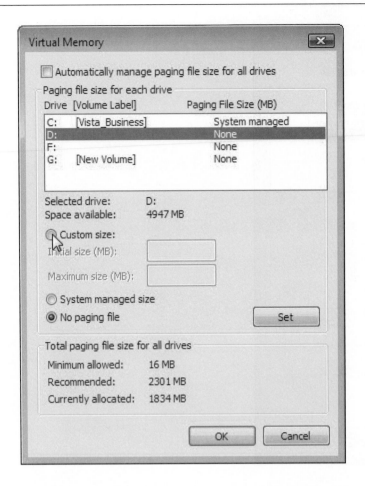

What Drive [Volume Label] contains the paging file, is system managed?

Choose the **D:** drive.

Select the **Custom size** radio button.

Look at the "Recommended" size in the "Total paging file size for all drives" section of the "Virtual Memory" window.

Type the recommended file size in the **Initial size (MB):** field.

Type the recommended file size again in the **Maximum size (MB):** field.

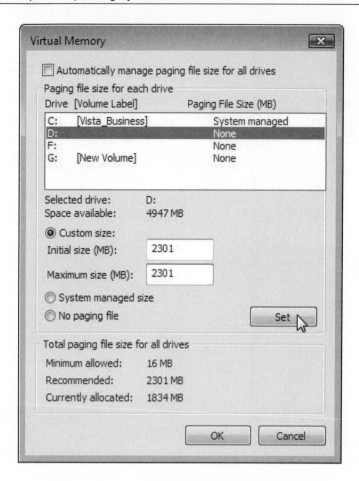

Click **Set**.

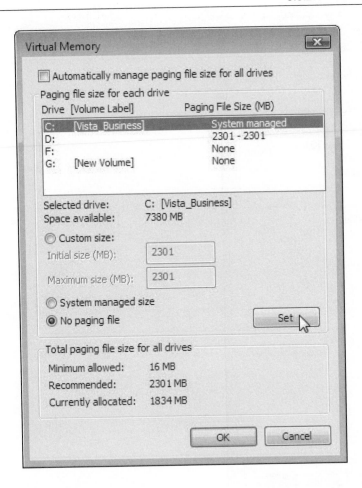

Select the **C:** drive.

Select the **No paging file** radio button, and then click **Set**.

The "System Properties" warning message appears.

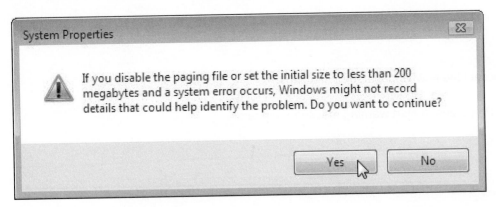

Click **Yes**.

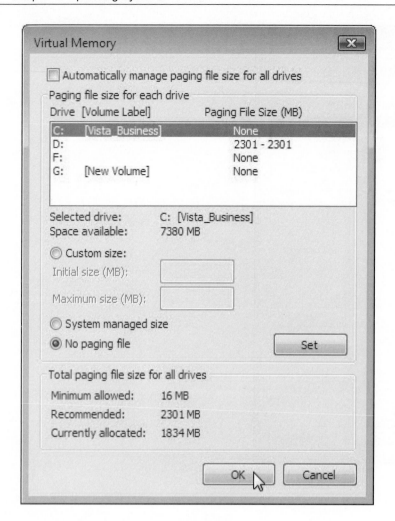

What is the paging file size (MB) for drive C:?

What is the paging file size (MB) for drive D:?

Click **OK** to accept the new virtual memory settings.

The "System Properties" restart warning message appears.

Click **OK**.

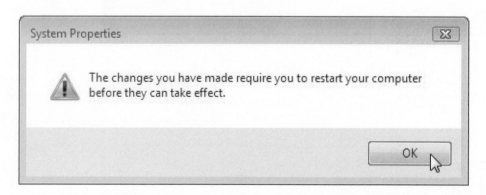

The "Performance Options" message window appears.

Click **OK**.

The "System Properties" message window appears.

Click **OK**.

The "You must restart your computer to apply these changes" message appears, click **Restart Now**.

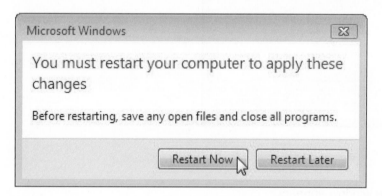

Step 3

Log on to Windows as an Administrator.

Open the "Virtual Memory" window.

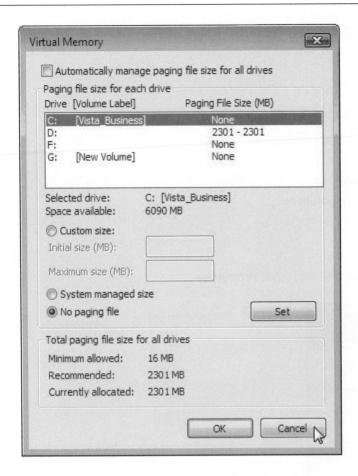

What Drive [Volume Label] contains the paging file?

Click **Cancel** to close all open windows.

Step 4

Reset virtual memory to be managed by the system.

Select drive **C: [Local Disk] > System managed size > Set**.

Next, select drive **E: > No paging file > Set**.

Place a check mark in **Automatically manage paging file size for all drives**.

Click **OK** when required.

Restart the computer and log off again.

5.3.2.18 Lab - Managing Virtual Memory in Windows XP

Introduction

In this lab, you will customize Virtual Memory settings.

Recommended Equipment
- A computer with Windows XP installed
- The hard drive must have two or more partitions

Step 1

Choose **Start >** right-click **My Computer**, and then click **Properties**.

The "System Properties" window opens.

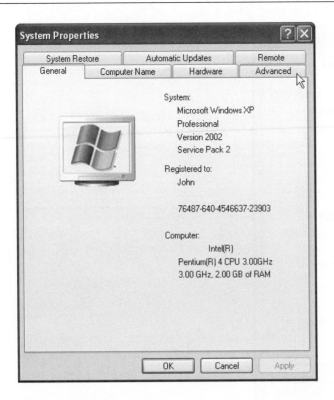

Click the **Advanced** tab.

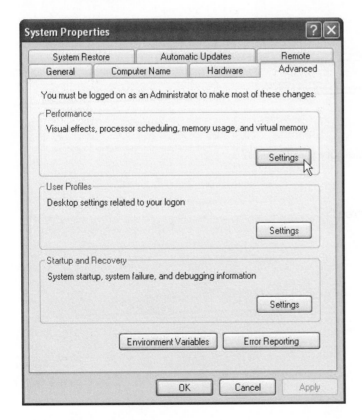

Click **Settings** in the "Performance" area.

Step 2

The "Performance Options" window opens.

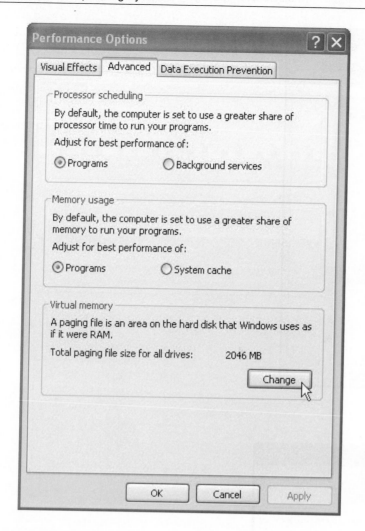

Click the **Advanced** tab.

What is the current size of the Virtual Memory (paging file)?

Click **Change** in the "Virtual Memory" area.

The "Virtual Memory" window opens.

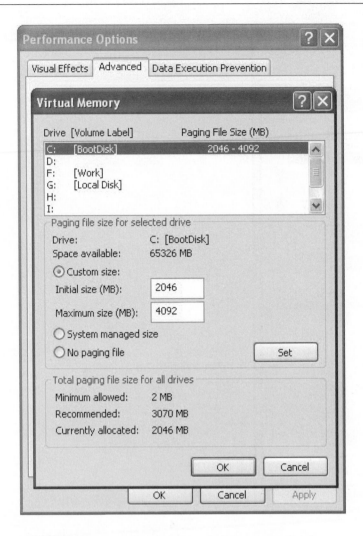

What Drive [Volume Label] contains the paging file?

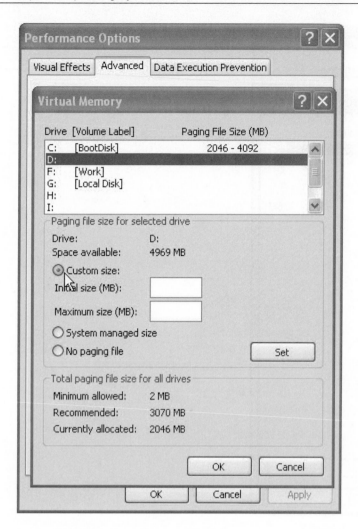

Choose the **D:** drive.

Select the **Custom size** radio button.

Look at the "Recommended" size in the "Total paging file size for all drives" section of the "Virtual Memory" window.

Type the recommended file size in the **Initial size (MB)**: field.

Type the recommended file size again in the **Maximum size (MB)**: field.

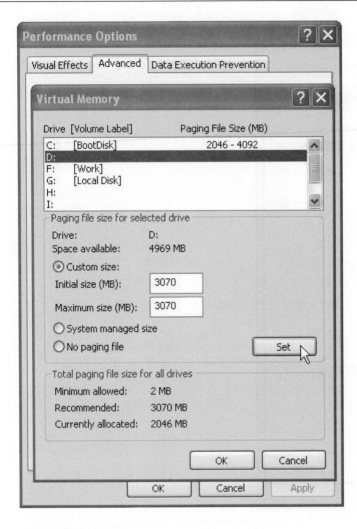

Click **Set**.

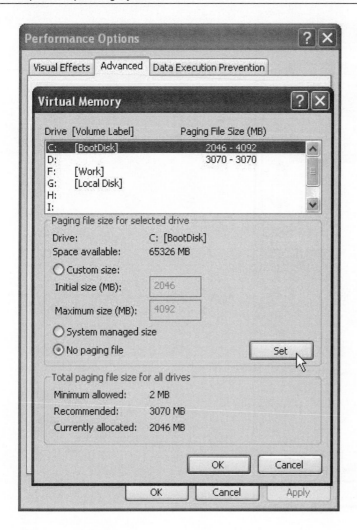

Choose the **C:** drive.

Click the **No paging file** radio button, and then click **Set**.

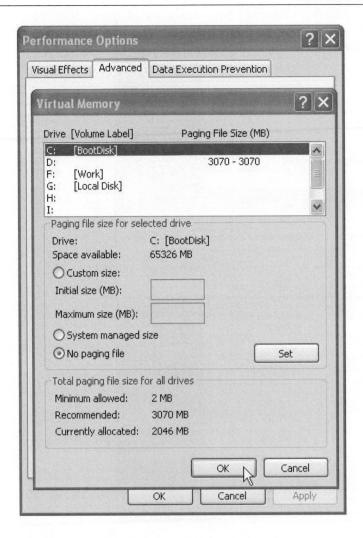

What is the paging file size (MB) for drive C:?

What is the paging file size (MB) for drive D:?

Click **OK**.

The "System Control Panel Applet" message window appears.

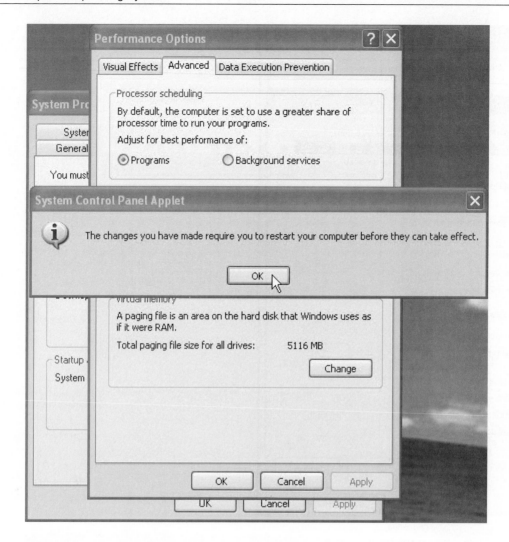

Click **OK** to close the information message window.

Click **OK** to close the "Performance Options" window.

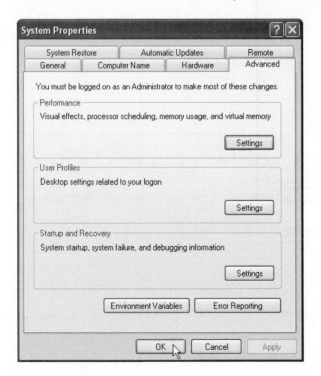

Click **OK** to close the "System Properties" window.

The "System Settings Change" window opens.

Click **Yes** to restart your computer now.

Step 3

Log on to Windows as an administrator.

Open the "Virtual Memory" window.

Which Drive [Volume Label] contains the paging file?

Step 4

Reset virtual memory to be managed by the system.

Select drive **D:**.

Select the radio button "System managed size", and then click **Set**.

Click **OK** to accept the message.

Select drive **C:**.

Select the radio button "System managed size", and then click **Set**.

Click **OK** to accept the message.

Restart the computer and log off again.

5.3.2.20 Lab - Managing Device Drivers with Device Manager in Windows 7

Introduction

In this lab, you will use Windows Device Manager to gather information about different drivers and learn how Device Manager manages drivers.

Recommended Equipment

The following equipment is required for this exercise:

- A computer running Windows 7

Step 1

Log on to the computer as an administrator.

Click **Start > Control Panel >** double-click the **System** icon.

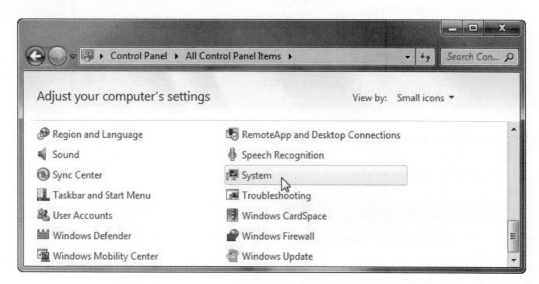

Step 2

The "System" window appears.

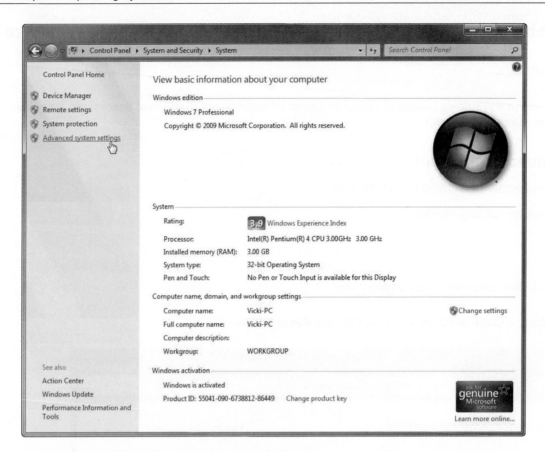

In the left pane, click **Advanced system settings**.

The "System Properties" window opens.

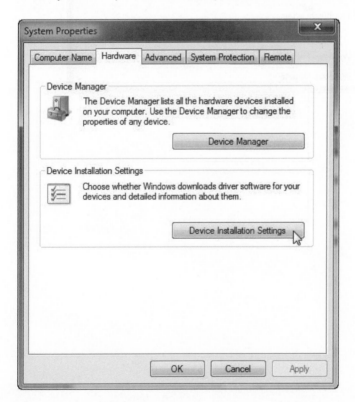

Click the **Hardware** tab **> Device Installation Settings** button.

The "Device Installation Settings" window opens.

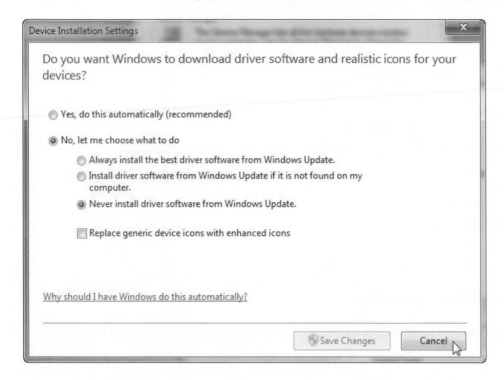

Accept the default setting and click **Cancel**.

Step 3

Click the **Device Manager** button.

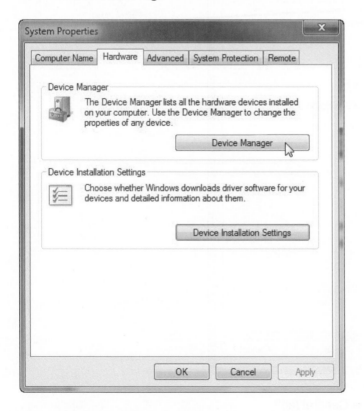

The "Device Manager" window opens.

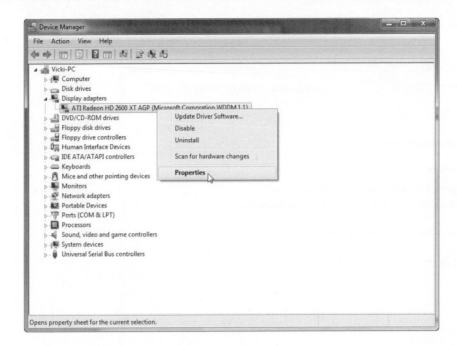

Select the **arrow** next to Display adapters. Right-click the adapter name and select **Properties**.

Step 4

The "Display adapters Properties" window opens.

What information is displayed under the General tab?

Step 5

Click the **Driver** tab.

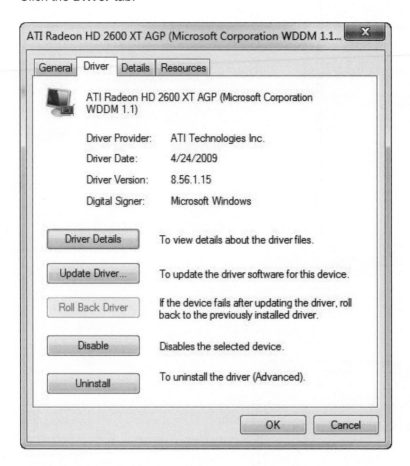

What functions can you accomplish from this page?

Step 6

Click the **Details** tab. This tab provides more details about the hardware.

Step 7

Click the **Resources** tab.

What information is displayed under the Resources tab?

Close the "Display adapters Properties" windows, and click **Cancel**.

Step 8

Navigate to the "Network adapter Properties" window by clicking the **arrow** next to Network adapters **>** right-click the adapter name **>** select **Properties**.

Which tabs are available?

Are there any extra tabs?

What is the purpose of the extra tabs?

Close the "Network adapters Properties" windows, and click **Cancel**.

Close all windows and log off.

5.3.2.21 Lab - Managing Device Drivers with Device Manager in Windows Vista

Introduction

In this lab, you will use Windows Device Manager to gather information about different drivers and learn how Device Manager manages drivers.

Recommended Equipment

The following equipment is required for this exercise:

> • A computer running Windows Vista

Step 1

Log on to the computer as an administrator.

Click **Start > Control Panel >** double-click the **System** icon.

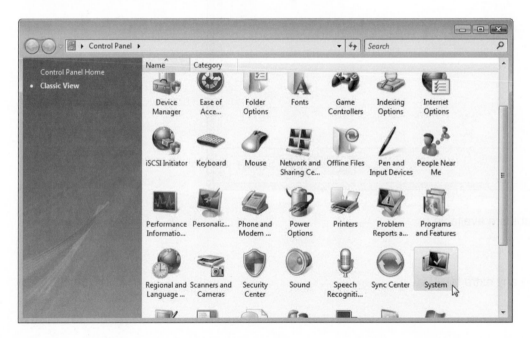

Step 2

The "System" window appears.

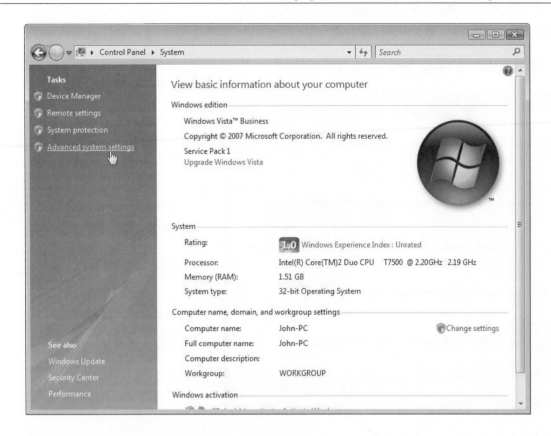

In the left pane, click **Advanced system settings**. If User Account Control appears, click **Continue**.

The "System Properties" window opens.

Click the **Hardware** tab **> Windows Update Driver Settings** button.

The "Windows Update Driver Settings" window opens.

Accept the default setting and click **OK**.

Step 3

Click the **Device Manager** button.

The "Device Manager" window opens.

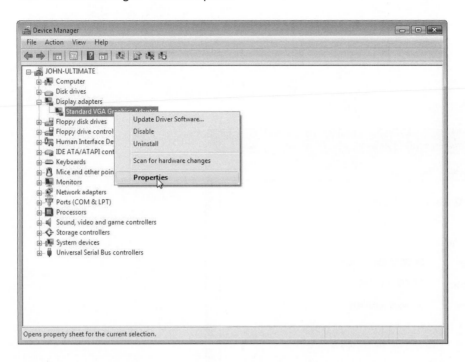

Select the **plus sign** next to Display adapters. Right-click the adapter name and select **Properties**.

Step 4

The "Display adapters Properties" window opens.

What information is displayed under the General tab?

Step 5

Click the **Driver** tab.

What functions can you accomplish from this page?

Step 6

Click the **Details** tab. This tab provides more details about the hardware.

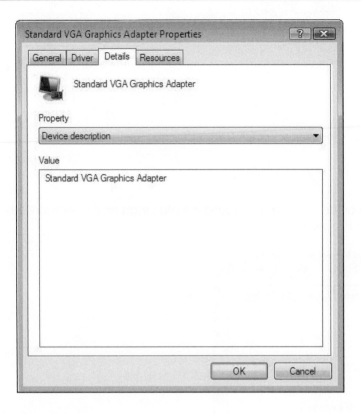

Step 7

Click the **Resources** tab.

What information is displayed under the Resources tab?

Close the "Display adapters Properties" windows, and click **Cancel**.

Step 8

Navigate to the "Network adapter Properties" window" by clicking the **plus sign** next to Network adapters > right-click the adapter name > select **Properties**.

Which tabs are available?

Are there any extra tabs?

What is the purpose of the extra tabs compared to the display adapter?

Close the "Network adapters Properties" windows, and click **Cancel**.

Close all windows and log off.

5.3.2.22 Lab - Managing Device Drivers with Device Manager in Windows XP

Introduction

In this lab, you will use Windows Device Manager to gather information about different drivers and learn how Device Manager manages drivers.

Recommended Equipment

The following equipment is required for this exercise:

• A computer running Windows XP Professional

Step 1

Log on to the computer as an administrator.

Click **Start > Control Panel** > double-click the **System** icon.

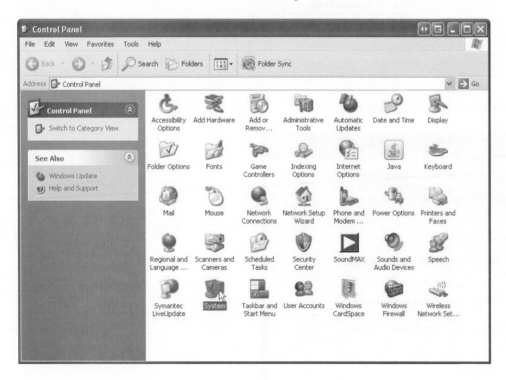

Step 2

The "System Properties" window opens.

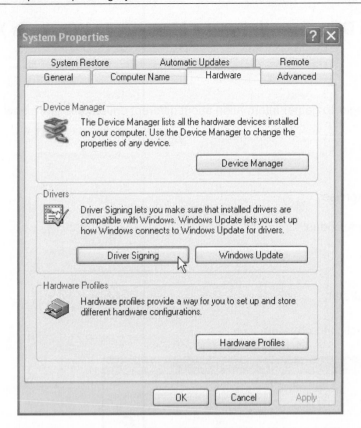

Click the **Hardware** tab **> Driver Signing** button.

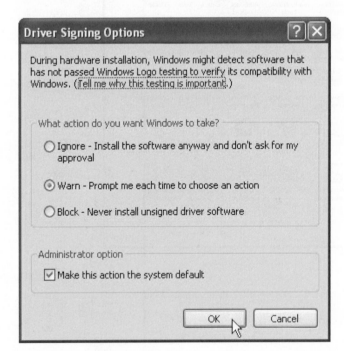

Accept the default setting and click **OK**.

Step 3

Click the **Device Manager** button.

The "Device Manager" window opens.

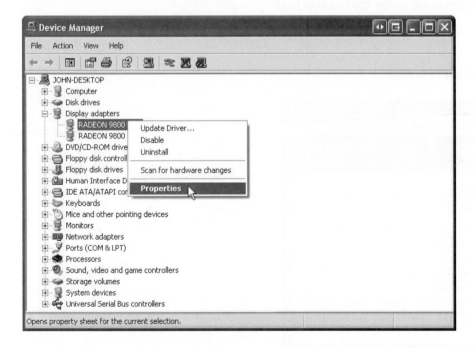

Select the **plus sign** next to "Display adapter" icon. Right-click the adapter name and select **Properties**.

Step 4

The "Display adapters Properties" window opens.

What information is displayed under the General tab?

Click the **Troubleshoot ...** button.

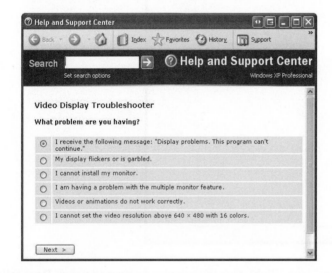

What window opens?

Close the "Help and support center" window.

Step 5

Click the **Driver** tab.

What functions can you accomplish from this page?

Step 6

Click the **Details** tab. This tab provides more details about the hardware.

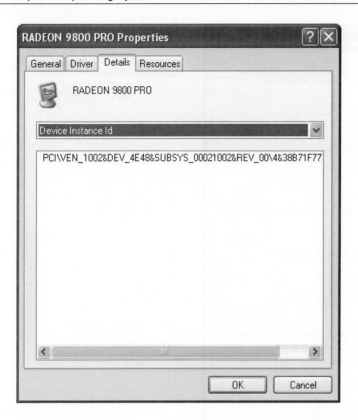

Step 7

Click the **Resources** tab.

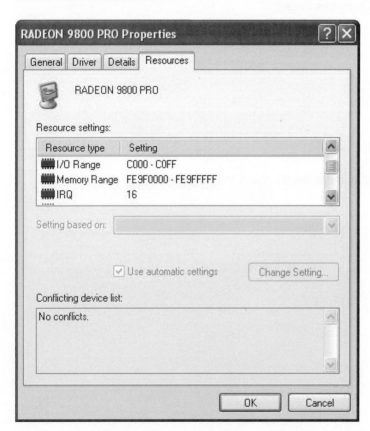

What information is displayed under the Resources tab?

Close the "Display adapters Properties" windows, click **Cancel**.

Step 8

Navigate to the "Network adapter Properties" window" by selecting the **plus sign** next to Network adapter **>** right-click the adapter name **>** select **Properties**.

Which tabs are available?

Are there any extra tabs compared to the display adapter?

What is the purpose of the extra tabs?

Close the "Network adapters Properties" windows, click **Cancel**.

Close all windows and log off.

5.3.2.24 Lab - Regional and Language Options in Windows 7

Introduction

In this lab, you will examine regional and language settings.

Recommended Equipment

The following equipment is required for this exercise:

   • A computer running Windows 7

Step 1

Log on to the computer.

Click **Start > Control Panel > Region and Language**.

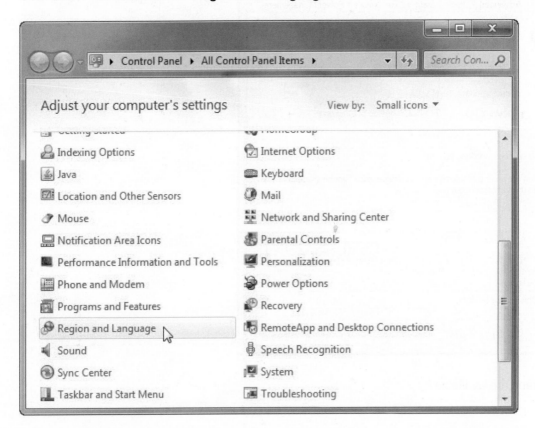

The "Regional and Language" window opens.

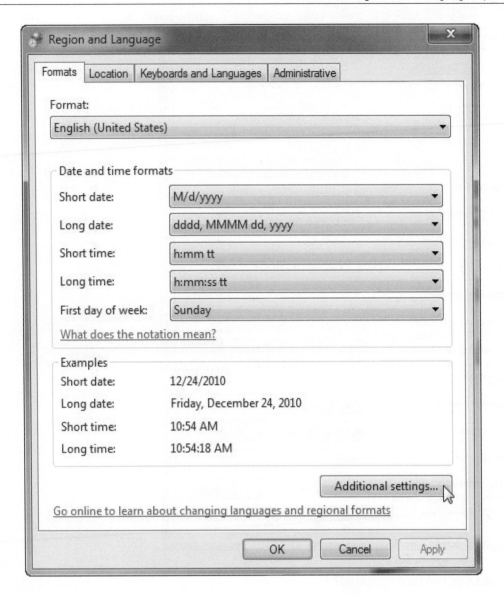

What regional format is being used?

Click **Additional settings**.

The "Customize Format" window opens.

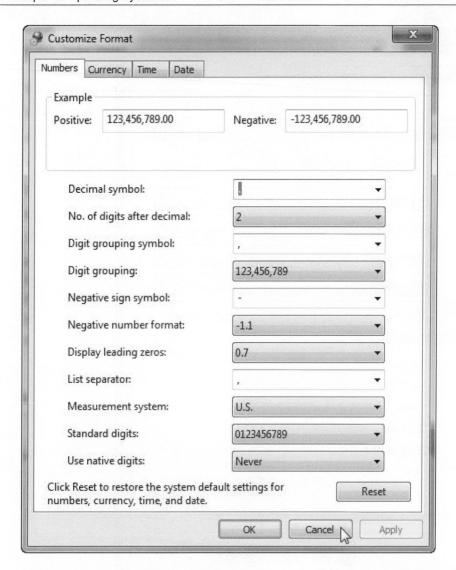

What are the tabs that can be customized?

Click **Cancel**.

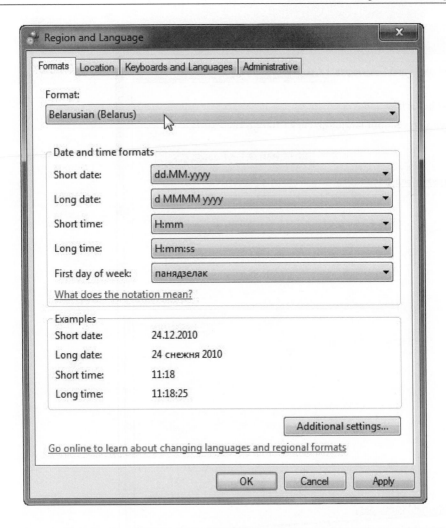

Click the drop-down menu in "Format" area. Select **Belarusian (Belarus)**.

Notice the changes to the output in the "Examples" area of how data is displayed using this format.

Click the drop-down menu in the "Format" area.

Return the setting to the original format.

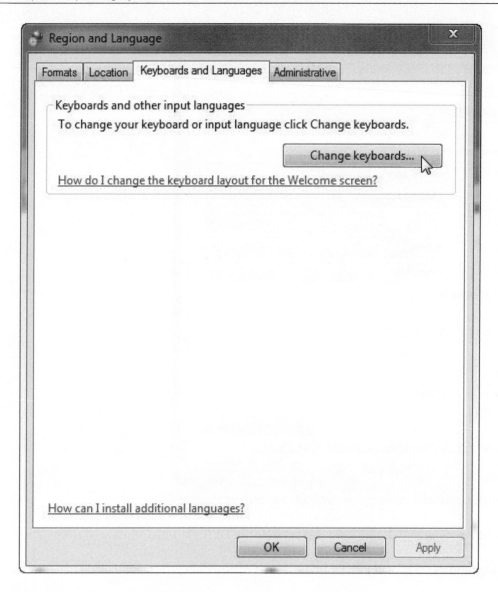

Click **Keyboards and Languages** tab **> Change keyboards**.

The "Text Services and Input Languages" window opens.

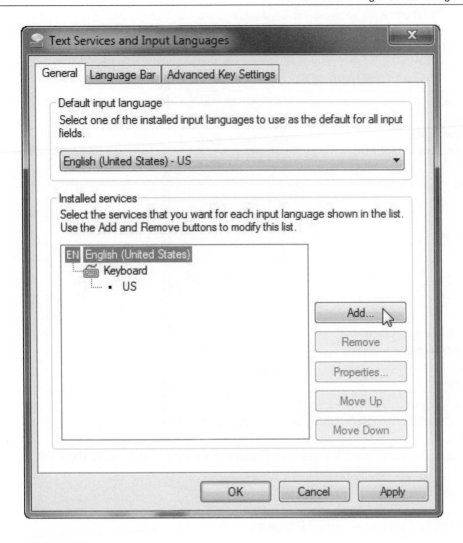

Click **Add**.

The "Add Input Language" window opens.

Scroll down the list of options and expand **Belarusian (Belarus) > Keyboard >** select **US > OK**.

Click **Apply** to accept the changes.

The "Text Services and Input Languages" window appears.

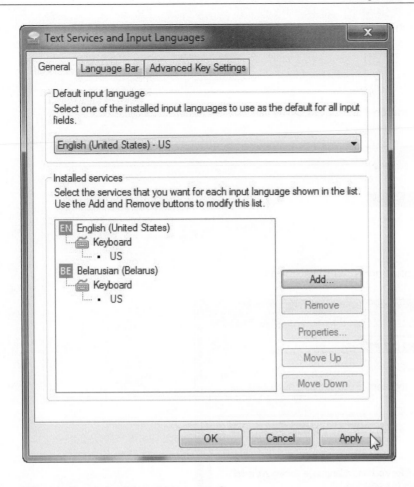

What is the default input language?

Close all opened windows

Step 2

Right-click the **Taskbar**.

Select **Toolbars > Language bar** to ensure that the Language bar is shown in the Taskbar.

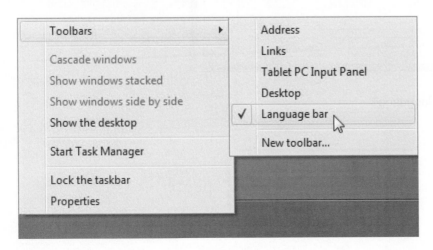

Right-click the **Language bar** in the Taskbar.

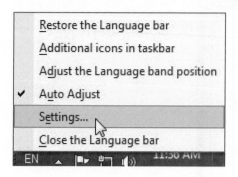

Select **Settings**.

The "Text Service and Input Languages" window opens.

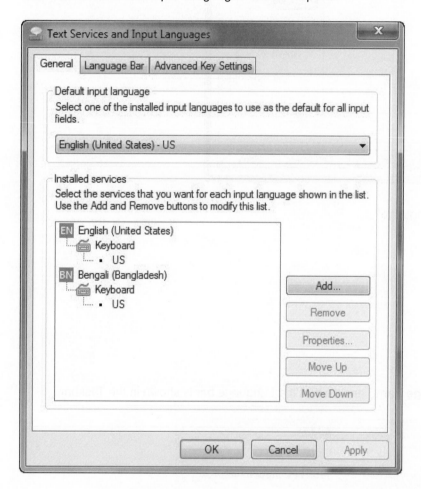

What is the Default input language?

Close all open windows.

5.3.2.25 Lab - Regional and Language Options in Windows Vista

Introduction

In this lab, you will examine regional and language settings.

Recommended Equipment

The following equipment is required for this exercise:

> • A computer running Windows Vista

Step 1

Log on to the computer.

Click **Start > Control Panel > Regional and Language Options**.

The "Regional and Language Options" window opens.

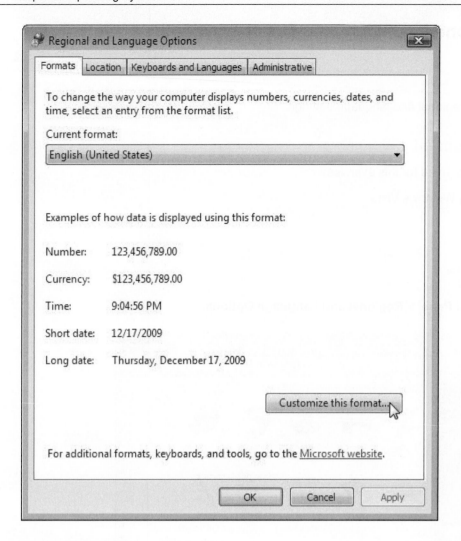

What regional options format is being used?

Click **Customize this format**.

The "Customize Regional Options" window opens.

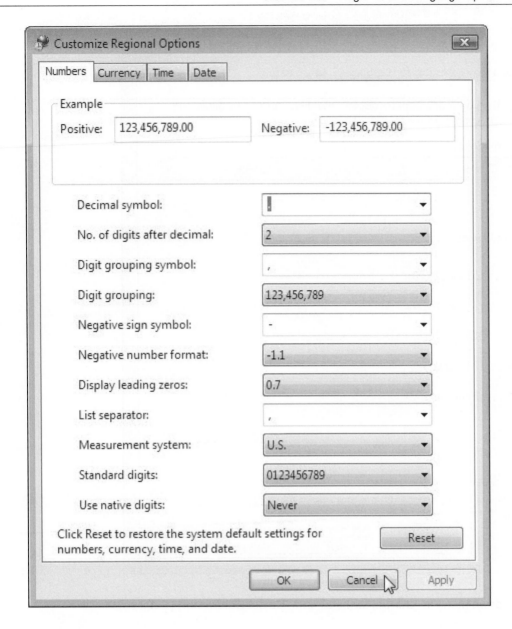

What are the tabs that can be customized?

Click **Cancel**.

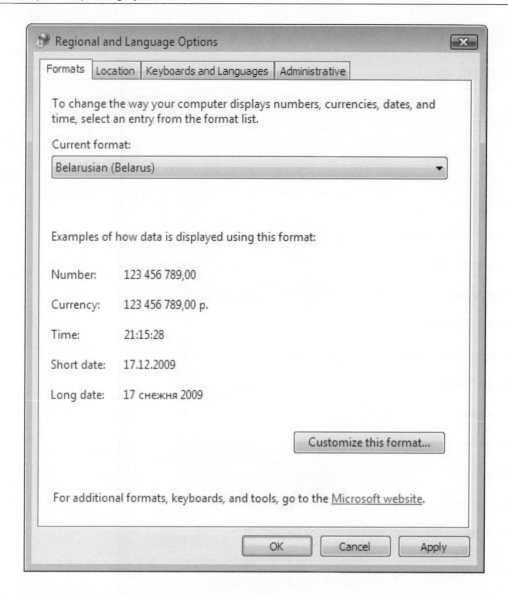

Click the drop-down menu in "Current formats" area. Select **Belarusian (Belarus)**.

Notice the changes to the output in the "Example of how data is displayed using this format:" fields.

Click the dropdown menu in the "Current format" area.

Return the setting to the original format.

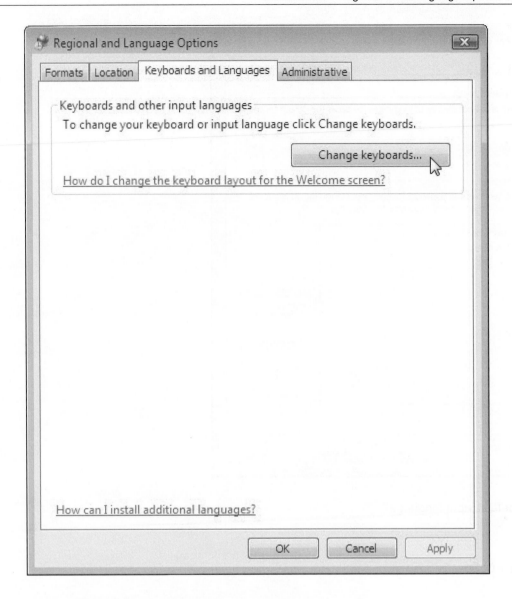

Click **Keyboard and Languages** tab **> Change keyboards**.

The "Text Services and Input Languages" window opens.

What is the default input language?

Click **Cancel > Cancel** to close all opened windows.

Step 2

Right-click the **Taskbar**.

Select **Toolbars > Language bar** to ensure that the Language bar is shown in the Taskbar.

Right-click the **Language bar** in the Taskbar.

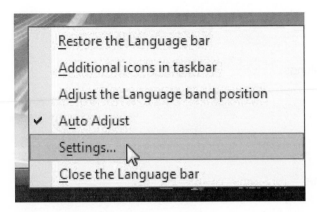

Select **Settings**.

The "Text Services and Input Languages" window opens.

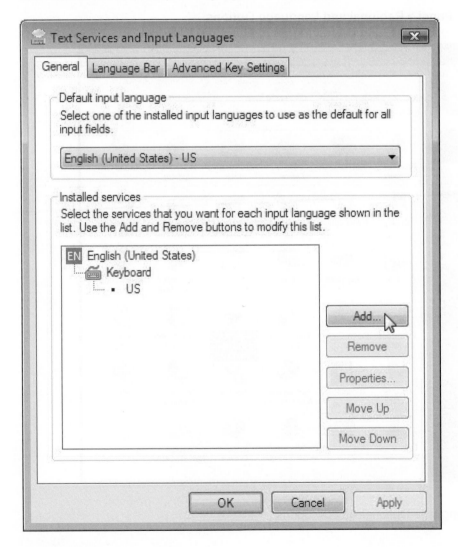

What is the Default input language?

Close all open windows.

5.3.2.26 Lab - Regional and Language Options in Windows XP

Introduction

In this lab, you will examine regional and language settings.

Recommended Equipment

The following equipment is required for this exercise:

 • A computer running Windows XP Professional

Step 1

Log on to the computer.

Click **Start > Control Panel > Regional and Language Options**.

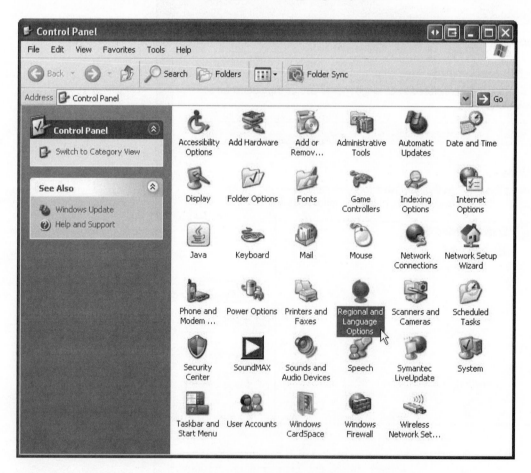

The "Regional and Language Options" window opens.

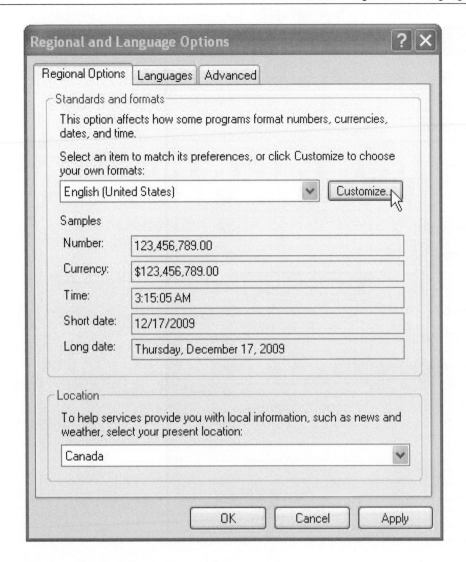

What regional options format is being used?

Click **Customize**.

The "Customize Regional Options" window opens.

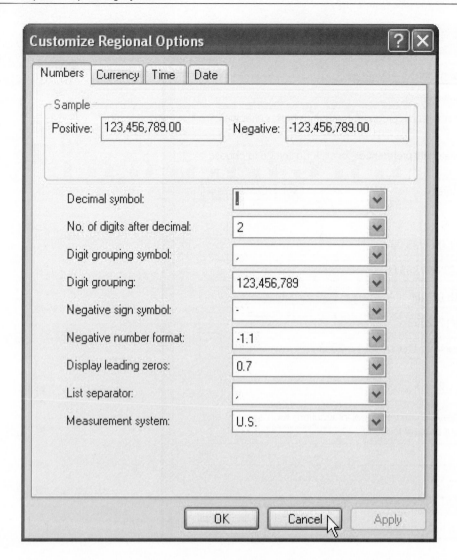

What are the tabs that can be customized?

Click **Cancel**.

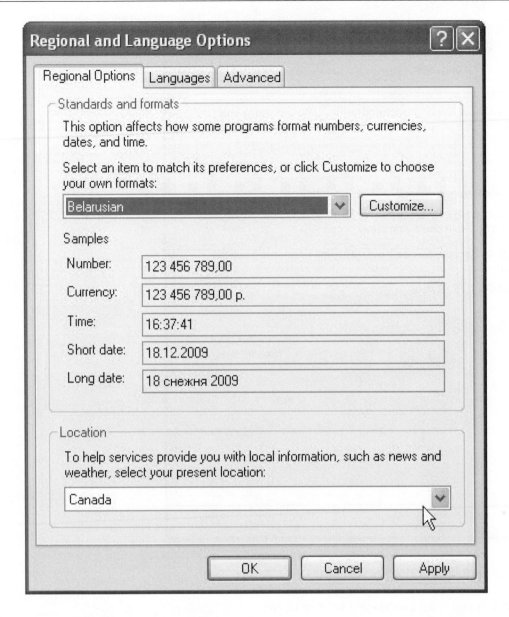

Click the drop-down menu in "Standards and formats" area. Select **Belarusian**.

Notice the changes to the output in the "Samples" fields.

Click the dropdown menu in the "Standards and formats" area.

Return the setting to the original format.

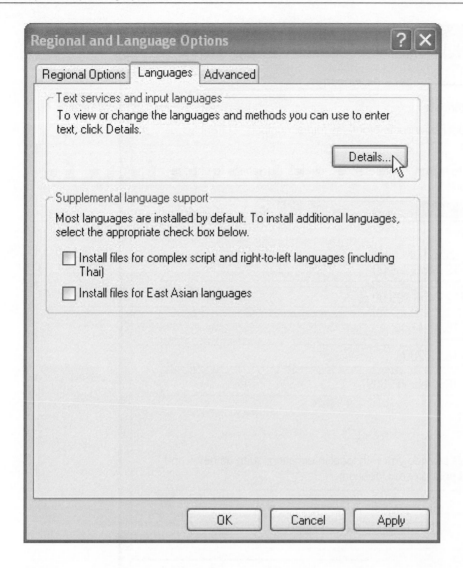

Click the **Languages** tab **> Details**.

The "Text Services and Input Languages" window opens.

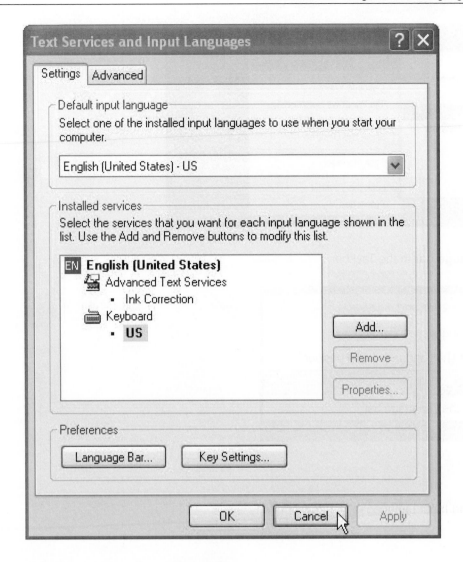

What is the default input language?

Click **Cancel > Cancel** to close all opened windows.

Step 2

Right-click the **Taskbar**.

Select **Toolbars > Language bar** to ensure that the Language bar is shown in the Taskbar.

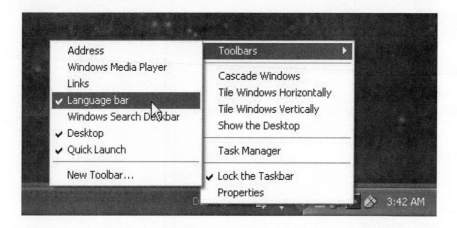

Right-click the **Language bar** in the Taskbar.

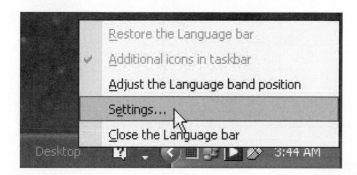

Select **Settings**.

The "Text Services and Input Languages" window opens.

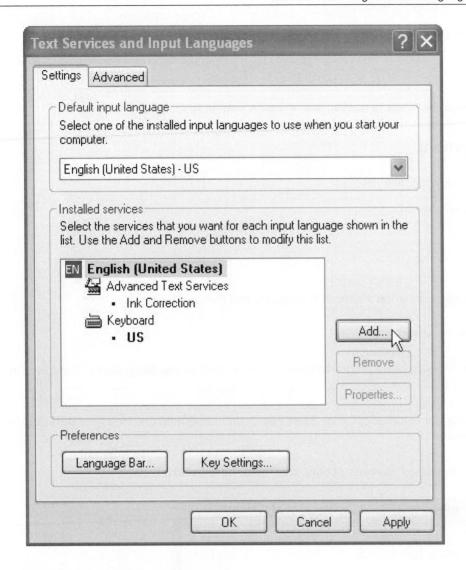

What is the Default input language?

Close all open windows.

5.3.3.5 Lab - Monitor and Manage System Resources in Windows 7

Introduction

In this lab, you will use administrative tools to monitor and manage system resources.

Recommended Equipment

The following equipment is required for this exercise:

- A computer running Windows 7
- Internet access

Step 1

You will explore what happens when a service is stopped, and then started.

Log on to Windows as an administrator.

Note: Some antivirus or antispyware programs must be uninstalled on the computer for Windows Defender to work.

To see if Windows Defender is turned off, click **Start >** in Search programs and files type **Defender >** select **Windows Defender**.

If the "This program is turned off" screen appears, click **click here to turn it on**.

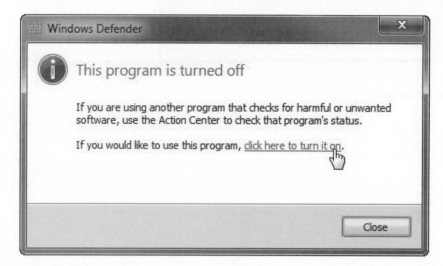

Windows Defender should start; if not, uninstall any antivirus or antispyware programs and then click **Start >** in Search programs and files type **Defender >** select **Windows Defender**.

Click **Start > Control Panel > Administrative Tools > Computer Management >** expand **Services and Applications >** select **Services**.

Close the Administrative Tools window.

Resize and position both windows so they can be seen at the same time.

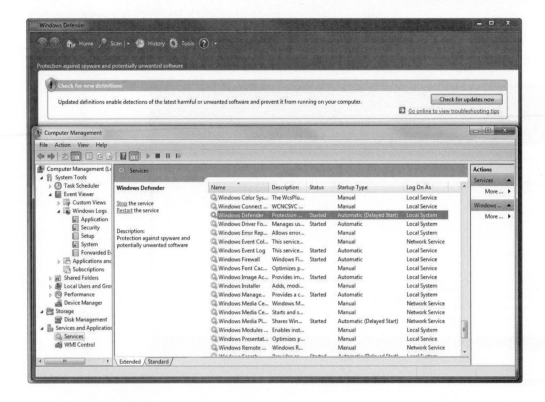

Can Windows Defender check for updates?

Scroll the "Computer Management" window so you see the "Windows Defender" service.

What is the Status of the service?

Right-click **Windows Defender** service **>** select **Stop**.

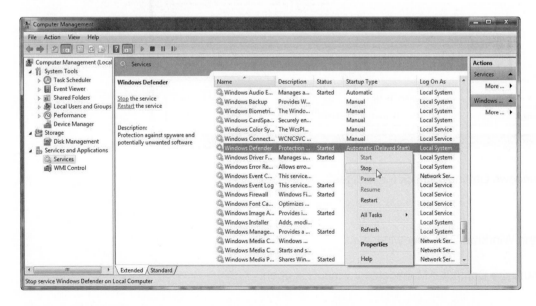

Note: The reason this service will be stopped is so you can easily see the results. When stopping a service, to free up system resources the service uses, it is important to understand how the overall system operation will be affected.

The "Service Control" window opens and closes.

Select the Windows Defender window so it is active.

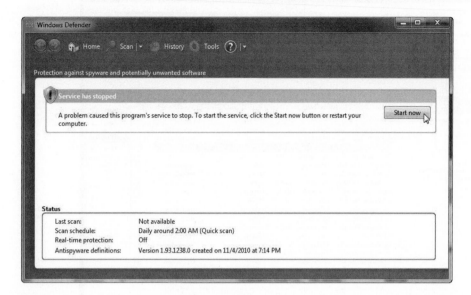

What must be done so Windows Defender can run?

Start the Windows Defender service; click **Start now**.

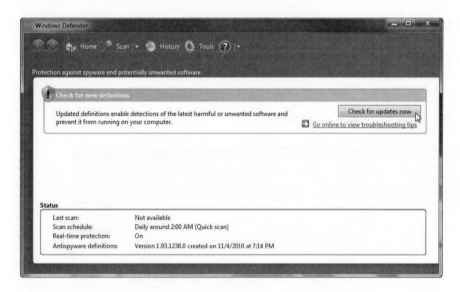

Can Windows Defender check for updates?

Close the Windows Defender window.

Make sure the Computer Management window is open.

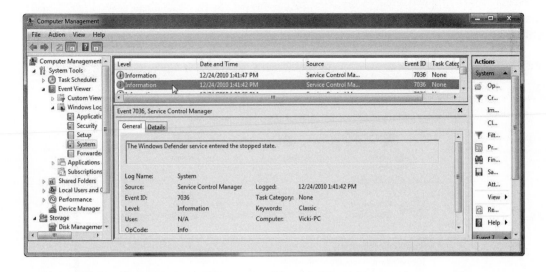

Expand **Event Viewer > Windows Logs >** select **System**.

Select the second event in the list.

Look below the General tab, and then explain what has happened to the Windows Defender service.

Click the up arrow button on the keyboard or select the event above the one you just viewed.

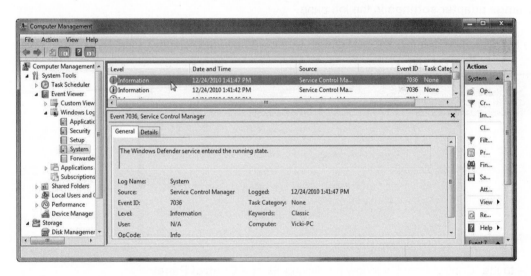

Look below the General tab, and then explain what has happened to the Windows Defender service.

Close all opened windows.

Step 2

You will explore what happens when a service is stopped, and then started.

Note: If Network is not shown in the Start menu, complete the following: Right-click **Start > Properties > Start Menu** tab. Click **Customize**, and then scroll down the list to Network. Place a check mark next to Network, and then click **OK > OK**.

Navigate to the "Network and Sharing Center" window by clicking **Start > Network > Network and Sharing Center**.

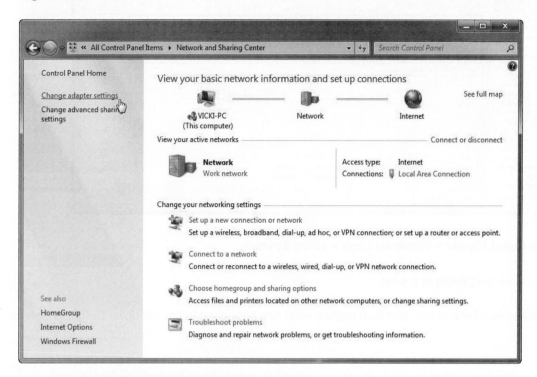

Click **Change adapter settings** in the left pane.

Reduce the size of the "Network Connections" window. Leave this window open.

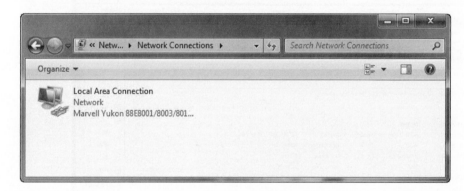

Navigate to the "Control Panel" window by clicking **Start > Control Panel**.

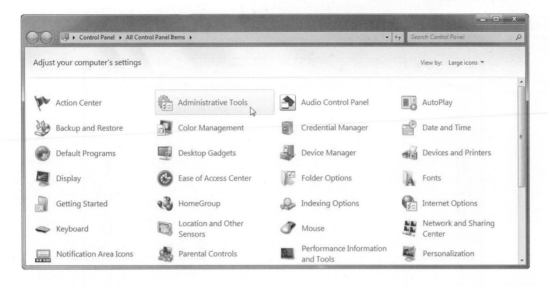

Click the **Administrative Tools** icon.

The "Administrative Tools" window opens.

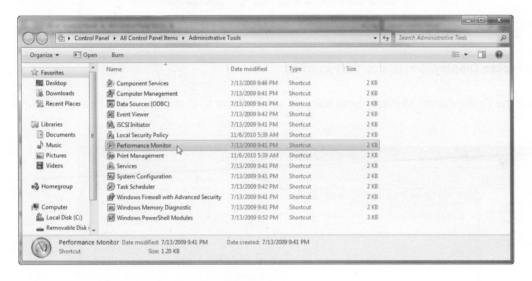

Double-click the **Performance Monitor** icon.

The "Performance Monitor" window appears. Make sure the Performance Monitor in the left pane is highlighted.

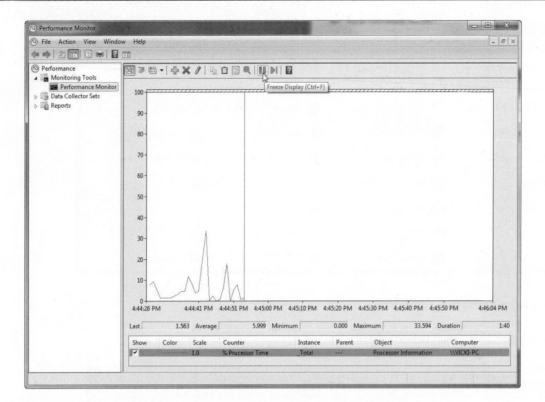

Click the **Freeze Display** icon to stop the recording.

Right-click the Performance Monitor menu bar and select **Clear** to clear the graph. Leave this window open.

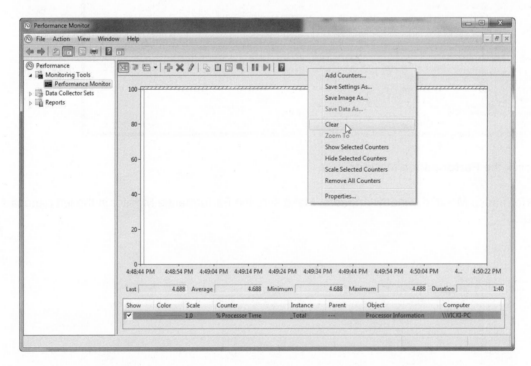

Navigate to the "Administrative Tools" window by clicking **Start > Control Panel > Administrative Tools**.

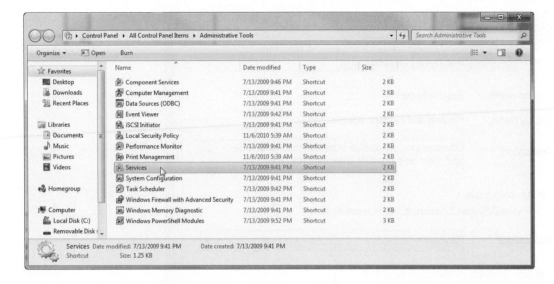

Double-click the **Services** icon.

Expand the width of the "Services" window so you have a clear view of the content. Scroll down in the right pane until you see the service Routing and Remote Access.

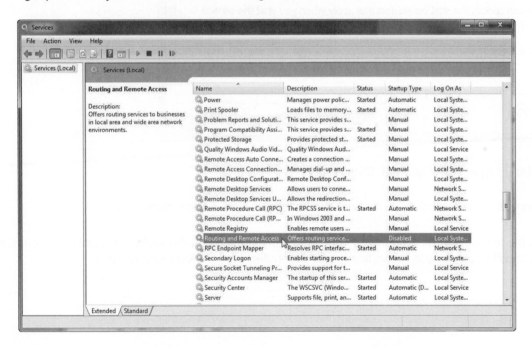

Double-click **Routing and Remote Access**.

The "Routing and Remote Access Properties (Local Computer)" windows opens.

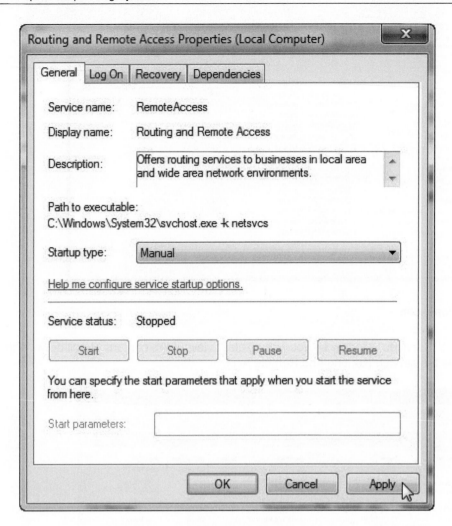

In the Startup type, select **Manual**. Click **Apply**.

The Start button is now active; do not click the button yet. Leave this window open.

Position the following three windows so you can clearly see them at the same time: Network Connections, Routing and Remote Access Properties (Local Computer), and Performance Monitor.

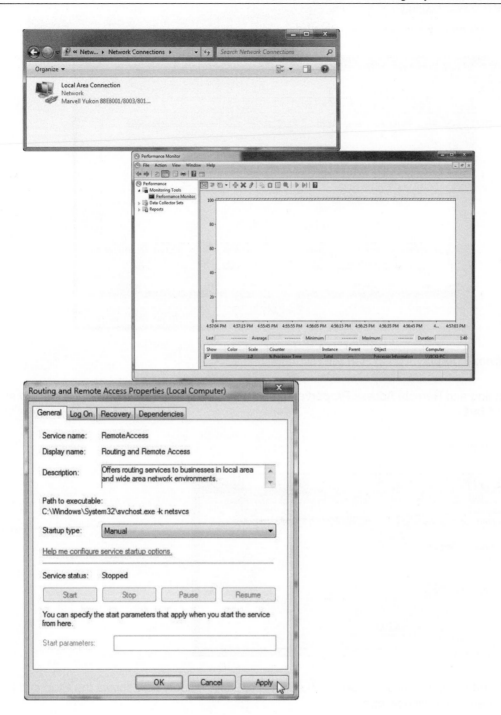

Click the "Performance Monitor" window so it is activated.

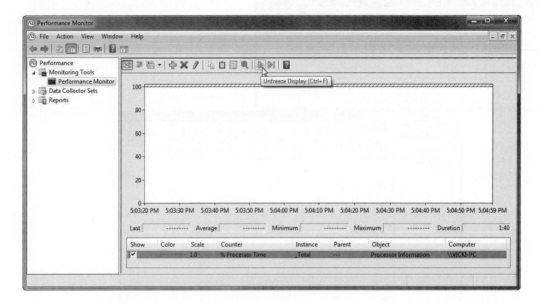

Click the **Unfreeze Display** icon to start the recording.

Click the "Routing and Remote Access Properties (Local Computer)" window so it is activated. To start the Service, click **Start**.

A window with a progress bar opens.

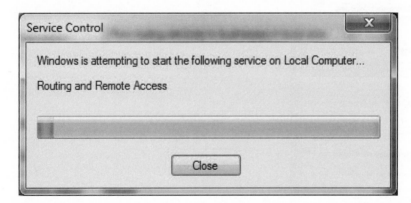

The "Routing and Remote Access Properties (Local Computer)" window now shows the Stop and Pause button active. Leave this window open.

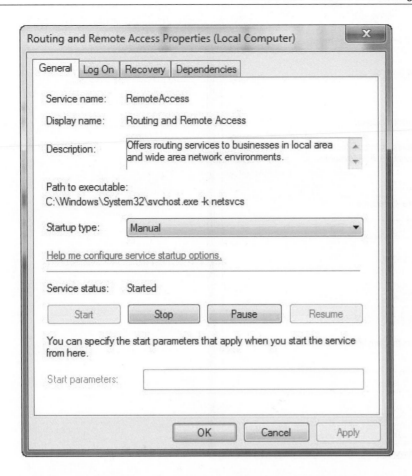

Click the "Network Connections" window so it is activated.

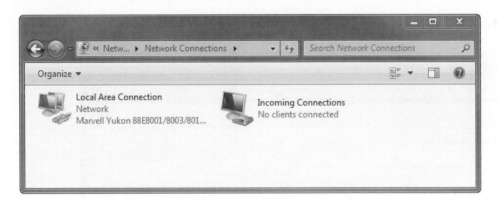

Press function key **F5** to refresh the content.

What changes appear in the right pane, after starting the Routing and Remote Access service?

Click the "Routing and Remote Access Properties (Local Computer)" window so it is activated.

Click **Stop**.

Click the "Network Connections" window so it is activated.

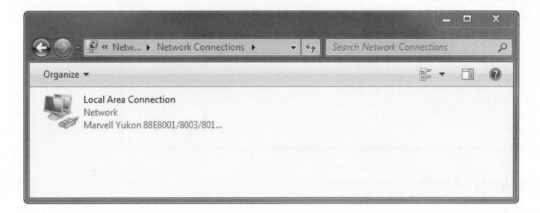

What changes appear in the right pane, after stopping the Routing and Remote Access service?

Click the "Performance Monitor" window so it is activated.

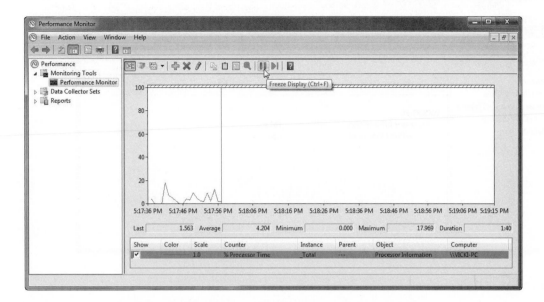

Click the **Freeze Display** icon to stop the recording.

Which Counter is being recorded the most in the graph (hint: look at the graph color and Counter color)?

Click the Change graph type drop-down menu, select **Report**.

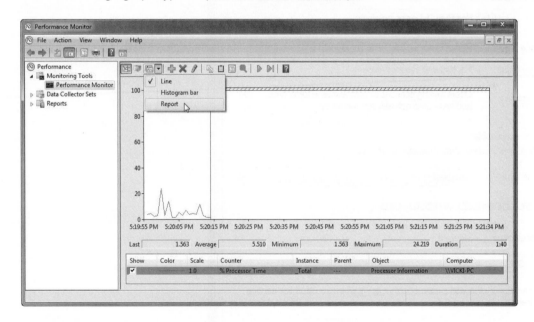

The display changes to report view.

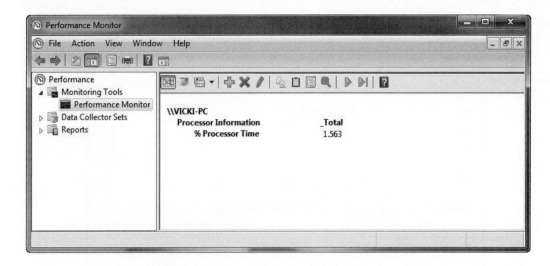

List the values of the counter.

Click the "Routing and Remote Access Properties (Local Computer)" window so it is activated.

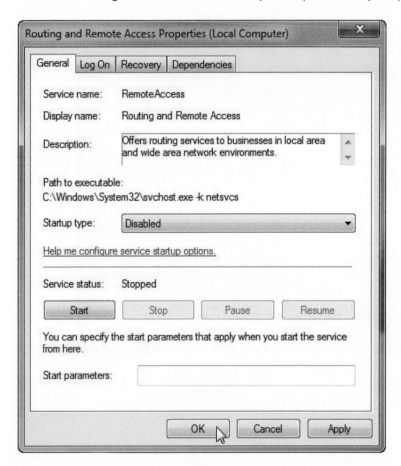

In the Startup type, select **Disabled**. Click **OK**.

Click the "Services" window so it is activated.

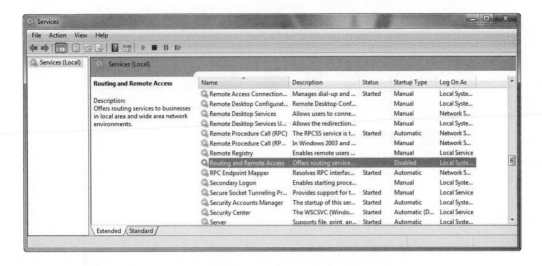

What is the Status and Startup Type for Routing and Remote Access?

Click the "Performance Monitor" window so it is activated.

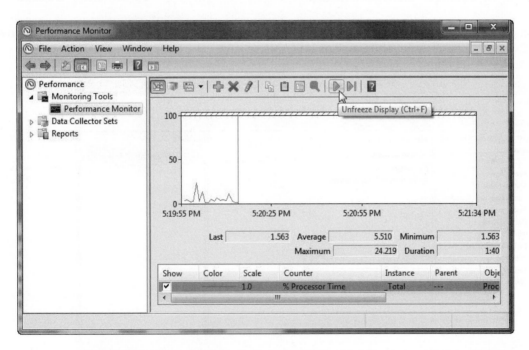

Click the **Unfreeze Display** icon to start the recording.

Close all open windows.

Navigate to the "Administrative Tools" window by clicking **Start > Control Panel > Administrative Tools**.

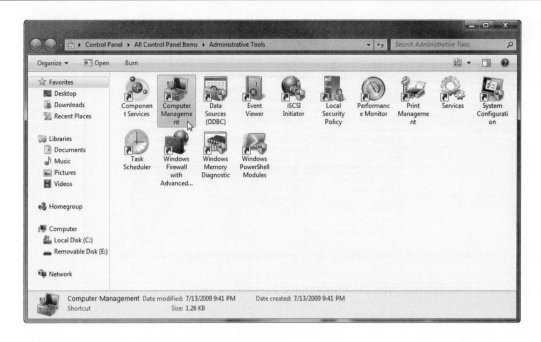

Double-click the **Computer Management** icon.

The "Computer Management" window appears. Expand the three categories by clicking on the **arrow** next to: System Tools, Storage, and Services and Applications.

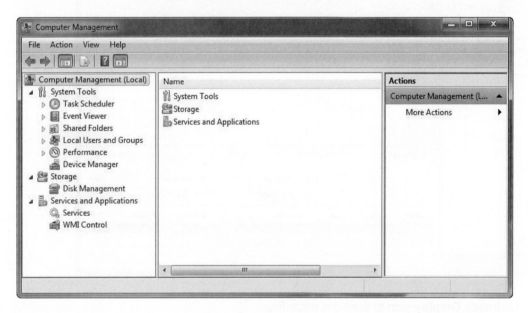

Click the **arrow** next to Event Viewer; then click the **arrow** next to Windows Logs.

Click the **green arrow** icon to start the data collection set.

Notice a green arrow is placed on top of the Memory Logs icon.

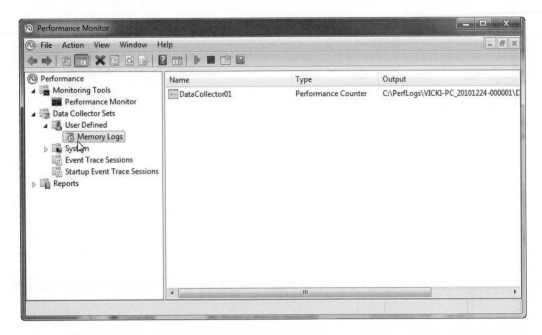

To force the computer to use some of the available memory, open and close a browser.

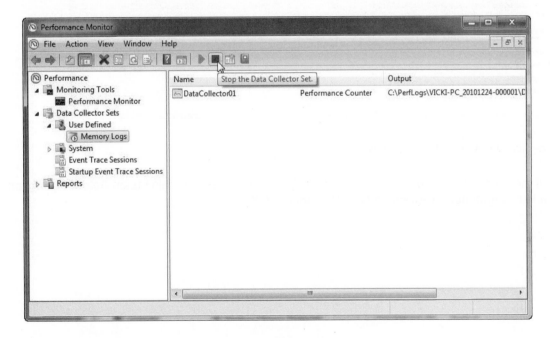

Click the **black box** icon to stop the data collection set.

What change do you notice for the Memory Logs icon?

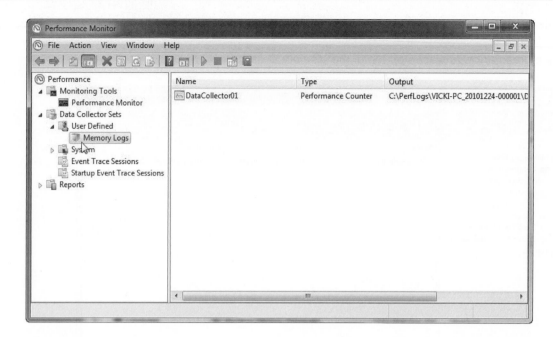

Click **Start > Computer >** double-click drive **C: > PerfLogs > Continue > VICKI-PC_20101224-00001 > Continue**.

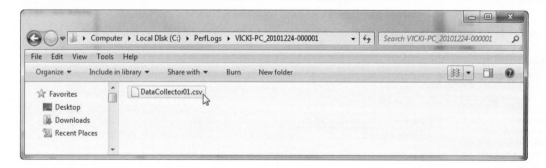

Double-click **DataCollector01.csv** file.

Note: If the "Windows cannot open the file:" message appears, select radio button **Select a program from a list of installed programs > OK > Notepad > OK**.

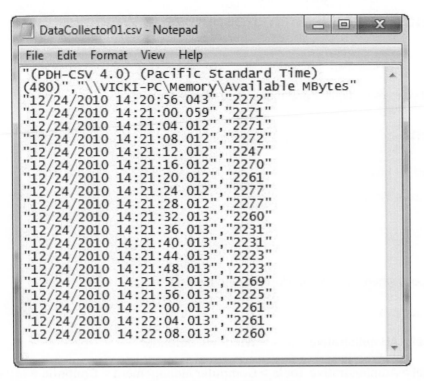

What does the column farthest to the right show?

Close the **DataCollector01.csv** file and the window with the PerfLogs folder.

Select the "Performance Monitor" window.

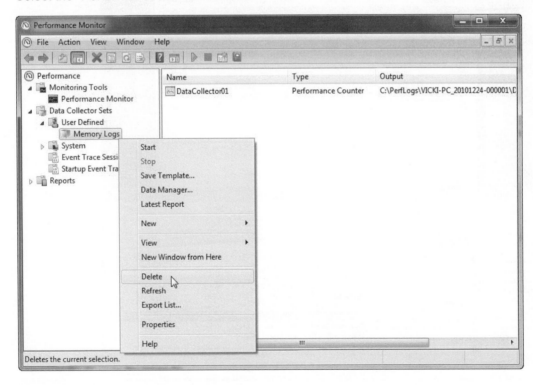

Right-click **Memory Logs > Delete > Yes**.

Open drive **C: > PerfLogs** folder > right-click **VICKI-PC_20101224-000001 > Delete > Yes**.

Close all open windows.

5.3.3.6 Lab - Monitor and Manage System Resources in Windows Vista

Introduction

In this lab, you will use administrative tools to monitor and manage system resources.

Recommended Equipment

The following equipment is required for this exercise:

- A computer running Windows Vista
- Internet access

Step 1

You will explore what happens when a service is stopped, and then started.

Log on to Windows as an administrator.

Click **Start > Control Panel > Administrative Tools > Windows Defender**.

Click **Start > Control Panel > Administrative Tools > Computer Management > Continue >** expand **Services and Applications >** select **Services**.

Close the Administrative Tools window.

Resize and position both windows so they can be seen at the same time.

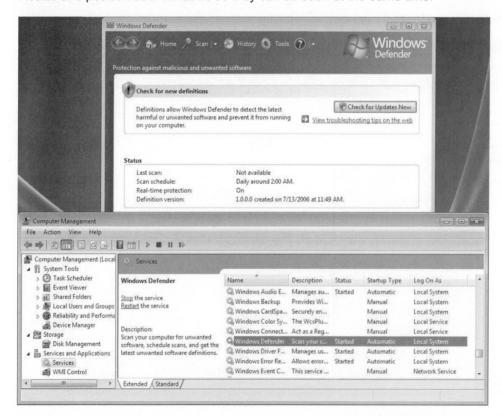

Can Windows Defender check for updates?

Scroll the Computer Management window so you see the "Windows Defender" service.

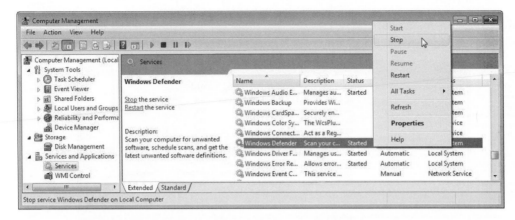

What is the Status of the service?

Right-click **Windows Defender** service **>** select **Stop**.

Note: The reason this service will be stopped is so you can easily see the results. When stopping a service, to free up system resources the service uses, it is important to understand how the overall system operation will be affected.

The "Service Control" window opens and closes.

Select the "Windows Defender" window so it is active.

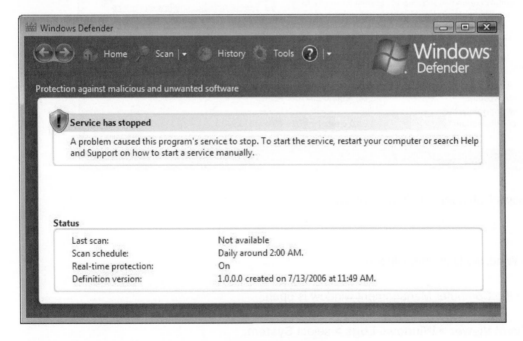

What must be done so Windows Defender can run?

What step must be followed to start the Windows Defender service?

Start the Windows Defender service.

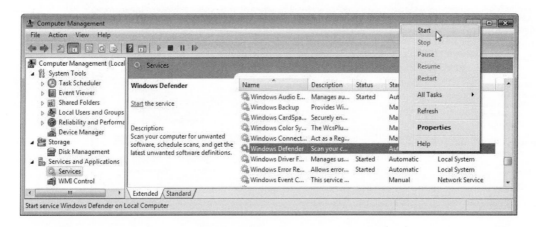

Select the "Windows Defender" window so it is active.

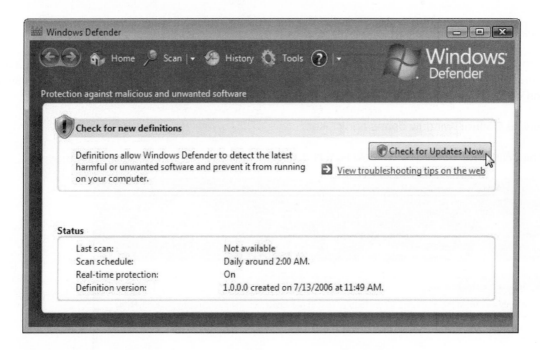

Can Windows Defender check for updates?

Close the Windows Defender window.

Make sure the Computer Management window is open.

Expand **Event Viewer > Windows Logs >** select **System**.

Select the second event in the list.

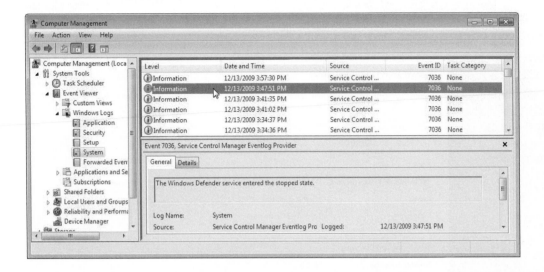

Look below the General tab; then explain what has happened to the Windows Defender service.

Click the up arrow button on the keyboard or select the event above the one you just viewed.

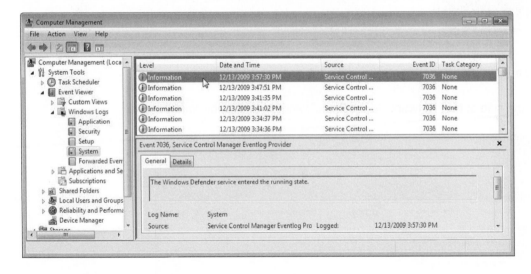

Look below the General tab; then explain what has happened to the Windows Defender service.

Close all opened windows.

Step 2

You will explore what happens when a service is stopped, and then started.

Navigate to the "Network and Sharing Center" window by clicking **Start > Network and Sharing Center**.

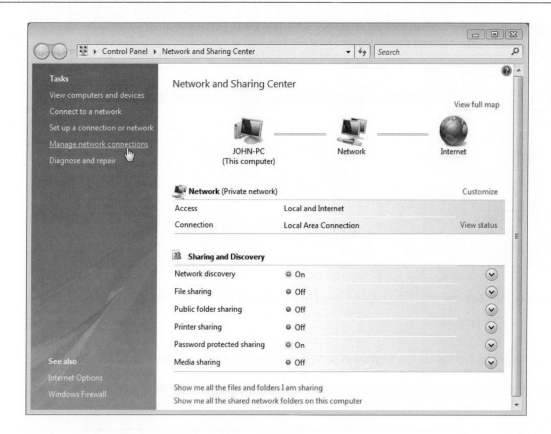

Click **Manage network connections** in the left pane.

Reduce the size of the "Network Connections" window. Leave this window open.

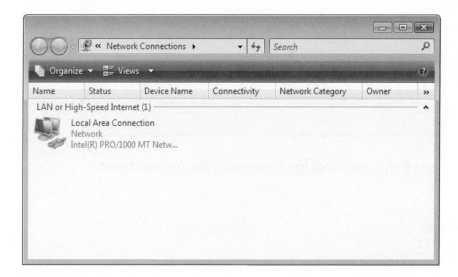

Navigate to the "Control Panel" window by clicking **Start > Control Panel**.

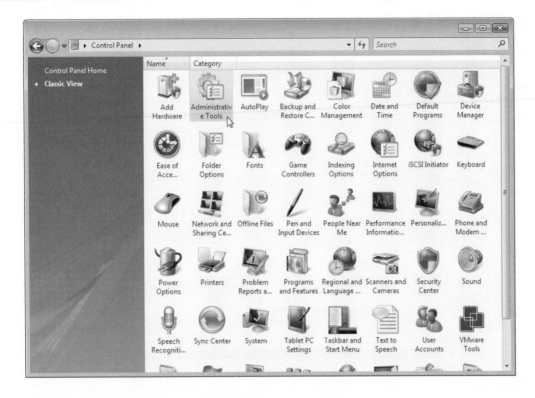

Double-click the **Administrative Tools** icon.

The "Administrative Tools" window opens.

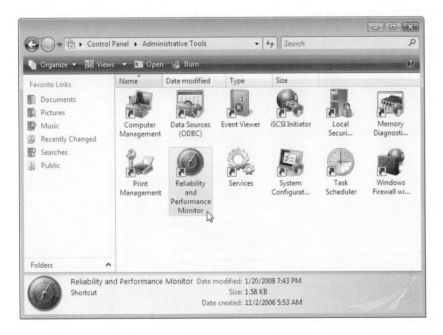

Double-click the **Reliability and Performance Monitor** icon > **Continue**.

The "Reliability and Performance Monitor" window opens. Make sure the Performance Monitor in the left pane is highlighted.

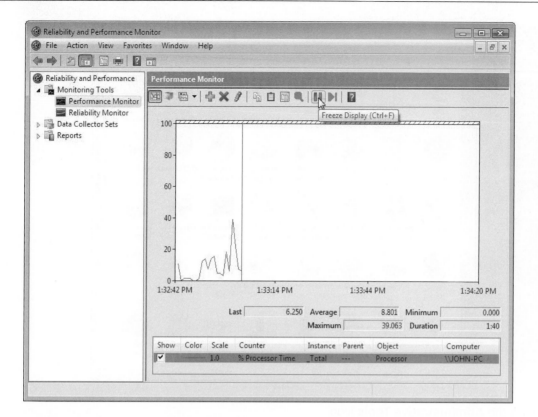

Click the **Freeze Display** icon to stop the recording.

Right-click the **Performance Monitor** menu bar.

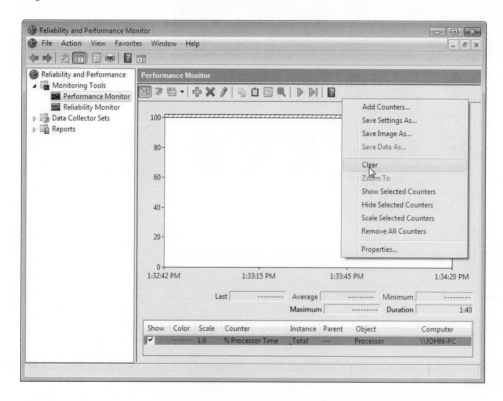

Select **Clear** to clear the graph. Leave this window open.

Navigate to the "Administrative Tools" window by clicking **Start > Control Panel > Administrative Tools**.

Double-click the **Services** icon > **Continue**.

Expand the width of the "Services" window so you have a clear view of the content. Scroll down in the right pane until you see the service Routing and Remote Access.

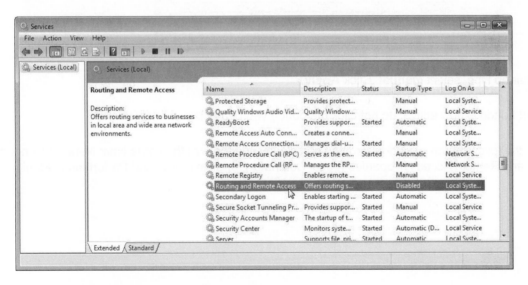

Double-click **Routing and Remote Access**.

The "Routing and Remote Access Properties (Local Computer)" windows opens.

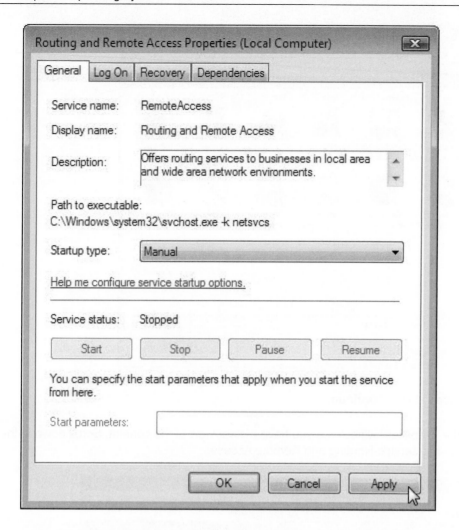

In the Startup type, select **Manual**. Click **Apply**.

The Start button is now active; do not click the button yet. Leave this window open.

Position the following three windows so you can clearly see them at the same time: Network Connections, Routing and Remote Access Properties (Local Computer), and Reliability and Performance Monitor.

Click the "Reliability and Performance Monitor" window so it is activated.

512 Chapter 5: Operating Systems

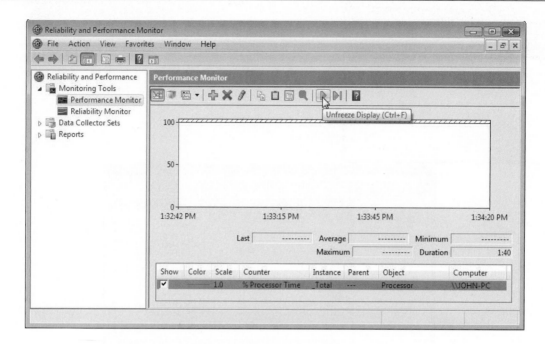

Click the **Unfreeze Display** icon to start the recording.

Click the "Routing and Remote Access Properties (Local Computer)" window so it is activated. To start the Service, click **Start**.

A window with a progress bar opens.

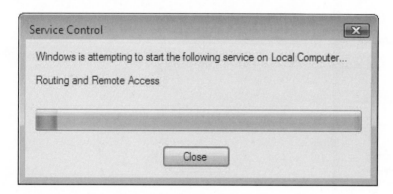

The "Routing and Remote Access Properties (Local Computer)" window now shows the Stop and Pause button active. Leave this window open.

Click the "Network Connections" window so it is activated.

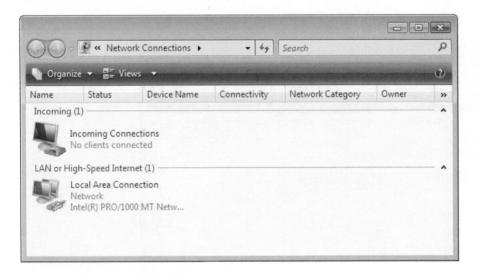

Press function key **F5** to refresh the content.

What changes appear in the right pane, after starting the Routing and Remote Access service?

Click the "Routing and Remote Access Properties (Local Computer)" window so it is activated.

Click **Stop**.

Click the "Network Connections" window so it is activated.

What changes appear in the right pane, after stopping the Routing and Remote Access service?

Click the "Reliability and Performance Monitor" window so it is activated.

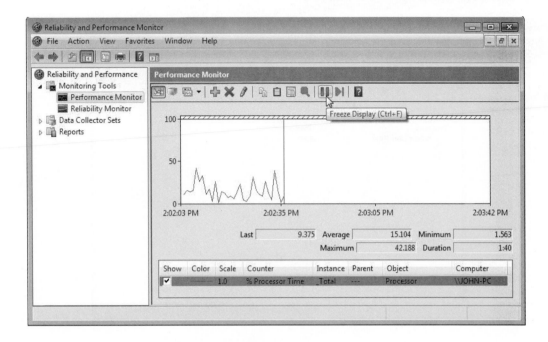

Click the **Freeze Display** icon to stop the recording.

Which Counter is being recorded the most in the graph (hint: look at the graph color and Counter color)?

Click the **Change graph type** drop-down menu, select **Report**.

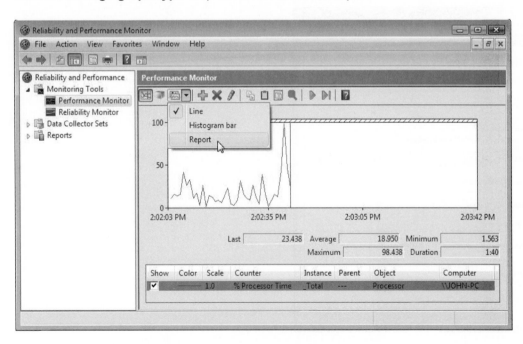

The display changes to report view.

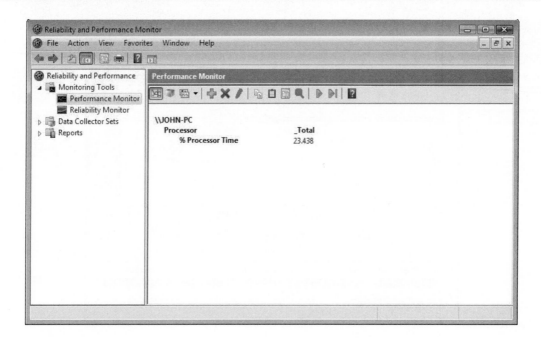

List the values of the counter.

Click the "Routing and Remote Access Properties (Local Computer)" window so it is activated.

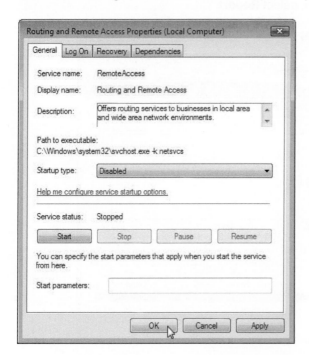

In the Startup type, select **Disabled > OK**.

Click the "Services" window so it is activated.

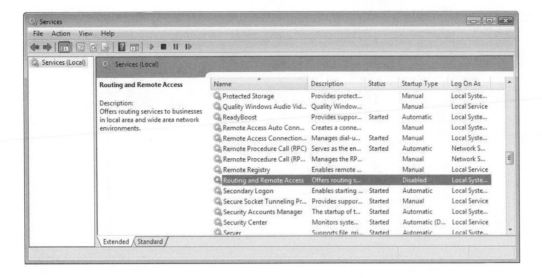

What is the Status and Startup Type for Routing and Remote Access?

Click the "Reliability and Performance Monitor" window so it is activated.

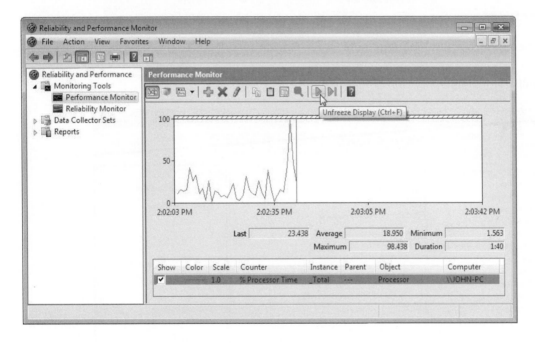

Click the **Unfreeze Display** icon to start the recording.

Close all open windows.

Navigate to the "Administrative Tools" window by clicking **Start > Control Panel > Administrative Tools**.

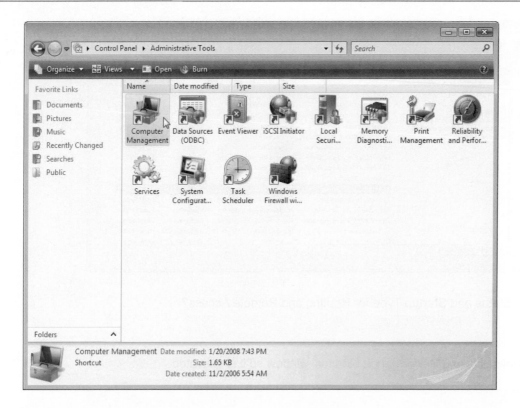

Double-click the **Computer Management** icon **> Continue**.

The "Computer Management" window appears.

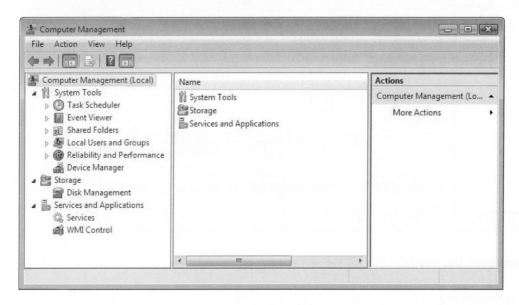

Expand the three categories by clicking on the **arrow** next to: System Tools, Storage, and Services and Applications.

Click the **arrow** next to Event Viewer; then click the **arrow** next to Windows Logs.

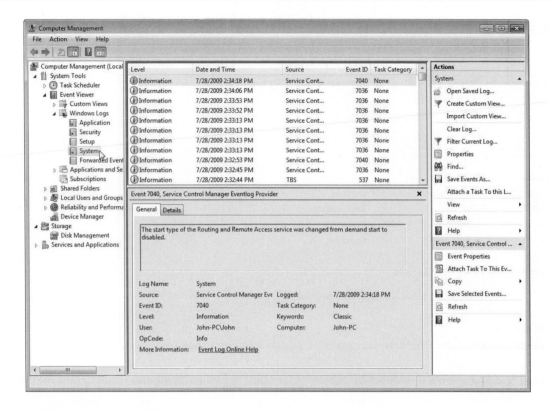

Select **System**.

Double-click the first event in the window.

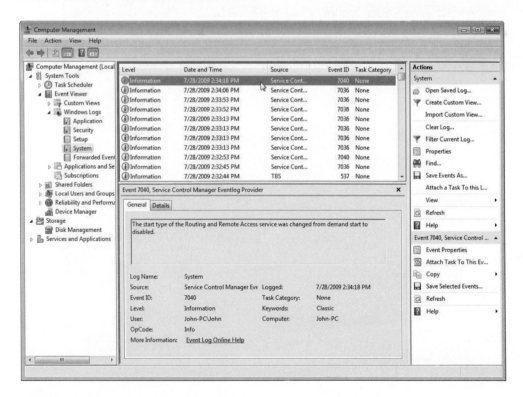

The "Event Properties" window opens for the event.

Click the down arrow key to locate an event for **Routing and Remote Access**.

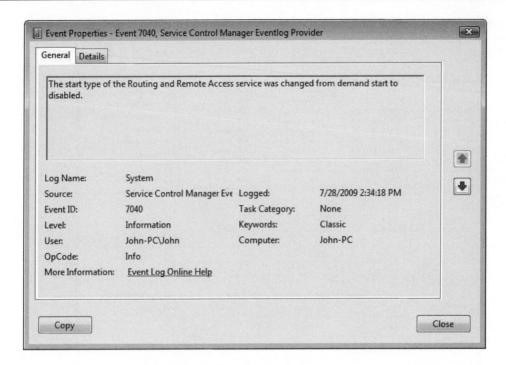

You should find four events that describe the order for starting and stopping the Routing and Remote access service.

Write down the description for each of the four events.

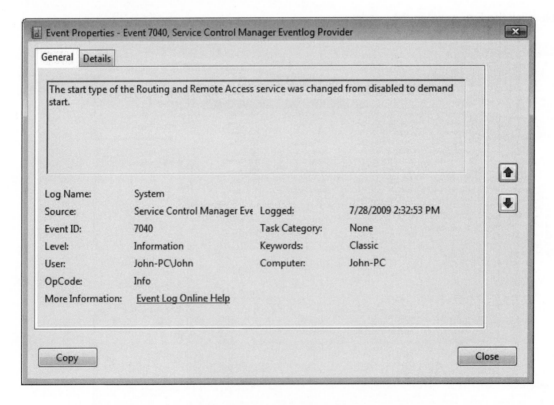

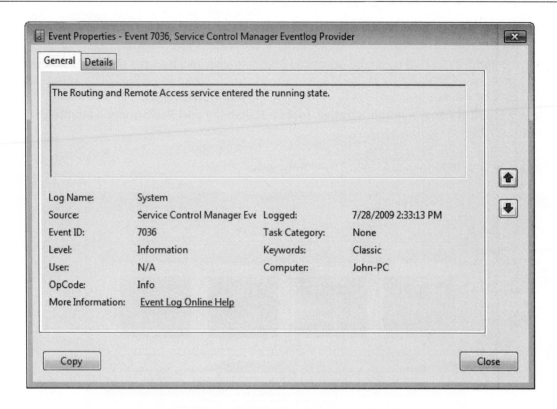

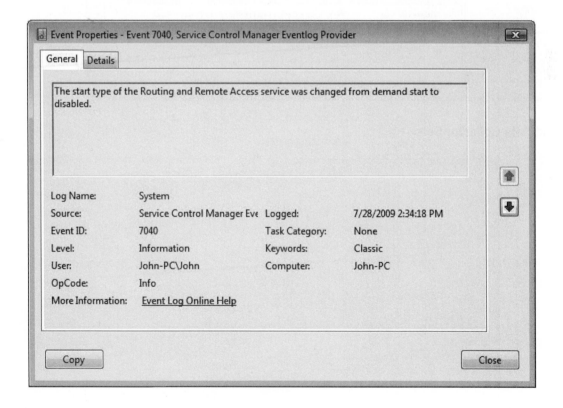

Close all open windows.

Step 3

For the rest of this lab, you will configure advanced Administrative Tool features and monitor how this affects the computer system.

Click **Start > Control Panel > Administrative Tools > Reliability and Performance Monitor > Continue**.

The "Reliability and Performance Monitor" window opens.

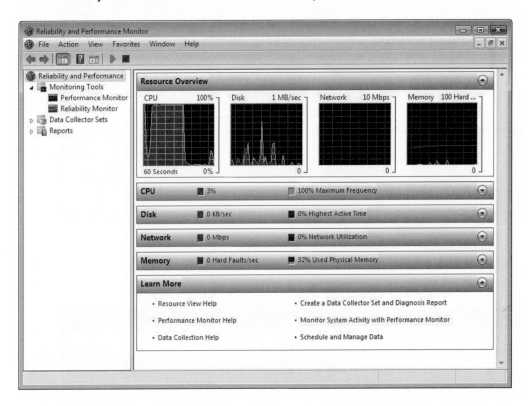

Expand **Data Collector Sets**.

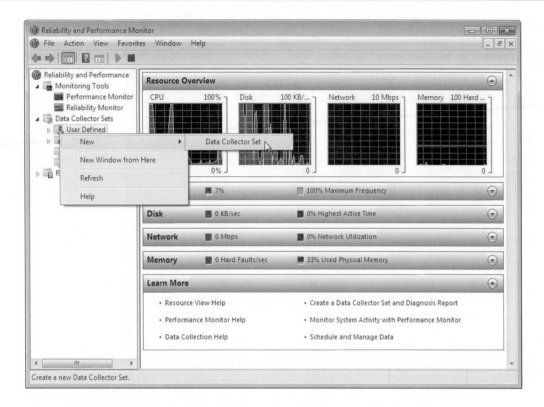

Right-click **User Defined > New > Data Collector Set**.

The "Create new Data Collector Set" window opens.

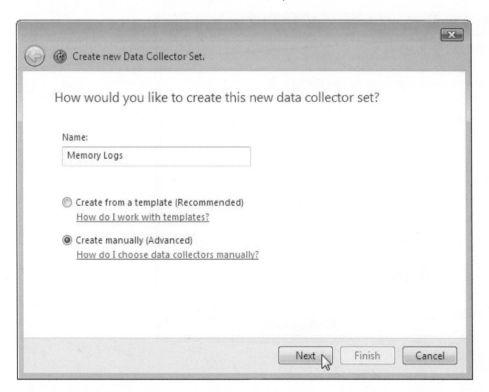

In the Name field, type **Memory Logs**. Select the **Create manually (Advanced)** radio button **> Next**.

The "What type of data do you want to include?" screen appears.

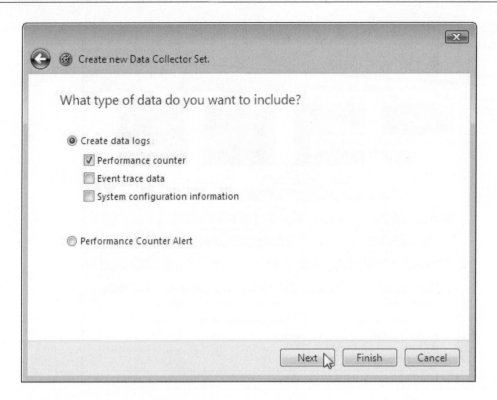

Select **Performance counter > Next**.

The "Which performance counter would you like to log?" screen appears.

Click **Add**.

From the list of available counters, locate and expand **Memory**.

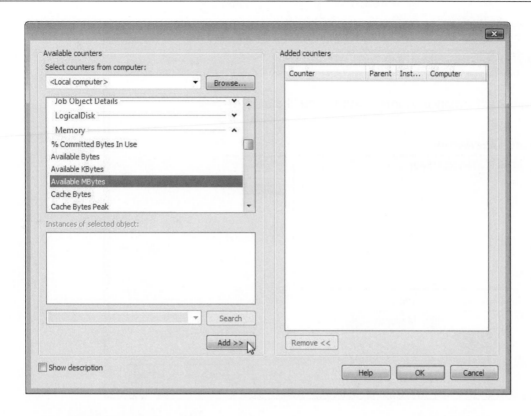

Select **Available MBytes > Add**.

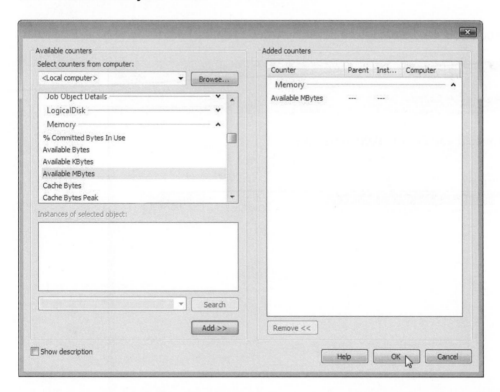

Click **OK**.

Set the Sample interval field to **4** seconds.

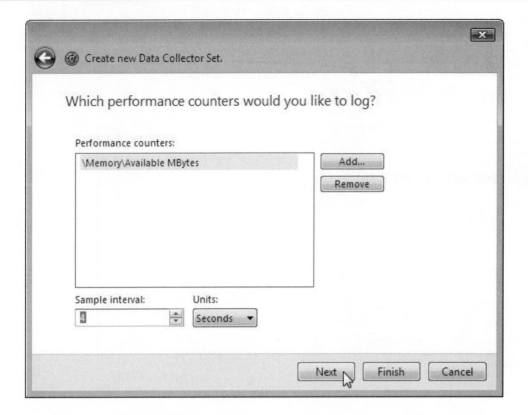

Click **Next**.

The "Where would you like the data to be saved?" screen appears.

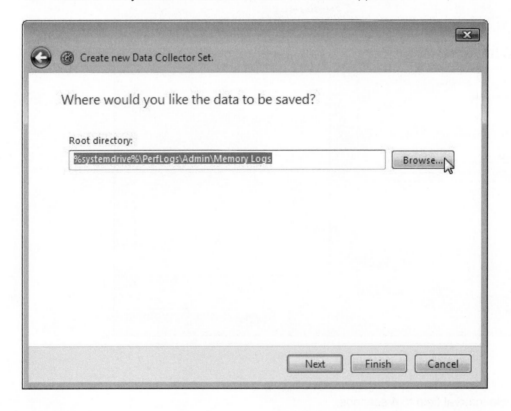

Click **Browse**.

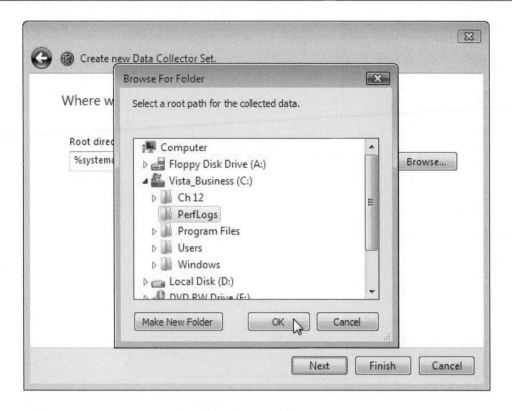

Select drive **(C:) > Make New Folder >** type **PerfLogs > OK**.

The "Create new Data Collector Set" window appears.

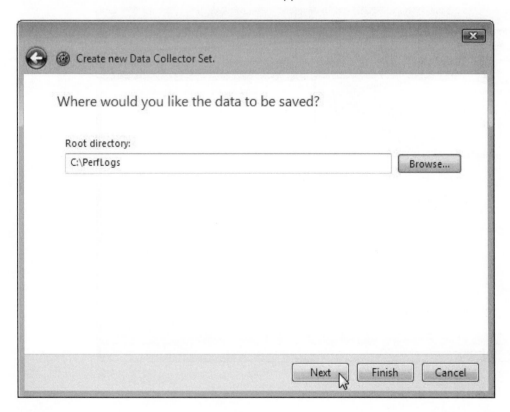

Click **Next**.

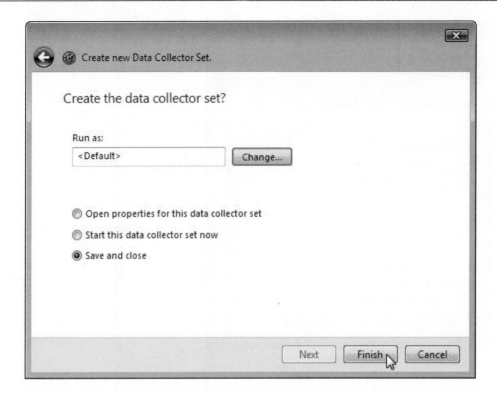

Click **Finish**.

Expand **User Defined** > select **Memory Logs** > right-click **Data Collector01** > **Properties**.

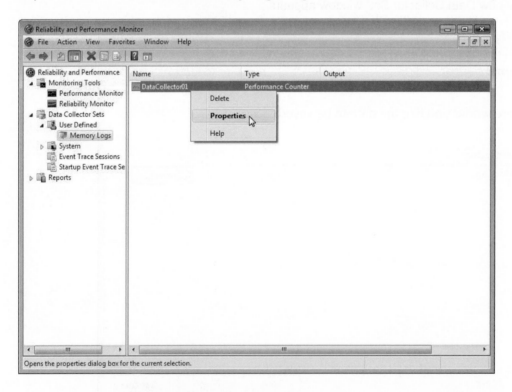

The "DataCollector01 Properties" window opens.

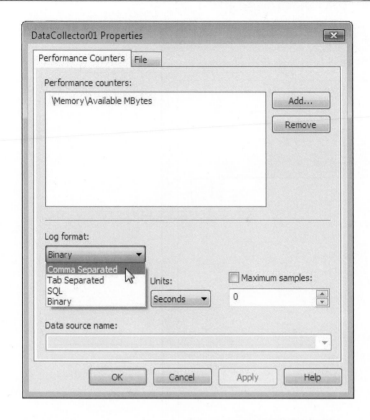

Change the "Log format:" field to **Comma Separated**.

Click the **File** tab.

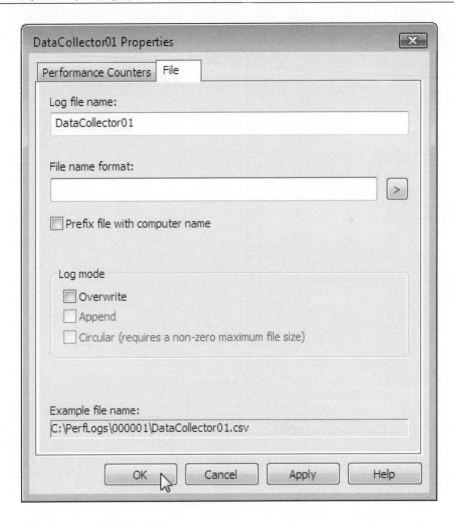

What is the full path name to the example file name?

Click **OK**.

Select the **Memory Logs** icon in the left pane of the "Reliability and Performance Monitor" window.

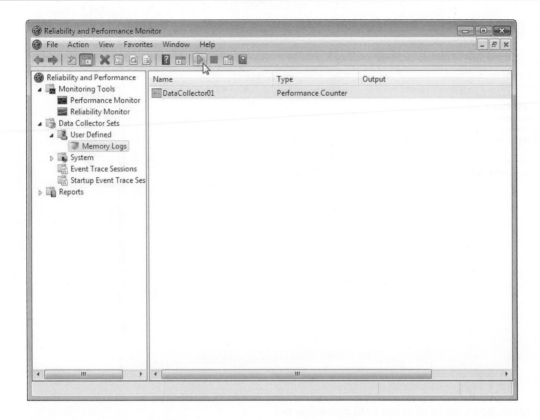

Click the **green arrow** icon to start the data collection set.

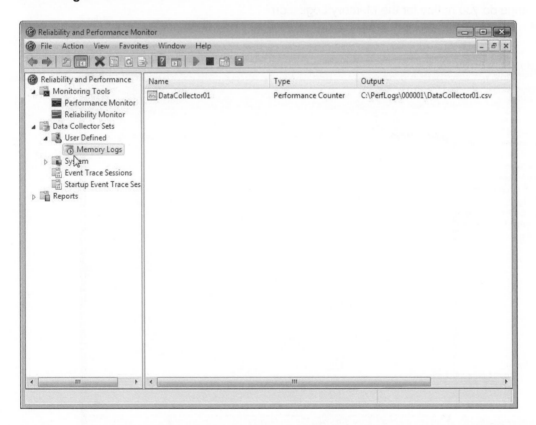

To force the computer to use some of the available memory, open and close a browser.

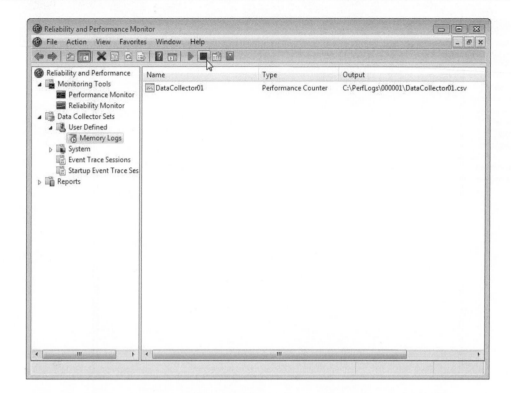

Click the **black box** icon to stop the data collection set.

What change do you notice for the Memory Logs icon?

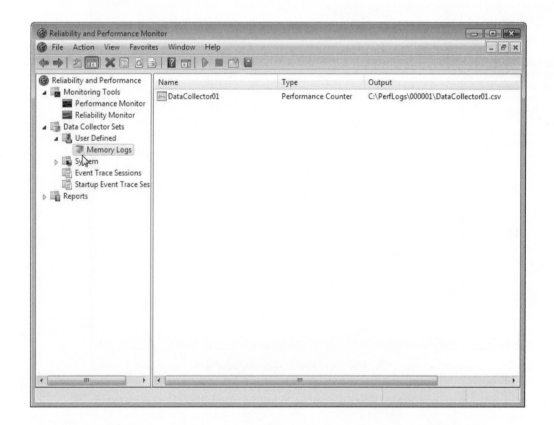

Click **Start > Computer >** double-click drive **C: > PerfLogs > 00001 > Continue**.

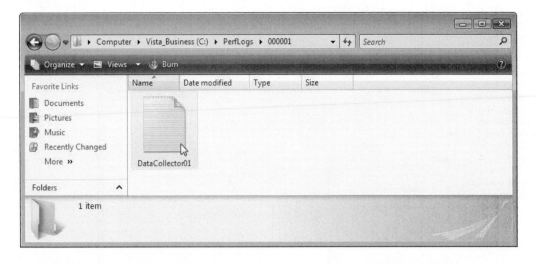

Double-click **DataCollector01** text file.

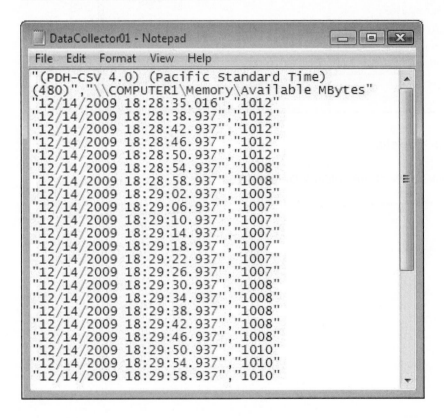

What does the column farthest to the right show?

Close the DataCollector01 text file and the window with the PerfLogs folder.

Select the Reliability and Performance Monitor window.

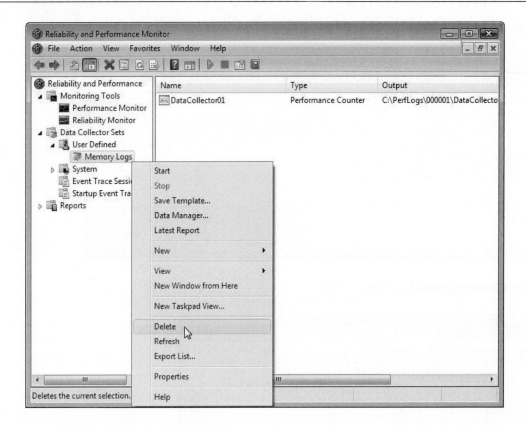

Right-click **Memory Logs > Delete**.

Open drive **C: >** right-click the **PerfLogs** folder **> Delete > Yes**.

Close all open windows.

5.3.3.7 Lab - Monitor and Manage System Resources in Windows XP

Introduction

In this lab, you will use administrative tools to monitor and manage system resources.

Recommended Equipment

The following equipment is required for this exercise:

- A computer running Windows XP Professional
- Internet access

Step 1

You will explore what happens when a service is stopped, and then started.

Log on to Windows as an administrator.

Click **Start > Control Panel > Administrative Tools > Computer Management >** expand **Services and Applications**.

Select **Services**.

Expand the **Computer Management** window so you see the "Help and Support" service.

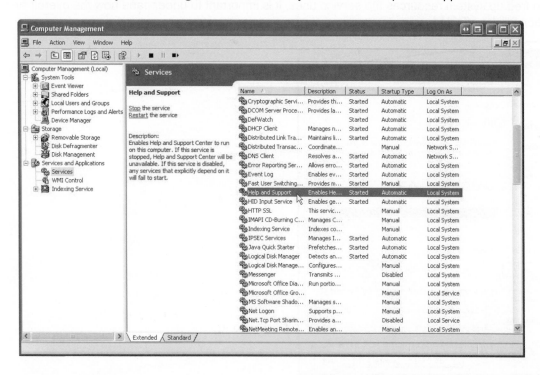

What is the Status of the service?

Right-click the **Help and Support** service > **Properties**.

The "Help and Support Properties (Local Computer)" window opens.

Click **Stop**.

Note: The reason this service will be stopped is so you can easily see the results. When stopping a service, to free up system resources the service uses, it is important to understand how the overall system operation will be affected.

When the Service Control window closes, set the Startup type field to **Disabled**, and then click **Apply**.

Click **Start > Help and Support**.

The "Help and Support Error" window opens.

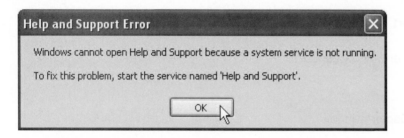

Why will Help and Support not start?

What must be done to correct the error?

Click **OK**.

What steps must be followed to start the Help and Support service?

Next, you will start up the Help and Support service.

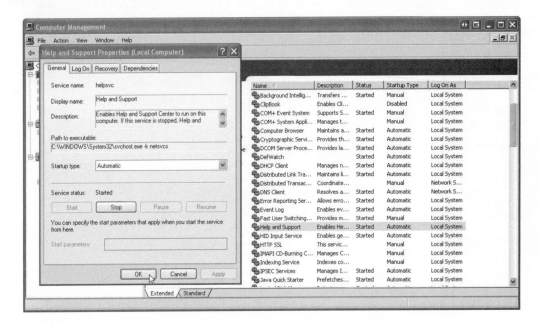

Set "Startup type" to **Automatic**, and then click **OK**.

Click **Start > Help and Support**.

Did the Help and Support Center window appear?

Close the "Help and Support Center" window.

Make sure the Computer Management window is open.

Expand Event Viewer, and then select **System**.

Double-click the most recent Error event. Error events are displayed as a white X in a red circle icon.

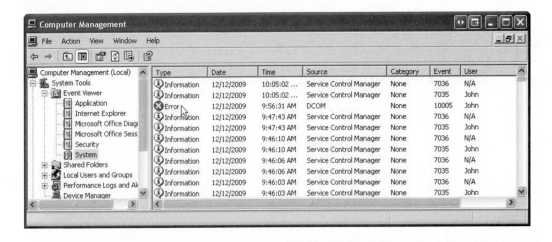

The "Event Properties" window opens.

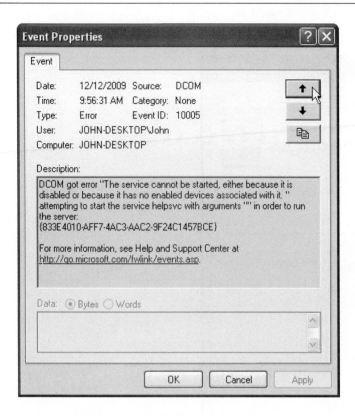

Why was helpsvc not started?

Click the up arrow button.

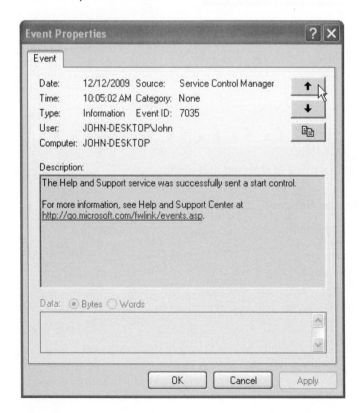

What has happened to the Help and Support service?

Click the up arrow button.

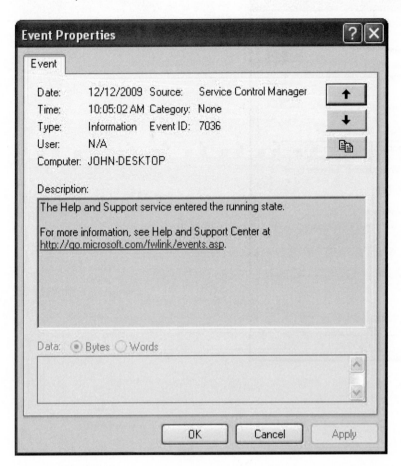

What has happened to the Help and Support service?

Close all open windows.

Step 2

You will now monitor what happens when a service is stopped and started.

Click **Start > Control Panel**. Double-click the **Network Connections** icon.

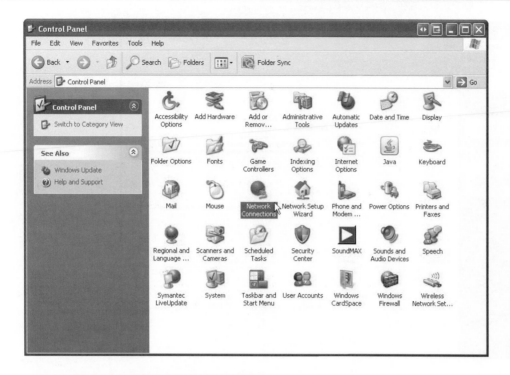

The "Network Connection" window opens.

Reduce the size of the "Network Connections" window. Leave this window open.

Once again navigate to the "Control Panel" window by clicking **Start > Control Panel**. Double-click the **Administrative Tools** icon.

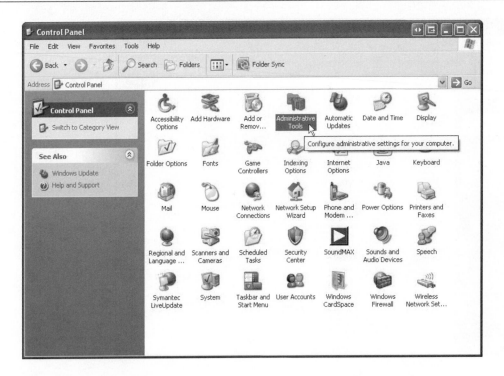

The "Administrative Tools" window opens.

Double-click the **Performance** icon.

The "Performance" window opens.

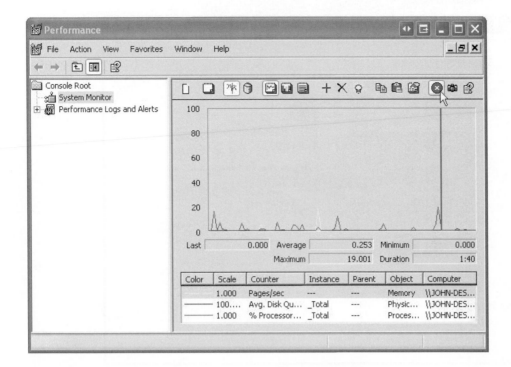

Make sure the System Monitor in the left pane is highlighted.

Click the **Freeze Display** icon to stop the recording.

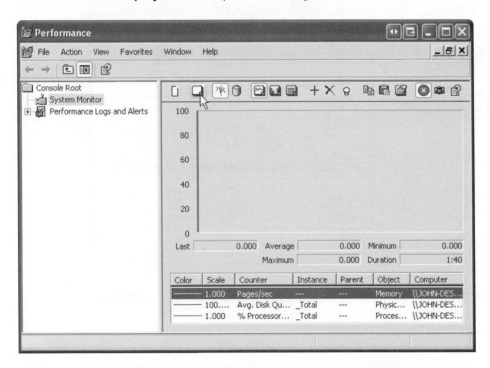

Click the **Clear Display** icon to clear the graph. Leave this window open.

Navigate to the "Administrative Tools" window by clicking **Start > Control Panel > Administrative Tools**. Double-click the **Services** icon.

Expand the width of the "Services" window so you have a clear view of the content.

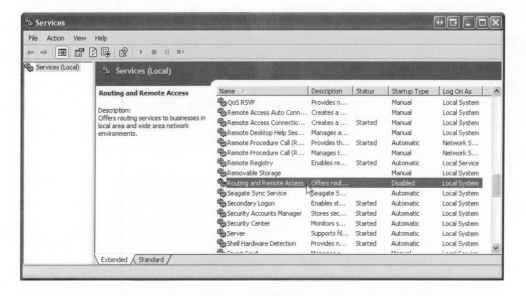

Scroll down in the right pane until you see the service Routing and Remote Access.

Double-click **Routing and Remote Access**.

The "Routing and Remote Access Properties (Local Computer)" windows opens.

In the Startup type, select **Manual**. Click **Apply**.

The Start button is now active; do not click the button yet. Leave this window open.

Position the following three windows so you can clearly see them at the same time: Network Connections, Routing and Remote Access Properties (Local Computer), and Performance.

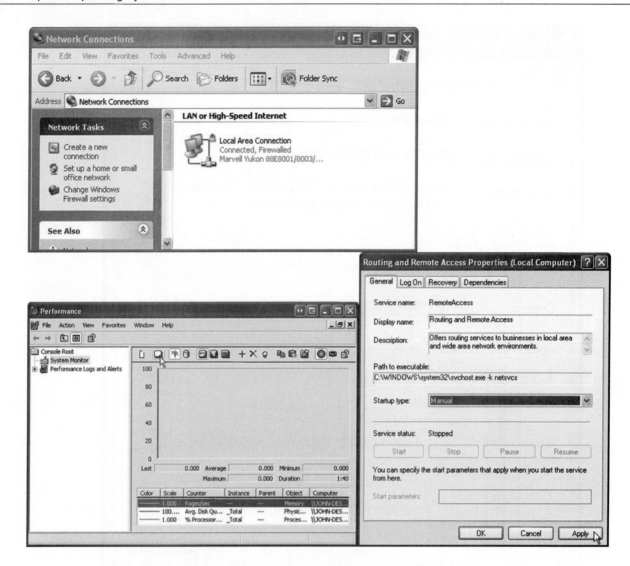

Click the "Performance" window so it is activated. Click the **Freeze Display** icon to start the recording.

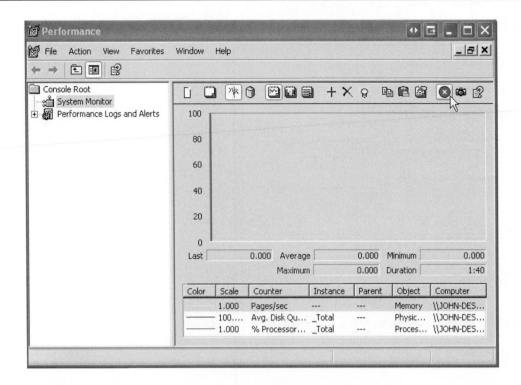

Click the "Routing and Remote Access Properties (Local Computer)" window so it is activated. To start the Service, click **Start**.

A window with a progress bar opens.

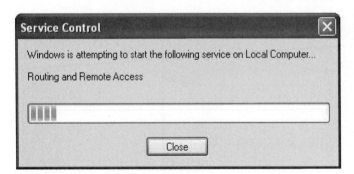

The "Routing and Remote Access Properties (Local Computer)" window now shows the Stop and Pause button active. Leave this window open.

Click the "Network Connections" window so it is activated.

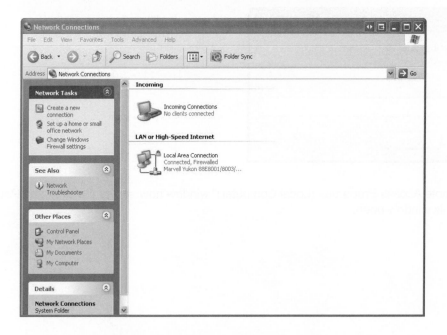

What changes appear in the right pane, after starting the Routing and Remote Access service?

Click the "Routing and Remote Access Properties (Local Computer)" window so it is activated. Click **Stop**.

Click the "Network Connections" window so it is activated.

What changes appear in the right pane, after stopping the Routing and Remote Access service?

Click the "Performance" window so it is activated. Click the **Freeze Display** icon to stop the recording.

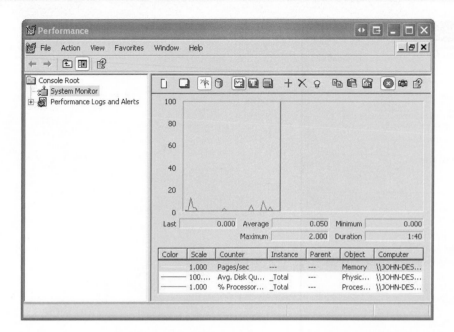

Which Counter is being recorded the most in the graph (hint: look at the graph color and Counter color)?

Click the **View Report** icon.

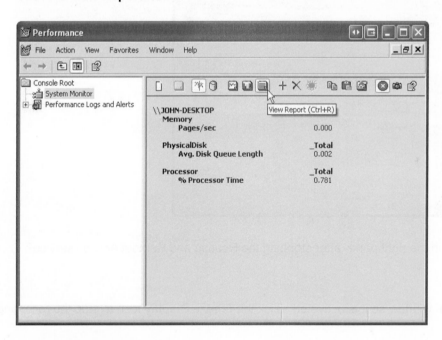

List the values of the three counters.

Click the "Routing and Remote Access Properties (Local Computer)" window so it is activated.

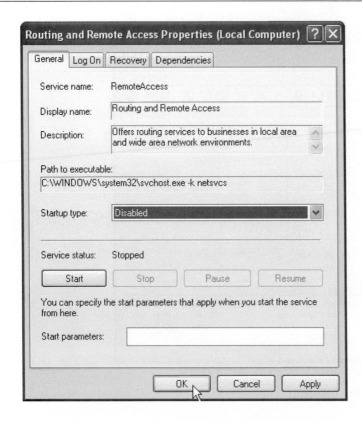

In the Startup type, select **Disabled** and then click **OK**.

Click the "Services" window so it is activated.

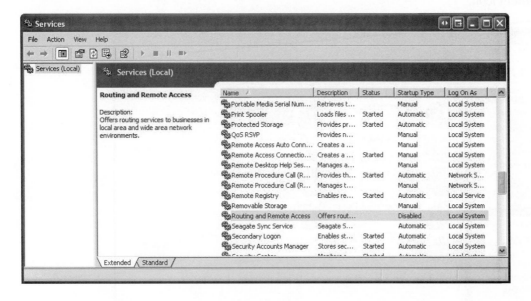

1.   What is the Status and Startup Type for Routing and Remote Access?

Click the "Performance" window so it is activated.

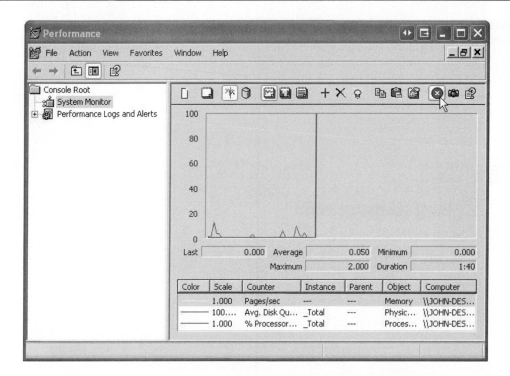

Click the **Freeze Display** icon to start the recording.

Close all open windows.

Navigate to the "Control Panel" window by clicking **Start > Control Panel**. Double-click the **Computer Management** icon.

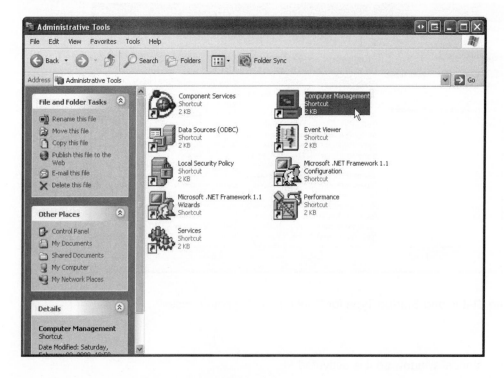

The "Computer Management" window opens.

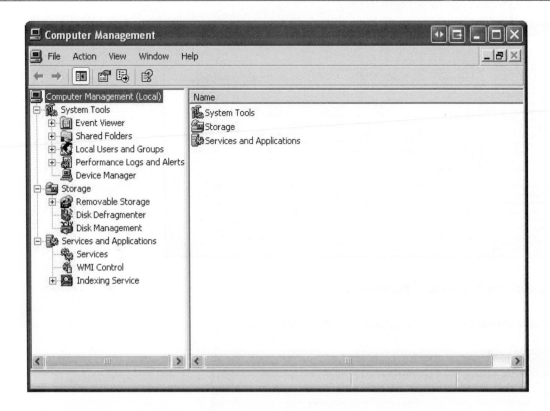

Expand the three categories by clicking on the **plus sign** next to: System Tools, Storage and Services, and Applications.

Click the **plus sign** next to Event Viewer.

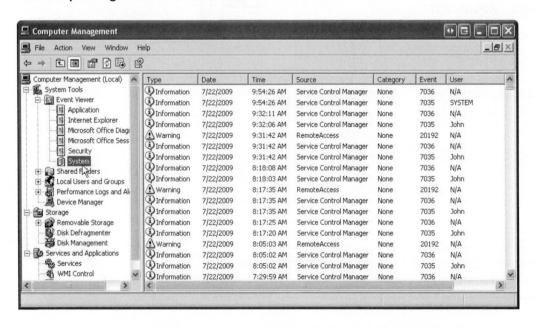

Then select **System**.

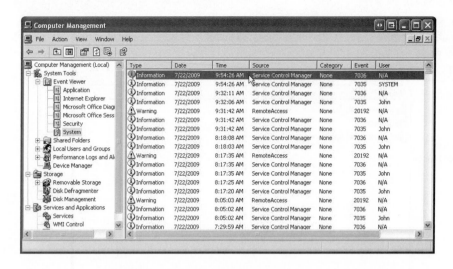

Double-click the first event in the window.

The "Event Properties" window appears for the event.

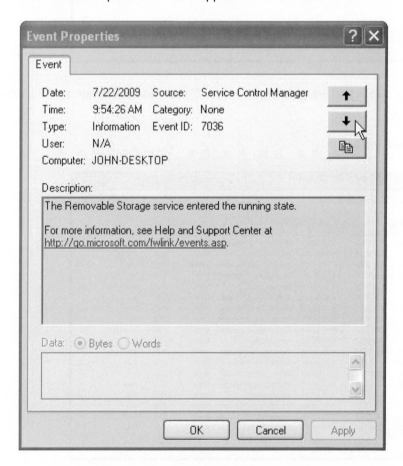

Click the down arrow key to locate an event for Routing and Remote Access.

You should find four events that describe the order for starting and stopping the Routing and Remote Access service.

Write down the description for each of the four events. Do not include any URL information.

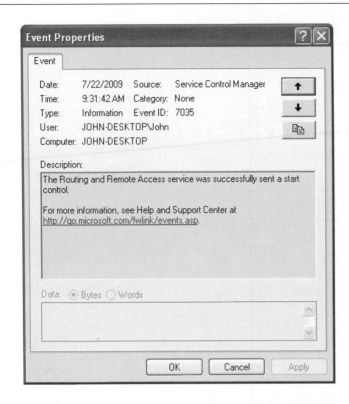

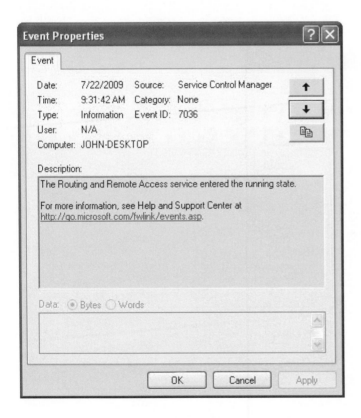

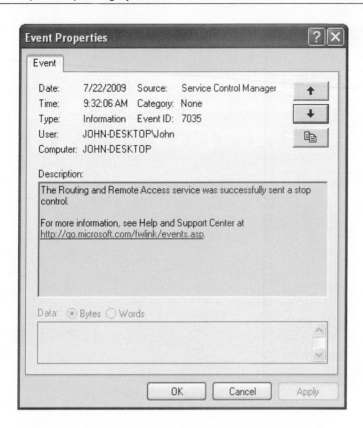

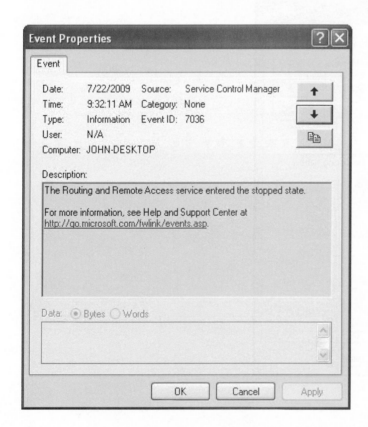

Close all open windows.

Step 3

For the rest of this lab, you will configure advanced Administrative Tool features and monitor how this affects the computer system.

Press **Ctrl-Alt-Delete**. When the "Windows Task Manager" window opens, select the **Performance** tab.

Click **Start > Control Panel > Administrative Tools**. Open the following tools: Event Viewer and Performance.

Close the "Administrative Tools" window.

Resize and position all three windows so they can be seen at the same time.

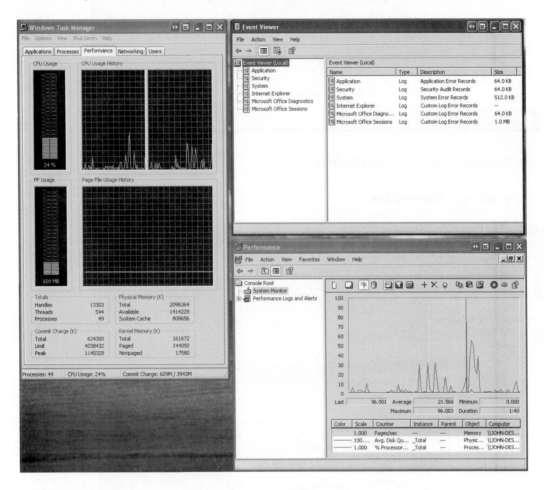

Select the "Performance" window.

Expand "Performance Logs and Alerts".

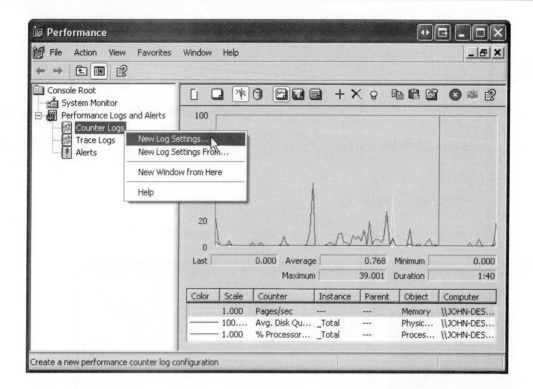

Right-click **Counter Logs > New Log Settings**.

In the Name field, type **Memory Counter**.

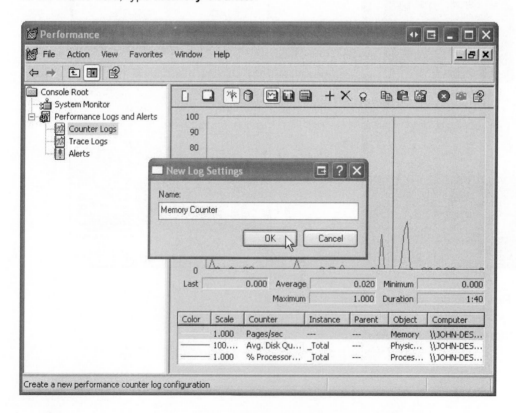

Click **OK**.

When the "Memory Counter" window appears, click **Add Counters**.

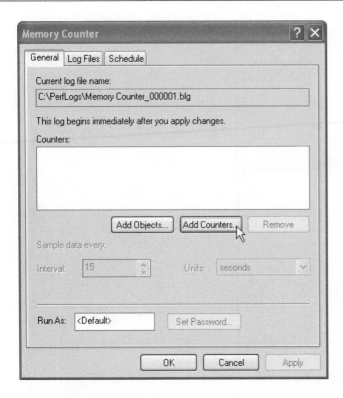

The "Add Counters" window opens.

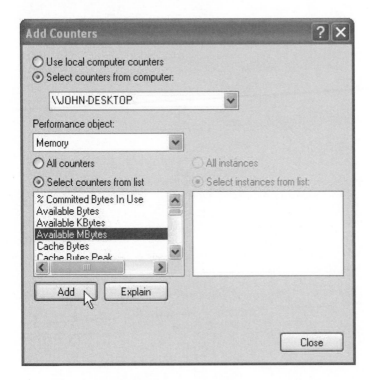

Set the Performance object field to **Memory**.

Set the "Select counters from list" field to **Available Mbytes**, and then click **Add > Close**.

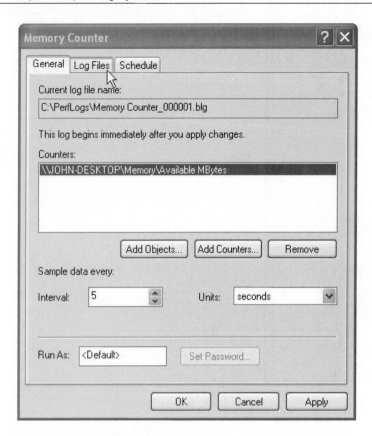

Change the Interval field to **5**.

Select the **Log Files** tab.

Set the Log file type field to **Text File (Tab delimited)**.

Click **Configure**.

What is the default location for the log files?

Click **OK** to close the "Configure Log Files" window.

A folder not found information window opens. Click **Yes** to create the folder.

Click the **Schedule** tab.

Keep the default settings and click **OK**.

The "Performance" window opens.

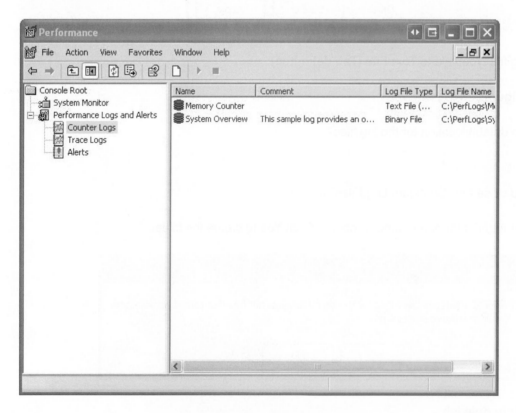

In the "Performance" window, select **Counter Logs**.

The Memory Counter log icon turns green once it has started.

Select the "Windows Task Manager" window.

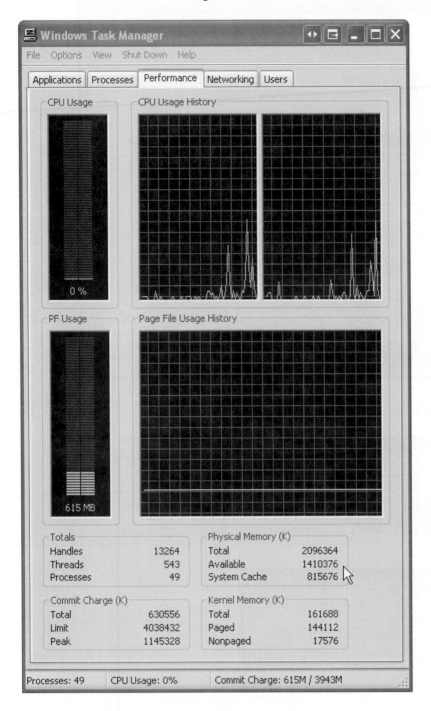

What amount of Physical Memory (K) is available?

Subtract about 10 MB of the available memory. Example: 1410376 – 10000 = 1400376.

How much available memory is left over?

Make sure the "Performance" window is active.

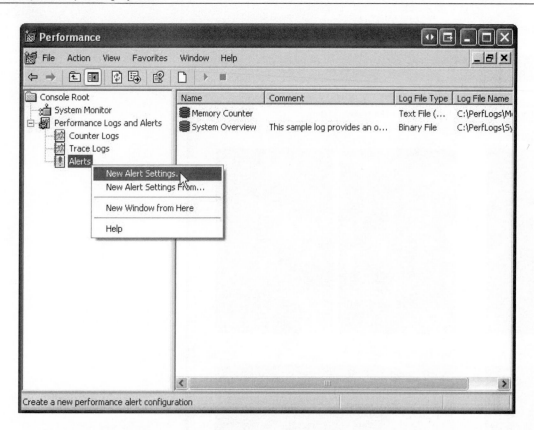

Right-click **Alerts > New Alert Settings**.

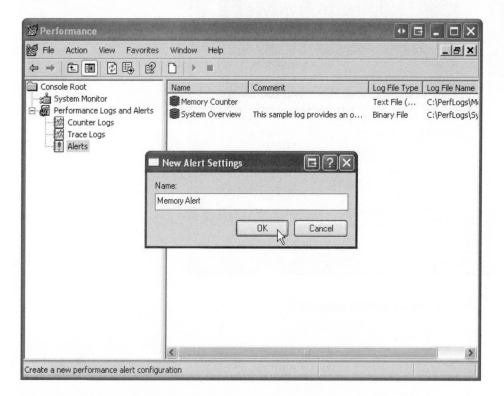

In the Name field, type **Memory Alert**; then click **OK**.

The "Memory Alert" window appears.

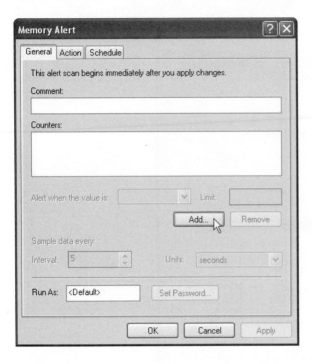

Click **Add**.

The "Add Counters" window opens.

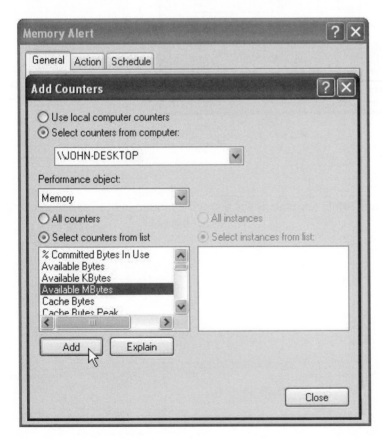

Set the "Performance object" field to **Memory**.

Set the "Select counters from list" field to **Available MBytes**. Click **Add > Close**.

Fill in the window fields.

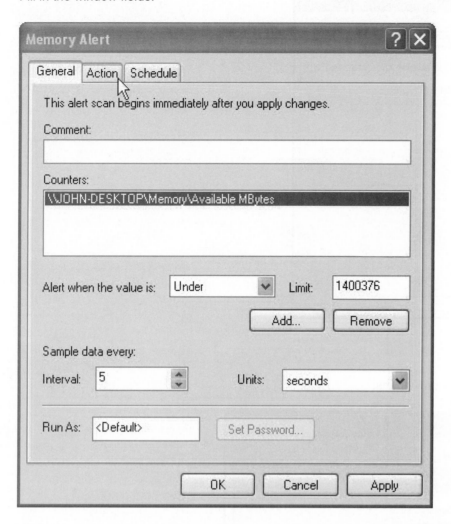

Set the following field values for the General tab:

Alert when the value is: **Under**

Limit: **enter physical memory minus 10MB** (use the physical memory found in the Task Manager earlier in this lab). Example – 1400376

Interval: **5**

Units: **seconds**

Click the **Action** tab.

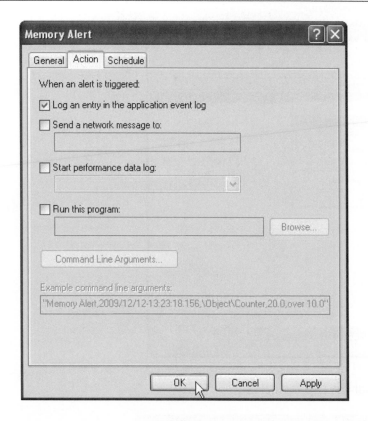

Click **OK** to keep default settings.

In the "Performance" window, select **Alerts**.

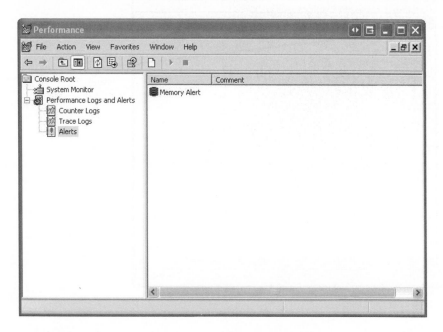

How can you tell that the Memory Alert has started?

To force the computer to use some of the available memory, open and close a browser. Example: Internet Explorer or FireFox.

Right-click the **Memory Alert** icon **> Stop**.

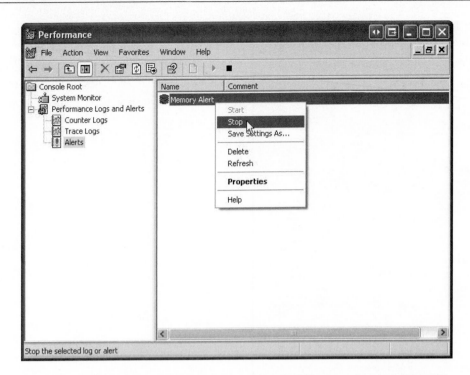

Notice the "Memory Alert" icon has changed to a red color.

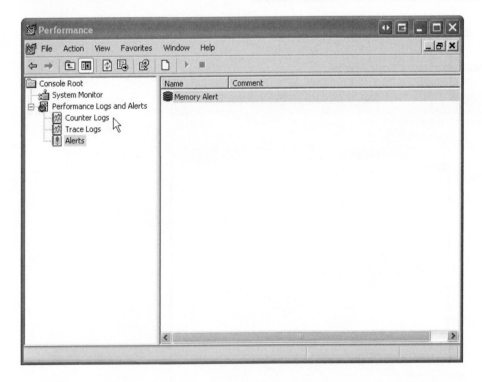

Select **Counter Logs**.

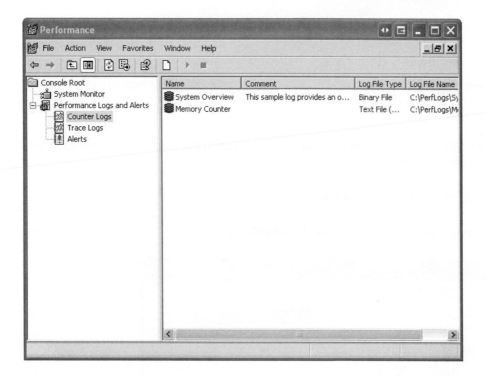

Right-click the **Memory Counter** icon and select **Stop**.

How can you tell the Memory Counter has stopped?

Make sure the "Event Viewer" window is active.

Select **Application**, and double-click the event at the top of the list.

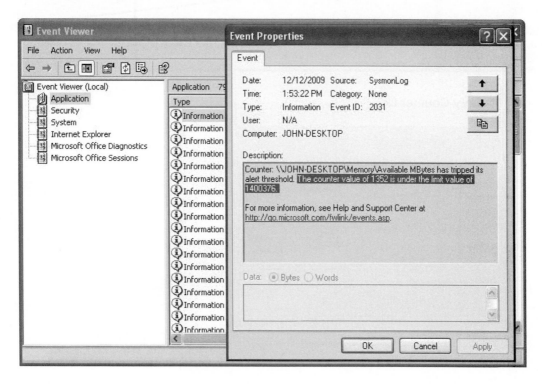

Does the event indicate that the available MBytes has tripped the alert threshold?

If you answered yes to the above question, what was the counter value that tripped the alert event?

If you answered no, click the down arrow a few times until you find the alert event. If you do not find an alert event, ask the instructor for assistance.

Close the "Event Properties" window, click **OK**.

Click **Start > My Computer >** double-click drive **C: > PerfLogs**.

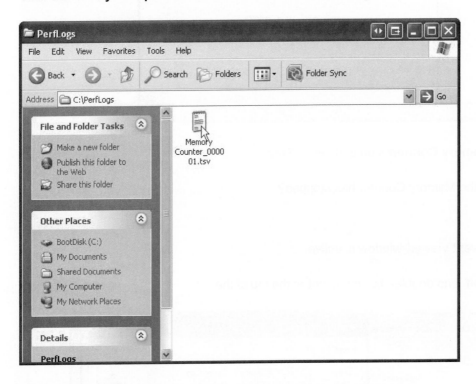

Double-click **Memory Counter** file.

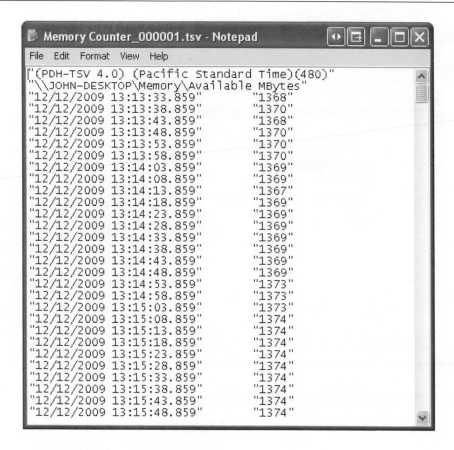

What does the column on the right show?

Close the Memory Counter file, PerfLogs folder, and Windows Task Manager.

In the "Event Viewer" window, click **Application > Action > Clear All Events**. Click **No** when you are asked to save the events to a file.

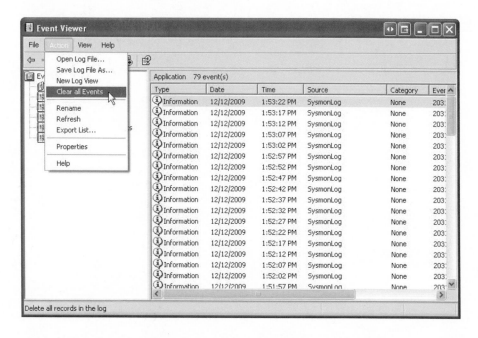

In the "Performance" window, click **Counter Logs >** right-click **Memory Counter > Delete**.

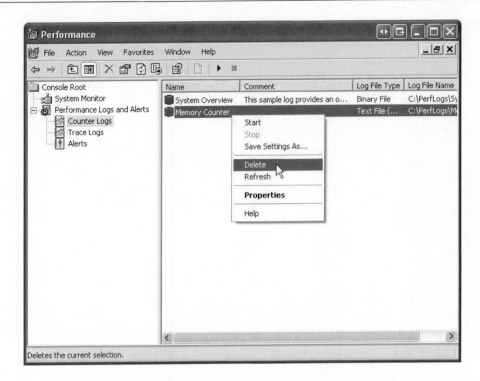

Select **Alerts > Memory Alert >** right-click **Memory Alert > Delete**.

Open drive **C:**.

Right-click the **PerfLogs** folder.

Click **Delete > Yes**.

Close all open windows.

5.3.4.2 Lab - Hard Drive Maintenance in Windows 7

Introduction

In this lab, you will examine the results after using Disk Check and Disk Defragmenter on a hard drive.

Recommended Equipment

The following equipment is required for this exercise:

- A computer running Windows 7
- Two or more partitions on the hard drive.

Step 1

Log on to Windows as an administrator.

Start > Computer > double-click **New Volume (G:)**.

Note: Substitute volume and drive (G:) for the letter used in your computer.

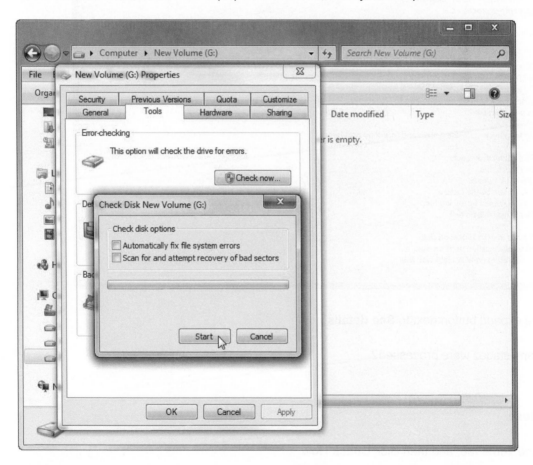

Right-click anywhere in the white space of the folder area for drive **G: > Properties > Tools** tab **> Check Now**.

The "Check Disk New Volume (G:)" window opens.

Make sure there is not a check mark in either checkbox; then click **Start**.

The "Your device or disk was successfully scanned" screen appears.

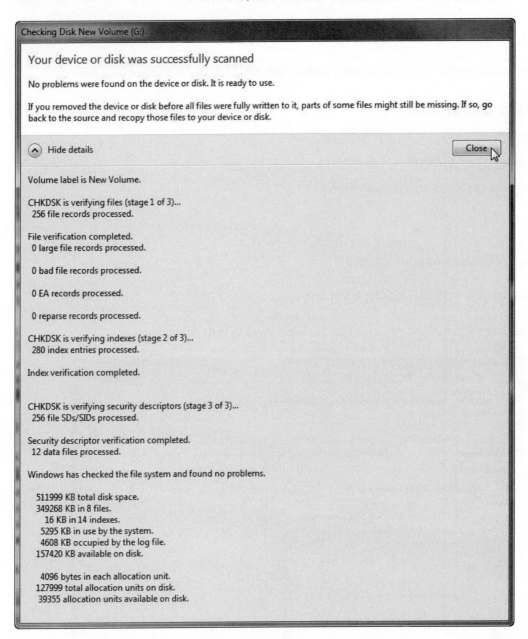

Click the expand button next to **See details**.

How many stages were processed?

Click **Close**.

Select the **Tools** tab, and then click **Check Now**.

Remove the check mark next to **Automatically fix file system errors**.

Place a check mark in the checkbox next to **Scan for and attempt recovery of bad sectors > Start**.

The "Your device or disk was successfully scanned" screen appears.

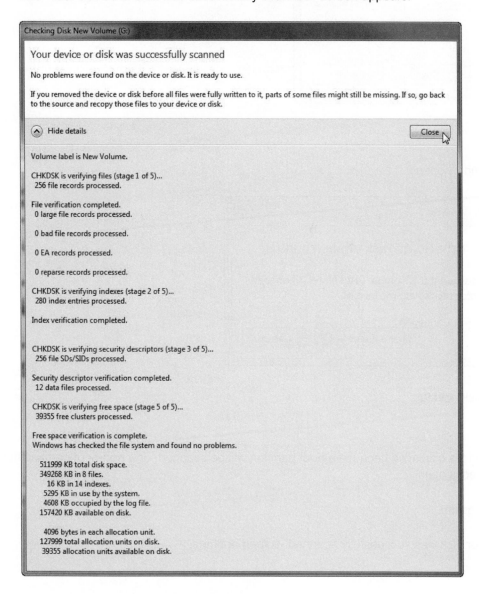

Click the expand button next to **See details**.

What stages were processed?

Click **Close**.

Select the **Tools** tab **> Check Now**.

Place a check mark in both checkboxes.

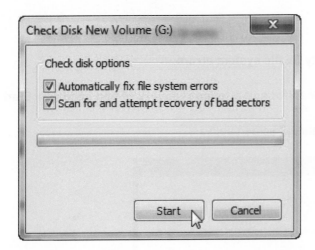

Click **Start**.

An information window opens.

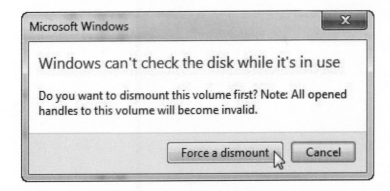

Why will Check Disk not start?

Note: This message is displayed because a boot partition will be scanned, or a non-boot partition that is going to be scanned is open.

Click **Force a dismount**.

The "Your device or disk was successfully scanned" screen appears.

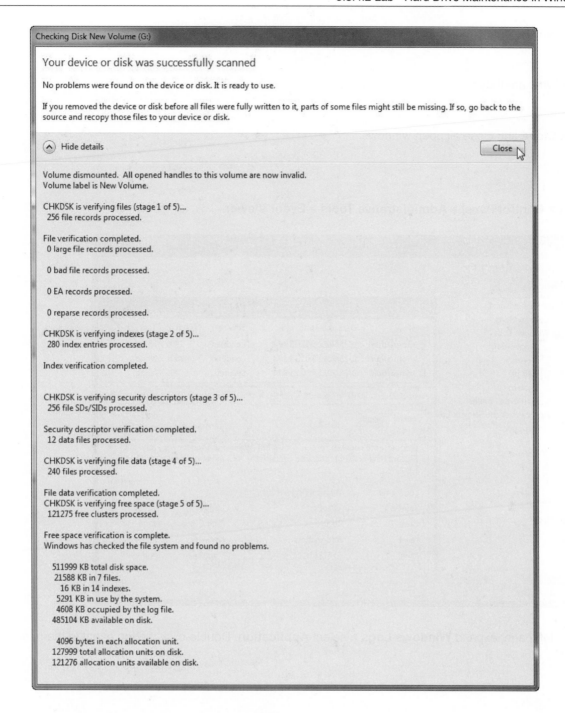

Checking Disk New Volume (G:)

Your device or disk was successfully scanned

No problems were found on the device or disk. It is ready to use.

If you removed the device or disk before all files were fully written to it, parts of some files might still be missing. If so, go back to the source and recopy those files to your device or disk.

⌃ Hide details   Close

Volume dismounted. All opened handles to this volume are now invalid.
Volume label is New Volume.

CHKDSK is verifying files (stage 1 of 5)...
  256 file records processed.

File verification completed.
  0 large file records processed.

  0 bad file records processed.

  0 EA records processed.

  0 reparse records processed.

CHKDSK is verifying indexes (stage 2 of 5)...
  280 index entries processed.

Index verification completed.

CHKDSK is verifying security descriptors (stage 3 of 5)...
  256 file SDs/SIDs processed.

Security descriptor verification completed.
  12 data files processed.

CHKDSK is verifying file data (stage 4 of 5)...
  240 files processed.

File data verification completed.
CHKDSK is verifying free space (stage 5 of 5)...
  121275 free clusters processed.

Free space verification is complete.
Windows has checked the file system and found no problems.

  511999 KB total disk space.
   21588 KB in 7 files.
      16 KB in 14 indexes.
    5291 KB in use by the system.
    4608 KB occupied by the log file.
  485104 KB available on disk.

    4096 bytes in each allocation unit.
  127999 total allocation units on disk.
  121276 allocation units available on disk.

Click the expand button next to **See details**.

What stages were processed?

What is being verified in each of the stages?

Were any problems found with the volume?

If so, what are they?

Click **Close** and close all open windows.

Step 2

Start > Control Panel > Administrative Tools > Event Viewer.

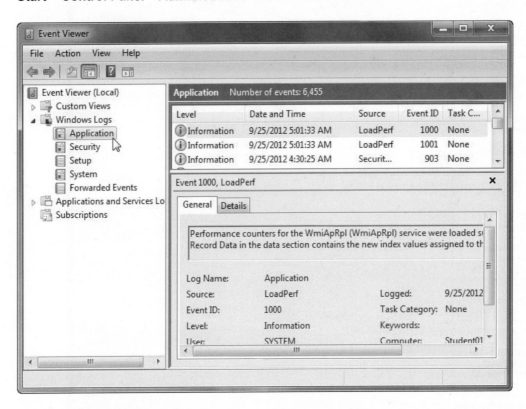

In the left pane, expand **Windows Logs >** select **Application**. Double-click the top event in the middle pane.

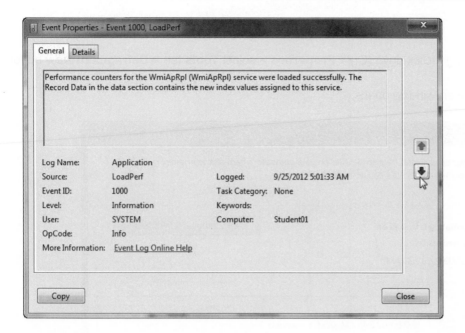

If the displayed event is not Chkdsk, click the black down arrow until the Chsdsk event appears.

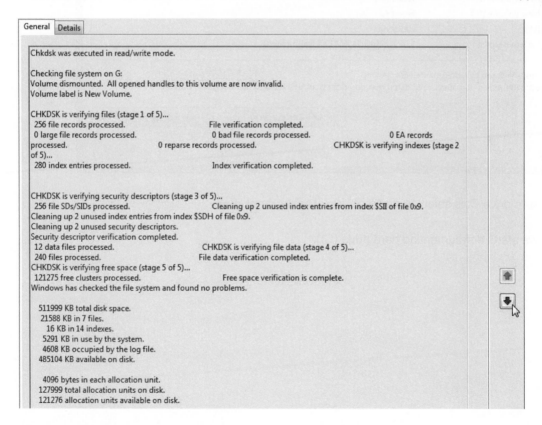

Which stages are shown as completed?

Close all open windows.

Step 3

Start > Computer > right-click drive **(C:) > Properties >** select **Tools** tab **> Defragment Now** button.

The "Disk Defragmenter" window opens.

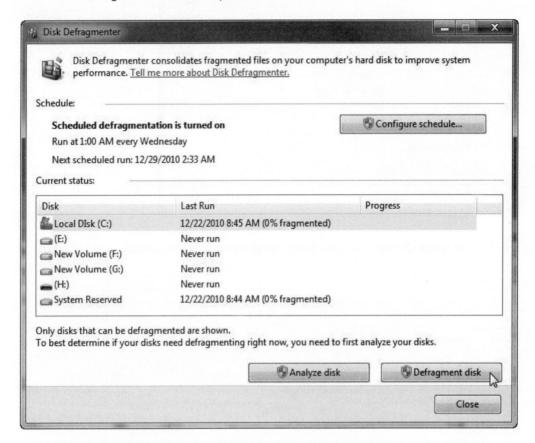

Make sure drive C: is selected and then click **Defragment disk**.

Windows starts defragmenting hard drive (C:).

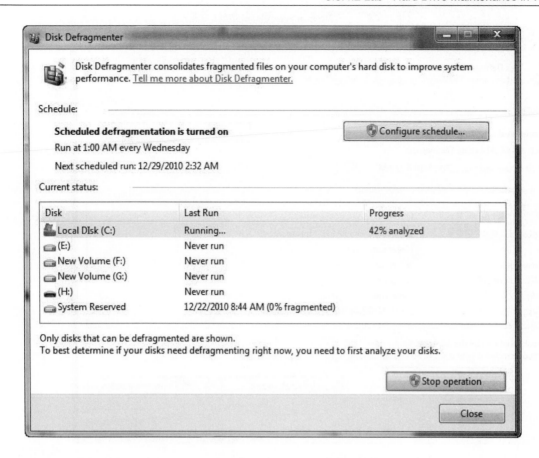

What is the first process during defragmenting (See "Progress" column)?

What are the three tasks performed for each Pass (See "Progress" column)?

How many passes did it take to defragment drive C:?

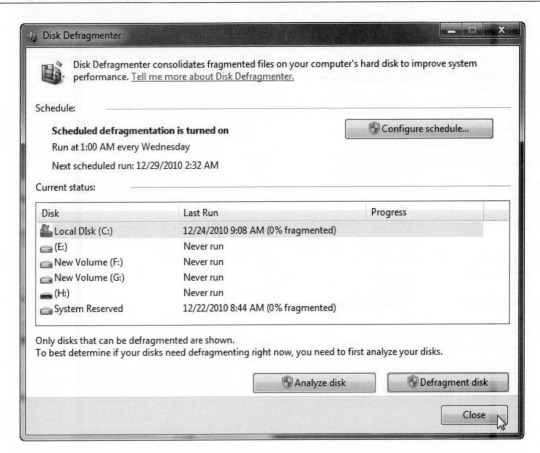

When defragmenting is completed click **Close**.

Close all windows.

Note: It is not possible to view the detail of the defragmented hard drive through the GUI version of defragmenter.

5.3.4.3 Lab - Hard Drive Maintenance in Windows Vista

Introduction

In this lab, you will examine the results after using Disk Check and Disk Defragmenter on a hard drive.

Recommended Equipment

The following equipment is required for this exercise:

- A computer running Windows Vista

- Two or more partitions on the hard drive.

Step 1

Log on to Windows as an administrator.

Start > Computer > double-click **New Volume (G:)**.

Note: Substitute volume and drive (G:) for the letter used in your computer.

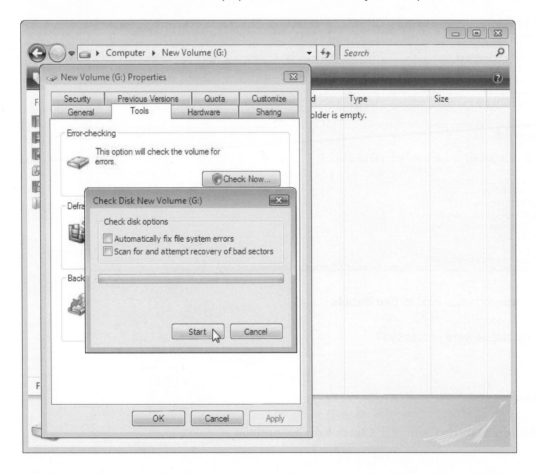

Right-click anywhere in the white space of the folder area for drive **G: > Properties > Tools** tab **> Check Now > Continue**.

The "Check Disk New Volume (G:)" window opens.

Make sure there is not a check mark in either check box; then click **Start**.

The "Your device or disc was successfully scanned" screen appears.

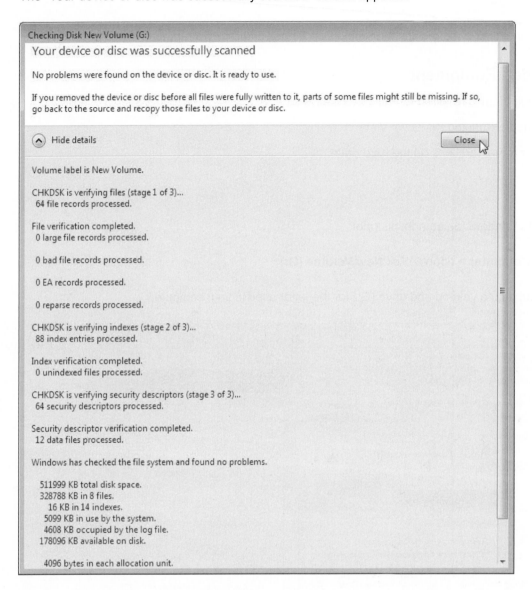

Click the expand button next to **See details**.

How many stages were processed?

Click **Close**.

Select the **Tools** tab, and then click **Check Now > Continue**.

Remove the check mark next to **Automatically fix file system errors**.

Place a check mark in the check box next to **Scan for and attempt recovery of bad sectors > Start**.

The "Your device or disc was successfully scanned" screen appears.

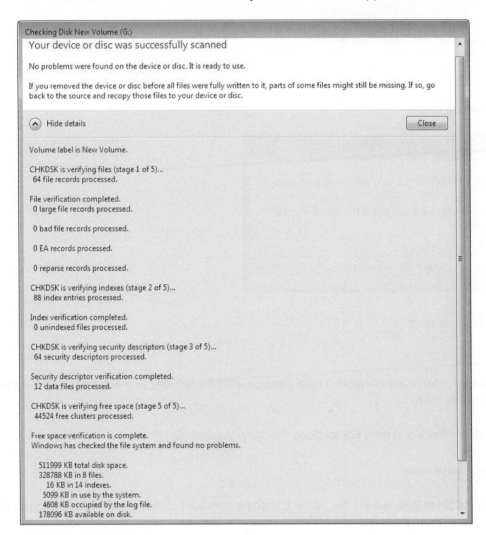

Click the expand button next to **See details**.

What stages were processed?

Click **Close**.

Select the **Tools** tab **> Check Now**.

Place a check mark in both check boxes.

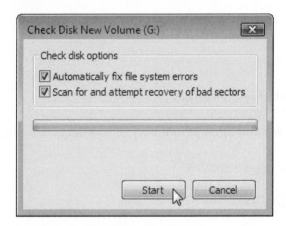

Click **Start**.

An information window opens.

Why will Check Disk not start?

Note: This message is displayed because a boot partition will be scanned, or a non-boot partition that is going to be scanned is open.

Click **Schedule disk check** and then **OK** to close the "New Volume (G:) Properties" window.

Make sure drive G: stays open.

Note: To force CHKDSK to create a log file, when it scans a non-boot partition with no bad sectors, the non-boot partition drive must be open.

Click **Start >** hover over the right arrow button **> Restart**.

Step 2

The "Checking file system on G:" screen appears.

```
Checking file system on G:
The type of the file system is NTFS.
Volume label is New Volume.

A disk check has been scheduled.
Windows will now check the disk.

CHKDSK is verifying files (stage 1 of 5)...
  64 file records processed.
File verification completed.
  0 large file records processed.
  0 bad file records processed.
  0 EA records processed.
  0 reparse records processed.
CHKDSK is verifying indexes (stage 2 of 5)...
  88 index entries processed.
Index verification completed.
  0 unindexed files processed.
CHKDSK is verifying security descriptors (stage 3 of 5)...
  64 security descriptors processed.
Security descriptor verification completed.
  12 data files processed.
CHKDSK is verifying file data (stage 4 of 5)...
  48 files processed.
File data verification completed.
CHKDSK is verifying free space (stage 5 of 5)...
  121324 free clusters processed.
Free space verification is complete.
Windows has checked the file system and found no problems.

    511999 KB total disk space.
     21588 KB in 7 files.
        16 KB in 14 indexes.
         0 KB in bad sectors.
      5099 KB in use by the system.
      4608 KB occupied by the log file.
    485296 KB available on disk.

      4096 bytes in each allocation unit.
    127999 total allocation units on disk.
    121324 allocation units available on disk.
Windows has finished checking the disk.
.....
```

How many stages in the scan are there?

What is being verified in each of the stages?

Were any problems found with the volume?

If so what are they?

Step 3

Log on to Windows as an administrator.

Start > Control Panel > Administrative Tools > Event Viewer > Continue.

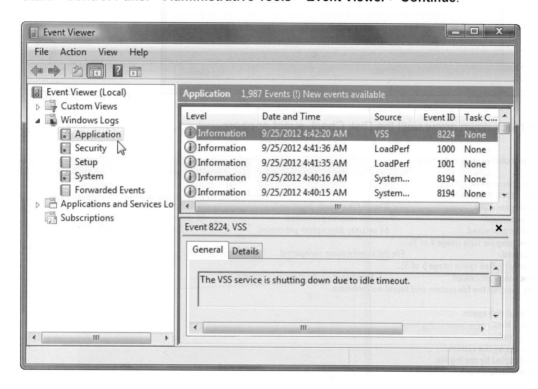

In the left pane, expand **Windows Logs >** select **Application**. Double-click the top event in the right pane.

The "Event Properties" window opens.

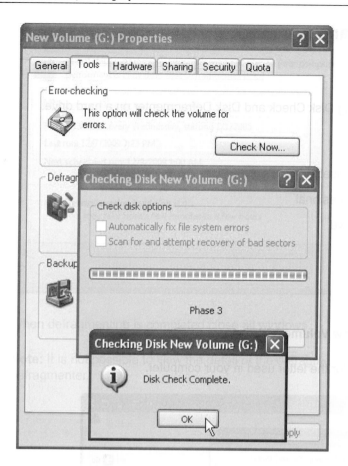

How many phases were checked?

Click **OK**.

Select the **Tools** tab, and click **Check Now**.

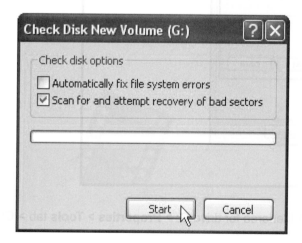

Place a check mark in the check box next to **Scan for and attempt recovery of bad sectors > Start**.

The "Disk Check Complete" window appears.

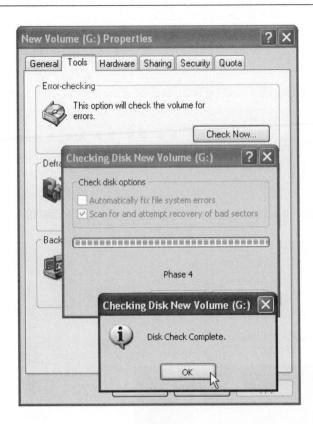

How many phases were checked?

Click **OK**.

Select the **Tools** tab, and click **Check Now**.

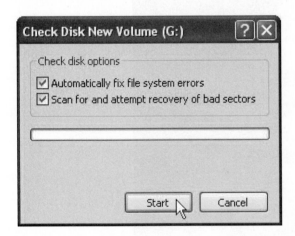

Place a check mark in both check boxes and click **Start**.

An information window opens.

Why will CHKDSK not start?

Note: This message is displayed because a boot partition will be scanned, or a non-boot partition that is going to be scanned is open.

Click **Yes** and then **OK** to close the "New Volume (G:) Properties" window.

Make sure drive G: stays open.

Note: To force CHKDSK to create a log file, when it scans a non-boot partition with no bad sectors, the non-boot partition drive must be open.

Click **Start > Shutdown > Restart**.

Step 2

The "Checking file system on G:" window appears.

How many stages in the scan are there?

What is being verified in each of the stages?

Were any problems found with the volume?

If so, what are they?

Step 3

Log on to Windows as an administrator.

Start > Control Panel > Administrative Tools > Event Viewer > in the left pane, select **Application**.

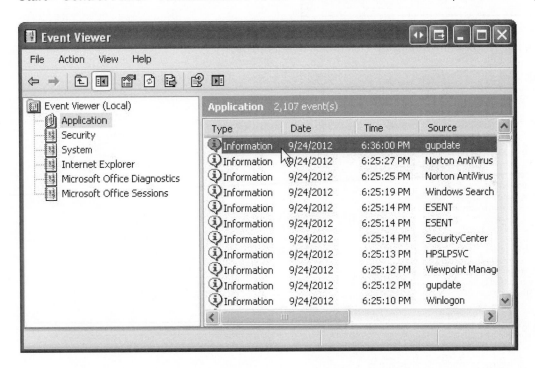

Double-click the top event in the right pane.

The "Event Properties" window opens.

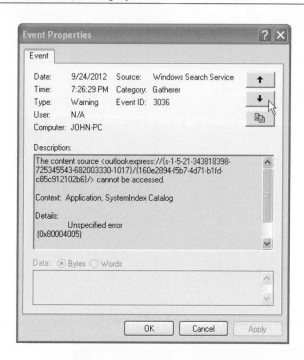

Click the black down arrow until the disk check event appears.

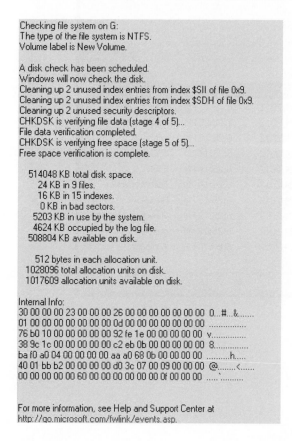

Which stages are shown as completed?

Close all open windows.

Step 4

Start > My Computer > right-click drive **(C:) > Properties > Tools** tab **> Defragment Now**.

The "Disk Defragmenter" window appears. Notice drive (C:) is selected.

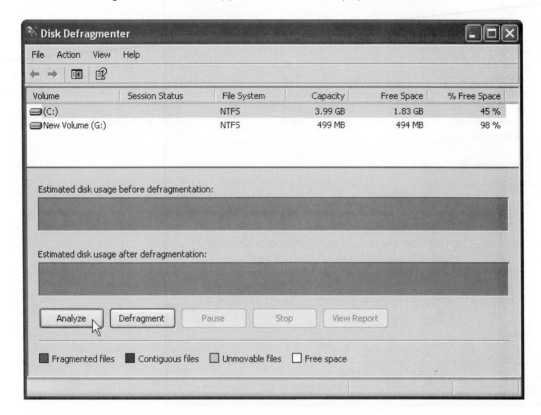

What are the file types and colors, grouped by Disk Defragmenter?

Click **Analyze**.

When the Analysis is complete for: (C:) window appears, click **View Report**.

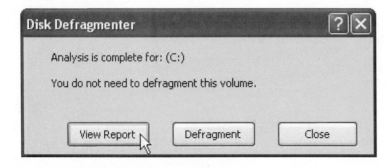

The "Analysis Report" window opens.

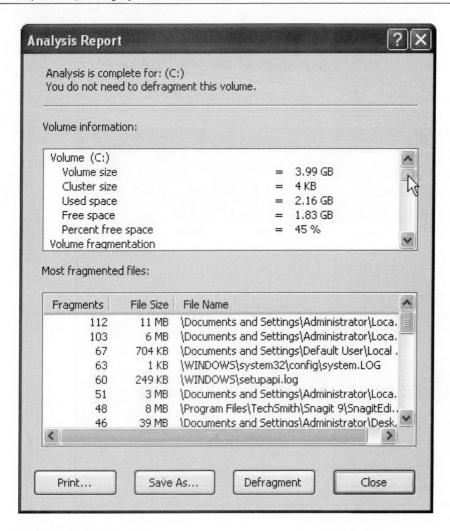

Does the volume need defragmenting?

Click on the scroll down bar to view volume information.

```
Volume (C:)
    Volume size                    =   3.99 GB
    Cluster size                   =   4 KB
    Used space                     =   2.16 GB
    Free space                     =   1.83 GB
    Percent free space             =   45 %
Volume fragmentation
    Total fragmentation            =   10 %
    File fragmentation             =   20 %
    Free space fragmentation       =   0 %
File fragmentation
    Total files                    =   10,655
    Average file size              =   246 KB
    Total fragmented files         =   634
    Total excess fragments         =   2,046
    Average fragments per file     =   1.19
Pagefile fragmentation
    Pagefile size                  =   768 MB
    Total fragments                =   1
Folder fragmentation
    Total folders                  =   748
    Fragmented folders             =   17
    Excess folder fragments        =   118
Master File Table (MFT) fragmentation
    Total MFT size                 =   11 MB
    MFT record count               =   11,420
    Percent MFT in use             =   99
    Total MFT fragments            =   2
```

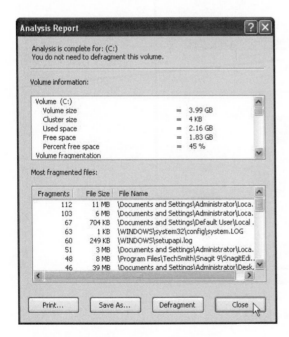

Click the **Close** button.

Drive (C:) has what percentage of free space?

The "Disk Defragmenter" window opens.

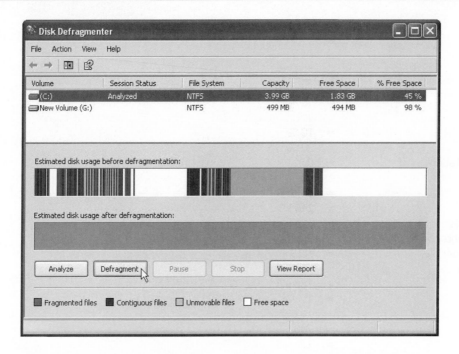

Click the **Defragment** button.

The defragmenting process begins.

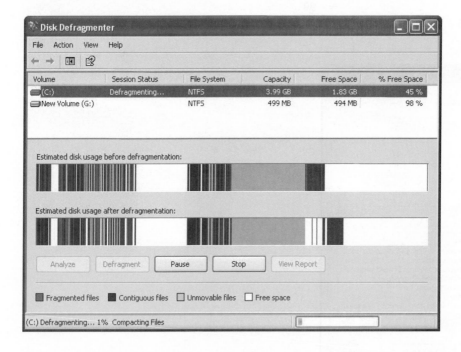

The "Defragmentation is complete for: (C:)" window appears.

Click **View Report**.

Click on the scroll down bar to view volume information.

```
Volume  (C:)
    Volume size                          =   3.99 GB
    Cluster size                         =   4 KB
    Used space                           =   2.15 GB
    Free space                           =   1.84 GB
    Percent free space                   =   46 %
Volume fragmentation
    Total fragmentation                  =   0 %
    File fragmentation                   =   0 %
    Free space fragmentation             =   0 %
File fragmentation
    Total files                          =   10,673
    Average file size                    =   245 KB
    Total fragmented files               =   0
    Total excess fragments               =   0
    Average fragments per file           =   1.00
Pagefile fragmentation
    Pagefile size                        =   768 MB
    Total fragments                      =   1
Folder fragmentation
    Total folders                        =   748
    Fragmented folders                   =   1
    Excess folder fragments              =   0
Master File Table (MFT) fragmentation
    Total MFT size                       =   11 MB
    MFT record count                     =   11,438
    Percent MFT in use                   =   99
    Total MFT fragments                  =   2
```

Volume (C:) has what percentage of free space?

Close all open windows.

5.3.4.6 Lab - Managing System Files with Built-in Utilities in Windows 7

Introduction

In this lab, you will use Windows built-in utilities to gather information about the system and to troubleshoot system resources.

Recommended Equipment

The following equipment is required for this exercise:

- A computer running Windows 7

Step 1

Log on to the computer as an administrator.

To add Run to the Start menu, right-click **Start > Properties** > **Start Menu** tab **> Customize....**

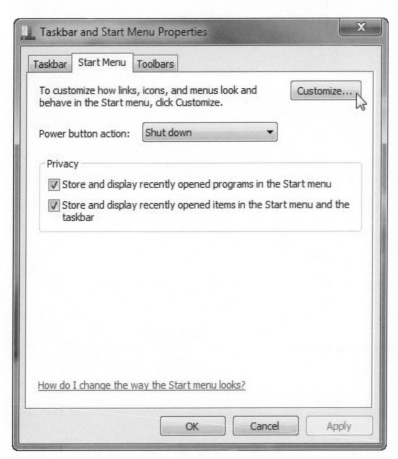

Scroll down until you see the Run command. Click in the box next to Run command. Click **OK**.

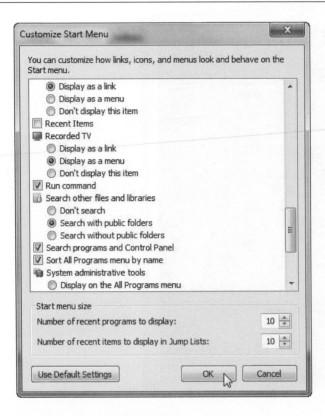

Click **Apply > OK** to close the "Taskbar and Start Menu Properties" window.

Open the command prompt by clicking **Start > Run >** type **cmd >** click **OK**.

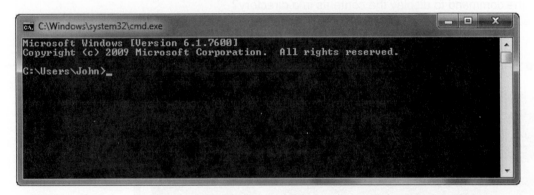

What is the drive path shown?

Type **help** and press **Enter**.

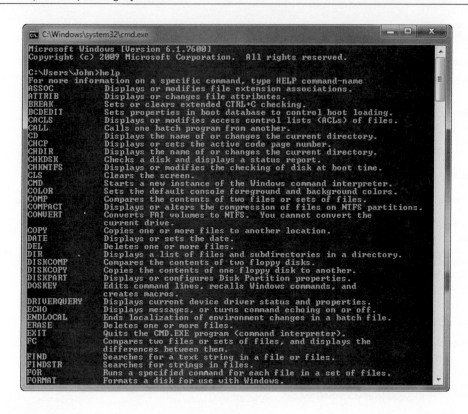

What is the command to change directory?

What is the command to display the contents in a directory?

Type **cd ..** and press **Enter**.

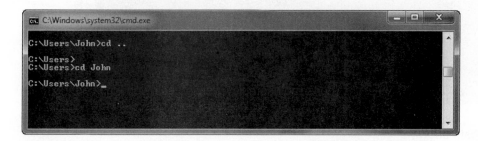

What is the drive path shown?

Change back to original drive path.

Example: Type **cd John** and press **Enter**.

What is the drive path shown?

Type **dir /?** and press **Enter**.

If asked, press any key to continue.

Which switch displays a wide list format?

Type **dir** and press **Enter**.

Type **dir /w** and press **Enter**.

What is the difference between these two commands?

Type **VOL**.

What is the volume name for drive C?

Close the Command prompt window.

Step 2

Open System Information by clicking **Start > Run >** type **msinfo32 >** click **OK**.

Click the **plus sign** next to Hardware Resources, Components, and Software Environment. Expand the window so you can see all the content.

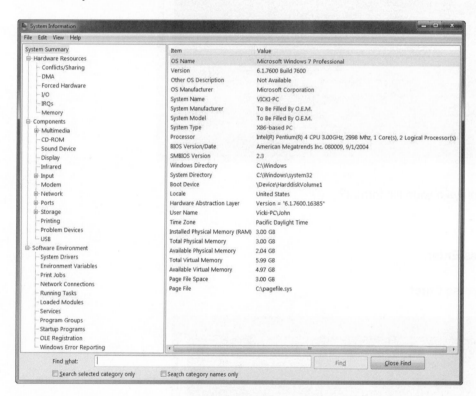

Under the System Summary heading, locate and list the following:

Processor

BIOS Version/Date

Total Physical Memory

Under the Hardware Resources heading, locate and list the following:

DMA channels and the device using the resources.

I/O address range for these devices.

Printer Port (LPT1)

Communications Port (COM1)

Communications Port (COM2)

IRQ address for these devices.

System timer

Communications Port (COM1)

Communications Port (COM2)

Under the Components heading and Software heading, look around to see what information is provided in these areas.

Close the System Information window.

Step 3

Open System Configuration by clicking **Start > Run >** type **msconfig >** click **OK**.

Note: It is very important that you do not make any changes in this utility without instructor permission.

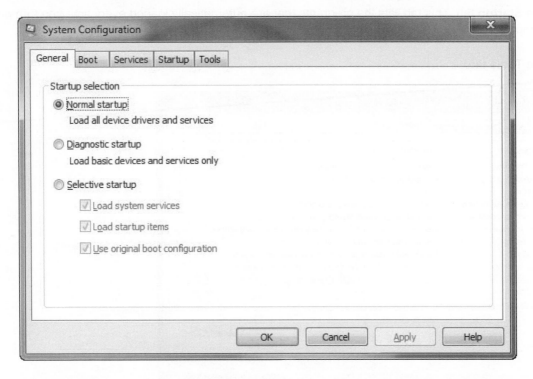

Click the **General** tab if it is not already active.

What are the startup options?

Click the **Boot** tab. This tab is for modifying boot options.

Click the **Services** tab. This tab lists the computers' services and their status.

Can you enable and disable services at this tab?

Click the **Startup** tab. This tab lists the programs that are automatically loaded every time you turn on your computer.

Click the **Tools** tab.

What can you do in this tab?

Click **Cancel** to close the "System Configuration" window.

Step 4

Open the DirectX Diagnostic Tool by clicking **Start > Run >** type **dxdiag >** click **OK**.

If you are asked to have DirectX check driver signatures, click **No**.

Note: When the DirectX Diagnostic Tool first opens, it may take a minute to load all information. Your DirectX Diagnostic Tool may not appear exactly as shown in this lab.

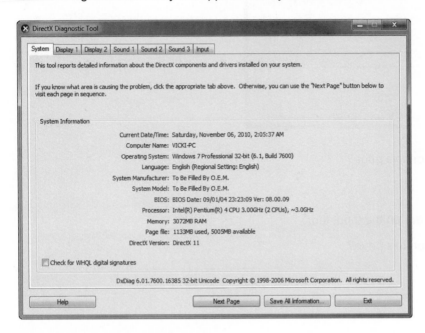

Make sure the System tab is active.
What does this tool report?

Click **Next Page** until you are at the Display tab.

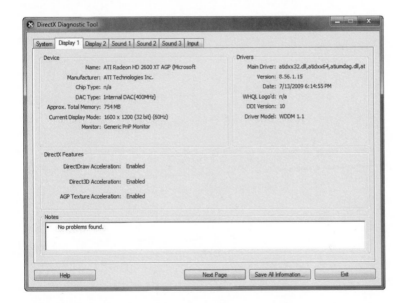

What information is listed on this page?

Click **Next Page** until you are at the Sound tab.

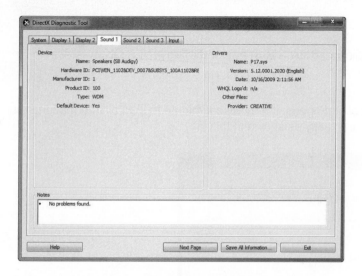

What information is listed on this page?

Click **Next Page** until you are on the Input tab.

What information is listed on this page?

Click **Exit**.

5.3.4.7 Lab - Managing System Files with Built-in Utilities in Windows Vista

Introduction

In this lab, you will use Windows built-in utilities to gather information about the system and to troubleshoot system resources.

Recommended Equipment

The following equipment is required for this exercise:

   • A computer running Windows Vista

Step 1

Log on to the computer as an administrator.

To add Run to the Start menu, right click **Start > Properties** > **Start Menu** tab **> Customize** ….

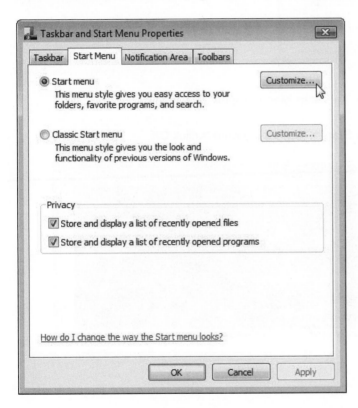

Scroll down until you see the Run command. Click in the box next to Run command. Click **OK**.

Click **Apply > OK** to close the "Taskbar and Start Menu Properties" window.

Open the command prompt by clicking **Start > Run >** type **cmd >** click **OK**.

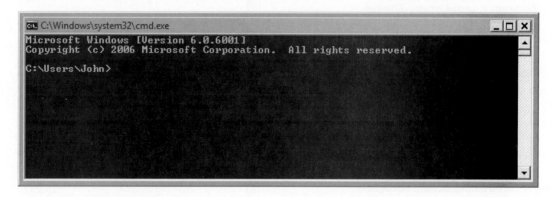

What is the drive path shown?

Type **help** and press **Enter**.

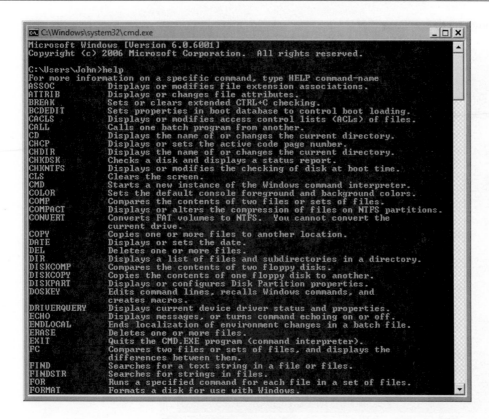

What is the command to change directory?

What is the command to display the contents in a directory?

Type **cd ..** and press **Enter**.

What is the drive path shown?

Change back to original drive path.

Example: Type **cd John** and press **Enter**.

What is the drive path shown?

Type **dir /?** and press **Enter**.

If asked, press any key to continue.

Which switch displays a wide list format?

Type **dir** and press **Enter**.

Type **dir /w** and press **Enter**.

What is the difference between these two commands?

Type **VOL**.

What volume is drive C in?

Close the Command prompt window.

Step 2

Open System Information by clicking **Start > Run >** type **msinfo32 >** click **OK**.

Click the **plus sign** next to Hardware Resources, Components, and Software Environment. Expand the window so you can see all the content.

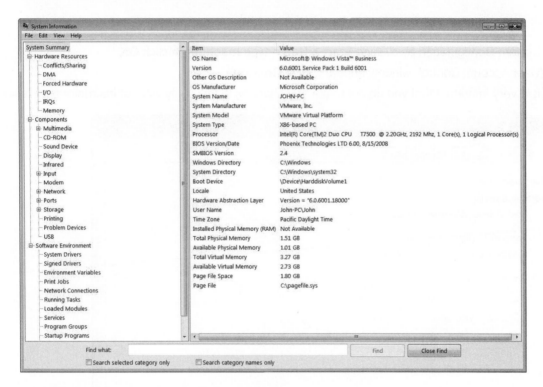

Under the System Summary heading, locate and list the following:

Processor

BIOS Version/Date

Total Physical Memory

Under the Hardware Resources heading, locate and list the following:

DMA channels and the device using the resources.

I/O address range for these devices.

Printer Port (LPT1)

Communications Port (COM1)

Communications Port (COM2)

IRQ address for these devices.

System timer

Communications Port (COM1)

Communications Port (COM2)

Under the Components heading and Software heading, look around to see what information is provided in these areas.

Close the System Information window.

Step 3

Open System Configuration by clicking **Start > Run >** type **msconfig >** click **OK**.

If the "User Account Control" window appears, click **Continue**.

Note: It is very important that you do not make any changes in this utility without instructor permission.

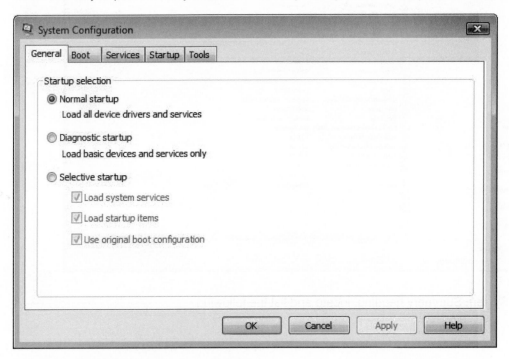

Click the **General** tab if not all ready active.

What are the startup options?

Click the **BOOT** tabs. This tab is for modifying boot options.

Click the **Service** tab. This tab lists the computers' services and their status.

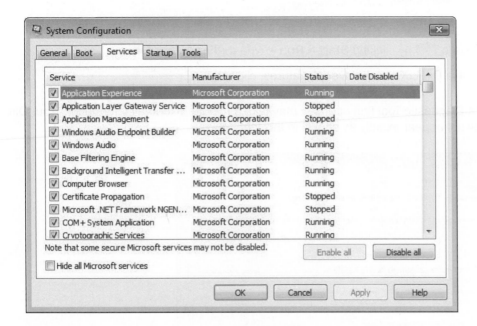

Can you enable and disable services at this tab?

Click the **Startup** tab. This tab lists the programs that are automatically loaded every time you turn on your computer.

Click the **Tools** tab.

What can you do in this tab?

Click **Cancel** to close the "System Configuration" window.

Step 4

Open DirectX Diagnostic Tool by clicking **Start > Run >** type **dxdiag >** click **OK**.

If you are asked to have DirectX check driver signatures, click **No**.

Note: When DirectX Diagnostic Tool first opens, it may take a minute to load all information. Your DirectX Diagnostic Tool may not appear exactly as shown in this lab.

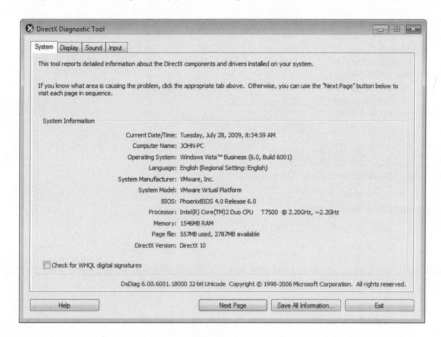

Make sure the System tab is active.

What does this tool report?

Click **Next Page** until you are at the Display tab.

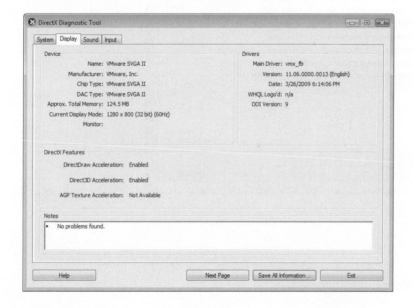

What information is listed on this page?

Click **Next Page** until you are at the Sound tab.

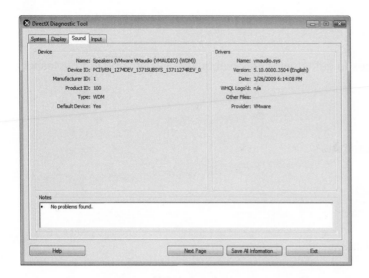

What information is listed on this page?

Click **Next Page** until you are on the Input tab.

What information is listed on this page?

Click **Exit**.

5.3.4.8 Lab - Managing System Files with Built-in Utilities in Windows XP

Introduction

In this lab, you will use Windows built-in utilities to gather information about the system and to troubleshoot system resources.

Recommended Equipment

The following equipment is required for this exercise:

- A computer running Windows XP

Step 1

Log on to the computer as an administrator.

Open the command prompt by clicking **Start > Run >** type **cmd >** click **OK**.

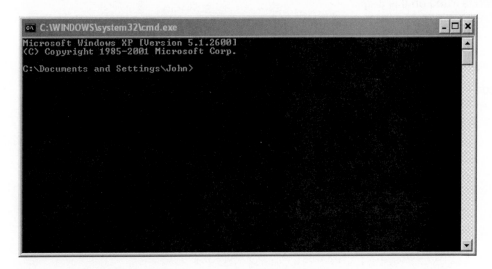

What is the drive path shown?

Type **help** and press **Enter**.

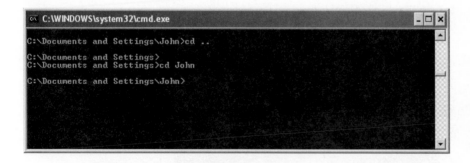

What is the command to change directory?

What is the command to display the contents in a directory?

Type **cd ..** and press **Enter**.

```
C:\WINDOWS\system32\cmd.exe                                    _ □ ×

C:\Documents and Settings\John>cd ..

C:\Documents and Settings>
C:\Documents and Settings>cd John

C:\Documents and Settings\John>
```

What is the drive path shown?

Change back to original drive path.

Example: Type **cd John** and press **Enter**.

What is the drive path shown?

Type **dir /?** and press **Enter**.

If asked, press any key to continue.

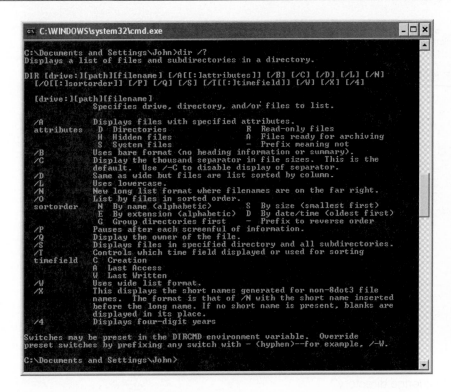

Which switch displays a wide list format?

Type **dir** and press **Enter**.

Type **dir /w** and press **Enter**.

What is the difference between these two commands?

Type **VOL**.

What volume is drive C in?

Close the Command prompt window.

Step 2

Open System Information by clicking **Start > Run >** type **msinfo32 >** click **OK**.

Click the **plus sign** next to Hardware Resources, Components, and Software Environment. Expand the window so you can see all the content.

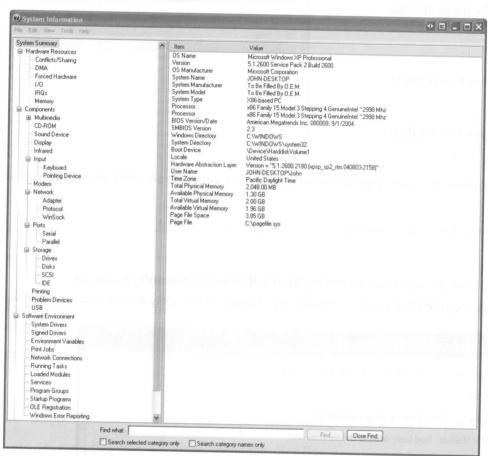

Under the System Summary heading, locate and list the following:
Processor

BIOS Version/Date

Total Physical Memory

Under the Hardware Resources heading, locate and list the following:
DMA channels and the device using the resources.

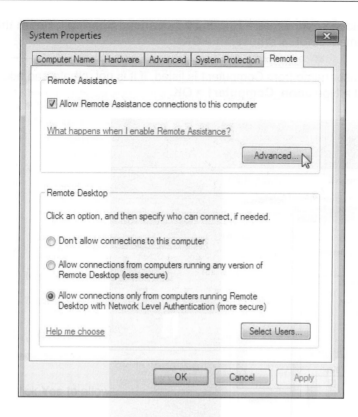

Notice "Remote Assistance" is activated by default.

Click **Advanced**.

The "Remote Assistance Settings" window opens.

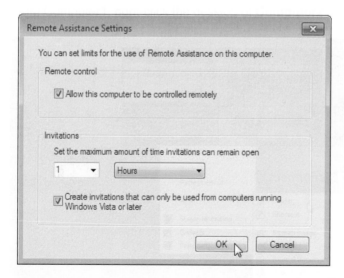

Make sure there is a check mark in the **Allow this computer to be controlled remotely** checkbox, set the invitation to **1 Hours**, place a check mark in the **Create invitations that can only be used from computers running Windows Vista or later** checkbox, and then click **OK**.

When the "System Properties" window appears, click **Apply**.

Step 5

On Computer2, click **Start > All Programs > Maintenance > Windows Remote Assistance**.

The "Do you want to ask for or offer help?" screen appears.

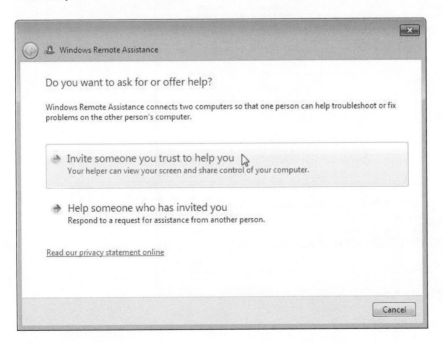

Click **Invite someone you trust to help you**.

The "How do you want to invite your trusted helper?" screen appears.

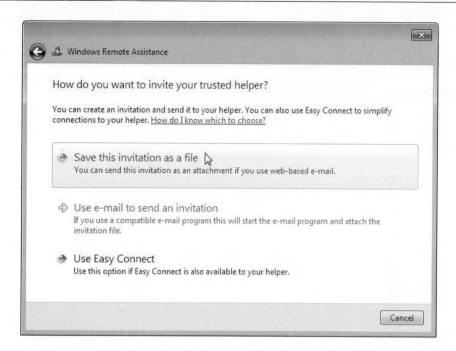

Which methods can you use to contact someone for assistance?

Click the **Save this invitation as a file**.

Locate the shared Remote Permission folder, and name the file **Invitation to Computer1**.

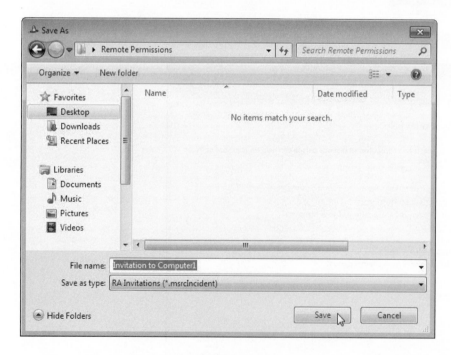

What type of extension does the file have?

Click **Save**.

When the "Windows Remote Assistance" window opens, record the invitation password.

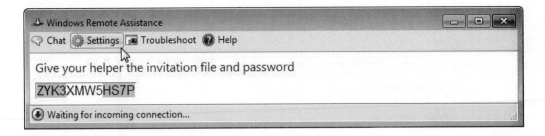

Example: ZYK3XMW5HS7P

Click **Settings**.

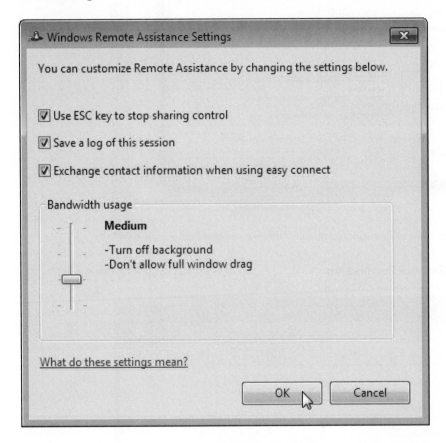

Make sure there is a check mark next to **Use ESC key to stop sharing control**.

Set the Bandwidth usage to **Medium**.

Which features are disabled with a Medium bandwidth usage?

Click **OK**.

Step 6

On Computer1, click **Start > Control Panel > Network and Sharing Center > See full map > Click here to see all other devices >** double-click **Computer2**.

If you are asked to log on, use the user account from Computer1.

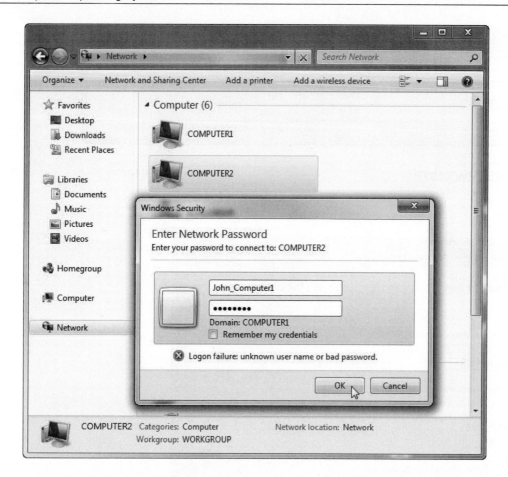

Double-click the folder **Remote Permission**.

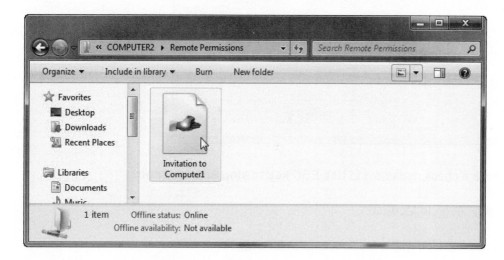

Double-click the file **Invitation to Computer1**.

The "Remote Assistance" window appears.

Type in the password recorded in Step 5. **Example: ZYK3XMW5HS7P**

Click **OK**.

Step 7

From Computer2, answer **Yes** to allow access to the computer.

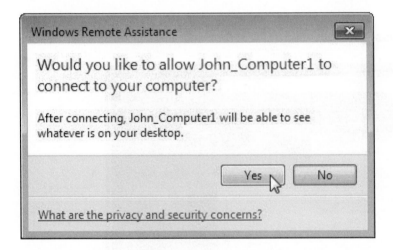

Select the "Windows Remote Assistance – Being helped by John_Computer1" window so it is activated.

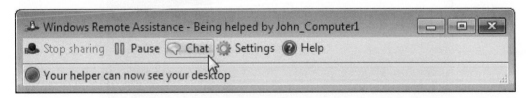

Click **Chat**.

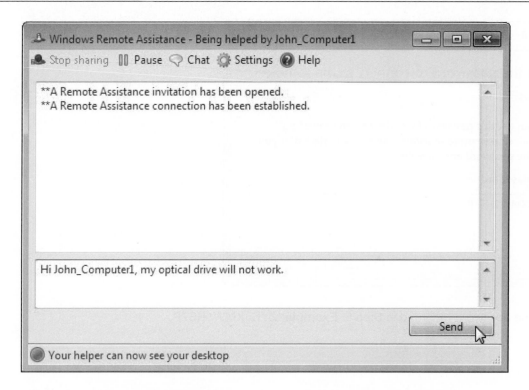

In the chat field, type **Hi John_ Computer1, my optical drive will not work.**. Click **Send**.

Step 8

From Computer1, click the **Request control** button in "Windows Remote Assistance" main menu.

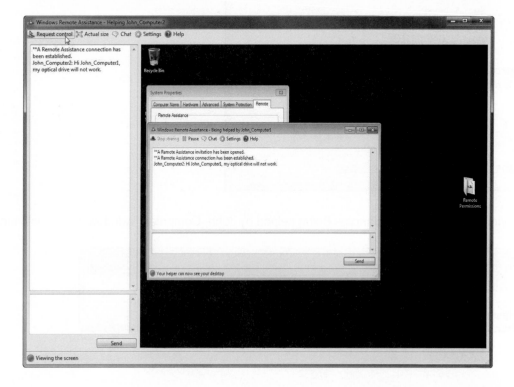

Step 9

From Computer2, click the **Allow John_Computer1 to respond to User Account Control prompts** checkbox.

Click **Yes**.

Step 10

From Computer1, select "System Properties" window for Computer2.

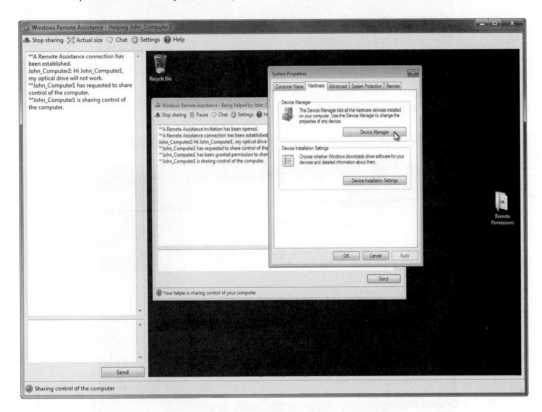

Note: If the Computer2 System Properties window is closed, you need to open it before you continue.

Click **Hardware** tab **> Device Manager**.

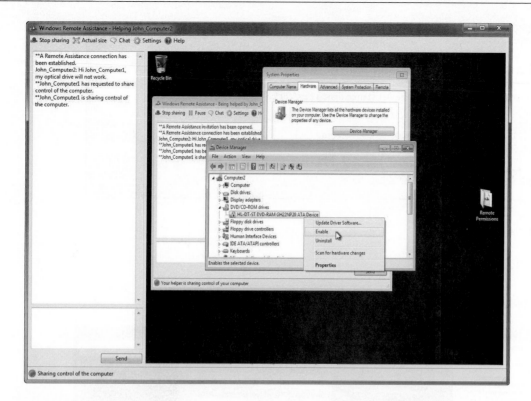

Right-click the optical drive that has a **black down arrow**. Select **Enable**.

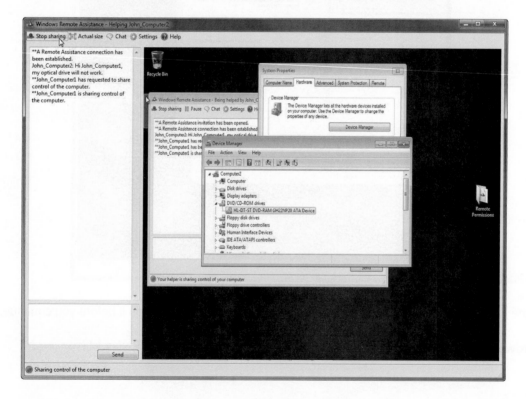

Click the **Stop sharing** button in "Windows Remote Assistance" main menu.

Click the **red X** button to close the "Windows Remote Assistance" connection.

Close all open windows and log off Computer1.

Step 11

On Computer2, click on **Device Manager** so it is activated.

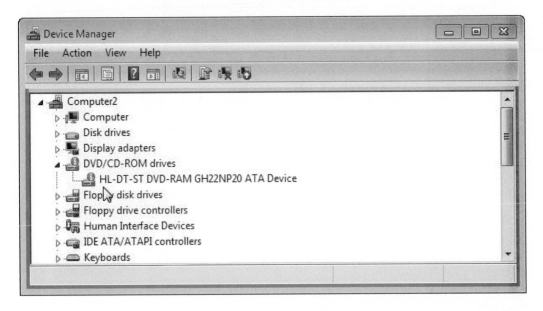

Dose the optical drive have a black arrow?

Close the Device Manager window and the Windows Remote Assistance window.

Delete the Remote Permission folder and empty the Recycle Bin.

Select the **System Properties** window.

Select the **Remote** tab and place a check mark next to **Don't allow connection to this computer > OK**.

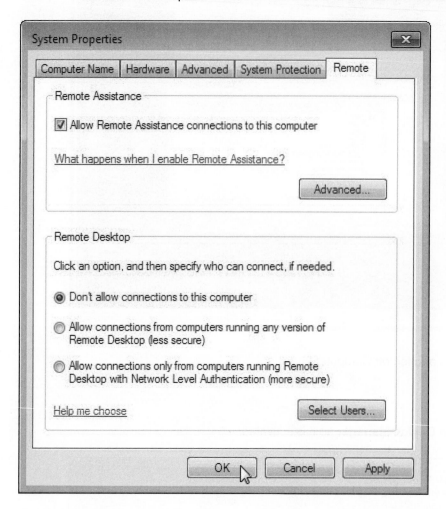

Log off Computer2.

5.3.5.3 Lab - Remote Desktop and Remote Assistance in Windows Vista

Introduction

In this lab, you will remotely connect to a computer, examine device drivers, and provide remote assistance.

Recommended Equipment

The following equipment is required for this exercise:

- Two computers running Windows Vista that are directly connected to each other or through a switch or hub.
- The two computers must be part of the same Workgroup and on the same subnet.

Step 1

Log on to Computer2 as a member of the administrator group. Ask your instructor for the user name.

Click **Start > Control Panel > System > Remote Settings**.

In the Remote Desktop area, select the radio button next to **Allow connections only from computers running Remote Desktop with Network Level Authentication (more secure)**.

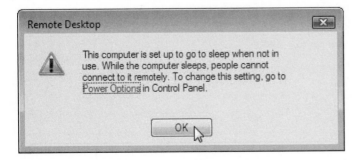

If a message appears warning the computer is set to go to sleep, click the **Power Options** link and then change the settings to **Never > Save** changes.

Click **OK** to close the warning message.

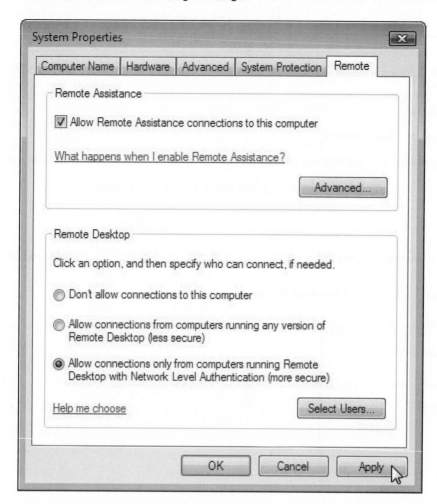

Click **Apply** in the "System Properties" window.

In the Remote Desktop area, click the **Select Users** button.

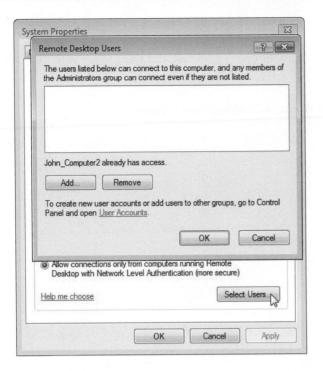

Which user already has remote access?

Since you will use this account to gain remote access, you do not need to add any users, click **Cancel**.

Click **Start > Control Panel > Windows Firewall > Change Settings**.

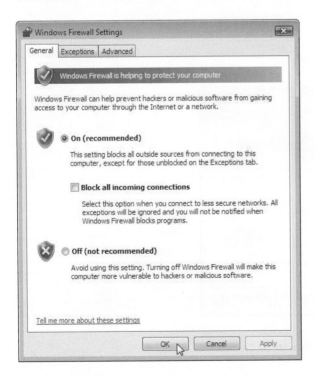

Make sure the **On (recommended)** radio button is selected, and then click **OK**.

Close the Control Panel window, the Windows Firewall window, and move to Computer1.

Step 2

Log on to Computer1 as an administrator or a member of the administrator group. Ask your instructor for the user name.

Click **Start > All Programs > Accessories > Remote Desktop Connection**.

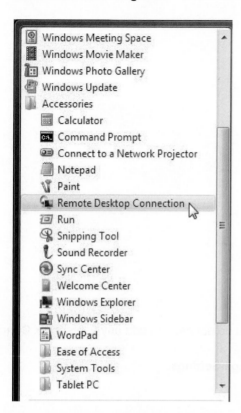

The "Remote Desktop Connection" window opens.

Type **Computer2** in the Computer field and click **Connect**.

In the "User name" field, type the account name you used to log on to Computer2. For example: **John_Computer2**.

In the "Password" field, type the password for the user.

Note: The user account must have a password.

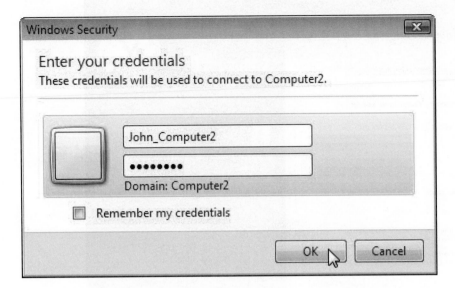

Click **OK**.

What happened to the desktop of Computer2?

What happened to the desktop of Computer1?

Step 3

From Computer1, right-click the desktop of **Computer2 > New > Folder >** name the folder **Remote Permission**.

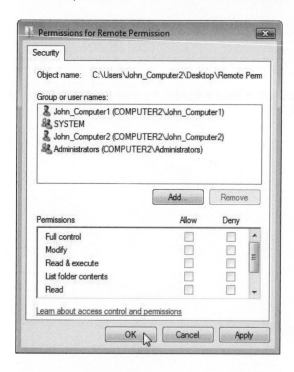

Right-click the **Remote Permission** folder > **Sharing** > **Advanced Sharing** > **Share this folder** check-box > keep the default name **Remote Permission** > **OK**.

Click the **Security** tab. Make sure the user name from Computer1 is listed in Computer2. If it is not, create and add the user name.

Click **OK** > **Close**.

Click **Start > Disconnect**.

Step 4

Log on to Computer2.

Click **Start > Control Panel > System > Remote settings**.

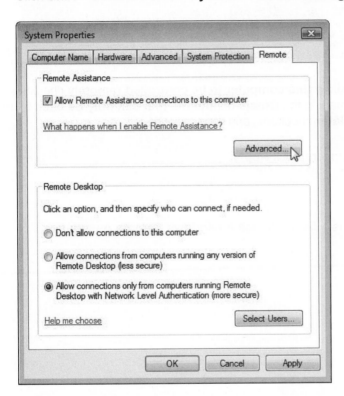

Notice Remote Assistance is activated by default.

Click **Advanced**.

The "Remote Assistance Settings" window opens.

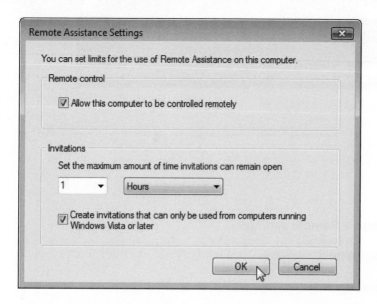

Make sure there is a check mark in the **Allow this computer to be controlled remotely** checkbox, set the invitation to **1 Hours**, place a check mark in the **Create invitations that can only be used from computers running Windows Vista or later** checkbox, and then click **OK**.

When the "System Properties" window appears, click **Apply**.

Step 5

On Computer2, click **Start > All Programs > Maintenance > Windows Remote Assistance**.

The "Do you want to ask for or offer help?" screen appears.

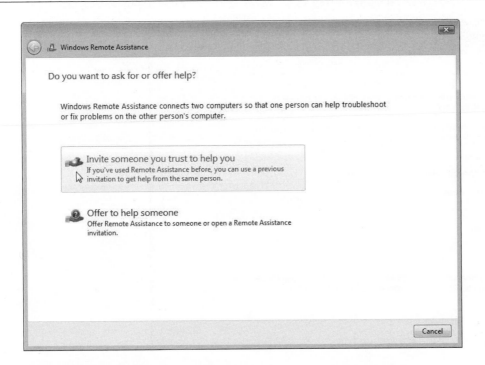

Click **Invite someone you trust to help you**.

The "How do you want to invite someone to help you?" screen appears.

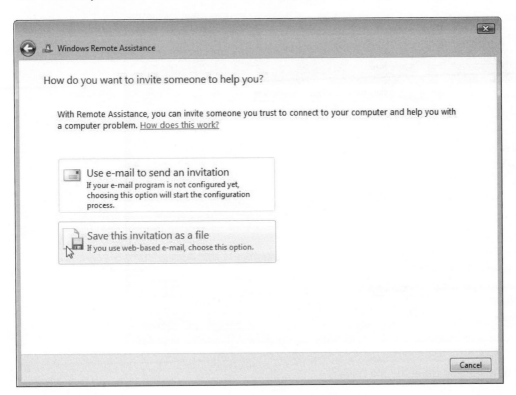

Which methods can you use to contact someone for assistance?

Click **Save this invitation as a file**.

The "Save the invitation as a file" screen appears.

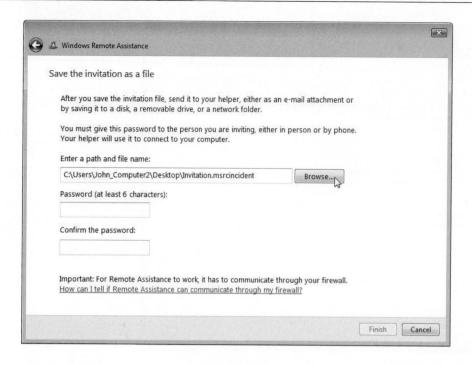

Click **Browse**.

Locate the shared Remote Permission folder, and name the file **Invitation to Computer1**.

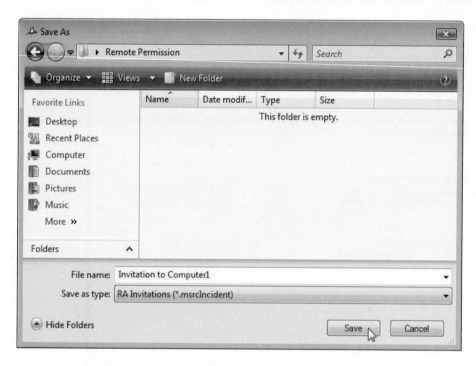

What type of extension does the file have?

Click **Save**.

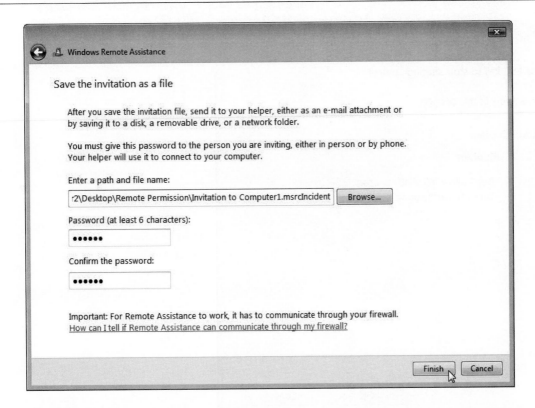

When the "Save the invitation as a file" screen appears, type the password **HelpMe** and confirm the password **HelpMe**. Click **Finish**.

When the Waiting for incoming connection screen appears, click **Settings**.

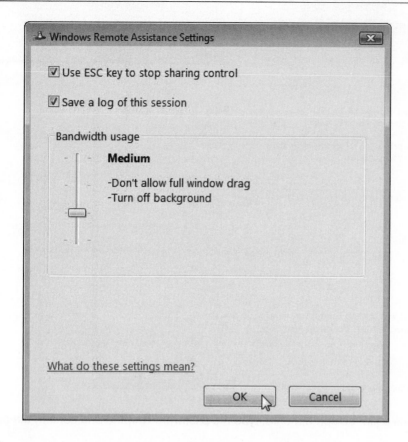

What key must you press to stop sharing control?

Which features are disabled with a Medium bandwidth usage?

Click **OK**.

Step 6

On Computer1, click **Start > Network >** double-click **Computer2**.

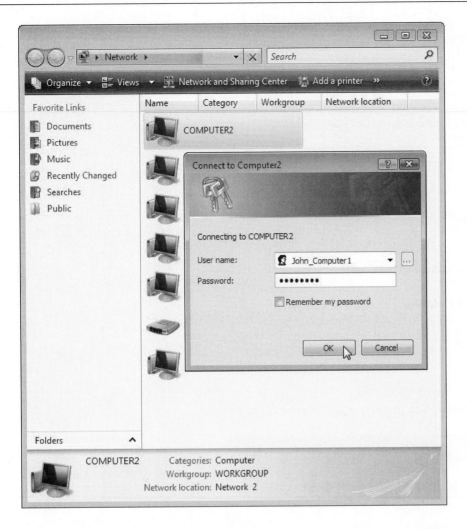

Log on with the user account from Computer1. Double-click the folder **Remote Permission** on Computer2.

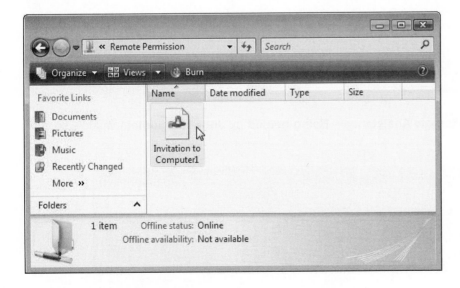

Double-click the file **Invitation to Computer1**.

The "Windows Remote Assistance" window opens.

Type in the password **HelpMe**.

Click **OK**.

Step 7

From Computer2, answer **Yes** to allow access to the computer.

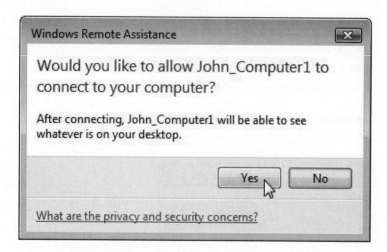

Select the **Windows Remote Assistance – Being helped by John_Computer1** window so it is activated.

Click **Chat**.

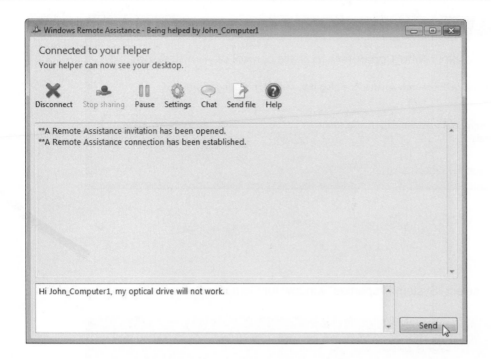

In the chat field, type **Hi John_ Computer1, my optical drive will not work.**. Click **Send**.

Step 8

From Computer1, click the **Request control** button in "Windows Remote Assistance" main menu.

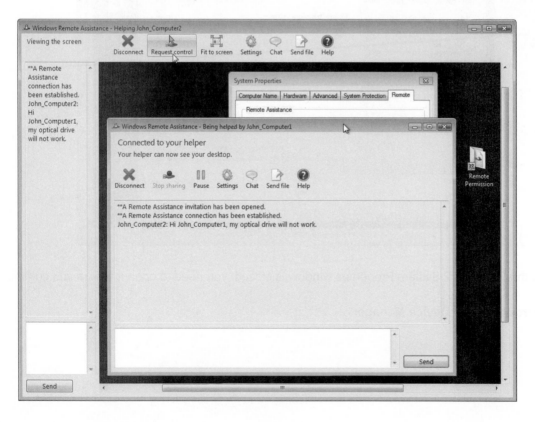

Step 9

From Computer2, click the **Allow John_Computer1 to respond to User Account Control prompts** checkbox.

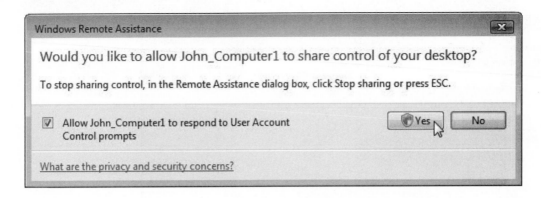

Click **Yes**.

Step 10

From Computer1, select "System Properties" window for Computer2.

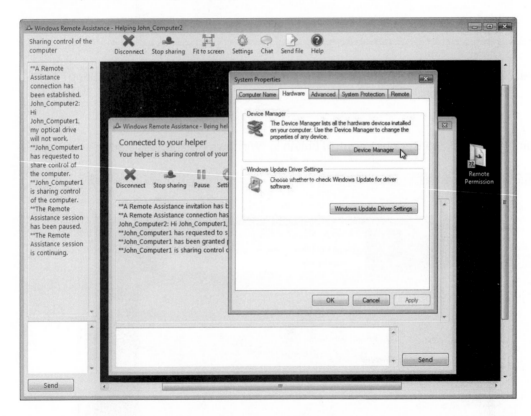

Note: If the Computer2 System Properties window is closed, you need to open it before you continue.

Click **Hardware** tab **> Device Manager**.

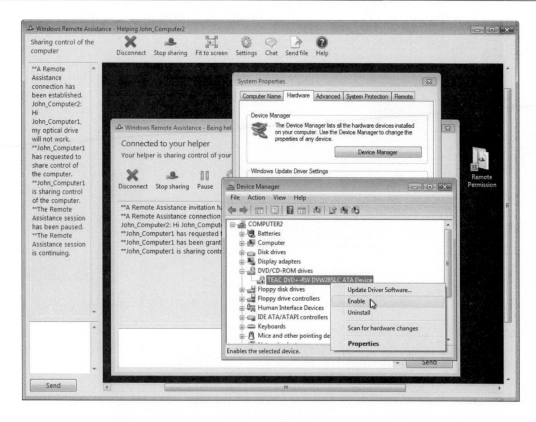

Right-click the optical drive that has a **black down arrow**. Select **Enable**.

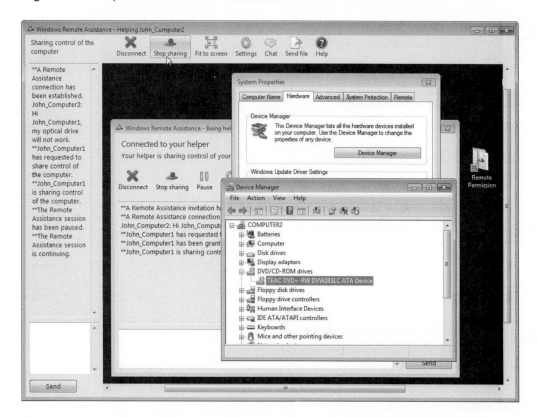

Click the **Stop sharing** button in "Windows Remote Assistance" main menu.

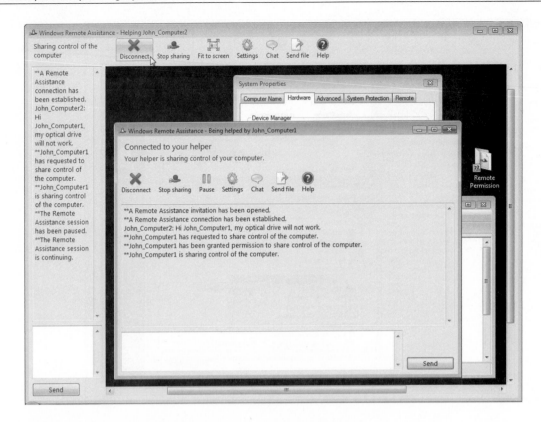

Click the **Disconnect** button in "Windows Remote Assistance" main menu.

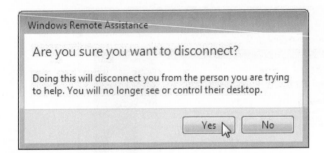

Click **Yes**.

Close all open windows and log off Computer1.

Step 11

On Computer2, click **Yes**.

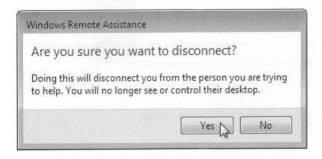

Click on **Device Manager** so it is activated.

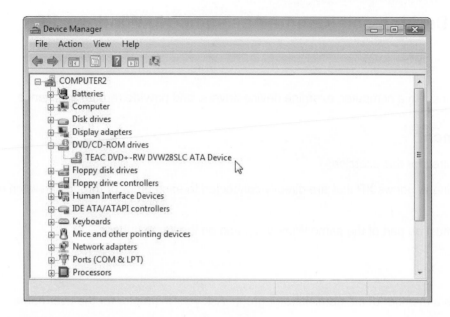

Dose the optical drive have a black arrow?

Close the Device Manager window and the Windows Remote Assistance window.

Delete the Remote Permission folder.

Select the "System Properties" window. Place a check mark next to **Don't allow connection to this computer > OK**.

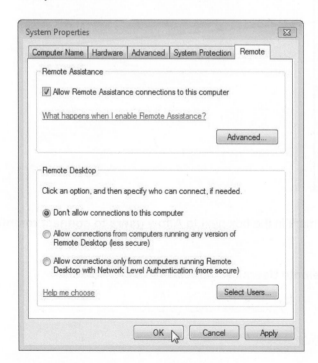

Log off Computer2.

5.3.5.4 Lab - Remote Desktop and Remote Assistance in Windows XP

Introduction

In this lab, you will remotely connect to a computer, examine device drivers, and provide remote assistance.

Recommended Equipment

The following equipment is required for this exercise:

- Two computers running Windows XP that are directly connected to each other or through a switch or hub.
- The two computers must be part of the same Workgroup and on the same subnet.

Step 1

Log on to Computer2 as a member of the administrator group. Ask your instructor for the user name.

Click **Start > Control Panel > System > Remote** tab.

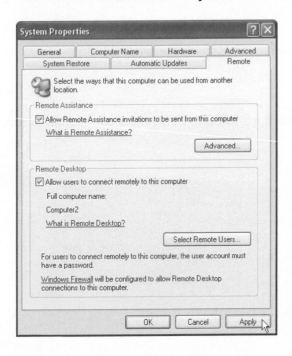

In the "Remote Desktop" area, place a check mark in the box next to **Allow users to connect remotely to this computer**, and click **Apply**.

In the "Remote Desktop" area, click **Select Remote Users**.

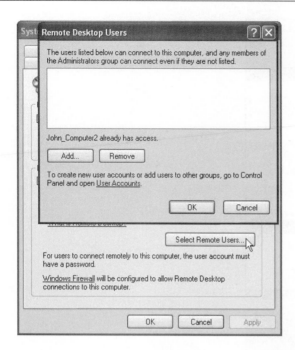

Which user already has remote access?

Since you will use this account to gain remote access, you do not need to add any users, click **Cancel**.

Close the Control Panel window.

Move to Computer1.

Step 2

Log on to Computer1 as a member of the administrator group. Ask your instructor for the user name.

Click **Start > All Programs > Accessories > Remote Desktop Connection**.

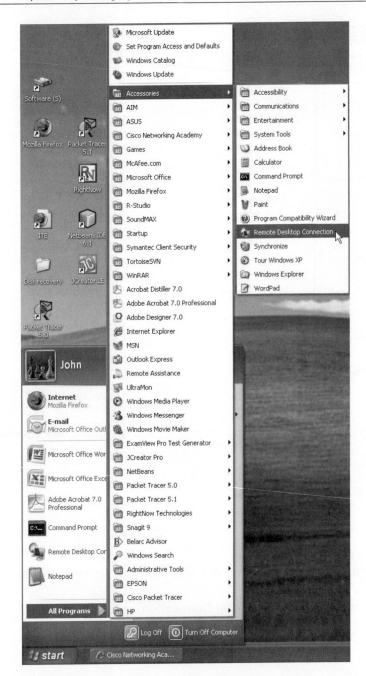

The "Remote Desktop Connection" window opens.

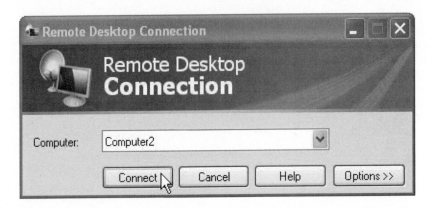

Type Computer2 in the Computer field and click **Connect**.

Next enter the credentials to access the remote computer.

In the User name field, type in the account name you used to log on to Computer2. For example: **John_Computer2**.

In the Password field, type the password for John_Computer2.

Note: The user account must have a password.

Click **OK**.

What happened to the desktop of Computer2?

What happened to the desktop of Computer1?

Step 3

On Computer1, right-click the desktop of **Computer2 > New > Folder >** name the folder **Remote Permission**.

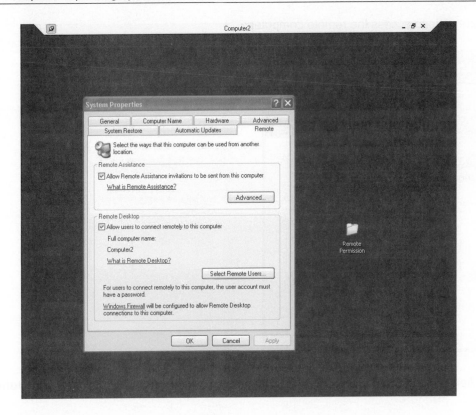

Right-click the **Remote Permission** folder > **Sharing and Security**.

Select the **Share this folder radio** button. Click **Apply**.

Click the **Security** tab. Make sure the user name from Computer1 is listed in Computer2. If it is not, create and add the user name.

Click **OK**.

Click **Start > Disconnect**.

The "Disconnect Windows" window opens.

Click **Disconnect**.

The "Your Remote Desktop session has ended" message appears.

Click **OK**.

Click **Close** to exit the "Remote Desktop Connection" window.

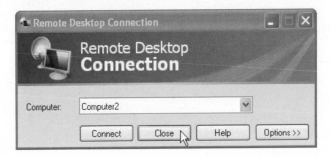

Step 4

Log on to Computer2.

Click **Start > Control Panel > System> Remote**.

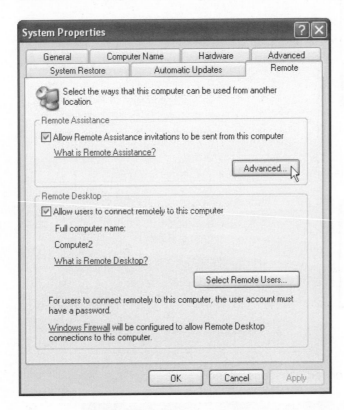

Click **Advanced**.

The "Remote Assistance Settings" window opens.

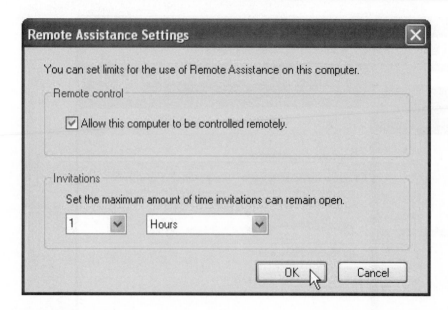

Make sure there is a check mark in the **Remote control** checkbox, set the invitation to **1 Hours**, and then click **OK**.

When the "System Properties" window appears, click **Apply**.

Step 5

On Computer2, click **Start > All Programs > Remote Assistance**.

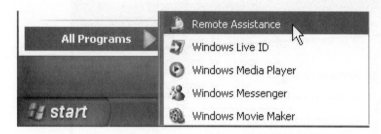

The "Help and Support Center" window opens.

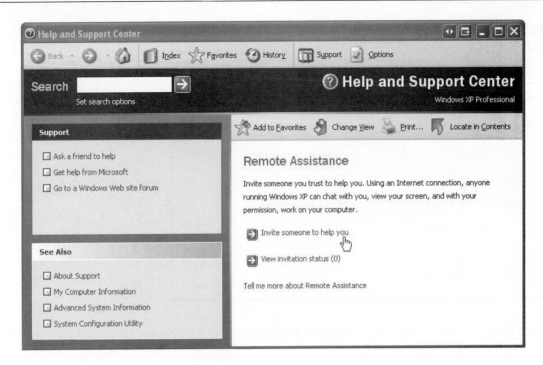

Click the **Invite someone to help you** link.

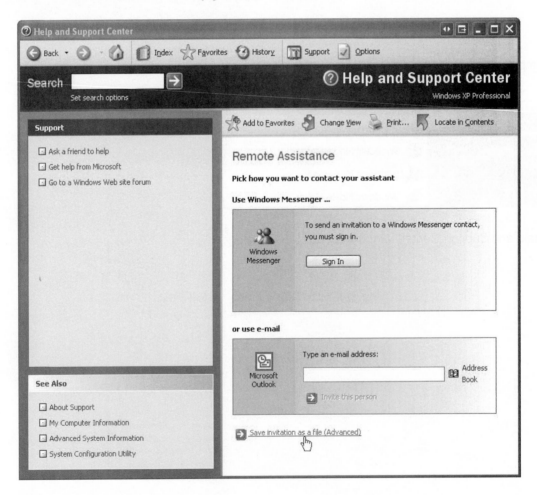

Which methods can you use to contact someone for assistance?

Click the **Save invitation as a file (Advanced)** link.

The "Remote Assistance – Save Invitation" screen appears.

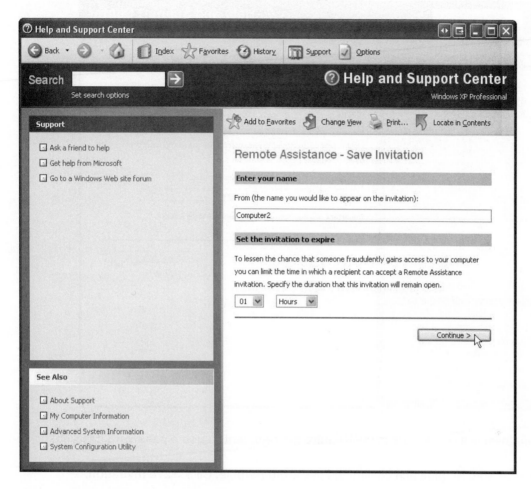

Type **Computer2** in the Enter your name field.

How long will the invitation remain open?

Click **Continue**.

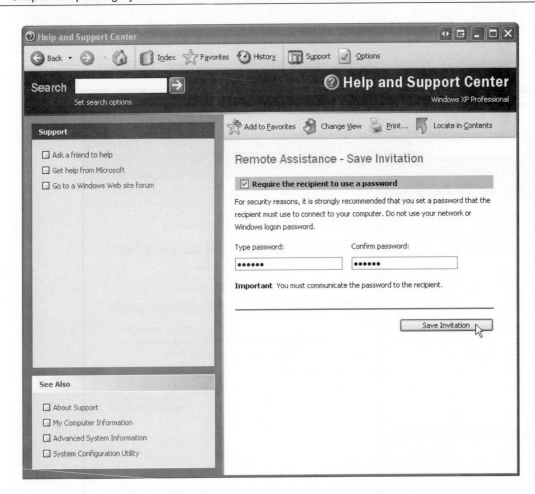

Make sure there is a check mark in the **Require the recipient to use a password** checkbox.

Type the password **HelpMe** and confirm the password **HelpMe**. Click **Save Invitation**.

Navigate to the folder Remote Permission.

What is the default file name?

What file type extension does the file have?

Click **Save**.

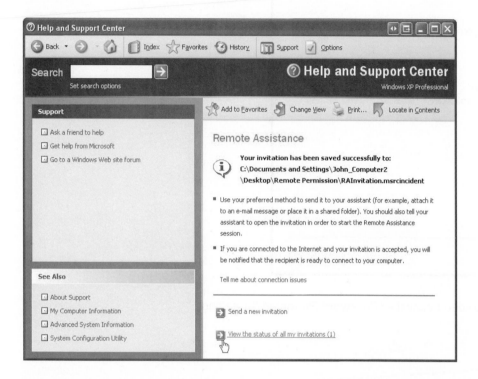

When the "Remote Assistance" window appears, click the **View the status of all my invitations (1)** link.

The "View or change your invitation" window appears.

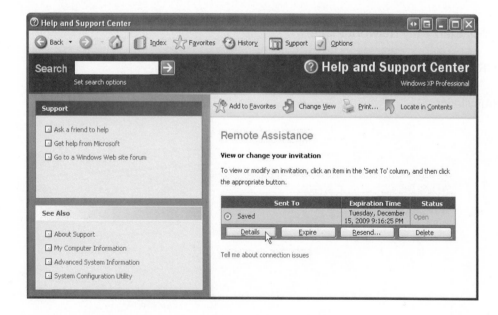

Select the **Saved** radio button. Click **Details**.

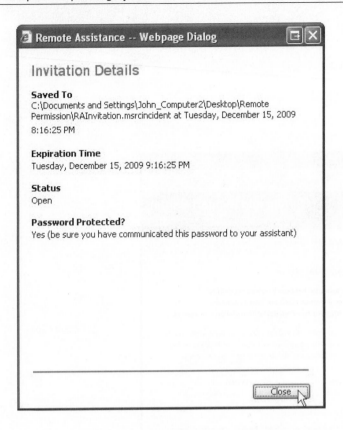

What advice is provided below the "Password Protected?" heading?

Click **Close**.

Close the Help and Support Center window.

Step 6

On Computer1, click **Start > My Network Place**.

Open the folder "Remote Permission" on Computer2.

Open the file "RAInvitation".

The "Remote Assistance" window opens.

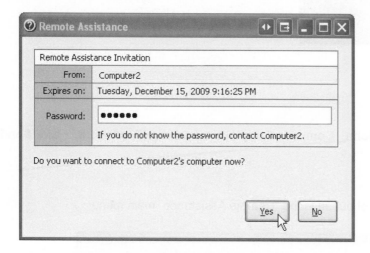

Type in the password **HelpMe**, and click **Yes**.

Step 7

On Computer2, answer **Yes** to allow access to the computer.

Read the message in the "Connection Status" area.

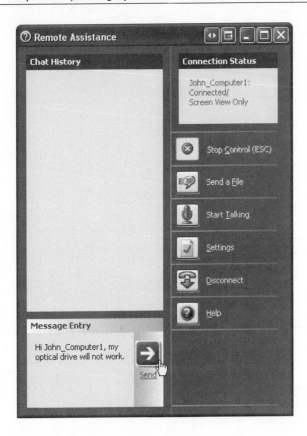

What is the connection status?

In the Message Entry field, type **Hi John_ Computer1, my optical drive will not work**. > click **Send**.

Step 8

On Computer1, click the **Take Control** button in the "Remote Assistance" main menu.

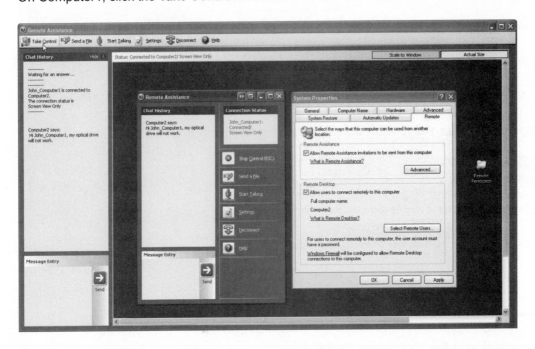

Step 9

On Computer2, click **Yes**.

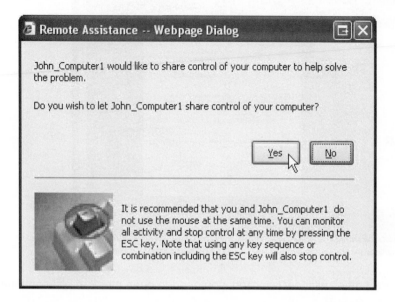

Step 10

Computer1:

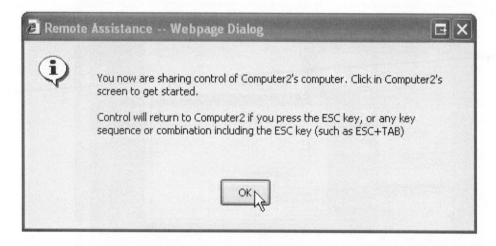

What must you do to activate the screen for Computer2?

What key must you press to return control back to Computer2?

Click **OK**.

Select the "System Properties" window for Computer2.

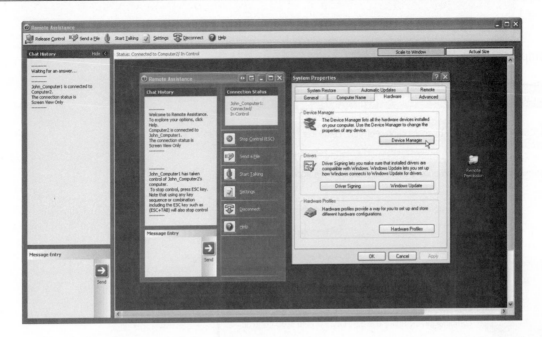

Note: If the Computer2 System Properties window is closed, you need to open it before you continue.

On the Hardware tab, click **Device Manager**.

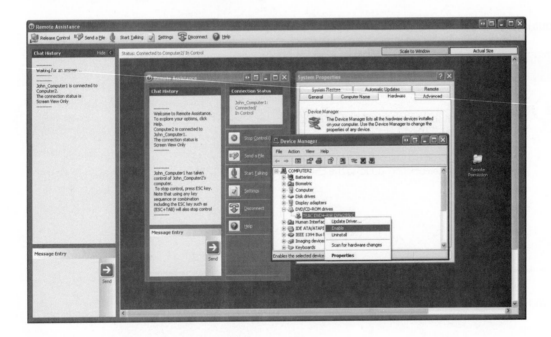

Right-click the optical drive with a **red X > Enable**.

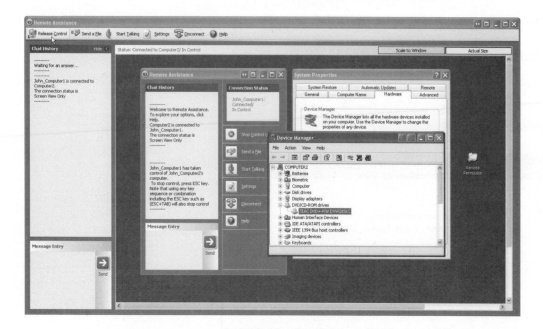

Click the **Release Control** button in the "Remote Assistance" main menu.

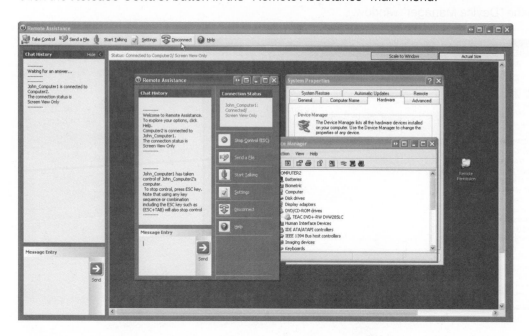

Click the **Disconnect** button in "Remote Assistance" main menu.

Click **OK**.

Close all open windows.

Step 11

On Computer2, click **OK**.

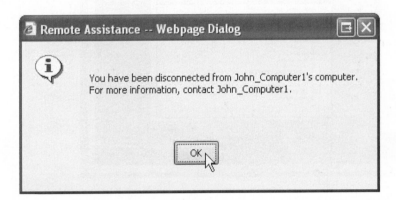

Click on the "Device Manager" window.

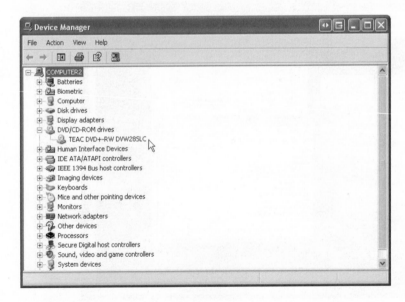

Does the optical drive have a red X?

Close the Device Manager window and the Remote Assistance window.

Delete the Remote Permission folder.

Select the "System Properties" window.

Remove the check mark from **Allow users to connect remotely to this computer > OK**.

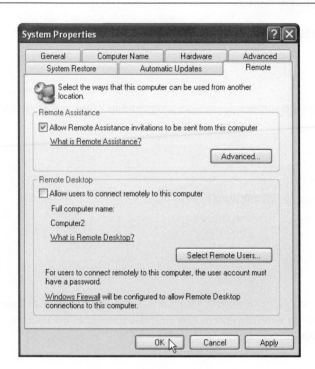

5.3.7.2 Lab - Working with CLI Commands in Windows

Introduction

In this lab, you will use Windows CLI commands to manage folders, files, and programs in Windows 7/Vista/XP.

Recommended Equipment

The following equipment is required for this exercise:

 • A computer running Windows 7, Windows Vista, or Windows XP

Step 1

Logon to the computer as an administrator.

Note: If you logon with a user account other than "Administrator", you will need to substitute that user account name with the "Administrator" account name when typing in commands. Example: **cd Users\ Administrator** replaced with **cd Users\Braxton**

For Windows 7 and Vista:

Navigate to the "Run" window by clicking **Start**. Type **cmd** and then press **Enter**.

For Windows XP:

Navigate to the "Run" window by clicking **Start > Run**. Type **cmd** and click **OK**.

Step 2

The command window opens.

What directory are you at?

Explain what the following commands do:

ATTRIB:

CD or CHDIR:

CLS:

COPY:

DEL:

DIR:

EXIT:

MD or MKDIR:

Move:

RD or RMDIR:

ROBOCOPY (Note, this command only works in Windows Vista and Windows 7):

XCOPY:

Step 4

At the command prompt, type **dir** and then press **Enter**.

Note: For Windows XP, replace Users with Documents and Settings. You will need to do this for the rest of the lab.

Is there a directory (DIR) called Users?

At the command prompt, type **cd users** and then press **Enter**.

At the command prompt, type **dir** and then press **Enter**.

Is there a directory listed for the account you are logged on to the computer with?

What is that account name?

At the command prompt, change to the account name in which you are logged on. Example: Type **cd administrator**, and then press **Enter**.

```
Administrator: C:\Windows\system32\cmd.exe
 Directory of c:\Users

09/11/2012  03:35 PM    <DIR>          .
09/11/2012  03:35 PM    <DIR>          ..
09/07/2012  01:36 PM    <DIR>          Administrator
09/11/2012  03:35 PM    <DIR>          DefaultAppPool
04/11/2011  07:21 PM    <DIR>          Public
06/18/2012  02:27 PM    <DIR>          SBC
               0 File(s)              0 bytes
               6 Dir(s)   451,973,898,240 bytes free

c:\Users>cd administrator

c:\Users\Administrator>
```

At the command prompt, type **dir** and then press **Enter**.

```
Administrator: C:\Windows\system32\cmd.exe
c:\Users\Administrator>dir
 Volume in drive C has no label.
 Volume Serial Number is 8A89-4C5F

 Directory of c:\Users\Administrator

09/07/2012  01:36 PM    <DIR>          .
09/07/2012  01:36 PM    <DIR>          ..
09/04/2012  09:13 PM    <DIR>          .android
10/03/2012  12:48 PM               192 .packettracer
10/03/2012  01:12 PM    <DIR>          Aspire-CANA
09/07/2012  01:41 PM    <DIR>          Cisco Packet Tracer 5.3.3
09/14/2012  11:57 AM    <DIR>          Contacts
10/03/2012  08:35 PM    <DIR>          Desktop
09/11/2012  05:28 PM    <DIR>          Documents
09/17/2012  08:57 PM    <DIR>          Downloads
09/14/2012  11:57 AM    <DIR>          Favorites
09/14/2012  11:57 AM    <DIR>          Links
09/11/2012  09:02 PM    <DIR>          Music
07/11/2012  09:47 AM    <DIR>          Pictures
09/14/2012  11:57 AM    <DIR>          Saved Games
09/14/2012  11:57 AM    <DIR>          Searches
07/11/2012  09:47 AM    <DIR>          Videos
               1 File(s)            192 bytes
              16 Dir(s)   451,973,804,032 bytes free

c:\Users\Administrator>
```

Notice there is a directory called "Desktop".

At the command prompt, type **cd desktop** and then press **Enter**.

```
Administrator: C:\Windows\system32\cmd.exe
c:\Users\Administrator>cd desktop

c:\Users\Administrator\Desktop>
```

At the command prompt, type **cd c:** and then press **Enter**.

```
Administrator: C:\Windows\system32\cmd.exe
c:\Users\Administrator>cd desktop
c:\Users\Administrator\Desktop>cd c:\
c:\>
```

At the command prompt, type **cd user/administrator/desktop** and then press **Enter**.

Note: Change "administrator" with the name you are logged onto the computer.

```
Administrator: C:\Windows\system32\cmd.exe
c:\>cd users\administrator\desktop
c:\Users\Administrator\Desktop>
```

Step 5

At the command prompt, type **md ITEfolder1** and then press **Enter**.

```
Administrator: C:\Windows\system32\cmd.exe
c:\>cd users\administrator\desktop
c:\Users\Administrator\Desktop>md ITEfolder1
c:\Users\Administrator\Desktop>
```

Look at the "Desktop".

What do you see?

Make another folder at the "Desktop".

At the command prompt, type **md ITEfolder2** and then press **Enter**.

Do you now have two folders at the "Desktop" labeled "ITEfolder1" and "ITEfolder2"?

If not, ask the instructor for assistance.

Step 6

At the command prompt, type **cls** and then press **Enter**.

What happened?

Now you will make a file and save it to ITEfolder1.

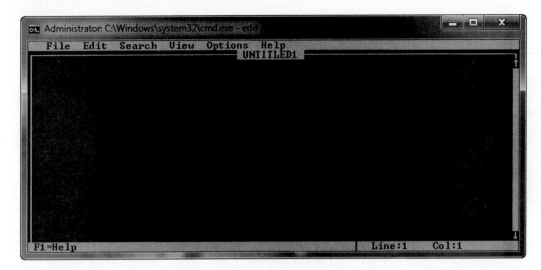

At the command prompt, type **edit** and then press **Enter**.

In the DOS editor, type **This file belongs in ITEfolder1**.

Press the following key combination **Alt** and **F** at the same time.

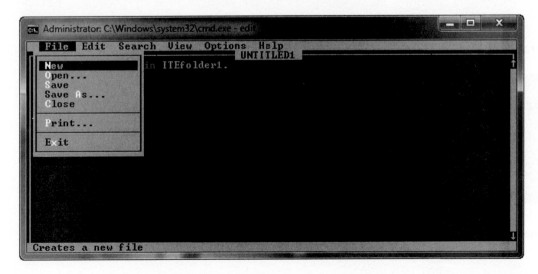

When the "File" menu opens, press the **A** key.

Press the following key combination **Alt** and **D**, and then press the down arrow key until the folder **ITEfolder1** is selected.

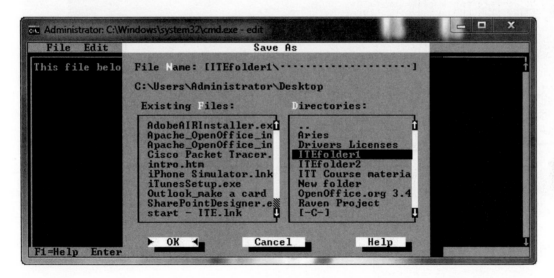

Press **Enter**.

Press the **Tab** key four times, until the curser is located at the "File Name:" field.

Type the "File Name:" **ITEfile1**.

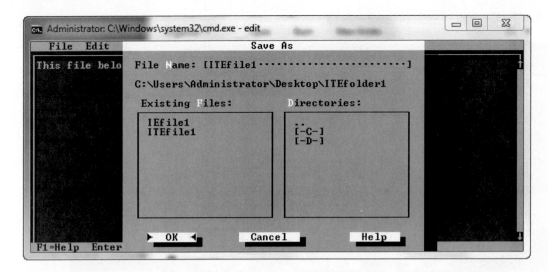

Press **Enter**.

Where is the file saved?

Press **Alt** and **F**, and then press **X**.

Open the "ITEfolder1" on the "Desktop".

What do you notice?

Step 7

At the command prompt, type **cls** and then press **Enter**.

At the command prompt, type **cd ITEfolder1**, press **Enter**, and then type **dir**.

How many files are listed?

What is the size of the file?

At the command prompt, type **cd ..** and then press **Enter**.

Type **cd ITEfolder2** and then press **Enter**.

Type **dir** and then press **Enter**.

How many files are listed?

Step 8

Type **cd ..** and then press **Enter**.

Type **cd ..** and then press **Enter**.

At the command prompt, type **cls**.

At the command prompt, type **xcopy ITEfolder1\ITEfile1 ITEfolder2**.

How many files were copied?

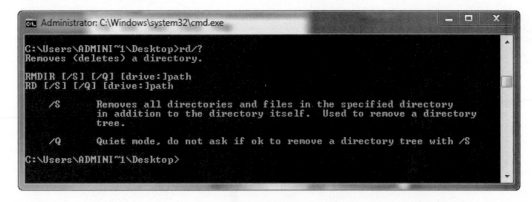

What letter can you add to "RD" so all files and the directory are removed?

Type **rd ITEfolder1 /s** and then press **Enter**.

When prompted, type **Y** and press **Enter**.

Is folder "ITEfolder1" shown on the "Desktop"?

Step 13

At the command prompt, type **cls** and then press **Enter**.

Type **start notepad.exe** and press **Enter**.

What happens?

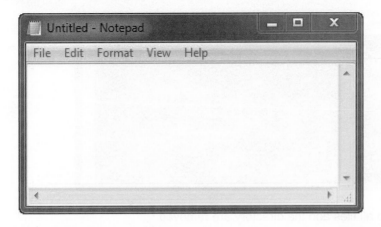

At the command prompt, type **tasklist** and then press **Enter**.

Is Notepad listed?

Type **taskkill /im notepad.exe** and press **Enter**.

What happens?

5.3.7.4 Lab - Run Line Utilities in Windows 7

Introduction

In this lab, you will use Windows Run line utilities to access and use tools to configure settings in Windows 7.

Recommended Equipment

The following equipment is required for this exercise:

 • A computer running Windows 7

Step 1

Navigate to the "Run" window by clicking **Start > Run**. Type **mmc** and click **OK**.

If the "User Account Control" window appears, click **Yes**.

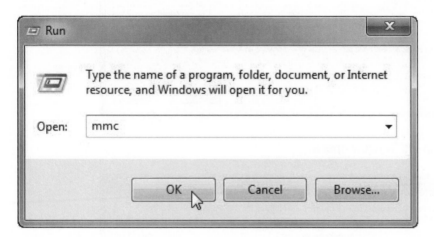

Step 2

The "Console1 - [Console Root]" (console number may vary) window opens.

Step 3

To build your own custom console, click **File > Add/Remove Snap-in**.

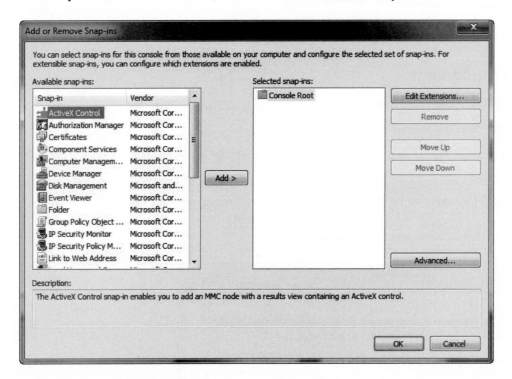

The "Add or Remove Snap-ins" window opens.

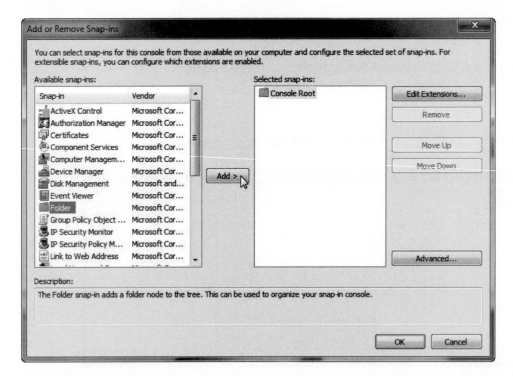

To add a folder snap-in so that you can organize all your snap-ins, scroll down until you see the Folder snap-in. Select **Folder >** click **Add**.

To add the "Link to Web Address" snap-in, scroll down until you see the snap-in. Select **Link to Web Address >** click **Add**. The "Link to Web Address" wizard opens. In the Target box, type **http://www.cisco. com**.

Click **Next**.

In the "Friendly name for the Link to Web Address snap-in" box, type **Cisco**.

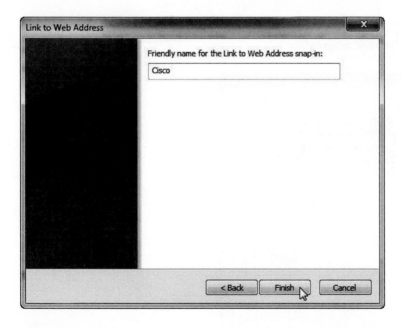

Click **Finish**.

Step 4

To add snap-ins to the folder snap-in, click **Advanced**.

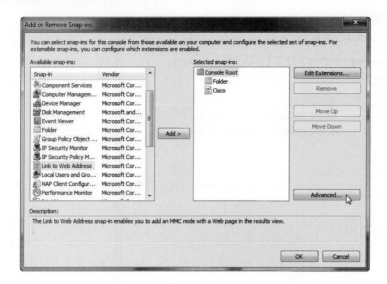

Check the **box** next to Allow changing the parent snap-in.

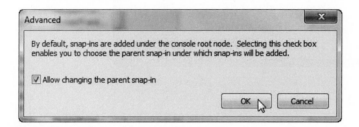

Click **OK**.

A drop-down menu appears for "Parent snap-in".

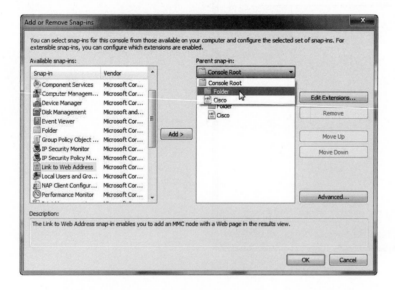

In the "Parent snap-in" box, select **Folder**.

Add the following snap-ins: Computer Management, Device Manager, and Disk Management.

Note: When you are asked what computer the snap-in will manage, select the default by clicking **Finish**. Click **OK** to accept all changes.

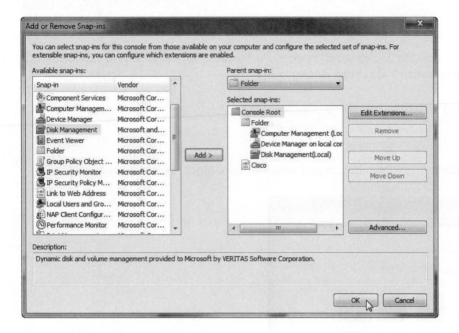

Step 5

The "Console1" window appears. Right-click the Folder icon and select **Rename**. Change the name of the folder to "Management Tools".

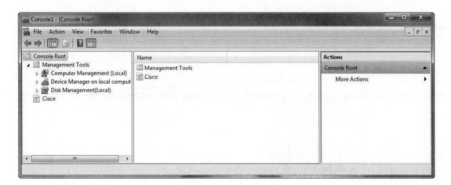

To save the custom console, click **File > Save As**. Change the file name to your name. Example: **John's Console**. Change the "Save in" box to **Desktop**. Click **Save**.

Step 6

Close all open windows.

On the desktop, double-click the **Console** icon to re-open the console with your snap-ins.

Step 7

Open the "Choose your desktop background" page in Personalize appearance and sounds by right-clicking the **Desktop > Personalize > Desktop Background**.

What is the Background picture?

Click the **Picture location** drop-down button and select **Solid Colors**. Select a **blue** color.

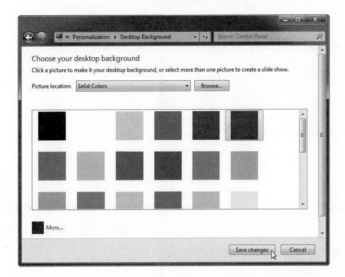

Click **Save changes**.

The computer screen should now have a blue background. If not, ask the instructor for assistance.

Step 8

Open Registry Editor by clicking **Start > Run >** type **regedit >** click **OK**.

If the "User Account Control" window appears, click **Yes**.

Note: Do not make any changes in the Registry Editor without instructor permission.

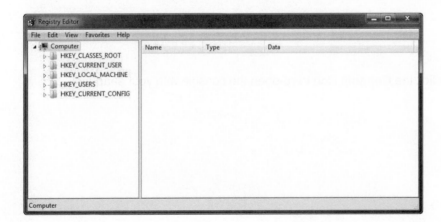

Click the **HKEY_CURRENT_USER** icon.

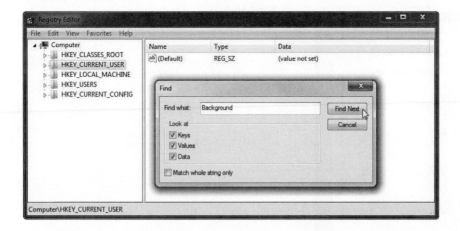

To search for the desktop Background key, click **Edit > Find >** type **Background >** click **Find Next**.

The Background value is located. Leave this window open.

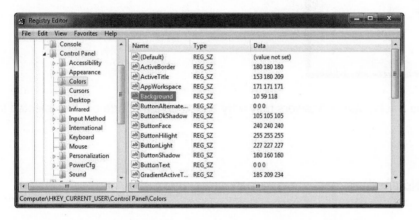

In which folder is the Background located?

What is the data value of the Background (hint – it has three numbers that correspond to red, green, and blue)? Answers may vary based on the shade of blue selected in Choose your desktop background.

Step 9

We will now export the **HKEY_CURRENT_USER\Control Panel\Colors** folder.

In the left pane, click the **Colors** folder.

Click **File > Export**. Save the file to the Desktop with the name **BlueBKG**.

At the desktop, right-click the **BlueBKG.reg** icon **> Edit**.

What is the data value of the Background? Answers may vary based on the shade of blue selected in Display Properties.

Close the **BlueBKG.reg – Notepad** window.

Step 10

Open the "Choose your desktop background" page in Personalize appearance and sounds by right-clicking the **Desktop > Personalize > Desktop Background**.

Click the **Location** drop-down button and select **Solid Colors**. Select a **red** color.

Click **Save changes**.

In a few seconds, the desktop will turn to red.

Click the **Registry Editor** window so it is activated.

On your keyboard, press **F5** to refresh the "Registry Editor" window.

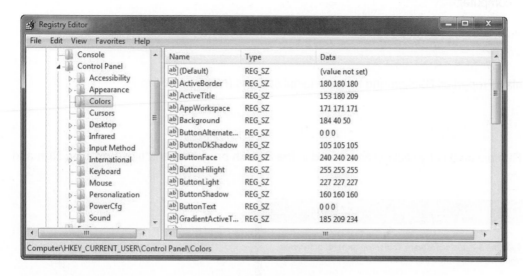

What is the data value of the Background? Answers may vary based on the shade of red selected in Display Properties.

Step 11

We will now import **BlueBKG.reg** file.

Click the "Registry Editor" window so it is activated.

Click **File > Import**. Locate and click the **BlueBKG.reg** icon, and then click **Open**.

Click **OK**.

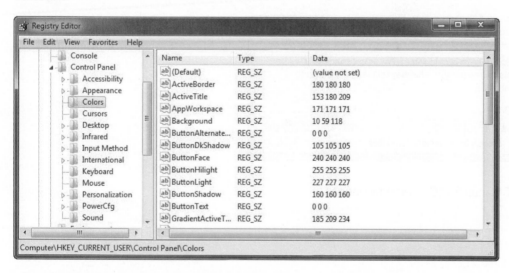

Click the Registry Editor window so it is activated.

What is the data value of the Background? Answers may vary based on the shade of blue selected in Display Properties.

What is the color of the desktop?

Restart the computer.

What is the color of the desktop?

Reset Display Properties Background to the original settings (hint – see Step 7).

Step 12

Open the Run dialog box by clicking **Start**, and in the Search programs and files box, type **Run** and press **Enter**.

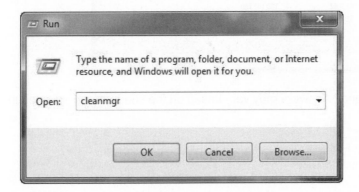

Type **cleanmgr** in the "Open:" field.

Click **OK**.

The "Disk Cleanup" window opens and calculates available free space.

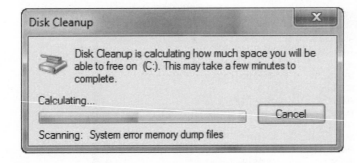

The "Disk Cleanup for (C:)" window opens.

Make sure only Downloaded Program Files and Temporary Internet Files are selected.

Click the **OK** button.

Why should disk cleanup be performed regularly?

5.3.7.5 Lab - Run Line Utilities in Windows Vista

Introduction

In this lab, you will use Windows Run line utilities to access and use tools to configure settings in Windows Vista.

Recommended Equipment

The following equipment is required for this exercise:

- A computer running Windows Vista

Step 1

Navigate to the "Run" window by clicking **Start > Run**. Type **MMC** and click **OK**.

If the "User Account Control" window appears, click **Continue**.

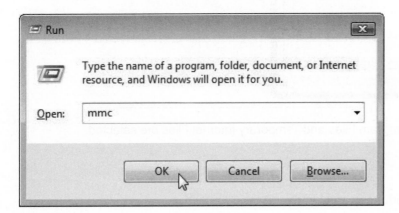

Step 2

The "Console1 [Console Root]" (console number may vary) window opens.

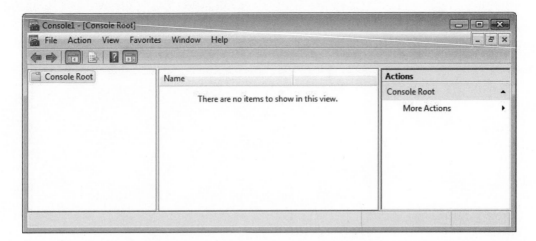

Step 3

To build your own custom console, click **File > Add/Remove Snap-in**.

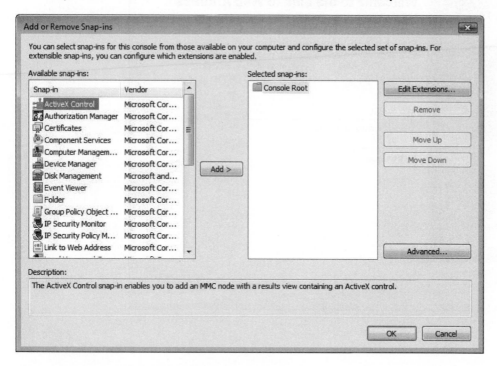

The "Add or Remove Snap-in" window opens.

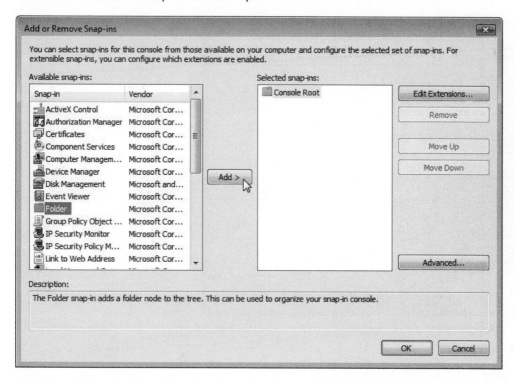

To add a folder snap-in so that you can organize all your snap-ins, scroll down until you see the Folder snap-in. Select **Folder >** click **Add**.

To add the "Link to Web Address" snap-in, scroll down until you see the snap-in. Select **Link to Web Address >** click **Add**. The "Link to Web Address" wizard opens. In the Target box, type **http://www.cisco. com**.

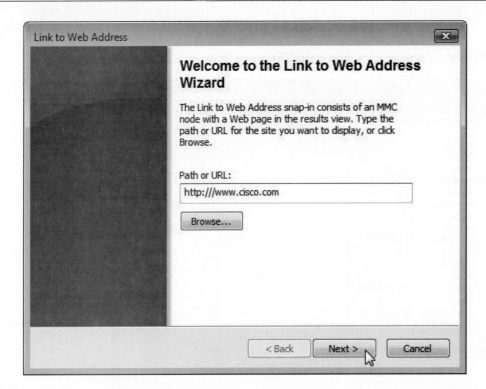

Click **Next**.

In the "Friendly name for the Link to Web Address snap-in" box, type **Cisco**.

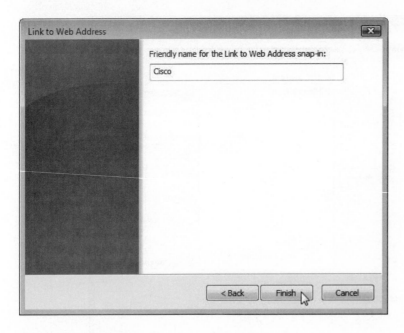

Click **Finish**.

Step 4

To add snap-ins to the folder snap-in, click **Advanced**.

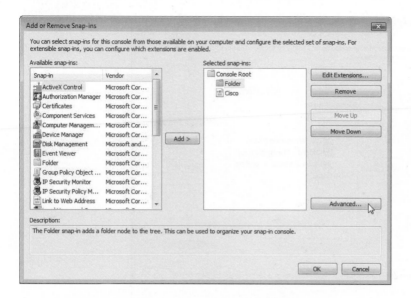

Click in the **box** next to Allow changing the parent snap-in.

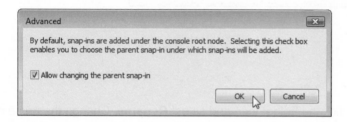

Click **OK**.

A drop-down menu appears for "Parent snap-in".

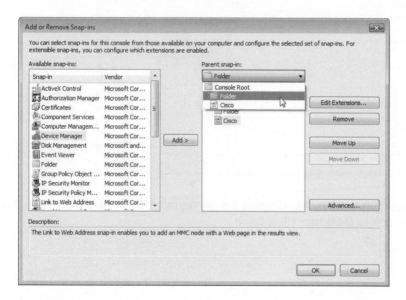

In the "Parent snap-in" box, select **Folder**.

Add the following snap-ins: Computer Management, Device Manager, and Disk Management.

Note: When asked what computer the snap-in will manage, select the default by clicking **Finish**.

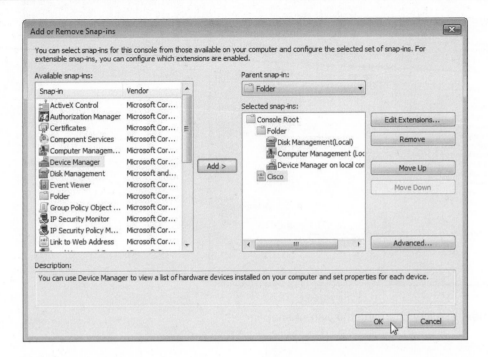

Click **OK** to accept all changes.

Step 5

The "Console1" window appears. Right-click the Folder icon and select **Rename**. Change the name of the folder to Management Tools.

To save the custom console, click **File > Save As**. Change the file name to your name. Example: **John's Console**. Change the "Save in" box to **Desktop**. Click **Save**.

Step 6

Close all open windows.

On the desktop, double-click the **Console** icon to re-open the console with your snap-ins.

Step 7

Open the "Choose a desktop background" page in Personalize appearance and sounds by right-clicking the **Desktop > Personalize > Desktop Background**.

What is the Background picture?

Click the Location dropdown button and select **Solid Colors**. Select a **blue** color.

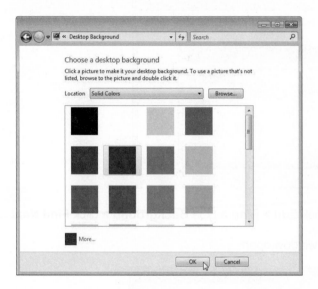

Click **OK**.

The computer screen should now have a blue background. If not, ask the instructor for assistance.

Step 8

Open Registry Editor by clicking **Start > Run >** type **regedit >** click **OK**.

If the "User Account Control" window appears, click **Continue**.

Note: Do not make any changes in the Registry Editor without instructor permission.

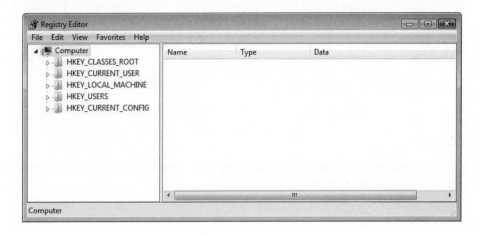

Click the **HKEY_Current_User** icon.

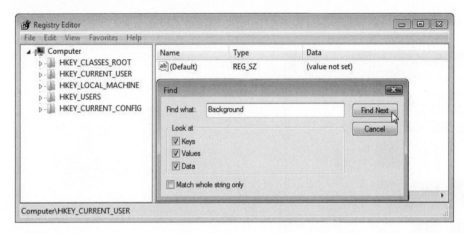

To search for the desktop Background key, click **Edit > Find >** type **Background >** click **Find Next**.

The Background value is located. Leave this window open.

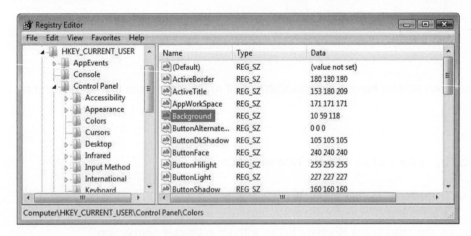

In which folder is the Background located?

What is the data value of the Background (hint – it has three numbers that correspond to red, green, and blue)? Answers may vary based on the shade of blue selected in Choose a desktop background.

Step 9

We will now export **HKEY_CURRENT_USER\Control Panel\Colors** folder.

In the left pane, click the **Colors** folder.

Click **File > Export**. Save the file to the Desktop. File name: **BlueBKG**

At the desktop, right-click the **BlueBKG.reg** icon **> Edit**.

What is the data value of the Background? Answers may vary based on the shade of blue selected in Display Properties.

Close **BlueBKG.reg – Notepad** window.

Step 10

Open the "Choose a desktop background" page in Personalize appearance and sounds by right-clicking the **Desktop > Personalize > Desktop Background**.

Click the **Location** drop-down button and select **Solid Colors**. Select a **red** color.

Click **OK**.

In a few second, the desktop will turn to red.

Click the "Registry Editor" window so it is activated.

On your keyboard, press **F5** to refresh the "Registry Editor" window.

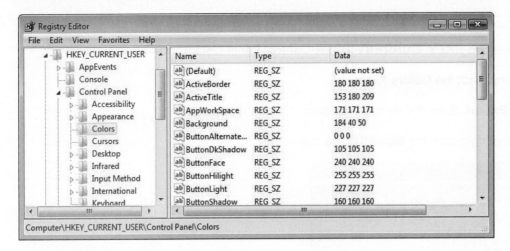

What is the data value of the Background? Answers may vary based on the shade of red selected in Display Properties.

Step 11

We will now import **BlueBKG.reg** file.

Click the "Registry Editor" window so it is activated.

Click **File > Import**. Locate and click the **BlueBKG.reg** icon, and then click **Open**.

Click **OK**.

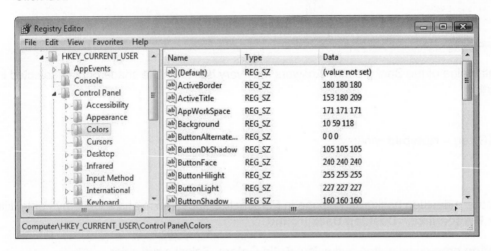

Click the Registry Editor window so it is activated.

What is the data value of the Background? Answers may vary based on the shade of blue selected in Display Properties.

What is the color of the desktop?

Restart the computer.
What is the color of the desktop?

Reset Display Properties Background to the original settings (hint – see Step 7).

Step 12

Open the Run dialog box by clicking **Start >** in the Start Search box, type **Run**.

Type **cleanmgr** in the "Open:" field.

Click **OK**.

The "Disk Cleanup Options" window opens.

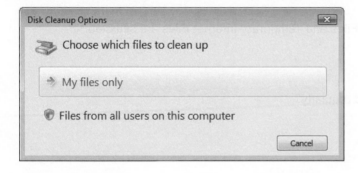

Click **My files only**.

Note: Clicking **Files from all users on this computer** will display the **User Account Control** window to ask for permission.

The "Disk Cleanup for (C:)" window opens.

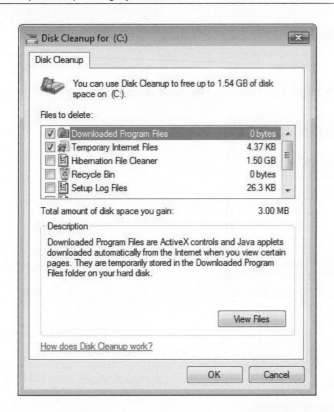

Make sure only Downloaded Program Files and Temporary Internet Files are selected.

Click the **OK** button.

Why should disk cleanup be performed regularly?

5.3.7.6 Lab - Run Line Utilities in Windows XP

Introduction

In this lab, you will use Windows Run line utilities to access and use tools to configure settings in Windows XP.

Recommended Equipment

The following equipment is required for this exercise:

• A computer running Windows XP

Step 1

Navigate to the "Run" window by clicking **Start > Run**. Type **MMC** and click **OK**.

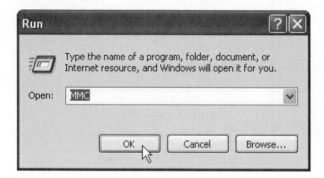

Step 2

The "Console1" (console number may vary) window and the "Console Root" window open.

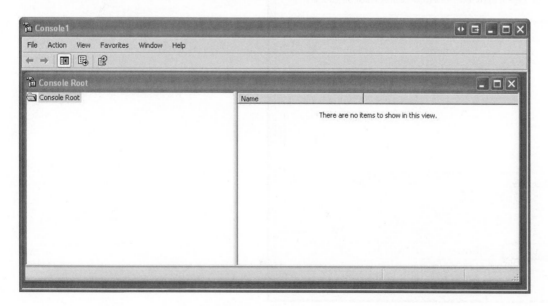

Step 3

To build your own custom console, click **File > Add/Remove Snap-in**.

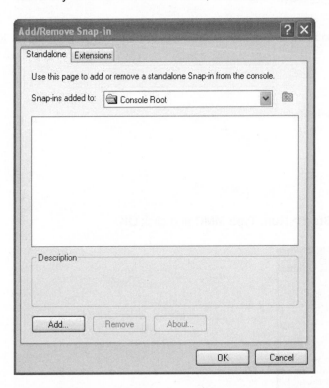

The "Add/Remove Snap-in" window opens.

To add a snap-in, click **Add**.

The "Add Standalone Snap-in" window appears. To add a folder snap-in so that you can organize all your snap-ins, scroll down until you see the Folder snap-in.

Select **Folder** > click **Add**.

To add the "Link to Web Address" snap-in, scroll down until you see the snap-in. Select **Link to Web Address** > click **Add**.

The "Link to Web Address" wizard opens.

In the Target box, type **http://www.cisco.com/**. Click **Next**.

In the "Select a name for the URL reference" box, type **Cisco**.

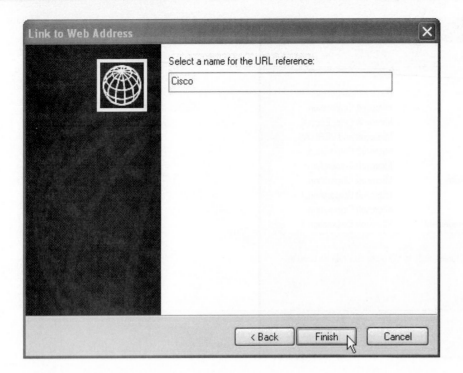

Click **Finish**.

Click **Close**.

Step 4

Click the "Add/Remove Snap-in" window so it is activated. In the "Snap-ins added to" box, select **Folder**.

Click **Add**.

Add the following snap-ins: Disk Defragmenter, Disk Management, and Removable Storage Management.

Note: When asked which computer the snap-in will manage, select the default by clicking **Finish**.

To close the "Add Standalone Snap-in" window, click **Close**.

Click the "Add/Remove Snap-in" window so it is activated.

Click **OK**.

Step 5

The "Console1" window appears. Right-click the Folder icon and select **Rename**.

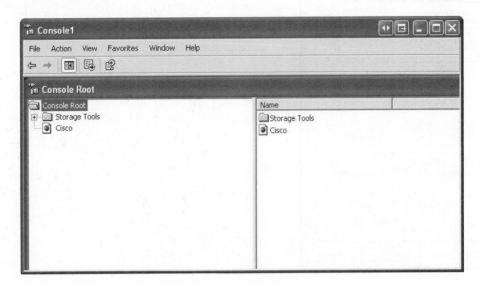

Change the name of the folder to "Storage Tools".

To save the custom console, click **File > Save As**. Change the file name to your name. Example: **John's Console**. Change the "Save in" box to **Desktop**. Click **Save**.

Step 6

Close all open windows.

On the desktop, double-click the **Console** icon to re-open the console with your snap-ins.

Step 7

Open the Desktop tab in Display Properties by right-clicking the **desktop > Properties > Desktop** tab.

What is the Background picture?

Set the background image to (None). If the **Color** drop-down button is not blue, click the **Color** drop-down menu and select **blue**.

Click **OK**.

The computer screen should now have a blue background. If not, ask the instructor for assistance.

Step 8

Open Registry Editor by clicking **Start > Run >** type **regedit >** click **OK**.

Note: Do not make any changes in the Registry Editor without instructor permission.

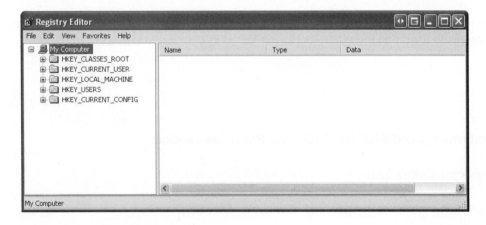

Click the **HKEY_Current_User** icon.

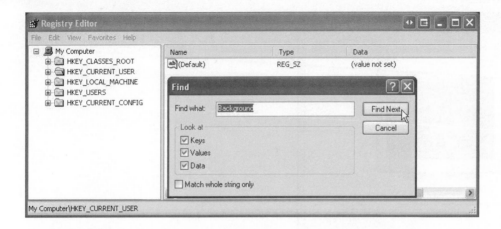

To search for the desktop Background key, click **Edit > Find >** type **Background >** click **Find Next**.

The Background value is located. Leave this window open.

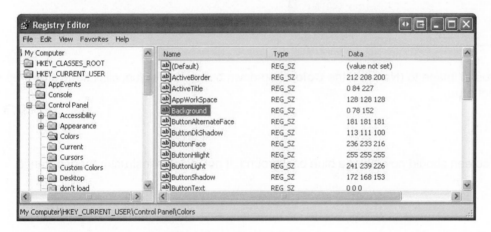

In which folder is the Background located?

What is the data value of the Background (hint – it has three numbers that correspond to red, green, and blue)? Answers may vary based on the shade of blue selected in Display Properties.

Step 9

We will now export **HKEY_CURRENT_USER\Control Panel\Colors** folder.

In the left pane, click the **Colors** folder.

Click **File > Export**. Save the file to the Desktop. File name: **BlueBKG**

At the desktop, right-click the **BlueBKG.reg** icon > **Edit**.

What is the data value of the Background? Answers may vary based on the shade of blue selected in Display Properties.

Close **BlueBKG.reg – Notepad** window.

Step 10

Open the Desktop tab in Display Properties by right-clicking the **desktop > Properties > Desktop** tab.

Click the **Color** drop-down button, select **red**.

Click **OK**.

In a few seconds, the desktop will turn to red.

Click the Registry Editor window so it is activated.

On your keyboard, press **F5** to refresh the Registry Editor window.

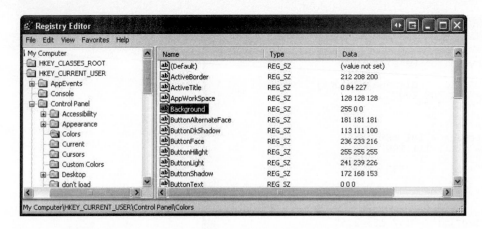

What is the data value of the Background? Answers may vary based on the shade of red selected in Display Properties.

Step 11

We will now import **BlueBKG.reg** file.

Click the "Registry Editor" window so it is activated.

Click **File > Import**. Locate and click the **BlueBKG.reg** icon and then click **Open**. Click **OK**.

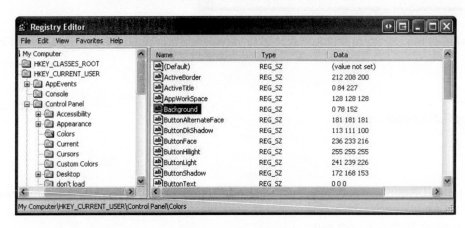

Click the "Registry Editor" window so it is activated.

What is the data value of the Background? Answers may vary based on the shade of red selected in Display Properties.

What is the color of the desktop?

Restart the computer.

What is the color of the desktop?

Reset Display Properties Background to the original settings (hint – see Step 7).

Step 12

Open the Run dialog box by clicking **Start > Run....**

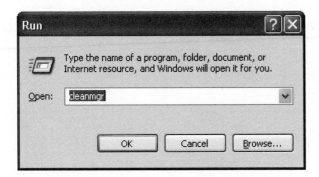

Type **cleanmgr** in the "Open:" field.

Click **OK**.

The "Disk Cleanup for (C:)" window opens.

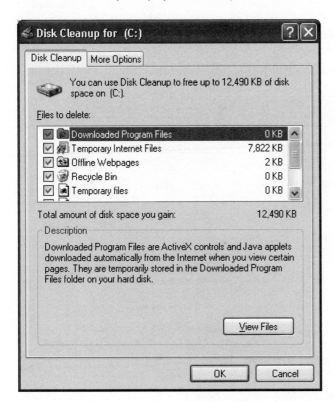

Click the **OK** button.

Why should disk cleanup be performed regularly?

5.4.1.4 Lab - Install Virtual PC

Introduction

In this lab, you will install and Configure XP Mode in Windows 7. You will then run a Windows XP-based application in XP Mode.

Recommended Equipment

The following equipment is required for this exercise:

- A computer system that is using Windows 7

- The following application downloaded to the Desktop of the computer: Hardware-Assisted Virtualization detection tool, Windows XP Mode, and Windows Virtual PC

- A USB flash drive with a Windows XP application

Step 1

Log on to the computer with the Administrator account.

As instructed by the instructions, locate Windows Hardware-Assisted Virtualization (HAV) detection tool.

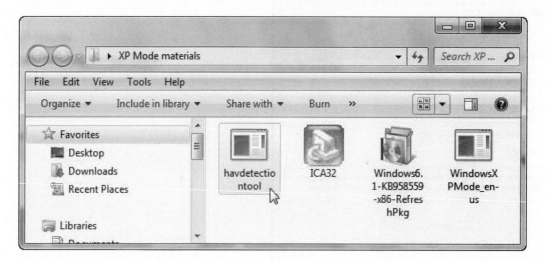

Double-click **havdetectiontool** application icon.

The "Hardware-Assisted Virtualization Detection Tool" window opens.

Does the computer meet the processor requirements to run Windows Virtual PC?

If you answered no to the question, ask the instructor for assistance.

Click OK.

Step 2

Double-click **WindowsXPMode-en-us** application icon.

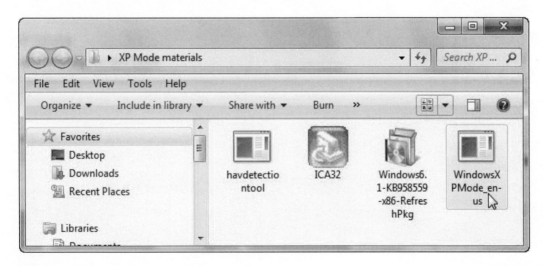

If the "Security Warning" window opens, click **Run**.

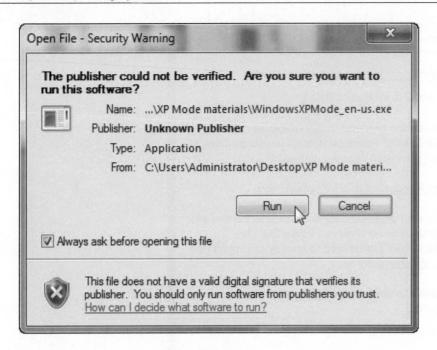

The "Extracting Files" window opens.

The "Windows XP Mode" window opens.

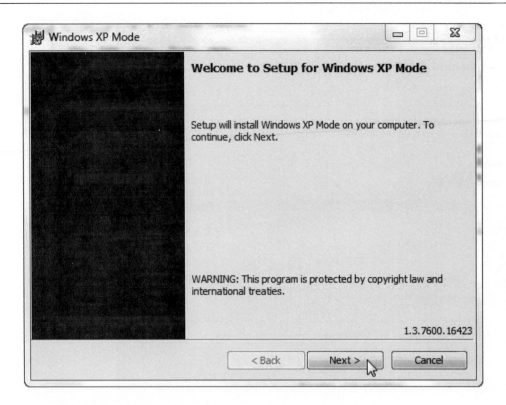

Click **Next**.

The "Location" screen appears.

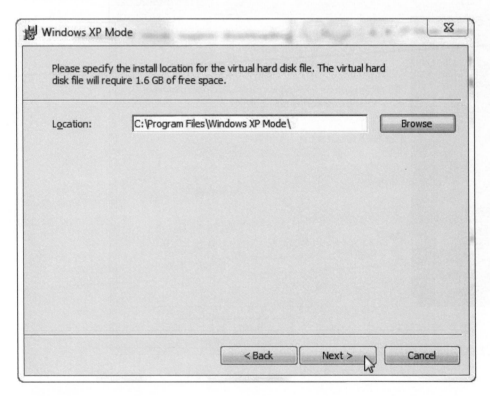

Click **Next**.

The "Installing virtual hard disk files for Windows XP Mode" screen appears.

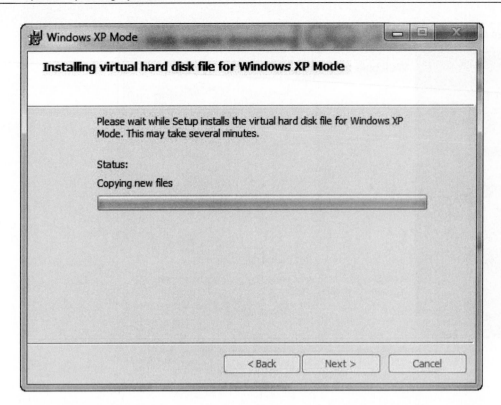

The "Setup Completed" screen appears.

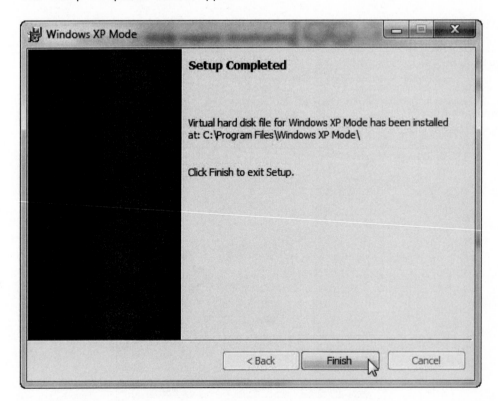

Click **Finish**.

Step 3

Double-click **Windows XP Mode** (Note: file may be different: Windows6.1-KB958559-x86-RefreshPkg) application icon.

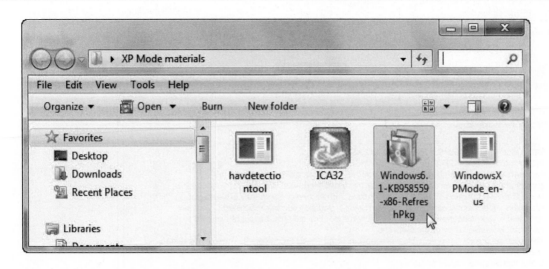

The "Windows Update Standalone Installer" window opens.

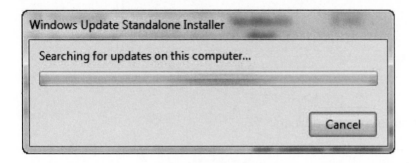

The "Do you want to install the following Windows software update?" screen appears.

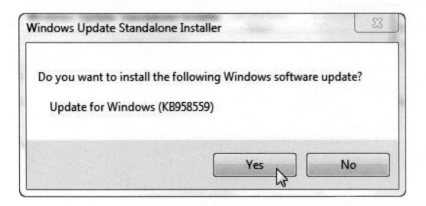

Click **Yes**.

The "Download and Install Updates" window opens.

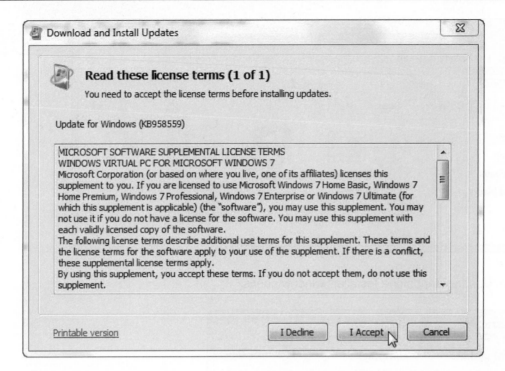

Click **I Accept**.

The "The updates are being installed" screen appears.

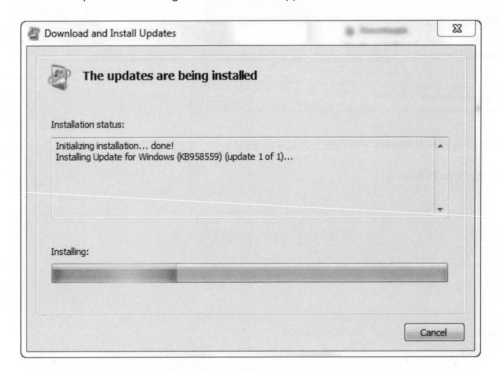

The "Installation complete" screen appears.

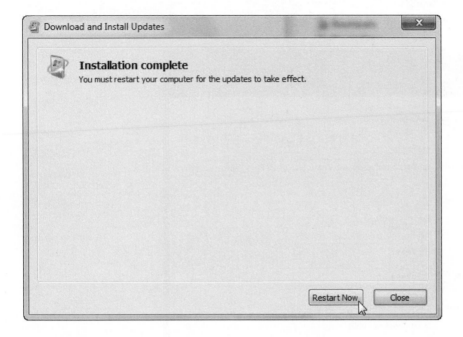

Click **Restart Now**.

Step 4

When the computer restarts, logon as an Administrator.

Click **Start > All Programs > Windows Virtual PC > Windows XP Mode**.

The "Windows XP Mode Setup" window opens.

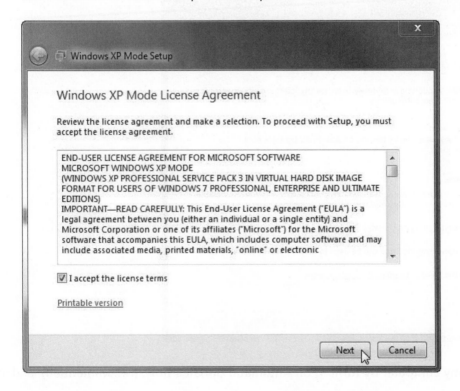

Select the **I accept the license terms** box and then click **Next**.

The "Installation folder and credentials" screen appears.

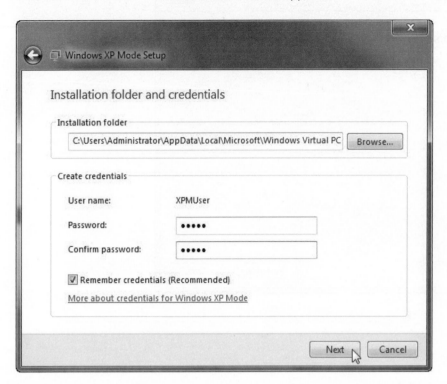

Type **ITEv5** as the password, retype the password, and then click **Next**.

The "Help protect your computer" screen appears.

Select **Help protect my computer by turning on Automatic Updates now. (recommended)**, and then click **Next**.

The "Setup will share the drive on this computer with Windows XP Mode" screen appears.

Click **Start Setup**.

After a few seconds, the "Windows XP Mode – Windows Virtual PC" window starts up.

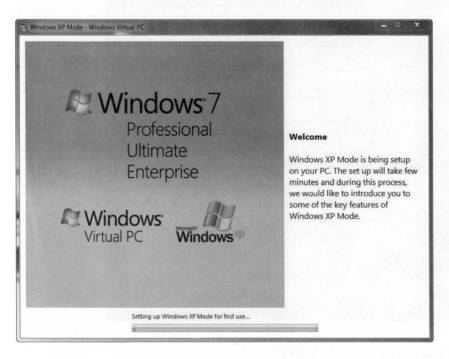

After a few minutes, the "Starting the virtual machine" indicator appears.

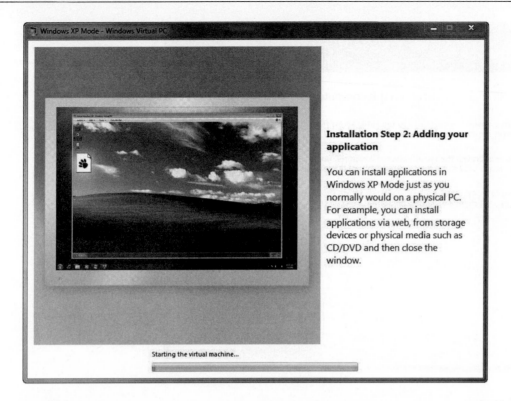

The "Windows Virtual PC" window opens with a black screen.

Windows "XP Mode" loads into "Windows Virtual PC".

Step 5

Plug the USB flash drive with the Windows XP application into a USB port on the computer.

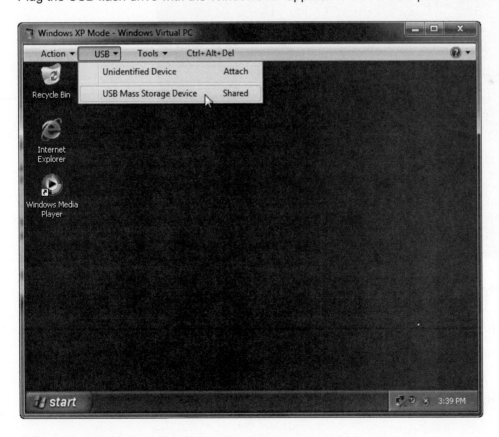

Click the **USB** menu **> USB Mass Storage Device**.

The "Attach a shared USB device" screen opens.

Click **Yes**.

The "Found New Hardware" message appears.

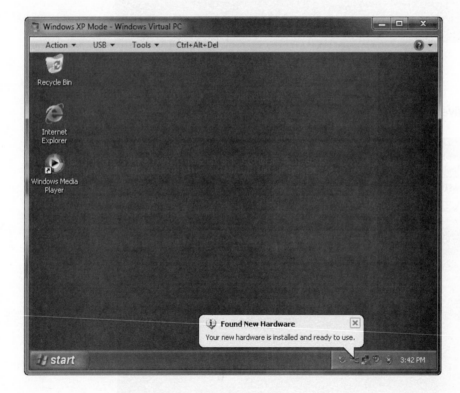

Click **Start > My Computer >** double-click **Removable Disk**.

The "USB flash drive" opens.

Step 6

Note: If installing a different Windows XP application, follow the install instructions provided by the instructor.

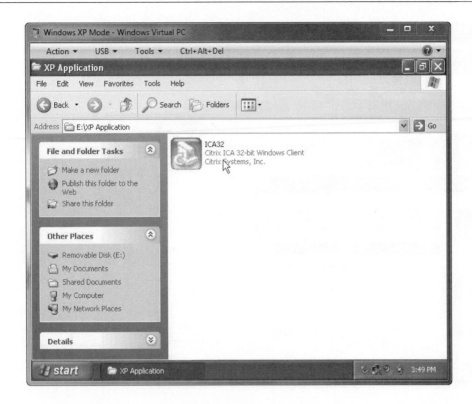

Double-click the "Windows XP application".

The "InstallShield Wizard" opens.

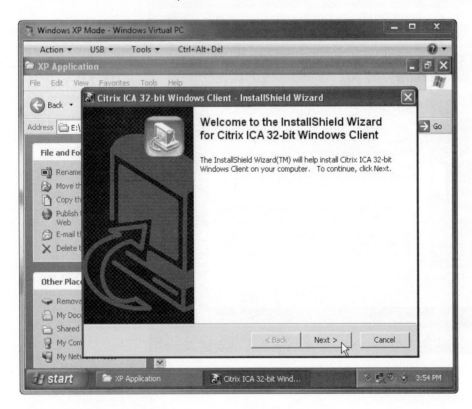

Click **Next**.

The "Setup" window opens.

The "Welcome" window opens.

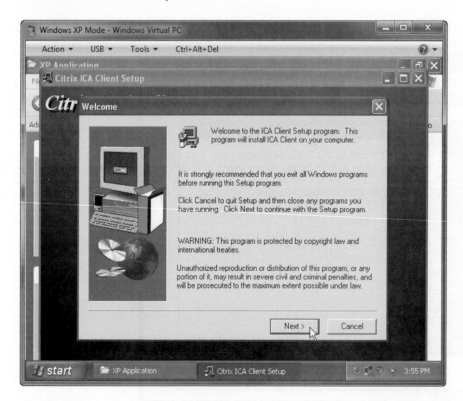

Click **Next**.

The "Citrix License Agreement" window opens.

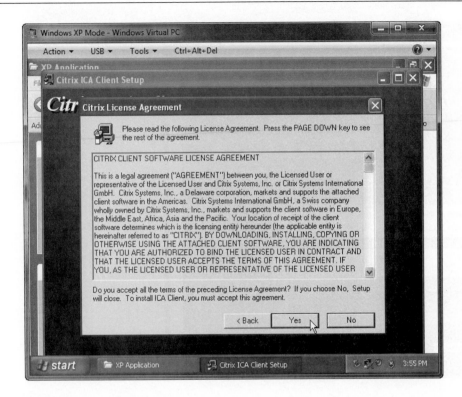

Click **Yes**.

The "Choose Destination Location" window opens.

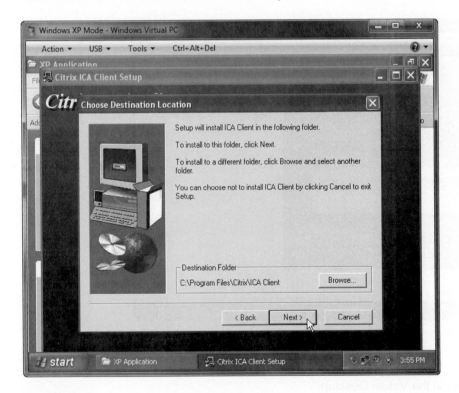

Click **Next**.

Continue clicking **Next** to accept all default settings.

The "Citrix ICA Client Setup" window opens.

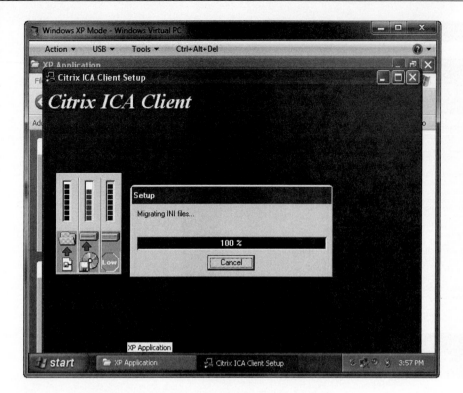

Notice the flashing icon in the Task Bar. Click the icon.

The "Information" window opens.

Click **OK**.

Close all open windows in the Virtual Desktop.

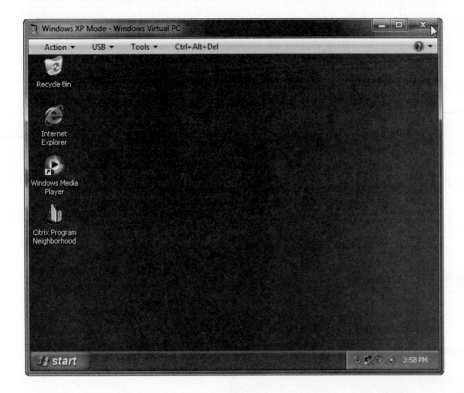

To close the Virtual PC, click the **red X** at the top-right corner of the screen.

The "Hibernating the virtual machine" screen appears.

Step 7

From Windows 7, click **Start > All Programs > Windows Virtual PC > Windows XP Mode Applications >** select the program you installed.

The "'Windows XP Mode' was closed with a user logged on" window opens.

Click **Continue**.

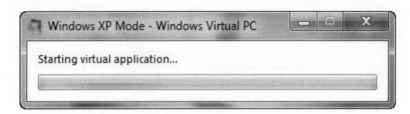

The "Starting virtual application" screen appears.

The application does not open in "XP Mode". It is running in its own window as if it were native to Windows 7.

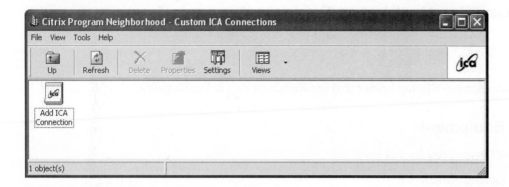

Step 8

Close all open windows

Click **Start > Control Panel > Programs and Features**. Find and select **Windows XP Mode > Uninstall**.

Click **Yes** to remove the program and all files.

Click **Yes** to restart the program.

5.5.1.2 Lab - Managing the Startup Folder in Windows 7

Introduction

In this lab, you will customize the Startup Folder and the RunOnce Key in the Registry.

Recommended Equipment

The following equipment is required for this exercise:

> • A computer running Windows 7

Step 1

> Click **Start > All Programs > Games >** right-click **FreeCell > Send To > Desktop (create shortcut)**.

Step 2

> Click and drag the shortcut **FreeCell** icon to the **Start** button.
>
> Do not release the shortcut icon.

The "Start menu" appears.

Drag the icon to **All Programs**.

The "All Programs" menu appears.

Drag the icon to the bottom of the Startup folder.

When a blue text Move to Startup appears next to the FreeCell shortcut icon, release the icon.

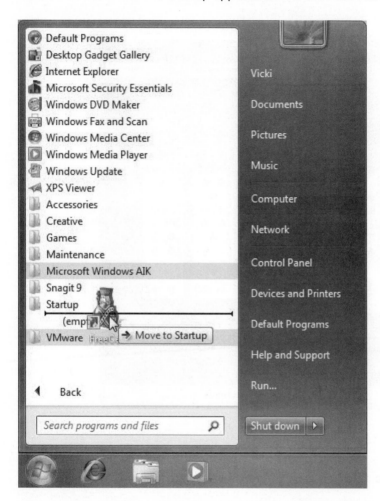

You should see the FreeCell icon listed below Startup.

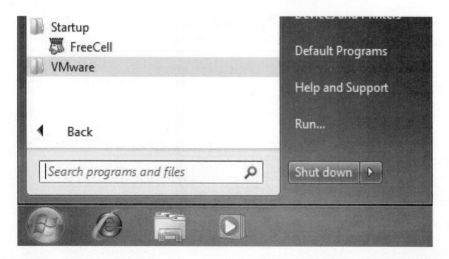

Step 3

Log off Windows.

Log on to Windows as an Administrator.

What happens when you log in?

Close the FreeCell application.

Step 4

Click **Start > Search for programs and files >** type **run > Enter**.

Type **regedit** in the "Open:" field **> OK > Yes**.

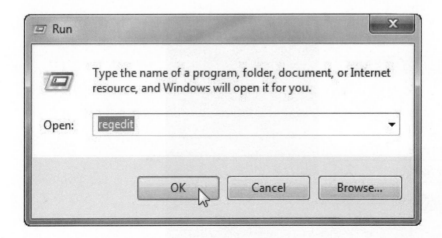

CAUTION: Incorrect changes to the registry can cause system errors and/or system instability.

The "Registry Editor" window opens.

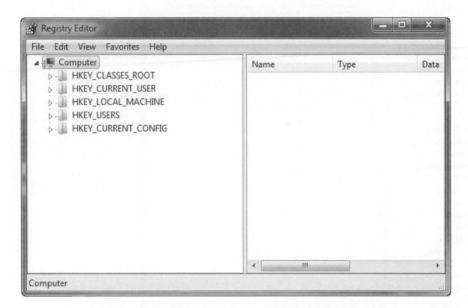

Expand the **HKEY_CURRENT_USER** Key.

Expand the **Software** Key.

Expand the **Microsoft** Key.

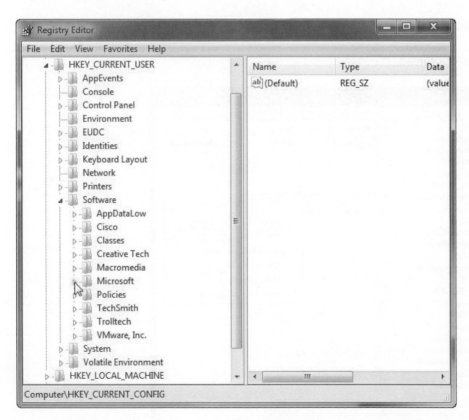

Expand the **Windows** Key.

Expand the **CurrentVersion** Key.

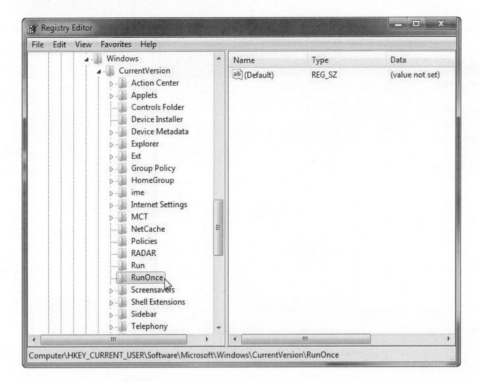

Select the **RunOnce** Key.

Right-click anywhere in the white space on the right side of the window.

Hover over **New** and select **String Value**.

A new "String Value" is created.

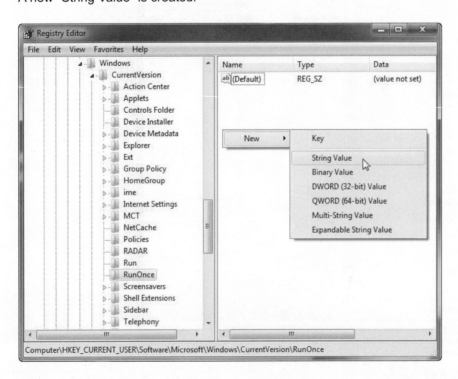

Click anywhere in the white space of the window.

Right-click **New Value #1 > Rename**.

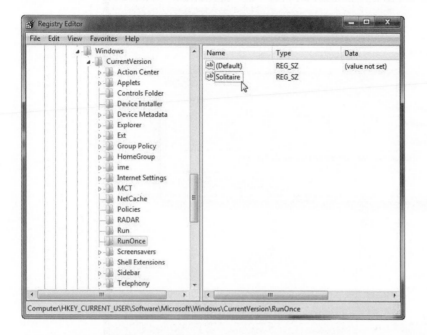

Type **Solitaire** and press **Enter**.

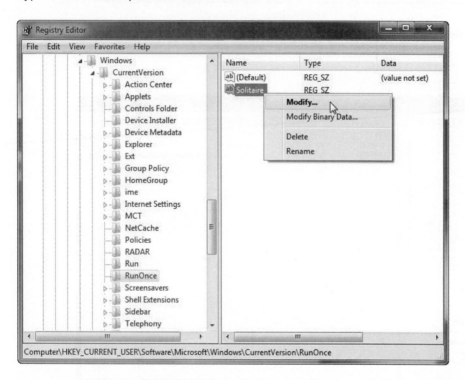

Right-click **Solitaire > Modify**.

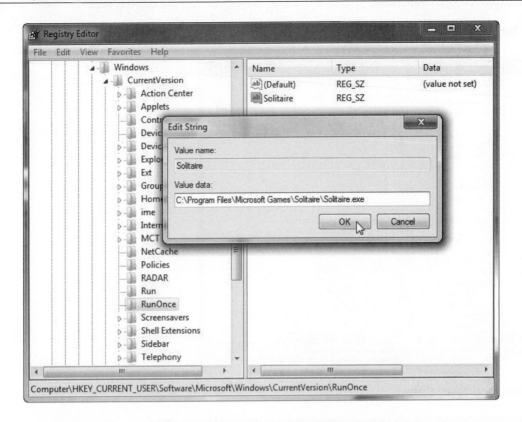

Type **C:\Program Files\Microsoft Games\Solitaire\Solitaire.exe** in the "Value data" field.

Click **OK**.

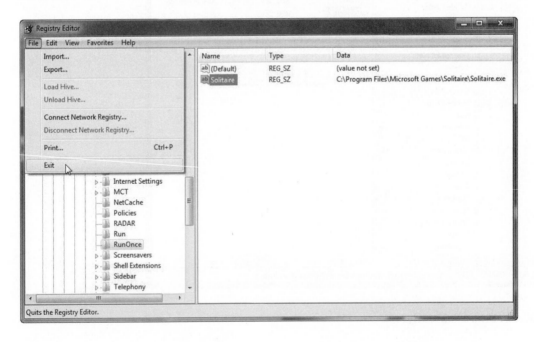

Close the "Registry Editor" window.

Step 5

Log off Windows.

Log on to Windows as an Administrator.

What happens when you log in?

Close all open Windows.

Remove FreeCell game from Startup.

Click **Start > All Programs > Startup** > right-click **FreeCell > Delete > Yes**.

5.5.1.3 Lab - Managing the Startup Folder in Windows Vista

Introduction

In this lab, you will customize the Startup Folder and the RunOnce Key in the Registry.

Recommended Equipment

The following equipment is required for this exercise:

• A computer running Windows Vista

Step 1

Click **Start > All Programs > Games >** right-click **FreeCell > Send To > Desktop (create shortcut)**.

Step 2

Click and drag the shortcut **FreeCell** icon to the **Start** button.

The "Start" menu appears.

Do not release the shortcut icon.

Drag the icon to **All Programs**.

The "All Programs" menu appears.

Drag the icon to the bottom of the **Startup** folder.

When a blue arrow appears next to the FreeCell shortcut icon, release the icon.

Click **Startup**.

You should see the FreeCell icon listed below Startup.

Step 3

Log off Windows.

Log on to Windows as an Administrator.

What happens when you log in?

Close the FreeCell application.

Step 4

Click **Start > Start Search >** type **run**.

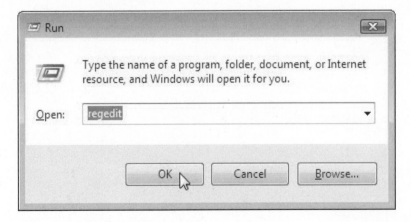

Type **regedit** in the "Open:" field **> OK > Continue**.

CAUTION: Incorrect changes to the registry can cause system errors and/or system instability.

The "Registry Editor" window opens.

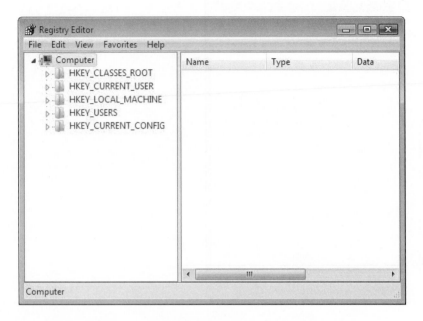

Expand the **HKEY_CURRENT_USER** Key.

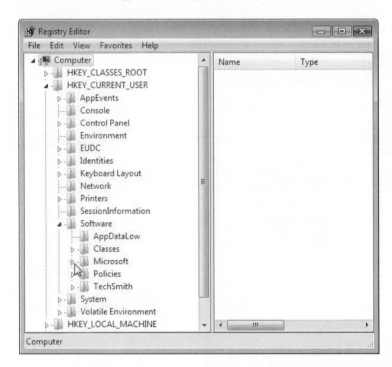

Expand the **Software** Key.

Expand the **Microsoft** Key.

Expand the **Windows** Key.

Expand the **CurrentVersion** Key.

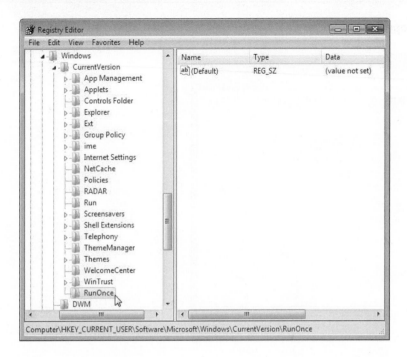

Select the **RunOnce** Key.

Right-click anywhere in the white space on the right side of the window.

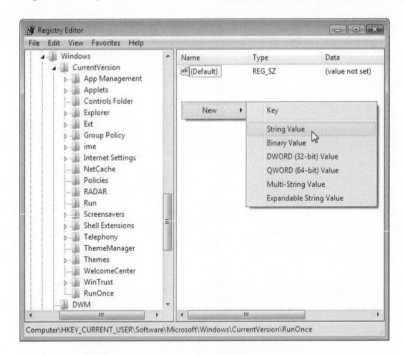

Hover over **New** and select **String Value**.

Click anywhere in the white space of the window.

A new "String Value" is created.

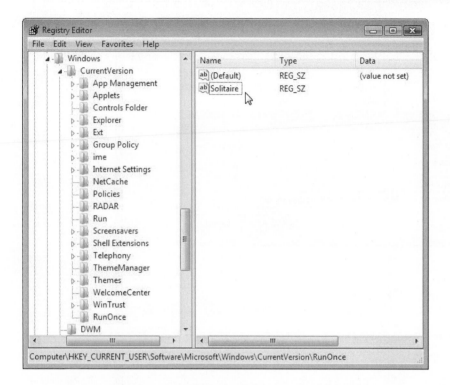

Right-click **New Value #1 > Rename**.

Type **Solitaire** and press **Enter**.

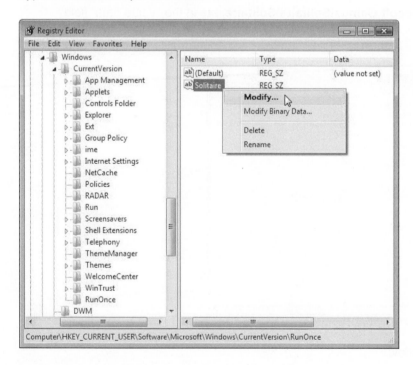

Right-click **Solitaire > Modify**.

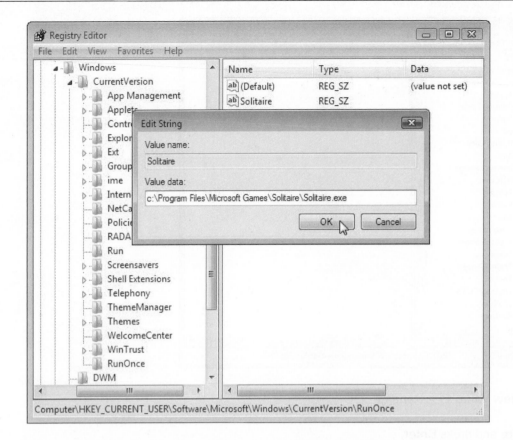

Type **C:\Program Files\Microsoft Games\Solitaire\Solitaire.exe** in the "Value data" field.

Click **OK**.

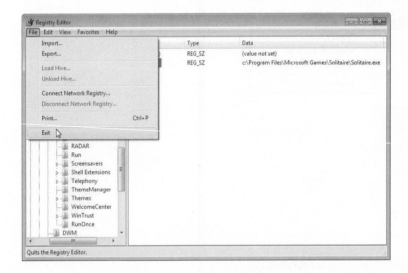

Close the Registry Editor window.

Step 5

Log off Windows.

Log on to Windows as an Administrator.

What happens when you log in?

Close all open Windows.

Remove FreeCell game from Startup.

Click **Start > All Programs > Startup >** right-click **FreeCell > Delete > Yes**.

5.5.1.4 Lab - Managing the Startup Folder in Windows XP

Introduction

In this lab, you will customize the Startup Folder and the RunOnce Key in the Registry.

Recommended Equipment

The following equipment is required for this exercise:

 • A computer running Windows XP Professional

Step 1

Log on to Windows as an administrator.

Choose **Start > All Programs > Games >** right-click **FreeCell > Send To > Desktop (create shortcut)**.

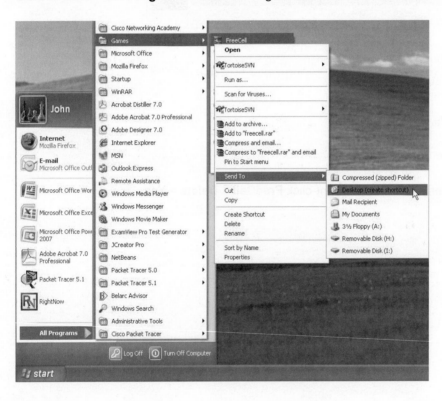

Step 2

Click and drag the **Freecell** to the **Start** button.

The "Start" menu appears.

Do not release the shortcut icon.

Drag the icon to **All Programs**.

The "All Programs" menu appears.

Drag the icon to **Startup**.

The "Startup" menu appears.

Drag the icon to the **Startup** menu.

Release the icon.

Step 3

Log off Windows.

Log on to Windows as an administrator.

What happens when you log in?

Close the Freecell application.

Step 4

Choose **Start > Run**.

Type **regedit** in the **Open:** field **> OK**.

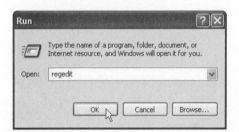

CAUTION: Incorrect changes to the registry can cause system errors and/or system instability.

The "Registry Editor" window opens.

Expand the **HKEY_CURRENT_USER** Key.

Expand the **Software** Key.

Expand the **Microsoft** Key.

Expand the **Windows** Key.

Expand the **CurrentVersion** Key.

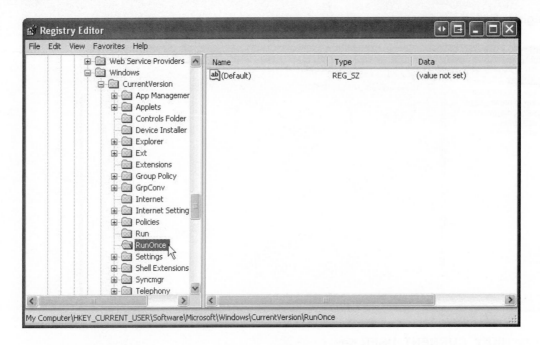

Select the **RunOnce** Key.

Right-click anywhere in the white space of the window.

Hover over **New** and then select **String Value**.

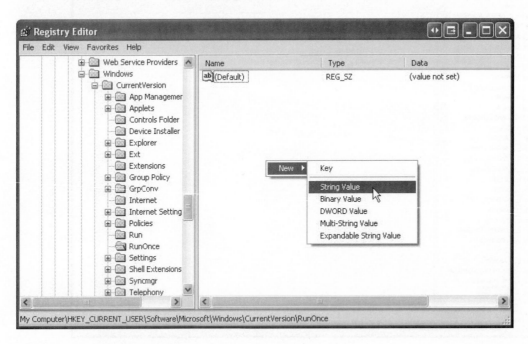

A new "String Value" is created.

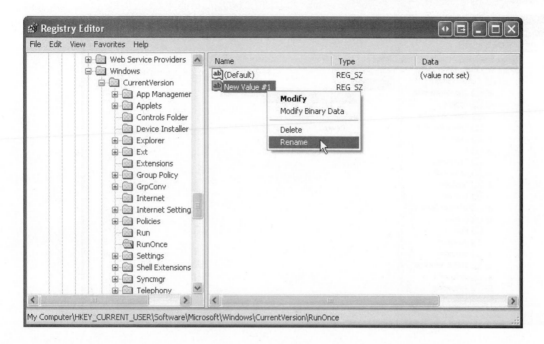

Right-click **New Value #1** and then choose **Rename**.

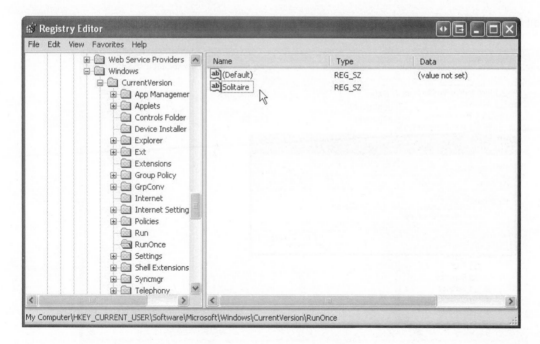

Type **Solitaire** and then press **Enter**.

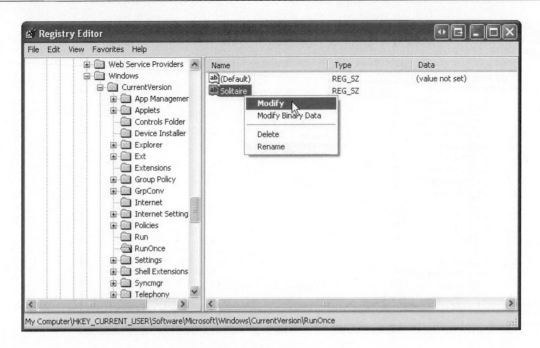

Right-click **Solitaire** and then choose **Modify**.

The "Edit String" window opens.

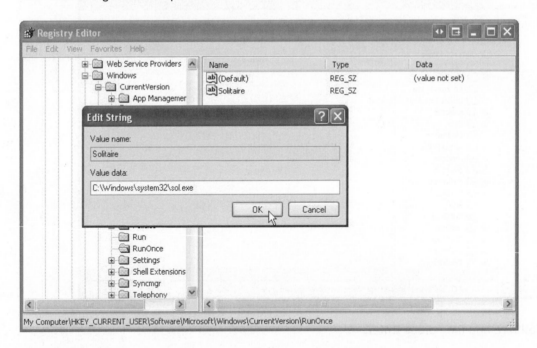

Type **C:\Windows\system32\sol.exe** in the "Value data" field.

Click **OK**.

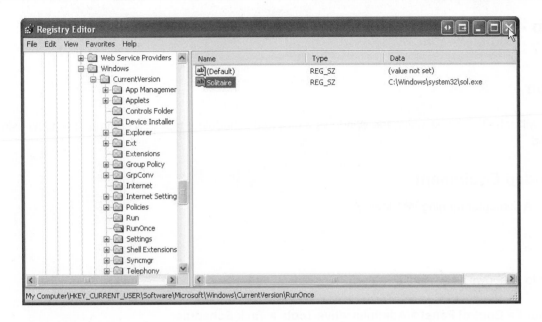

Close the Registry Editor window.

Step 5

Log off Windows.

Log on to Windows as an administrator.

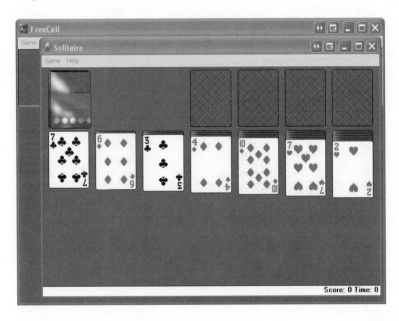

What happens when you log in?

Close all open Windows.

Remove FreeCell game from Startup.

Click **Start > All Programs > Startup >** right-click **FreeCell > Delete > Delete Shortcut**.

5.5.1.7 Lab - Schedule a Task Using the GUI and the at Command in Windows 7

Introduction

In this lab, you will schedule a task using the Windows 7 GUI and schedule a task in a command window using the **at** command.

Recommended Equipment

- A computer running Windows 7

Step 1

Log on to Windows as an Administrator.

Click **Start > Control Panel > Administrative Tools > Task Scheduler**.

Step 2

The "Task Scheduler" window opens.

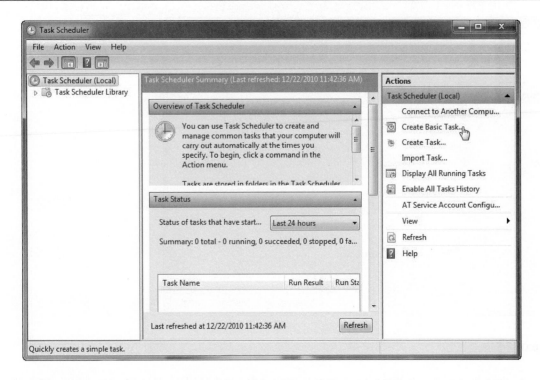

Click **Create Basic Task** in the Actions area.

Step 3

The "Create Basic Task Wizard" window opens.

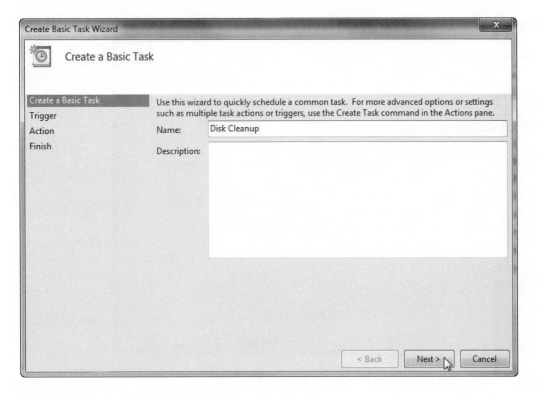

Type **Disk Cleanup** in the **Name:** field, and then click **Next**.

Select the **Weekly** radio button.

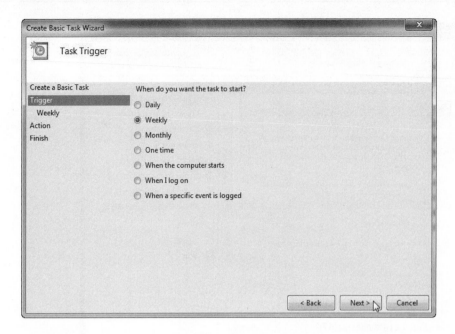

Click **Next**.

Click on the time field and select the hour, minute, seconds, and AM/PM. Use the scroll buttons in the **Start:** field to set the time to **6:00:00 PM**.

Set the **Recur every _ weeks on:** field to **1**.

Check the **Wednesday** checkbox.

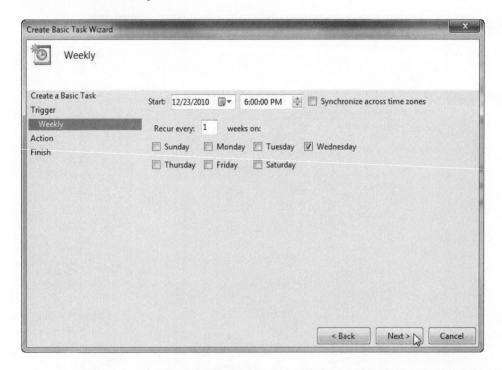

Click **Next**.

The "Action" screen opens.

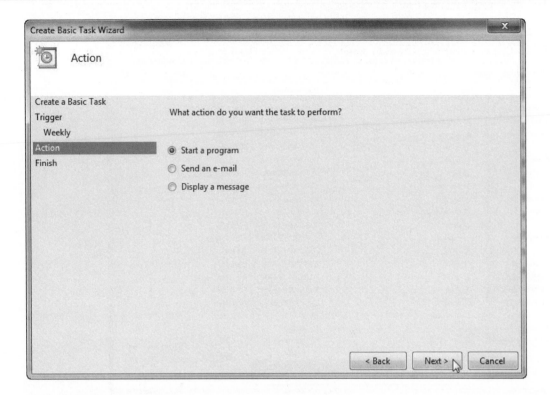

Make sure **Start a program** is selected, and then click **Next**.

The "Start a Program" screen appears.

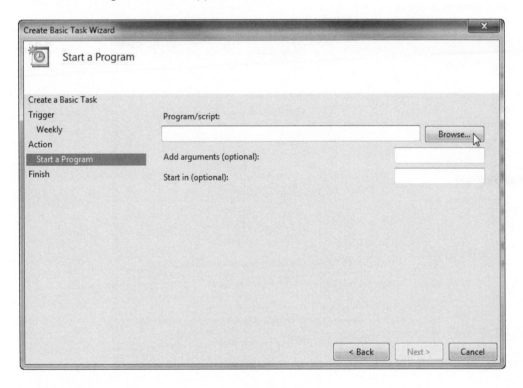

Click **Browse**.

Type **cle** in the **File name:** field, select **cleanmge.exe**, and then click **Open**.

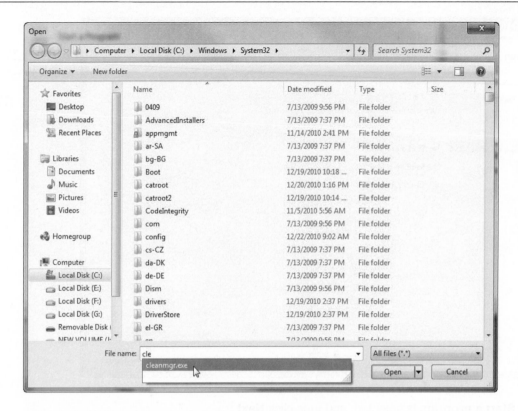

When the "Start a Program" screen re-opens, click **Next**.

The "Summary" screen appears.

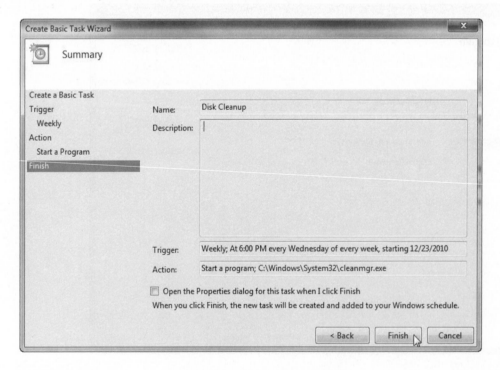

Click **Finish**.

Step 4

The "Task Scheduler" window opens.

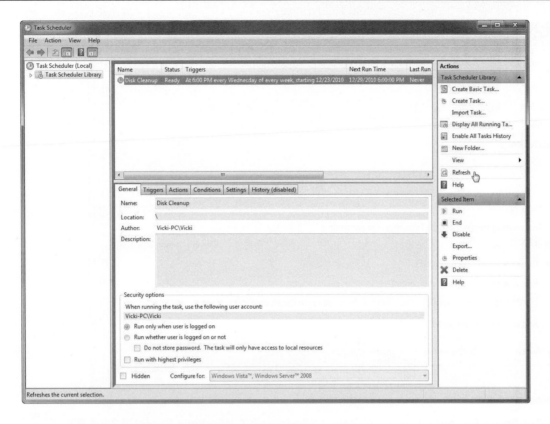

In the left pane, select **Task Scheduler Library**.

Next, in the right pane, click **Refresh** until you see the task **Disk Cleanup** you created.

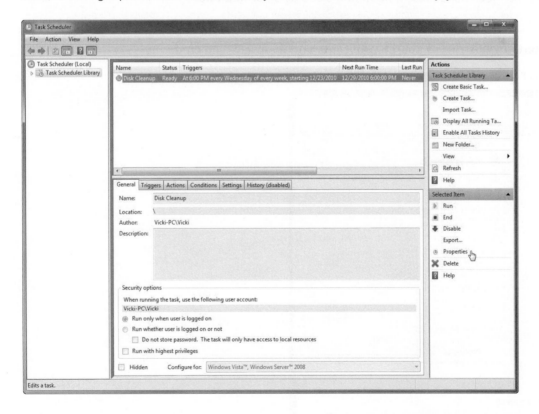

Select the task **Disk Cleanup**, and then in the right pane, click **Properties**.

The "Disk Cleanup Properties (Local Computer)" window appears.

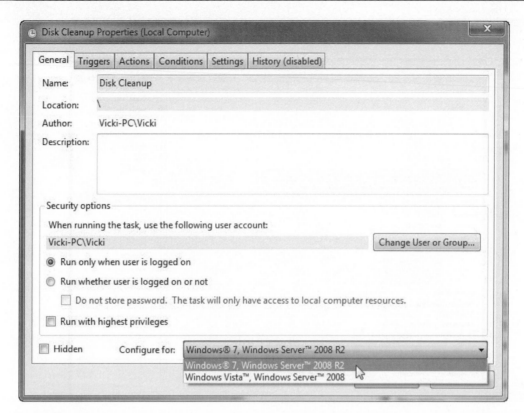

In the **Configure for:** drop-down menu select **Windows® 7, Windows Server™ 2008 R2**.

Click **OK**.

Minimize the "Task Scheduler" window and close all other windows.

Step 5

Click **Start**, and then in the **Search programs and files** field-type **cmd**.

Right-click **cmd > Run as administrator > Yes**.

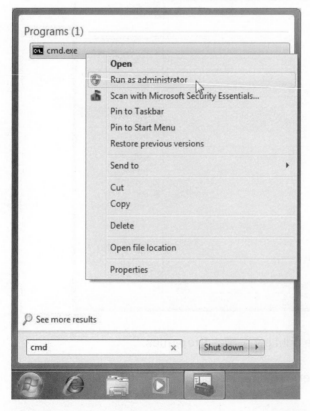

The "Administrator: C:\Windows\System32\cmd.exe" window opens.

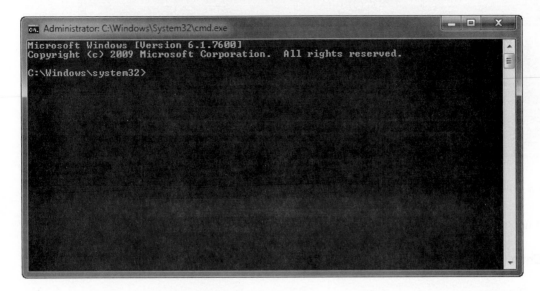

Type **at/?**, and then press the **Enter** key.

The **at** command options are displayed.

Type **at 20:00:00 /every:W backup**.

Note that the time must be military time.

Press **Enter**.

Added a new job with job ID = 1 is displayed.

Type **at \\computername**. For example, **at \\Vicki-PC**.

Press **Enter**.

The scheduled job appears.

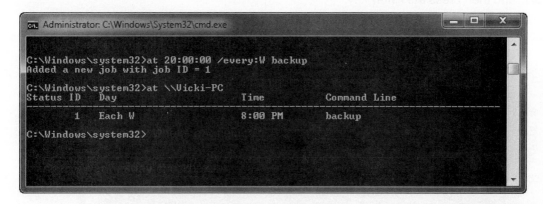

Which command would you enter to get the backup to run every Tuesday and Wednesday at 3:00 PM?

Type **exit**, and then press the **Enter** key.

Step 6

Open the "Scheduled Tasks" window.

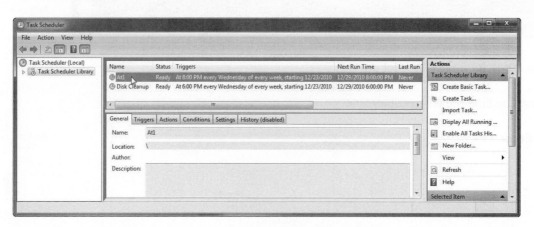

Click **Task Scheduler Library**. You may need to refresh the screen.

The task created using the **at** command is listed in the window.

Step 7

For the scheduled tasks that you have created, right-click the scheduled task and then click **Delete**.

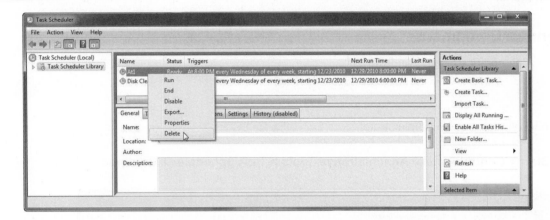

Click **Yes** to confirm you want to delete the task.

Make sure all scheduled tasks created by you are removed from the scheduled tasks window.

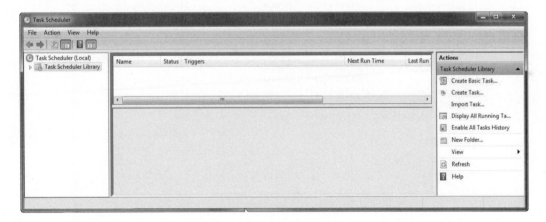

5.5.1.8 Lab - Schedule a Task Using the GUI and the at Command in Windows Vista

Introduction

In this lab, you will schedule a task using the Windows Vista GUI and schedule a task in a command window using the **at** command.

Recommended Equipment

- A computer running Windows Vista

Step 1

Log on to Windows as an Administrator.

Click **Start > Control Panel > Administrative Tools > Task Scheduler > Continue**.

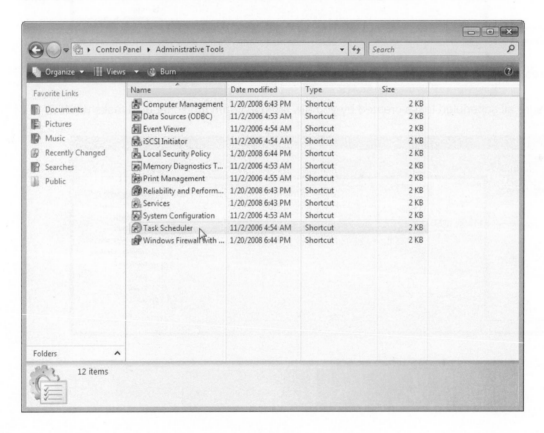

Step 2

The "Task Scheduler" window opens.

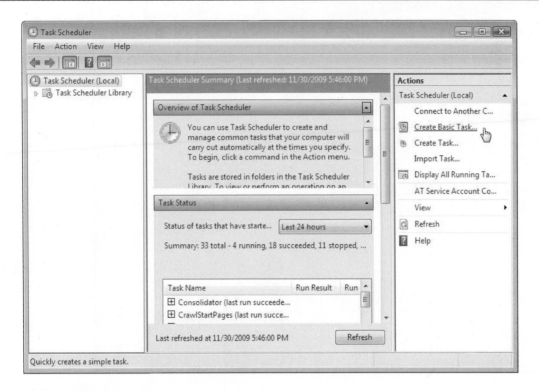

Click **Create Basic Task** in the Actions area.

Step 3

The "Create Basic Task Wizard" window opens.

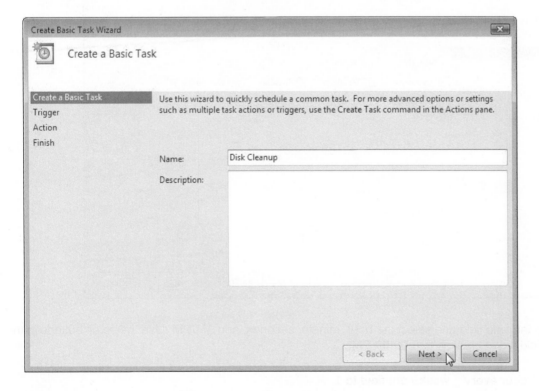

Type **Disk Cleanup** in the **Name** field, and then click **Next**.

Select the **Weekly** radio button.

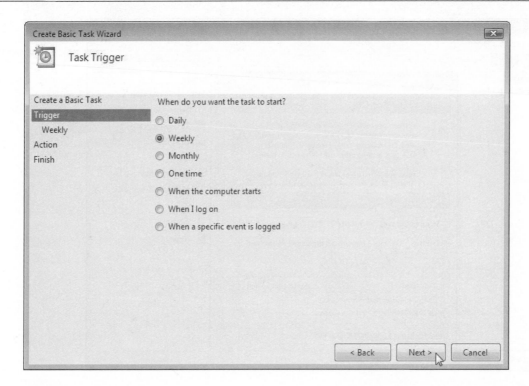

Click **Next**.

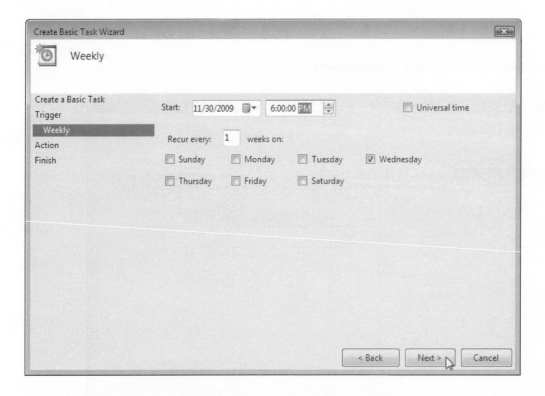

Click on the time field and select the hour, minute, seconds, and AM/PM. Use the scroll buttons in the **Start:** field to set the time to **6:00:00 PM**.

Set the **Recur every _ weeks on:** field to **1**.

Check the **Wednesday** check box, and then click **Next**.

The "Action" screen opens.

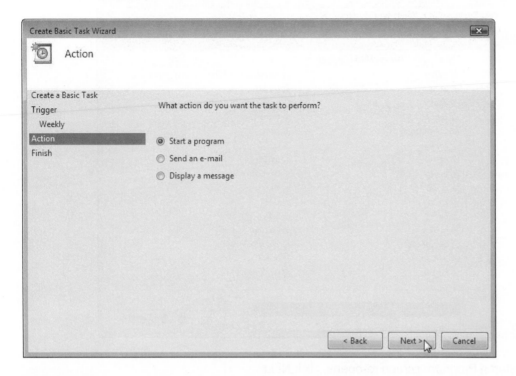

Make sure **Start a program** is selected, and then click **Next**.

The "Start a Program" screen appears.

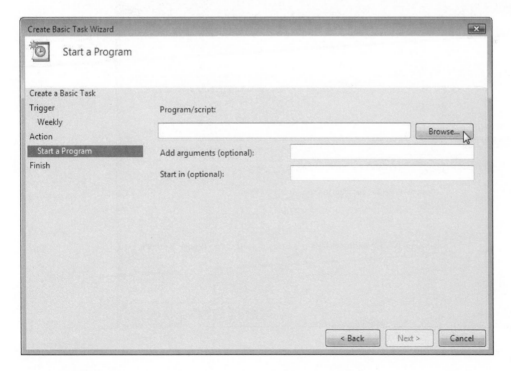

Click **Browse**.

Type **cle** in the **File name** field, select **cleanmge.exe**, and then click **Open**.

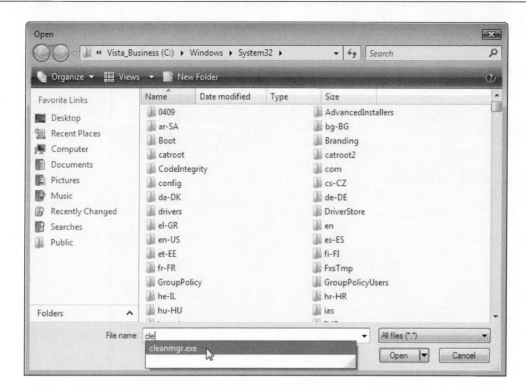

When the "Start a Program" screen re-opens, click **Next**.

The "Summary" screen appears.

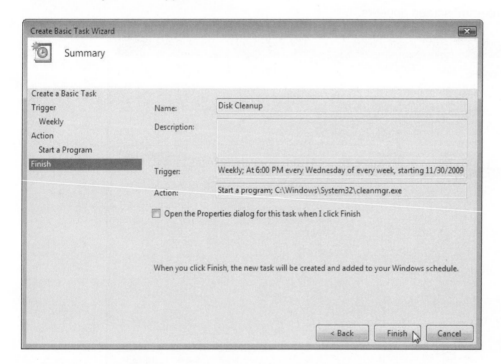

Click **Finish**.

Step 4

The "Task Scheduler" window opens.

Drag the center screen scroll bar to the bottom of the screen.

Next, drag the **Task Name** scroll bar down until you see the task **Disk Cleanup** you created.

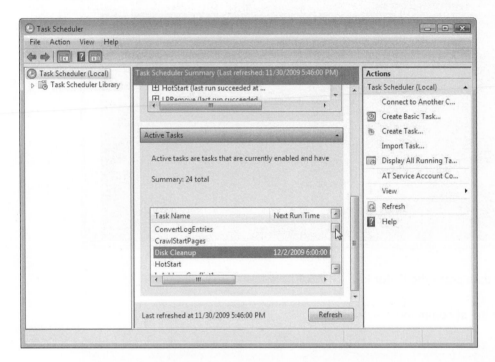

Minimize the "Task Scheduler" window and close all other windows.

Step 5

Click **Start**, and then in the **Start Search** field, type **cmd**.

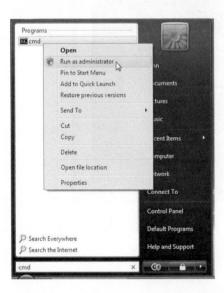

Right-click **cmd > Run as administrator > Continue**.

The "Administrator: C:\Windows\System32\cmd.exe" window opens.

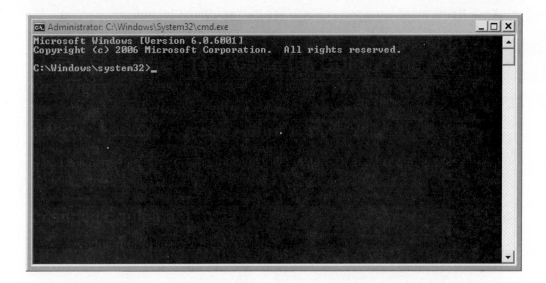

Type **at/?**, and then press the **Enter** key.

The options for the **at** command are displayed.

Type **at 20:00:00 /every:W backup**.

Note that the time must be military time.

Press **Enter**.

Added a new job with job ID = 1 is displayed.

Type **at** \\computername. For example, **at \\computer1**.

The scheduled job appears.

Which command would you enter to get the backup to run every Tuesday and Wednesday at 3:00 PM?

Type **exit**, and then press the **Enter** key.

Step 6

Open the "Scheduled Tasks" window.

Click **Task Scheduler Library**.

The task created using the **at** command is listed in the window.

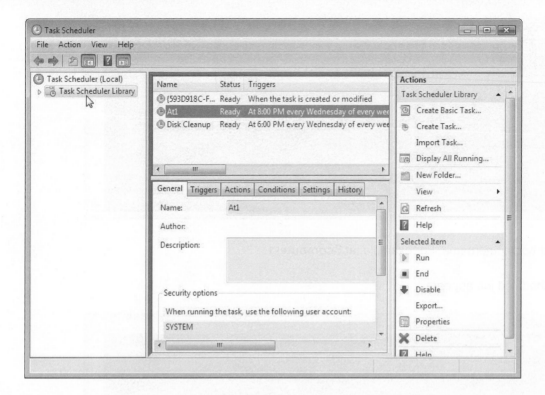

Step 7

For the scheduled tasks that you have created, right-click the scheduled task and then click **Delete**.

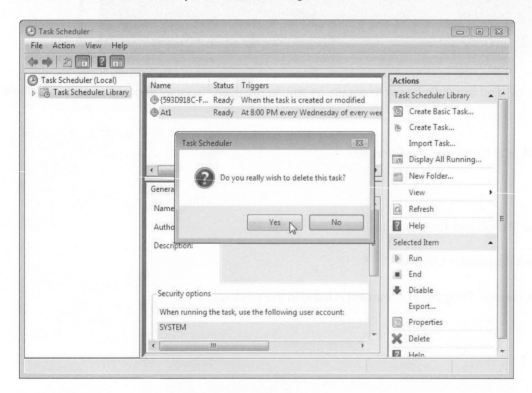

Click **Yes** to confirm you want to delete the task.

Both scheduled tasks created are removed from the scheduled tasks window.

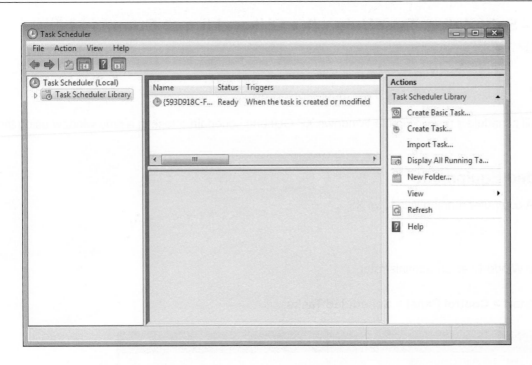

5.5.1.9 Lab - Schedule a Task Using the GUI and the at Command in Windows XP

Introduction

In this lab, you will schedule a task using the Windows XP GUI and schedule a task in a cmd window using the **at** command.

Recommended Equipment

- A computer running Windows XP

Step 1

Log on to Windows as an administrator.

Choose **Start > Control Panel > Scheduled Tasks**.

Step 2

The "Performance and Maintenance" window opens.

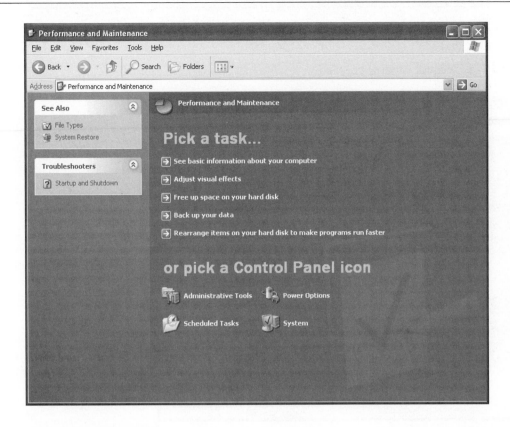

Click **Scheduled Tasks**.

Step 3

The "Scheduled Tasks" window appears.

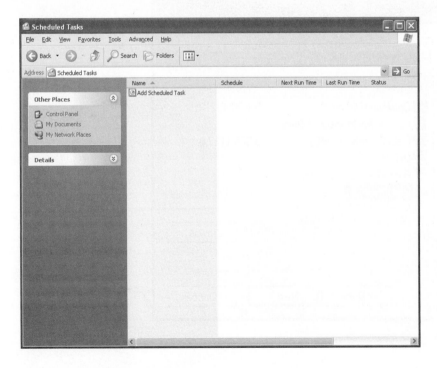

Double-click **Add Scheduled Task**.

Step 4

The "Scheduled Task Wizard" window opens.

Click **Next**.

Scroll down the Application window, and then select **Disk Cleanup**.

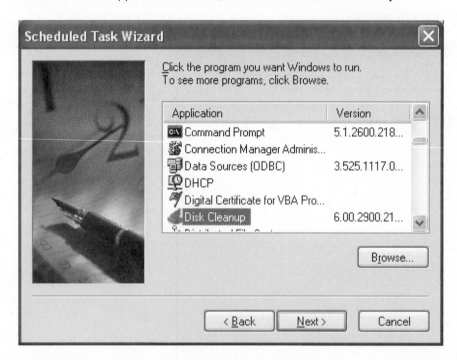

Click **Next**.

Type **Disk Cleanup** in the "Type a name for this task." field.

Select the **Weekly** radio button.

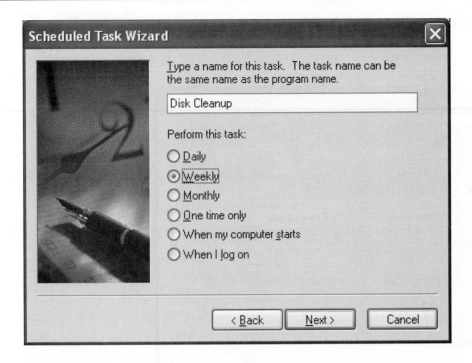

Click **Next**.

Use the scroll buttons in the "Start time:" field to select "6:00 PM".

Use the scroll buttons in the "Every _ weeks" field to select "1".

Check the "Wednesday" check box.

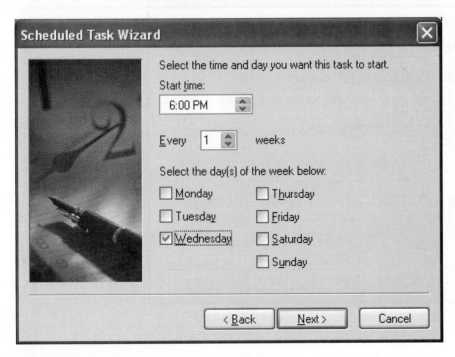

Click **Next**.

Enter your username and password in the appropriate fields.

Click **Next**.

The "You have successfully scheduled the following task:" window appears.

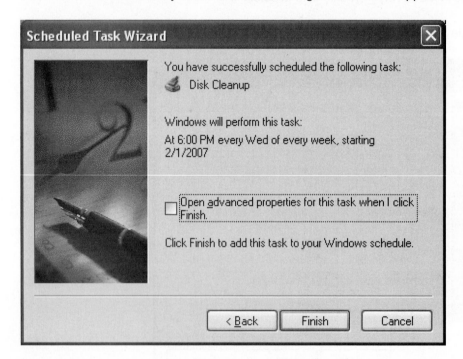

Click **Finish**.

Step 5

The scheduled task that you created appears in the "Scheduled Tasks" window.

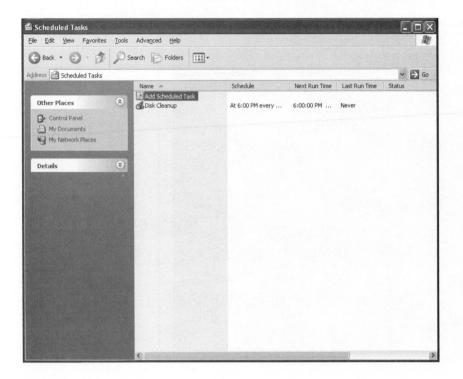

Step 6

Choose **Start > Run**.

Type **cmd**, and then click **OK**.

The "C:\WINDOWS\System32\cmd.exe" window opens.

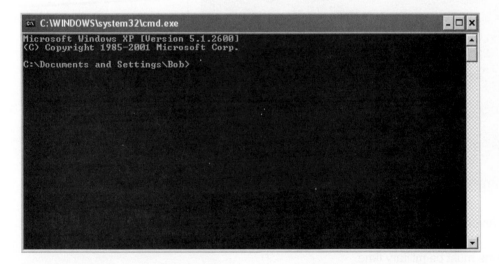

Type **at/?**, and then press the **Enter** key.

The options for the **at** command are displayed.

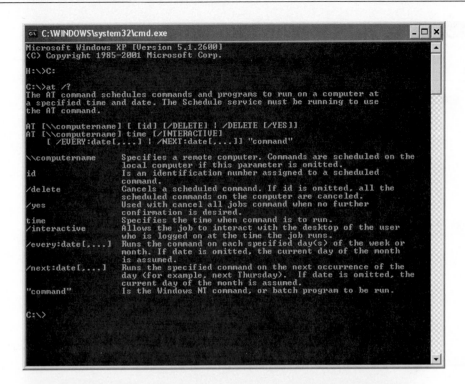

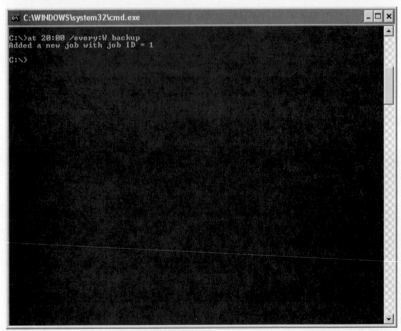

Type **at 20:00 /every:W backup**.

Note that the time must be military time.

"Added a new job with job ID = 1" is displayed.

Type **at \\computername**. For example, **at \\labcomputer**.

The scheduled job appears.

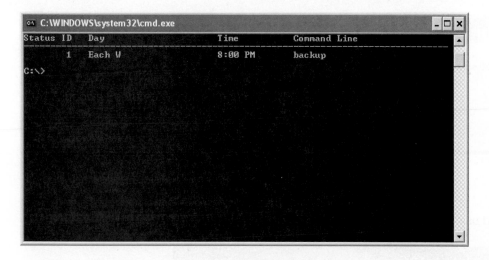

Which command would you enter to get the backup to run every Tuesday and Wednesday at 3:00 PM?

Type **exit**, and then press the **Enter** key.

Step 7

Open the Scheduled Tasks window.

The task created using the **at** command is listed in the window.

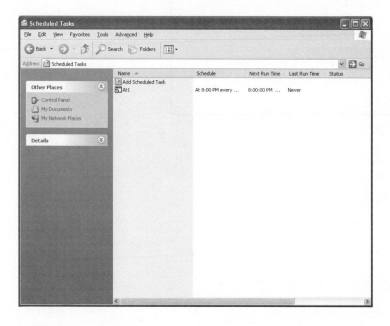

Step 8

Right-click your scheduled task.

Choose **File > Delete**.

The "Confirm File Delete" window appears.

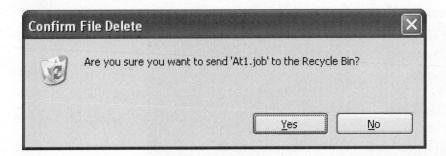

Click **Yes**.

The task created using the **at** command is removed from the scheduled tasks window.

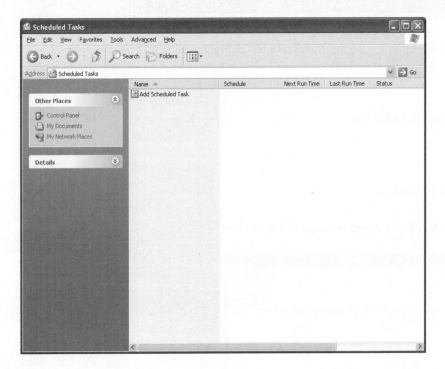

5.5.1.11 Lab - Use the System Restore Tool in Windows 7

Introduction

In this lab, you will create a restore point and return your computer back to that point in time.

Recommended Equipment

The following equipment is required for this exercise:

- A computer system running Windows 7

Step 1

Click **Start >** right-click **Computer > Properties**.

The "System" window opens.

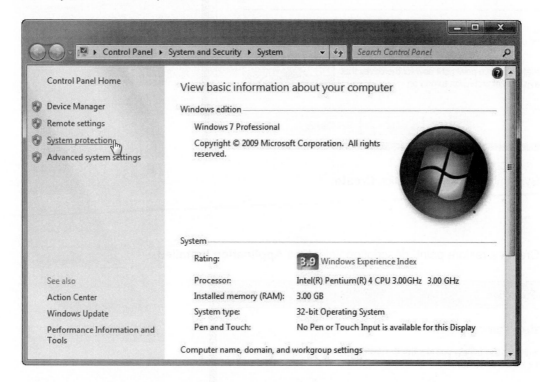

To create a restore point, click **System protection**.

Step 2

The "System Properties" window opens.

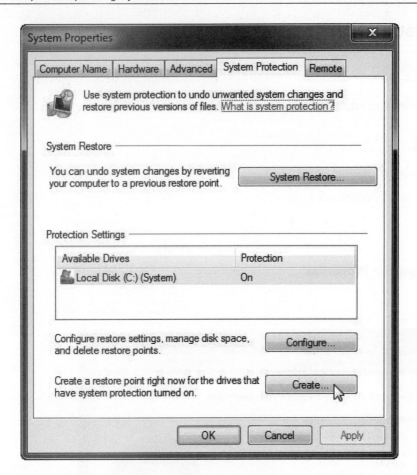

In the "System Protection" tab, click **Create**.

Step 3

In the "Create a restore point" description field, type **Application Installed**.

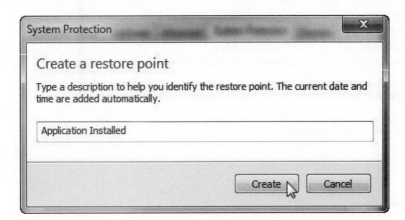

Click **Create**.

Step 4

After a period of time, a "The restore point was created successfully" message appears.

Click **Close**.

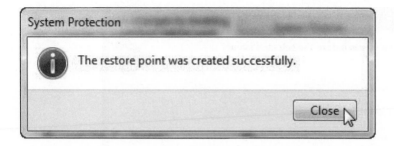

Click **OK** to close the "System Properties" window.

Step 5

Click **Start > All Programs > Accessories > System Tools > System Restore**.

When the "System Restore" Window opens, click **Next**.

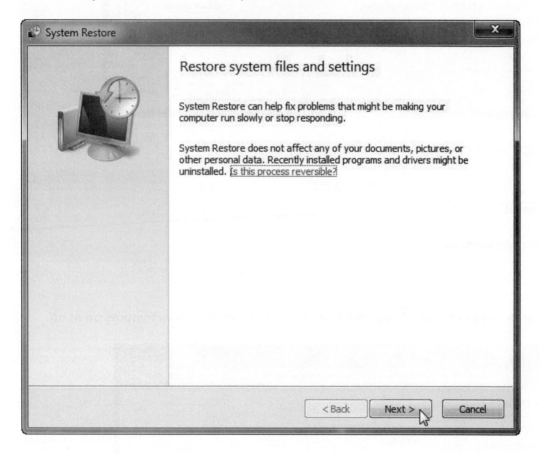

A list of restore points is displayed.

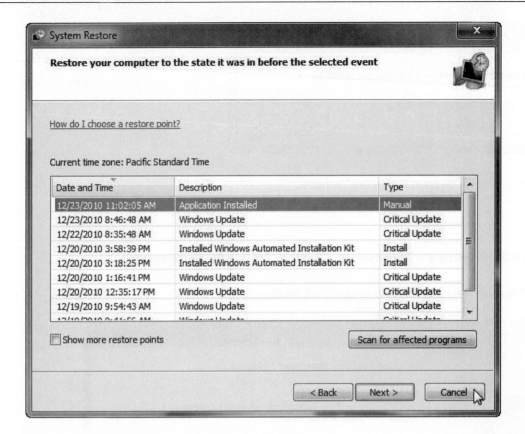

What "Type" is the restore point created by you?

Click **Cancel**.

Close all open windows.

Step 6

Click **Start > Control Panel > Programs and Features > Turn Windows features on or off**.

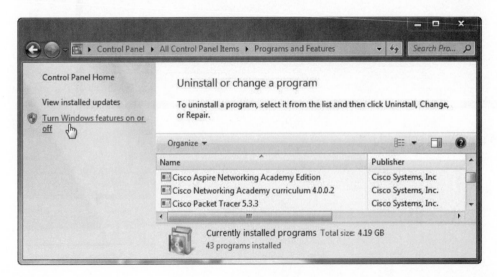

Step 7

The "Windows Features" window opens.

Click the **Internet Information Services** checkbox, and then click **OK**.

Step 8

The configuring features progress window opens.

The progress window will close on its own when the configuration is completed.

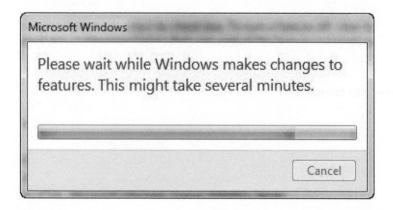

Step 9

When you navigate in a browser to localhost, you will see the new IIS default page.

Click **Start >** in "Search programs and files" type **http://localhost**.

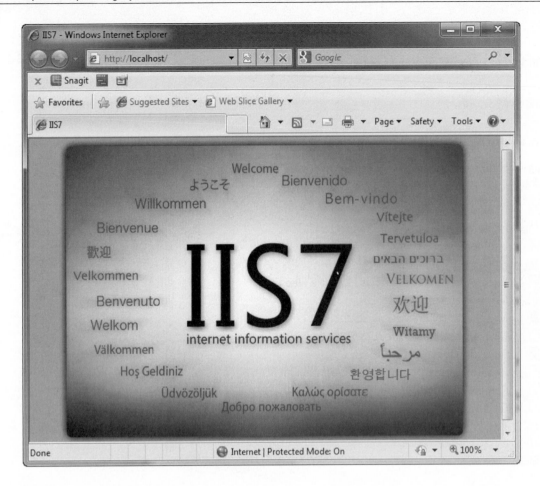

Close the browser.

Step 10

Open the Notepad application by clicking **Start > All Programs > Accessories > Notepad**.

Type **This is a test for a Restore Point** in the Notepad application.

Click **File > Save As…**.

Click **Documents**.

Type **Restore Point Test file** in the "File Name:" field.

Click **Save**.

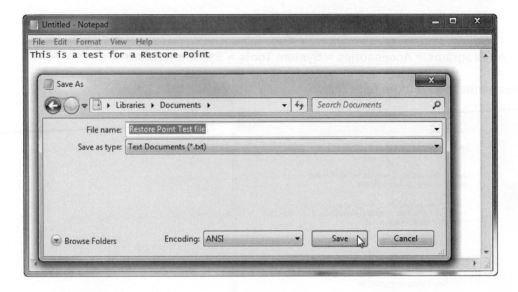

Click **File > Exit**.

Step 11

Open IIS to confirm that you have successfully installed this service.

Click **Start > Control Panel > System and Security > Administrative Tools > Internet Information Services (IIS) Manager**.

The "Internet Information Services (IIS) Manager" window opens.

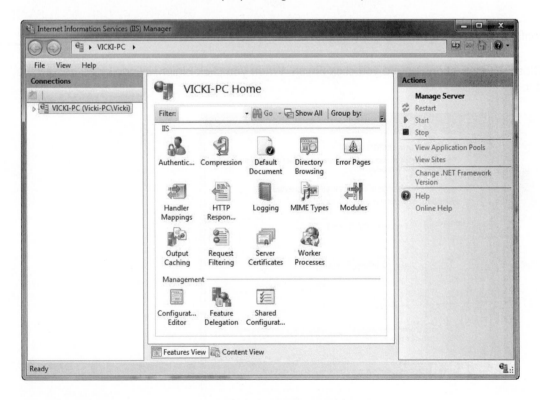

Click **File > Exit**.

Step 12

Click **Start > All Programs > Accessories > System Tools > System Restore**.

Select the **Recommended restore** radio button.

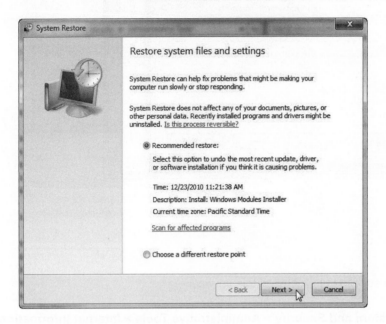

Click **Next**.

Step 13

The "Confirm your restore point" window appears.

Note: Close all applications before you click Finish. When you click Finish, Windows will restart the computer.

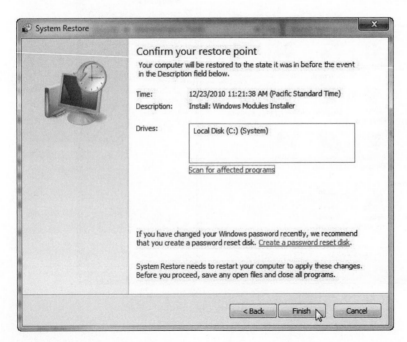

Click **Finish**.

Click **Yes** to confirm "System Restore".

The operating system restores to the point before the IIS application was installed. This can take several minutes to complete.

Step 14

Logon to the computer if required.

The "System Restore completed successfully" message appears.

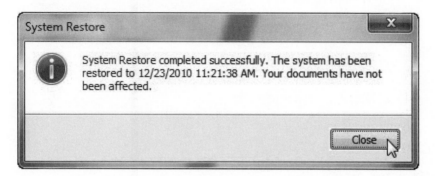

Click **Close**.

Step 15

Click **Start > Control Panel > System and Security > Administrative Tools**.

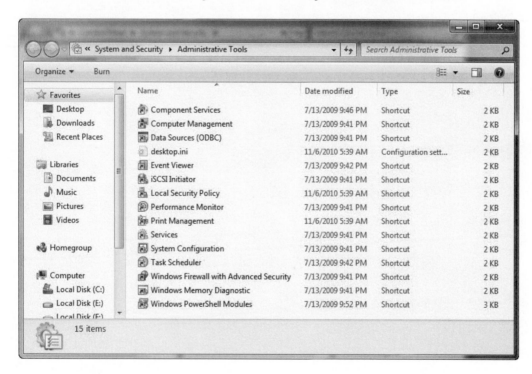

Is the IIS Manager application listed?

Step 16

Navigate to the "Documents" folder.

Open the "Restore Point Test file.txt" file.

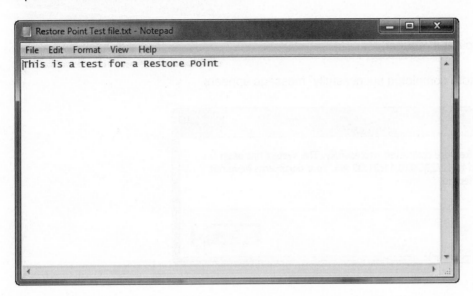

Are the contents the same?

5.5.1.12 Lab - Use the System Restore Tool in Windows Vista

Introduction

In this lab, you will create a restore point and return your computer back to that point in time.

Recommended Equipment

The following equipment is required for this exercise:

- A computer system running Windows Vista

Step 1

Click **Start > All Programs > Accessories > System Tools > System Restore**.

Click **Continue** if asked for permission.

The "System Restore" window opens.

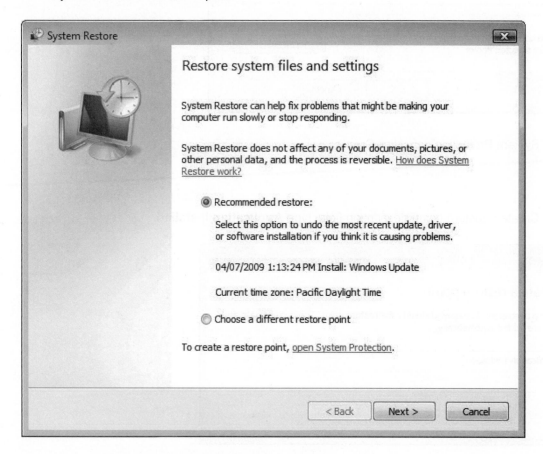

To create a restore point, click **open System Protection**.

Step 2

The "System Properties" window opens.

In the "System Protection" tab, click **Create**.

Step 3

In the "Create a restore point" description field, type **Application Installed**.

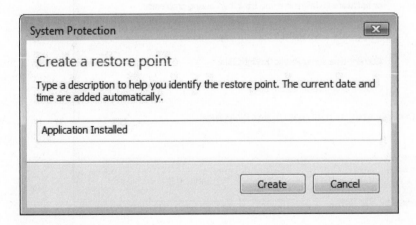

Click **Create**.

Step 4

After a period of time, a "The restore point was created successfully" message appears.

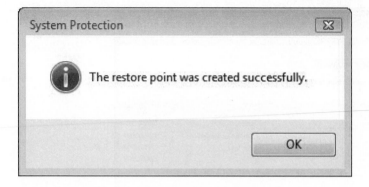

Click **OK**.

Step 5

The "System Properties" window with the "System Protection" tab selected appears. Notice in "Available Disks" area the new date below "Most recent restore point".

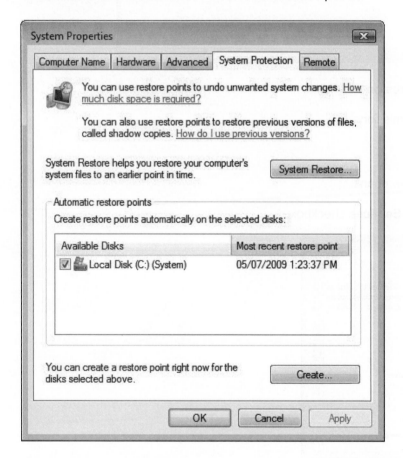

Click **OK**.

Close all open windows.

Step 6

Click **Start > Control Panel > Programs and Features**.

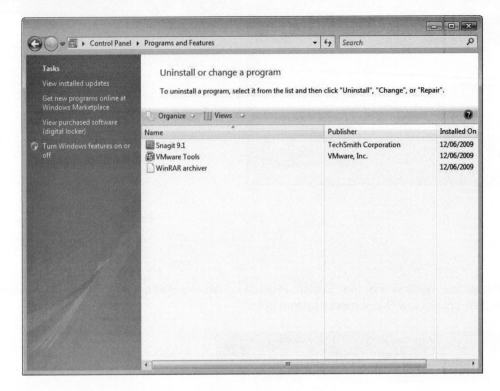

Click the **Turn Windows features on or off** link.

Click **Continue** if asked for permission.

Step 7

The "Windows Features" window opens.

Click the **Internet Information Services** checkbox.

Click **OK**.

Step 8

The configuring features progress window opens.

The progress windows will close on its own when the configuration is completed.

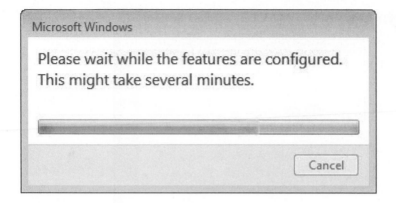

Step 9

When you navigate in a browser to localhost, you will see the new IIS default page.

Click **Start >** in **Start Search** type **http://localhost**.

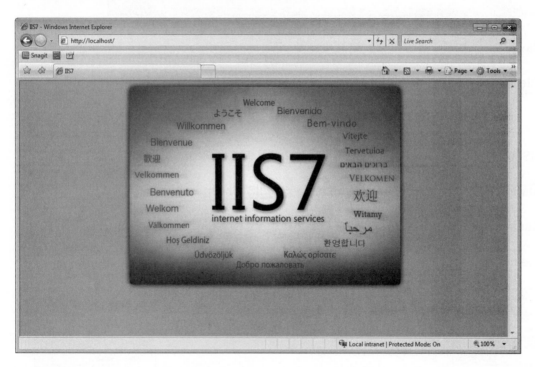

Close the browser.

Step 10

Open the Notepad application by clicking **Start > All Programs > Accessories > Notepad**.

Type **This is a test of the Restore Points** in the Notepad application.

Click **File > Save As…**.

Click **Documents**.

Type **Restore Point Test file** in the "File Name:" field.

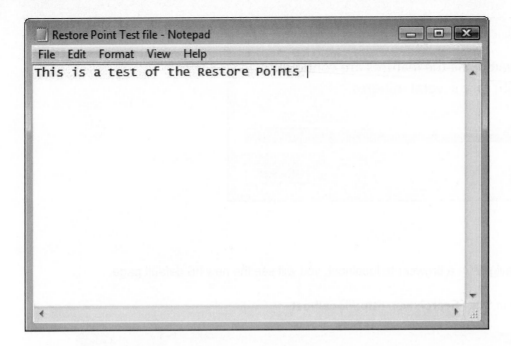

Click **Save**.

Click **File > Exit**.

Step 11

Open IIS to confirm that you have successfully installed this service.

Click **Start > All Programs > Administrative Tools > IIS Manager**.

Click **Continue** if asked for permission.

The "Internet Information Services (IIS) Manager" window opens.

Click **File > Exit**.

Step 12

Click **Start > All Programs > Accessories > System Tools > System Restore**.

Click **Continue** if asked for permission.

Select the **Recommended restore** radio button.

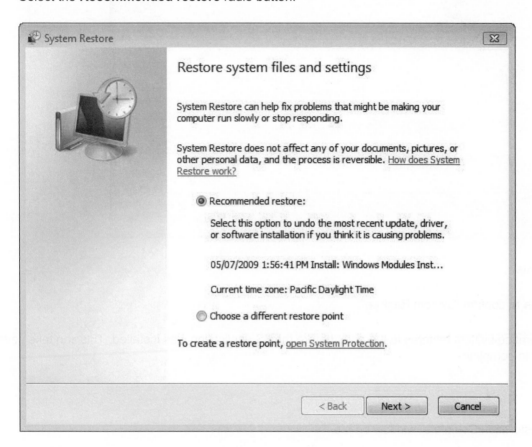

Click **Next**.

Step 13

The "Confirm your restore point" window appears.

NOTE: When you click Finish, Windows will restart the computer. Close all applications before you click Finish.

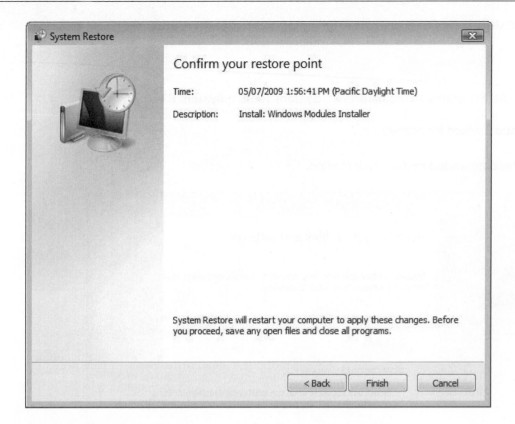

Click **Finish**.

Click **Yes** to confirm "System Restore".

The operating system restores to the point before the IIS application was installed. This can take several minutes to complete.

Step 14

The "Restoration Complete" window opens.

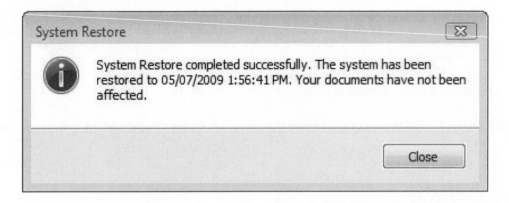

Click **Close**.

Step 15

Click **Start > Control Panel > Administrative Tools**.

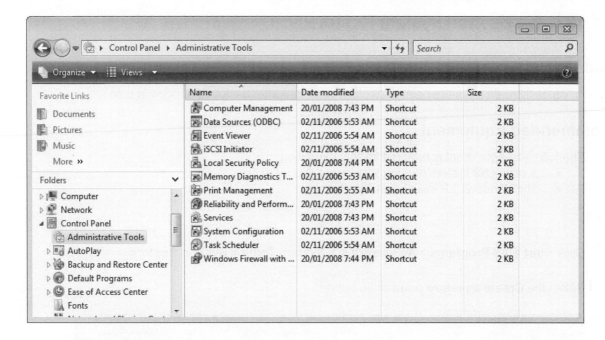

Is the IIS Manager application listed?

Step 16

Navigate to the "Documents" folder.

Open the "Restore Point Test file.txt" file.

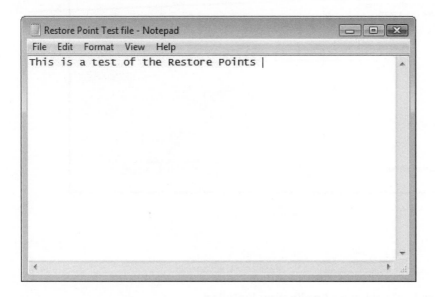

Are the contents the same?

5.5.1.13 Lab - Use the System Restore Tool in Windows XP

Introduction

In this lab, you will create a restore point and return your computer back to that point in time.

Recommended Equipment

The following equipment is required for this exercise:
- A computer system running Windows XP
- The Windows XP installation CD

Step 1

Click **Start > All Programs > Accessories > System Tools > System Restore**.

Select the **Create a restore point** radio button.

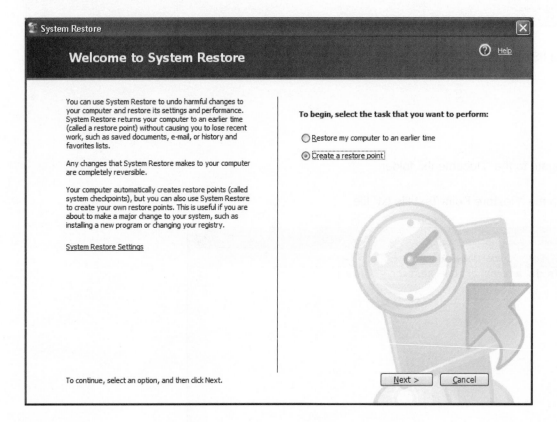

Click **Next**.

Step 2

In the "Restore point description" field, type **Application Installed**.

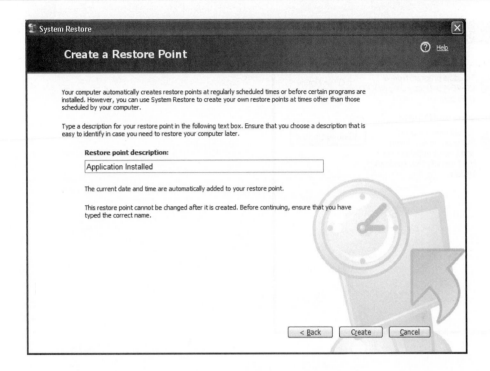

Click **Create**.

Step 3

The "Restore Point Created" window appears.

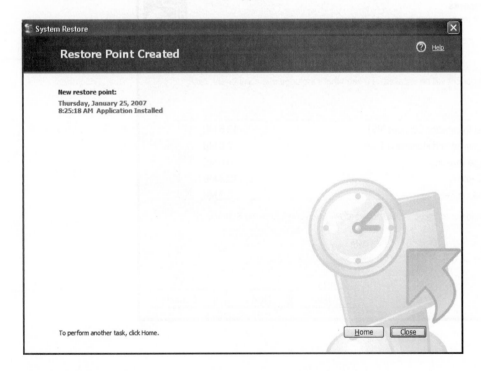

Click **Close**.

Step 4

Click **Start > Control Panel > Add or Remove Programs > Add/Remove Windows Components**.

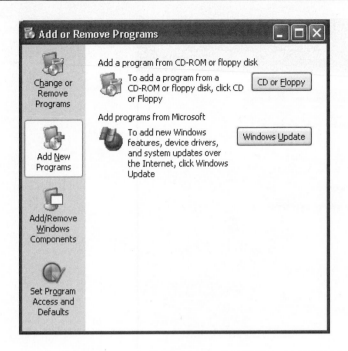

Step 5

Click the **Internet Information Services (IIS)** checkbox.

Click **Next**.

Step 6

Place the Windows XP installation CD into the optical drive.

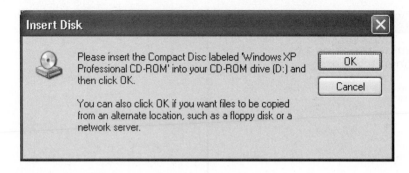

Click **OK**.

Step 7

The "Files Needed" window opens.

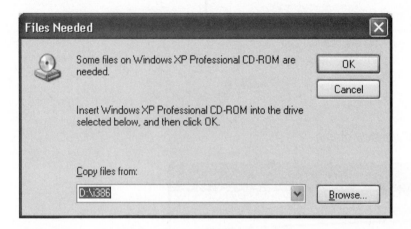

Click **OK**.

The "Configuring Components" progress window appears.

Step 8

The "Completing the Windows Components Wizard" window appears.

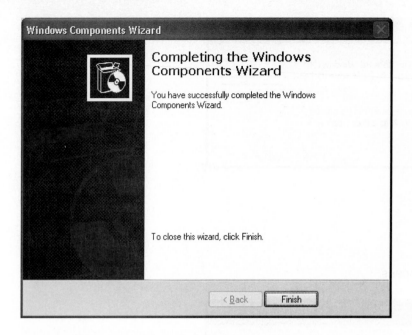

Click **Finish**.

Step 9

The "System Settings Change" window opens.

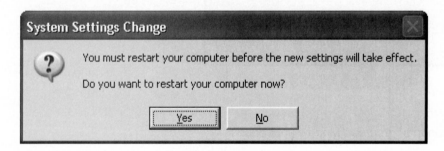

Remove the Windows XP installation disk from the optical drive.

Click **Yes**.

Step 10

Log on to Windows as yourself.

Open the Notepad application by clicking **Start > All Programs > Accessories > Notepad**.

Type **This is a test of the Restore Points** in the Notepad application.

Click **File > Save As…**.

Click **My Documents**.

Type **Restore Point Test file** in the "File Name:" field.

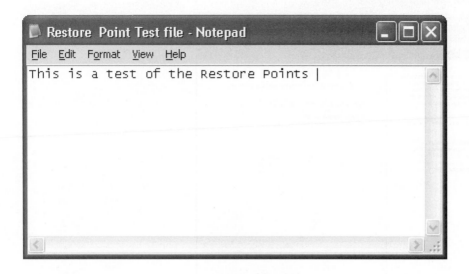

Click **Save**.

Click **File > Exit**.

Step 11

Open IIS to confirm that you have successfully installed this service.

Click **Start > All Programs > Administrative Tools > Internet Information Services**.

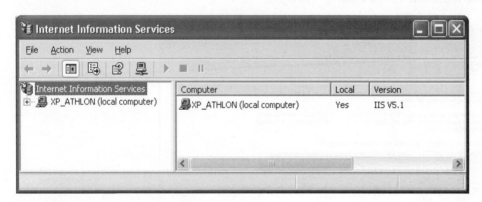

Click **File > Exit**.

Step 12

Click **Start > All Programs > Accessories > System Tools > System Restore**.

Select the **Restore my computer to an earlier time** radio button.

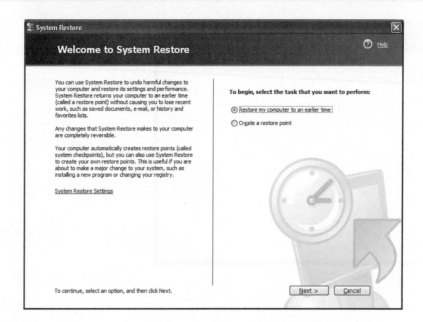

Click **Next**.

Step 13

Select today's date from the calendar on the left.

Select **Application Installed** from the list on the right.

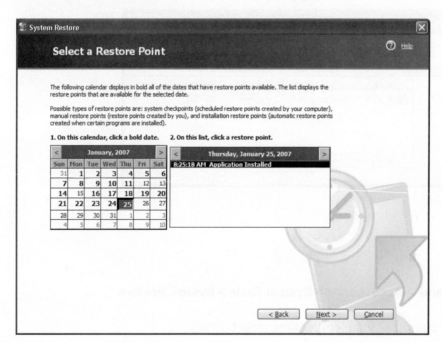

Click **Next**.

Step 14

The "Confirm Restore Point Selection" window appears.

NOTE: When you click Next, Windows will restart the computer. Close all applications before you click Next.

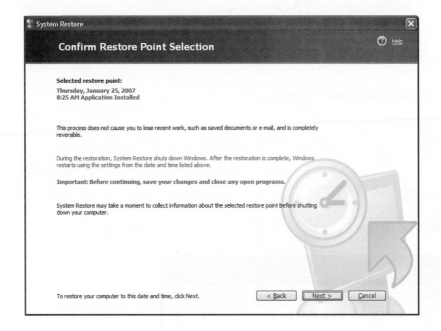

Click **Next**.

The operating system restores to the point before the IIS application was installed.

Step 15

The "Restoration Complete" screen appears.

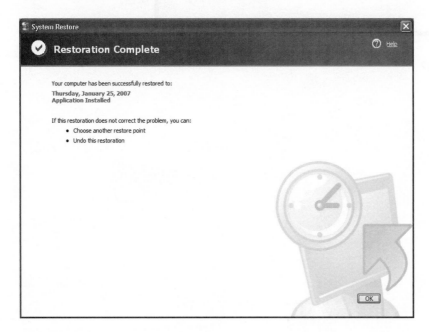

Click **OK**.

Step 16

Click **Start > All Programs > Administrative Tools**.

Is the Internet Information Services application listed?

Step 17

Navigate to the "My Documents" folder.

Open the "Restore Point Test file.txt" file.

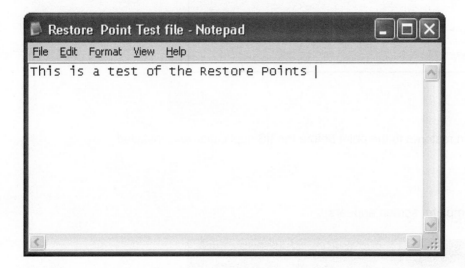

Are the contents the same?

Chapter 6: Networks

6.3.2.7 Lab - Configure a NIC to Use DHCP in Windows 7

Introduction

In this lab, you will configure an Ethernet NIC to use DHCP to obtain an IP address and test connectivity between two computers.

Recommended Equipment

- Linksys E2500 router

- Two computers running Window 7

- Ethernet patch cables

Step 1

For Host A, plug one end of the Ethernet patch cable into "Port 1" on the back of the router.

For Host A, plug the other end of the Ethernet patch cable into the network port on the NIC in your computer.

For Host B, plug one end of the Ethernet patch cable into "Port 2" on the back of the router.

For Host B, plug the other end of the Ethernet patch cable into the network port on the NIC in your computer.

Plug in the power cable of the router if it is not already plugged in.

Turn on both computers and log on to Windows in Host A as an administrator.

Click **Start** > **Control Panel > Network and Sharing Center**.

The "Network and Sharing Center" window opens.

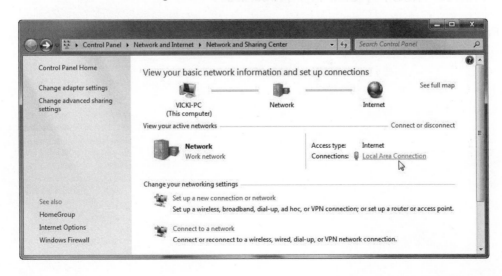

Step 2

Click **Local Area Connection > Properties**.

The "Local Area Connection Properties" window appears.

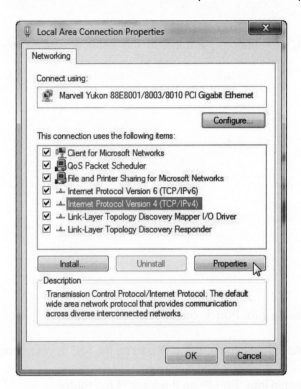

What is the name and model number of the NIC in the "Connect using:" field?

What are the items listed in the "This connection uses the following items:" field?

Step 3

Select **Internet Protocol Version 4 (TCP/IPv4) > Properties**.

The "Internet Protocol Version 4 (TCP/IPv4) Properties" window opens.

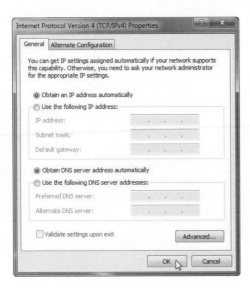

What is listed for the IP address, Subnet mask, and Default gateway in the fields of the "Use the following IP address:" area?

Select the **Obtain an IP address automatically** radio button, if it is not already selected.

Select the **Obtain DNS server address automatically** radio button, if it is not already selected.

Click **OK** to close the "Internet Protocol Version 4 (TCP/IPv4) Properties" window.

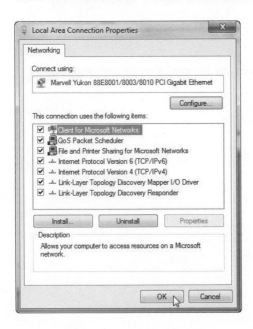

Click **OK** to close the "Local Area Connection Properties" window.

Click **Close** to close the "Local Area Connection Status" window.

Step 4

Check the lights on the back of the NIC. These lights will blink when there is network activity.

Click **Start**.

In **Search programs and files** box, type **cmd** and press **Enter** to open a command window.

Type **ipconfig /all**, and then press the **Enter** key.

What is the IP address of the computer?

What is the subnet mask of the computer?

What is the default gateway of the computer?

What are the DNS servers for the computer?

What is the MAC address of the computer?

Is DHCP enabled?

What is the IP address of the DHCP server?

On what date was the Lease Obtained?

On what date does the Lease Expire?

Step 5

Type **ping** *your IP address*. For example, **ping 192.168.1.112**.

```
C:\Windows\system32\cmd.exe

C:\Users\Vicki>ping 192.168.1.112

Pinging 192.168.1.112 with 32 bytes of data:
Reply from 192.168.1.112: bytes=32 time<1ms TTL=128
Reply from 192.168.1.112: bytes=32 time<1ms TTL=128
Reply from 192.168.1.112: bytes=32 time<1ms TTL=128
Reply from 192.168.1.112: bytes=32 time<1ms TTL=128

Ping statistics for 192.168.1.112:
    Packets: Sent = 4, Received = 4, Lost = 0 (0% loss),
Approximate round trip times in milli-seconds:
    Minimum = 0ms, Maximum = 0ms, Average = 0ms

C:\Users\Vicki>
```

Record one of the replies from your ping command.

If the ping was not successful, ask the instructor for assistance.

Step 6

Log in to Host B as an administrator and ensure the **Obtain an IP address automatically** and the **Obtain DNS server address automatically** radio buttons are selected.

Click **OK > OK**.

Open a command window.

Type **ipconfig /all**.

What is the IP address of the computer?

What is the subnet mask of the computer?

What is the default gateway of the computer?

What are the DNS servers for the computer?

What is the IP address of the DHCP server?

Step 7

Select the radio buttons **Use the following IP address** and **Use the following DNS server address**.

Enter in the IP address information for the NIC from the previous step.

Click **OK > OK.**

Open the command window.

Type **ping** *IP address for Host B.*

If the ping was not successful, ask the instructor for assistance.

Step 8

From Host B, type **ping** *IP address for Host A.*

Was the ping successful?

From Host A, type **ping** *IP address for Host B.*

Was the ping successful?

Step 9

Return configurations to the settings at the start of the lab, unless stated otherwise by the instructor.

Set the NIC to **Obtain an IP address automatically** and **Obtain DNS server address automatically**.

Click **OK > OK.**

6.3.2.8 Lab - Configure a NIC to Use DHCP in Windows Vista

Introduction

In this lab, you will configure an Ethernet NIC to use DHCP to obtain an IP address and test connectivity between two computers.

Recommended Equipment

- Linksys E2500 router

- Two computers running Window Vista

- Ethernet patch cables

Step 1

For Host A, plug one end of the Ethernet patch cable into "Port 1" on the back of the router.

For Host A, plug the other end of the Ethernet patch cable into the network port on the NIC in your computer.

For Host B, plug one end of the Ethernet patch cable into "Port 2" on the back of the router.

For Host B, plug the other end of the Ethernet patch cable into the network port on the NIC in your computer.

Plug in the power cable of the router if it is not already plugged in.

Turn on both computers and log on to Windows in Host A as an administrator.

Click **Start > Control Panel > Network and Sharing Center**.

The "Network and Sharing Center" window appears.

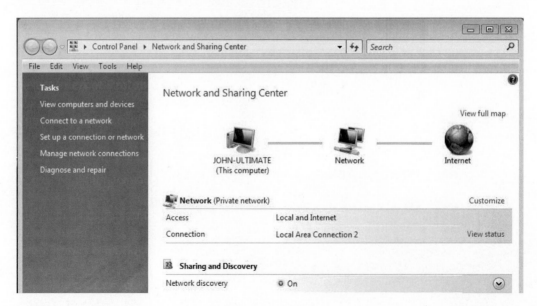

Step 2

Click **View status**, and then choose **Properties > Continue** if asked.

The "Local Area Connection Properties" window opens.

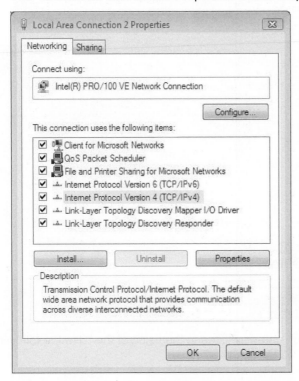

What is the name and model number of the NIC in the "Connect using:" field?

What are the items listed in the "This connection uses the following items:" field?

Step 3

Select **Internet Protocol Version 4 (TCP/IPv4)**.

Click **Properties**.

The "Internet Protocol Version 4 (TCP/IPv4) Properties" window opens.

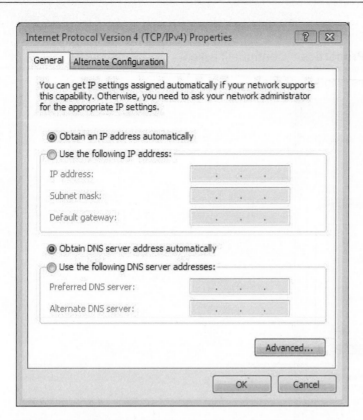

What is the IP address, Subnet mask, and Default gateway listed in the fields of the "Use the following IP address:" area?

Select the **Obtain an IP address automatically** radio button, if it is not already selected.

Select the **Obtain DNS server address automatically** radio button, if it is not already selected.

Click **OK**.

The "Internet Protocol Version 4 (TCP/IPv4) Properties" window closes.

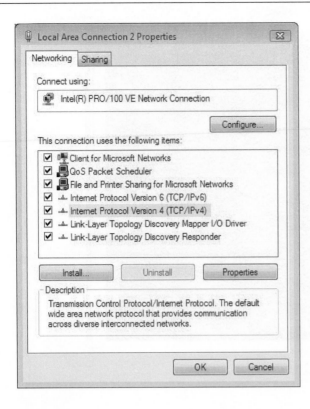

Click **OK**.

Step 4

Check the lights on the back of the NIC. These lights will blink when there is network activity.

Click **Start**.

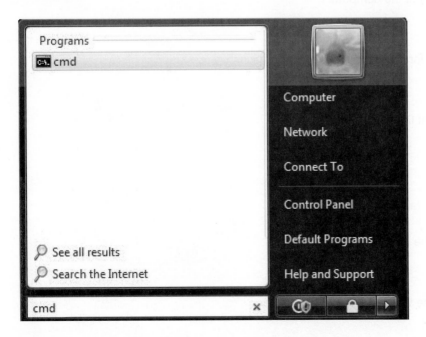

In **Start Search**, type **cmd** and press **Enter**.

The "cmd.exe" window opens.

```
C:\Windows\system32\cmd.exe                                              _ □ ×
Microsoft Windows [Version 6.0.6000]
Copyright (c) 2006 Microsoft Corporation.  All rights reserved.

C:\Users\John>ipconfig /all

Windows IP Configuration

   Host Name . . . . . . . . . . . . : John-Ultimate
   Primary Dns Suffix  . . . . . . . :
   Node Type . . . . . . . . . . . . : Hybrid
   IP Routing Enabled. . . . . . . . : No
   WINS Proxy Enabled. . . . . . . . : No
   DNS Suffix Search List. . . . . . : va.shawcable.net

Ethernet adapter Local Area Connection 2:

   Connection-specific DNS Suffix  . : va.shawcable.net
   Description . . . . . . . . . . . : Intel(R) PRO/100 UE Network Connection
   Physical Address. . . . . . . . . : 00-03-47-C1-EA-5D
   DHCP Enabled. . . . . . . . . . . : Yes
   Autoconfiguration Enabled . . . . : Yes
   Link-local IPv6 Address . . . . . : fe80::7cb1:a08a:7079:435d%9(Preferred)
   IPv4 Address. . . . . . . . . . . : 192.168.1.113(Preferred)
   Subnet Mask . . . . . . . . . . . : 255.255.255.0
   Lease Obtained. . . . . . . . . . : June-07-09 1:31:46 PM
   Lease Expires . . . . . . . . . . : June-08-09 1:31:46 PM
   Default Gateway . . . . . . . . . : 192.168.1.1
   DHCP Server . . . . . . . . . . . : 192.168.1.1
   DHCPv6 IAID . . . . . . . . . . . : 234881863
   DNS Servers . . . . . . . . . . . : 64.59.144.18
                                       64.59.144.19
   NetBIOS over Tcpip. . . . . . . . : Enabled
```

Type **ipconfig /all**, and then press **Enter**.

What is the IP address of the computer?

What is the subnet mask of the computer?

What is the default gateway of the computer?

What are the DNS servers for the computer?

What is the MAC address of the comptuer?

Is DHCP enabled?

What is the IP address of the DHCP server?

On what date was the Lease Obtained?

On what date does the Lease Expire?

Step 5

Type **ping** *your IP address*. For example, **ping 192.168.1.113**.

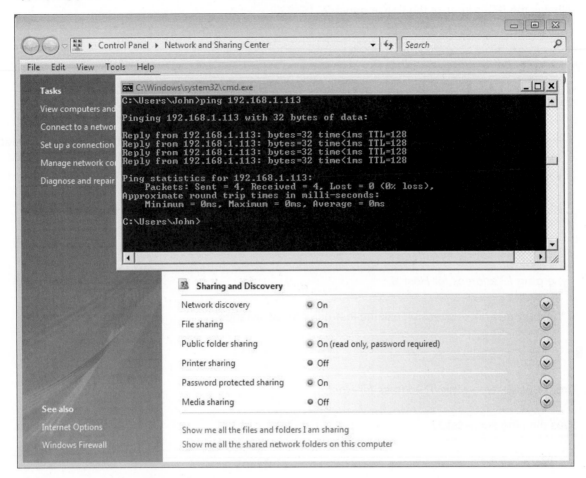

Record one of the replies of your ping command.

If the ping was not successful, ask the instructor for assistance.

Step 6

Login to Host B as an administrator and make sure the **Obtain an IP address automatically** and the **Obtain DNS server address automatically** radio buttons are selected.

Click **OK > OK**.

Open a command window.

Type **ipconfig /all** in the command window.

What is the IP address of the computer?

What is the subnet mask of the computer?

What is the default gateway of the computer?

What are the DNS servers for the computer?

What is the IP address of the DHCP server?

Step 7

Return to the "Internet Protocol Version 4 (TCP?IP4) Properties" window.

Select the radio buttons **Use the following IP address** and **Use the following DNS server address**.

Enter in the IP address information for the NIC.

Click **OK > OK**.

Open the command window.

Type **ping** *IP address for Host B*.

If the ping was not successful, ask the instructor for assistance.

Step 8

From Host B, type **ping** *IP address for Host A*.

Was the ping successful?

From Host A, type **ping** *IP address for Host B*.

Was the ping successful?

Step 9

Return configurations to the settings at the start of the lab, unless stated otherwise by the instructor.

Select the radio buttons **Obtain an IP address automatically** and **Obtain DNS server address automatically**.

Click **OK > OK**.

6.3.2.9 Lab - Configure a NIC to Use DHCP in Windows XP

Introduction

In this lab, you will configure an Ethernet NIC to use DHCP to obtain an IP address and test connectivity between two computers.

Recommended Equipment

- Linksys E2500 router

- Two computers running Window XP Professional

- Ethernet patch cables

Step 1

For Host A, plug one end of the Ethernet patch cable into "Port 1" on the back of the router.

For Host A, plug the other end of the Ethernet patch cable into the network port on the NIC in your computer.

For Host B, plug one end of the Ethernet patch cable into "Port 2" on the back of the router.

For Host B, plug the other end of the Ethernet patch cable into the network port on the NIC in your computer.

Plug in the power cable of the router if it is not already plugged in.

Turn on both computers and log on to Windows in Host A as an administrator.

Click **Start > Control Panel > Network Connections**.

The "Network Connections" window opens.

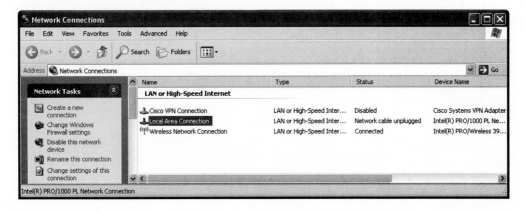

Step 2

Right-click **Local Area Connection**, and then choose **Properties**.

The "Local Area Connection Properties" window opens.

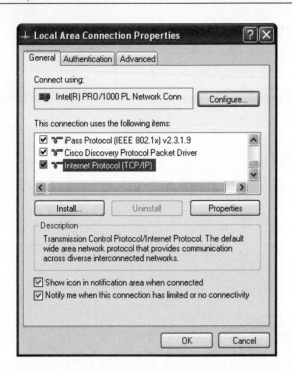

What is the name and model number of the NIC in the "Connect using:" field?

What are the items listed in the "This connection uses the following items:" field?

Step 3

Select **Internet Protocol (TCP/IP)**.

Click **Properties**.

The "Internet Protocol (TCP/IP) Properties" window opens.

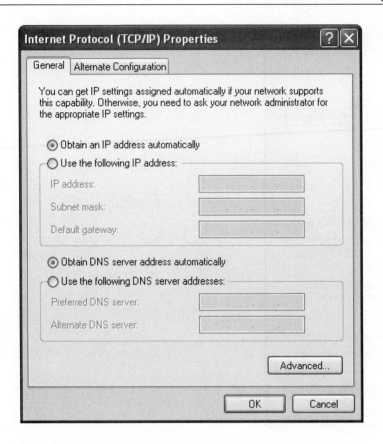

What is the IP address, Subnet mask, and Default gateway listed in the fields of the "Use the following IP address:" area?

Select the **Obtain an IP address automatically** radio button, if it is not already selected.

Select the **Obtain DNS server address automatically** radio button, if it is not already selected.

Click **OK**.

The "Internet Protocol (TCP/IP) Properties" window closes.

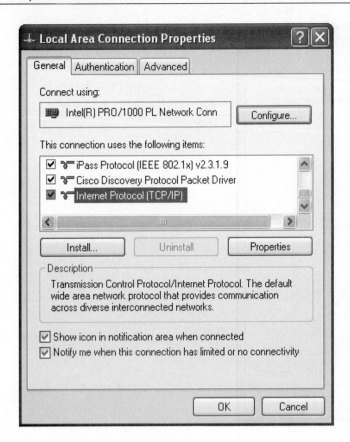

Click **OK**.

Step 4

Check the lights on the back of the NIC. These lights will blink when there is network activity.

Choose **Start > Run...**.

The "Run" window opens.

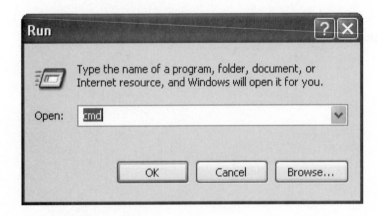

Type **cmd** and click **OK**.

The "cmd.exe" window opens.

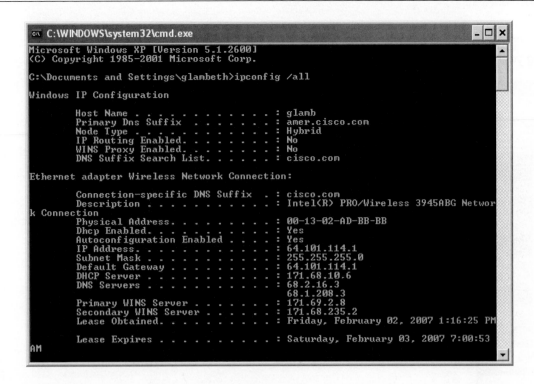

Type **ipconfig /all**, and then press the **Enter** key.

What is the IP address of the computer?

What is the subnet mask of the computer?

What is the default gateway of the computer?

What are the DNS servers for the computer?

What is the MAC address of the comptuer?

Is DHCP enabled?

What is the IP address of the DHCP server?

On what date was the Lease Obtained?

On what date does the Lease Expire?

Step 5

Type **ping** *your IP address*. For example, **ping 192.168.1.103**.

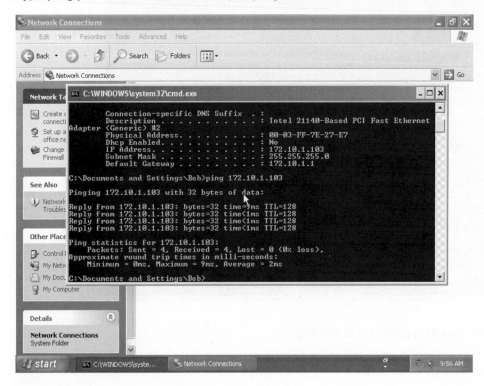

Write one of the replies of your ping command.

If the ping was not successful, ask the instructor for assistance.

Step 6

Login to Host B as an administrator and make sure the **Obtain an IP address automatically** and the **Obtain DNS server address automatically** radio buttons are selected.

Click **OK > OK**.

Open a command window.

Type **ipconfig /all**.

What is the IP address of the computer?

What is the subnet mask of the computer?

What is the default gateway of the computer?

What are the DNS servers for the computer?

What is the IP address of the DHCP server?

Step 7

Return to "Internet Protocol (TCP/IP) Properties" window.

Select the radio buttons **Use the following IP address** and **Use the following DNS server address**.

Enter in the IP address information for the NIC from the previous step.

Click **OK > OK**.

Open the command window.

Type **ping** *IP address for Host B.*

If the ping was not successful, ask the instructor for assistance.

Step 8

From Host B, type **ping** *IP address for Host A.*

Was the ping successful?

From Host A, type **ping** *IP address for Host B.*

Was the ping successful?

Step 9

Return configurations to the settings at the start of the lab, unless stated otherwise by the instructor.

Select the radio buttons **Obtain an IP address automatically** and **Obtain DNS server address automatically**.

Click **OK > OK**.

6.3.3.4 Worksheet - Protocol Definitions and Default Ports

In this worksheet, you will write the name of the protocol and the default port(s) for each protocol definition in the table.

Be prepared to discuss your answers.

Protocol Definition	Protocol	Default Port(s)
Provides connections to computers over a TCP/IP network		
Sends email over a TCP/IP network		
Translates URLs to IP address		
Transports Web pages over a TCP/IP network		
Automates assignment of IP address on a network		
Securely transports Web pages over a TCP/IP network		
Transports files over a TCP/IP network		
Manage and monitor devices on a network		
Download email from an email server		
Access information directories		
Remote access to computers (MSTSC)		
Secured file transfer system		
Provides shared access to file and printers		
Provides no Internet access in a workgroup network		

6.4.2.4 Lab - Building Straight-Through and Crossover UTP Cables

Introduction

In this lab, you will build and test straight-through and crossover Unshielded Twisted-Pair (UTP) Ethernet network cables.

Note: With a straight-through cable, the color of wire used by pin 1 on one end is the same color used by pin 1 on the other cable end, and similarly for the remaining seven pins. The cable will be constructed using either TIA/EIA T568A or T568B standards for Ethernet, which determines the color wire to be used on each pin. Straight-through patch cables are normally used to connect a host directly to a hub or switch or to a wall plate in an office area.

With a crossover cable, the second and third pairs on the RJ-45 connector at one end of the cable are reversed at the other end. The pin-outs for the cable are the T568A standard on one end and the T568B standard on the other end. Crossover cables are normally used to connect hubs and switches or can be used to directly connect two hosts to create a simple network.

Recommended Equipment

- Two 0.6 to 0.9m (2 to 3 ft.) lengths of cable, Category 5 or 5e
- A minimum of four RJ-45 connectors (more may be needed if mis-wiring occurs)
- An RJ-45 crimping tool
- Two computers with Windows 7, Windows Vista, or Windows XP.
- Wire cutters
- Wire stripper

Wire Diagrams

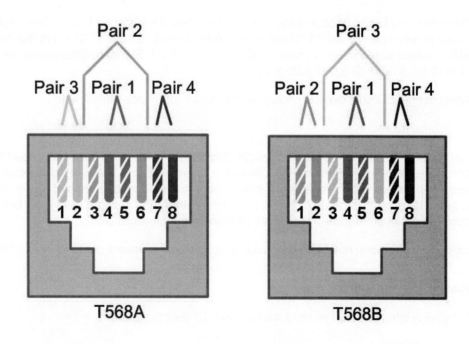

T568A Standard			
Pin No.	**Pair No.**	**Wire Color**	**Function**
1	3	White/Green	Transmit
2	3	Green	Transmit
3	2	White/Orange	Receive
4	1	Blue	Not used
5	1	White/Blue	Not used
6	2	Orange	Receive
7	4	White/Brown	Not used
8	4	Brown	Not used

T568B Standard			
Pin No.	**Pair No.**	**Wire Color**	**Function**
1	2	White/Orange	Transmit
2	2	Orange	Transmit
3	3	White/Green	Receive
4	1	Blue	Not used
5	1	White/Blue	Not used
6	3	Green	Receive
7	4	White/Brown	Not used
8	4	Brown	Not used

Build and test an Ethernet straight-through patch cable

Step 1: Obtain and prepare the cable

a. Determine the length of cable required. This could be the distance from a computer to a switch or between a device and an RJ-45 outlet jack. Add at least 30.48 cm (12 in.) to the distance. The TIA/EIA standard states the maximum length is 5 m (16.4 ft.). Standard Ethernet cable lengths are usually .6 m (2 ft.), 1.83 m (6 ft.), or 3.05 m (10 ft.).

b. Which length of cable did you choose and why did you choose this length?

c. Cut a piece of cable to the desired length. Stranded UTP cable is commonly used for patch cables (the cables between an end network device such as a PC and an RJ-45 connector) because it is more durable when bent repeatedly. It is called stranded because each of the wires within the cable is made up of many strands of fine copper wire, rather than a single solid wire. Solid wire is used for cable runs that are between the RJ-45 jack and a punch-down block.

d. Using wire strippers, remove 5.08 cm (2 in.) of the cable jacket from both ends of the cable.

Step 2: Prepare and insert the wires

a. Determine which wiring standard will be used. Circle the standard.

[T568A | T568B]

b. Locate the correct table or figure from the "Wire Diagrams" based on the wiring standard used.

c. Spread the cable pairs and arrange them roughly in the desired order based on the standard chosen.

d. Untwist a short length of the pairs and arrange them in the exact order needed by the standard moving left to right starting with pin 1. **It is very important to untwist as little as possible. The twists are important because they provide noise cancellation**.

e. Straighten and flatten the wires between your thumb and forefinger.

f. Ensure the cable wires are still in the correct order as the standard.

g. Cut the cable in a straight line to within 1.25 to 1.9 cm (1/2 to 3/4 in.) from the edge of the cable jacket. If it is longer than this, the cable will be susceptible to crosstalk (the interference of bits from one wire with an adjacent wire).

h. The key (the prong that sticks out from the RJ-45 connector) should be on the underside pointing downward when inserting the wires. Ensure the wires are in order from left to right starting with pin 1. Insert the wires firmly into the RJ-45 connector until all wires are pushed as far as possible into the connector.

Step 3: Inspect, crimp, and re-inspect

a. Visually inspect the cable and ensure the right color codes are connected to the correct pin numbers.

b. Visually inspect the end of the connector. The eight wires should be pressed firmly against the end of the RJ-45 connector. Some of the cable jacket should be inside the first portion of the connector. This provides strain relief for the cable. If the cable jacket is not far enough inside the connector, it may eventually cause the cable to fail.

c. If everything is correctly aligned and inserted properly, place the RJ-45 connector and cable into the crimper. The crimper will push two plungers down on the RJ-45 connector.

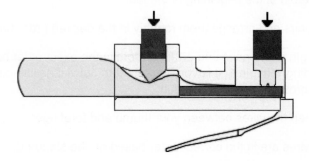

d. Visually re-inspect the connector. If improperly installed, cut the end off and repeat the process.

Step 4: Terminate the other cable end

a. Use the previously described steps to attach an RJ-45 connector to the other end of the cable.

b. Visually re-inspect the connector. If improperly installed, cut the end off and repeat the process.

c. Which standard [T568A | T568B] is used for patch cables in your school?

Step 5: Test the cable

a. Use the cable to connect a PC to a network.

b. Visually check the LED status lights on the NIC card. If they are on (usually green or amber), the cable is functional.

c. On the PC, open the command prompt.

     d.   Type **ipconfig**.

     e.   Write down the default gateway IP address.

     f.   From the command prompt, type **ping** *default gateway IP address*. If the cable is functional, the ping should be successful (provided that no other network problem exists and the default gateway router is connected and functional).

     g.   Was the ping successful?

     h.   If the ping fails, repeat the lab.

Build and test an Ethernet crossover cable

Step 1: Obtain and prepare the cable

     a.   Determine the length of cable required. This could be from a hub to a hub, hub to switch, switch to switch, computer to router, or from one computer to another computer. Add at least 30.48 cm (12 in.) to the distance. Which length of cable did you choose and why did you choose this length?

     b.   Cut a piece of cable to the desired length and, using wire strippers, remove 5.08 cm (2 in.) of the cable jacket from both ends of the cable.

Step 2: Prepare and insert the T568A wires

     a.   Locate the T568A table at the beginning of the lab.

     b.   Spread the cable pairs and arrange them roughly in the desired order based on the T568A standard.

     c.   Untwist a short length of the pairs and arrange them in the exact order needed by the standard moving left to right starting with pin 1. It is very important to untwist as little as possible. Twists are important because they provide noise cancellation.

     d.   Straighten and flatten the wires between your thumb and forefinger.

     e.   Ensure the cable wires are in the correct order based on the standard.

     f.   Cut the cable in a straight line to within 1.25 to 1.9 cm (1/2 to 3/4 in.) from the edge of the cable jacket. If it is longer than this, the cable will be susceptible to crosstalk (the interference of bits from one wire with an adjacent wire).

     g.   The key (the prong that sticks out from the RJ-45 connector) should be on the underside pointing downward when inserting the wires. Ensure the wires are in order from left to right starting with pin 1. Insert the wires firmly into the RJ-45 connector until all wires are pushed as far as possible into the connector.

Step 3: Inspect, crimp, and re-inspect

     a.   Visually inspect the cable and ensure the right color codes are connected to the correct pin numbers.

     b.   Visually inspect the end of the connector. The eight wires should be pressed firmly against the RJ-45 connector. Some of the cable jacket should be inside the first portion of the connector. This provides for cable strain relief which can eventually cause the cable to fail.

     c.   If everything is correctly aligned and inserted properly, place the RJ-45 connector and cable into the crimper. The crimper will push two plungers down on the RJ-45 connector.

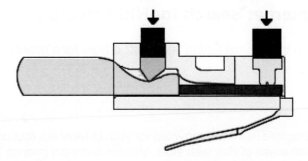

d. Visually re-inspect the connector. If improperly installed, cut the end off and repeat the process.

Step 4: Terminate the T568B cable end

a. On the other end, use the previously described steps (but use the T568B table and standard) to attach an RJ-45 connector to the cable.

b. Visually re-inspect the connector. If improperly installed, cut the end off and repeat the process.

c. Which standard [T568A | T568B] would you rather use at home if you have or would like to have a home network?

Step 5: Test the cable

a. Use the cable to connect two PCs.

b. Visually check the LED status lights on the NIC card. If they are on (usually green or amber), the cable is functional.

c. On both computers, open a command prompt.

d. On both computers, type **ipconfig**.

e. Write the IP address of both computers.

Computer 1:

Computer 2:

f. From the command prompt of one computer, type ping IP address of the other computer. If the cable is functional, the ping should be successful. Perform a ping from the other computer as well.

g. Was the ping successful?

h. If the ping fails, repeat the lab.

6.8.2.2 Worksheet - Internet Search for NIC Drivers

In this worksheet, you will search the Internet for the latest NIC drivers for a network card.

Complete the table below. An example has been provided for you. Drivers are routinely updated. Manufacturers often move driver files to different areas of their web sites. Version numbers change frequently. The driver in the example was found by visiting the manufacturer's (www.intel.com) web site. A search for the full name of the NIC was used to find the driver download file.

NIC	URL Driver Location and Latest Version Number
Cisco WMP600N Desktop Adapter for Windows 7	http://homesupport.cisco.com/en-us/support/adapters/WMP600N Ver. #3.2.7
Intel Gigabit CT Desktop Adapter for Windows 7	
Broadcom Ethernet NIC NetXtreme Desktop	

6.8.2.4 Lab - Install a Wireless NIC in Windows 7

Introduction

In this lab, you will install and configure a wireless NIC.

Recommended Equipment

- A computer with Windows 7 installed
- Empty PCI or PCIe slot on the motherboard
- A wireless PCI or PCIe NIC
- An antistatic wrist strap
- Tool kit

Step 1

Turn off your computer. If a switch is present on the power supply, set the switch to "0" or "off". Unplug the computer from the AC outlet. Remove the side panels from the case.

Put on the antistatic wrist strap and attach it to an unpainted metal surface of the computer case.

Choose an appropriate slot on the motherboard to install the new wireless NIC.

You may need to remove the metal cover near the slot on the back of the case.

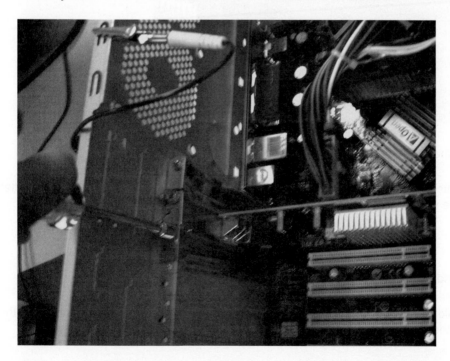

Make sure the wireless NIC is properly lined up with the slot. Push down gently on the wireless NIC.

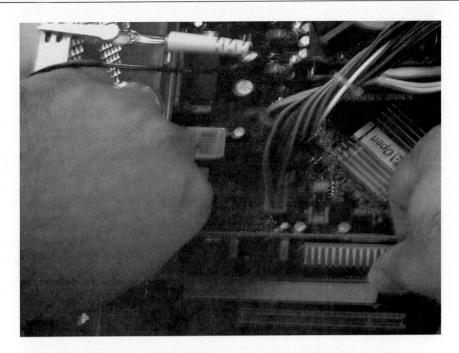

Secure the wireless NIC mounting bracket to the case with a screw.

Attach the antenna to the antenna connector on the back of the computer.

Disconnect the antistatic wrist strap. Replace the case panels. Plug the power cable into an AC outlet. If a switch is present on the power supply, set the switch to "1" or "on".

Step 2

Boot your computer, and then log on as an administrator.

The wireless NIC should be detected by Windows and drivers installed. If Windows does not have the required drivers, the "Add Hardware" screen will appear.

Click **Next**.

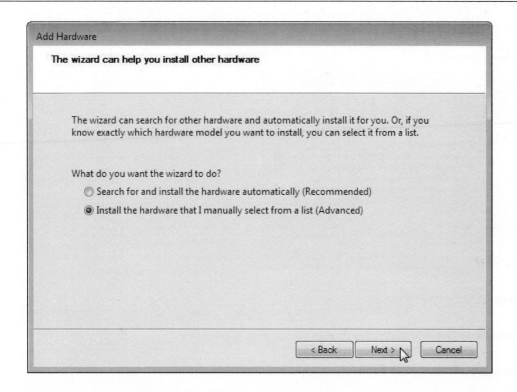

Select the **Install the hardware that I manually select from a list (Advanced)** radio button. Click **Next**.

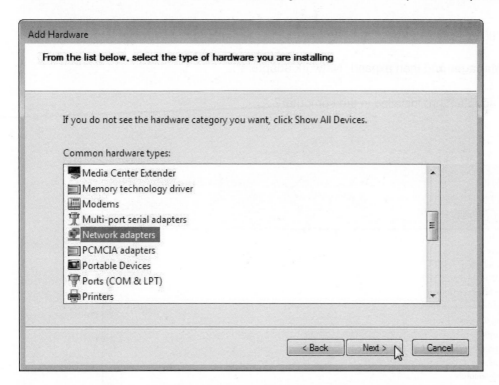

Scroll down the list, select **Network adapters**, and then click **Next**.

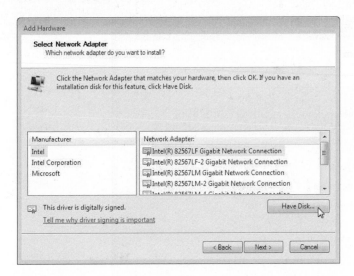

Click **Have Disk…**

Follow instruction to locate and install the drivers.

Once the drivers are installed, click **Finish** to complete the driver installation process.

Step 3

Click **Start >** right-click **Computer > Manage**.

Click **Device Manager** and then expand "Network adapters".

What network adapters are installed in the computer?

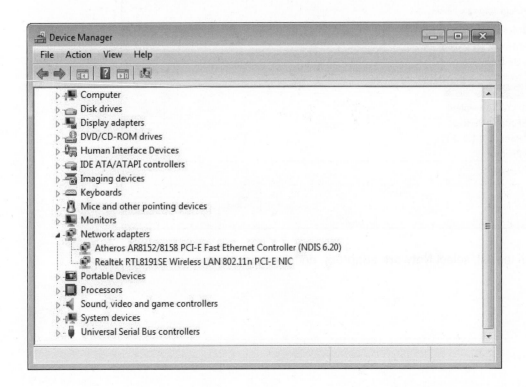

Step 4

Double-click on the network adapter you just installed to open the "Properties" window.

Click **Driver** tab **> Update Driver…**

The "Update Driver Software" window opens.

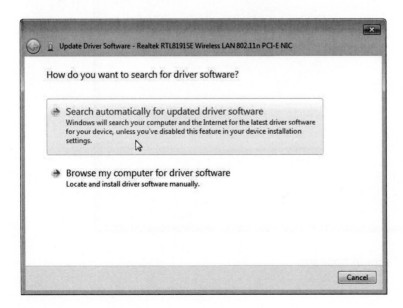

Select **Search automatically for updated driver software**.

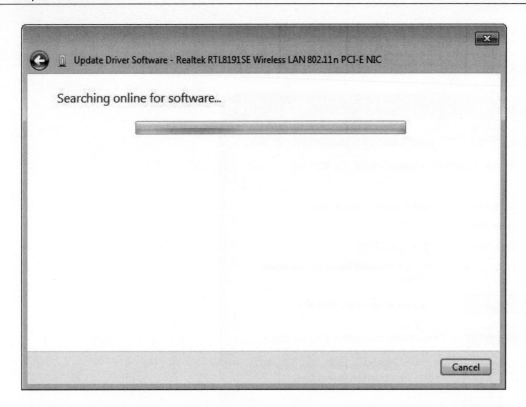

The "Searching online for software ..." screen appears.

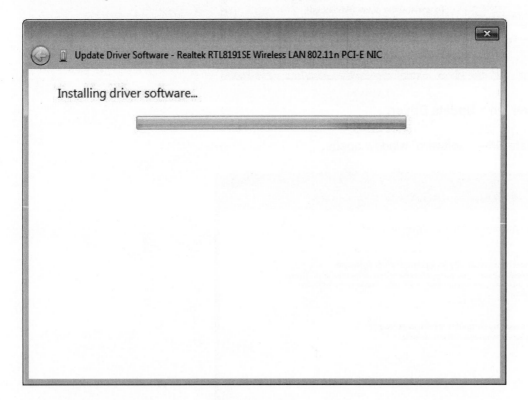

The "Installing driver software..." screen appears.

Once the software is installed, click **Close**.

Step 5

If required to reset the computer to the state at the start of the lab, complete the following tasks:

To uninstall the driver, click **Start > Control Panel > System > Device Manager >** expand "Network Adapters". Then right-click the newly install wireless NIC and select **Uninstall > OK**.

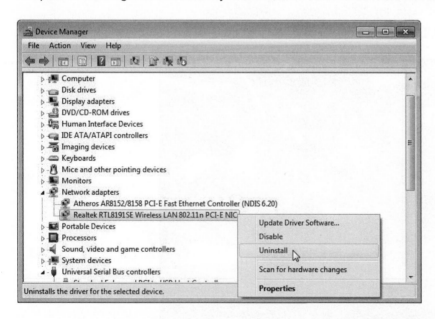

To remove software that was installed along with the wireless NIC driver, click **Start > Control Panel > Programs and Features >** select the software **> Uninstall**. Follow instructions to fully remove the software. Shut down the computer.

To remove the wireless NIC from the computer, use the steps from the start of this lab except for installing the wireless NIC.

6.8.2.5 Lab - Install a Wireless NIC in Windows Vista

Introduction

In this lab, you will install and configure a wireless NIC.

Recommended Equipment

- A computer with Windows Vista installed
- Empty PCI or PCIe slot on the motherboard
- A wireless PCI or PCIe NIC
- An antistatic wrist strap
- Tool Kit

Step 1

Turn off your computer. If a switch is present on the power supply, set the switch to "0" or "off". Unplug the computer from the AC outlet. Remove the side panels from the case.

Put on the antistatic wrist strap and attach it to an unpainted metal surface of the computer case.

Choose an appropriate slot on the motherboard to install the new wireless NIC.

You may need to remove the metal cover near the slot on the back of the case.

Make sure the wireless NIC is properly lined up with the slot. Push down gently on the wireless NIC.

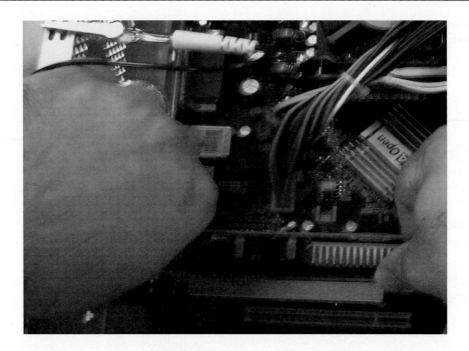

Secure the wireless NIC mounting bracket to the case with a screw.

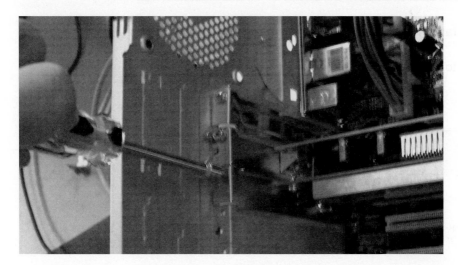

Attach the antenna to the antenna connector on the back of the computer.

Disconnect the antistatic wrist strap. Replace the case panels. Plug the power cable into an AC outlet. If a switch is present on the power supply, set the switch to "1" or "on".

Step 2

Boot your computer, and then log on as an administrator.

The wireless NIC will be detected by Windows. The "Found New Hardware" window will open.

Click **Locate and install driver software (recommended)**. Click **Continue**.

You will be prompted to insert the manufacturer's CD.

Insert the CD.

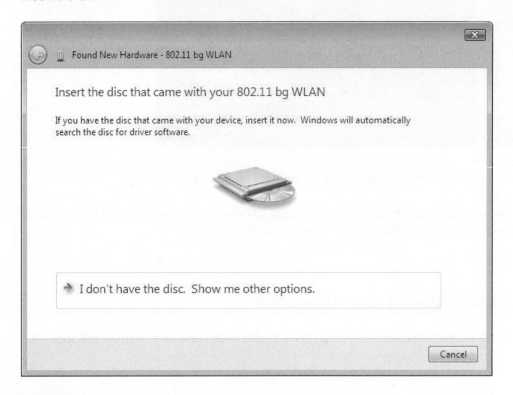

Once the drivers are installed, click **Close** to complete the driver installation process.

Step 3

Click **Start** > right-click **Computer** > **Manage** > **Continue**.

Click **Device Manager**, and then expand "Network Adapters".

What network adapters are installed in the computer?

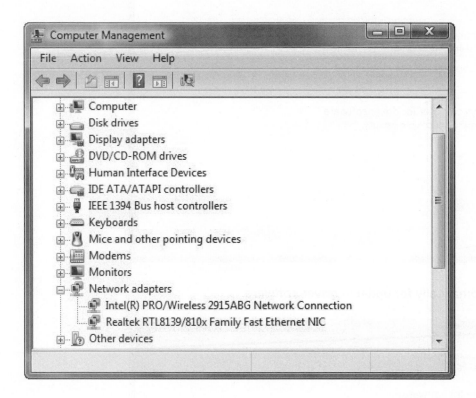

Step 4

Double click on the network adapter you just installed to open the "Properties" window.

Select **Driver** tab > **Update Driver...**

The "Update Driver Software" window opens.

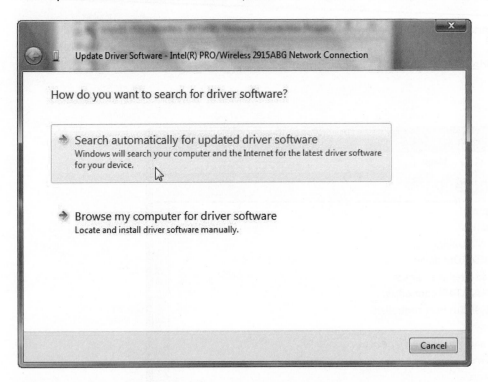

Select **Search automatically for updated driver software**.

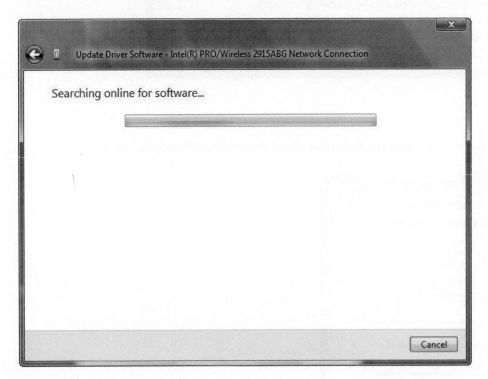

The "Searching online for software ..." screen appears.

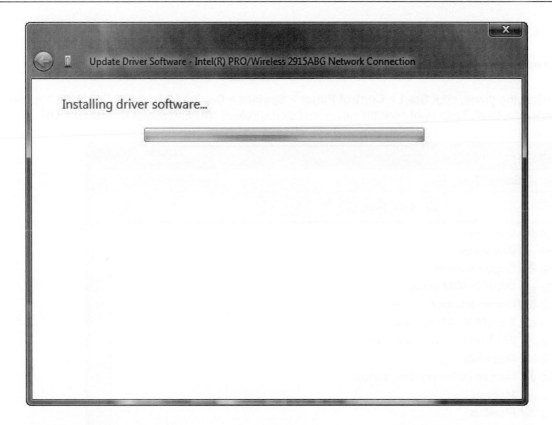

The "Installing driver software…" screen appears.

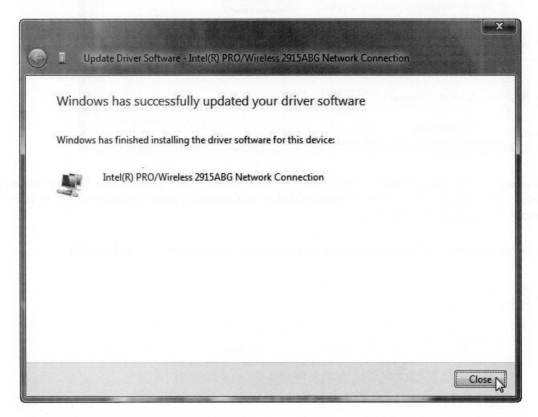

Once the software is installed, click **Close**.

Step 5

If required to reset the computer to the state at the start of the lab, complete the following tasks:

To uninstall the driver, click **Start > Control Panel > System > Device Manager > Continue >** expand "Network Adapters". Then right-click the newly installed wireless NIC and select **Uninstall > OK**.

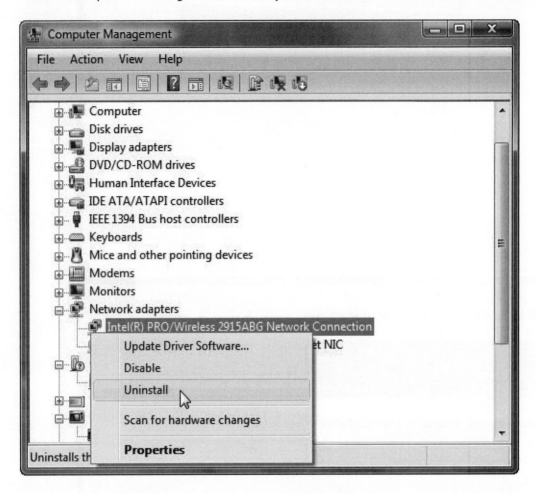

To remove software that was installed along with the wireless NIC driver, click **Start > Control Panel > Programs and Features >** select the software > **Uninstall/Change**. Follow instructions to fully remove the software. Shut down the computer.

To remove the wireless NIC from the computer, reverse the steps from the start of this lab.

6.8.2.6 Lab - Install a Wireless NIC in Windows XP

Introduction

In this lab, you will install and configure a wireless NIC.

Recommended Equipment

- A computer with Windows XP installed
- Empty PCI or PCIe slot on the motherboard
- A wireless PCI or PCIe NIC
- An antistatic wrist strap
- Tool kit

Step 1

Turn off your computer. If a switch is present on the power supply, set the switch to "0" or "off". Unplug the computer from the AC outlet. Remove the side panels from the case.

Put on the antistatic wrist strap and attach it to an unpainted metal surface of the computer case.

Choose an appropriate slot on the motherboard to install the new wireless NIC.

You may need to remove the metal cover near the slot on the back of the case.

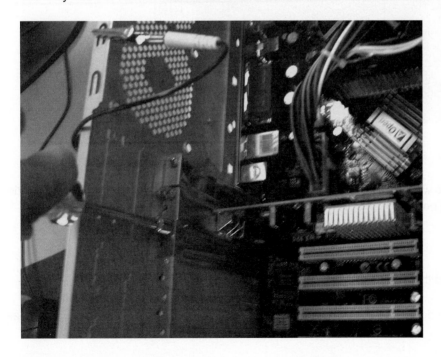

Make sure the wireless NIC is properly lined up with the slot. Push down gently on the wireless NIC.

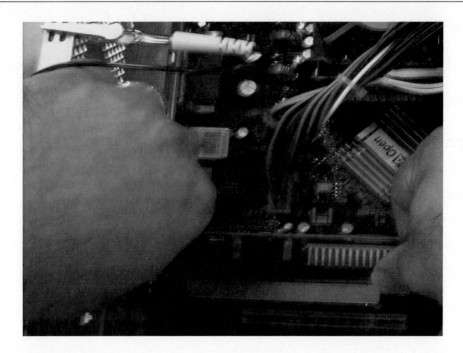

Secure the wireless NIC mounting bracket to the case with a screw.

Attach the antenna to the antenna connector on the back of the computer.

Disconnect the antistatic wrist strap. Replace the case panels. Plug the power cable into an AC outlet. If a switch is present on the power supply, set the switch to "1" or "on".

Step 2

Boot your computer, and then log on as an administrator.

The wireless NIC will be detected by Windows. The "Found New Hardware Wizard" window will open.

Select the **Yes, this time only** radio button, and then click **Next**.

Insert the manufacturer's CD.

Select the **Install the software automatically (Recommended)** radio button, and then click **Next**.

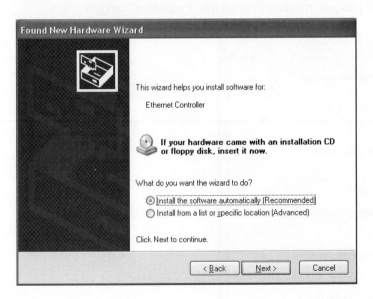

Step 3

Right-click **My Computer**, and choose **Manage**.

Choose **Device Manager**, and then expand "Network Adapters".

What network adapters are installed in the computer?

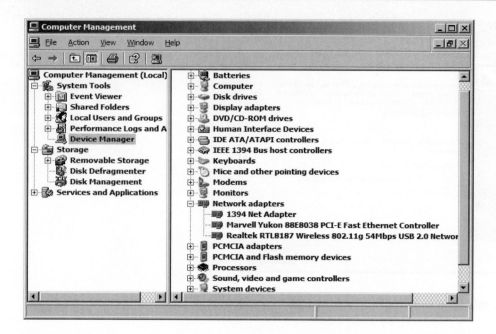

Step 4

Double-click on the network adapter you just installed to open the "Properties" window.

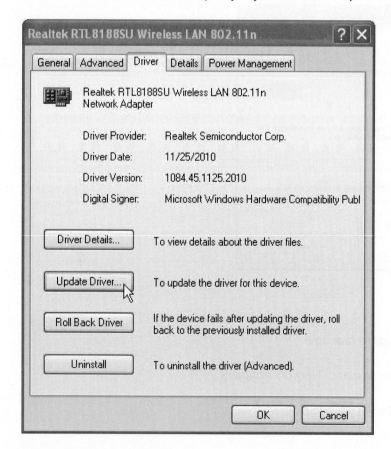

Click **Driver** tab > **Update Driver…**

The "Hardware Update Wizard" starts.

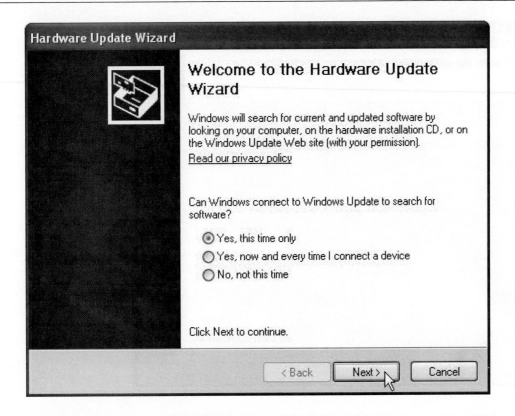

Select **Yes, this time only > Next**.

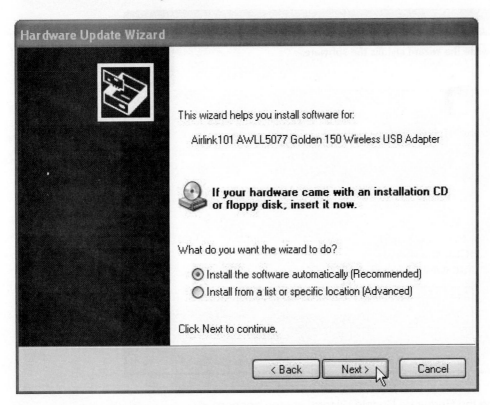

Select **Install the software automatically (Recommended) > Next**.

The "Please wait while the wizard searches…" screen appears.

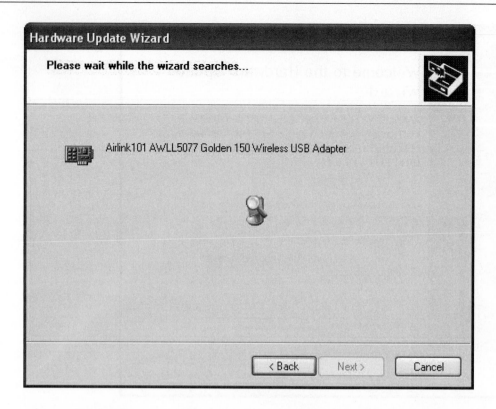

The "Please wait while the wizard installs the software…" screen appears.

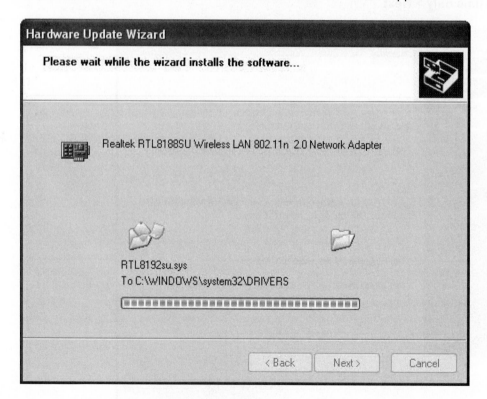

The "Completing the Hardware Update Wizard" screen appears.

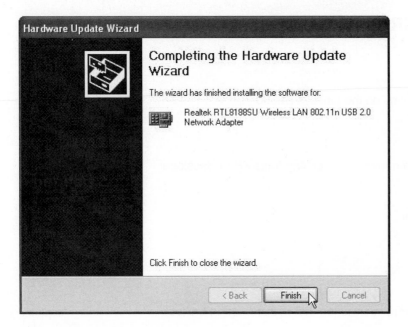

Once the software is installed, click **Finish**.

Step 5

If required to reset the computer to the state at the start of the lab, complete the following tasks:

To uninstall the driver, click **Start > Control Panel > System > Hardware** tab **> Device Manager >** expand "Network Adapters". Then right-click the newly install wireless NIC and select **Uninstall > OK**.

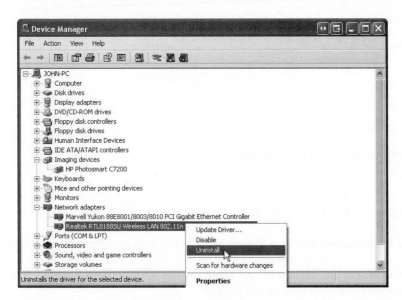

To remove software that was installed along with the wireless NIC driver, click **Start > Control Panel > Add or Remove Programs >** select the software **> Change/Remove**. Follow instructions to fully remove the software. Shut down the computer.

To remove the wireless NIC from the computer, reverse the steps from the start of this lab.

6.8.3.5 Lab - Connect to a Router for the First Time

Introduction

In this lab, you will configure basic settings on the Linksys E2500.

Recommended Equipment

- A computer with Windows 7, Windows Vista, or Windows XP Professional
- An Ethernet NIC installed
- Linksys E2500 Wireless Router
- Ethernet patch cable

Step 1

Ask the instructor for the following information that is used during the lab.

Router Address Information:

IP address _____

Subnet mask _____

Router name _____

DHCP Server Setting Information:

Start IP address _____

Maximum number of users _____

Static DNS 1 (optional) _____

Router Access:
Router Password _____

Important: Only use configurations assigned by the instructor.

Step 2

Plug in the power of the wireless router. Boot the computer and log in as an administrator.

Connect the computer to one of the **Ethernet** ports on the wireless router with an Ethernet patch cable.

Note: If this is the first time connecting to the lab router, complete the following. Follow these instructions to set a network location. This will be explained later in the course.

The "Set Network Location" window opens.

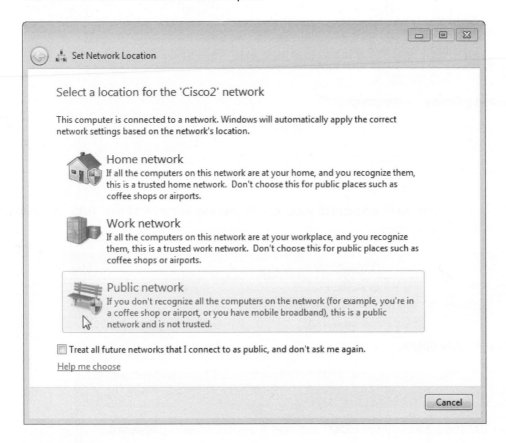

Select **Public network**.

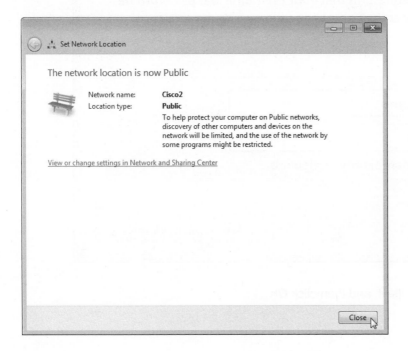

Click **Close** to accept the network location Public.

Step 3

Open the command prompt.

Type **ipconfig /renew**.

What is the default gateway for the computer?

Step 4

Open Internet Explorer. Type the IP address of your default gateway in the "Address" field, and then press **Enter**.

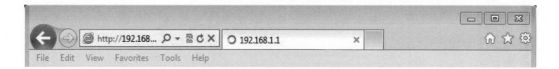

The "Connect to" window opens.

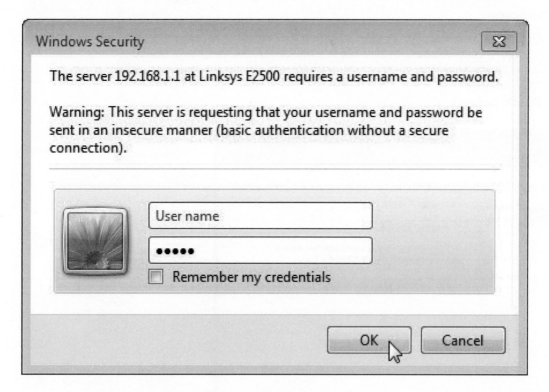

Type **admin** in the "Password:" field, and then click **OK**.

The "Setup screen" appears.

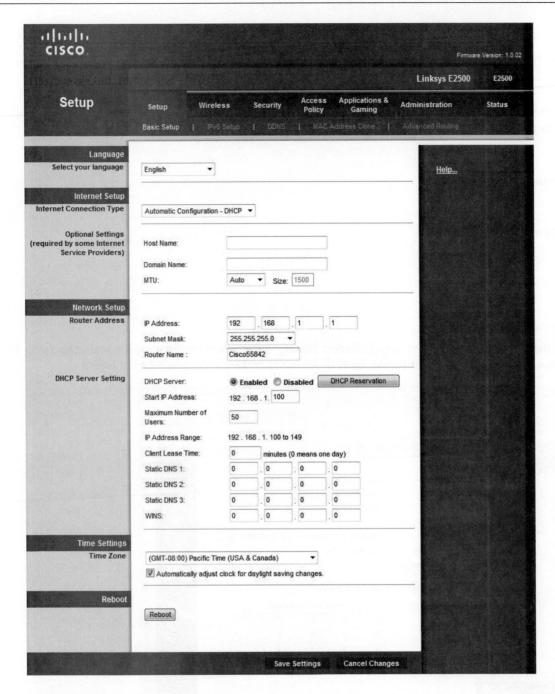

Internet Setup

What is the "Internet Connection Type" assigned to the router?

Make sure the "Internet Connection Type" is set to **Automatic Configuration – DHCP**.

Network Setup

What is the following for the "Router Address":

IP Address

Subnet Mask

Router Name

What is the following for the "DHCP Server Setting":
Start IP Address

Maximum Number of Users

IP Address Range

Make sure DHCP is enabled.

Step 5

Enter the "Router Address" and "DHCP Server Setting" information provided by the instructor (step 1): IP Address, Subnet Mask, Router Name, Start IP Address, and Maximum Number of Users.

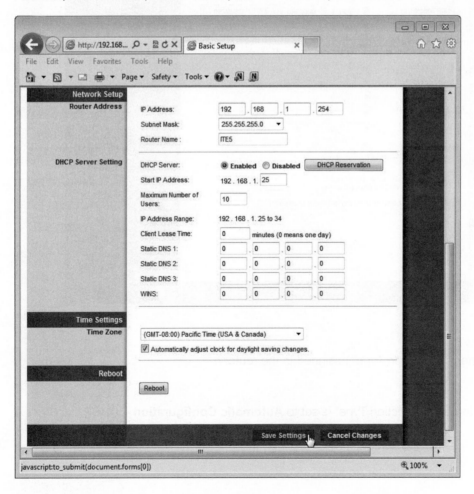

Click **Save Settings**.

The "Your Settings have been successfully saved. A system reboot is in progress and may take up to 60 seconds." screen appears.

Click **Continue**.

After the router reboots, you may need to log back into the router.

Step 6

Open the command prompt.

Type **ipconfig /all**, and record the following information.

Computer IP information:

IP address _____

Subnet mask _____

Gateway _____

DNS (optional) _____

Open the "Internet Protocol Version 4 (TCP/IPv4) Properties" window.

Use the recorded information to configure the NIC with static IP information.

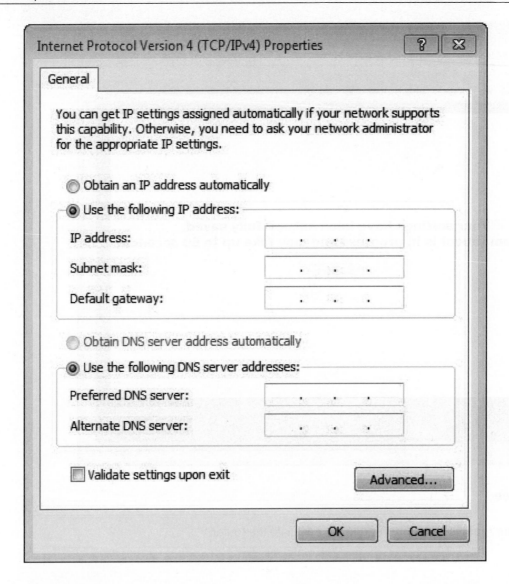

Click **OK > OK**.

Step 7

Click the **Application & Gaming** tab and then select **QoS**.

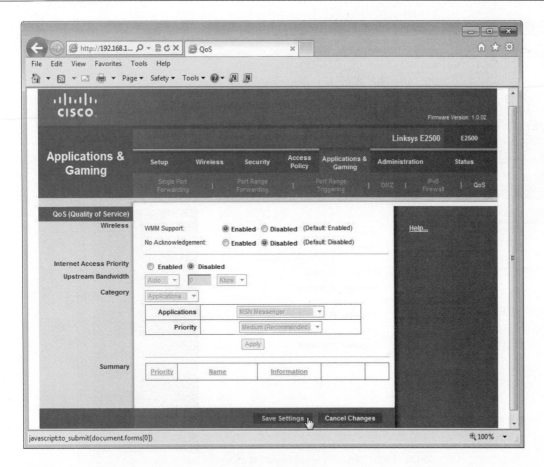

Make sure **WMM Support** is enabled. Click **Help** for more information about QoS settings.

Click **Save Settings > Continue**, if any changes were made.

Step 8

Click the **Administration** tab and then select **Management**.

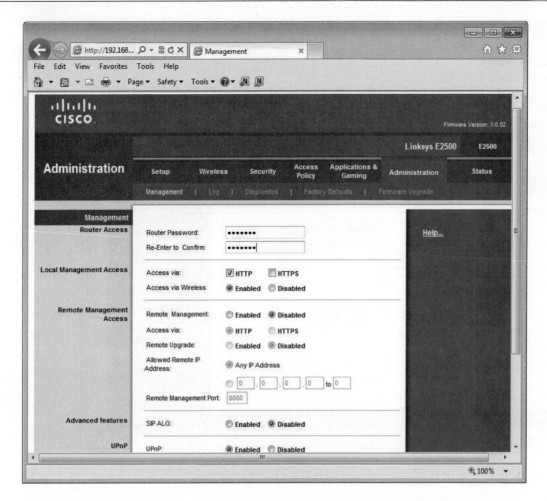

Type **Network** in the "Router Password:" and "Re-Enter to Confirm:" fields.

Click **Save Settings > Continue**.

Close Internet Explorer.

Open up a new browser and log back into the router.

What IP address did you enter into the URL field of the browser?

_____

What password did you use to access the router GUI?

_____

Step 9

Return configurations to the following settings, unless stated otherwise by the instructor.

Connect the computer to one of the **Ethernet** ports on the wireless router with an Ethernet patch cable.

Router Address Information:

      IP address _____192.168.1.1_____

      Subnet mask _____255.255.255.0_____

      Router name _____Linksys_____

DHCP Server Setting Information:

      Start IP address _____192.168.1.100_____

      Maximum number of users _____50_____

      Static DNS 1 (optional) _____ blank _____

Router Access:
      Router Password _____Admin_____

Close the browser and log off the computer.

6.8.3.8 Lab - Configure Wireless Router in Windows 7

Introduction

In this lab, you will configure and test the wireless settings on the Linksys E2500.

Recommended Equipment

- A computer with Windows 7
- A Wireless NIC installed
- An Ethernet NIC installed
- Linksys E2500 Wireless Router
- Ethernet patch cable

Note: All wireless settings in this lab are for a 2.4 GHz wireless connection. Follow the same steps for setting up a 5 GHz wireless connection or when setting up both 2.4 GHz and 5 GHz connections.

Step 1

Ask the instructor for the following information that is used during the lab.

Router Address Information:

IP address _____

Subnet mask _____

Router name _____

DHCP Server Setting Information:

Start IP address _____

Maximum number of users _____

Static DNS 1 (optional) _____

SSID Values:

New SSID _____

Channel number:
Channel _____

Router Access:
Router Password _____

Wireless Security:

Passphase key _____

Important: Only use configurations assigned by the instructor.

Step 2

Plug in the power of the wireless router. Boot the computer and log in as an administrator.

Connect the computer to one of the **Ethernet** ports on the wireless router with an Ethernet patch cable.

Note: If this is the first time connecting to the lab router, complete the following. Follow these instructions to set a network location. This will be explained later in the course.

The "Set Network Location" window opens.

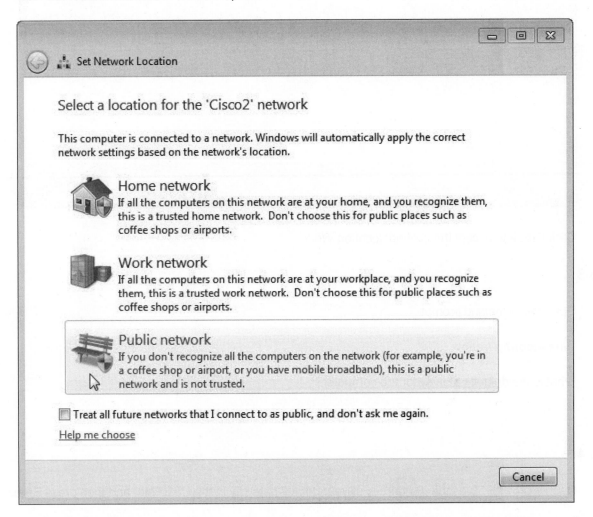

Select **Public network**.

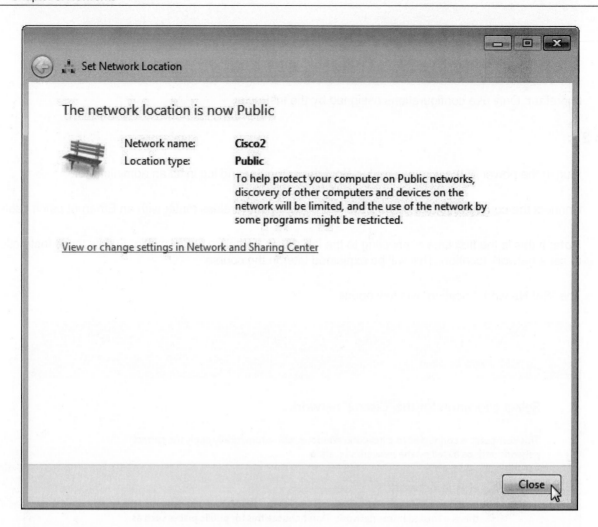

Click **Close** to accept the network location Work.

Step 3

Open the command prompt.

Type **ipconfig /renew**.

What is the default gateway for the computer?

Step 4

Open a browser. Type the IP address of your default gateway in the URL field, and then press **Enter**.

The "Connect to" window appears.

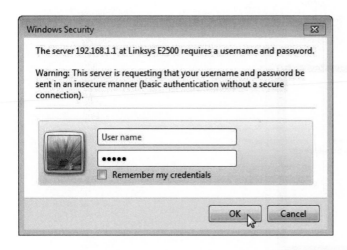

Type the password provided by the instructor in the "Password:" field, and then click **OK**.

Step 5

The Setup screen appears.

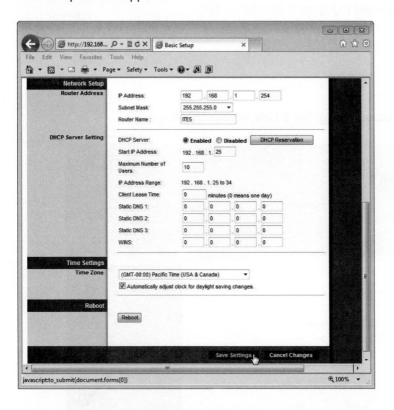

Enter the following "Router Address" and "DHCP Server Setting" information provided by the instructor (step 1): IP Address, Subnet Mask, Router Name, Start IP Address, and Maximum Number of Users.

Click **Save Settings**.

The "Your settings have been successfully saved. A system reboot is in progress and may take up to 60 seconds." screen appears.

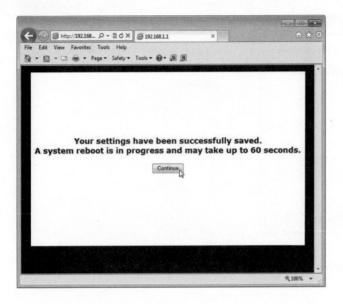

Click **Continue**.

After the router reboots, you may need to log back into the router.

Step 6

Click the **Wireless** tab.

Click the **Network Mode** drop-down menu for the 5 GHz Wireless Settings.

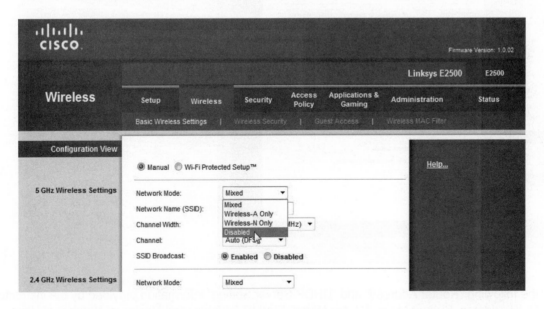

What 802.11 technologies are supported?

Click the **Channel** drop-down menu for the 5 GHz Wireless Settings.

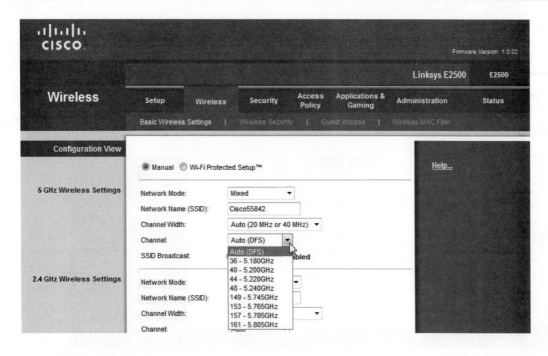

What channels are listed?

Disable Network Mode for the 5 GHz Wireless Settings, unless informed otherwise by the instructor.

Click the **Network Mode** drop-down menu for the 2.4 GHz Wireless Settings.

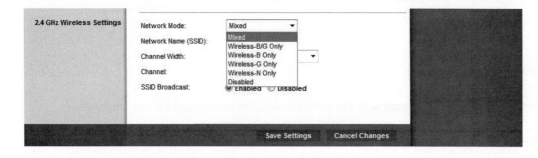

What 802.11 technologies are supported?

Choose **Mixed** in the "Network Mode:" drop-down box.

What is the default SSID for the wireless router?

Type **cisco#** in the "Network Name (SSID):" field, where # is the number assigned by the instructor.

Click the **Channel** drop-down menu for the 2.4GHz Wireless Settings.

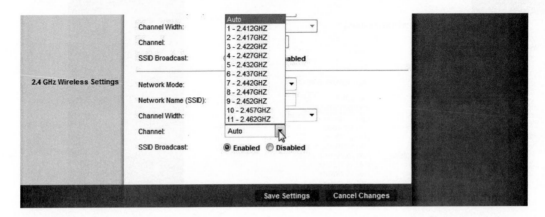

What channels are listed?

Select the Channel number that was provided by the instructor.

Click **Save Settings > Continue** then close the browser.

Step 7

Unplug the Ethernet cable from the computer.

View wireless networks associated with the wireless adapter configured for the computer.

Click **Start > Control Panel > Network and Sharing Center > Connect to a network**.

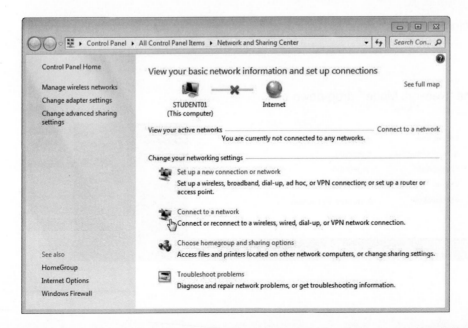

A list of available wireless networks is displayed.

What wireless network(s) are available?

Choose **cisco#**, where # is the number assigned by the instructor, make sure **Connect automatically** is selected, and then click the **Connect** button.

When the "Set Network Location" window opens, select **Public network > Close**.

Step 8

Open a browser. Type the IP address of your default gateway in the URL field, and then press **Enter**.

The "Connect to" window appears.

Type the password provided by the instructor in the "Password:" field.

The Setup screen appears.

Navigate to "Basic Wireless Settings". Select **Disable** for the 2.4 GHz SSID broadcast.

Click **Save Settings > Continue**.

Why would you disable SSID broadcast?

Close all opened Windows: Network and Sharing Center, browser, command prompt, etc.

View wireless networks associated with the wireless adapter configured to the computer.

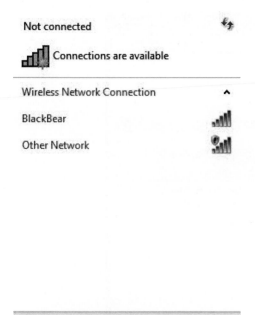

What wireless network(s) are available?

Click **Open Network and Sharing Center**.

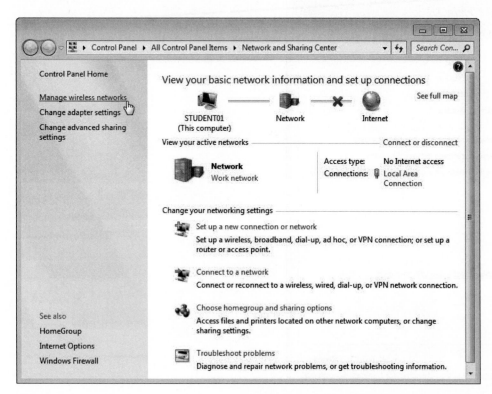

When the "Network and Sharing Center" window opens, click **Manage wireless networks**.

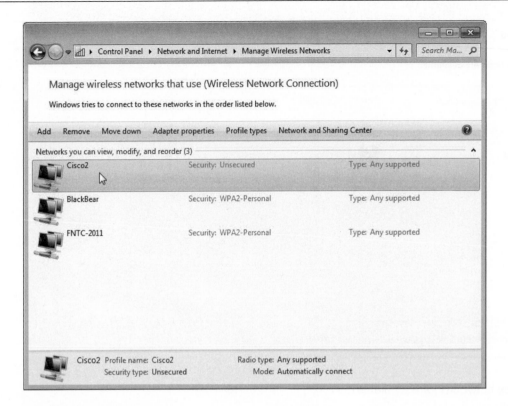

When the "Manage Wireless Networks" window opens, double click **Cisco#,** where # is the number assigned to you.

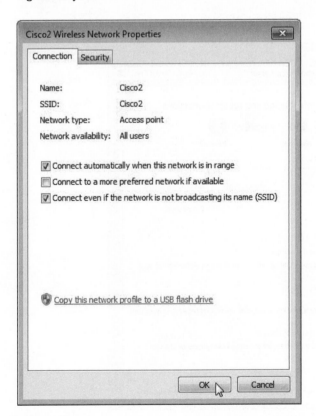

Select the check box **Connect even if the network in not broadcasting its name (SSID)**, and then click **OK**.

View wireless networks associated with the wireless adapter configured for the computer.

What wireless network(s) are available?

Step 9

Connect to **cisco#**, where # is the number assigned by the instructor and log into the router.

Use a browser to logon to the router.

Click the **Wireless** tab and then select **Wireless Security**.

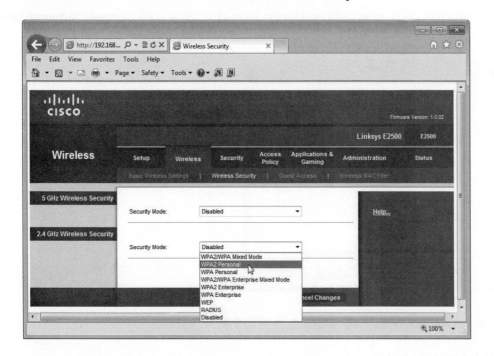

In the **Security Mode** drop-down box, for the "2.4GHz Wireless Security", select **WPA2 Personal**.

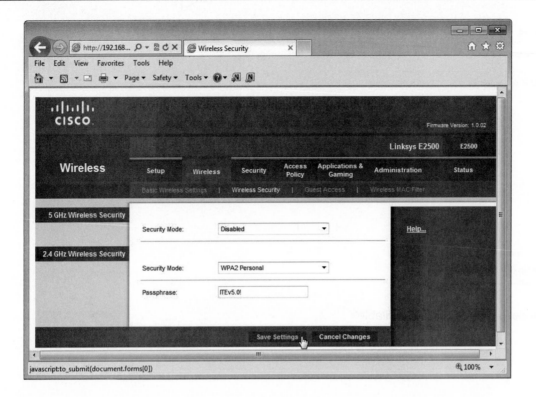

Type **ITEv5.0!** for the Passphrase and click **Save Settings > Continue**.

Step 10

View wireless networks associated with the wireless adapter configured to the computer.

Choose **cisco#**, where # is the number assigned by the instructor, make sure **Connect automatically** is selected, and then click the **Connect** button.

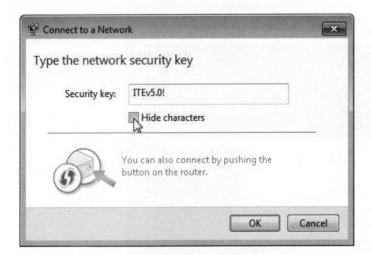

When the "Connect to a Network" window opens, type **ITEv5.0!** for the "Security key," and then click **OK**.

Use a browser to logon to the router

If you cannot access the GUI of the router, contact the instructor.

Step 11

Return configurations to the following settings, unless stated otherwise by the instructor.

Connect the computer to one of the **Ethernet** ports on the wireless router with an Ethernet patch cable.

Router Address Information:

        IP address _____ 192.168.1.1 _____

        Subnet mask _____ 255.255.255.0 _____

        Router name _____ Linksys _____

DHCP Server Setting Information:

        Start IP address _____ 192.168.1.100 _____

        Maximum number of users _____ 50 _____

        Static DNS 1 (optional) _____ blank _____

SSID Values:

        Network Name (SSID) _____ Linksys _____

        SSID Broadcast _____ Disabled _____

Channel number:
        Channel _____ Auto _____

Router Access:
        Router Password _____ admin _____

Wireless Security:

        Security Mode _____ Disable _____

Close the browser and logoff the computer.

6.8.3.9 Lab - Configure Wireless Router in Windows Vista

Introduction

In this lab, you will configure and test the wireless settings on the Linksys E2500.

Recommended Equipment

- A computer with Windows Vista
- A Wireless NIC installed
- An Ethernet NIC installed
- Linksys E2500 Wireless Router
- Ethernet patch cable

Note: All wireless settings in this lab are for a 2.4 GHz wireless connection. Follow the same steps for setting up a 5 GHz wireless connection or when setting up both 2.4 GHz and 5 GHz connections.

Step 1

Ask the instructor for the following information that is used during the lab.

Router Address Information:

IP address _____

Subnet mask _____

Router name _____

DHCP Server Setting Information:

Start IP address _____

Maximum number of users _____

Static DNS 1 (optional) _____

SSID Values:

New SSID _____

Channel number:
Channel _____

Router Access:
Router Password _____

Wireless Security:
Passphase key _____

Important: Only use configurations assigned by the instructor.

Step 2

Plug in the power of the wireless router. Boot the computer and log in as an administrator.

Connect the computer to one of the **Ethernet** ports on the wireless router with an Ethernet patch cable.

Note: If this is the first time connecting to the lab router, complete the following. Follow these instructions to set a network location. "Set Network Location" will be explained later in the course.

The "Set Network Location" window opens.

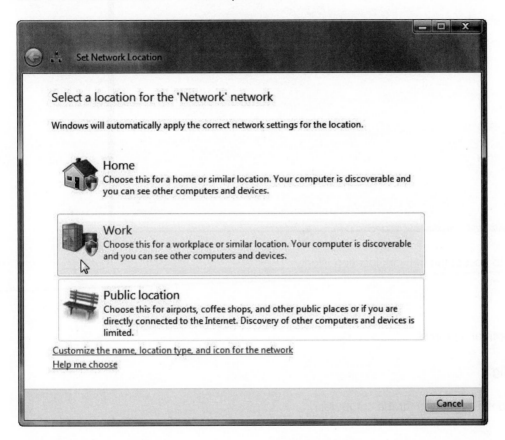

Select **Work > Continue**.

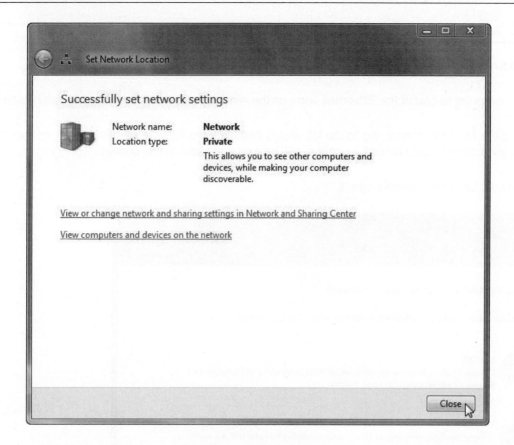

Click **Close** to accept the network location Work.

Step 3

Open the command prompt.

Type **ipconfig**.

What is the default gateway for the computer?

Step 4

Open a browser. Type the IP address of your default gateway in the url field, and then press **Return**.

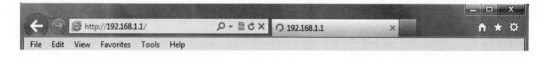

The "Connect to" window appears.

Type the password provided by the instructor in the "Password:" field, and then click **OK**.

Step 5

The Setup screen appears.

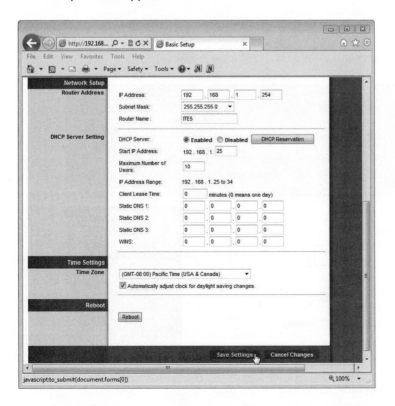

Enter the following "Router Address" and "DHCP Server Setting" information provided by the instructor (step 1): IP Address, Subnet Mask, Router Name, Start IP Address, and Maximum Number of Users.

Click **Save Settings**.

The "Your Settings have been successfully saved." screen appears.

Click **Continue**.

Step 6

Click the **Wireless** tab.

Click the **Network Mode** drop-down menu for the 5 GHz Wireless Settings.

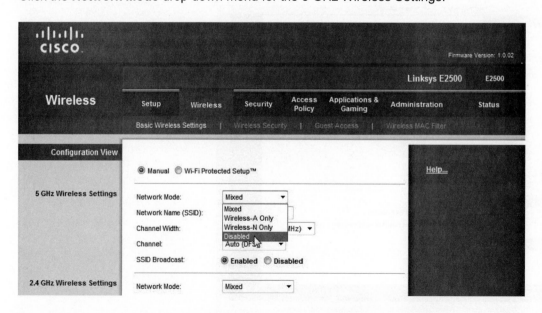

What 802.11 technologies are supported?

Click the **Channel** drop-down menu for the 5 GHz Wireless Settings.

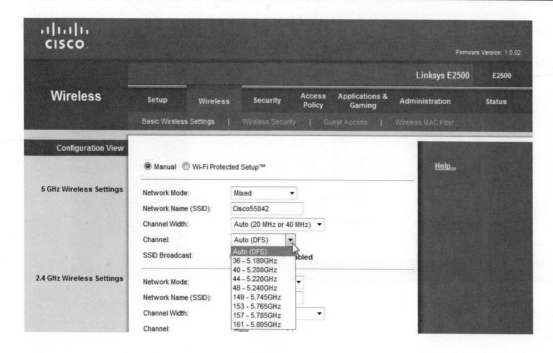

What channels are listed?

Disable Network Mode for the 5 GHz Wireless Settings, unless informed otherwise by the instructor.

Click the **Network Mode** drop-down menu for the 2.4 GHz Wireless Settings.

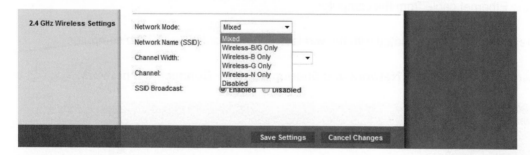

What 802.11 technologies are supported?

Choose **Mixed** in the "Network Mode:" drop-down box.

What is the default SSID for the wireless router?

Type **cisco#** in the "Network Name (SSID):" field, where # is the number assigned by the instructor.

Click the **Channel** drop-down menu for the 2.4GHz Wireless Settings.

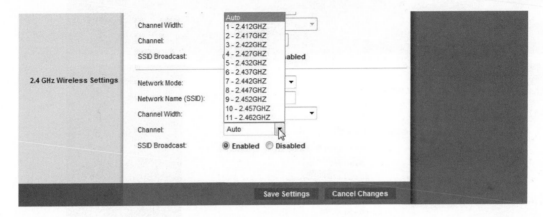

What channels are listed?

Select the Channel number that was provided by the instructor.

Click **Save Settings > Continue**, and then close the browser.

Step 7

Unplug the Ethernet cable from the computer.

View wireless networks associated with the wireless adapter configured for the computer.

Click **Start > Control Panel > Network and Sharing Center > Connect to a network**.

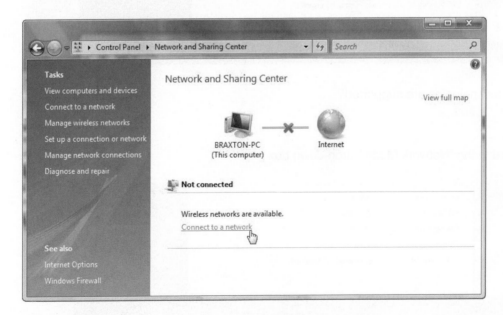

A list of available wireless networks is displayed.

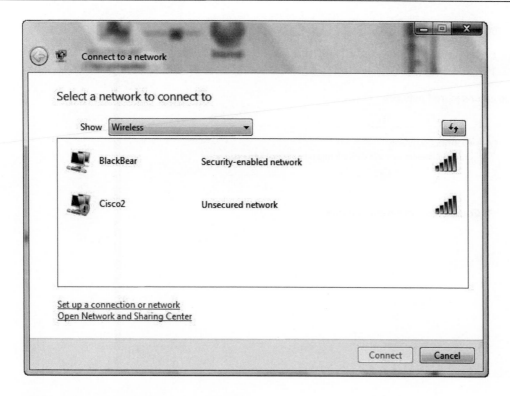

What wireless network(s) are available?

Choose **cisco#**, where # is the number assigned by the instructor and then click the **Connect** button.

The "Getting information from Cisco#" screen appears.

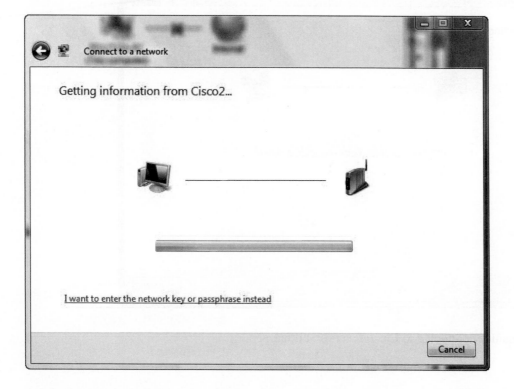

The "Cisco# is an unsecured network" screen appears.

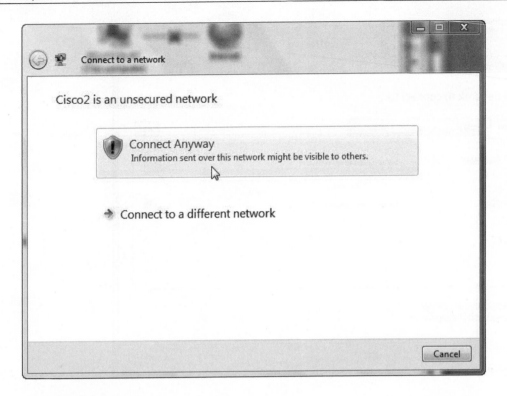

Click **Connect Anyway**.

The "Connecting to Cisco#" screen appears.

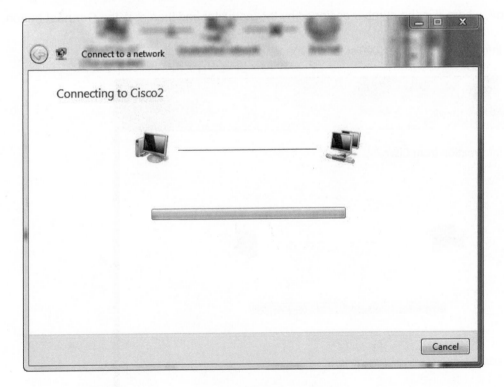

The "Successfully connected to Cisco#" screen appears.

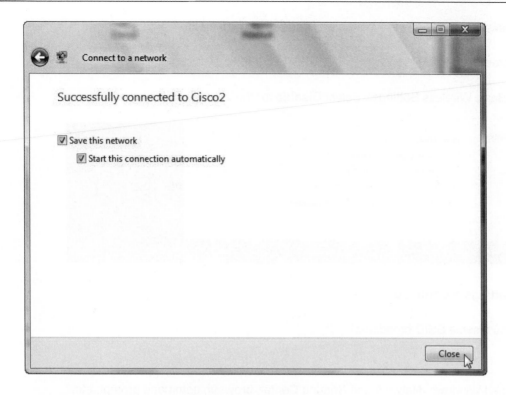

Click the **Save this network** box and then click **Close**.

When the "Set Network Location" window opens, select **Work > Continue > Close**.

Step 8

Open a browser. Type the IP address of your default gateway in the url field, and then press **Return**.

The "Connect to" window appears.

Type the password provided by the instructor in the "Password:" field.

The Setup screen appears.

Navigate to "Basic Wireless Settings". Select **Disable** for the 2.4 GHz SSID broadcast.

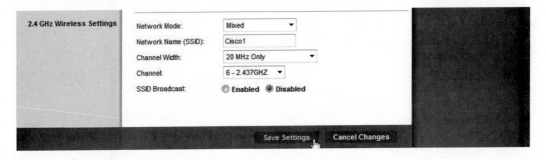

Click **Save Settings > Continue**.

Why would you disable SSID broadcast?

Close all opened Windows: Network and Sharing Center, browser, command prompt, etc.

View wireless networks associated with the wireless adapter configured to the computer. Click **Start > Control Panel > Network and Sharing Center > Manage network connections**.

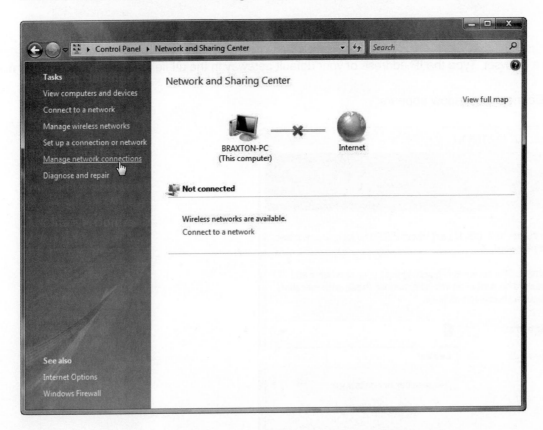

Right-click the wireless adapter icon and then select **Connect/Disconnect**.

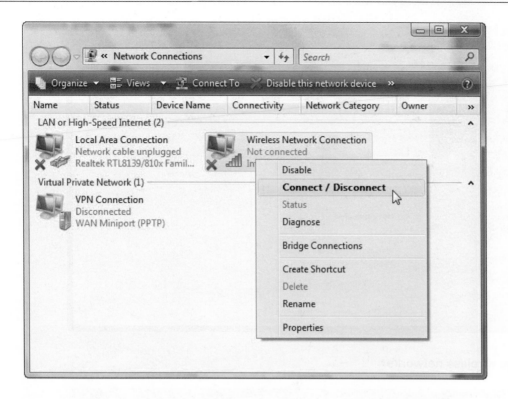

A list of wireless connection is displayed. Click the refresh button a few times.

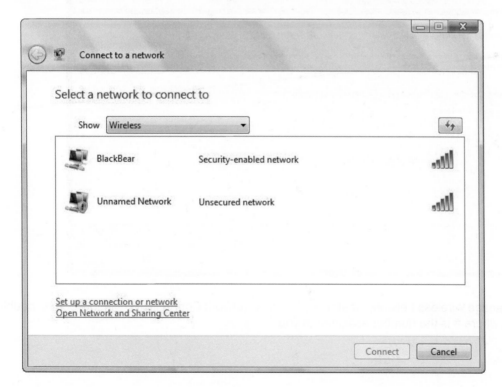

What wireless network(s) are available?

Close the "Select a network to connect to" window.

Click **Open Network and Sharing Center**.

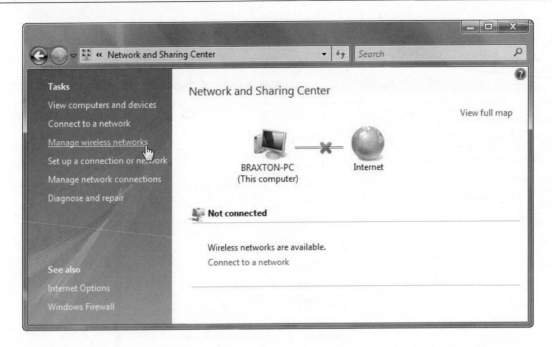

Click **Manage wireless networks**.

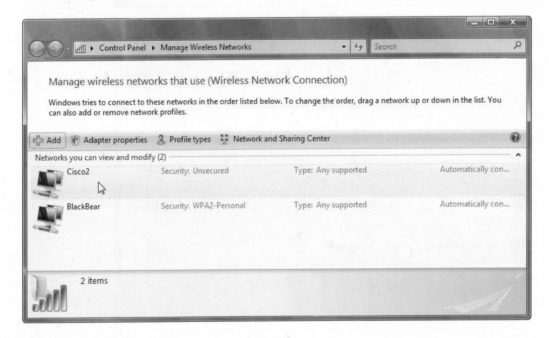

When the "Manage wireless networks that use (Wireless Network Connection)" window opens, double-click **Cisco#,** where # is the number assigned to you.

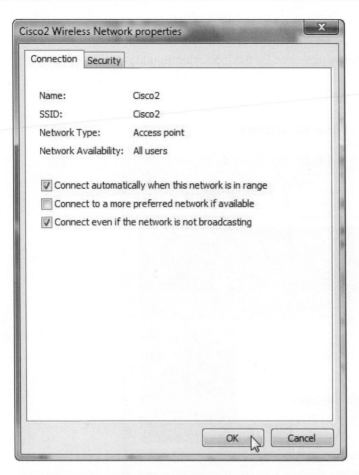

Select the check box **Connect even if the network in not broadcasting**, and then click **OK**.

View wireless networks associated with the wireless adapter configured for the computer.

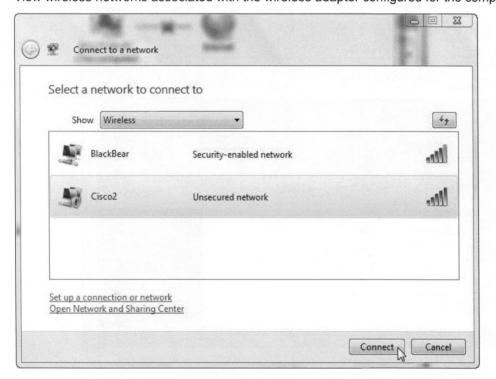

What wireless network(s) are available?

Step 9

Connect to **cisco#**, where # is the number assigned by the instructor, and log into the router.

Use a browser to logon to the router.

Click the **Wireless** tab and then select **Wireless Security**.

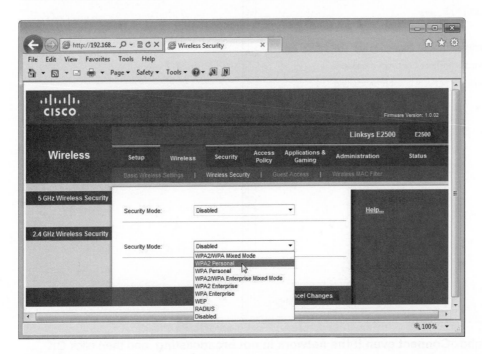

In the Security Mode drop-down box, for the "2.4GHz Wireless Security", select **WPA2 Personal**.

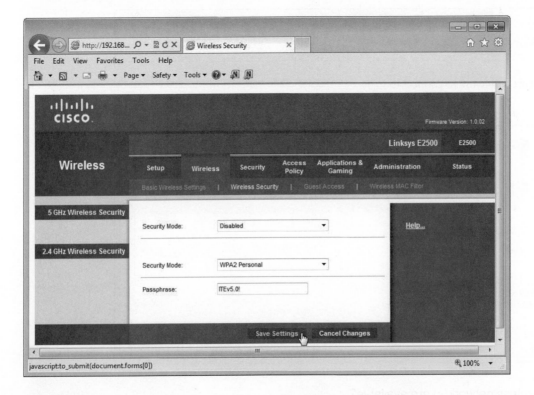

Type **ITEv5.0!** for the Passphrase and click **Save Settings > Continue**.

Step 10

View wireless networks associated with the wireless adapter configured to the computer.

Open "Network and Sharing Center," and then click **Connect to a network**.

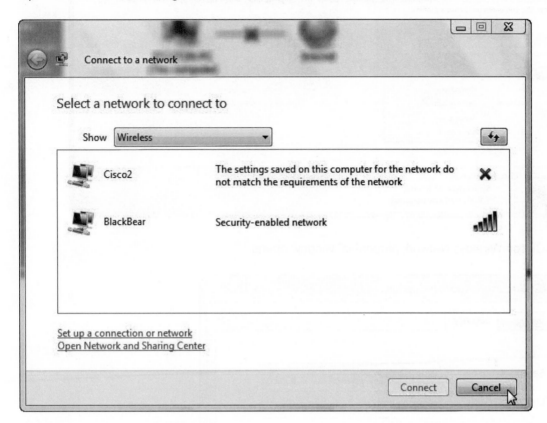

Why can you not connect to Cisco#?

Click **Cancel**.

When the "Network and Sharing Center" windows opens, click **Manage Wireless Networks**, and right-click **Cisco# > Properties**.

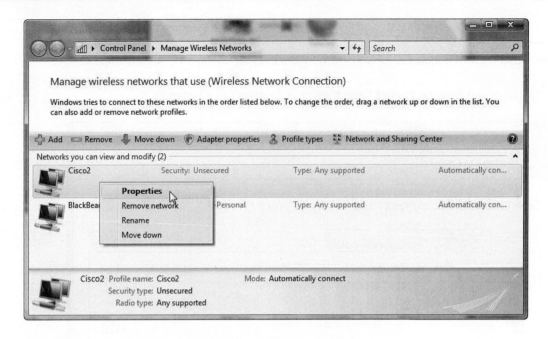

The "Cisco# Wireless Network properties" window opens.

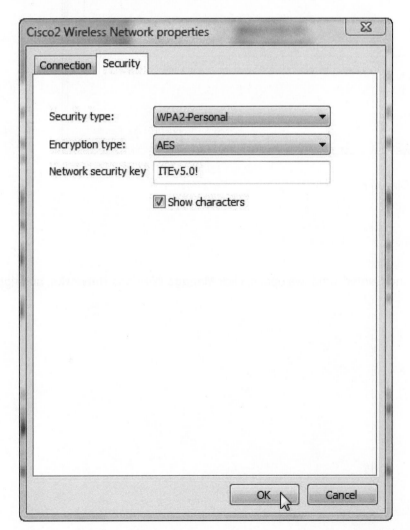

Select the Security tab and then set the "Security type:" to **WPA2 –Personal**, type in **ITEv5.0!** for the "Network security key", and then click **OK**.

When the "Set Network Location" window opens, select **Work > Continue > Close**.

Use a browser to logon to the router

If you cannot access the GUI of the router, contact the instructor.

Step 11

Return configurations to the following settings, unless stated otherwise by the instructor.

Connect the computer to one of the **Ethernet** ports on the wireless router with an Ethernet patch cable.

Router Address Information:
      IP address _____ 192.168.1.1 _____

      Subnet mask _____ 255.255.255.0 _____

      Router name _____ Linksys _____

DHCP Server Setting Information:
      Start IP address _____ 192.168.1.100 _____

      Maximum number of users _____ 50 _____

      Static DNS 1 (optional) _____ blank _____

SSID Values:
      Network Name (SSID) _____ Linksys _____

      SSID Broadcast _____ Disabled _____

Channel number:
      Channel _____ Auto _____

Router Access:
      Router Password _____ admin _____

Wireless Security:
      Security Mode _____ Disable _____

Close the browser and log off the computer.

6.8.3.10 Lab - Configure Wireless Router in Windows XP

Introduction

In this lab, you will configure and test the wireless settings on the Linksys E2500.

Recommended Equipment

- A computer with Windows XP
- A Wireless NIC installed
- An Ethernet NIC installed
- Linksys E2500 Wireless Router
- Ethernet patch cable

Note: All wireless settings in this lab are for a 2.4 GHz wireless connection. Follow the same steps for setting up a 5 GHz wireless connection or when setting up both 2.4 GHz and 5 GHz connections.

Step 1

Ask the instructor for the following information that is used during the lab.

Router Address Information:
IP address _____

Subnet mask _____

Router name _____

DHCP Server Setting Information:
Start IP address _____

Maximum number of users _____

Static DNS 1 (optional) _____

SSID Values:
New SSID _____

Channel number:
Channel _____

Router Access:
Router Password _____

Wireless Security:
Passphase key _____

Important: Only use configurations assigned by the instructor.

Step 2

Plug in the power of the wireless router. Boot the computer and log in as an administrator.

Connect the computer to one of the **Ethernet** ports on the wireless router with an Ethernet patch cable.

Step 3

Open the command prompt.

Type **ipconfig /renew**.

What is the default gateway for the computer?

Step 4

Open a browser. Type the IP address of your default gateway in the URL field, and then press **Enter**.

The "Connect to" window appears.

Type the password provided by the instructor in the "Password:" field, and then click **OK**.

Step 5

The Setup screen appears.

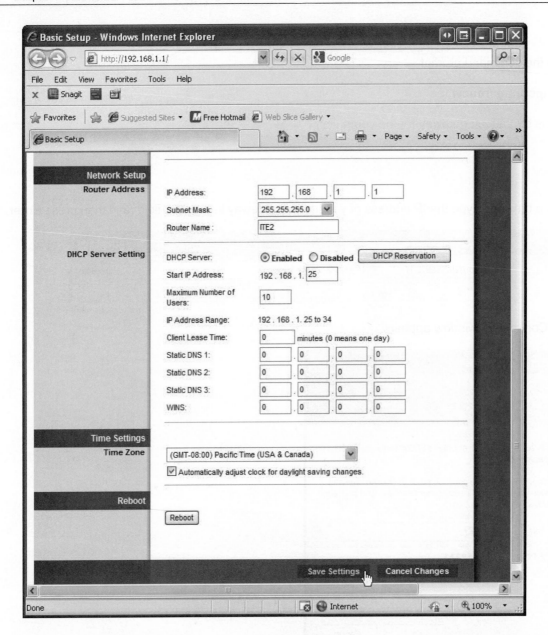

Enter the following "Router Address" and "DHCP Server Setting" information provided by the instructor (step 1): IP Address, Subnet Mask, Router Name, Start IP Address, and Maximum Number of Users.

Click **Save Settings**.

The "Your settings have been successfully saved." screen appears.

Click **Continue**.

After the router reboots, you may need to log back into the router.

Step 6

Click the **Wireless** tab.

Click the **Network Mode** drop-down menu for the 5 GHz Wireless Settings.

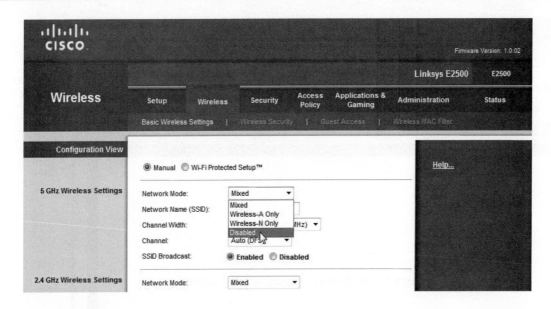

What 802.11 technologies are supported?

Click the **Channel** drop-down menu for the 5 GHz Wireless Settings.

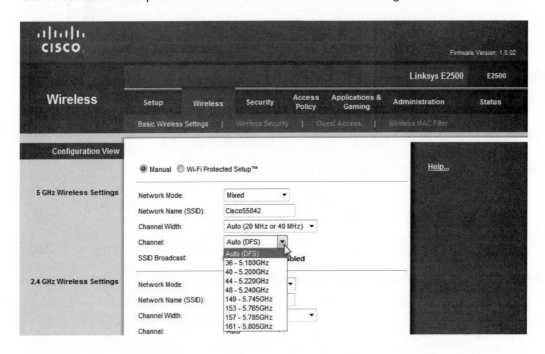

What channels are listed?

Disable Network Mode for the 5 GHz Wireless Settings, unless informed otherwise by the instructor.

Click the **Network Mode** drop-down menu for the 2.4 GHz Wireless Settings.

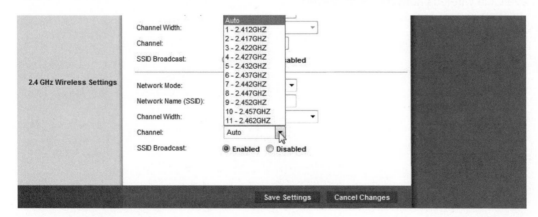

What 802.11 technologies are supported?

Choose **Mixed** in the "Network Mode:" drop-down box.

What is the default SSID for the wireless router?

Type **cisco#** in the "Network Name (SSID):" field, where # is the number assigned by the instructor.

Click the **Channel** drop-down menu for the 2.4 GHz Wireless Settings.

What channels are listed?

Select the Channel number that was provided by the instructor.

Click **Save Settings > Continue**, and then close the browser.

Step 7

Unplug the Ethernet cable from the computer.

View wireless networks associated with the wireless adapter configured for the computer.

Click **Start > Control Panel > Network Connections >** right-click the wireless adapter, and select **View Available Wireless Networks**.

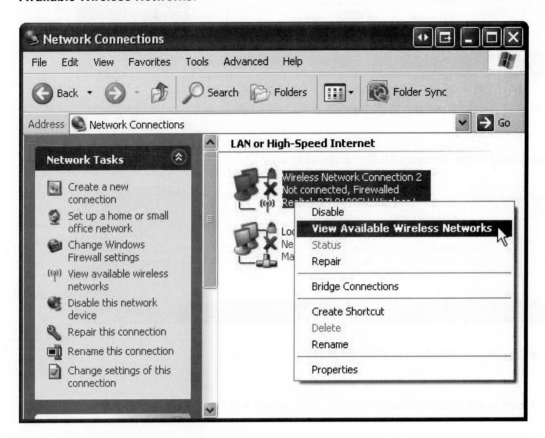

A list of available wireless networks is displayed.

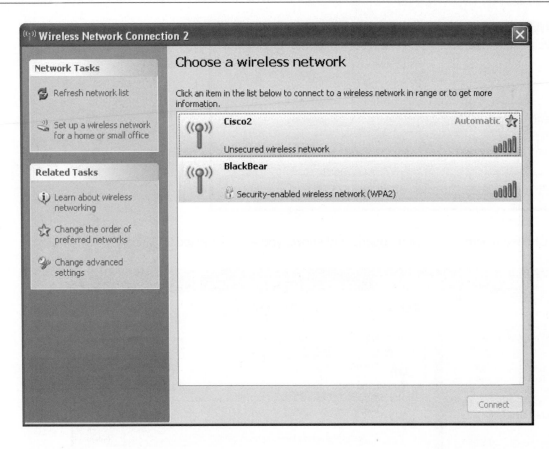

What wireless network(s) are available?

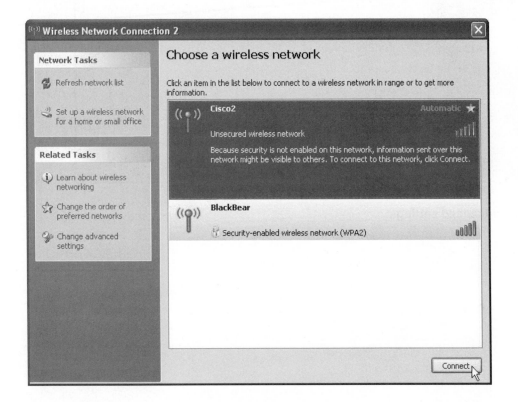

Choose **cisco#**, where # is the number assigned by the instructor, and then click the **Connect** button.

The "Please wait while Windows connects to 'Cisco#' network" screen appears.

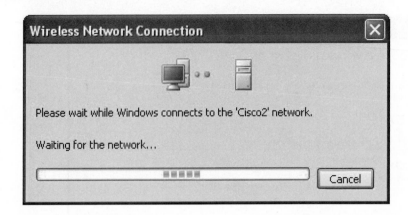

The "Choose a wireless network" opens and shows you are connected to Cisco#.

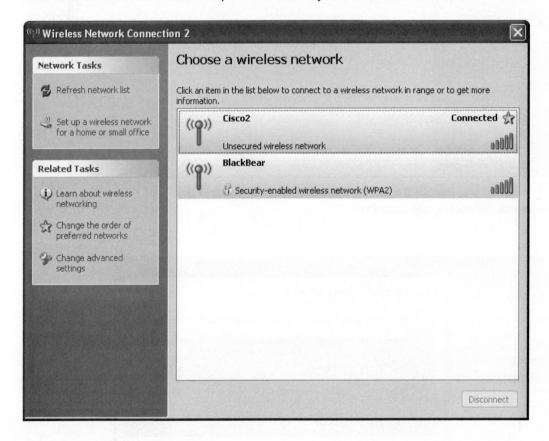

Click **Change advanced settings**.

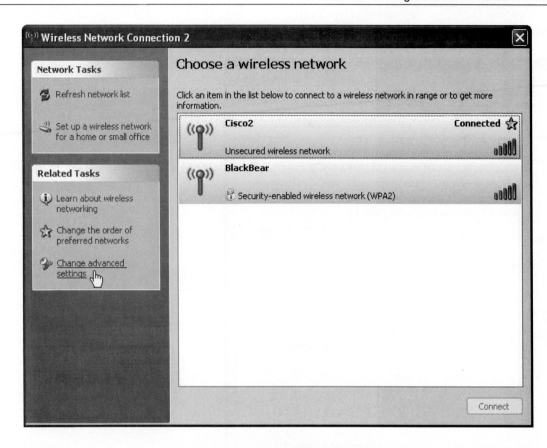

The "Wireless Network Connection Properties" window opens.

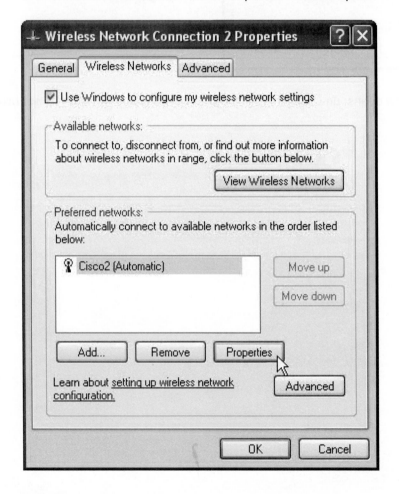

Click **Wireless Networks** tab > **Cisco# (Automatic)** > **Properties**.

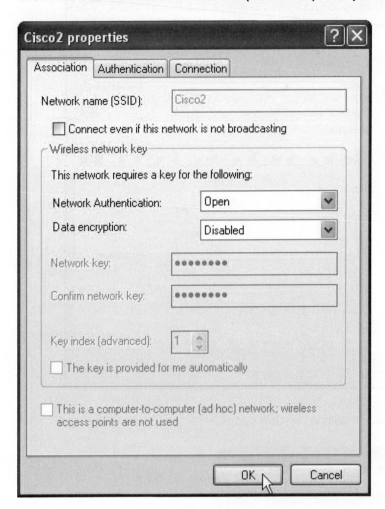

When "Cisco# properties" window opens, un-check the box **Connect even if this network in not broadcasting > OK**.

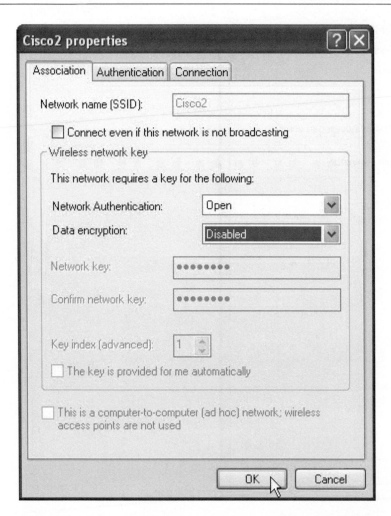

When the warring message appears, click **Continue Anyway**.

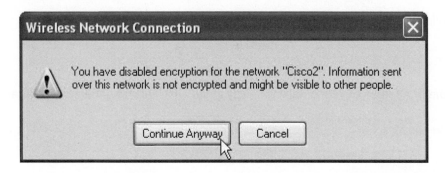

Select **Connection** tab > un-check the box **Connect when this network is in range** > **OK**.

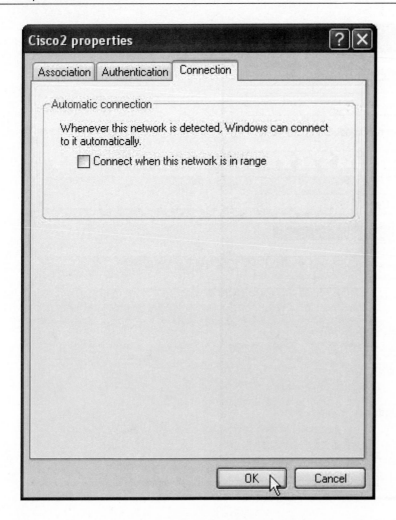

When the warring message appears, click **Continue Anyway**.

Click **OK** to close the "Wireless Network Connection Properties" window.

Step 8

Open a browser. Type the IP address of your default gateway in the URL field, and then press **Enter**.

The "Connect to" window appears.

Type the password provided by the instructor in the "Password:" field.

The Setup screen appears.

Navigate to "Basic Wireless Settings". Select **Disable** for the 2.4 GHz SSID broadcast.

Click **Save Settings > Continue**.

Why would you disable SSID broadcast?

View wireless networks associated with the wireless adapter configured to the computer.

Click **Start > Control Panel > Network Connections >** right-click the wireless adapter, and select **View Available Wireless Networks**.

Note: You may need to refresh the list every 30 seconds until the Cisco# connection is no longer listed.

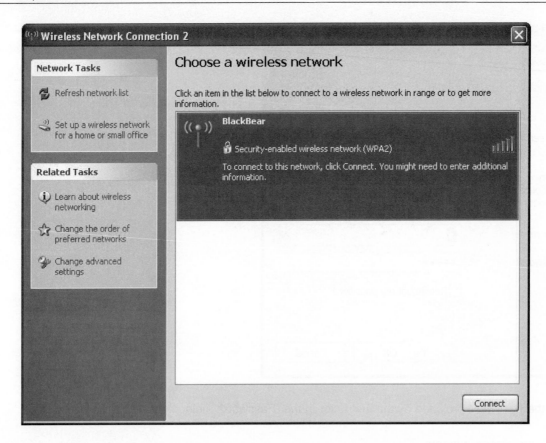

What wireless network(s) are available?

Click **Start > Control Panel > Network Connections >** right-click the wireless adapter **> Properties > View Networks** tab > select **Cisco# (On Demand) > Properties**.

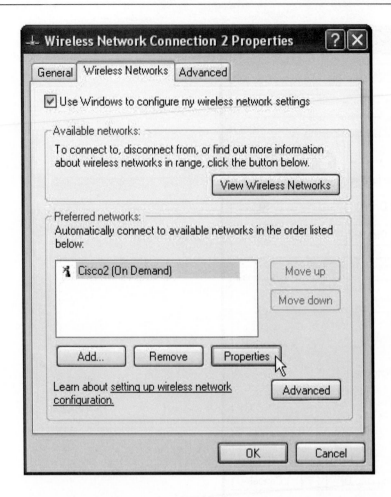

When the "Cisco# properties" window opens, place a check mark in the box next to **Connect even if this network in not broadcasting > OK**.

Select **Connection** tab > place a check mark in the box next to **Connect when this network is in range > OK > OK**.

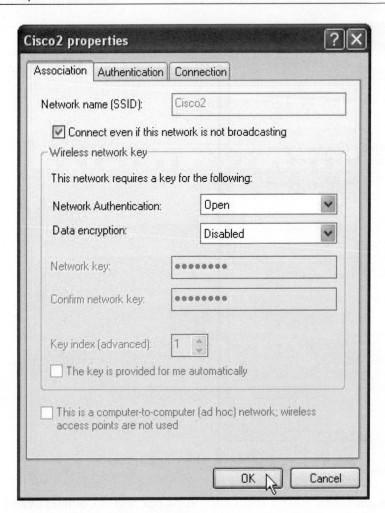

When the "Network Connections" window opens, click **View available wireless networks**.

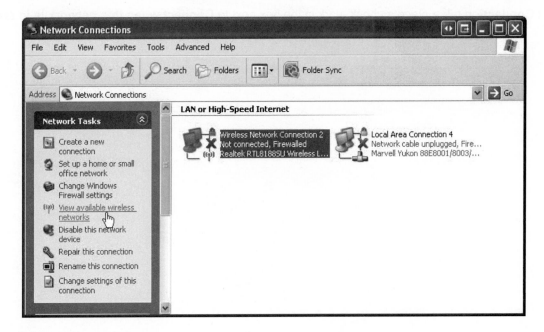

Press **Refresh network list** until Cisco# appears in the list.

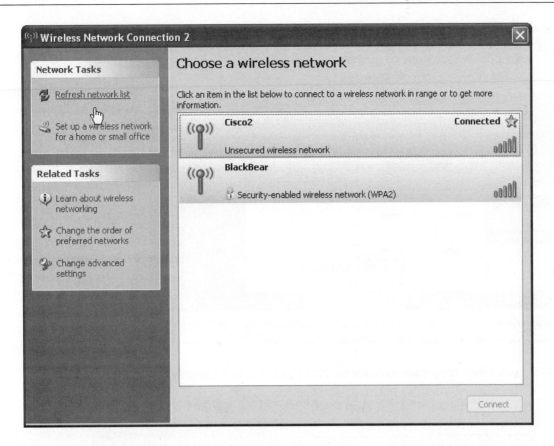

What wireless network(s) are available?

Step 9

Connect to **cisco#**, where # is the number assigned by the instructor and log into the router.

Use a browser to logon to the router.

Click the **Wireless** tab and then select **Wireless Security**.

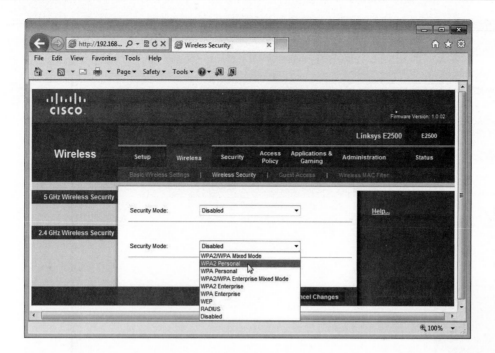

In the Security Mode drop-down box, for the "2.4 GHz Wireless Security", select **WPA2 Personal**.

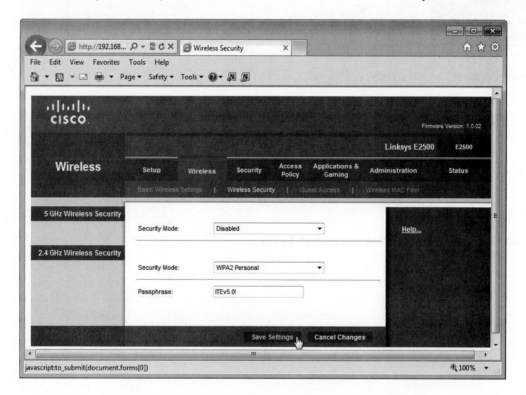

Type **ITEv5.0!** for the Passphrase and click **Save Settings > Continue**.

Step 10

View wireless networks associated with the wireless adapter configured to the computer.

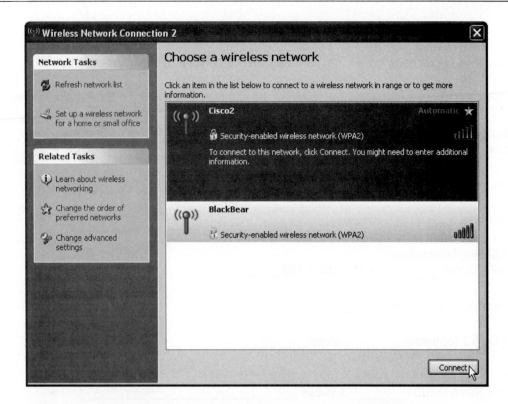

Choose **cisco#**, where # is the number assigned by the instructor, and then click the **Connect** button.

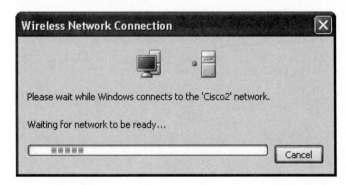

When the security screen appears, type **ITEv5.0!** for the "Network key", confirm the key, and then click **Connect**.

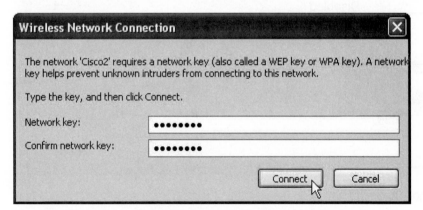

The "Please wait while Windows connects to the "Cisco#" network." screen appears.

When the screen closes, use a browser to logon to the router

If you cannot access the GUI of the router, contact the instructor.

Step 11

Return configurations to the following settings, unless stated otherwise by the instructor.

Connect the computer to one of the **Ethernet** ports on the wireless router with an Ethernet patch cable.

Router Address Information:

        IP address _____ 192.168.1.1 _____

        Subnet mask _____ 255.255.255.0 _____

        Router name _____ Linksys _____

DHCP Server Setting Information:

        Start IP address _____ 192.168.1.100 _____

        Maximum number of users _____ 50 _____

        Static DNS 1 (optional) _____ blank _____

SSID Values:

        Network Name (SSID) _____ Linksys _____

        SSID Broadcast _____ Disabled _____

Channel number:

        Channel _____ Auto _____

Router Access:

        Router Password _____ admin _____

Wireless Security:

        Security Mode _____ Disable _____

Close the browser and logoff the computer.

6.8.3.14 Lab - Test the Wireless NIC in Windows 7

Introduction

In this lab, you will check the status of your wireless connection, investigate the availability of wireless networks, and test connectivity.

Recommended Equipment

- A computer with Windows 7 installed
- A wireless NIC installed
- An Ethernet NIC installed
- Linksys E2500 Wireless Router
- Internet connectivity

Step 1

Disconnect the Ethernet cable from your computer.

An "orange dot" appears over the "Connections" icon.

Hover over the "Connections" icon in the tray.

What is the name of the wireless connection?

Connect to a wireless network.

Open a command window.

Ping **127.0.0.1**.

How many replies did you receive?

Use the **ipconfig** command.

What is the IP address of the default gateway?

Ping the default gateway.

A successful ping indicates that there is a connection between the computer and the default gateway.

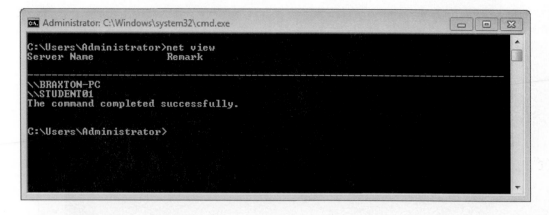

Type **net view**.

List the computer names that are displayed.

If you have an external connection, try the following commands.

Use the **tracert** command along with your school's Web site or the Cisco Networking Academy Web site. Example: type **tracert www.netacad.com**.

What IP address was returned?

Use the **nslookup** command with the IP address you just discovered.

Type **nslookup 72.163.6.233**.

What name was returned?

Step 2

Open a web browser.

Type **www.cisco.com** in the "Address" field, and then press **Enter**.

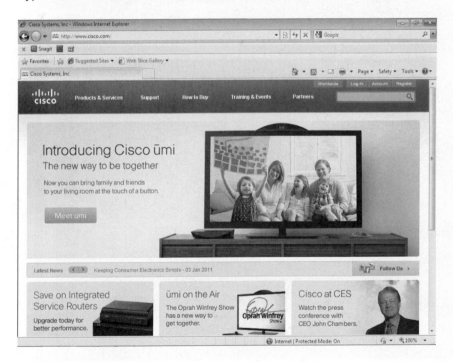

Step 3

Open the **Network Connections** window.

Right-click the **Wireless Network Connection** icon > **Status**.

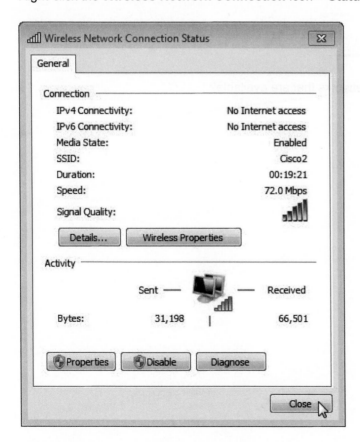

The "Wireless Network Connection Status" window opens.

Click **Close**.

Right-click the wireless connection and select **Connect / Disconnect**.

Select **All** from the Show drop-down menu.

Click the **Refresh** button.

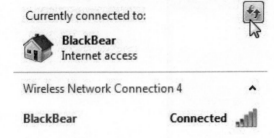

Open Network and Sharing Center

What are the names of the wireless networks that are available?

6.8.3.15 Lab - Test the Wireless NIC in Windows Vista

Introduction

In this lab, you will check the status of your wireless connection, investigate the availability of wireless networks, and test connectivity.

Recommended Equipment

- A computer with Windows Vista installed
- A wireless NIC installed
- An Ethernet NIC installed
- Linksys E2500 Wireless Router
- Internet connectivity

Step 1

Disconnect the Ethernet cable from your computer.

A red "X" appears over the "Local Area Connection" icon.

Connect to a wireless network.

Hover over the "Wireless Network Connection" icon in the tray.

What is the name of the wireless connection?

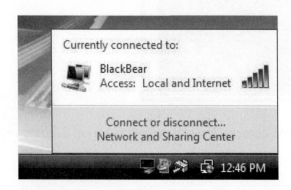

Open a command window.

Ping 127.0.0.1.

```
C:\Windows\system32\cmd.exe                                    _ □ X

C:\>ping 127.0.0.1

Pinging 127.0.0.1 with 32 bytes of data:
Reply from 127.0.0.1: bytes=32 time=9ms TTL=128
Reply from 127.0.0.1: bytes=32 time<1ms TTL=128
Reply from 127.0.0.1: bytes=32 time<1ms TTL=128
Reply from 127.0.0.1: bytes=32 time<1ms TTL=128

Ping statistics for 127.0.0.1:
    Packets: Sent = 4, Received = 4, Lost = 0 (0% loss),
Approximate round trip times in milli-seconds:
    Minimum = 0ms, Maximum = 9ms, Average = 2ms

C:\>_
```

How many replies did you receive?

Use the **ipconfig** command.

```
C:\Windows\system32\cmd.exe                                    _ □ X

C:\>ipconfig

Windows IP Configuration

Ethernet adapter Local Area Connection:

   Connection-specific DNS Suffix  . :
   Link-local IPv6 Address . . . . . : fe80::e016:96c0:2623:8f16%11
   IPv4 Address. . . . . . . . . . . : 192.168.1.195
   Subnet Mask . . . . . . . . . . . : 255.255.255.0
   Default Gateway . . . . . . . . . : 192.168.1.1
```

What is the IP address of the default gateway?

Ping the default gateway.

```
C:\Windows\system32\cmd.exe                                    _ □ X

C:\>ping 192.168.1.1

Pinging 192.168.1.1 with 32 bytes of data:
Reply from 192.168.1.1: bytes=32 time=30ms TTL=64
Reply from 192.168.1.1: bytes=32 time=3ms TTL=64
Reply from 192.168.1.1: bytes=32 time=3ms TTL=64
Reply from 192.168.1.1: bytes=32 time=2ms TTL=64

Ping statistics for 192.168.1.1:
    Packets: Sent = 4, Received = 4, Lost = 0 (0% loss),
Approximate round trip times in milli-seconds:
    Minimum = 2ms, Maximum = 30ms, Average = 9ms

C:\>_
```

A successful ping indicates that there is a connection between the computer and the default gateway.

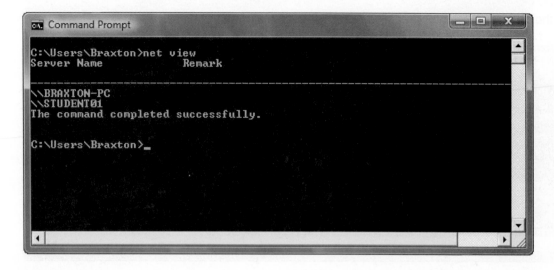

Type **net view**.

List the computer names that are displayed.

If you have an external connection, try the following commands.

Use the **tracert** command along with your school's Web site or the Cisco Networking Academy Web site. Example: type **tracert www.netacad.net**.

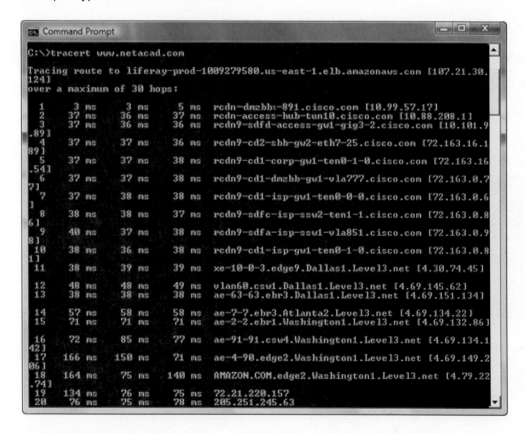

What IP address was returned?

Use the **nslookup** command with the IP address you just discovered.

Type **nslookup 72.163.6.233**.

What name was returned?

Step 2

Open a web browser.

Type **www.cisco.com** in the "Address" field, and then press **Enter**.

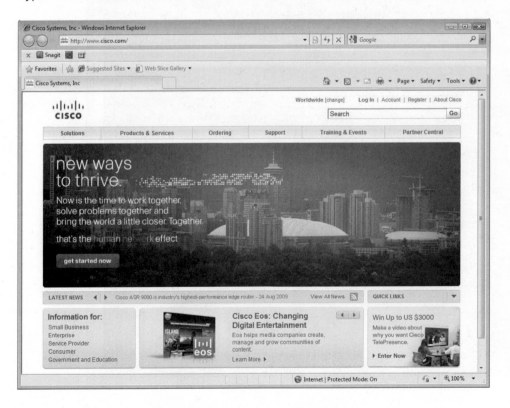

Step 3

Open the **Network Connections** window.

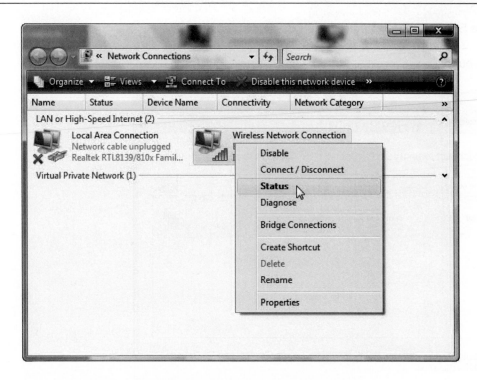

Right-click the **Wireless Network Connection** icon > **Status**.

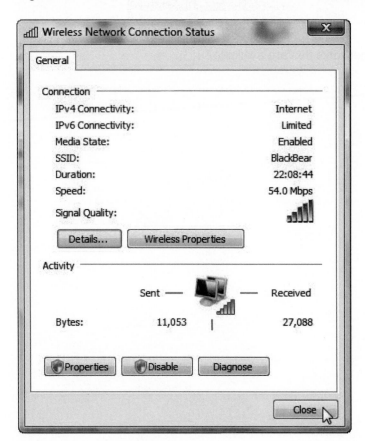

The "Wireless Network Connection Status" window opens.

Click **Close**.

Right-click the wireless connection and select **Connect / Disconnect**.

Select **All** from the Show drop-down menu.

Click the **Refresh** button.

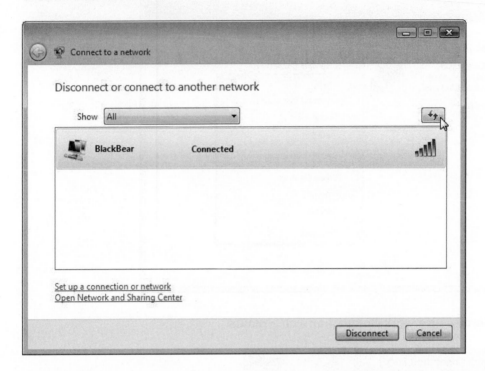

What are the names of the wireless networks that are available?

6.8.3.16 Lab - Test the Wireless NIC in Windows XP

Introduction

In this lab, you will check the status of your wireless connection, investigate the availability of wireless networks, and test connectivity.

Recommended Equipment

- A computer with Windows XP installed
- A wireless NIC installed
- An Ethernet NIC installed
- Linksys E2500 Wireless Router
- Internet connectivity

Step 1

Disconnect the Ethernet patch cable from your computer.

A red "X" appears over the "Local Area Connection" icon.

Hover over the "Wireless Network Connection" icon in the tray.

What is the speed and signal strength?

Open a command window.

Ping 127.0.0.1.

How many replies did you receive?

```
C:\WINDOWS\system32\cmd.exe

C:\>ping 127.0.0.1

Pinging 127.0.0.1 with 32 bytes of data:

Reply from 127.0.0.1: bytes=32 time<1ms TTL=128
Reply from 127.0.0.1: bytes=32 time<1ms TTL=128
Reply from 127.0.0.1: bytes=32 time<1ms TTL=128
Reply from 127.0.0.1: bytes=32 time<1ms TTL=128

Ping statistics for 127.0.0.1:
    Packets: Sent = 4, Received = 4, Lost = 0 (0% loss),
Approximate round trip times in milli-seconds:
    Minimum = 0ms, Maximum = 0ms, Average = 0ms

C:\>
```

Use the **ipconfig** command.

What is the IP address of the default gateway?

```
C:\WINDOWS\system32\cmd.exe

C:\>ipconfig

Windows IP Configuration

Ethernet adapter Local Area Connection:

        Media State . . . . . . . . . . . : Media disconnected

Ethernet adapter Wireless Network Connection:

        Connection-specific DNS Suffix  . :
        IP Address. . . . . . . . . . . . : 192.168.2.3
        Subnet Mask . . . . . . . . . . . : 255.255.255.0
        Default Gateway . . . . . . . . . : 192.168.2.1

C:\>
```

Ping the default gateway.

```
C:\WINDOWS\system32\cmd.exe

C:\>ping 192.168.2.1

Pinging 192.168.2.1 with 32 bytes of data:

Reply from 192.168.2.1: bytes=32 time=1ms TTL=64
Reply from 192.168.2.1: bytes=32 time=1ms TTL=64
Reply from 192.168.2.1: bytes=32 time=1ms TTL=64
Reply from 192.168.2.1: bytes=32 time=1ms TTL=64

Ping statistics for 192.168.2.1:
    Packets: Sent = 4, Received = 4, Lost = 0 (0% loss),
Approximate round trip times in milli-seconds:
    Minimum = 1ms, Maximum = 1ms, Average = 1ms

C:\>
```

A successful ping indicates that there is a connection between the computer and the default gateway.

Type **net view**.

List the computer names that are displayed.

If you have an external connection, try the following commands.

Use the **tracert** command along with your school's Web site or the Cisco Networking Academy Web site. Example: type **tracert www.netacad.com**.

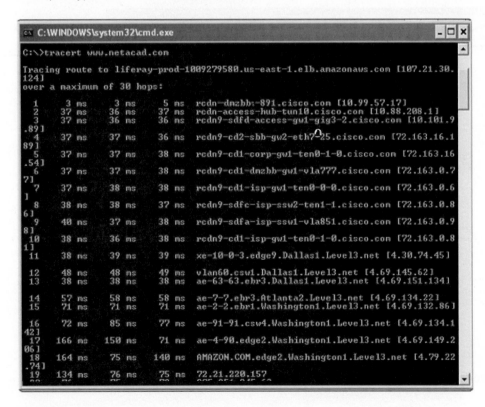

What IP address was returned?

Use the **nslookup** command with the IP address you just discovered.

Type **nslookup 72.163.6.233**.

What name was returned?

Step 2

Open a web browser.

Type **www.cisco.com** in the "Address" field, and then press **Return**.

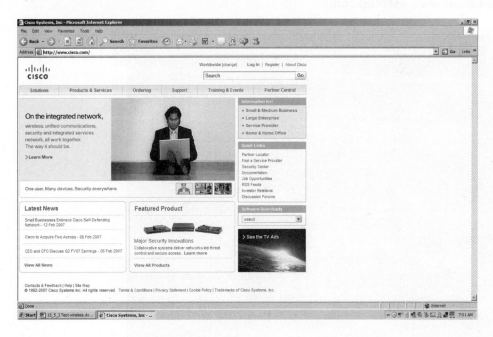

Step 3

Open the **Network Connections** window.

Right-click the **Wireless Network Connection** icon > **Status**.

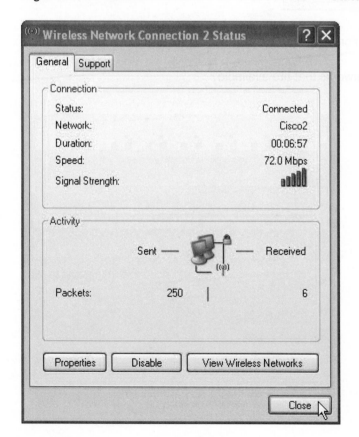

The "Wireless Network Connection Status" window opens.

Click **Close**.

Right-click the wireless connection and select **Properties**.

Click the **Wireless Networks** tab.

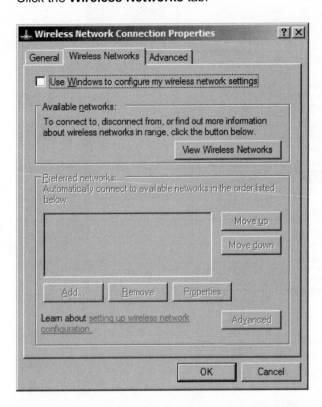

Click the **View Wireless Networks** button.

What are the names of the wireless networks that are available?

6.8.4.7 Lab - Share a Folder, Create a Homegroup, and Map a Network Drive in Windows 7

Introduction

In this lab, you will create and share a folder, set permissions for the shares, create a homegroup to share resources, and map a network drive.

Recommended Equipment

- Two computers running Windows 7 that are directly connected to each other or through a switch or hub.

- To better identify which steps should be done on a computer, the lab will refer to them as computer01, computer02, or both. Only change which computer you are working on when informed within the instructions.

Step 1

Workgroup Information:

Workgroup name _____

Complete the following steps on both computers.

Click **Start** > right-click **Computer** > **Properties**.

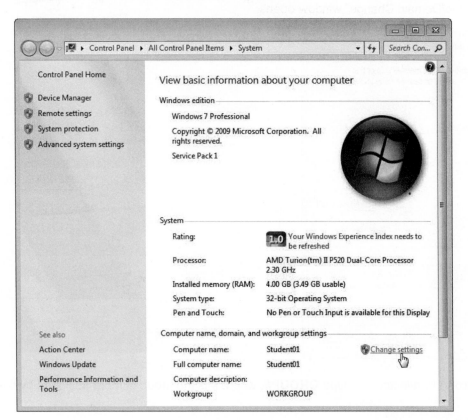

Click **Change settings**.

The "System Properties" window opens.

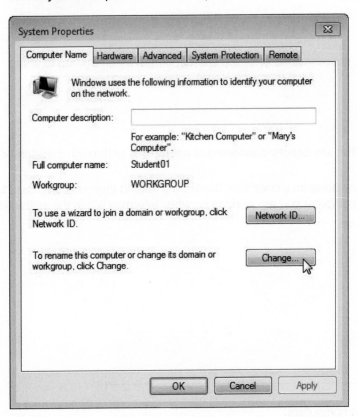

Click the **Change** button.

The "Computer Name/Domain Change" window opens.

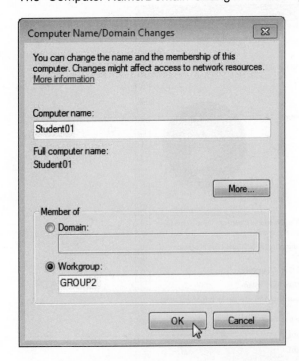

Make sure **Workgroup** is selected and type **GROUP#**, where # is the group number assigned by the instructor.

Click **OK**.

Click **OK** when the "Welcome to the GROUP# workgroup" screen opens.

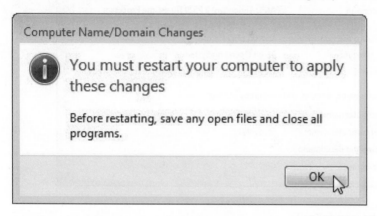

Click **OK** to restart the computer.

Close all opened windows and programs.

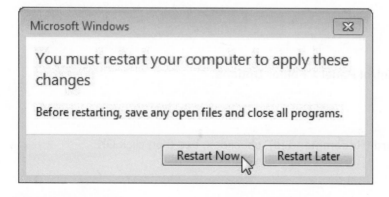

Click **Restart Now**.

Step 2

Complete the following steps on both computers.

Click **Start > right-click Computer > Properties**.

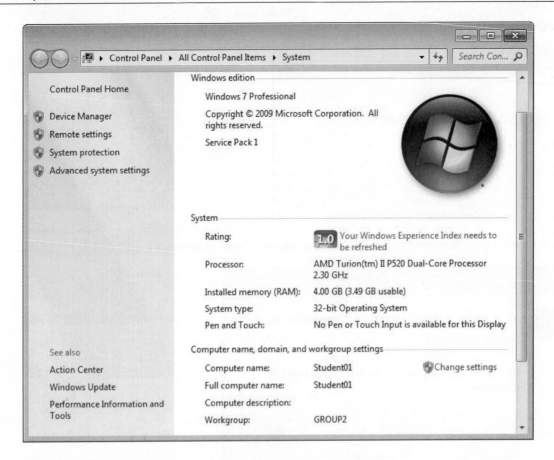

What is the Workgroup name for the computer?

Close the "System" window.

Step 3

On computer01, click **Start > Control Panel > Folder Options**.

Click the **View** tab.

Uncheck the "**Use Sharing Wizard (Recommended)**" checkbox, and then click **OK**.

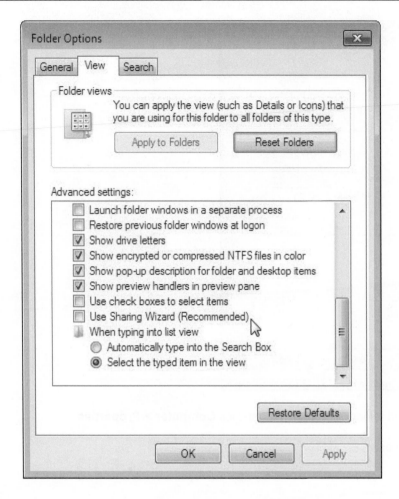

Step 4

On computer01, right-click the **desktop**, and then choose **New > Folder**.

Type **Example** to name the folder, and then press the **Enter** key.

Open Notepad. Type "**This is an example document**".

Save the file in the "Example" folder with the name "Brief", and then close Notepad.

Step 5

On computer01, right-click the **Example** folder, and then choose **Sharing with > Advanced Sharing > Advanced Sharing**.

Select the **Share this folder** checkbox, and then click **OK**.

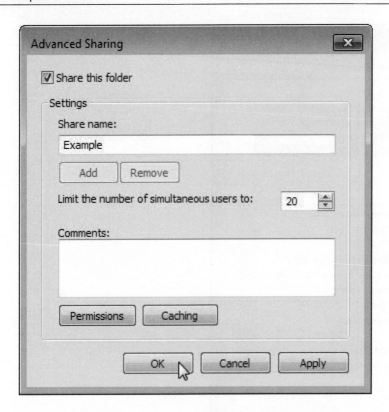

On the computer with the shared folder, click **Start** > right-click **Computer** > **Properties**.

What is the name of the computer?

Step 6

On computer02, choose **Start > Search programs and files**.

Type **\\computername\Example**, where computername is the name of the computer with the "Example" folder, and then press the **Enter** key.

Can you open the "Brief" file?

Can you delete the "Brief" file?

What happens?

Click **Cancel**.

Step 7

Return to the computer with the shared folder, computer01.

Right-click **Example** folder > **Sharing with** > **Advanced sharing** > **Advanced Sharing** > **Permissions**.

What are the default permissions?

Close all open windows.

Delete the shared folder.

Step 8

On both computers, click **Start > Control Panel > HomeGroup**.

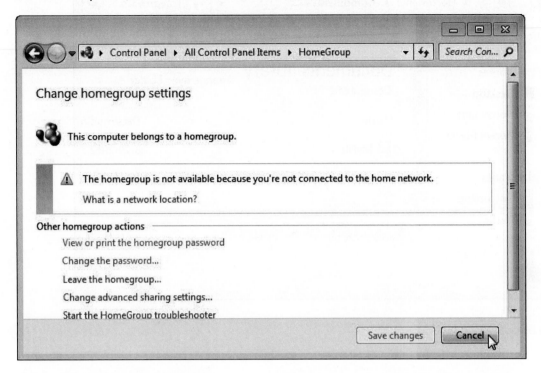

Why is homegroup not available?

Click **Cancel**.

Step 9

On both computers, click **Start > Documents**.

On computer01, create a folder, in Document library, called Computer01.

On computer02, create a folder, in Document library, called Computer02.

For both computers, open notepade and type the following text: "**This file is shared in a homegroup**". Next, save the file as "MyFile" inside the folder you just created.

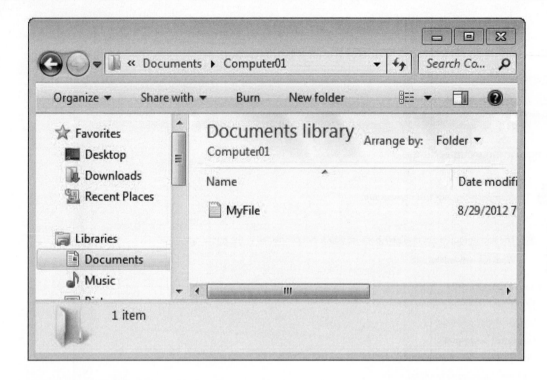

Close all open windows.

Step 10

On computer01, click **Start > Control Panel > Network and Sharing Center > Public network**.

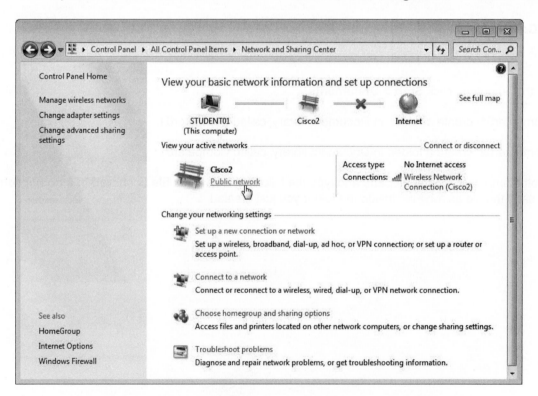

The "Set Network Location" window opens.

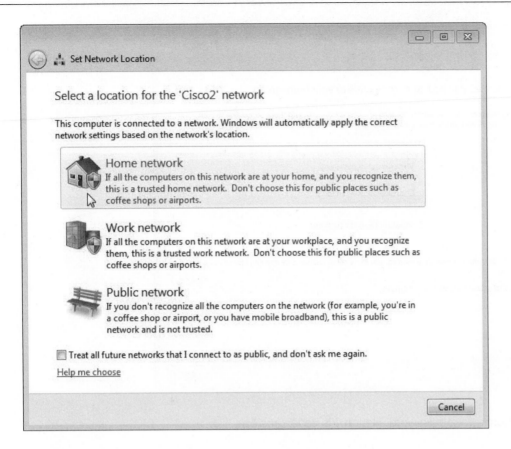

Click **Home network**.

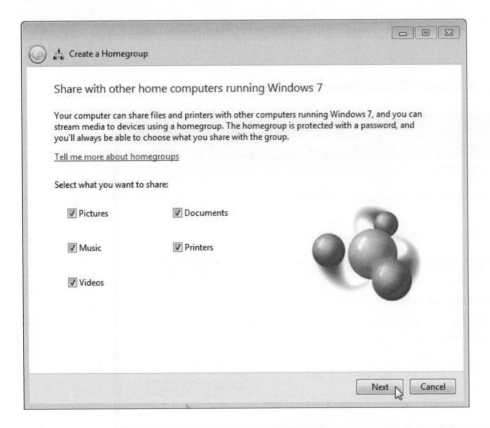

Make sure **Documents** is checked, and then click **Next**.

Record the homegroup password. Notice it is case sensitive.

Click **Finish**.

Step 11

On computer02, click **Start > Control Panel > HomeGroup**.

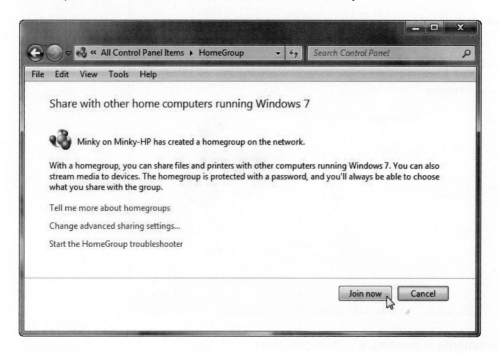

Click **Join now**.

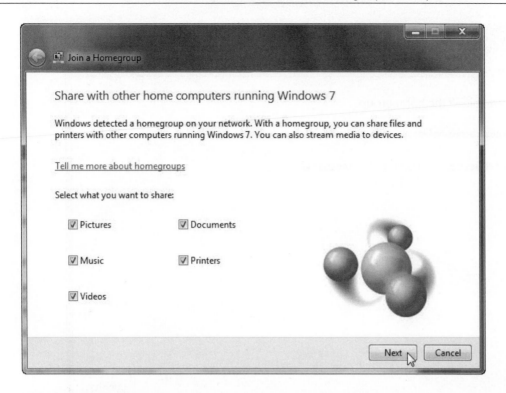

Make sure **Documents** is checked, and then click **Next**.

Enter the password you record when the Homegroup was created, and then click **Next**.

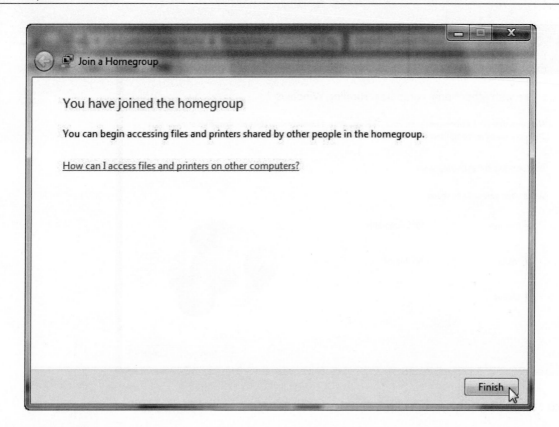

Click **Finish**.

Step 12

On both computers, complete the following if it is not already configured on the computer.

Right-click **Start > Properties > Start Menu** tab **> Customize**.

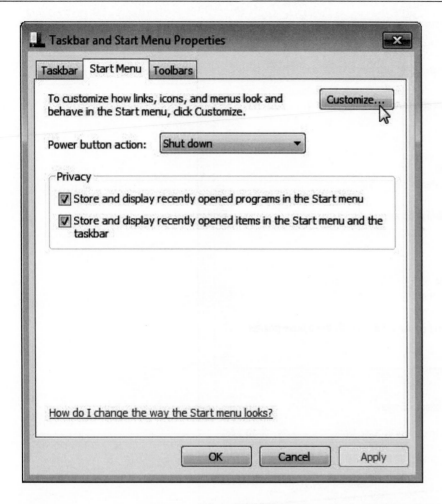

Scroll down until you see both the" Homegroup" and "Network" icons.

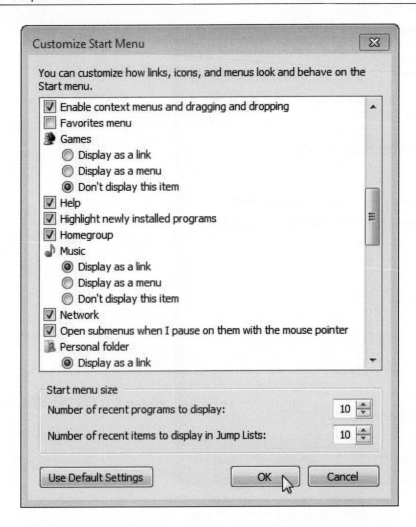

Place a check mark in each, if this is not already done, and then click **OK > OK**.

Step 13

On both computers, click **Start**, and then the **Homegroup** icon in the start menu.

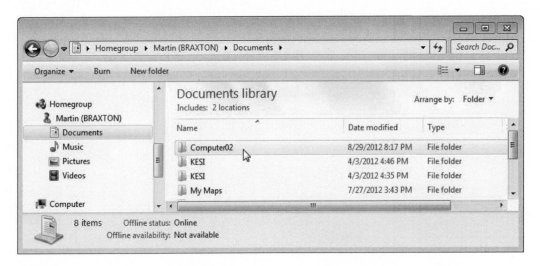

Locate the Homegroup icon, click the expand arrow next to the other computer name, click **Documents**, and then double-click **Computer#** (where # is the number of the folder located on the other computer).

Can you delete the file located on the other computer?

Right-click on the file > **Properties** > **Security** tab > select **HomeUsers**.

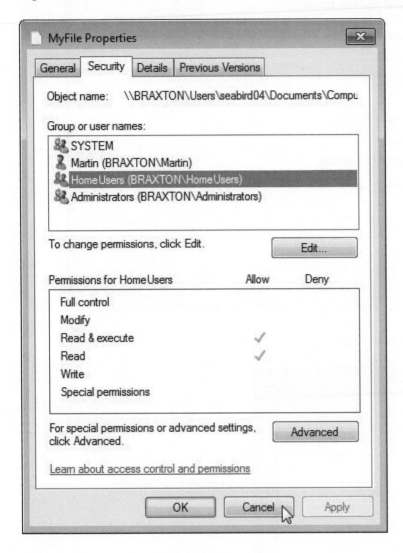

What are the "Permissions for HomeUsers"?

Click **Cancel**.

Close all open windows.

Step 14

On both computers, click **Start** > right-click **Network** > **Map network drive**.

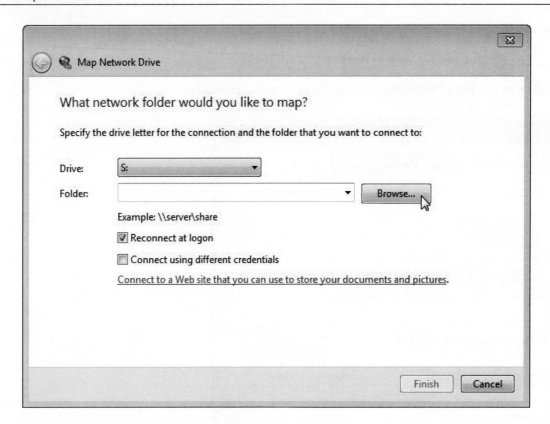

Set the Drive to "**S**" and then click **Browse...**

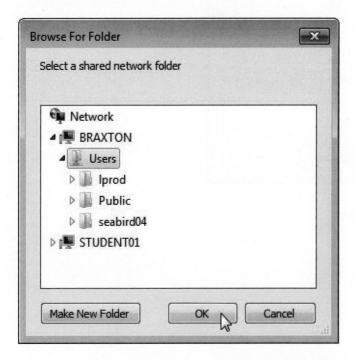

Once the window is populated, expand the other computer and select **Users > OK**.

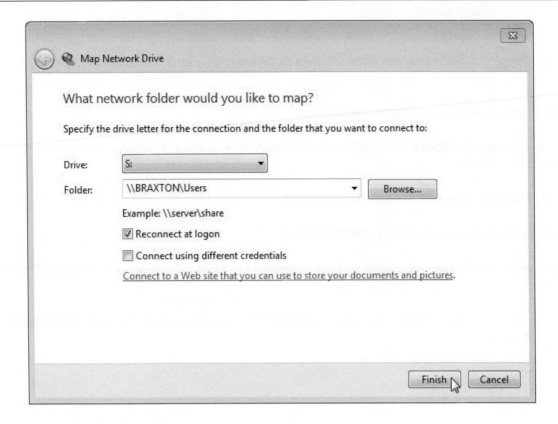

Click **Finish**.

Close all open windows.

Click **Start > Computer**.

Which Network Location drive do you see?

Step 15

On both computers, return configurations to the following settings, unless stated otherwise by the instructor.

Delete all folders and files created on the computer.

Leave the homegroup. **Start > Control Panel > Homegroup > Leave the homegroup > Leave the homegroup > Finish**.

Set the network location type back to **Public** network.

Change the Workgroup name back to **WORKGROUP**.

Place a check next to **Use sharing Wizard (Recommended)**. **Start > Control Panel > Folder Options > View** tab.

Delete any mapped drives. **Start >** right-click **Network > Disconnect network drive >** select network drive **> OK**.

6.8.4.8 Lab - Share a Folder and Map a Network Drive in Windows Vista

Introduction

In this lab, you will create and share a folder, set permissions for the shares, and map a network drive.

Recommended Equipment

- Two computers running Windows Vista that are directly connected to each other or through a switch or hub
- To better identify which steps should be done on a computer, the lab will refer to them as computer01, computer02, or both. Only change which computer you are working on when informed within the instructions.

Step 1

Workgroup Information:
      Workgroup name _____

Complete the following steps on both computers. Logon as the administrator.

Click **Start** > right-click **Computer** > **Properties**.

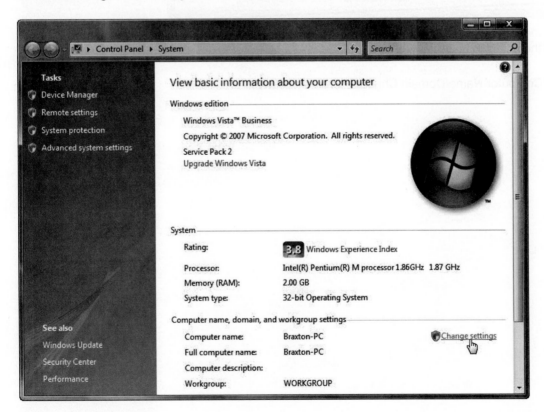

Click **Change settings** > **Continue**.

The "System Properties" window opens.

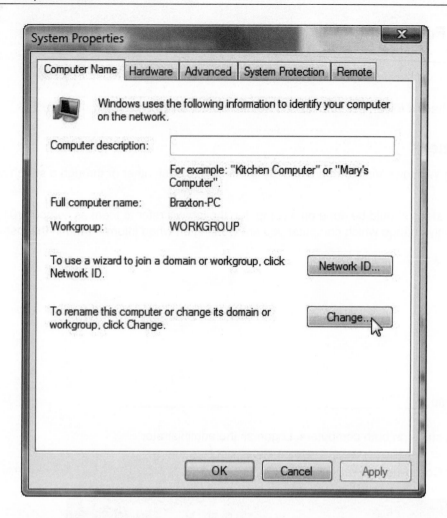

Click the **Change** button.

The "Computer Name/Domain Change" window opens.

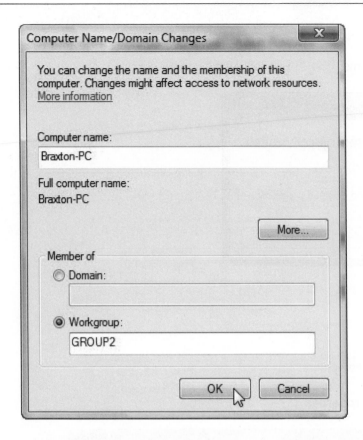

Make sure **Workgroup** is selected and type **GROUP#**, where # is the group number assigned by the instructor.

Click **OK**.

Click **OK** when the "Welcome to the GROUP# workgroup" screen opens.

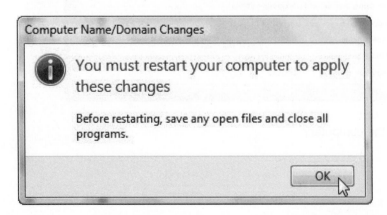

Click **OK** to restart the computer.

Close all opened windows and programs.

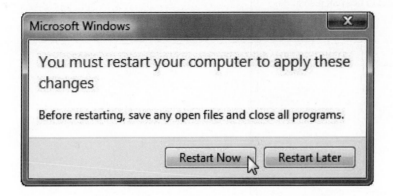

Click **Restart Now**.

Step 2

Complete the following steps on both computers.

Click **Start** > right-click **Computer** > **Properties**.

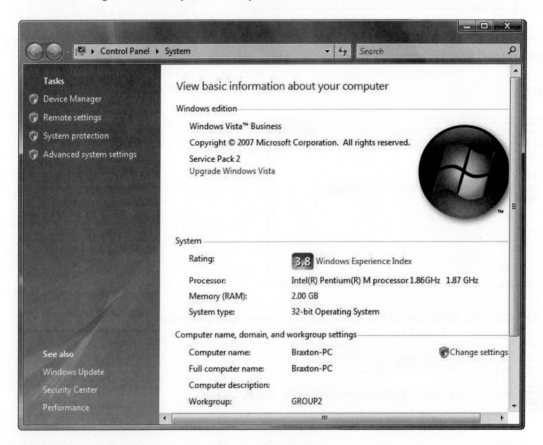

What is the Workgroup name for the computer?

Close the "System" window.

Step 3

On computer01, click **Start > Control Panel >** double-click **Folder Options**.

Click the **View** tab.

Uncheck the "**Use Sharing Wizard (Recommended)**" checkbox, and then click **OK**.

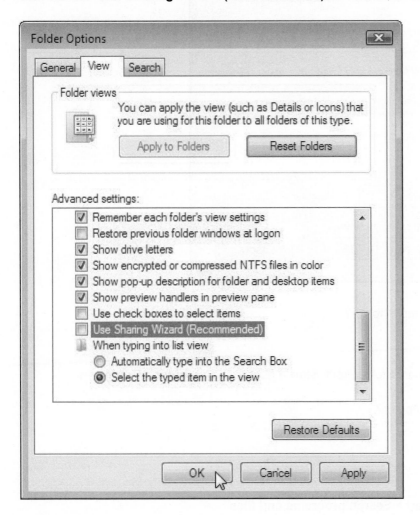

Step 4

On computer01, click right-click the **desktop**, and then choose **New > Folder**.

Type **Example**, and then press the **Enter** key.

Open WordPad. Type **"This is an example document."**.

Save the file in the "Example" folder with the name "Brief.doc", and then close WordPad.

Step 5

On computer01, right-click the **Example** folder, and then choose **Share > Advanced Sharing > Continue**.

Select the **Share this folder** radio button, and then click **OK**.

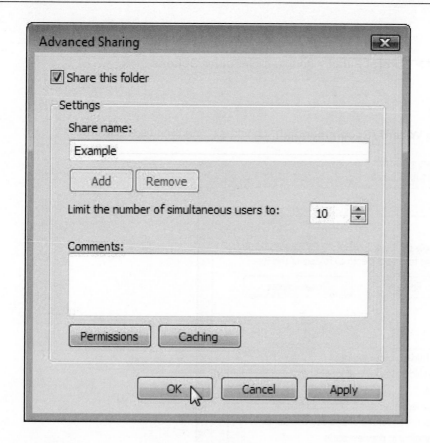

What is the icon of the "Example" folder?

On the computer with the shared folder, click **Start** > right-click **Computer** > **Properties**.

What is the name of the computer?

Step 6

On computer02, choose **Start** > **Search programs and files**.

Type **\\computername\Example**, where computername is the name of the computer with the "Example" folder, and then press the **Enter** key.

Open the "Brief.doc" file.

Delete the text in the "Brief.doc" file, and then choose **File > Save**.

What happens?

Click **OK**.

Close WordPad, and then choose **Don't Save** when prompted to save changes to the file.

Step 7

Return to the computer with the shared folder, computer01.

Right-click **Example** folder **> Sharing**, and then click **Advanced Sharing > Continue > Permissions**.

What are the default permissions?

Step 8

On both computers, complete the following if it is not already configured on the computer.

Right-click **Start > Properties > Start Menu** tab **> Customize**.

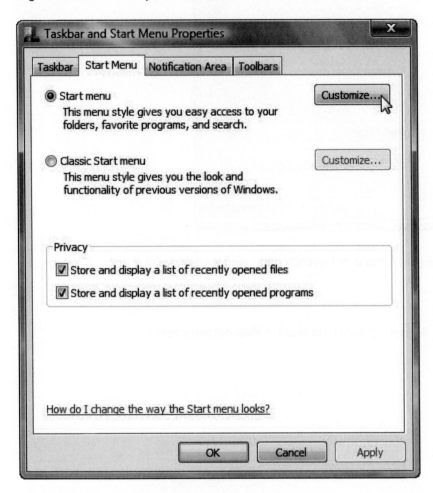

Scroll down until you see both the "Network" icons.

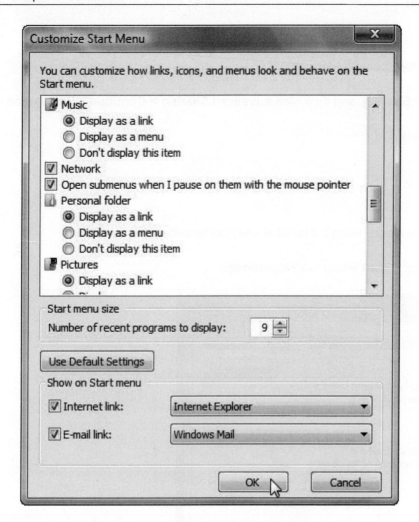

Place a check mark in the box, if this is not already done, and then click **OK > OK**.

Step 9

On both computers, click **Start >** right-click **Network > Map network drive**.

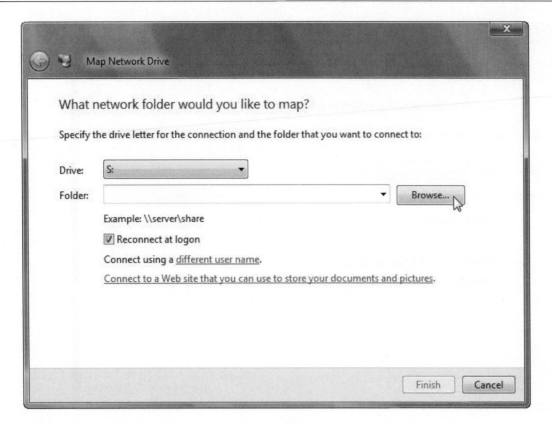

Set the Drive to "**S**" and then click **Browse…**

Once the window is populated, expand the other computer and select **Users > OK**.

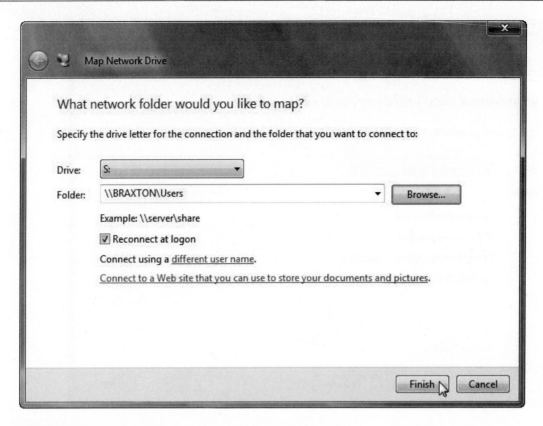

Click **Finish**.

Close all open windows.

Click **Start > Computer**.

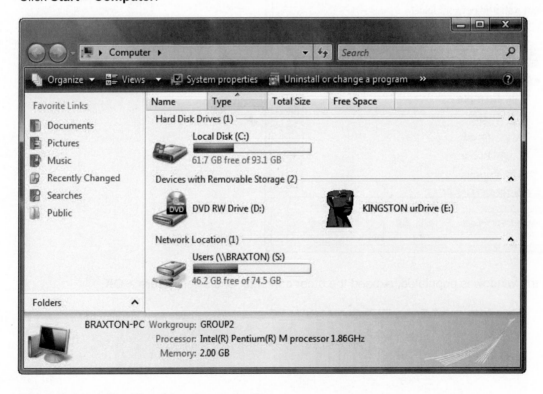

Which Network Location drive do you see?

Step 10

On both computers, return configurations to the following settings, unless stated otherwise by the instructor.

Delete all folders and files created on the computer.

Leave the homegroup. **Start > Control Panel > Homegroup > Leave the homegroup > Leave the homegroup > Finish**.

Set the network location type back to **Public** network.

Change the Workgroup name back to **WORKGROUP**.

Place a check next to **Use sharing Wizard (Recommended)**. **Start > Control Panel > Folder Options > View** tab.

Delete any mapped drives. **Start >** right-click **Network > Disconnect network drive >** select network drive **> OK**.

6.8.4.9 Lab - Share a Folder and Map a Network Drive in Windows XP

Introduction

In this lab, you will create and share a folder, set permissions for the shares, and map a network drive.

Recommended Equipment

- Two computers running Windows XP that are directly connected to each other or through a switch or hub.
- To better identify which steps should be done on a computer, the lab will refer to them as computer01, computer02, or both. Only change which computer you are working on when informed within the instructions.

Step 1

Workgroup Information:

Workgroup name _____

Complete the following steps on both computers. Logon as the administrator.

Click **Start** > right-click **My Computer** > **Properties** > **Computer Name** tab.

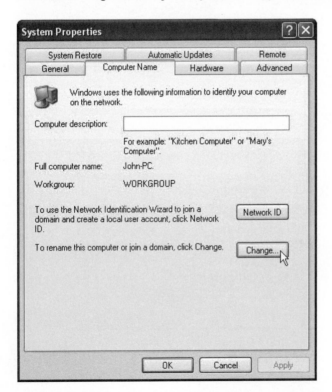

Click **Change**.

The "Computer Name Changes" window opens.

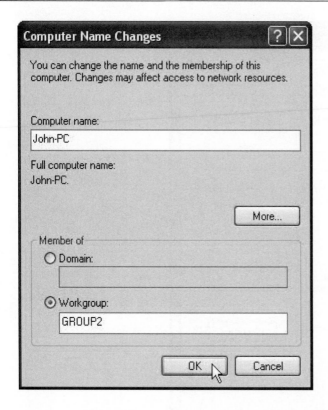

Make sure **Workgroup** is selected and type **GROUP#**, where # is the group number assigned by the instructor.

Click **OK**.

Click **OK** when the "Welcome to the GROUP# workgroup" screen opens.

Click **OK** to restart the computer.

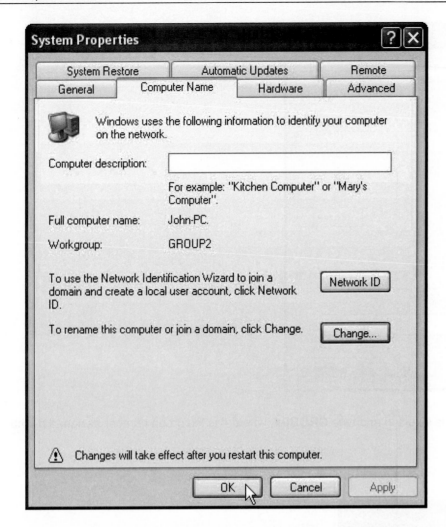

Bring the "System Properties" window to the foreground and click **OK**.

Close all opened windows and programs.

Click **Yes** to restart the computer.

Step 2

Complete the following steps on both computers.

Click **Start** > right-click **My Computer** > **Properties** > **Computer Name** tab.

6.9.1.8 Worksheet - ISP Connection Types

In this worksheet, you will determine the best ISP type for your customer.

Be prepared to discuss your answers.

Scenario 1

The customer lives in a remote area deep in a valley and cannot afford broadband.

Scenario 2

The customer can only receive television using satellite but lives in an area where high-speed Internet access is available.

Scenario 3

The customer is a sales-person who travels most of the time. A connection to the main office is required almost 24 hours a day.

Scenario 4

The customer works from home, needs the fastest possible upload and download speeds to access the company's FTP server, and lives in a very remote area where DSL and cable are not available.

Scenario 5

The customer wants to bundle television, Internet access, and phone all through the same company, but the local phone company does not offer all the services.

Scenario 6

The customer works downtown in a large city and requires a fast reliable connection that is not easily disrupted by large buildings.

Chapter 7: Laptops

7.1.1.6 Worksheet - Research Docking Stations

In this activity, you will use the Internet, a newspaper, or a local store to gather information and then enter the specifications for a laptop docking station onto this worksheet. Be prepared to discuss your decisions regarding the docking station you select.

1. Research a docking station compatible with a laptop. What is the model number of the docking station?

2. What is the approximate cost?

3. What are the dimensions of the docking station?

4. How does the laptop connect to the docking station?

5. List the features available with this docking station.

6. Is this docking station compatible with other laptop models?

7.3.1.3 Worksheet - Match ACPI Standards

Enter the ACPI standard next to the matching power management state description.

S0	S1	S2	S3	S4	S5

ACPI Standard	Power Management States
	The CPU is off, but the RAM is refreshed to maintain the contents.
	The CPU and RAM are off. The contents of RAM have been saved to a temporary file on the hard disk.
	The CPU is not executing instructions; however, the CPU and RAM are still receiving power.
	The CPU is off, and the RAM is set to a slow refresh rate.
	The computer is off and any content that has not been saved will be lost.
	The computer is on and the CPU is running at full power.

7.5.1.4 Worksheet - Laptop RAM

In this activity, you will use the Internet, a newspaper, or a local store to gather information about expansion memory for a laptop.

1. Research the manufacturer specifications for the memory in a laptop. List the specifications in the table below:

Memory Specifications	Laptop Expansion Memory
Form Factor	
Type	
Size (MB)	
Manufacturer	
Speed	
Slots	

2. Shop around, and in the table below, list the features and costs for expansion memory for a laptop.

Memory Specifications	Expansion Memory
Form Factor	
Type	
Size (MB)	
Manufacturer	
Speed	
Retail Cost	

3. In your research, did you find any reason to select a particular type of expansion memory over another?

4. Is the new expansion memory compatible with the existing memory installed in the laptop? Why is this important?

7.5.2.3 Worksheet - Laptop Batteries

In this activity, you will use the Internet, a newspaper, or a local store to gather information and then enter the specifications for a laptop battery onto this worksheet.

1. List the specifications for a laptop battery. Please ask your instructor for the laptop model to research.

2. Shop around, and in the table below, list the features and cost for a generic and a laptop battery from the manufacturer of the laptop.

Battery Specifications	Generic	Manufacturer
Voltage requirements		
Battery cell configuration-ex: 6-Cell, 9-Cell		
Compatibility		
Dimensions		
Hours of life		
Approxmate cost		

3. Based on your research, which battery would you select? Be prepared to discuss your decisions regarding the battery you select.

7.5.2.5 Worksheet - Laptop Screens

In this activity, you will use the Internet, a newspaper, or a local store to gather information and then enter the specifications for a laptop display onto this worksheet.

1. Research and list the specifications for a laptop screen with a 14.1" display. Please ask your instructor for the laptop model to research.

Screen Specifications	Display Screen
Type	
Size	
Resolution	
Manufacturer	
Backlight Type	

2. When replacing a laptop screen, the replacement screen must match many, if not all, specifications of the original screen. Research and list which specifications must match the original display screen.

3. Shop around, and in the table below, list the features and cost of two replacement screens for a laptop.

Screen Specifications	Replacement #1	Replacement #2
Type		
Size		
Resolution		
Manufacturer		
Backlight Type		
Approximate Cost		
Warranty		

4. Based on your research, which replacement screen would you select? Be prepared to discuss your decisions regarding the screen you select.

7.5.2.7 Worksheet - Laptop Hard Drives

In this activity, you will use the Internet, a newspaper, or a local store to gather information about expansion memory for a laptop.

1. Research the manufacturer specifications for the hard drive in the laptop. List the specifications in the table below:

Hard Drive Specifications	Hard Drive
Form Factor	
Type	
Size (GB)	
Manufacturer	
Port Type	
Speed	

2. Shop around, and in the table below list the features and costs of two replacement hard drives for a laptop.

Hard Drive Specifications	Replacement Hard Drive #1	Replacement Hard Drive #2
Form Factor		
Type		
Size (GB)		
Manufacturer		
Port Type		
Retail Cost		

3. In your research, did you find any reason to select a particular hard drive over another?

4. Is the new hard drive compatible with other components in the laptop? Why is this important?

7.5.2.13 Worksheet - Build a Specialized Laptop

In this worksheet, you will use the Internet, a newspaper, or a local store to gather information about building a specialized laptop that supports hardware and software that allows a user to perform tasks that an off-the-shelf system cannot perform. Be prepared to discuss your selections.

For this worksheet, assume the customer's system will be compatible with the parts you order.

1. The customer runs an audio and video editing workstation to record music, create music CDs, CD labels, and to create home movies. The customer wishes to upgrade the components listed in the table.

Brand and Model Number	Features	Cost
Audio card		
Video card		
Hard drive		
External monitors		

Provide reasons for the components purchased. How will they support the customer's needs?

2. The customer runs computer-aided design (CAD) or computer-aided manufacturing (CAM) software and wishes to upgrade the components listed in the table.

Brand and Model Number	Features	Cost
CPU		
Video card		
RAM		

Provide reasons for the components purchased. How will they support the customer's needs?

3. The customer uses virtualization technologies to run several different operating systems to test software compatibility. The customer wishes to upgrade the components listed in the table.

Brand and Model Number	Features	Cost
RAM		
CPU		

Provide reasons for the components purchased. How will they support the customer's needs?

7.7.2.2 Worksheet - Research Laptop Problems

Laptops often use proprietary parts. To find information about the replacement parts, you may have to research the website of the laptop manufacturer.

Before you begin this worksheet, you need to know some information about the laptop.

Your instructor will provide you with the following information:

Laptop manufacturer:

Laptop model number:

Amount of RAM:

Size of the hard drive:

Use the Internet to locate the website for the laptop manufacturer. What is the URL for the website?

Locate the service section of the website and look for links that focus on your laptop. It is common for websites to allow you to search by the model number. The list below shows common links that you might find:

- FAQs

- WIKIs

- Service notices

- White papers

- Blogs

List the links you found specific to the laptop and include a brief description of the information in that link.

Briefly describe any service notices you found on the website. A service notice example is a driver update, a hardware issue, or a recall notice for a laptop component.

Open forums may exist for your laptop. Use an Internet search engine to locate any open forums that focus on your laptop by typing in the name and model of the laptop. Briefly describe the websites (other than the manufacturer website) that you located.

7.7.2.3 Worksheet – Gather Information from the Customer

In this worksheet, you will act as a call center technician and come up with closed-ended and open-ended questions to ask a customer about a laptop problem.

A customer complains that the network connection on the laptop is intermittent. The customer states that they are using a wireless PC card for network connectivity. The customer believes that the laptop may be too far from the wireless access point; however, he does not know where the wireless access point is located.

As a technician, you need to be able to ask questions that will be recorded on a work order. In the table below, record closed-ended question and open-ended question that you would ask a customer.

Closed-Ended Questions	Open-Ended Questions

7.7.2.4 Worksheet - Investigating Support Websites and Repair Companies

For this worksheet, you will investigate the services provided by a local laptop repair company or a laptop manufacturer support website. Use the Internet or a local phone directory to locate a local laptop repair company or laptop manufacturer support website. Answer the following questions.

Local Laptop Repair Company

1. What different types of services are offered by the repair company?

2. What brand(s) of laptop computers can be repaired at this repair company?

3. What type(s) of warranty is offered at this repair company?

4. Does the staff have industry certifications? If so, what are the certifications?

5. Is there a guaranteed completion time for repairs? If so, what are the details?

6. Does the repair company offer remote technical services?

Laptop Manufacturer Support Website

7. What steps are required for locating device drivers for a laptop?

8. What type(s) of support are offered for troubleshooting laptops?

9. Does the manufacturer website offer remote technical services, if so what type(s)?

10. What method(s) are used to located parts?

11. What steps are required for locating manuals for a laptop?

Chapter 8: Mobile Devices

8.2.2.3 Lab - Working with Android

Introduction

In this lab, you will place apps and widgets on the home screen and move them between different home screens. You will also create folders to which apps will be added and removed. Finally, you will uninstall apps from the Android device.

Recommended Equipment

The following equipment is required for this exercise:

- Android tablet or smartphone running Android version 4.0

Part 1 - Apps and Widgets

Step 1

Turn on the device and log in with the password, PIN, or other passcode, if necessary.

The main home screen appears.

Step 2

Apps can be installed using the "All Apps" icon.

Touch the **All Apps** icon.

The "All Apps" screen appears.

Touch and hold any app.

The main home screen becomes visible in the background.

Drag the app to any empty space and release it.

Step 3

Apps can also be installed directly from a home screen.

Touch and hold a blank area of a home screen.

The "Home screen" menu appears.

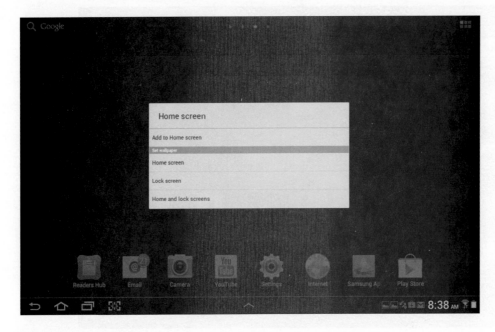

Touch **Add to Home screen**.

The "All Apps" screen appears.

Touch and hold any app.

The main home screen becomes visible in the background.

Drag the app to any empty space and release it.

Step 4

Widgets can be installed using the All Apps icon.

Touch the **All Apps** icon.

Touch the **Widgets** tab at the top of the screen.

The "Widgets" tab appears.

Touch and hold any widget.

The main home screen becomes visible in the background.

Drag the widget to any empty space and release it.

Step 5

Widgets can also be installed directly from a home screen.

Touch and hold a blank area of a home screen.

The "Home screen" menu appears.

Touch **Add to Home screen**.

Touch the **Widgets** tab.

Touch and hold any widget.

The main home screen becomes visible in the background.

Drag the widget to any empty space and release it.

Step 6

You can move apps to other home screens.

Touch and hold any app.

The home screen shifts to the background.

Drag the app to the edge of the screen.

The neighboring home screen appears in the background.

Drag the app to any empty space and release it.

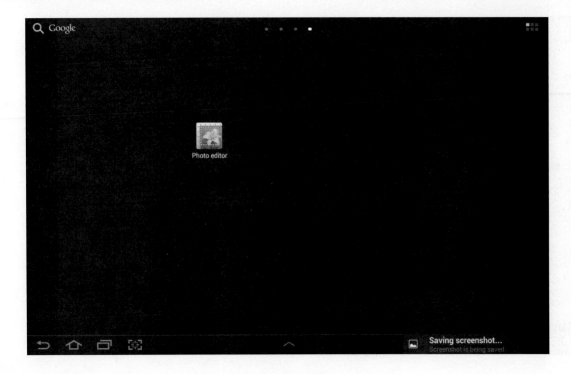

Step 7

Move another app from one home screen to another.

Step 8

Widgets can also be moved to other home screens in the same manner as apps.

Move a widget from one home screen to another.

Step 9

Move another widget from one home screen to another.

Part 2 – Folders

Step 1

Apps can be grouped together to create folders.

Place 5 apps on the same home screen.

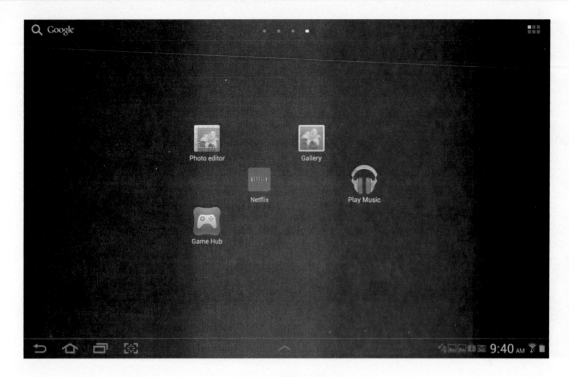

Step 2

Touch and drag one of the five apps onto the "folder" icon at the top of the screen.

Release the app.

A folder is created containing the app.

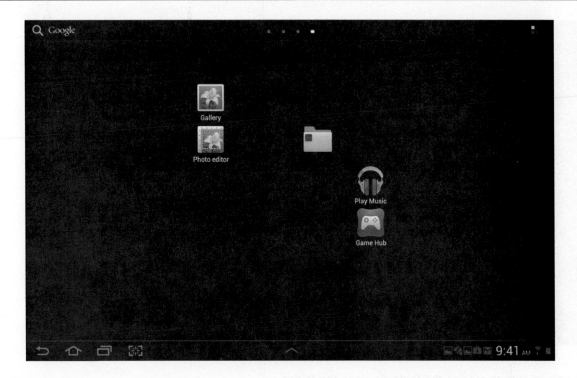

Step 3

Folders can be named to describe the contents.

Touch the folder.

Touch the words **Unnamed folder**.

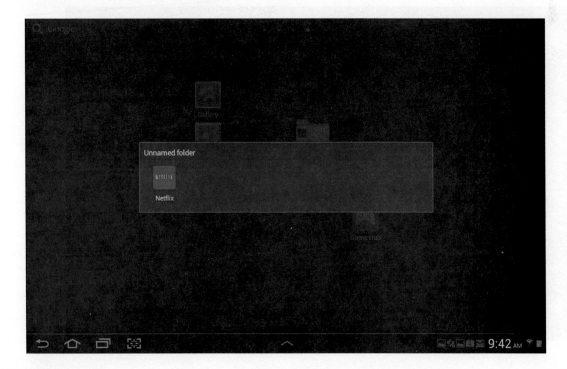

Type the name "New Folder" for the folder.

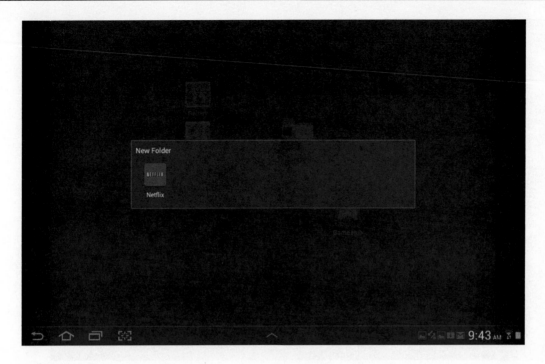

Touch anywhere outside the folder to close the folder.

Step 4

Create another folder containing three apps.

Name the folder **New Folder 2**.

Step 5

Apps can be removed from folders.

Touch and hold any app within the folder.

Drag the app to an empty area of the home screen.

Release the app.

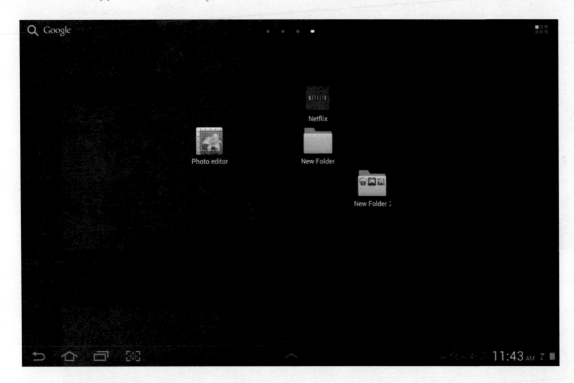

Remove the rest of the apps from the folder.

What happens to the folder?

Delete the folder in the same manner as deleting an app or a widget.

Part 3 - Uninstalling Apps

Step 1

Touch the **All Apps** icon.

Touch the **menu** icon.

The "All Apps" menu appears.

Touch **Uninstall**.

Touch any icon that has a circle with a red dash in it. Apps without the red dash circle are default apps and cannot be uninstalled.

CAUTION: If you complete the next step, the app will be uninstalled from the device. You will need to reinstall the app from the Google Play Store.

Step 2

Touch **OK**.

8.2.3.3 Lab - Working with iOS

Introduction

In this lab, you will place apps on the home screen and move them between different home screens. You will also create folders to which apps will be added and removed. Finally, you will uninstall apps from the iOS device.

Recommended Equipment

The following equipment is required for this exercise:

- iOS tablet or smartphone running iOS version 5.0

Part 1 - Apps

Step 1

Turn on the device and log in with the password, PIN, or other passcode, if necessary.

The main home screen appears.

Step 2

Default apps appear on the home screen of an iOS device.

Touch and hold any app until it starts to jiggle.

Drag the app to the desired location and release it.

You can move apps to other home screens.

Touch and hold any app.

Drag the app to the edge of the screen on the left or right in order to place it on a different **home screen**. This operation will also create a new home screen if there are no others.

Press the home button when all applications are in the desired location.

Part 2 - Folders

Step 1

Apps can be grouped together to create folders.

Place five apps on the same home screen.

Step 2

Touch and drag one of the apps onto another app.

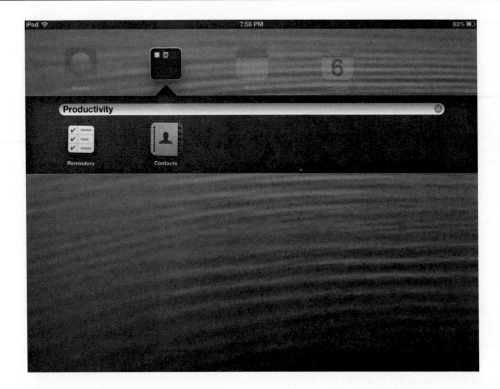

Release the app.

A folder is created containing the apps.

The default folder name is determined by the types of apps placed in the folder.

Step 3

Folders can be named to describe the contents.

Touch the words that appear in the text box.

Type the name **New Folder** for the folder.

Touch anywhere outside the folder to close the folder.

Step 4

Create another folder containing three apps.

Name the folder **New Folder 2**.

Step 5

Apps can be removed from folders.

Touch **New Folder 2** to open the folder.

Touch and hold any app within the folder.

Drag the app to an empty area of the home screen outside of the folder.

Release the app.

Remove the rest of the apps from the folder.

What happens to the folder?

Part 3 - Uninstalling Apps

Step 1

Touch and hold an app.

Touch any icon that has a circle with a white x in it. Apps without the white x circle are default apps and cannot be uninstalled.

CAUTION: If you complete the next step, the app will be uninstalled from the device. You will need to reinstall the app from the App Store.

Step 2

Touch **Delete**.

8.2.4.3 Lab - Mobile Device Features - Android and iOS

Introduction

In this lab, you will set the autorotation, brightness, and turn GPS on and off.

Recommended Equipment

The following equipment is required for this exercise:

- Android tablet or smartphone running Android version 4.0

- iOS tablet or smartphone running iOS version 5.0

Part 1 - Android Auto Rotation

Step 1

Turn on the device and log in with the password, PIN, or other passcode, if necessary.

The main home screen appears.

Step 2

Touch the **notification and system** icons.

The "notification" area appears.

Touch the **Settings** icon.

The "Settings" menu appears.

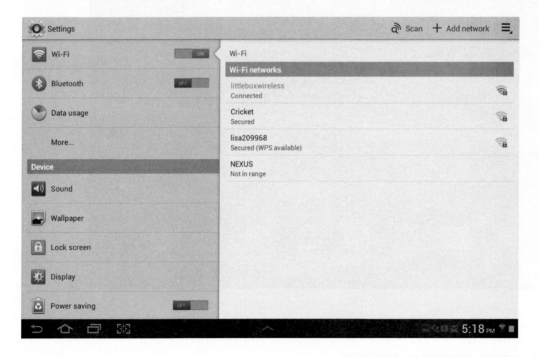

Step 3

Touch **Display**.

The "Display" menu appears.

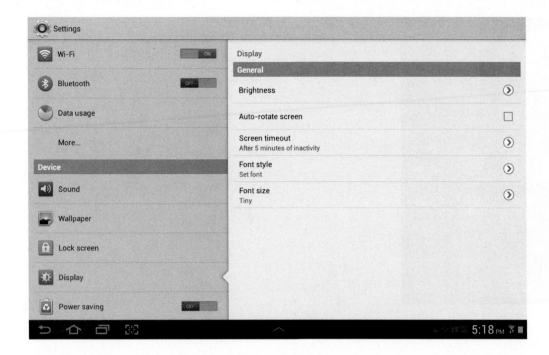

Touch the checkbox next to **Auto-rotate screen** repeatedly until there is no check in the box.

Rotate the device 90 degrees clockwise.

What happens to the screen?

Rotate the device 90 degrees counter-clockwise.

Touch the checkbox next to **Auto-rotate screen**.

Rotate the device 90 degrees clockwise.

What happens to the screen?

Touch the **Home** button to return to the home screen.

Part 2 - iOS Auto Rotation

Step 1

Turn on the device and log in with the password, PIN, or other passcode, if necessary.

The main home screen appears.

Step 2

Double-click the **Home** button.

The "Multitasking Bar" appears.

Scroll from left to right until the "Orientation" icon appears.

Step 3

Touch the **Orientation** icon to lock the screen in portrait orientation.

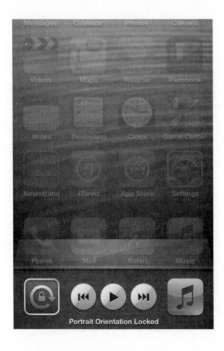

Click the **Home** button.

Touch **Calendar**.

Rotate the device 90 degrees clockwise.

What happens to the screen?

Double-click the **Home** button.

Scroll left to right.

Touch the **Orientation** icon to unlock portrait orientation.

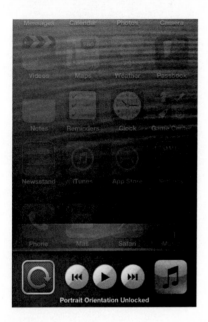

Rotate the device 90 degrees clockwise.

What happens to the screen?

Click the **Home** button to return to the home screen.

Part 3 – Android Brightness

Step 1

Touch the **notification and system** icons.

The "notification" area appears.

Touch the **Settings** icon.

The "Settings" menu appears.

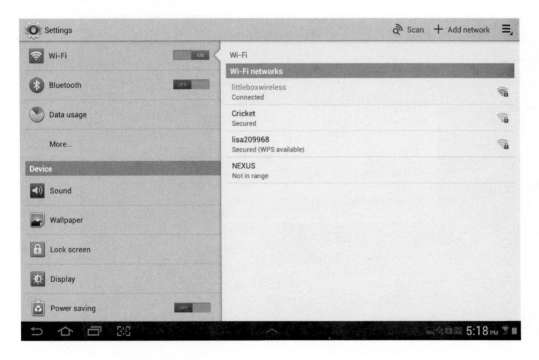

Step 2

Touch **Display**.

The "Display" menu appears.

Touch **Brightness**.

The "Brightness" menu appears

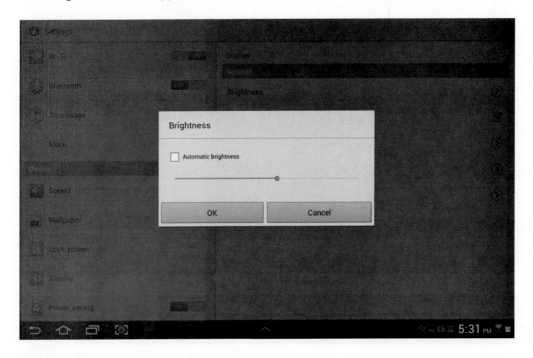

Move the slider all the way to the right.

What happens?

Touch the **Automatic brightness** checkbox repeatedly until there is a check in the box.

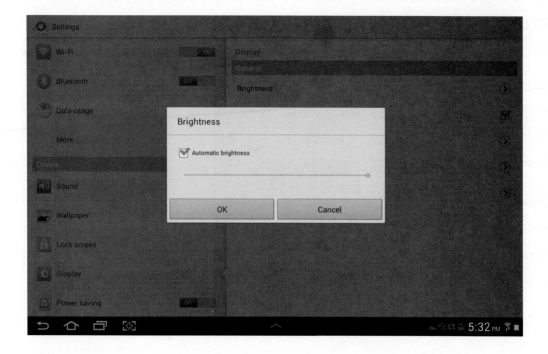

What happens?

Touch the **Automatic brightness** checkbox.

Move the slider all the way to the left.

What happens?

Touch the **Automatic brightness** checkbox.

What happens?

Touch the **Home** button to return to the home screen.

Part 4 – iOS Brightness

Step 1

Touch the **Settings** icon.

The "Settings" menu appears.

Step 2

Touch **Brightness and Wallpaper**.

The "Brightness and Wallpaper" screen appears.

Turn off **Auto-Brightness**.

Move the slider all the way to the right.

What happens?

Turn on **Auto-Brightness**.

What happens?

Turn off **Auto-Brightness**.

Move the slider all the way to the right.

What happens?

Turn on **Auto-Brightness**.

What happens?

Part 5 – Android GPS

Step 1

Touch the **notification and system** icons.

The "notification" area appears.

Touch the **Settings** icon.

The "Settings" menu appears.

Touch **Location Services**.

The "Location Services" menu appears.

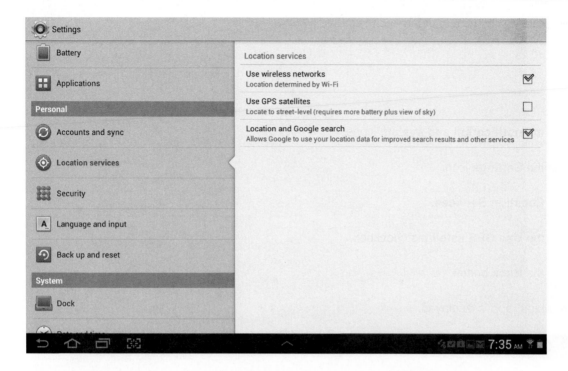

Make sure that only the **Use GPS satellites** checkbox is not checked.

Touch the **Home** button.

Step 2

Touch the **All Apps** button.

Touch the **Maps** app icon.

The "Maps" app is opened.

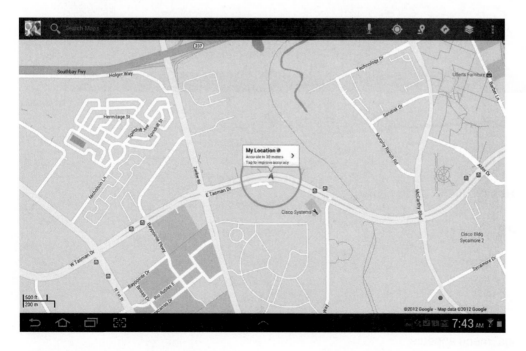

What is the accuracy of the location?

How is the device able to determine the location?

Step 3

Touch the **notification and system** icons.

Touch the **Settings** icon.

Touch **Location Services**.

Touch the **Use GPS satellites** checkbox.

Touch the **Back** button.

The "Maps" app is displayed.

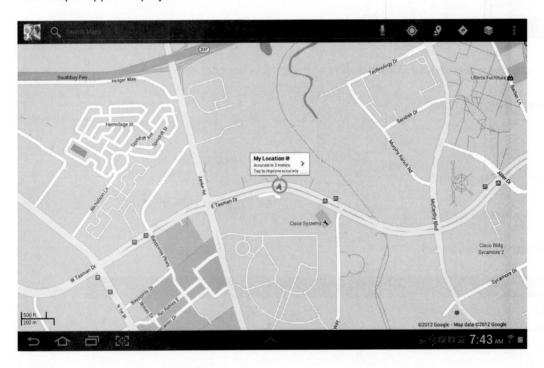

What is the accuracy of the location?

Touch the **Home** button.

Part 6 – iOS GPS

Step 1

Touch the **Settings** icon.

The "Settings" menu appears.

Step 2

Touch **Privacy**.

The "Privacy" menu appears.

Touch **Location Services**.

The "Location Services" menu appears.

What apps are using Location Services?

Turn **Location Services** off.

Click the **Home** button.

Step 3

Touch the **Map** app icon.

The "Map" app opens.

Touch the **Current Location** icon.

What happens?

Select **Services**.

Turn **Location Services** on.

Touch the **Home** button.

Touch the **Map** app icon.

The "Map" app is opened.

Touch the **Current Location** icon.

What is the accuracy of the location?

Click the **Home** button.

8.2.4.4 Worksheet – Mobile Device Information

In this activity, you will use the Internet, a newspaper, or a local store to gather information and then enter the specifications for an Android and iOS device onto this worksheet. For both devices, you will identify common operating system features. Be prepared to discuss your decisions regarding the devices you select.

Instructor: You may choose another Android and iOS device to research. The answers below are specific to the Samsung Galaxy S III and the Apple iPhone 5.

1. Select an Android and iOS device to research. Record the hardware specifications in the boxes below.

Specifications:	Android Device: Selection:	iOS Device: Selection:
Manufacturer		
Operating System		
Available Memory		
Battery Information		
Screen Size and Resolution		
Size and Weight		

For each device, specify the pathway to the given operating system feature and list available options for that feature.

2. The **About** Screen

Device	Pathway	Features/Information

3. **Software Updates**

Device	Pathway	Features/Information

4. **Reset** Options

Device	Pathway	Features/Information

5. **Cellular Usage**

Device	Pathway	Features/Information

6. **Date and Time**

Device	Pathway	Features/Information

7. Based on your research, which mobile device would you select? Be prepared to discuss your decisions regarding the mobile device you select.

8.3.1.2 Lab - Mobile Wi-Fi - Android and iOS

Introduction

In this lab, you will turn the Wi-Fi radio on and off, forget a found Wi-Fi network, and find and connect to a Wi-Fi network.

Recommended Equipment

The following equipment is required for this exercise:

- Android tablet or smartphone running Android version 4.0
- iOS tablet or smartphone running iOS version 5.0

Part 1 - Configure Wi-Fi Settings on an Android Device

Step 1

Turn on the device and log in with the password, pin code, or other passcode, if necessary.

The main home screen appears.

Step 2

Touch the **notification and system** icons.

The "notification" area appears.

8.4.1.2 Lab - Passcode Locks - Android and iOS

Introduction

In this lab, you will set a passcode lock, change a passcode lock, and fail passcode authentication. You will also remove a passcode lock.

Recommended Equipment

The following equipment is required for this exercise:

- Android tablet or smartphone running Android version 4.0
- iOS tablet or smartphone running iOS version 5.0

Part 1 - Configure Passcode Settings on an Android Device

Step 1

Turn on the device and log in with the password, PIN, or other passcode, if necessary.

The main home screen appears.

Step 2

Touch the **notification and system** icons.

The "notification" area appears.

Touch the **Settings** icon.

The "Settings" menu appears.

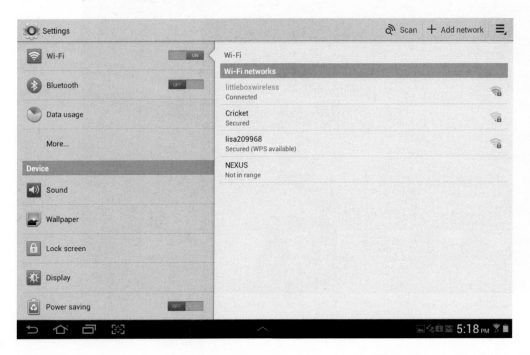

Step 3

Touch **Security**.

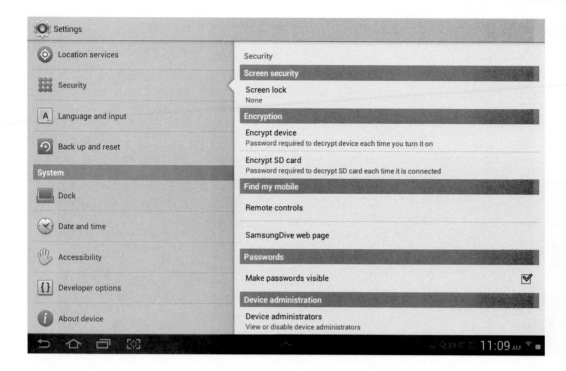

Touch **Screen Lock**.

Touch **PIN**.

Type **1234**.

Touch **Continue**.

Type **1234** to confirm the PIN.

Touch **OK**.

Step 4

Press the **power** button to lock the screen.

Press the **power** button to unlock the screen.

Type **1234**.

Touch **OK**.

What happens?

Step 5

Press the **power** button to lock the screen.

Press the **power** button to unlock the screen.

Type **4321**.

Touch **OK**.

What happens?

Enter the incorrect PIN four more times.

What happens?

Step 6

After 30 seconds, enter the correct PIN.

Touch **Screen Lock**.

What happens?

Why?

Type the correct PIN.

Touch **Continue**.

Touch **None**.

Press the **power** button to lock the screen.

Press the **power** button to unlock the screen.

What happens?

Part 2 - Set a Passcode Lock on an iOS Device

Step 1

Turn on the device and log in with the password, PIN, or other passcode, if necessary.

The main home screen appears.

Step 2

Touch the **Settings** icon.

The "Settings" screen appears.

Touch **General**.

The "General" menu appears.

Step 3

Touch **Passcode Lock**.

The "Passcode Lock" screen appears.

Touch **Turn Passcode On**.

The "Set Passcode" screen appears.

Type **1234**.

Re-enter **1234** to confirm the PIN.

Step 4

Press the **power** button to lock the screen.

Press the **power** button to unlock the screen.

Slide to unlock the screen.

Type **1234**.

What happens?

Step 5

Press the **power** button to lock the screen.

Press the **power** button to unlock the screen.

Type **4321**.

Touch **OK**.

What happens?

Enter the incorrect PIN five more times.

What happens?

Step 6

After 1 minute, enter the correct PIN.

Touch **Passcode Lock**.

What happens?

Why?

Type the correct PIN.

Touch **Turn Passcode Off**.

Type the correct PIN.

Press the **power** button to lock the screen.

Press the **power** button to unlock the screen.

What happens?

Touch the **Settings** icon.

The "Settings" menu appears.

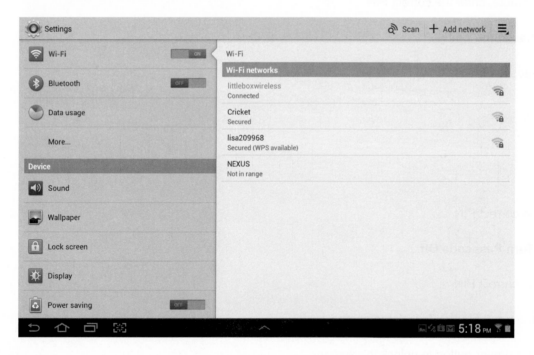

Step 7

Touch the **Wi-Fi** switch until it is set to **Off**.

Touch the **Wi-Fi** switch again.

Touch the name of the network to which the device is connected.

The "Wi-Fi details" window appears.

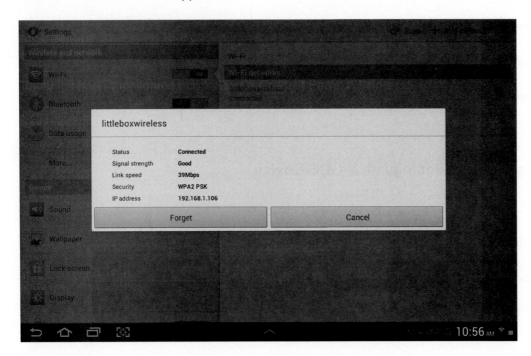

Touch **Forget**.

What happens?

Step 8

Touch the network to which the device used to be connected.

Type the Wi-Fi password.

Touch **Done**.

Touch **Connect**.

What happens?

Part 2 - Configure Wi-Fi Settings on an iOS Device

Step 1

Turn on the device and log in with the password, pin code, or other passcode, if necessary.

The main home screen appears.

Step 2

Touch the **Settings** icon.

The "Settings" menu appears.

Step 3

Touch **Wi-Fi**.

The "Wi-Fi" menu appears

Slide the Wi-Fi switch until it is **OFF**.

Slide the Wi-Fi switch until it is **On**.

Touch the name of the network to which the device is connected

The "Wi-Fi details" window opens.

Touch **Forget**.

What happens?

Step 4

Touch the network to which the device used to be connected.

Type the Wi-Fi password.

Touch **Join**.

What happens?

8.5.2.2 Lab – Troubleshooting Mobile Devices

Introduction

In this lab, you will analyze scenarios involving common problems for mobile devices and identify the solutions. You have been provided with a list of solutions for common problems. Each solution may be used more than once.

After the solutions have been identified, you will research and list the steps for implementing them.

Recommended Equipment

The following equipment is required for this exercise:

- Android tablet or smartphone running Android version 4.0
- iOS tablet or smartphone running iOS version 5.0

Solutions for Common Problems

• Perform a hard shutdown	• Pull the battery	• Complete a Factory Restore/ Reset
• Force the app to close	• Replace the SIM card	
• Insert or replace the memory card	• Delete unnecessary files or uninstall apps	• Reconfigure network settings
		• Clean the phone

Select one solution from the box above for each common problem listed below. Each solution may be used more than once.

1) You have been using a social networking app on your phone without any problems. Suddenly the application freezes up while trying to upload a photo.

   a) Which solution should be used to solve this common problem? Explain your answer.

   b) Research and list the steps for implementing the solution.

2) The passcode, or passcode pattern, has been forgotten.

   a) Which solution should be used to solve this common problem? Explain your answer.

   b) Research and list the steps for implementing the solution.

3) A phone has been powered on, but it proceeds to loop through the startup process repeatedly.

   a) Which solution should be used to solve this common problem? Explain your answer.

   b) Research and list the steps for implementing the solution.

4) You have had your Android smartphone for five months and have not experienced any problems. Suddenly, a "No SIM Card" message begins appearing regularly. You check your SIM card and there are no problems with the contacts on the SIM card and the SIM card is locked into place.

   a) Which solution should be used to solve this common problem? Explain your answer.

   b) Research and list the steps for implementing the solution.

5) Friends and family have recently begun complaining about how hard it is to hear you during calls. You have already tried a hard reset for your phone, but that has not solved the problem.

   a) Which common solution should be used to solve the problem?

   b) Research and list the steps for implementing the solution.

6) The phone is entirely unresponsive.

   a) Which common solution should be used to solve the problem?

   b) Research and list the steps for implementing the solution.

7) The mobile device cannot send or receive email.

   a) Which common solution should be used to solve the problem?

   b) Research and list the steps for implementing the solution.

8) The phone cannot install additional apps or save photos.

   a) Which common solution should be used to solve the problem?

   b) Research and list the steps for implementing the solution.

Chapter 9: Printers

9.3.1.2 Lab - Install a Printer in Windows 7

Introduction

In this lab, you will install a printer. You will find, download, and update the driver and the software for the printer.

Recommended Equipment

- A computer running Windows 7
- Internet connection
- Printer

Step 1

If you are installing a USB printer, plug the printer into the computer using a USB cable. Plug the printer power cord into an AC outlet if necessary. Unlock the printer if it is locked.

Step 2

Windows detects the new hardware and attempts to load the appropriate driver.

The "Installing device driver software" bubble opens.

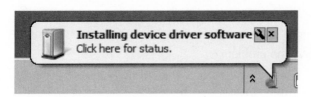

Click on the bubble.

The "Driver Software Installation" window opens.

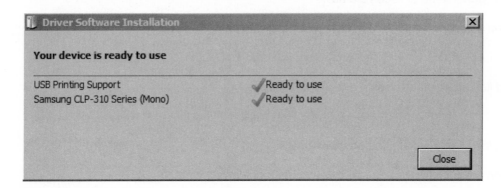

Click **Close**.

Step 3

In order to ensure that your computer has the most up-to-date driver, find the manufacturer and the model number of the printer.

Visit the manufacturer's web site and navigate to the product downloads or support page. Download the most recent driver and software for the model of printer device that you have installed. The software and driver must be compatible with your operating system.

Download the driver and extract to a temporary folder on your desktop.

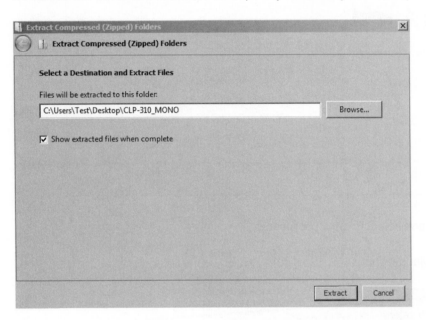

Step 4

To manually install the driver, select **Start > Devices and Printers**.

The "Devices and Printers" window opens.

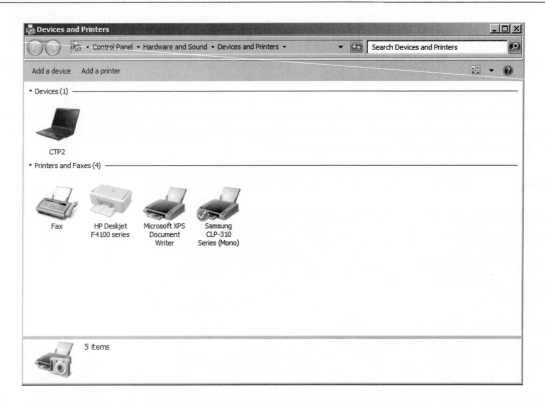

Right click on the printer, and select **Printer properties**.

The "Printer Properties" window opens.

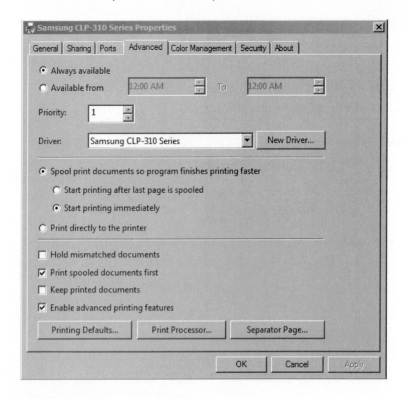

Click **Advanced > New Driver**.

The "Add Printer Driver Wizard" window opens.

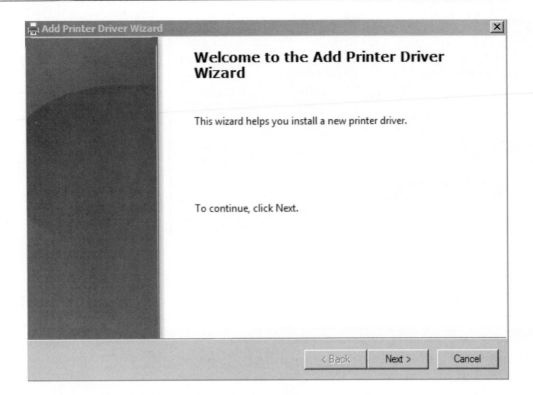

Click **Next**.

The "Printer Driver Selection" screen appears.

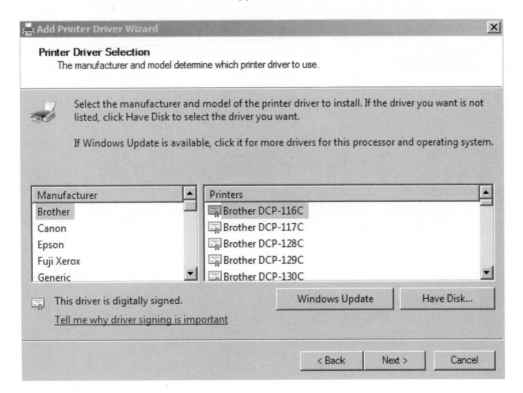

Click **Have Disk**.

The "Install from Disk" window opens.

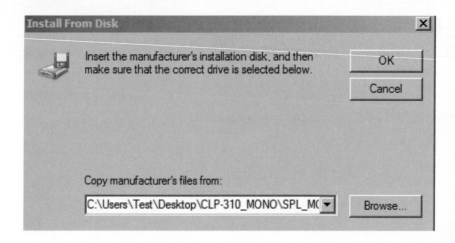

Browse and select the downloaded driver and click **OK**.

The "Printer Driver Selection" screen appears.

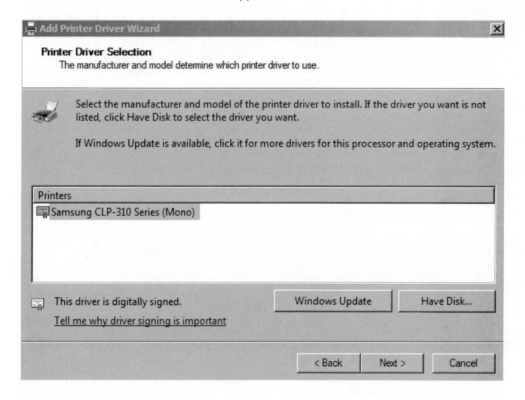

Click **Next**.

The "Completing the Add Printer Driver" screen appears.

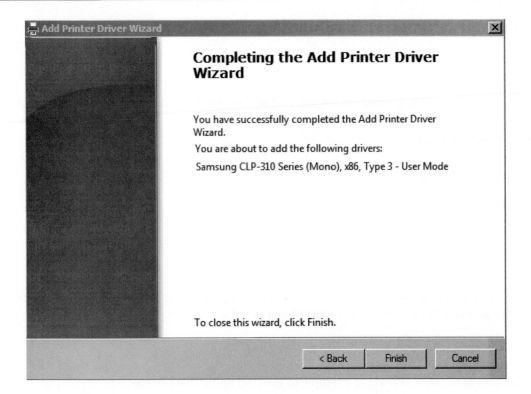

Click **Finish**.

Step 5

To verify printer functionality, click **Start > Devices and Printers**.

Right-click the printer and then select **Printer Properties**.

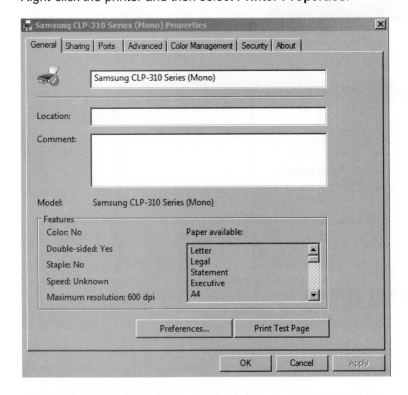

Click **Print Test Page**.

9.3.1.3 Lab - Install a Printer in Windows Vista

Introduction

In this lab, you will install a printer. You will find, download, and update the driver and the software for the printer.

Recommended Equipment

- A computer running Windows Vista
- Internet connection
- Printer

Step 1

If you are installing a USB printer, plug the printer into the computer using a USB cable. Plug the printer power cord into an AC outlet if necessary. Unlock the printer if it is locked.

Step 2

Windows detects the new hardware and attempts to load the appropriate driver.

The "Installing device driver software" bubble opens.

The "The software for the device has been successfully installed" screen appears.

Click **Close**.

Step 3

In order to ensure that your computer has the most up-to-date driver, find the manufacturer and the model number of the printer.

Visit the manufacturer's web site and navigate to the product downloads or support page. Download the most recent driver and software for the model of printer device that you have installed. The software and driver must be compatible with your operating system.

Download the driver and extract to a temporary folder on your desktop.

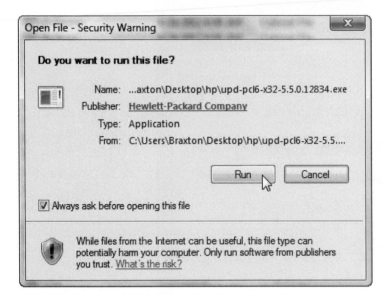

Step 4

To manually install the driver, select **Start > Control Panel > Printers**.

The "Printers" window opens.

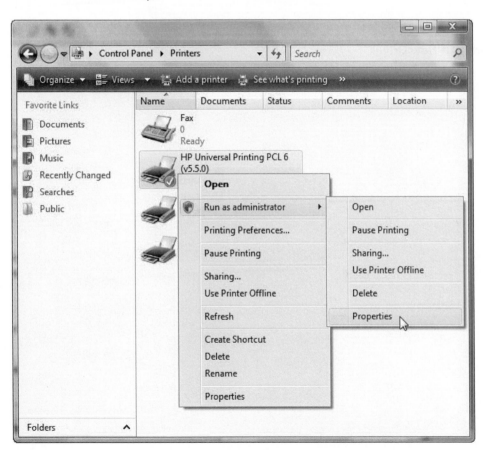

Right-click on the printer, and select **Run as administrator > Properties**.

The "Printer Properties" window opens.

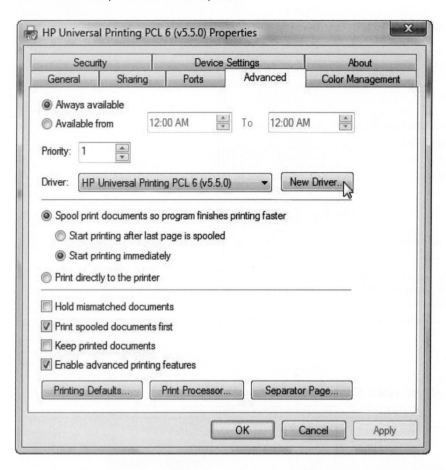

Click **Advanced** tab **> New Driver**.

The "Add Printer Driver Wizard" opens.

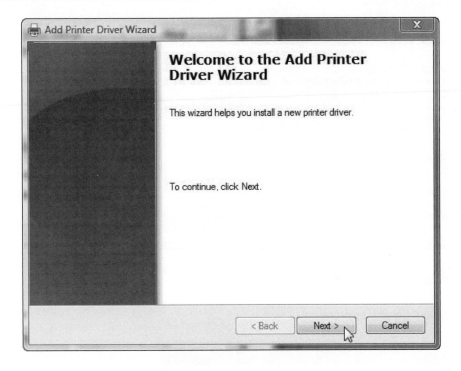

Click **Next**.

The "Printer Driver Selection" screen appears.

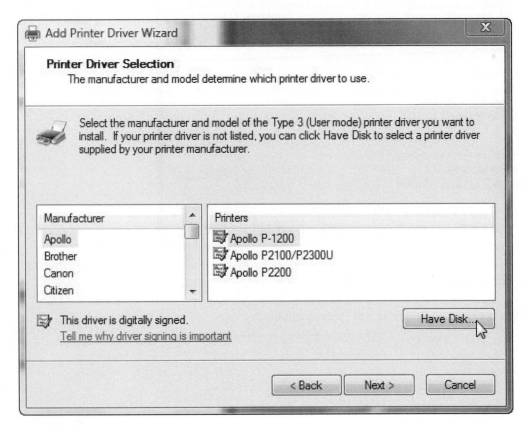

Click **Have Disk**.

The "Install From Disk" window opens.

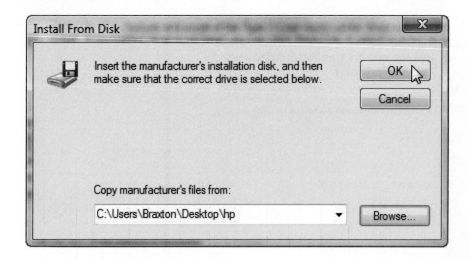

Click **Browse** and select the downloaded driver and click **OK**.

The "Printer Driver Selection" screen appears.

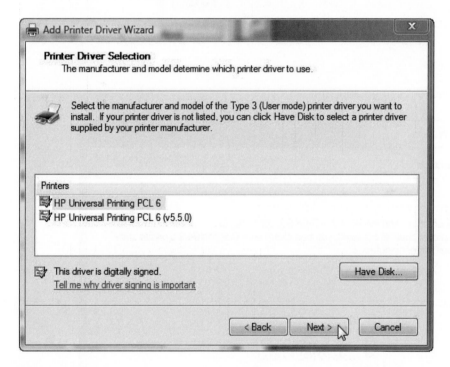

Select the correct driver and then click **Next**.

The "Completing the Add Printer Driver" screen appears.

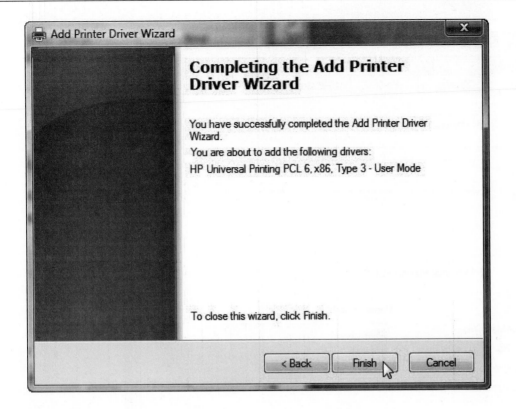

Click **Finish**.

Step 5

To verify printer functionality, click **Start > Control Panel > Printers**.

Right-click the printer and then select **Properties**.

Click **Print Test Page**.

9.3.1.4 Lab - Install a Printer in Windows XP

Introduction

In this lab, you will install a printer. You will find, download, and update the driver and the software for the printer.

Recommended Equipment

- A computer running Window XP Professional
- Internet connection
- Printer

Step 1

If you are installing a printer that connects to a parallel port, shut down the computer and connect the cable to the printer and computer using a parallel cable. Plug the printer power cord into an AC outlet and unlock the printer if necessary. Restart your computer.

If you are installing a USB printer, plug the printer into the computer using a USB cable. Plug the printer power cord into an AC outlet if necessary. Unlock the printer if it is locked.

Step 2

Windows detects the new hardware.

The "Found New Hardware Wizard" window opens.

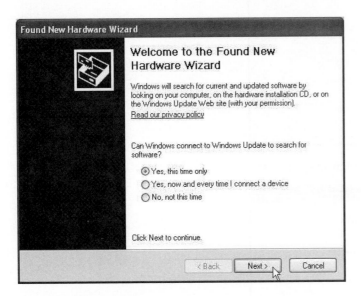

Select the **Yes, this time only** radio button, and then click **Next**.

The second screen of the Found New Hardware Wizard appears.

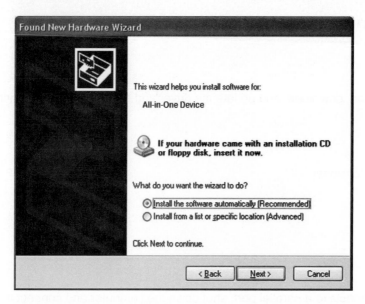

The default is "Install the software automatically (Recommended)".

Click **Next**.

The "Please wait while the wizard searches" screen appears.

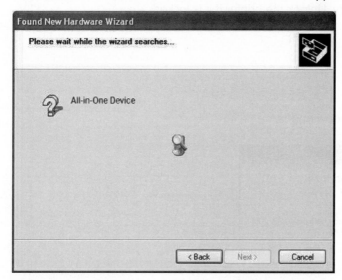

The "Cannot Install this Hardware" window may appear.

If this happens, click **Finish**.

Step 3

If the computer does not detect the printer, right-click **My Computer**, and then select **Manage > Device Manager**.

Under "Other Devices," double-click the printer device you are trying to install.

Step 4

The "Properties" window for the printer device appears.

The "Device Status" area shows that "The drivers for this device are not installed. (Code 28)".

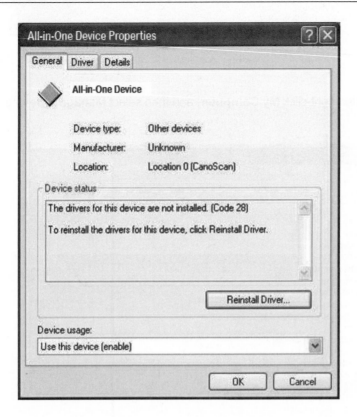

Do not click "Reinstall Driver..." at this time.

Click **Cancel**.

Step 5

Find the manufacturer and the model number of the printer.

Visit the manufacturer's web site and navigate to the product downloads or support page. Download the most recent driver and software for the model of printer device that you have installed. The software and driver must be compatible with your operating system.

Download the driver to a temporary folder on your desktop.

Double-click the installation file that you downloaded.

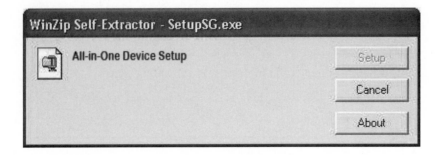

Step 6

Unplug the printer device, and plug it back in.

The Windows XP operating system detects the new device and installs the new drivers.

To verify, right-click **My Computer**, and then select **Manage > Device Manager**.

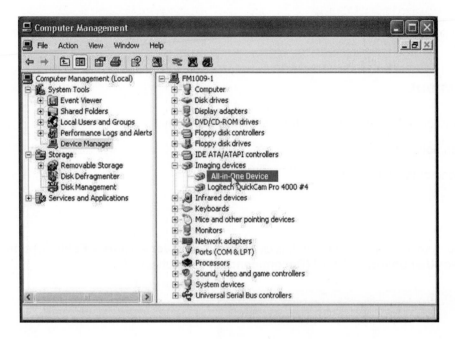

You should now see the printer device installed under "Imaging devices" on the right side of the window.

Step 7

To verify printer functionality, click **Start > Printers and Faxes**.

Right-click the printer, and then select **Properties**.

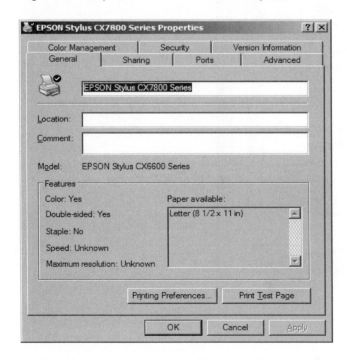

Click the **Print Test Page** button.

9.4.2.3 Lab - Share a Printer in Windows 7

Introduction

In this lab, you will share a printer, configure the printer on a networked computer, and print a test page from the remote computer.

Recommended Equipment

- Two computers directly connected or connected through a hub or switch
- Windows 7 installed on both computers
- A printer installed on one of the computers

Step 1

Log on to the computer with the printer connected, click **Start > Computer > Tools > Folder options > View**, and then uncheck **Use Sharing Wizard (Recommended)** if it is checked.

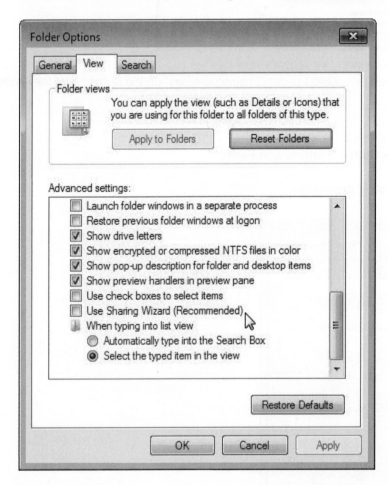

Click **OK**.

Step 2

Click **Start > Control Panel > Network and Sharing Center > Choose homegroup and sharing options > Change advanced sharing settings**.

The "Change sharing options for different network profiles" screen appears.

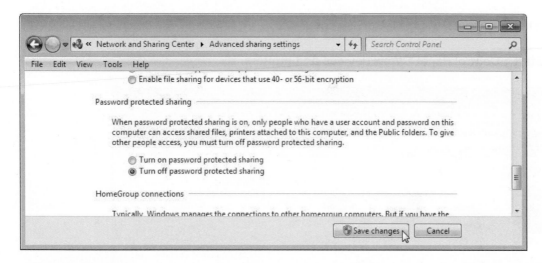

For the current profile, scroll down to **Password protected sharing** and then check **Turn off password protected sharing**.

Click **Save changes**.

Close any open windows.

Step 3

Click **Start > Control Panel > View devices and printers**.

Right-click the printer, and then select **Printer properties**.

The "Printer Properties" window opens.

Click the **Sharing** tab.

Select **Share this printer**. Name the new share **All-in-One Printer**, and then click **OK**.

Step 4

Log on to the computer without the printer connected.

Click **Start > Control Panel > View devices and printers**.

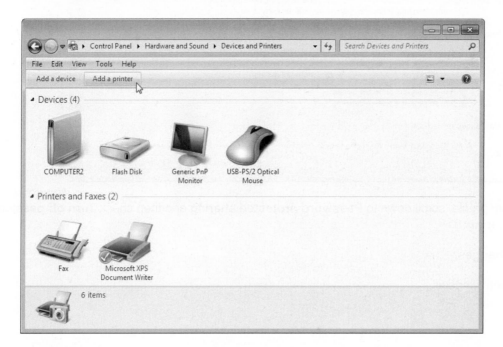

Add a printer.

The "Add Printer" window appears.

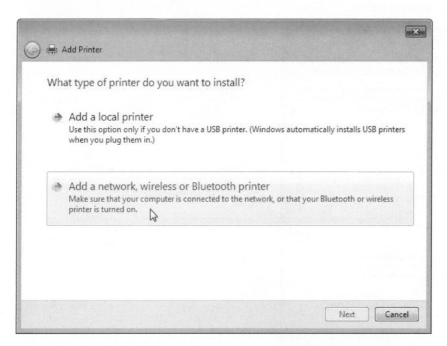

Click **Add a network, wireless or Bluetooth printer**.

The "Searching for available Printers" screen appears.

When all printers are discovered, the "Select a printer" screen appears.

If displayed in the search list, select *Printer* on *Computername*.

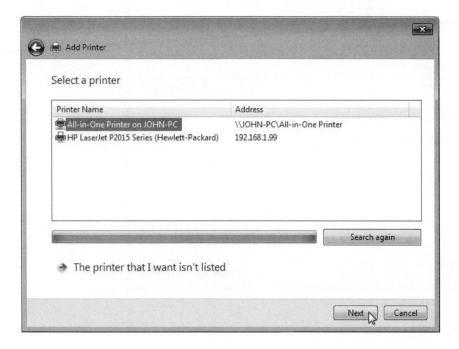

Click **Next**.

Or to find a printer by name or TCP/IP address, select **The printer that I want isn't listed**.

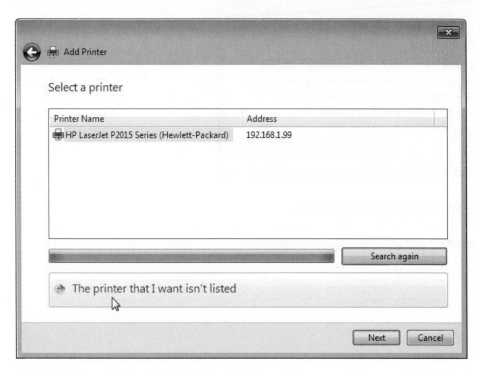

Select the radio button **Select a shared printer by name** and type **\\computername\printer**, where computername is the name of the computer with the connected printer and printer is the name of the printer.

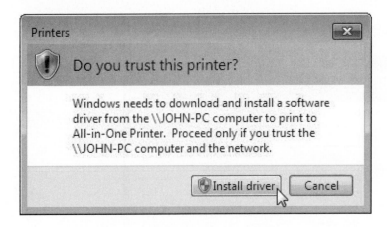

Click **Next**.

If prompted to install drivers, click **Install driver**.

If User Account Control appears, click **Continue**.

The "You've successfully added a printer" screen appears.

After the printer successfully installs, click **Next**.

Click **Finish** to close the "Add Printer" window.

Step 5

In the Devices and Printers window, right-click the printer, and then select **Printer properties**.

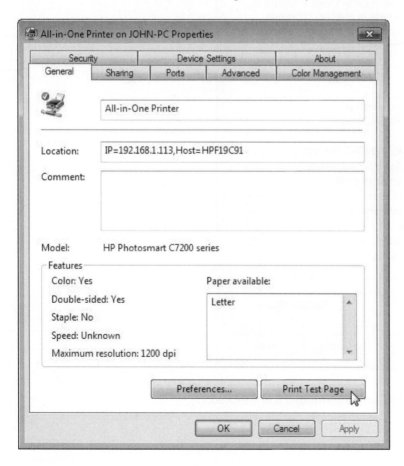

Click **Print Test Page**.

9.4.2.4 Lab - Share a Printer in Windows Vista

Introduction

In this lab, you will share a printer, configure the printer on a networked computer, and print a test page from the remote computer.

Recommended Equipment

- Two computers directly connected or connected through a hub or switch
- Windows Vista installed on both computers
- A printer installed on one of the computers

Step 1

Log on to the computer with the printer connected and click **Start > Computer > Tools > Folder Options > View** tab.

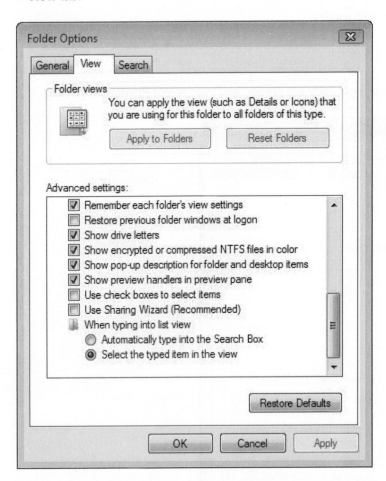

Uncheck **Use Sharing Wizard (Recommended)** if it is checked.

Click **OK**.

Step 2

Click **Start > Control Panel > Network and Sharing Center > Password protected sharing**.

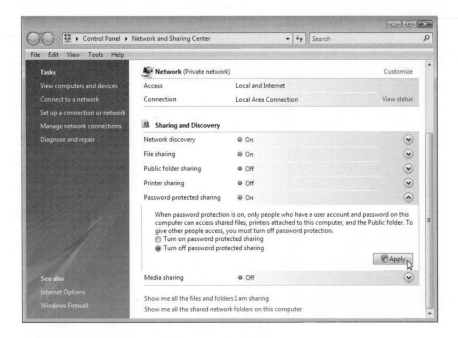

Check **Turn off password protected sharing**.

Click **Apply**. If User Account Control appears, click **Continue**.

Step 3

Click **Start > Control Panel** and double-click **Printers**.

Right-click the printer, and then select **Properties > Sharing** tab.

Click **Change sharing options**. If User Account Control appears, click **Continue**.

Select **Share this printer**.

Name the new share **Example**, and then click **OK**.

Step 4

Log on to the computer without the printer connected, and then click **Start > Control Panel > Printers**.

Click **Add a printer**.

The "Add Printer" window opens.

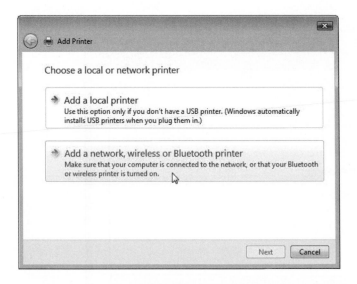

Click **Add a network, wireless or Bluetooth printer**.

The "Searching for Available Printers" screen appears.

When all printers are discovered, the "Select a printer" screen appears.

If displayed in the search list, select *Printer* on *Computername* and then click **Next**.

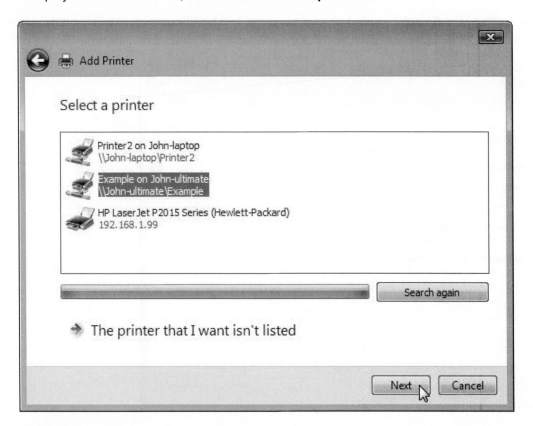

Or to find a printer by name or TCP/IP address, select **The printer that I want isn't listed**.

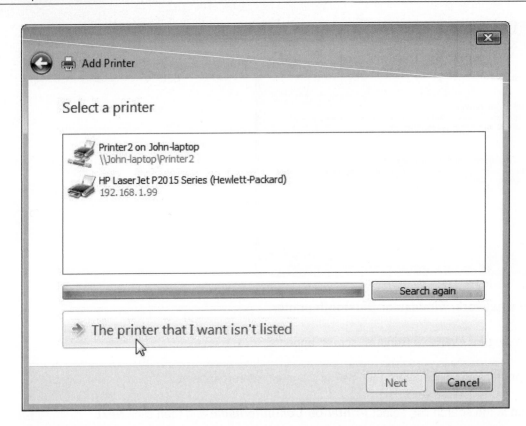

Select the radio button **Select a shared printer by name** and type **\\computername\printer**, where computername is the name of the computer with the connected printer and printer is the name of the printer.

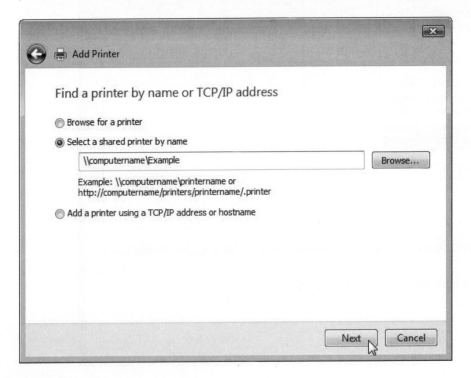

Click **Next**.

If prompted to install drivers, click **Install driver**. If User Account Control appears, click **Continue**.

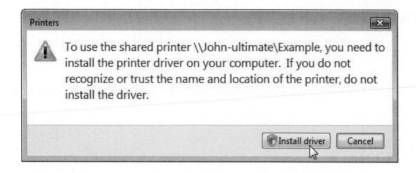

Accept all default settings, click **Next** and then click **Finish**.

Step 5

Click **Start > Control Panel** and double-click **Printers**.

Right-click the printer, and then select **Properties**.

Click **Print Test Page**.

9.4.2.5 Lab - Share a Printer in Windows XP

Introduction

In this lab, you will share a printer, configure the printer on a networked computer, and print a test page from the remote computer.

Recommended Equipment

- Two computers directly connected or connected through a hub or switch
- Windows XP installed on both computers
- A printer installed on one of the computers

Step 1

Log on to the computer with the printer connected, and click **My Computer > Tools > Folder Options > View** tab.

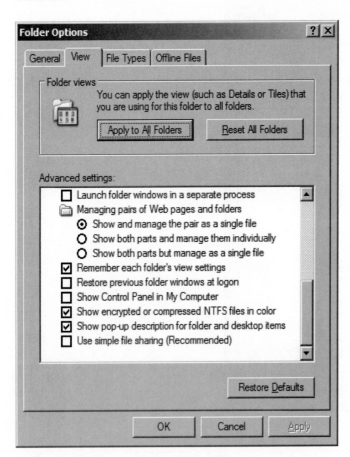

Uncheck **Use Simple File Sharing (Recommended)**.

Click **OK**.

Step 2

Click **Start > Printers and Faxes**.

Right-click the printer, and then select **Properties > Sharing** tab.

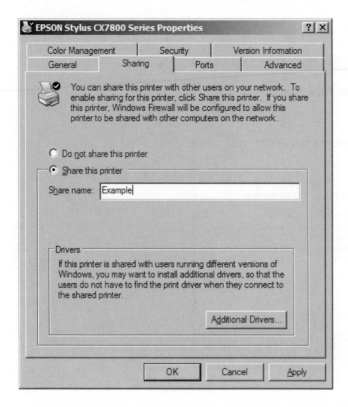

Select **Share this printer**.

Name the new share **Example**, and then click **Apply**.

Click **OK**.

Step 3

Log on to the computer without the printer connected.

Click **Start > Printers and Faxes**.

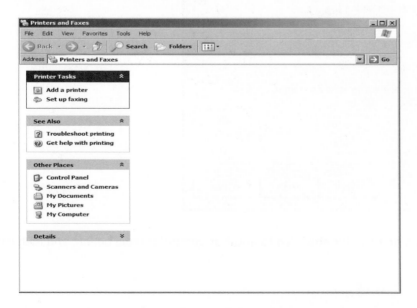

Click **Add a printer**.

The "Add Printer Wizard" window opens.

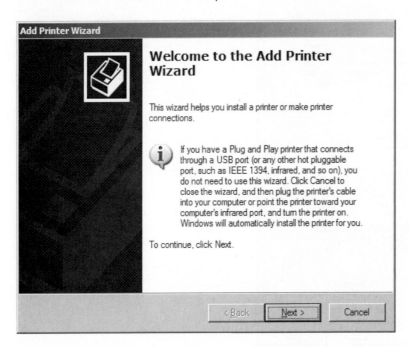

Click **Next**.

The "Local or Network Printer" screen appears.

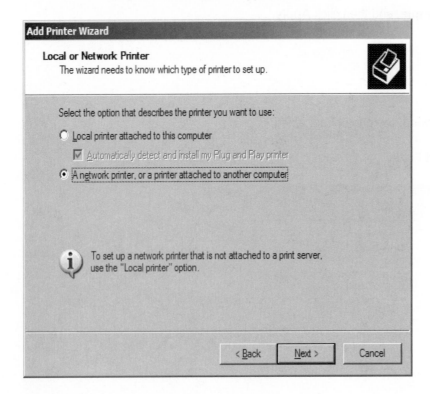

Select the **A network printer, or a printer attached to another computer** radio button, and then click **Next**.

Type **\\computername\printer** in the **Connect to this printer (or to browse for a printer, select Browse for a printer** radio button), where computername is the name of the computer with the connected printer and printer is the name of the printer.

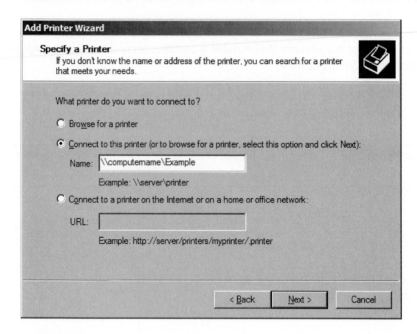

Click **Next**.

Step 4

Click **Start > Printers and Faxes**.

Right-click the printer, and then select **Properties**.

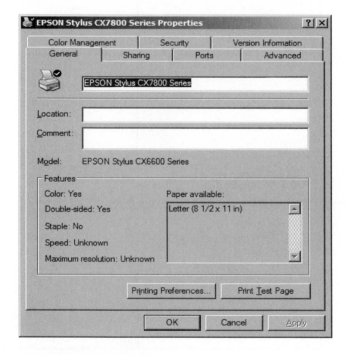

Click **Print Test Page**.

9.5.1.5 Worksheet - Search for Certified Printer Technician Jobs

In this activity, you will use the Internet to gather information about becoming a certified printer technician.

In the table below, list the name of three printer manufacturers, any certification programs available, the required skills of the certification, and make and model of the printers that require a certified technician. An example has been provided for you. Be prepared to discuss your answers.

Printer Manufacturer	Certification Programs	Required Skills	Printer Make/Model

Chapter 10: Security

10.1.1.7 Worksheet - Security Attacks

In this activity, you will use the Internet, a newspaper, or magazines to gather information to help you become familiar with computer crime and security attacks in your area. Be prepared to discuss your research with the class.

1. Briefly describe one article dealing with computer crime or a security attack.

    Based on your research, could this incident have been prevented? List the precautions that might have prevented this attack.

10.2.1.2 Worksheet - Answer Security Policy Questions

In this activity, you will answer security questions regarding the IT Essentials classroom.

1. List the person(s) responsible for each piece of network equipment that is used in your classroom (for example, routers, switches, and wireless access points).

2. List the person(s) responsible for the computers that are used in your classroom.

3. List the person(s) responsible for assigning permissions to use the network resources.

4. Which Internet web sites do you have permission to access?

5. What type of Internet web sites are not permitted to be accessed in the classroom?

6. List activities that could damage the network or the computers attached to the network with malware.

7. Should anyone, other than the network administrator, be allowed to attach modems or wireless access points to the network? Please explain why or why not.

10.2.1.7 Lab - Securing Accounts, Data, and the Computer in Windows 7

In this lab, you will explore how to secure accounts, data, and the computer in Windows 7.

Recommended Equipment

The following equipment is required for this exercise:

- A computer system running Windows 7 is required for this exercise

Step 1

Boot the computer and enter the key(s) required to enter the "BIOS Setup Utility" window.

Note: Since there are several arrangements and features in different BIOSs, you may need to search for the features talked about in the lab. Also, if your BIOS does not support the feature talked about in the lab, move to the next feature.

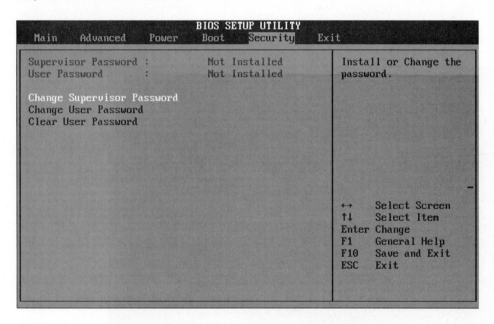

Click the **Security** tab.

To set the User password:

Select **Change User Password**, and then press **Enter**.

Type the password **us3rIT**, and then press **Enter**.

To confirm the new password, type **us3rIT**, and then press **Enter > OK**.

To set the Supervisor password:

Select **Change Supervisor Password**, and then press **Enter**.

Type the password **sup3IT**, and then press Enter.

To confirm the new password, type **sup3IT**, and then press **Enter > OK**.

To set the User access level:

Select **User Access Level**, and then press **Enter**.

Select **No Access**, and then press **Enter**.

Select **Exit > Exit Saving Changes > OK**.

Step 2

When the computer restarts, enter the key(s) required to enter the "BIOS Setup Utility" window.

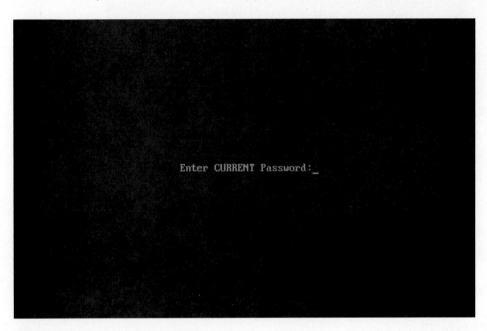

Enter the User password **us3rIT**.

Did you gain access to the BIOS?

Restart the computer if needed; enter the key(s) required to enter the "BIOS Setup Utility" window.

Enter the Supervisor password **sup3IT**.

Did you gain access to the BIOS?

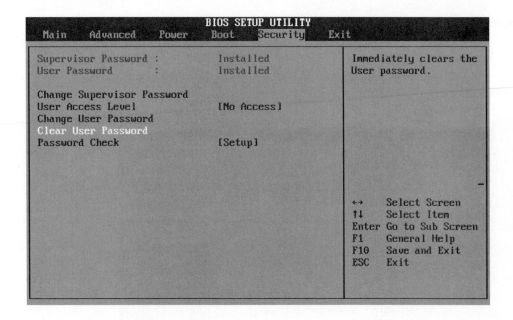

Click the **Security** tab.

To clear the User password:

Select **Clear User Password**, and then press **Enter > OK**.

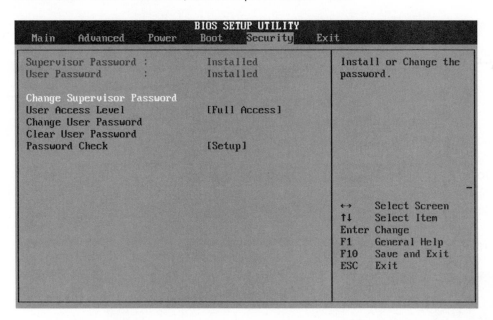

To remove the Supervisor password:

Select **Change Supervisor Password**, and then press **Enter >** type **sup3IT > Enter**.

For the new password, press **Enter**.

What message appeared?

Press Enter for **OK**.

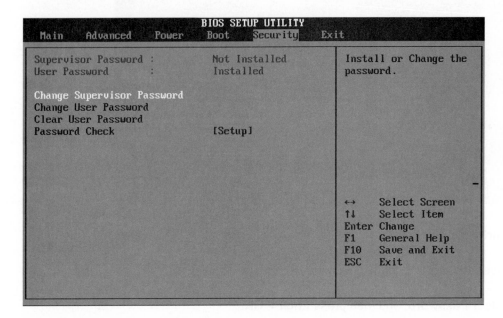

All passwords should now be removed.

Select **Exit > Exit Saving Changes > OK**.

Step 3

Log on to the computer with the Administrator account.

Click **Start > Computer > Local Disk (C:)**. Select **New folder >** name the folder **No Access**.

Click **Start > Control Panel > Administrative Tools > Computer Management**.

The "Computer Management" Window opens.

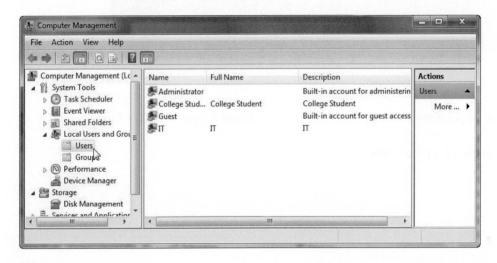

Expand the arrow next to **Local Users and Groups >** select **Users**.

Right-click **Guest > Properties >** place a check mark next to **Account is disabled > OK**.

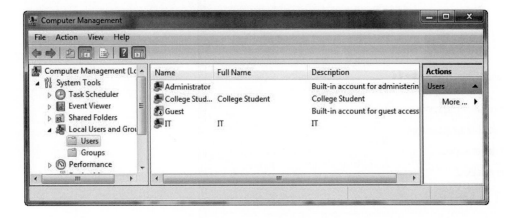

What do you notice about the Guest account icon?

Step 4

Right-click in an open area in the middle panel of the "Computer Management" window.

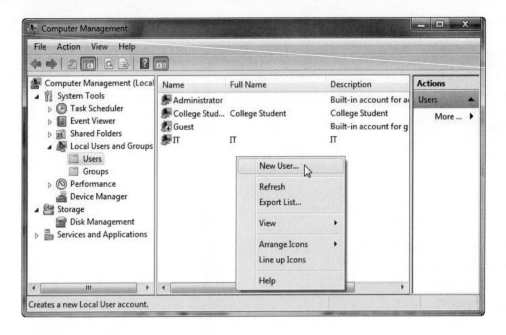

Select **New User**.

The "New User" window opens.

Enter the following account information:

User name: **ITE Cisco**

Full name: **ITE Cisco**

Description: **ITE Student**

Password and confirm password: **Tc!15Kwz**

Remove the check mark next to **User must change password at the next logon**.

Place a check mark next to **User cannot change password**.

Click **Create > Close**.

Step 5

The "Computer Management" Window opens.

Expand the arrow next to **Local Users and Groups** > select **Groups**.

Right-click in an open area in the middle panel and select **New Group**.

The "New Group" window opens.

Enter the following information:

Group name: **Temp Account**

Description: **Temporary Users**

Click **Add**.

The "Select Users" window opens.

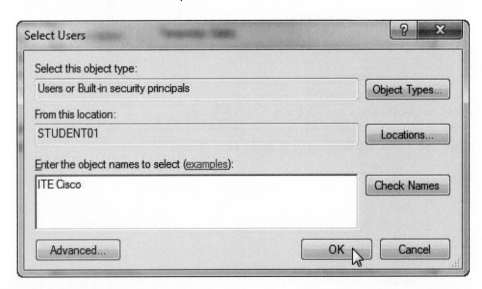

In the **Enter the object names to select** field, type **ITE Cisco > OK**.

The "New Group" window opens.

Where has the ITE Cisco account been added to?

Click **Create > Close**.

Double-click the **Users** group.

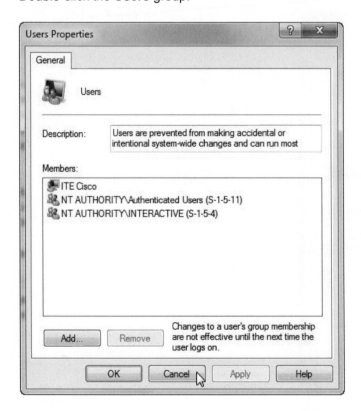

Notice that ITE Cisco was added by default to this group.

Click **Cancel** to close the window.

Close all open windows.

Step 6

Navigate to and right-click the **No Access** folder > **Properties** > **Security** tab > **Edit** > **Add**.

The "Select Users or Groups" window opens.

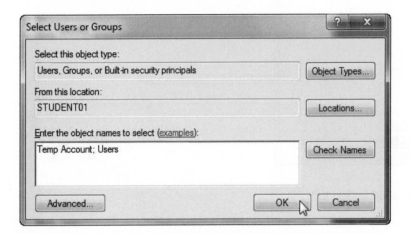

Type **Temp Account; Users > OK**.

The "Permissions for No Access" window opens.

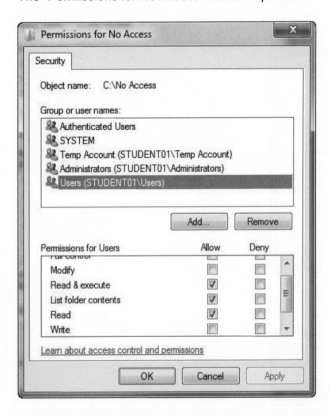

What Permissions for Temp Account Group and Users Group are activated by default?

Select the **Temp Account** group.

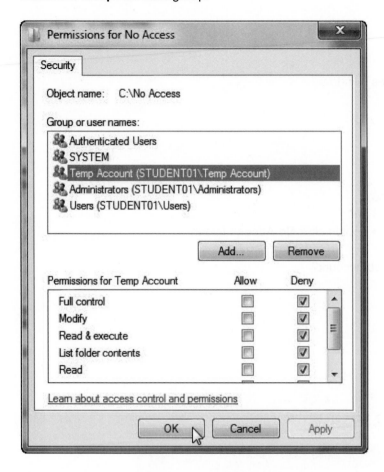

Select **Deny** for Full control.

What happens?

Click **OK**.

The "Windows Security" window opens.

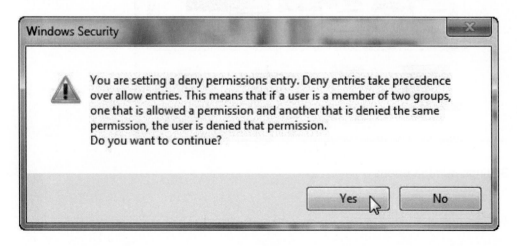

What would happen if a member of the Temp Account group belonged to another group that was allowed access to the No Access folder?

Click **Yes**.

Click **OK** to close the "No Access Properties" window.

Close all open windows.

Step 7

Logoff the computer and logon as ITE Cisco

Click **Start > Computer > Local Disk (C:) >** double-click **No Access** folder.

Can you access the folder with the ITE Cisco account?

Close any open windows.

Step 8

Right-click on the **Desktop > Personalize > Screen saver**.

The "Screen Saver Settings" window opens.

Select a Screen saver from the drop-down list and place a check mark in the box for **On resume, display logon screen**.

Make sure Wait is set to 1 minute.

Click **OK**.

Wait one minute.

What happens?

Step 9

Navigate back to the "Screen Saver Settings" window.

Set the Screen saver to **(None)** and remove the check mark from **On resume, display logon screen > OK**.

Logoff the computer.

Logon to the computer as an Administrator.

Click **Start > Computer > Local Disk (C:)**. Right-click **No Access** folder **> Delete > Yes**.

Click **Start > Control Panel > Administrative Tools > Computer Management** > expand the arrow next to **Local Users and Groups**.

Select **Users** > right-click **ITE Cisco > Delete > Yes**.

Right-click **Guest** account **> Properties >** remove check mark from **Account is disabled > OK**.

Select **Groups** > right-click **Temp Account > Delete > Yes**.

10.2.1.8 Lab - Securing Accounts, Data, and the Computer in Windows Vista

In this lab, you will explore how to secure accounts, data, and the computer in Windows Vista.

Recommended Equipment

The following equipment is required for this exercise:

- A computer system running Windows Vista is required for this exercise.

Step 1

Boot the computer and enter the key(s) required to enter the "BIOS Setup Utility" window.

Note: Since there are several arrangements and features in different BIOSs, you may need to search for the features talked about in the lab. Also, if your BIOS does not support the feature talked about in the lab, move to the next feature.

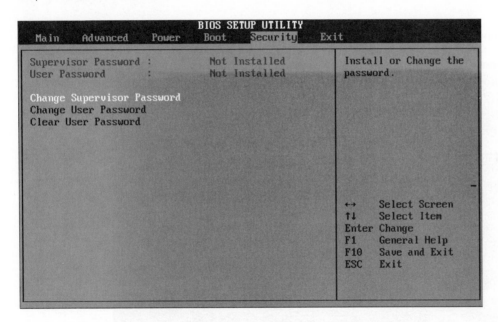

Click the **Security** tab.

To set the User password:

Select **Change User Password**, and then press **Enter**.

Type the password **us3rIT**, and then press **Enter**.

To confirm the new password, type **us3rIT**, and then press **Enter > OK**.

To set the Supervisor password:

Select **Change Supervisor Password**, and then press **Enter**.

Type the password **sup3IT**, and then press Enter.

To confirm the new password, type **sup3IT**, and then press **Enter > OK**.

To set the User access level:

Select **User Access Level**, and then press **Enter**.

Select **No Access**, and then press **Enter**.

Select **Exit > Exit Saving Changes > OK**.

Step 2

When the computer restarts, enter the key(s) required to enter the "BIOS Setup Utility" window.

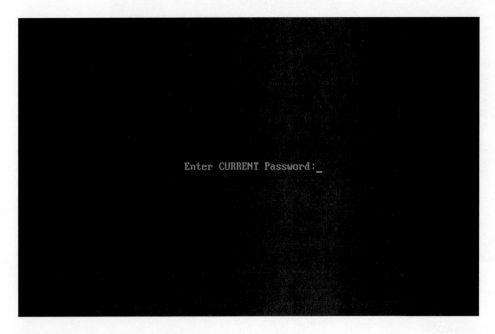

Enter the User password **us3rIT**.

Did you gain access to the BIOS?

Restart the computer if needed; enter the key(s) required to enter the "BIOS Setup Utility" window.

Enter the Supervisor password **sup3IT**.

Did you gain access to the BIOS?

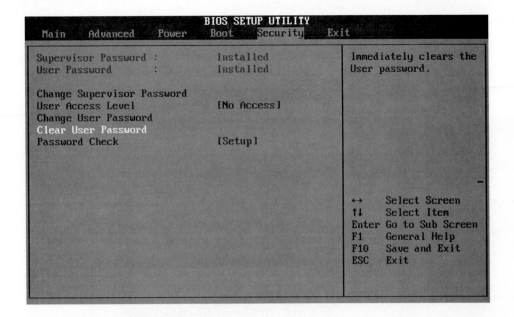

Click the **Security** tab.

To clear the User password:

Select **Clear User Password**, and then press **Enter > OK**.

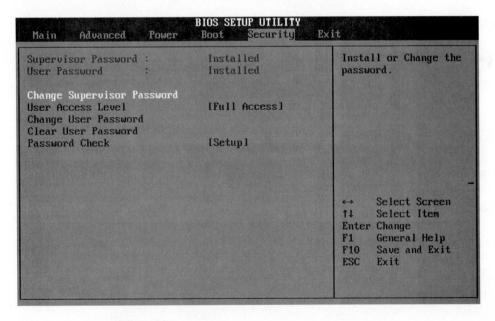

To remove the Supervisor password:

Select **Change Supervisor Password**, and then press **Enter >** type **sup3IT > Enter**.

For the new password, press **Enter**.

What message appeared?

Press Enter for **OK**.

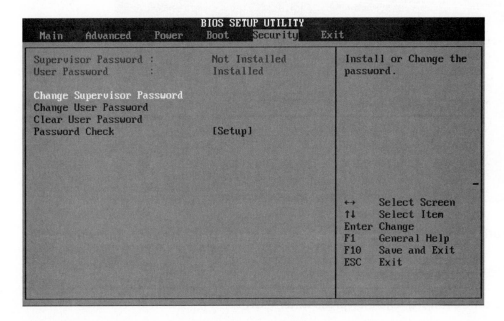

All passwords should now be removed.

Select **Exit > Exit Saving Changes > OK**.

Step 3

Log on to the computer with the Administrator account.

Click **Start > Computer > Local Disk (C:)**. Create a **New folder >** name the folder **No Access**.

Click **Start > Control Panel > Administrative Tools > Computer Management**.

The "Computer Management" Window opens.

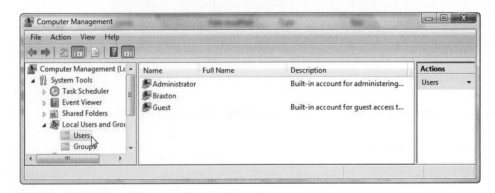

Expand the arrow next to **Local Users and Groups >** select **Users**.

Right-click **Guest > Properties >** place a check mark next to **Account is disabled > OK**.

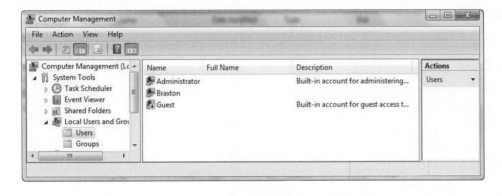

What do you notice about the Guest account icon?

Step 4

Right-click in an open area in the middle panel of the "Computer Management" window.

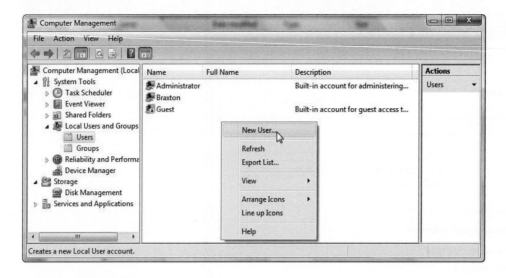

Select **New User**.

The "New User" window opens.

Enter the following account information:

User name: **ITE Cisco**

Full name: **ITE Cisco**

Description: **ITE Student**

Password and confirm password: **Tc!15Kwz**

Remove the check mark next to **User must change password at the next logon**.

Place a check mark next to **User cannot change password**.

Click **Create > Close**.

Step 5

The "Computer Management" Window opens.

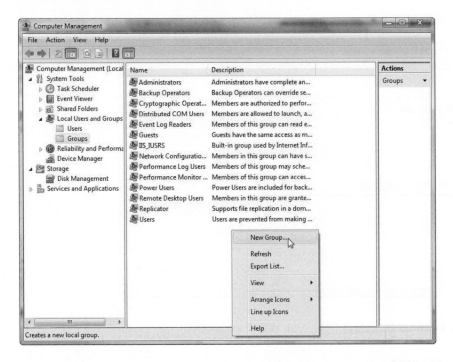

Expand the arrow next to **Local Users and Groups** > select **Groups**.

Right-click in an open area in the middle panel and select **New Group**.

The "New Group" window opens.

Enter the following information:

Group name: **Temp Account**

Description: **Temporary Users**

Click **Add**.

The "Select Users" window opens.

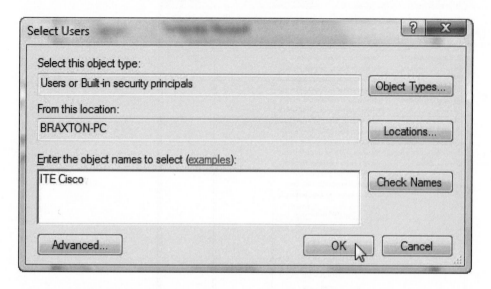

In the **Enter the object names to select** field, type **ITE Cisco > OK**.

The "New Group" window opens.

Where has the ITE Cisco account been added to?

Click **Create > Close**.

Double-click the **Users** group.

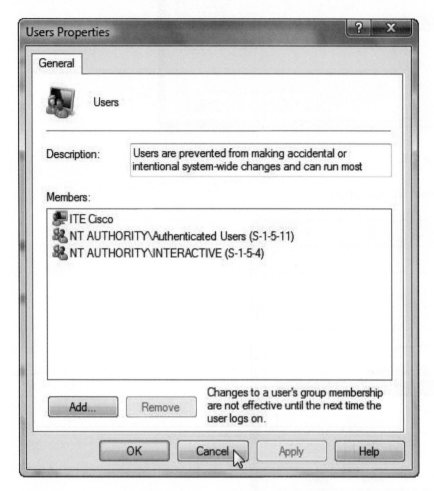

Notice that ITE Cisco was added by default to this group.

Click **Cancel** to close the window.

Close all open windows.

Step 6

Navigate to and right-click the **No Access** folder **> Properties > Security** tab **> Edit > Add**.

The "Select Users or Groups" window opens.

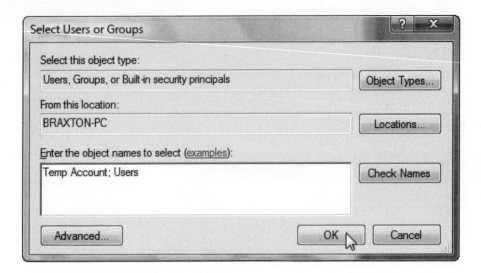

Type **Temp Account; Users > OK**.

The "Permissions for No Access" window opens.

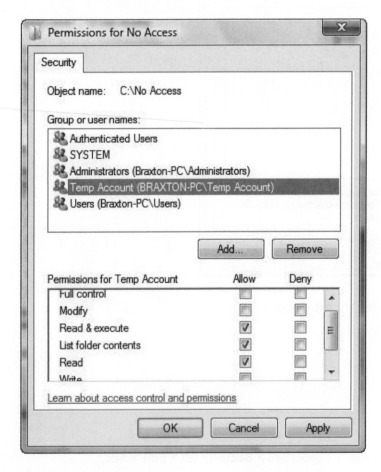

What Permissions for Temp Account Group and Users Group are activated by default?

Select the **Temp Account** group.

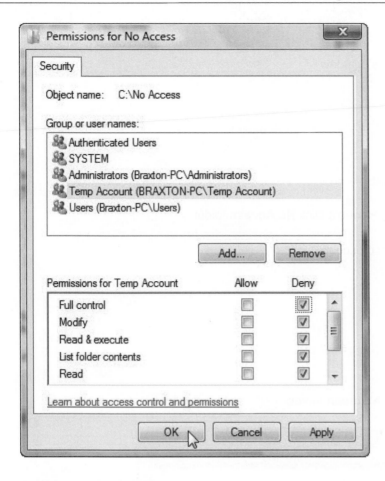

Select **Deny** for Full control.

What happens?

Click **OK**.

The "Windows Security" window opens.

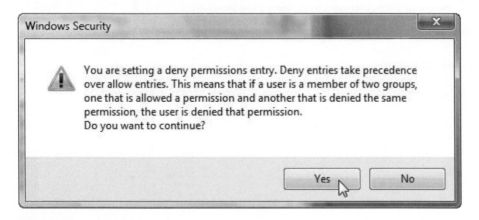

What would happen if a member of the Temp Account group belonged to another group that was allowed access to the No Access folder?

Click **Yes**.

Click **OK** to close the "No Access Properties" window.

Close all open windows.

Step 7

Logoff the computer and logon as ITE Cisco

Click **Start > Computer > Local Disk (C:) >** double-click **No Access** folder.

Can you access the folder with the ITE Cisco account?

Close any open windows.

Step 8

Right-click on the **Desktop > Personalize > Screen saver**.

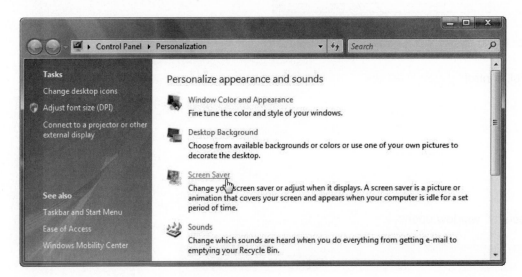

The "Screen Saver Settings" window opens.

Select a Screen saver from the drop-down list and place a check mark in the box for **On resume, display logon screen**.

Make sure Wait is set to 1 minute.

Click **OK**.

Wait one minute.

What happens?

Step 9

Navigate back to the "Screen Saver Settings" window.

Set the Screen saver to **(None)** and remove the check mark from **On resume, display logon screen > OK**.

Logoff the computer.

Logon to the computer as an Administrator.

Click **Start > Computer > Local Disk (C:)**. Right-click **No Access** folder **> Delete > Yes**.

Click **Start > Control Panel > Administrative Tools > Computer Management** > expand the arrow next to **Local Users and Groups**.

Select **Users** > right-click **ITE Cisco > Delete > Yes**.

Right-click **Guest** account **> Properties >** remove check mark from **Account is disabled > OK**.

Select **Groups** > right-click **Temp Account > Delete > Yes**.

10.2.1.9 Lab - Securing Accounts, Data, and the Computer in Windows XP

In this lab, you will explore how to secure accounts, data, and the computer in Windows XP.

Recommended Equipment

The following equipment is required for this exercise:

- A computer system running Windows XP is required for this exercise

Step 1

Boot the computer and enter the key(s) required to enter the "BIOS Setup Utility" window.

Note: Since there are several arrangements and features in different BIOSs, you may need to search for the features talked about in the lab. Also, if your BIOS does not support the feature talked about in the lab, move to the next feature.

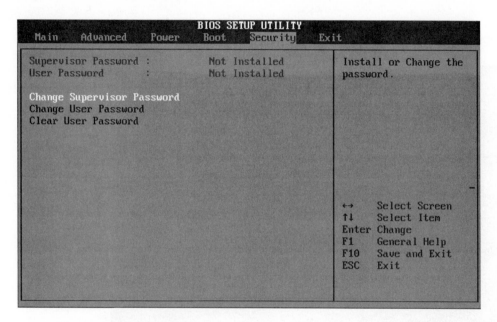

Click the **Security** tab.

To set the User password:

Select **Change User Password**, and then press **Enter**.

Type the password **us3rIT**, and then press **Enter**.

To confirm the new password, type **us3rIT**, and then press **Enter > OK**.

To set the Supervisor password:

Select **Change Supervisor Password**, and then press **Enter**.

Type the password **sup3IT**, and then press Enter.

To confirm the new password, type **sup3IT**, and then press **Enter > OK**.

To set the User access level:

Select **User Access Level**, and then press **Enter**.

Select **No Access**, and then press **Enter**.

Select **Exit > Exit Saving Changes > OK**.

Step 2

When the computer restarts, enter the key(s) required to enter the "BIOS Setup Utility" window.

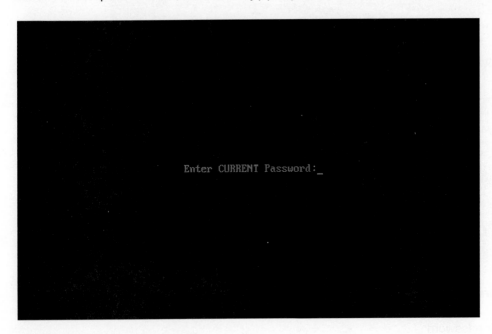

Enter the User password **us3rIT**.

Did you gain access to the BIOS?

Restart the computer if needed; enter the key(s) required to enter the "BIOS Setup Utility" window.

Enter the Supervisor password **sup3IT**.

Did you gain access to the BIOS?

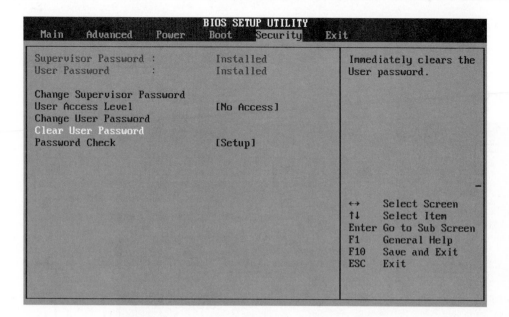

Click the **Security** tab.

To clear the User password:

Select **Clear User Password**, and then press **Enter > OK**.

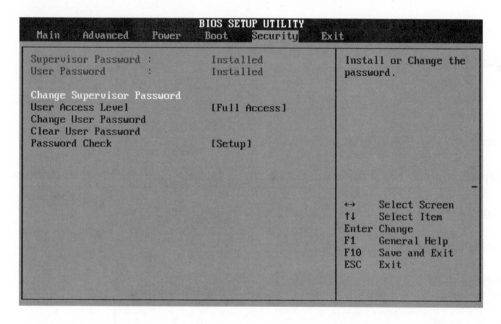

To remove the Supervisor password:

Select **Change Supervisor Password**, and then press **Enter** > type **sup3IT > Enter**.

For the new password, press **Enter**.

What message appeared?

Press Enter for **OK**.

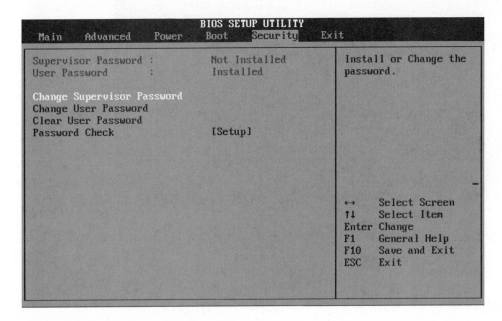

All passwords should now be removed.

Select **Exit > Exit Saving Changes > OK**.

Step 3

Log on to the computer with the Administrator account.

Click **Start > My Computer > Local Disk (C:)**. Create a **New folder >** name the folder **No Access**.

Click **Start > Control Panel > Administrative Tools > Computer Management**.

The "Computer Management" Window opens.

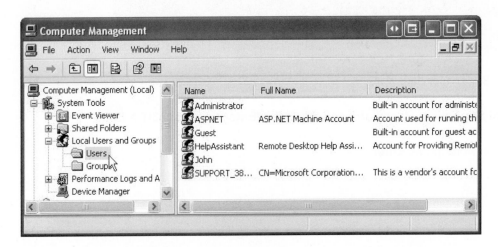

Expand the arrow next to **Local Users and Groups >** select **Users**.

Right-click **Guest > Properties >** place a check mark next to **Account is disabled > OK**.

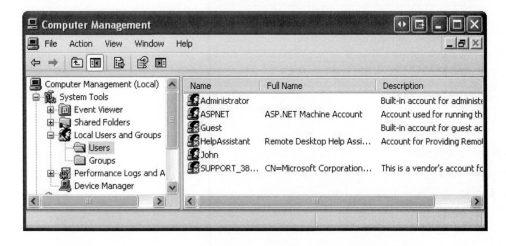

What do you notice about the Guest account icon?

Step 4

Right-click in an open area in the middle panel of the "Computer Management" window.

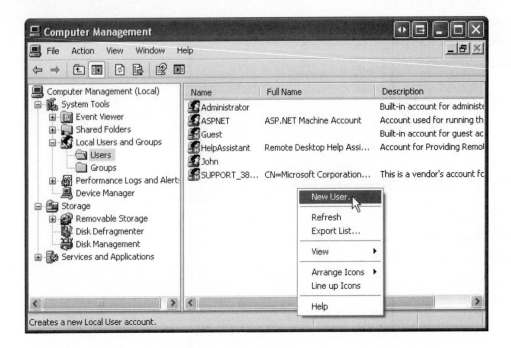

Select **New User**.

The "New User" window opens.

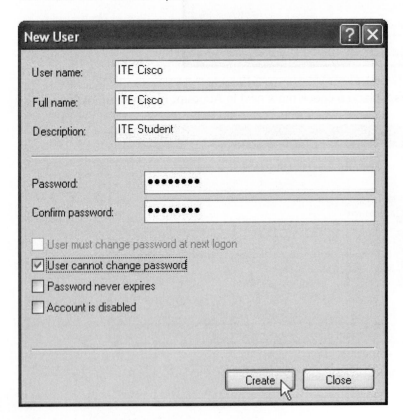

Enter the following account information:

User name: **ITE Cisco**

Full name: **ITE Cisco**

Description: **ITE Student**

Password and confirm password: **Tc!15Kwz**

Remove the check mark next to **User must change password at the next logon**.

Place a check mark next to **User cannot change password**.

Click **Create > Close**.

Step 5

The "Computer Management" Window opens.

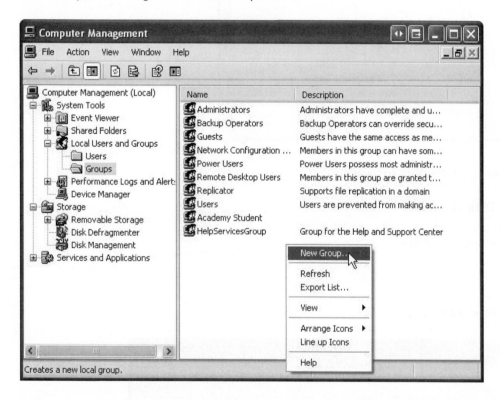

Expand the arrow next to **Local Users and Groups** > select **Groups**.

Right-click in an open area in the middle panel and select **New Group**.

The "New Group" window opens.

Enter the following information:

Group name: **Temp Account**

Description: **Temporary Users**

Click **Add**.

The "Select Users" window opens.

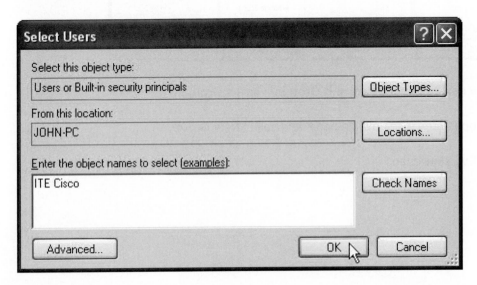

In the **Enter the object names to select** field, type **ITE Cisco > OK**.

The "New Group" window opens.

Where has the ITE Cisco account been added to?

Click **Create > Close**.

Double-click the **Users** group.

Notice that ITE Cisco was added by default to this group.

Click **Cancel** to close the window.

Close all open windows.

Step 6

Navigate to and right-click the **No Access** folder **> Properties > Security** tab **> Add**.

The "Select Users or Groups" window opens.

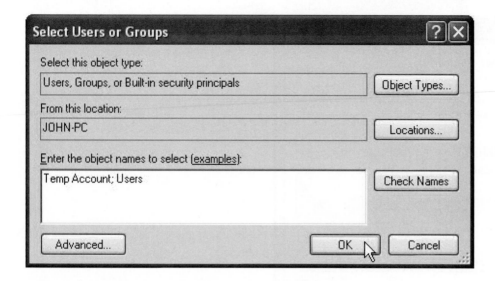

Type **Temp Account; Users > OK**.

The "No Access Properties" window opens.

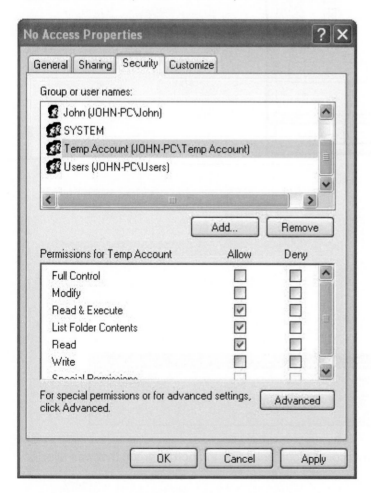

What Permissions for Temp Account Group and Users Group are activated by default?

Select the **Temp Account** group.

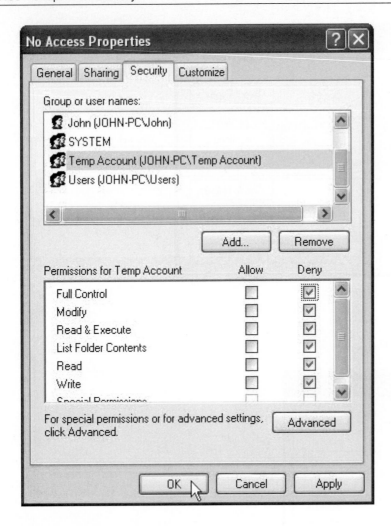

Select **Deny** for Full control.

What happens?

Click **OK**.

The "Windows Security" window opens.

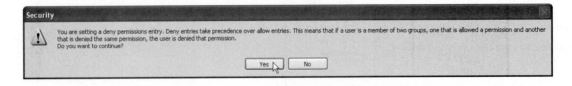

What would happen if a member of the Temp Account group belonged to another group that was allowed access to the No Access folder?

Click **Yes**.

Close all open windows.

Step 7

Logoff the computer and logon as ITE Cisco

Click **Start > Computer > Local Disk (C:) >** double-click **No Access** folder.

Can you access the folder with the ITE Cisco account?

Close any open windows.

Step 8

Right-click on the **Desktop > Properties > Screen saver** tab.

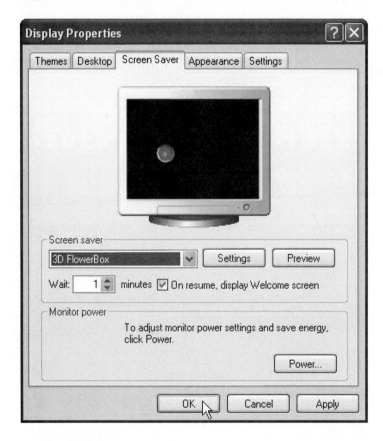

Select a Screen saver from the drop-down list and place a check mark in the box for **On resume, display logon screen**.

Make sure Wait is set to 1 minute.

Click **OK**.

Wait one minute.

What happens?

Step 9

Navigate back to the "Screen Saver Settings" window.

Set the Screen saver to **(None)** and remove the check mark from **On resume, display logon screen > OK**.

Logoff the computer.

Logon to the computer as an Administrator.

Click **Start > Computer > Local Disk (C:)**. Right-click **No Access** folder **> Delete > Yes**.

Click **Start > Control Panel > Administrative Tools > Computer Management** > expand the arrow next to **Local Users and Groups**.

Select **Users** > right-click **ITE Cisco > Delete > Yes**.

Right-click **Guest** account **> Properties >** remove check mark from **Account is disabled > OK**.

Select **Groups** > right-click **Temp Account > Delete > Yes**.

10.2.3.2 Worksheet - Third-Party Antivirus Software

Print and complete this activity.

In this activity, you will use the Internet, a newspaper, or a local store to gather information about third-party anti-virus software.

1. Using the Internet, research two different anti-virus software applications. Based on your research, complete the table below.

Company/Software Name Website URL	Software Features Subscription Length (Month/Year/Lifetime) Cost

2. Which anti-virus software would you purchase? List reasons for your selection.

10.2.4.8 Worksheet - Research Firewalls

Print and complete this activity.

In this activity, you will use the Internet, a newspaper, or a local store to gather information about hardware and software firewalls.

1. Using the Internet, research two different hardware firewalls. Based on your research, complete the table below.

Company/Hardware Name	Website URL	Cost	Subscription Length (Month/Year/Lifetime)	Hardware Features

2. Which hardware firewall would you purchase? List reasons for your selection.

3. Using the Internet, research two different software firewalls. Based on your research, complete the table below.

Company/Software Name	Website URL	Cost	Subscription Length (Month/Year/Life-time)	Software Features

4. Which software firewall would you purchase? List reasons for your selection.

10.2.4.10 Lab - Configure Wireless Security

Introduction

In this lab, you will configure and test the wireless settings on the Linksys E2500.

Recommended Equipment

- Two computers with Windows 7 or Windows Vista or Windows XP

- An Ethernet NIC installed in computer 1

- A Wireless NIC installed in computer 2

- Linksys E2500 Wireless Router

- Ethernet patch cable

Step 1

Ask the instructor for the following information that is used during the lab.

Default Login Information:

User Name (if any): _____

Password: _____

Basic Wireless Settings:

Network Name (SSID): _____

Network Mode: _____

Channel: _____

Important: Only use configurations assigned by the instructor.

Note: Use computer 1 for all lab instructions unless stated.

Step 2

Connect computer 1 to an **Ethernet** ports on the wireless router with an Ethernet patch cable.

Plug in the power of the wireless router. Boot the computer and log in as an administrator.

Step 3

Open the command prompt.

Type **ipconfig**.

What is the IP address for the computer?

What is the default gateway for the computer?

Step 4

Open Internet Explorer and connect to the wireless router.

Type "**admin**" in the "Password:" field.

The "Setup screen" appears.

Click **Wireless** tab.

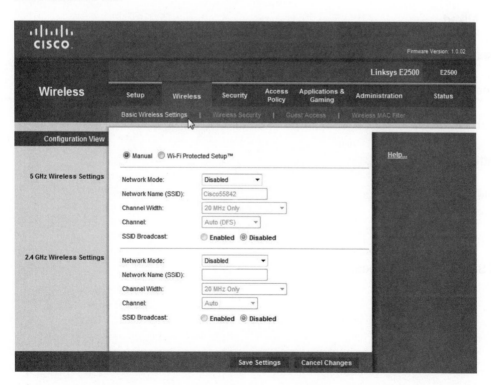

Under the Wireless tab, click **Basic Wireless Settings** if it is not selected.

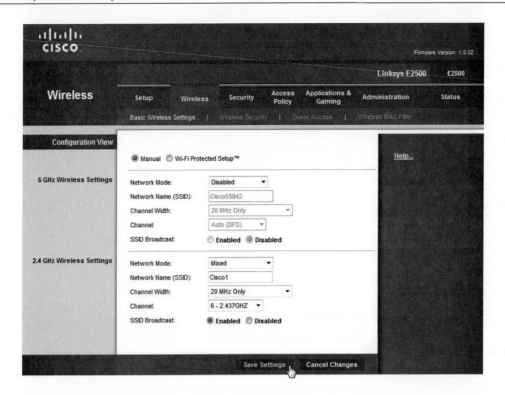

Enter the following information for the 2.4 GHz wireless settings, unless stated otherwise by the instructor:

Network Mode: **Mixed**

Network Name (SSID): **Cisco#**, where # is a number assigned by the instructor

Channel: **#**, where # is a number assigned by the instructor

SSID Broadcast: **Enabled**

Click **Save Settings > Continue**.

Click the **Wireless Security** sub-tab.

Step 5

The "Wireless Security" screen appears.

Enter the following information for the 2.4 GHz wireless security settings, unless stated otherwise by the instructor:

Security Mode: **WPA2 Personal**.

Passphrase: **C!scoL&b102410**

Click **Save Settings > Continue**.

Keep Internet Explorer open to the Linksys router.

Step 6

Log in to computer 2, the wireless computer, as the administrator.

Connect to the wireless network. If asked for a security key or passphase, enter: **C!scoL&b102410**.

Open the command prompt.

Type **ipconfig /all**.

What is the IP address of the wireless NIC?

What is the physical address of the wireless NIC?

Type **ping** *IPaddress*. Where *IPaddress* is the IP address of computer 1.

Was the ping successful?

Keep the command prompt window open.

Step 7

From computer 1, make sure Internet Explorer is active.

Under the Wireless tab, click **Guest Access**.

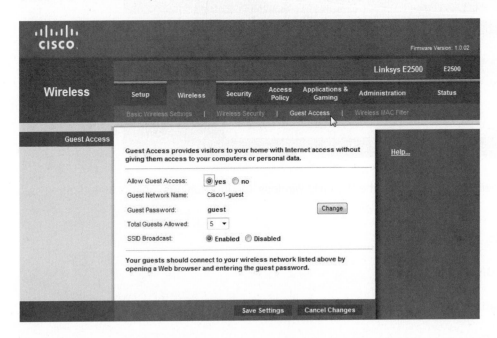

Why would you allow guest access?

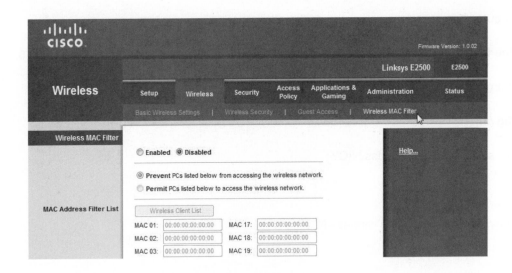

Under the Wireless tab, click **Wireless MAC Filter**.

Step 8

The "Wireless MAC Filter" screen appears.

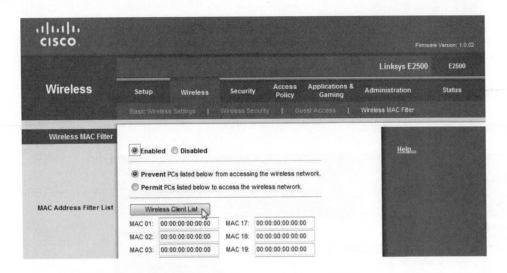

Select **Enabled > Prevent >** click **Wireless Client List**.

The "Wireless Client List" screen appears.

Select **Save to MAC Address Filter List** check box for computer 2.

Click **Add**.

What MAC address is now listed?

Click **Save Settings > Continue**.

Step 9

From computer 2:

In the command prompt window, type **ping *IPaddress***. Where ***IPaddress*** is the IP address of computer 1.

Was the ping successful?

Step 10

From computer 1, click the **browser** so it is activated.

Click **Administration** on the main tab bar.

The "Management" screen appears.

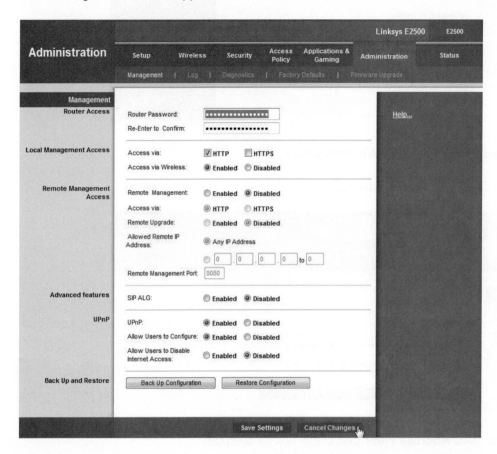

Highlight the Router Password and type **ITEv5.0**. Type the same password in Re-Enter to Confirm.

Click **Cancel Changes**. Do not save the new password.

Click **Security** on the main tab bar.

Step 11

The "Firewall" screen appears.

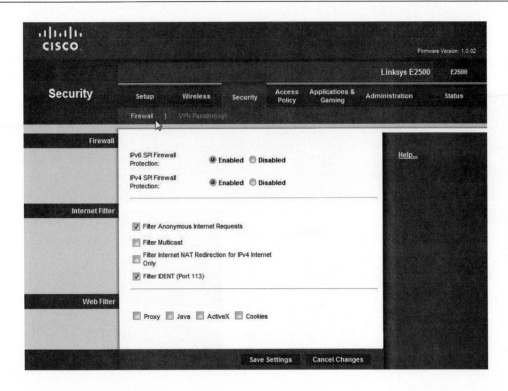

By default, SPI Firewall Protection is enabled.

What Internet Filters are available?

What Web Filters are available?

Click **Applications & Gaming** on the main tab bar.

Step 12

The "Applications & Gaming" screen appears.

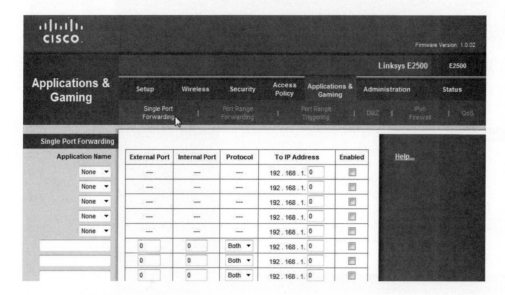

Click **Single Port Forwarding**.

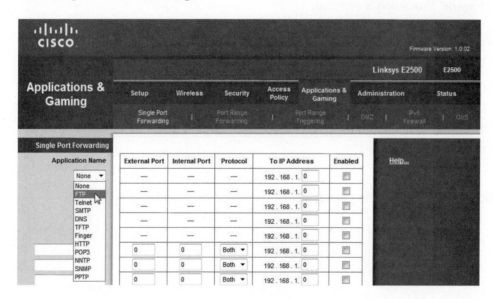

To forward an otherwise blocked port to a specific computer, select **Application Name** > **FTP**.

Type the last octet of the IP address for the computer and then click **Enabled** checkbox.

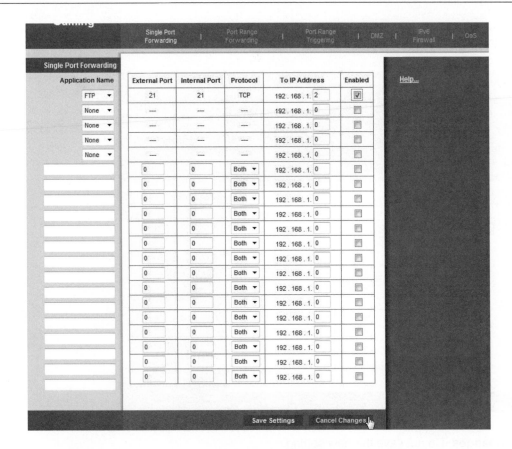

Click **Cancel Changes**. Do not save the new setting.

Click **Port Range Triggering**.

Step 13

The "Port Range Triggering" screen appears.

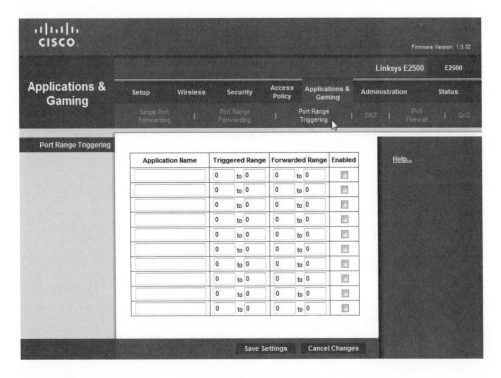

To open an otherwise blocked port, type in the application name **IRC**. Then type the Triggered Range **6660 to 7000**, Forwarded Range **113 to 113**, and then click **Enabled** checkbox.

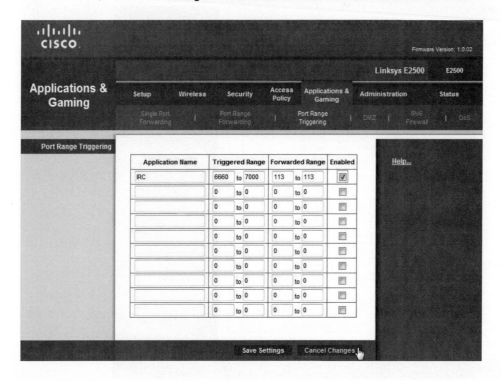

Click **Cancel Changes**. Do not save the new setting.

Click **Access Policy**.

Step 14

The "Parental Controls" screen appears.

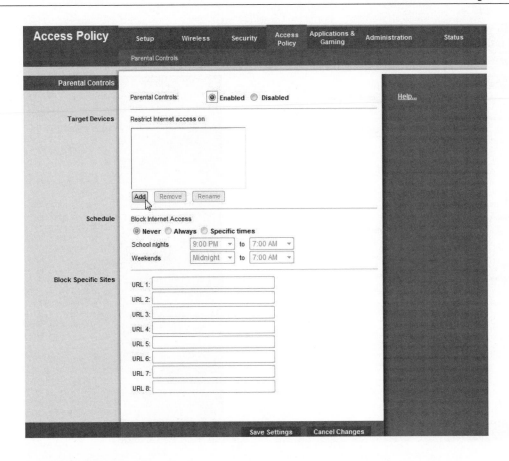

Select **Enable > Add**.

The "Set up parental control for:" window opens.

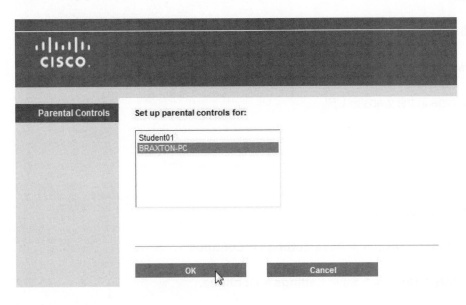

Select a computer name, **Computer2 > OK**.

The "Parental Controls" screen re-appears.

Set a schedule to block Internet access.

Select **Specific times**.

School nights: **5:30 PM to 7:00AM**

Weekends: **8:00 PM to 7:00 AM**

Block specific sites: type in the website URL.

Click **Cancel Changes**.

Step 15

From computer 1, click **Wireless** tab.

Click **Wireless MAC Filter** > **Disable** > **Save Settings** > **Continue**.

Click **Wireless Security** > **Disable** > **Save Settings** > **Continue**.

Click **Basic Wireless Settings** > **Disable** > **Save Settings** > **Continue**.

10.3.1.2 Worksheet - Operating System Updates in Windows

In this activity, you will use the Internet to research operating system updates. Be prepared to discuss your research with the class.

1. Which operating system (OS) is installed on your computer?

2. List the configuration options available for important updates for the OS.

3. Which configuration option would you use to update the OS? List the reason for choosing a particular option.

4. List any other configuration options available for updating the OS.

5. If the instructor gives you permission, begin the update process for the OS. List all security updates available.

10.3.1.4 Lab - Data Backup and Recovery in Windows 7

Introduction

In this lab, you will back up data. You will also perform a recovery of the data.

Recommended Equipment

The following equipment is required for this exercise:

- A computer system running Windows 7 is required for this exercise.

Step 1

Log on to the computer as an administrator.

Create a text file on the desktop called **Backup File One**. Open the file and type the text "**The text in this file will not be changed.**"

Create another text file on the desktop called **Backup File Two**. Open the file and type the text "**The text in this file will be changed.**"

Note: Remove all extra folders and files from the computers Desktop. This will help to reduce the length of time to complete the backup for this lab.

Step 2

Click **Start > All Programs > Maintenance > Backup and Restore**.

The "Back up or restore your files" screen appears.

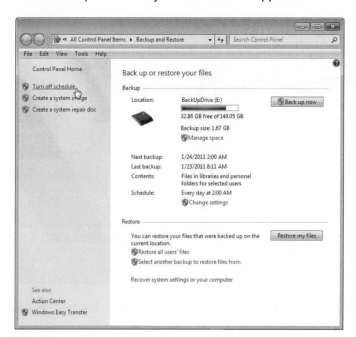

If a backup is scheduled to run, click **Turn off schedule**.

Step 3

Click **Change settings**.

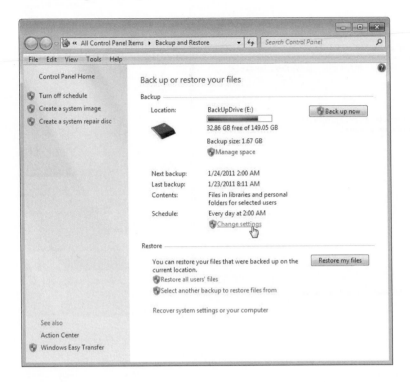

Select the location where the backup will be stored. In this example, an external hard drive is used.

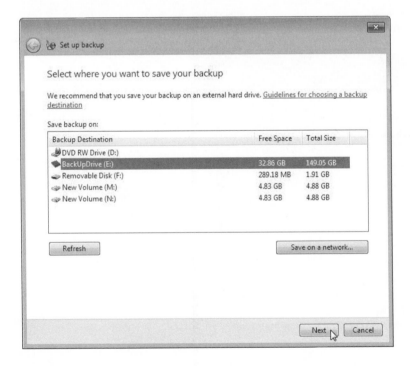

Click **Next**.

The "What do you want to back up?" screen appears.

Select **Let me choose**.

Click **Next**.

Step 4

Expand the current user account so you can view the different locations.

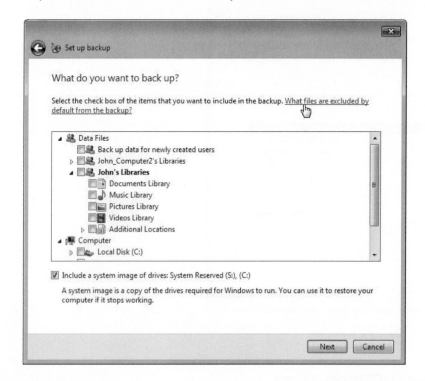

Which libraries can be backed up?

Click **What files are excluded by default from the backup?**.

The "Windows Help and Support" window opens.

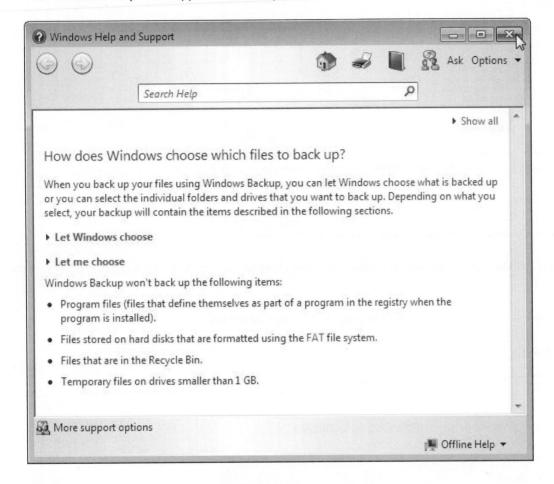

Windows Backup will not back up which items?

Close the "Windows Help and Support" window.

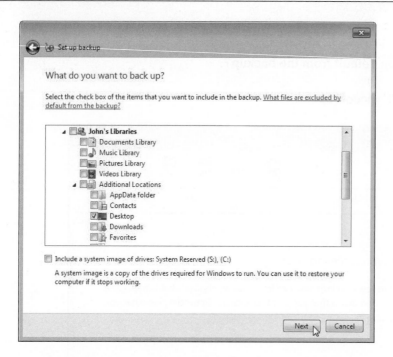

Expand **Additional Locations** and make sure only **Desktop** is selected. Make sure no other location is selected.

Remove the check mark from **Include a system image of drives:**.

Click **Next**.

Step 5

The "Review your backup settings" screen appears.

Click **Change schedule**.

The "How often do you want to back up?" screen appears.

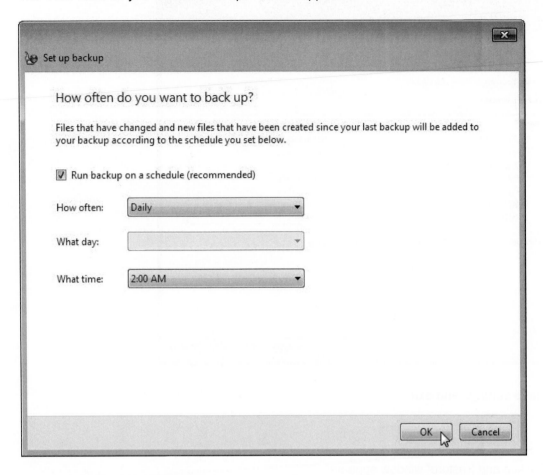

Place a check mark in the checkbox **Run backup on a schedule (recommended)**.

Set the following conditions:

How often: **Daily**

What day: **blank**

What time: **2:00 AM**

Which files will be backed up?

Click **OK**.

The "Review your backup settings" screen appears.

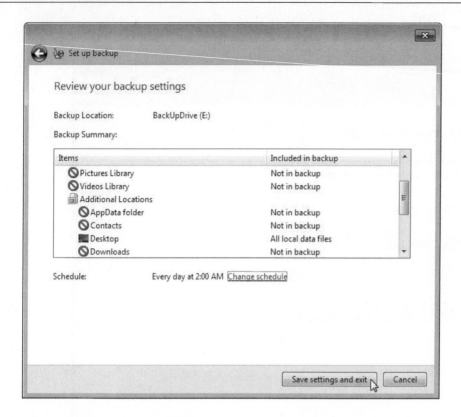

Click **Save settings and exit**.

Step 6

The "Backup and Restore" window appears.

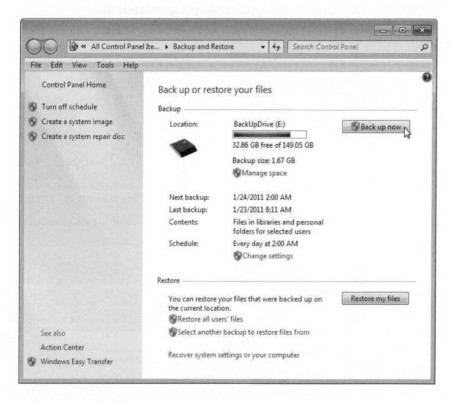

When will the next backup take place?

What is the state of the schedule, on or off?

Click **Back up now > View Details**.

The "Windows Backup is currently in progress" screen appears.

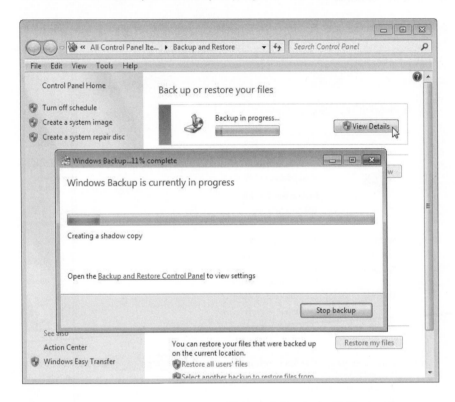

The "Windows Backup has completed successfully" screen appears.

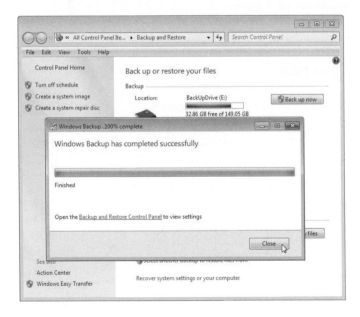

Click **Close**.

Step 7

Navigate to the Desktop. Delete **Backup File One** and **Backup File Two**.

Empty the Recycle Bin.

Step 8

Click on the "Backup and Restore" window.

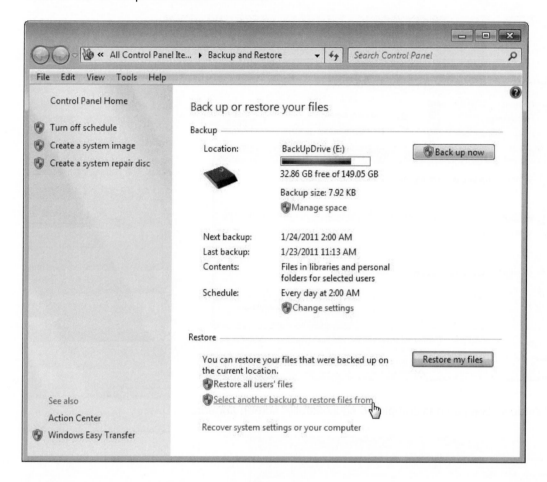

Click **Select another backup to restore files from**.

The "Select the backup that you want to restore files from" screen appears.

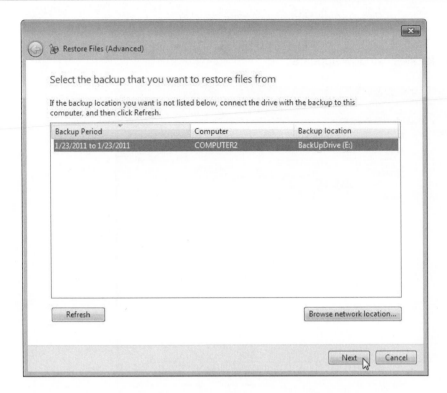

Select the location the files are stored at, and then click **Next**.

Step 9

The "Browse or search your backup for files and folders to restore" screen appears.

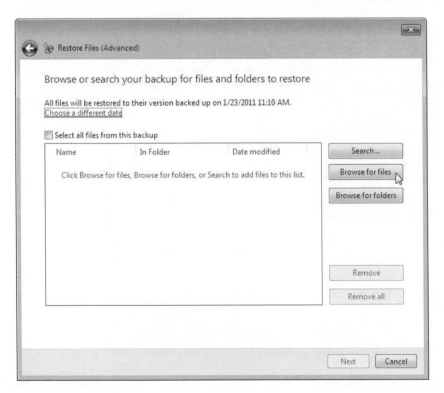

Click **Browse for files**.

Step 10

The "Browse the backup for files" window appears.

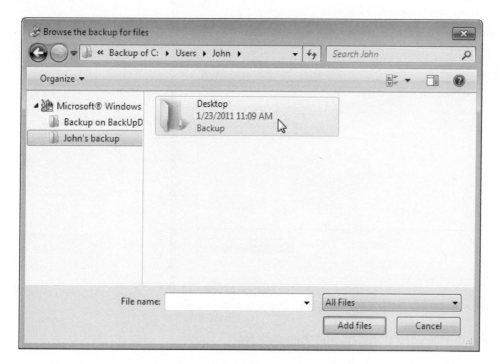

Click the current user's backup. Example: **John's backup**.

Double-click **Desktop** and locate files **Backup File One** and **Backup File Two**.

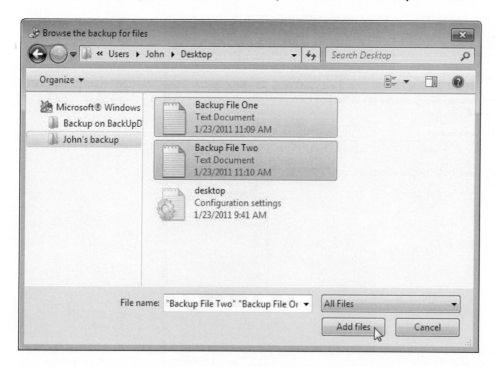

Select both files by clicking **Backup File One** and then holding down the Ctrl key while clicking **Backup File Two**. Click **Add files**.

The two files should show up in the "Browse or search your backup for files and folders to restore" screen.

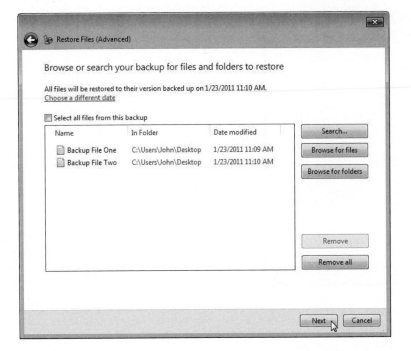

Click **Next**.

Step 11

The "Where do you want to save the restored files?" screen appears.

Select **In the original location**, and then click **Restore**.

The "Your files have been restored" screen appears.

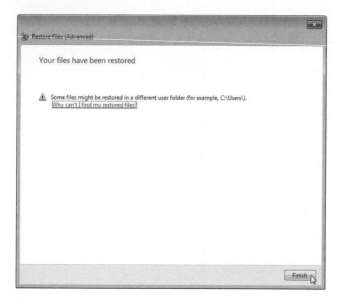

Click **Finish**.

Step 12

Navigate to the Desktop.

Are the two files restored to the Desktop?

Step 13

Open file **Backup File Two**. Add the following text "More text added." to the file. Save the file.

Step 14

Click on the "Backup and Restore" window so it is active.

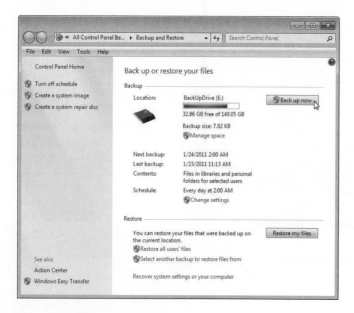

Click **Back up now**.

Step 15

Navigate to the Desktop. Delete **Backup File Two**.

Empty the Recycle Bin.

Step 16

Click on the "Backup and Restore" window so it is activated.

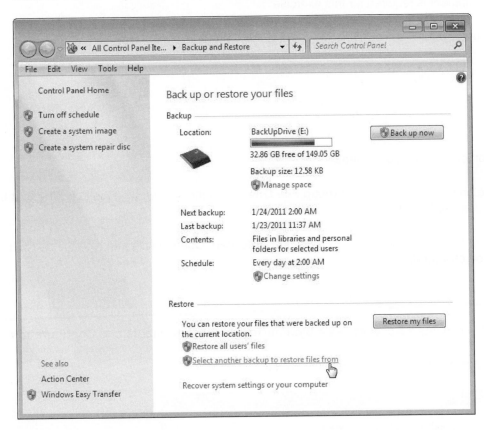

Click **Select another backup to restore files from**.

Select the location the files are stored at and then click **Next > Browse for files > user's backup > Desktop**.

Restore **Backup File Two**.

Step 17

Navigate to the Desktop. Open file **Backup File Two**.

What text is in the file?

Step 18

Delete the following from the Desktop: **Backup File One** and **Backup File Two**.

Empty the Recycle Bin.

10.3.1.5 Lab - Data Backup and Recovery in Windows Vista

Introduction

In this lab, you will back up data. You will also perform a recovery of the data.

Recommended Equipment

The following equipment is required for this exercise:

- A computer system running Windows Vista is required for this exercise.

Step 1

Log on to the computer as an administrator.

Create a text file on the desktop called **Backup File One**. Open the file and type the text "**The text in this file will not be changed.**"

Create another text file on the desktop called **Backup File Two**. Open the file and type the text "**The text in this file will be changed.**"

Step 2

Click **Start > All Programs > Accessories > System Tools > Backup Status and Configuration**.

The "Backup Status and Configuration" window appears.

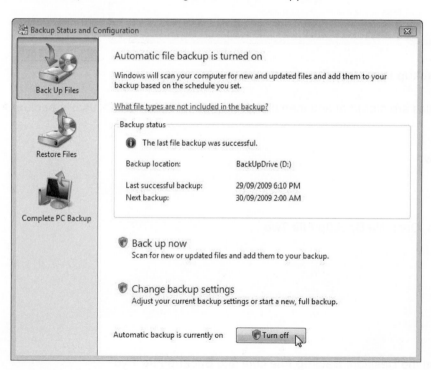

If automatic backup is turned on, click **Turn Off > Continue**.

Step 3

Click **Change backup settings > Continue**.

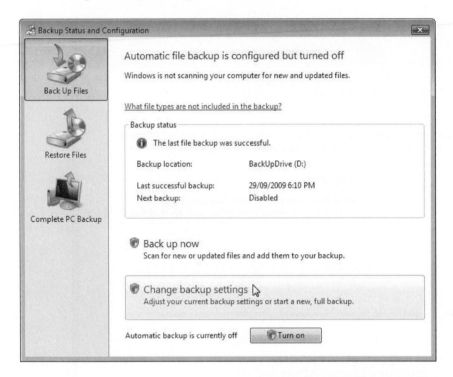

The "Where do you want to save your backup?" screen appears.

Select the location where the backup will be stored. In this example, an external hard drive is used.

Click **Next**.

Step 4

The "Which file types do you want to back up?" screen appears.

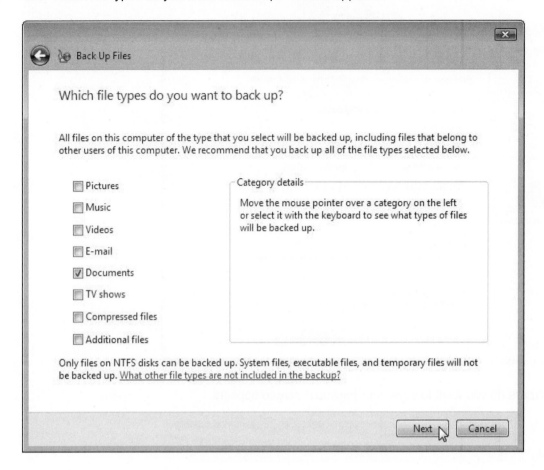

What file type can be backed up?

What file types will not be backed up?

Only files on what type of disk can be backed up?

Make sure only file type **Documents** is selected.

Click **Next**.

Step 5

The "How often do you want to create a backup?" screen appears.

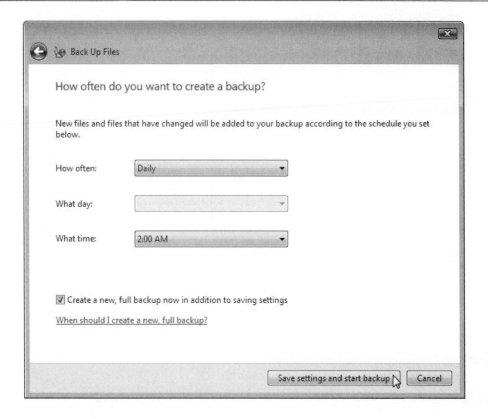

Set the following conditions:

How often – Daily

What day – blank

What time – 2:00 AM

Which files will be backed up?

_____

Place a check mark in the checkbox **Create a new, full backup now in addition to saving settings**.

Click **Save settings and start backup**.

The "Creating a shadow copy" progress screen appears.

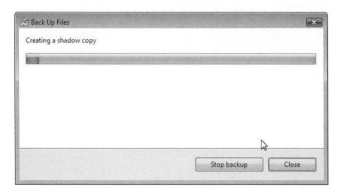

The "The backup has finished successfully" screen appears.

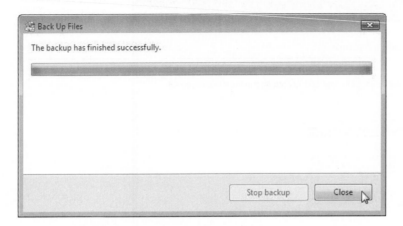

When the backup is finished, click **Close**.

Step 6

The "Backup Status and Configuration" window appears.

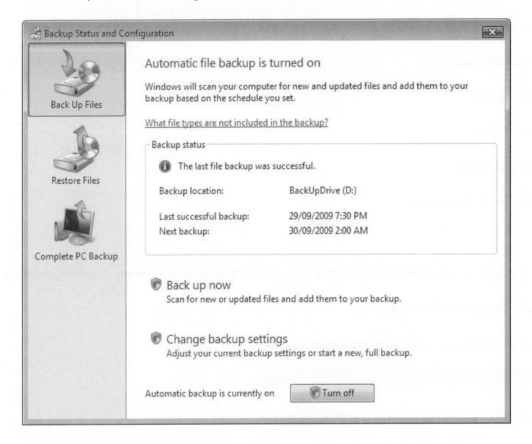

When will the next backup take place?

What is the state of automatic backup?

Step 7

Navigate to the Desktop. Delete **Backup File One** and **Backup File Two**.

Empty the Recycle Bin.

Step 8

Click on the "Backup Status and Configuration" window so it is active.

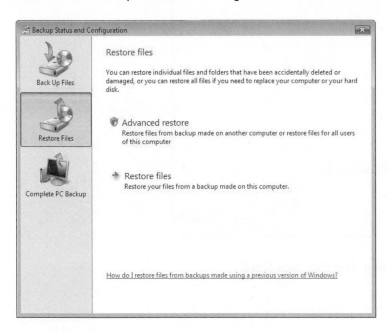

Click **Restore Files** icon on the left panel.

Step 9

Click **Restore files**.

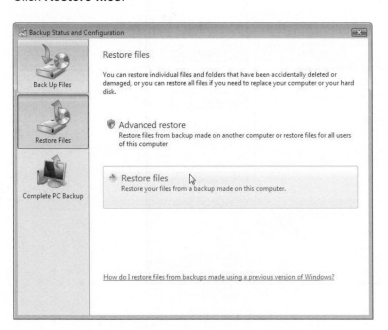

Step 10

The "What do you want to restore?" screen appears.

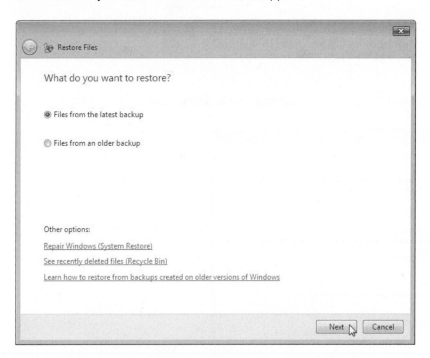

Select **Files from the latest backup**, and then click **Next**.

Step 11

The "Select the files and folders to restore" screen appears.

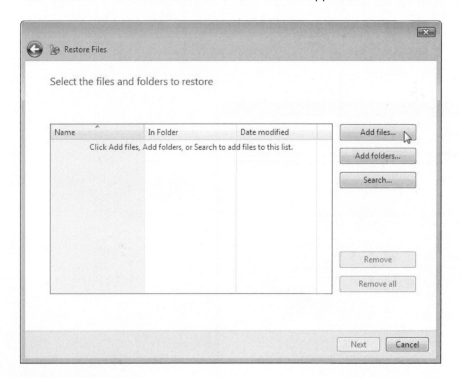

Click **Add files**.

Navigate to the Desktop and locate files **Backup File One** and **Backup File Two**.

Select both files by clicking **Backup File One** and then holding down the Ctrl key while clicking **Backup File Two**.

Click **Add**.

The two files should show up in the "Select the files and folders to restore" screen.

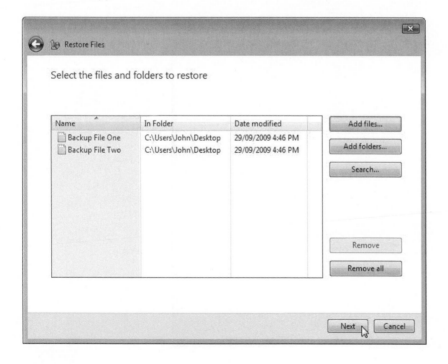

Click **Next**.

Step 12

The "Where do you want to save the restored files?" screen appears.

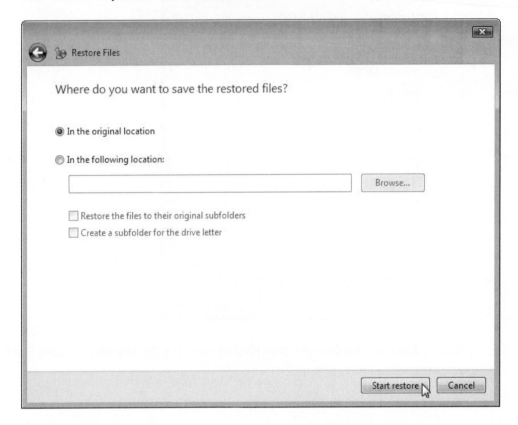

Select **In the original location**, and then click **Start restore**.

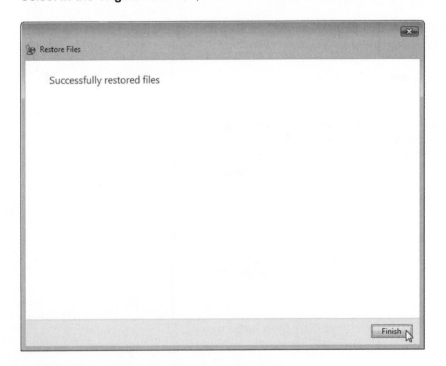

When the "Successfully restored files" screen appears, click **Finish**.

Step 13

Navigate to the Desktop.

Are the two files restored to the Desktop?

Step 14

Open file **Backup File Two**. Add the following text "More text added." to the file. Save the file.

Step 15

Click on the "Backup Status and Configuration" window so it is active.

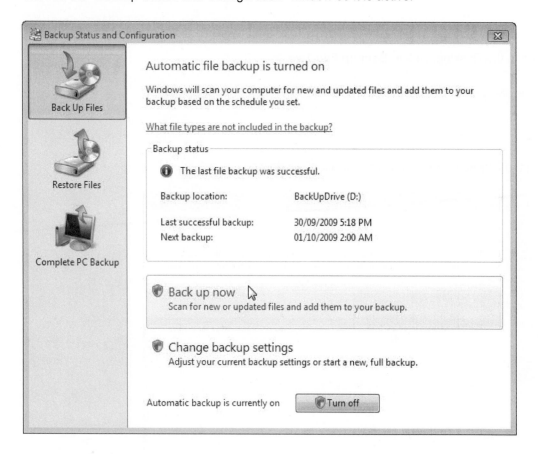

Click **Back Up Files**.

Which files will be backed up?

To where will the files be backed up?

Click **Back up now > Continue**.

The progress bar appears.

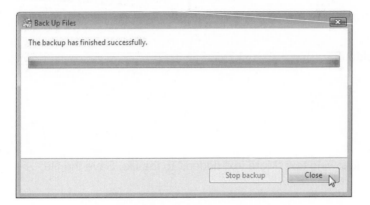

When the backup is completed, click **Close**.

Step 16

Navigate to the Desktop. Delete **Backup File Two**.

Empty the Recycle Bin.

Step 17

Click on the "Backup Status and Configuration" window so it is activated.

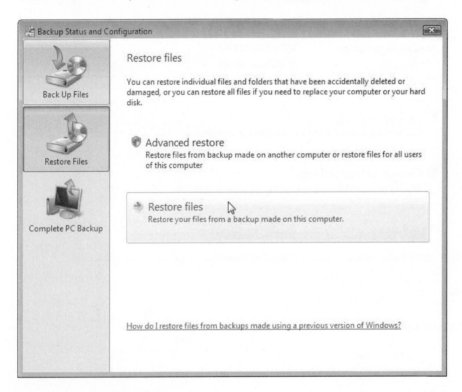

Click **Restore Files** icon.

Click **Restore files**.

Restore both **Backup File One** and **Backup File Two**.

Step 18

Navigate to the Desktop. Open file **Backup File Two**.

What text is in the file?

Step 19

Delete the following from the Desktop: **Backup File One** and **Backup File Two**.

Empty the trash.

10.3.1.6 Lab - Data Backup and Recovery in Windows XP

Introduction

In this lab, you will back up data. You will also perform a recovery of the data.

Recommended Equipment

The following equipment is required for this exercise:

- A computer system running Windows XP is required for this exercise.

Step 1

Log on to the computer as an administrator.

Navigate to the location where backed-up files will be stored. For example, use the external hard drive H:\. Create a folder called **Backup Location**.

Create a text file on the desktop called **Backup File One**. Open the file and type the text "**The text in this file will not be changed.**"

Create another text file on the desktop called **Backup File Two**. Open the file and type the text "**The text in this file will be changed.**"

Step 2

Click **Start > All Programs > Accessories > System Tools > Backup**.

The "Backup or Restore Wizard" window appears.

Click **Advanced Mode**.

Step 3

The "Backup Utility" window appears.

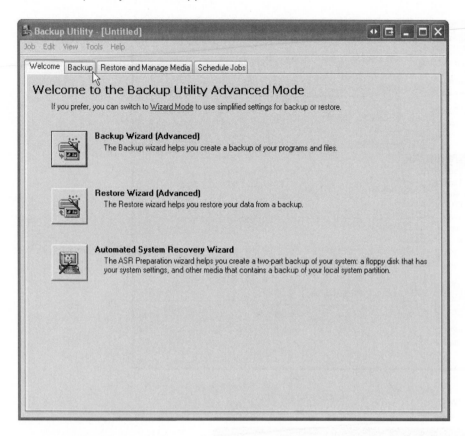

Click the **Backup** tab.

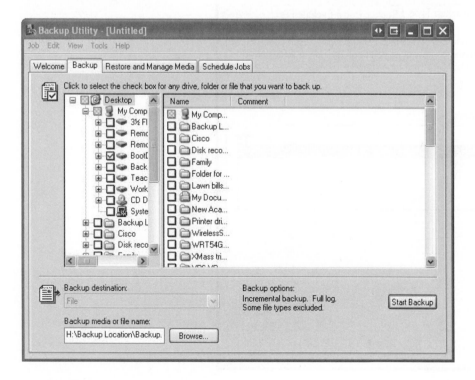

Step 4

From the menu, select **Tools > Options**.

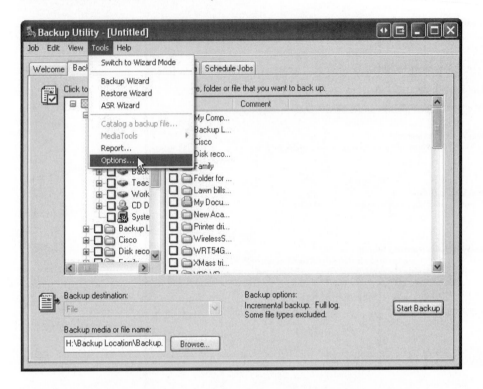

The "Options" window opens.

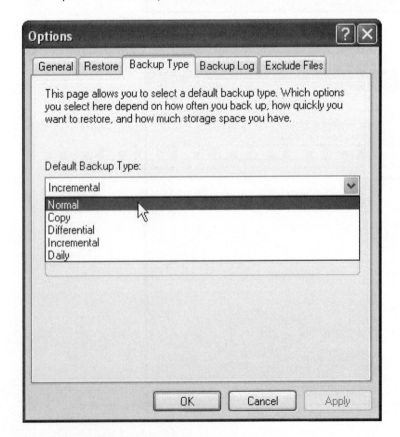

Click the **Backup Type** tab.

Select the Default Backup Type to **Normal**.

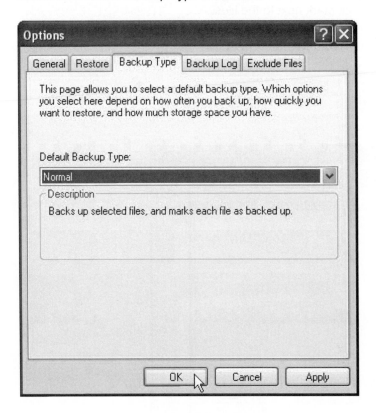

What is the description of a normal backup?

Click **OK**.

Step 5

The "Backup" tab screen re-appears.

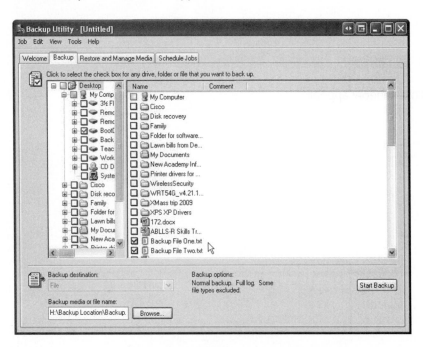

Click the **Desktop:** icon in the left panel. Then locate in the right panel the files named **Backup File One** and **Backup File Two**, and place a check mark next to the files.

Click the **Browse** button. If asked to insert a disk into drive A, click **Cancel**.

Step 6

The "Save As" window opens.

Locate the **Drive H:** folder called **Backup Location**. Select the **Backup Location** folder and click **Open**. Click **Save**.

Step 7

The "Backup" tab screen re-appears.

Click **Start Backup** button.

The "Backup Job Information" window appears.

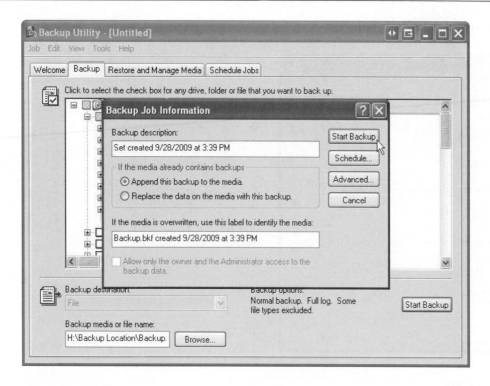

Keep the default settings.

What is the default label for the backup file?

Click **Start Backup**.

The "Backup Progress" window appears.

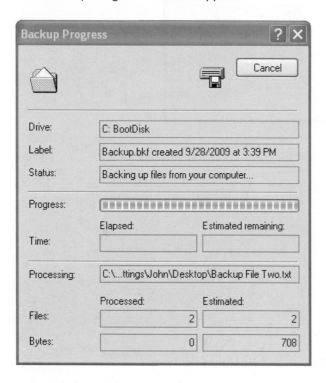

When the backup is finished, click **Report**.

A backup log file opens.

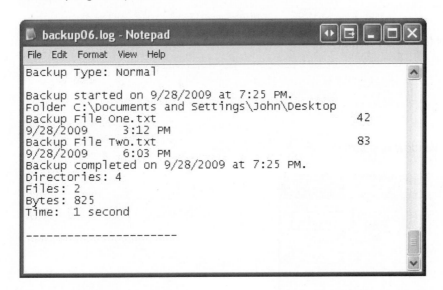

Scroll to the bottom of the file.

What files were backed up?

Close the notepad document.

Click **Close** to exit Backup Progress.

Step 8

Navigate to the Desktop. Delete **Backup File One** and **Backup File Two**.

Empty the Recycle Bin.

Step 9

Click on the **Backup Utility** window so it is activated.

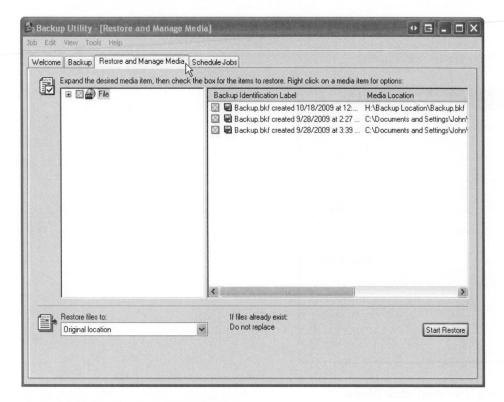

Click the **Restore and Manage Media** tab.

In the left panel, expand the most recent backup file.

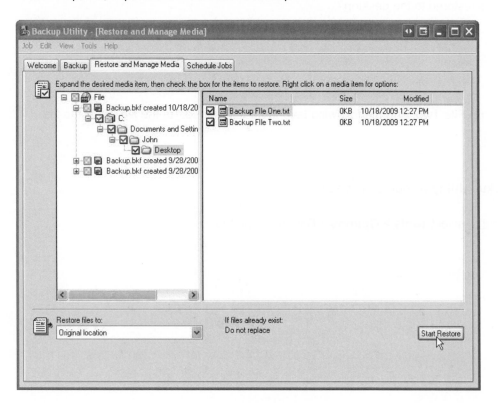

Place a check mark in the checkbox.

Make sure the "Restore file to" is set to **Original location**.

Click **Start Restore > OK**.

The "Restore Progress" window opens.

When the restore is finished, click **Close**.

Navigate to the desktop.

Are the two files restored to the desktop?

Step 10

Open file **Backup File Two**. Add the following text "More text added." to the file. Save the file.

Step 11

Click the **Backup Utility** window so it is active.

In the main menu, select **Tools > Options > Backup Type** tab.

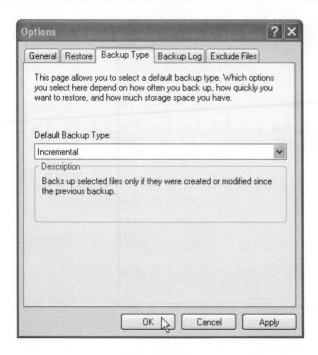

Change the Default Backup Type to **Incremental**.

What is the description of an incremental backup?

Click **OK**.

Step 12

Click the **Backup Tab**. Click the **Desktop** icon in the left panel. Locate in the right panel the file named **Backup File One** and **Backup File Two**. Place a check mark next to the files.

Click **Start Backup** button.

The Backup Job Information window appears. Keep the default settings.

What is the default label for the backup file?

Click **Start Backup**.

When the backup is finished, click **Report**.

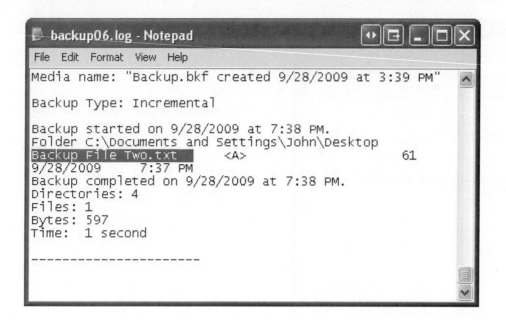

Scroll to the bottom of the file.

What file(s) were backed up?

Close the notepad document.

Click **Close** to exit Backup Progress.

Step 13

The "Backup Utility" window re-appears.

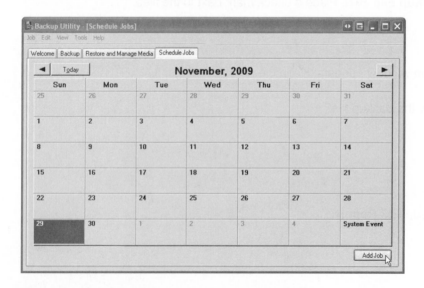

Click the **Schedule Job** tab.

Click **Add Job > Next**.

Select **Back up selected files, drivers, or network data**.

Click **Next**.

Locate and place a check mark next to files **Backup File One** and **Backup File Two**.

Click **Next**.

Click the **Browse** button; then locate and select the **Backup Location** folder. Click **Open > Save**.

Click **Next**.

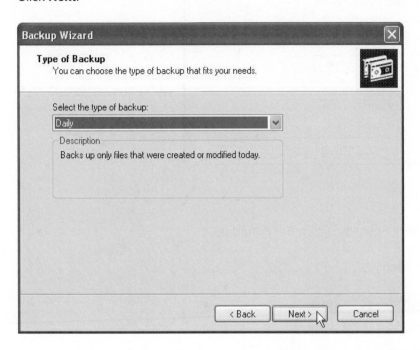

Set backup type to **Daily**.

What is the description of a daily backup?

Click **Next > Next > Next**.

The "When to Back Up" screen appears.

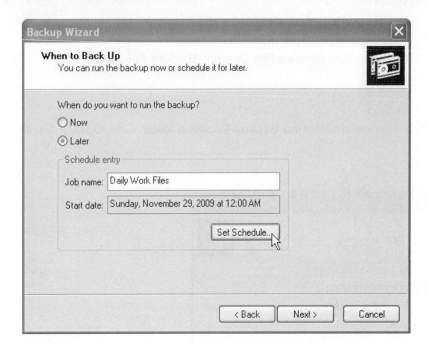

Select **Later**.

For Job name, type **Daily Work Files**; then click **Set Schedule**.

The "Schedule Job" window opens.

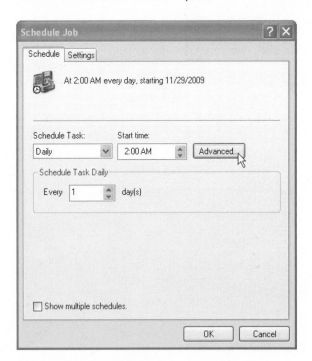

Set Schedule Task to **Daily**, Start time to **2:00 AM**, Schedule Task Daily Every **1** day(s), and then click the **Advanced** button.

The "Advanced Schedule Options" window opens.

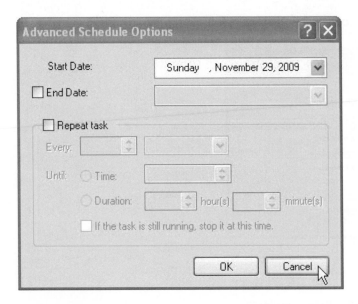

Click **Cancel**.

The "Schedule Job" window re-appears.

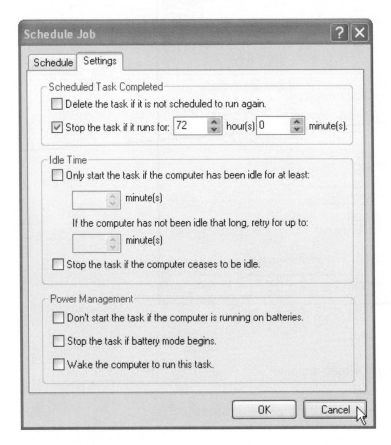

Click the **Settings** tab.

What is the default maximum time allowed to run a backup?

Click **OK**.

Enter the administrator password and confirm the password.

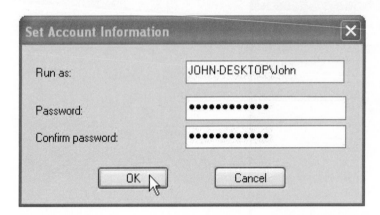

Click **OK**.

The "When to Back Up" screen appears with new settings.

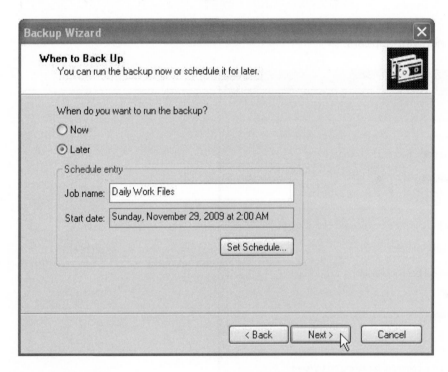

Click **Next > OK**.

The "Completing the Backup Wizard" screen appears.

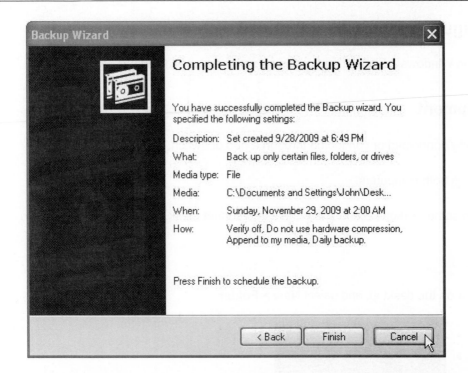

Click **Cancel**. Do not save the scheduled backup. Close the **Backup Utility [Schedule Jobs]** window.

Step 14

Delete the following from the Desktop: **Backup File One** and **Backup File Two**.

Delete the **Backup Location** folder from Drive H:.

Empty the trash.

10.3.1.8 Lab - Configure a Windows 7 Firewall

In this lab, you will explore the Windows 7 Firewall and configure some advanced settings.

Recommended Equipment

- Two computers directly connected or connected through a hub or switch.

- Windows 7 installed on both computers.

- Computers are in the same workgroup and share the same subnet mask.

Step 1

For computer 1, right-click on the desktop, and select **New > Folder**.

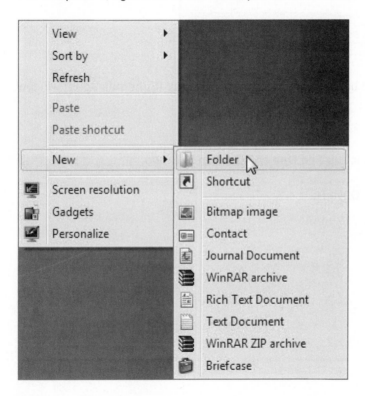

Name the folder Cisco.

Right-click on the **Cisco** folder, and then select **Share with > Advanced sharing > Advanced Sharing**.

The "Advanced Sharing" window opens.

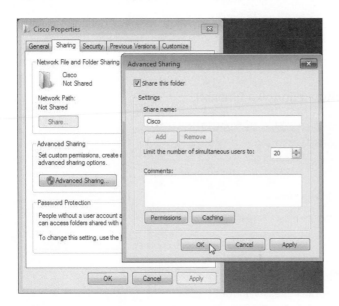

Share the folder; use the default name **Cisco**.

From computer 2, click **Start > Control Panel > Network and Sharing Center > Network** icon.

Double-click **computer 1**.

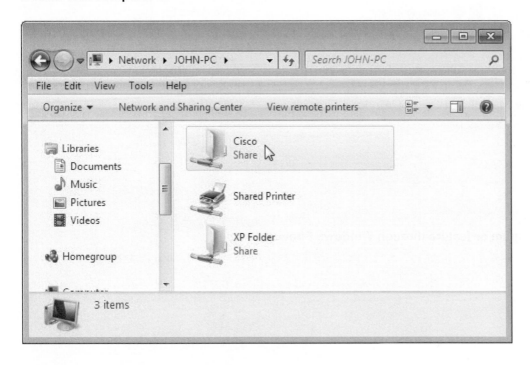

Can you see the shared folder Cisco?

Note: If you answered no, ask the instructor for help.

Close **Network**.

Note: Use computer 1 for the rest of the lab unless otherwise stated.

Step 2

Navigate to the Windows 7 Firewall:

Click **Start > Control Panel > System and Security > Windows Firewall**.

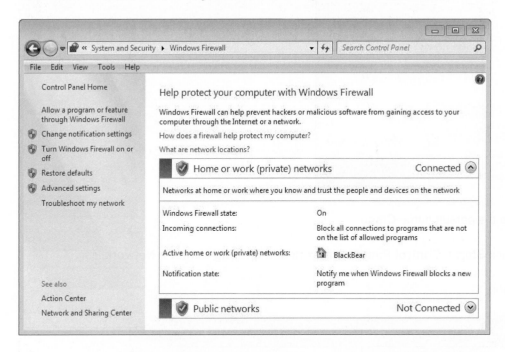

The Firewall indicator shows the status of the firewall. The normal setting is "**On**".

In the space below, state the benefits of Windows Firewall.

Step 3

Click **Allow a program or feature through Windows Firewall**.

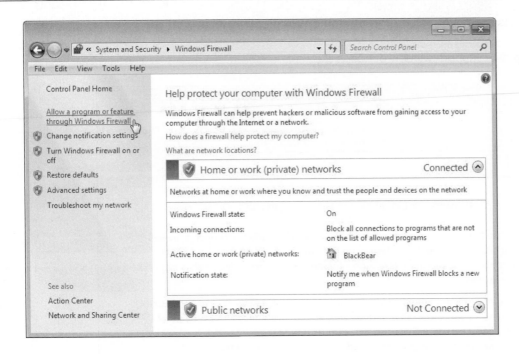

Step 4

The "Allowed Programs" window opens.

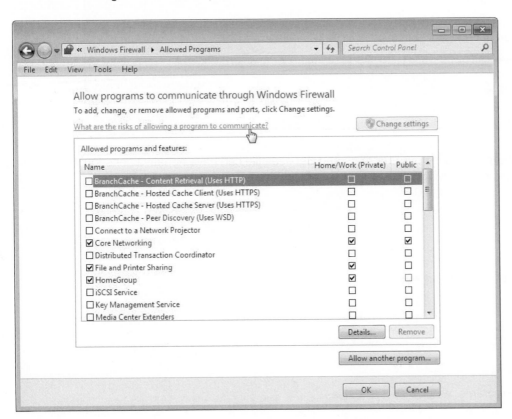

Programs and services that Windows Firewall is not blocking will be listed with a check mark.

You can add applications to this list. This may be necessary if your customer has an application that requires outside communications but for some reason the Windows Firewall cannot perform the configuration automatically. You must be logged on to this computer as an administrator to complete this procedure.

Click **What are the risks of allowing a program to communicate?**.

The "Windows Help and Support" window opens.

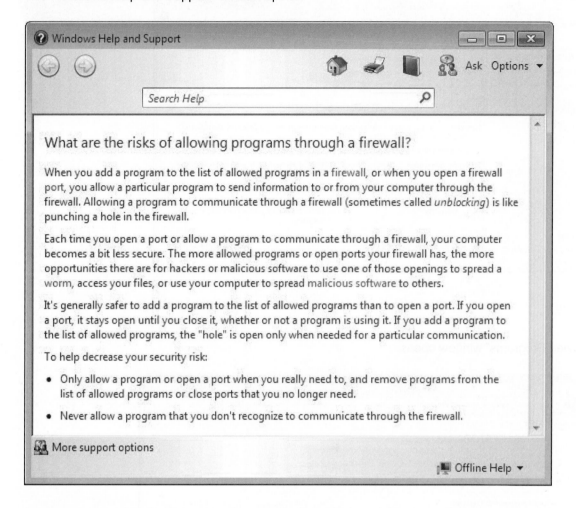

Creating too many exceptions in your Programs and Services file can have negative consequences. Describe a negative consequence of having too many exceptions.

Close Windows Help and Support window.

Step 5

From computer 1:

Click on "Allowed Programs" window so it is active.

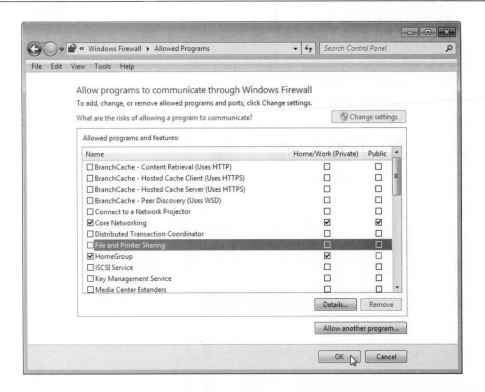

To turn off an exception, remove the check mark from **File and Printer Sharing > OK**.

From computer 2:

Open the network connect to computer 1.

Click **Start > Control Panel > Network and Sharing Center > Network** icon.

Can you connect to computer 1?

From computer 1:

To turn on an exception, add a check mark to **File and Printer Sharing > OK**.

From computer 2:

Refresh **Network** screen and connect to computer 1.

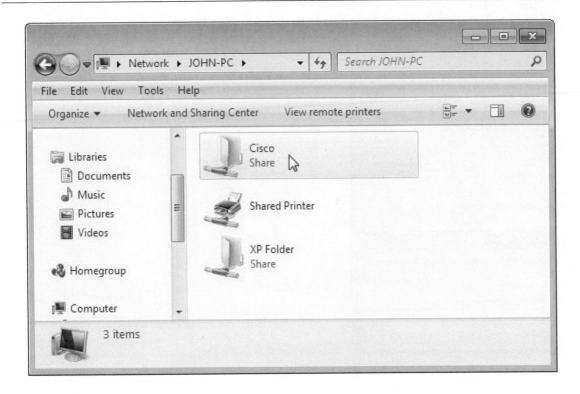

Can you connect to computer 1?

Log off computer 2. Use computer 1 for the rest of the lab.

Step 6

Click **Start > Control Panel > System and Security > Administrative Tools > Windows Firewall with Advanced Security > Inbound Rules**.

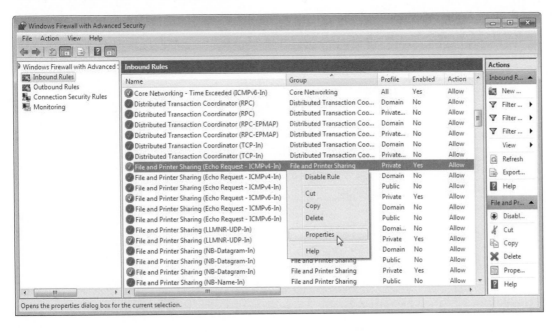

Expand the window so you can see the full name of the Inbound rules. Locate Files and Printer Sharing (Echo Request – ICMPv4-In).

Right-click on the rule and select **Properties > Advanced** tab **> Customize**.

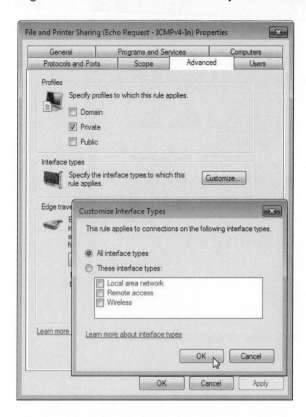

The Advance tab displays the profile(s) used by the computer and the "Customize Interface Types" window displays the different connections configured for your computer.

Click **OK**.

Click **Programs and Services** tab.

The "Customize Service Settings" window opens.

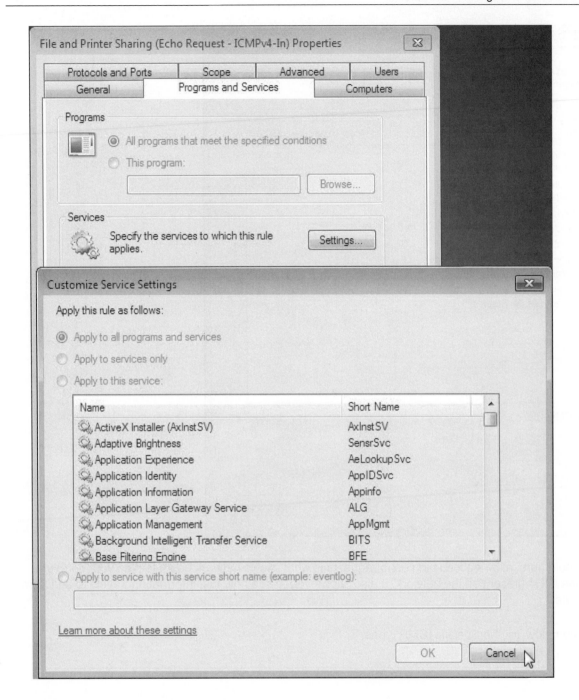

In the space below, list the short name of four services that are available.

Click **Cancel**.

Step 7

There are many applications that users do not normally see that also need to get through the Windows Firewall to access your computer. These are the network-level commands that direct traffic on the network and the Internet.

Click **Protocols and Ports** tab. For the ICMP settings, click the **Customize** button. You will see the menu where ICMP exceptions are configured.

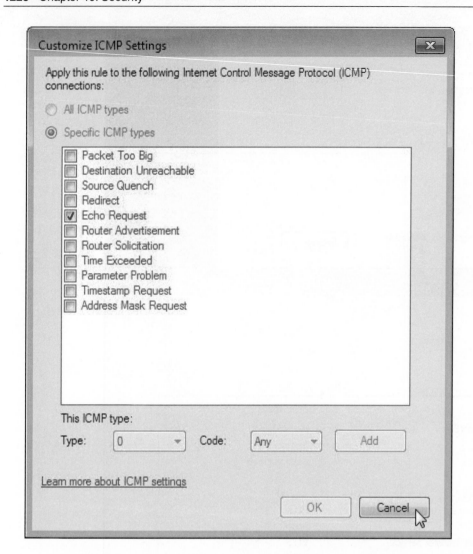

In the example here, allowing incoming echo requests is what allows network users to ping your computer to determine if it is present on the network. It also allows you to see how fast information travels to and from your computer.

In the space below, list the Specific ICMP types.

Close all windows.

10.3.1.9 Lab - Configure a Windows Vista Firewall

In this lab, you will explore the Windows Vista Firewall and configure some advanced settings.

Recommended Equipment

- Two computers directly connected or connected through a hub or switch.

- Windows Vista installed on both computers.

- Computers are in the same workgroup and share the same subnet mask.

Step 1

For computer 1, right-click on the desktop, and select **New > Folder**.

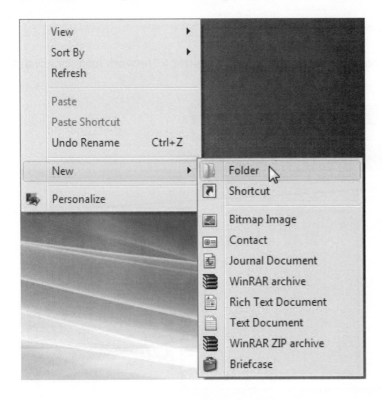

Name the folder Cisco.

Right-click on the Cisco folder, and then select **Share > Continue**.

The "Advanced Sharing" window opens.

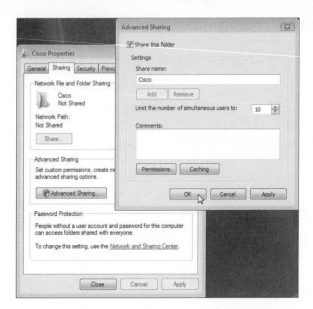

Share the folder; use the default name **Cisco**.

From computer 2, click **Start > Control Panel > Network and Sharing Center > Network** icon (icon with the network name you are connected to).

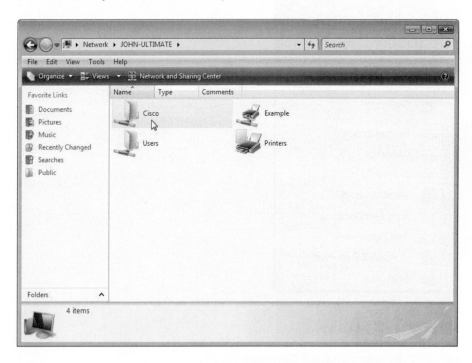

Double-click **computer 1**.

Can you see the shared folder Cisco?

Note: If you answered no, ask the instructor for help.

Close **Network**.

Note: Use computer 1 for the rest of the lab unless otherwise stated.

Step 2

Navigate to the Windows Vista Firewall.

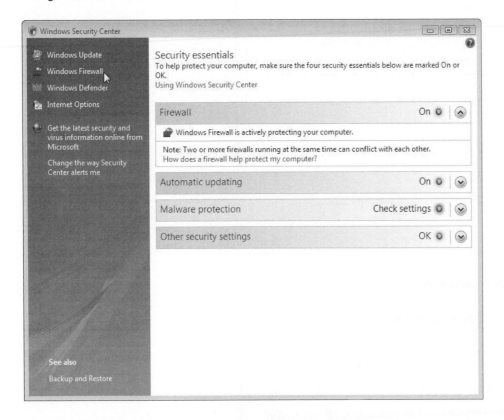

Click **Start > Control Panel > Security Center**.

The Firewall indicator shows the status of the firewall. The normal setting is "**On**".

Access Windows Firewall by clicking **Firewall** at the right side of the window.

Step 3

The "Windows Firewall" window opens.

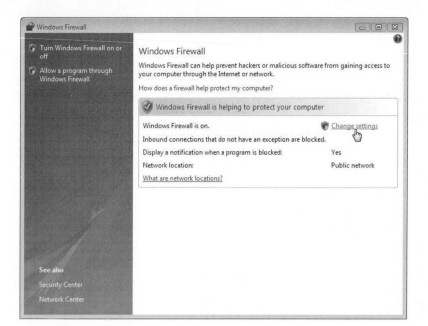

Click **Change settings > Continue**.

The "Windows Firewall Settings" window opens.

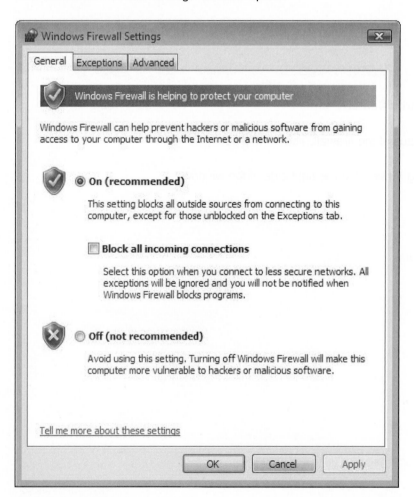

In the space below, state why turning off the Windows Firewall is not advised.

Step 4

From the Windows Firewall Settings window, select the **Exceptions** tab.

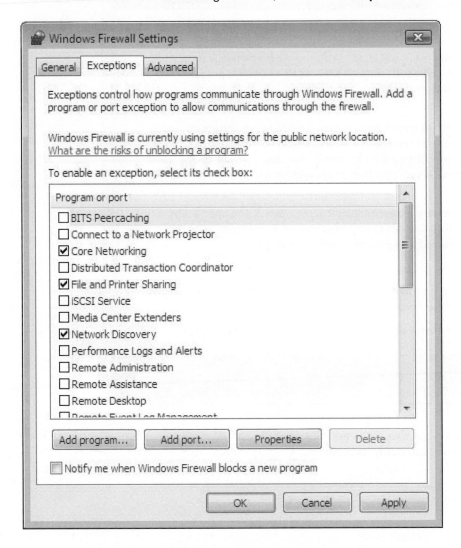

Programs and services that Windows Firewall is not blocking will be listed with a checkmark.

You can add applications to this list. This may be necessary if your customer has an application that requires outside communications but for some reason the Windows Firewall cannot perform the configuration automatically. You must be logged on to this computer as an administrator to complete this procedure.

Click **What are the risks of unblocking a program?**.

The "Window Help and Support" window opens.

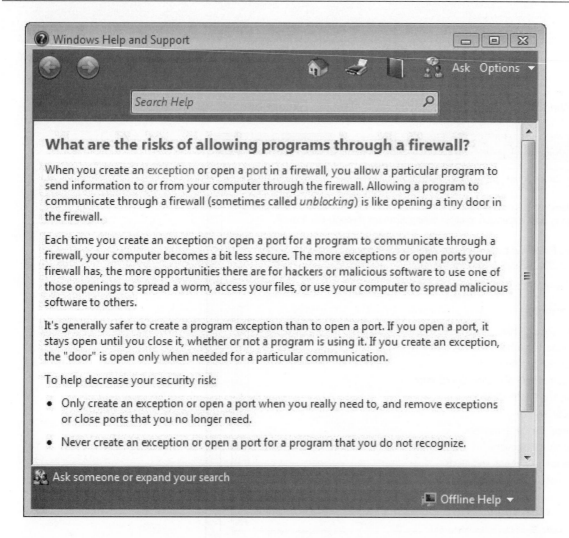

Creating too many exceptions in your Programs and Services file can have negative consequences. Describe a negative consequence to having too many exceptions.

Close the Windows Help and Support window.

Step 5

From computer 1:

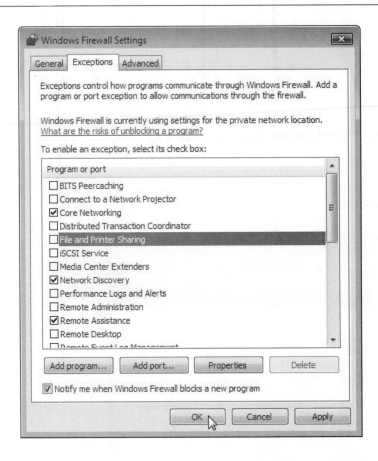

To turn off an exception, remove the check mark from **File and Printer Sharing > OK**.

From computer 2:

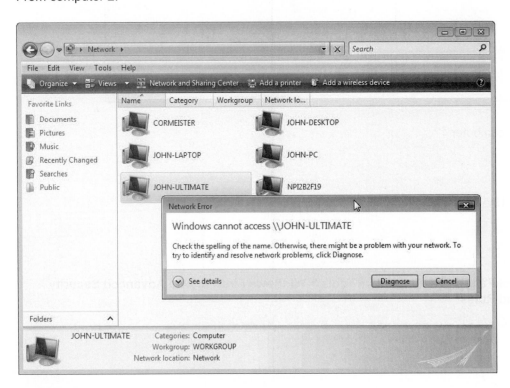

Click **Start > Control Panel > Network and Sharing Center > Network** icon (icon with the network name you are connected to) and connect to computer 1.

Can you connect to computer 1?

From computer 1:

To turn on an exception add a check mark to **File and Printer Sharing > OK**.

From computer 2:

Refresh **Network** screen and connect to computer 1.

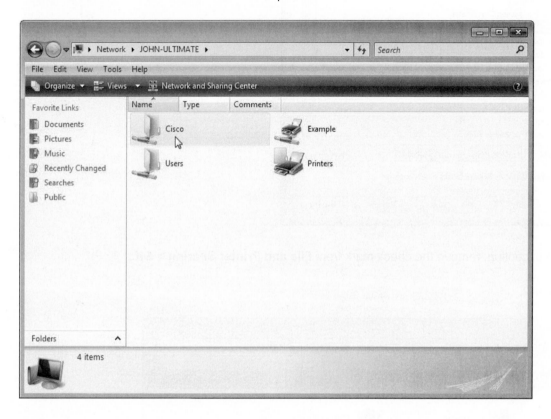

Can you connect to computer 1?

Log off computer 2. Use computer 1 for the rest of the lab.

Step 6

Click **Start > Control Panel > Administrative Tools > Windows Firewall with Advanced Security > Continue > Inbound Rules**.

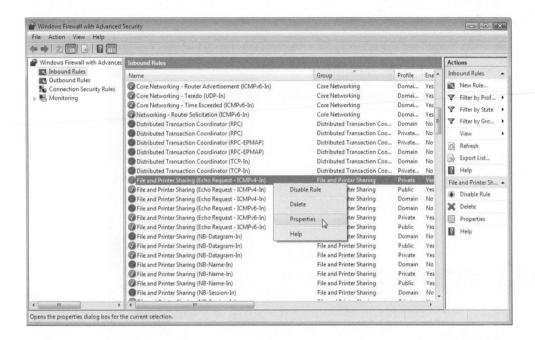

Expand the window so you can see the full name of the Inbound rules. Locate Files and Printer Sharing (Echo Request – ICMPv4-In).

Right-click on the rule and select **Properties > Advanced** tab **> Customize**. The Advanced tab displays the profile(s) used by the computer and the "Customize Interface Types" window displays the different connections configured for your computer.

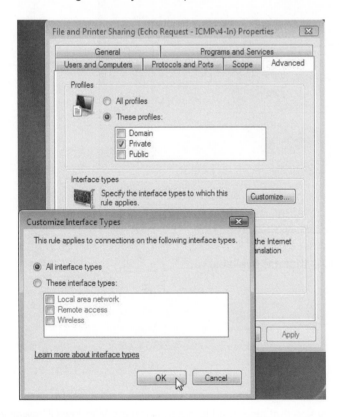

Click **OK**.

Click **Programs and Services** tab.

The "Customize Service Settings" window opens.

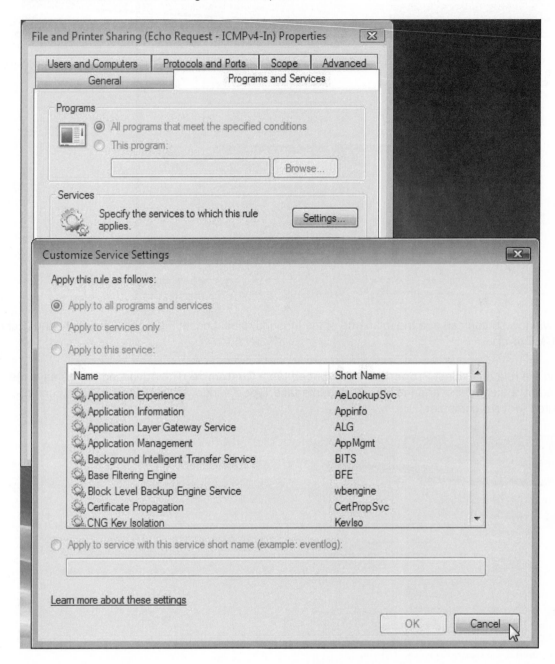

In the space below, list the short name of four services that are available.

Click **Cancel**.

Step 7

There are many applications that users do not normally see that also need to get through the Windows Firewall to access your computer. These are the network-level commands that direct traffic on the network and the Internet.

Click **Protocols and Ports** tab. For the ICMP settings, click the **Customize** button. You will see the menu where ICMP exceptions are configured.

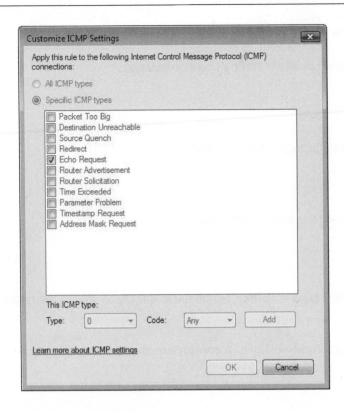

In the example here, allowing incoming echo requests is what allows network users to ping your computer to determine if it is present on the network. It also allows you to see how fast information travels to and from your computer.

In the space below, list the requests for information that your computer will respond to.

Close all windows.

10.3.1.10 Lab - Configure a Windows XP Firewall

In this lab, you will explore the Windows XP Firewall and configure some advanced settings.

Recommended Equipment

- Two computers directly connected or connected through a hub or switch.

- Windows XP installed on both computers.

- Computers are in the same workgroup and share the same subnet mask.

Step 1

From computer 1, right-click the **Desktop**, and select **New > Folder**. Name the folder Cisco. Share the folder; use the default name Cisco.

From computer 2, open **My Network Place >** select **View workgroup computers** and connect to computer 1.

Can you see the shared folder Cisco?

Note: If you answered no, ask the instructor for help.

Close **My Network Place**.

Note: Use computer 1 for the rest of the lab unless otherwise stated.

Step 2

Navigate to the Windows XP Firewall.

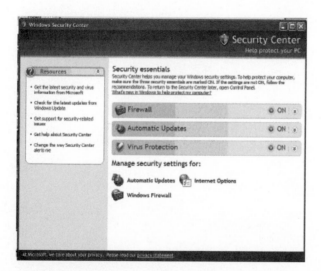

Click **Start > Control Panel > Security Center**.

The Firewall indicator shows the status of the firewall. The normal setting is "**ON**".

Access Windows Firewall by clicking **Windows Firewall** at the bottom of the window.

Step 3

The "Windows Firewall" window opens.

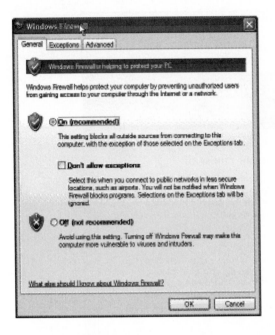

In the space below, state why turning off the Windows Firewall is not advised.

Step 4

From the Windows Firewall window, select the **Exceptions** tab. Programs and services that Windows Firewall is not blocking will be listed with a checkmark.

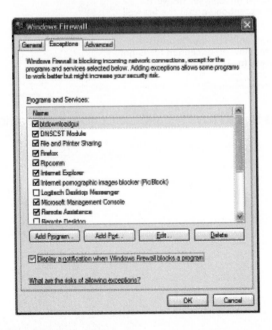

You can add applications to this list. This may be necessary if your customer has an application that requires outside communications, but for some reason the Windows Firewall cannot perform the configuration automatically. You must be logged on to this computer as an administrator to complete this procedure.

Click **What are the risks of allowing exceptions?**.

The "Help and Support Center" window opens.

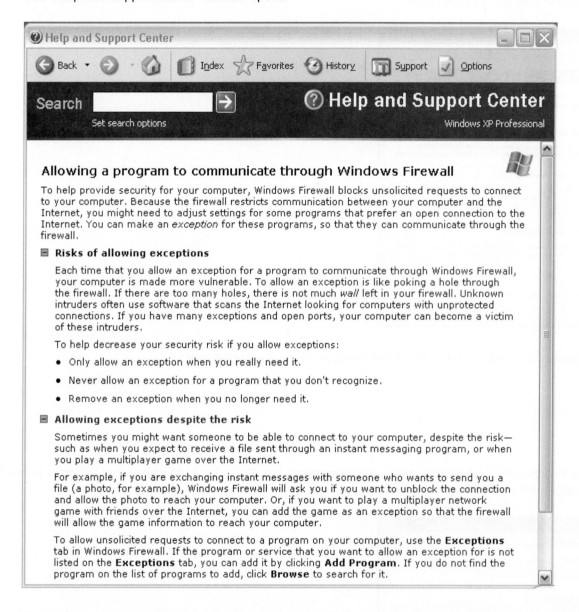

Creating too many exceptions in your Programs and Services file can have negative consequences. Describe a negative consequence to having too many exceptions.

Close the Help and Support Center window.

Step 5

From computer 1:

To turn off an exception, remove the check mark from **File and Printer Sharing > OK**.

From computer 2:

Open **My Network Place > View workgroup computers** and connect to computer 1.

Can you connect to computer 1?

From computer 1:

To turn on an exception, add a check mark to **File and Printer Sharing > OK**.

From computer 2:

Refresh **My Network Place** and connect to computer 1.

Can you connect to computer 1?

Log off computer 2. Use computer 1 for the rest of the lab.

Step 6

From the Windows Firewall control menu, select the **Advanced** tab to view the **Network Connection Settings**. Network Connection Settings displays the different connections configured for your computer.

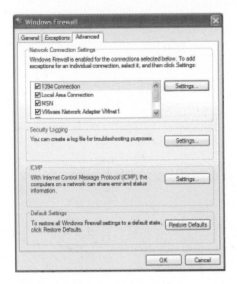

Click the **Settings** button in the Network Connection Settings area. The Advanced Settings window has two tabs: Services and ICMP. Click the **Services** tab.

In the space below, list the services that are available.

Step 7

There are many applications that users do not normally see that also need to get through the Windows Firewall to access your computer. These are the network-level commands that direct traffic on the network and the Internet.

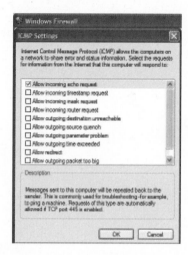

Under the ICMP heading, click the **Settings** button. You will see the menu where ICMP exceptions are configured.

In the example here, allowing incoming echo requests is what allows network users to ping your computer to determine if it is present on the network and how fast information travels to and from it.

In the space below, list the requests for information that your computer will respond to.

Close all windows.

10.4.2.2 Worksheet - Gather Information from the Customer

(Student Technician Sheet)

Gather data from the customer (a partner that has been assigned by your instructor) to begin the troubleshooting process. Document the customer's problem in the work order below.

Work Order

Company Name: _____

Contact: _____

Company Address: _____

Company Phone: _____

Category _____   Closure Code_____   Status_____

Type_____   Escalated_____   Pending_____

Item_____   Pending Until Date_____

Business Impacting? O Yes O No

Summary_____

_____

Case ID#_____   Connection Type_____

Priority_____   Environment_____

User Platform_____

Problem Description: _____
_____
_____
_____

Problem Solution: _____
_____
_____
_____

(Student Customer Sheet)

Use the contact information and problem description below to report the following information to a level-one technician.

Contact Information

Company Name: Organization of Associated Chartered Federations, Inc.

Contact: Braxton Jones

Company Address: 123 E. Main Street

Company Phone: 480-555-1234

Category: Security

Problem Description

I am not able to login. I was able to login yesterday and all days previously. I tried to login with a different computer but was unsuccessful there also. I received an email last week about changing my password, but I have not changed my password yet.

(NOTE: Once you have given the level-one tech the problem description, use the Computer Configuration to answer any follow up questions the technician may ask.)

Computer Configuration

- Windows 7

- I do not know when it was last updated.

- There is some kind of antivirus program that used to run when I started the computer, but I haven't seen it recently.

Chapter 11: The IT Professional

11.1.1.3 Worksheet - Technician Resources

In this worksheet, you will use the Internet to find online resources for a specific computer component. Search online for resources that can help you troubleshoot the component. In the table below, list a least one website for each of the following types of resources: online FAQs, online manuals, online troubleshooting/help site, and blogs. Give a brief description of the content on the site. Be prepared to discuss the usefulness of the resources you found.

Component to research: _____

Type of Resources	Website Address

Chapter 12: Advanced Troubleshooting

12.1.1.4 Lab - Repair Boot Problem

Introduction

In this lab, you will troubleshoot and repair a computer that does not boot.

Recommended Equipment

- A computer running Windows 7
- Antistatic wrist strap
- Tool kit

Scenario

The computer will not start up. The computer beeps constantly.

Step 1

Unplug the power cable from the computer. Check the other external cables. Make sure all other external cables are in the correct position and the connections are secure. Make sure any power switches are set to "off" or "0".

Step 2

Open the case and check all internal data and power cable connections. Check the adapter cards and RAM modules to make sure they are seated completely.

Step 3

Remove your antistatic wrist strap. If there is a power switch on the power supply, turn it to "on" or "1". Turn on the computer.

What steps did you perform to fix the computer?

12.1.1.5 Lab - Remote Technician - Repair Boot Problem

(Student Technician Sheet)

In this lab, you will gather data from the customer, and then instruct the customer on how to fix a computer that does not boot. Document the customer's problem in the work order below.

Company Name: JH Travel, Inc.
Contact: Dan Handy
Company Address: 204 N. Main Street
Company Phone: 1-866-555-0998

| **Work Order** |

Generating a New Ticket

Category <u>Hardware</u>   Closure Code ____   Status <u>Open</u>

Type: _____   Escalated <u>Yes</u>   Pending _____

Item _____   Pending Until Date _____

                    Business Impacting? X Yes   O No

Summary <u>The computer will not start up. The computer beeps constantly.</u>

_____

Case ID#_____   Connection Type _____

Priority _____2_____   Environment _____

User Platform <u>Windows 7</u>

Problem Description: <u>Computer will not boot. Customer does not know the</u> <u>manufacturer of the BIOS. Cannot identify error from beep sequence. Customer</u> <u>did not hear any strange sounds from the computer. Customer does not smell</u> <u>smoke or burning electronics.</u>

<u>Problem Solution</u>

_____

_____

_____

_____

_____

_____

(Student Customer Sheet)

Use the contact information and problem description below to report the following information to a level-two technician:

Contact Information

Company Name: JH Travel, Inc.

Contact: Dan Handy

Company Address: 204 N. Main Street

Company Phone: 1-866-555-0998

Problem Description

Ok, so I work with cars all the time and I know how they work, but I do not know how my computer works. This morning was pretty slow because I guess more and more people are using those Internet travel sites. So, after my morning coffee, I decided to figure out what makes my computer work. I opened up the case and just started looking at the different things inside. When I put everything back together, everything seemed to fit and I didn't see any leftover parts. Now it does not work at all. It beeps at me all the time.

(NOTE: Once you have given the level-two tech the problem description, use the Additional Information to answer any follow-up questions the technician may ask.)

Additional Information

- Windows 7.
- Computer has no new hardware.
- Computer has not been moved recently.
- Except for the beeping, I did not hear any other strange sounds from the computer.
- I do not smell any electronics burning or smoke.
- Computer looks the same as it did yesterday.

12.1.1.6 Lab - Troubleshooting Hardware Problems in Windows 7

Introduction

In this lab, the instructor will introduce various hardware problems, and you will diagnose the cause of these problems, and then fix them.

Recommended Equipment

The following equipment is required for this exercise:

*   A computer running Windows 7

Scenario

You must solve hardware problems for a customer. You may need to troubleshoot both software and hardware used by the computer. Make sure you document and solve the problems, and then document the solutions.

There are several possible errors. Solve one problem at a time until you can successfully start the computers and all devices are fully functional. You may need to ask the instructor for hardware when needed.

Step 1

Start the computer.

Did the computer boot successfully?

If the computer started Windows 7, log on with the Administrator account.

Test all internal and external hardware devices.

Did all devices operate properly?

If the computer successfully started and all devices are fully functional, you have successfully solved all hardware problems. Hand the lab into your instructor.

If you could not successfully start the computer and all devices are not fully functional, continue troubleshooting the problem.

Students start by troubleshooting the computer for problems. Answer the following questions after each problem is solved. The instructor may inform you of the number of troubleshooting problems to complete.

Problem 1

What problem did you find?

What steps did you take to determine the problem?

What is causing the problem?

List the steps taken to fix the problem.

Problem 2

What problem did you find?

What steps did you take to determine the problem?

What is causing the problem?

List the steps taken to fix the problem.

Problem 3

What problem did you find?

What steps did you take to determine the problem?

What is causing the problem?

List the steps taken to fix the problem.

Problem 4

What problem did you find?

What steps did you take to determine the problem?

What is causing the problem?

List the steps taken to fix the problem.

Problem 5

What problem did you find?

What steps did you take to determine the problem?

What is causing the problem?

List the steps taken to fix the problem.

Problem 6

What problem did you find?

What steps did you take to determine the problem?

What is causing the problem?

List the steps taken to fix the problem.

Problem 7

What problem did you find?

What steps did you take to determine the problem?

What is causing the problem?

List the steps taken to fix the problem.

Problem 8

What problem did you find?

What steps did you take to determine the problem?

What is causing the problem?

List the steps taken to fix the problem.

Problem 9

What problem did you find?

What steps did you take to determine the problem?

What is causing the problem?

List the steps taken to fix the problem.

Problem 10

What problem did you find?

What steps did you take to determine the problem?

What is causing the problem?

List the steps taken to fix the problem.

12.1.1.7 Lab - Troubleshooting Hardware Problems in Windows Vista

Introduction

In this lab, the instructor will introduce various hardware problems, and you will diagnose the cause of these problems, and then fix them.

Recommended Equipment

The following equipment is required for this exercise:

- A computer running Windows Vista

Scenario

You must solve hardware problems for a customer. You may need to troubleshoot both software and hardware used by the computer. Make sure you document and solve the problems, and then document the solutions.

There are several possible errors. Solve one problem at a time until you can successfully start the computers and all devices are fully functional. You may need to ask the instructor for hardware when needed.

Step 1

Start the computer.

Did the computer boot successfully?

If the computer started Windows Vista, log on with the Administrator account.

Test all internal and external hardware devices.

Did all devices operate properly?

If the computer successfully started and all devices are fully functional, you have successfully solved all hardware problems. Hand the lab into your instructor.

If you could not successfully start the computer and all devices are not fully functional, continue troubleshooting the problem.

Students start by troubleshooting the computer for problems. Answer the following questions after each problem is solved. The instructor may inform you of the number of troubleshooting problems to complete.

Problem 1

What problem did you find?

What steps did you take to determine the problem?

What is causing the problem?

List the steps taken to fix the problem.

Problem 2

What problem did you find?

What steps did you take to determine the problem?

What is causing the problem?

List the steps taken to fix the problem.

Problem 3

What problem did you find?

What steps did you take to determine the problem?

What is causing the problem?

List the steps taken to fix the problem.

Problem 4

What problem did you find?

What steps did you take to determine the problem?

What is causing the problem?

List the steps taken to fix the problem.

Problem 5

What problem did you find?

What steps did you take to determine the problem?

What is causing the problem?

List the steps taken to fix the problem.

Problem 6

What problem did you find?

What steps did you take to determine the problem?

What is causing the problem?

List the steps taken to fix the problem.

Problem 7

What problem did you find?

What steps did you take to determine the problem?

What is causing the problem?

List the steps taken to fix the problem.

Problem 8

What problem did you find?

What steps did you take to determine the problem?

What is causing the problem?

List the steps taken to fix the problem.

Problem 9

What problem did you find?

What steps did you take to determine the problem?

What is causing the problem?

List the steps taken to fix the problem.

Problem 10

What problem did you find?

What steps did you take to determine the problem?

What is causing the problem?

List the steps taken to fix the problem.

12.1.1.8 Lab - Troubleshooting Hardware Problems in Windows XP

Introduction

In this lab, the instructor will introduce various hardware problems. The student will diagnose the causes and solve the problems.

Recommended Equipment

The following equipment is required for this exercise:

- A computer running Windows XP

Scenario

You must solve hardware problems for a customer. You may need to troubleshoot both software and hardware used by the computer. Make sure you document and solve the problems, and then document the solutions.

There are several possible errors. Solve one problem at a time until you can successfully start the computer and all devices are fully functional.

Step 1

Start the computer.

Did the computer boot successfully?

If the computer started Windows XP, log on with the Administrator account.

Test all internal and external hardware devices.

Did all devices operate properly?

If the computer successfully started and all devices are fully functional, you have successfully solved all hardware problems. Hand the lab into your instructor.

If you could not successfully start the computer and all devices are not fully functional, continue trouble-shooting the problem.

Students start by troubleshooting the computer for problems. Answer the following questions after each problem is solved. The instructor may inform you of the number of troubleshooting problems to complete.

Problem 1

What problem did you find?

What steps did you take to determine the problem?

What is causing the problem?

List the steps taken to fix the problem.

Problem 2

What problem did you find?

What steps did you take to determine the problem?

What is causing the problem?

List the steps taken to fix the problem.

Problem 3

What problem did you find?

What steps did you take to determine the problem?

What is causing the problem?

List the steps taken to fix the problem.

Problem 4

What problem did you find?

What steps did you take to determine the problem?

What is causing the problem?

List the steps taken to fix the problem.

Problem 5

What problem did you find?

What steps did you take to determine the problem?

What is causing the problem?

List the steps taken to fix the problem.

Problem 6

What problem did you find?

What steps did you take to determine the problem?

What is causing the problem?

List the steps taken to fix the problem.

Problem 7

What problem did you find?

What steps did you take to determine the problem?

What is causing the problem?

List the steps taken to fix the problem.

Problem 8

What problem did you find?

What steps did you take to determine the problem?

What is causing the problem?

List the steps taken to fix the problem.

Problem 9

What problem did you find?

What steps did you take to determine the problem?

What is causing the problem?

List the steps taken to fix the problem.

Problem 10

What problem did you find?

What steps did you take to determine the problem?

What is causing the problem?

List the steps taken to fix the problem.

12.2.1.4 Lab - Fix an Operating System Problem

Introduction

In this lab, you will troubleshoot and fix a computer that does not connect to the network.

Recommended Equipment

- A computer running Windows

- Linksys E2500 wireless router

- Ethernet patch cable

Scenario

The computer will not connect to the Internet, network shares, or network printers.

Step 1

Open a command line and use command line tools to determine the ip address, subnet mask, and default gateway of the computer.

Step 2

Use Windows tools to determine the status of the Ethernet NIC.

Step 3

Repair the Ethernet connection by restoring the computer.

Step 4

What steps did you perform to fix the network?

12.2.1.5 Lab - Remote Technician - Fix an Operating System Problem

(Student Technician Sheet)

In this lab, you will gather data from the customer, and then instruct the customer on how to fix a computer that does not connect to the network. Document the customer's problem in the work order below.

Company Name: Main Street Stoneworks

Contact: Karin Jones

Company Address: 4252 W Main St.

Company Phone: 1-888-774-4444

<table>
<tr><td colspan="2">

Work Order

</td></tr>
</table>

Generating a New Ticket

Category Operating System   Closure Code ____   Status Open _____

Type: _____   Escalated Yes   Pending _____

Item _____   Pending Until Date _____

Business Impacting? X Yes   O No

Summary Customer cannot connect to the network or the Internet. _____

Case ID#_____   Connection Type Ethernet _____

Priority ____2_____   Environment _____

User Platform Windows 7 _____

Problem Description: Computer boots correctly. Network cable connected. Link lights not working. Network icon not visible in tray.

Problem Solution _____

_____

_____

_____

_____

_____

_____

(Student Customer Sheet)

Use the contact information and problem description below to report the following information to a level-two technician:

Contact Information

Company Name: Main Street Stoneworks

Contact: Karin Jones

Company Address: 4252 W. Main St.

Company Phone: 1-888-774-4444

Problem Description

When I came into the office today, I could not get my email. The Internet does not work either. I tried to restart my computer, but that did not help. None of the files that I need are available to me either. It is like someone pulled the plug, but the plug is still there. I need to get some files from my folder that I was working on yesterday. It is very important for me to get my files so that I can send them to my client. I do not know how to get the files or send them because my computer cannot find them. What do I do?

(NOTE: Once you have given the level-two tech the problem description, use the Additional Information to answer any follow-up questions the technician may ask.)

Additional Information

- Windows 7.

- Computer has not had any new hardware installed recently.

- There is no wireless network available at work.

- Computer detected new hardware at boot-up.

- Computer could not install new hardware.

12.2.1.6 Lab - Troubleshooting Operating System Problems in Windows 7

Introduction

In this lab, the instructor will introduce various operating system problems. The student will diagnose the causes and solve the problems.

Recommended Equipment

The following equipment is required for this exercise:

- Computer running Windows 7

Scenario

You must solve operating system problems for a customer. Make sure you document and solve the problems, and then document the solutions.

There are several errors. Solve one problem at a time until you can successfully boot the computer, the desktop contains the appropriate open programs, and the display is set to the native resolution or the resolution given to you by your instructor.

Step 1

Start the computer.

Does the computer boot to the desktop?

If the computer started Windows 7, log on to the computer with the Administrator account.

If the computer did not start Windows 7, troubleshoot the operating system until the computer successfully boots. Because all hardware is correctly connected, you do not need to troubleshoot hardware in this lab.

If the operating system is missing the required files to boot the computer, you can replace these files by booting the computer with the Windows 7 installation media. Use the Startup Repair option to replace any missing files.

Does the Calculator start automatically?

If the Calculator does not start automatically, configure Windows to start the Calculator every time Windows starts.

Is the resolution of the screen the native resolution or the resolution chosen by your instructor?

If the screen resolution is not native or the resolution chosen by your instructor, configure Windows to display the desktop at the native resolution of the monitor or the resolution chosen by your instructor.

If the computer successfully started, the desktop contains the appropriate open programs, and the display is set to the native resolution you have successfully solved all operating system problems. Hand the lab into your instructor.

If you could not successfully start the computer, the desktop does not contain the appropriate open programs, and the display is not set to the native resolution, continue troubleshooting the problems.

Students start by troubleshooting the computer for problems. Answer the following questions after each problem is solved. The instructor may inform you of the number of troubleshooting problems to complete.

Problem 1

What problem did you find?

What steps did you take to determine the problem?

What is causing the problem?

List the steps taken to fix the problem.

Problem 2

What problem did you find?

What steps did you take to determine the problem?

What is causing the problem?

List the steps taken to fix the problem.

Problem 3

What problem did you find?

What steps did you take to determine the problem?

What is causing the problem?

List the steps taken to fix the problem.

Problem 4

What problem did you find?

What steps did you take to determine the problem?

What is causing the problem?

List the steps taken to fix the problem.

Problem 5

What problem did you find?

What steps did you take to determine the problem?

What is causing the problem?

List the steps taken to fix the problem.

Problem 6

What problem did you find?

What steps did you take to determine the problem?

What is causing the problem?

List the steps taken to fix the problem.

Problem 7

What problem did you find?

What steps did you take to determine the problem?

What is causing the problem?

List the steps taken to fix the problem.

12.2.1.7 Lab - Troubleshooting Operating System Problems in Windows Vista

Introduction

In this lab, the instructor will introduce various operating system problems. The student will diagnose the causes and solve the problems.

Recommended Equipment

The following equipment is required for this exercise:

- Computer running Windows Vista

Scenario

You must solve operating system problems for a customer. Make sure you document and solve the problems, and then document the solutions.

There are several errors. Solve one problem at a time until you can successfully boot the computer, the desktop contains the appropriate open programs, and the display is set to the native resolution or the resolution given to you by your instructor.

Step 1

Start the computer.

Does the computer boot to the desktop?

If the computer started Windows Vista, log on to the computer with the Administrator account.

If the computer did not start Windows Vista, troubleshoot the operating system until the computer successfully boots. Because all hardware is correctly connected, you do not need to troubleshoot hardware in this lab.

If the operating system is missing the required files to boot the computer, you can replace these files by booting the computer with the Windows Vista installation media. Use the Startup Repair option to replace any missing files.

Does the Performance Monitor start automatically?

If the Performance Monitor does not start automatically, configure Windows to start the Performance Monitor every time Windows starts.

Is the resolution of the screen the native resolution or the resolution chosen by your instructor?

If the screen resolution is not native or the resolution chosen by your instructor, configure Windows to display the desktop at the native resolution of the monitor or the resolution chosen by your instructor.

If the computer successfully started, the desktop contains the appropriate open programs, and the display is set to the native resolution you have successfully solved all operating system problems. Hand the lab into your instructor.

If you could not successfully start the computer, the desktop does not contain the appropriate open programs, and the display is not set to the native resolution, continue troubleshooting the problems.

Students start by troubleshooting the computer for problems. Answer the following questions after each problem is solved. The instructor may inform you of the number of troubleshooting problems to complete.

Problem 1

What problem did you find?

What steps did you take to determine the problem?

What is causing the problem?

List the steps taken to fix the problem.

Problem 2

What problem did you find?

What steps did you take to determine the problem?

What is causing the problem?

List the steps taken to fix the problem.

Problem 3

What problem did you find?

What steps did you take to determine the problem?

What is causing the problem?

List the steps taken to fix the problem.

Problem 4

What problem did you find?

What steps did you take to determine the problem?

What is causing the problem?

List the steps taken to fix the problem.

Problem 5

What problem did you find?

What steps did you take to determine the problem?

What is causing the problem?

List the steps taken to fix the problem.

Problem 6

What problem did you find?

What steps did you take to determine the problem?

What is causing the problem?

List the steps taken to fix the problem.

Problem 7

What problem did you find?

What steps did you take to determine the problem?

What is causing the problem?

List the steps taken to fix the problem.

12.2.1.8 Lab - Troubleshooting Operating System Problems in Windows XP

Introduction

In this lab, the instructor will introduce various operating system problems. The student will diagnose the causes and solve the problems.

Recommended Equipment

The following equipment is required for this exercise:

• Computer running Windows XP

Scenario

You must solve operating system problems for a customer. Make sure you document and solve the problems, and then document the solutions.

There are several errors. Solve one problem at a time until you can successfully boot the computer, the desktop contains the appropriate open programs, and the display is set to the native resolution or the resolution given to you by your instructor.

Step 1

Start the computer.

Does the computer boot to the desktop?

If the computer started Windows XP, log on to the computer with the Administrator account.

If the computer did not start Windows XP, troubleshoot the operating system until the computer successfully boots. Because all hardware is correctly connected, you do not need to troubleshoot hardware in this lab.

If the operating system is missing the required files to boot the computer, you can replace these files by booting the computer with the Windows XP installation media. Start the Recovery Console and copy the missing files to the root of the C: drive.

Does the Performance Monitor start automatically?

If the Performance Monitor does not start automatically, configure Windows to start the Performance Monitor every time Windows starts.

Is the resolution of the screen the native resolution or the resolution chosen by your instructor?

If the screen resolution is not native or the resolution chosen by your instructor, configure Windows to display the desktop at the native resolution of the monitor or the resolution chosen by your instructor.

If the computer successfully started, the desktop contains the appropriate open programs, and the display is set to the native resolution, you have successfully solved all operating system problems. Hand the lab into your instructor.

If you could not successfully start the computer, the desktop does not contain the appropriate open programs, and the display is not set to the native resolution, continue troubleshooting the problems.

Students start by troubleshooting the computer for problems. Answer the following questions after each problem is solved. The instructor may inform you of the number of troubleshooting problems to complete.

Problem 1

What problem did you find?

What steps did you take to determine the problem?

What is causing the problem?

List the steps taken to fix the problem.

Problem 2

What problem did you find?

What steps did you take to determine the problem?

What is causing the problem?

List the steps taken to fix the problem.

Problem 3

What problem did you find?

What steps did you take to determine the problem?

What is causing the problem?

List the steps taken to fix the problem.

Problem 4

What problem did you find?

What steps did you take to determine the problem?

What is causing the problem?

List the steps taken to fix the problem.

Problem 5

What problem did you find?

What steps did you take to determine the problem?

What is causing the problem?

List the steps taken to fix the problem.

Problem 6

What problem did you find?

What steps did you take to determine the problem?

What is causing the problem?

List the steps taken to fix the problem.

Problem 7

What problem did you find?

What steps did you take to determine the problem?

What is causing the problem?

List the steps taken to fix the problem.

12.3.1.4 Lab - Fix a Network Problem

Introduction

In this lab, you will troubleshoot and fix a computer that does not connect to the network.

Recommended Equipment

- A computer running Windows 7
- Linksys E2500 wireless router
- Ethernet patch cable

Scenario

The computer will not connect to the Internet, network shares, or network printers.

Step 1

Open a command line and use command-line tools to determine the ip address, subnet mask, and default gateway of the computer.

Step 2

Use command-line tools to attempt to fix the network connection problem.

Step 3

Verify the settings in the wireless router configuration screens.

Step 4

What steps did you perform to fix the network?

12.3.1.5 Lab - Remote Technician - Fix a Network Problem

(Student Technician Sheet)

In this lab, you will gather data from the customer, and then instruct the customer on how to fix a computer that does not connect to the network. Document the customer's problem in the work order below.

Company Name: JH Paint Supply
Contact: Jill Henderson
Company Address: 114 W. Main Street
Company Phone: 1-888-555-2143

Work Order

Generating a New Ticket

Category Network   Closure Code ____   Status Open

Type: _____   Escalated Yes   Pending _____

Item _____   Pending Until Date _____

Business Impacting? X Yes   O No

Summary One computer cannot connect to the Internet, network shares, or

network printers.

Case ID#_____   Connection Type Wireless

Priority _____2_____   Environment _____

User Platform Windows 7

Problem Description: All computers boot up properly. Computer does not

connect to shares or the Internet. Computer has not been moved. Cables are

securely connected. Link lights are blinking.

Problem Solution:

_____

_____

_____

_____

_____

_____

_____

(Student Customer Sheet)

Use the contact information and problem description below to report the following information to a level-two technician:

Contact Information

Company Name: JH Paint Supply

Contact: Jill Henderson

Company Address: 114 W. Main Street

Company Phone: 1-888-555-2143

Problem Description

Well, the problem does not always seem to be there. Typically, not all computers on the network are used all of the time, so everything seems to be fine. On some busy days, every computer is being used and there is always one computer that cannot connect. I cannot figure out what the problem is because it is not usually on the same computer. When a computer cannot make connectivity, I check to make sure all cables and connections are fine.

(NOTE: Once you have given the level-two tech the problem description, use the Additional Information to answer any follow-up questions the technician may ask.)

Additional Information

- Windows 7.
- Computer has no new hardware.
- Computer has not been moved recently.
- An extra computer was added to the network recently.
- Computer looks the same as it did yesterday.

12.3.1.6 Lab - Troubleshooting Network Problems in Windows 7

Introduction

In this lab, the instructor will introduce various network problems. The student will diagnose the causes and solve the problems.

Recommended Equipment

The following equipment is required for this exercise:

- Two computers running Windows 7
- Linksys E2500 wireless router
- Two Ethernet cables
- Internet access

Scenario

You must solve network problems for a customer. You may need to troubleshoot both the router and two computers. Make sure you document and solve the problems, and then document the solutions.

There are several possible errors. Solve one problem at a time until you can successfully establish a connection between the two computers.

To better identify which steps should be done on a computer, the lab will refer to them as computer01, computer02, or both.

Step 1

List the computer name used for computer01 and computer02. Use these names whenever the lab refers to computer01 and computer01.

Computer01 name:

Computer02 name:

Complete the following from computer01.

Log on to the computer with the Administrator account.

Click **Start > Network**.

Do you see computer02?

If you answered yes, double-click computer 02.

Did the connection open?

Students start by troubleshooting the computer for problems. Answer the following questions after each problem is solved. The instructor may inform you of the number of troubleshooting problems to complete.

Problem 1

What problem did you find?

What steps did you take to determine the problem?

What is causing the problem?

List the steps taken to fix the problem.

Problem 2

What problem did you find?

What steps did you take to determine the problem?

What is causing the problem?

List the steps taken to fix the problem.

Problem 3

What problem did you find?

What steps did you take to determine the problem?

What is causing the problem?

List the steps taken to fix the problem.

Problem 4

What problem did you find?

What steps did you take to determine the problem?

What is causing the problem?

List the steps taken to fix the problem.

Problem 5

What problem did you find?

What steps did you take to determine the problem?

What is causing the problem?

List the steps taken to fix the problem.

Problem 6

What problem did you find?

What steps did you take to determine the problem?

What is causing the problem?

List the steps taken to fix the problem.

Problem 7

What problem did you find?

What steps did you take to determine the problem?

What is causing the problem?

List the steps taken to fix the problem.

Problem 8

What problem did you find?

What steps did you take to determine the problem?

What is causing the problem?

List the steps taken to fix the problem.

Problem 9

What problem did you find?

What steps did you take to determine the problem?

What is causing the problem?

List the steps taken to fix the problem.

Problem 10

What problem did you find?

What steps did you take to determine the problem?

What is causing the problem?

List the steps taken to fix the problem.

Problem 11

What problem did you find?

What steps did you take to determine the problem?

What is causing the problem?

List the steps taken to fix the problem.

12.3.1.7 Lab - Troubleshooting Network Problems in Windows Vista

Introduction

In this lab, the instructor will introduce various network problems. The student will diagnose the causes and solve the problems.

Recommended Equipment

The following equipment is required for this exercise:
- Two computers running Windows Vista
- Linksys E2500 wireless router
- Two Ethernet cables
- Internet access

Scenario

You must solve network problems for a customer. You may need to troubleshoot both the router and two computers. Make sure you document and solve the problems, and then document the solutions.

There are several possible errors. Solve one problem at a time until you can successfully establish a connection between the two computers.

To better identify which steps should be done on a computer, the lab will refer to them as computer01, computer02, or both.

Step 1

List the computer name used for computer01 and computer02. Use these names whenever the lab refers to computer01 and computer02.

Computer01 name:

Computer02 name:

Complete the following from computer01.

Log on to the computer with the Administrator account.

Click **Start > Network**.

Do you see computer02?

If you answered yes, double click computer02.

Did the connection open?

Students start by troubleshooting the computer for problems. Answer the following questions after each problem is solved. The instructor may inform you of the number of troubleshooting problems to complete.

Problem 1

What problem did you find?

What steps did you take to determine the problem?

What is causing the problem?

List the steps taken to fix the problem.

Problem 2

What problem did you find?

What steps did you take to determine the problem?

What is causing the problem?

List the steps taken to fix the problem.

Problem 3

What problem did you find?

What steps did you take to determine the problem?

What is causing the problem?

List the steps taken to fix the problem.

Problem 4

What problem did you find?

What steps did you take to determine the problem?

What is causing the problem?

List the steps taken to fix the problem.

Problem 5

What problem did you find?

What steps did you take to determine the problem?

What is causing the problem?

List the steps taken to fix the problem.

Problem 6

What problem did you find?

What steps did you take to determine the problem?

What is causing the problem?

List the steps taken to fix the problem.

Problem 7

What problem did you find?

What steps did you take to determine the problem?

What is causing the problem?

List the steps taken to fix the problem.

Problem 8

What problem did you find?

What steps did you take to determine the problem?

What is causing the problem?

List the steps taken to fix the problem.

Problem 9

What problem did you find?

What steps did you take to determine the problem?

What is causing the problem?

List the steps taken to fix the problem.

Problem 10

What problem did you find?

What steps did you take to determine the problem?

What is causing the problem?

List the steps taken to fix the problem.

Problem 11

What problem did you find?

What steps did you take to determine the problem?

What is causing the problem?

List the steps taken to fix the problem.

12.3.1.8 Lab - Troubleshooting Network Problems in Windows XP

Introduction

In this lab, the instructor will introduce various network problems. The student will diagnose the causes and solve the problems.

Recommended Equipment

The following equipment is required for this exercise:
- Two computers running Windows XP
- Linksys E2500 wireless router
- Two Ethernet cables
- Internet access

Scenario

You must solve network problems for a customer. You may need to troubleshoot both the router and two computers. Make sure you document and solve the problems, and then document the solutions.

There are several possible errors. Solve one problem at a time until you can successfully establish a connection between the two computers.

To better identify which steps should be done on a computer, the lab will refer to them as computer01, computer02, or both.

Step 1

List the computer name used for computer01 and computer02. Use these names whenever the lab refers to computer01 and computer02.

Computer01 name:

Computer02 name:

Complete the following from computer01.

Log on to the computer with the Administrator account.

Click **Start > My Network Places > View workgroup computers**.

Do you see computer02?

If you answered yes, double click computer02.

Did the connection open?

Students start by troubleshooting the computer for problems. Answer the following questions after each problem is solved. The instructor may inform you of the number of troubleshooting problems to complete.

Problem 1

What problem did you find?

What steps did you take to determine the problem?

What is causing the problem?

List the steps taken to fix the problem.

Problem 2

What problem did you find?

What steps did you take to determine the problem?

What is causing the problem?

List the steps taken to fix the problem.

Problem 3

What problem did you find?

What steps did you take to determine the problem?

What is causing the problem?

List the steps taken to fix the problem.

Problem 4

What problem did you find?

What steps did you take to determine the problem?

What is causing the problem?

List the steps taken to fix the problem.

Problem 5

What problem did you find?

What steps did you take to determine the problem?

What is causing the problem?

List the steps taken to fix the problem.

Problem 6

What problem did you find?

What steps did you take to determine the problem?

What is causing the problem?

List the steps taken to fix the problem.

Problem 7

What problem did you find?

What steps did you take to determine the problem?

What is causing the problem?

List the steps taken to fix the problem.

Problem 8

What problem did you find?

What steps did you take to determine the problem?

What is causing the problem?

List the steps taken to fix the problem.

Problem 9

What problem did you find?

What steps did you take to determine the problem?

What is causing the problem?

List the steps taken to fix the problem.

Problem 10

What problem did you find?

What steps did you take to determine the problem?

What is causing the problem?

List the steps taken to fix the problem.

Problem 11

What problem did you find?

What steps did you take to determine the problem?

What is causing the problem?

List the steps taken to fix the problem.

12.4.1.4 Lab - Fix a Laptop Problem

In this lab, you will troubleshoot and fix a laptop that has a second monitor connected which does not display anything.

Recommended Equipment

- Laptop running Windows 7

- Second monitor

Scenario

The second monitor will not display anything from the laptop.

Step 1

Verify that the video cable is properly plugged into the back of the second monitor.

Step 2

Verify second monitor is plugged in and has power.

Step 3

Verify that the Fn key along with the multi-purpose key to toggle to the external display will not work.

Step 4

What steps did you perform to fix the display problem?

12.4.1.5 Lab - Remote Technician - Fix a Laptop Problem

(Student Technician Sheet)

In this lab, you will gather data from the customer, and then instruct the customer on how to fix a laptop that will not display anything on a secondary monitor. Document the customer's problem in the work order below.

Company Name: Don's Delivery
Contact: Don Marley
Company Address: 11 E. Main Street
Company Phone: 1-800-555-0032

Work Order

Generating a New Ticket

Category Laptop

Closure Code ____

Status Open

Type: _____

Escalated Yes

Pending _____

Item _____

Pending Until Date _____

Business Impacting? X Yes   O No

Summary_____

_____

_____

Case ID#_____

Connection Type Ethernet

Priority ____2____

Environment _____

User Platform Windows 7

Problem Description: Laptop is powered on. Laptop screen shows Desktop properly. Second monitor plugged into laptop. Second monitor has a black screen.

Problem Solution: _____

_____

_____

_____

_____

(Student Customer Sheet)

Use the contact information and problem description below to report the following information to a level-two technician:

Contact Information

Company Name: Don's Delivery

Contact: Don Marley

Company Address: 11 E. Main Street

Company Phone: 1-800-555-0032

Problem Description

I am not able to view anything on my second monitor connected to a laptop. I tried turning the second screen off and back on, but the second monitor remains black. The second monitor worked fine yesterday, but now, nothing is displayed. Other employees use the laptop and second monitor during the day. What can I do to make my second monitor work?

(NOTE: Once you have given the level-two tech the problem description, use the Additional Information to answer any follow-up questions the technician may ask.)

Additional Information

- Laptop and second screen are not moved around.

- Tech support fixed a similar problem for a user last week.

12.4.1.6 Lab - Troubleshooting Laptop Problems in Windows 7

Introduction

In this lab, the instructor will introduce various laptop problems. The student will diagnose the causes and solve the problems.

Recommended Equipment

The following equipment is required for this exercise:

- A laptop computer running Windows 7

Scenario

You have been sent out to solve laptop problems for a customer. You may need to troubleshoot both software and hardware used by the laptop. Make sure you document and solve the problems, and then document the solutions.

There are several possible errors. Solve one problem at a time until the laptop boots without errors, plays audio, and the touchpad functions correctly.

Note: It is important that you solve only one problem at a time. Troubleshoot, solve, and document only one problem before moving onto the next problem.

Students start by troubleshooting the computer for problems. Answer the following questions after each problem is solved. The instructor may inform you of the number of troubleshooting problems to complete.

Problem 1

What problem did you find?

What steps did you take to determine the problem?

What is causing the problem?

List the steps taken to fix the problem.

Problem 2

What problem did you find?

What steps did you take to determine the problem?

What is causing the problem?

List the steps taken to fix the problem.

Problem 3

What problem did you find?

What steps did you take to determine the problem?

What is causing the problem?

List the steps taken to fix the problem.

Problem 4

What problem did you find?

What steps did you take to determine the problem?

What is causing the problem?

List the steps taken to fix the problem.

Problem 5

What problem did you find?

What steps did you take to determine the problem?

What is causing the problem?

List the steps taken to fix the problem.

Problem 6

What problem did you find?

What steps did you take to determine the problem?

What is causing the problem?

List the steps taken to fix the problem.

12.4.1.7 Lab - Troubleshooting Laptop Problems in Windows Vista

Introduction

In this lab, the instructor will introduce various laptop problems. The student will diagnose the causes and solve the problems.

Recommended Equipment

The following equipment is required for this exercise:

* A laptop computer running Windows Vista

Scenario

You have been sent out to solve laptop problems for a customer. You may need to troubleshoot both software and hardware used by the laptop. Make sure you document and solve the problems, and then document the solutions.

There are several possible errors. Solve one problem at a time until the laptop boots without errors, plays audio, and the touchpad functions correctly.

Note: It is important that you solve only one problem at a time. Troubleshoot, solve, and document only one problem before moving onto the next problem.

Students start by troubleshooting the computer for problems. Answer the following questions after each problem is solved. The instructor may inform you of the number of troubleshooting problems to complete.

Problem 1

What problem did you find?

What steps did you take to determine the problem?

What is causing the problem?

List the steps taken to fix the problem.

Problem 2

What problem did you find?

What steps did you take to determine the problem?

What is causing the problem?

List the steps taken to fix the problem.

Problem 3

What problem did you find?

What steps did you take to determine the problem?

What is causing the problem?

List the steps taken to fix the problem.

Problem 4

What problem did you find?

What steps did you take to determine the problem?

What is causing the problem?

List the steps taken to fix the problem.

Problem 5

What problem did you find?

What steps did you take to determine the problem?

What is causing the problem?

List the steps taken to fix the problem.

Problem 6

What problem did you find?

What steps did you take to determine the problem?

What is causing the problem?

List the steps taken to fix the problem.

12.4.1.8 Lab - Troubleshooting Laptop Problems in Windows XP

Introduction

In this lab, the instructor will introduce various laptop problems. The student will diagnose the causes and solve the problems.

Recommended Equipment

The following equipment is required for this exercise:

- A laptop computer running Windows XP

Scenario

You have been sent out to solve laptop problems for a customer. You may need to troubleshoot both software and hardware used by the laptop. Make sure you document and solve the problems, and then document the solutions.

There are several possible errors. Solve one problem at a time until the laptop boots without errors, plays audio, and the touchpad functions correctly.

Note: It is important that you solve only one problem at a time. Troubleshoot, solve, and document only one problem before moving onto the next problem.

Students start by troubleshooting the computer for problems. Answer the following questions after each problem is solved. The instructor may inform you of the number of troubleshooting problems to complete.

Problem 1

What problem did you find?

What steps did you take to determine the problem?

What is causing the problem?

List the steps taken to fix the problem.

Problem 2

What problem did you find?

What steps did you take to determine the problem?

What is causing the problem?

List the steps taken to fix the problem.

Problem 3

What problem did you find?

What steps did you take to determine the problem?

What is causing the problem?

List the steps taken to fix the problem.

Problem 4

What problem did you find?

What steps did you take to determine the problem?

What is causing the problem?

List the steps taken to fix the problem.

Problem 5

What problem did you find?

What steps did you take to determine the problem?

What is causing the problem?

List the steps taken to fix the problem.

Problem 6

What problem did you find?

What steps did you take to determine the problem?

What is causing the problem?

List the steps taken to fix the problem.

12.5.1.4 Lab - Fix a Printer Problem

In this lab, you will troubleshoot and fix a printer that does not print documents for a user.

Recommended Equipment

- At least two computers running Windows 7

- Printer connected and installed on one of the computers

- Printer installed as a network printer on other computer(s)

- Computers networked using switch, hub, or wireless router

Scenario

The printer will not print documents for a user.

Step 1

Verify printer hardware.

Step 2

Verify network printer installation on client computer(s).

Step 3

Verify network connectivity for computer that will not print.

Step 4

Verify installation of printer on directly-connected computer.

Step 5

What steps did you perform to fix the printer?

12.5.1.5 Lab - Remote Technician - Fix a Printer Problem

(Student Technician Sheet)

In this lab, you will gather data from the customer, and then instruct the customer on how to fix a printer that does not print documents for a user. Document the customer's problem in the work order below.

Company Name: Don's Delivery
Contact: Don Marley
Company Address: 11 E. Main Street
Company Phone: 1-800-555-0032

Work Order

Generating a New Ticket

Category Printer   Closure Code ____   Status Open

Type: _____   Escalated Yes   Pending _____

Item _____   Pending Until Date _____

Business Impacting? X Yes O No

Summary_____

_____

Case ID#_____   Connection Type Ethernet

Priority ____2____   Environment _____

User Platform Windows 7

Problem Description: Printer is powered on. Cables are securely connected.

Printer has ink and paper. Printer is installed as network printer on all client

computers. Other users are able to print to the printer.

Problem Solution:
_____
_____
_____
_____

(Student Customer Sheet)

Use the contact information and problem description below to report the following information to a level-two technician:

Contact Information

Company Name: Don's Delivery

Contact: Don Marley

Company Address: 11 E. Main Street

Company Phone: 1-800-555-0032

Problem Description

I am not able to print documents on our printer. I tried turning the printer off and then back on, but I am still unable to print. The printer worked fine yesterday, but now, no documents print. Nobody has touched the printer since yesterday, and I do not understand why it will not print. What can I do to make my documents print?

(NOTE: Once you have given the level-two tech the problem description, use the Additional Information to answer any follow-up questions the technician may ask.)

Additional Information

- Printer is hosted by dedicated computer on the network.

- Tech support fixed a similar problem for a user yesterday.

12.5.1.6 Lab - Troubleshooting Printer Problems in Windows 7

Introduction

In this lab, the instructor will introduce various printer problems. The student will diagnose the causes and solve the problems.

Recommended Equipment

The following equipment is required for this exercise:

- A computer running Windows 7

- A printer connected to the computer

Scenario

You must solve printer problems for a customer. You may need to troubleshoot both the printer and computer. Make sure you document and solve the problems, and then document the solutions.

There are several possible errors. Solve one problem at a time until you can successfully print a document from Notepad.

Step 1

Log on to the computer with the Administrator account.

Click **Start > Search programs and files >** type **Notepad >** press **Enter**.

In the Notepad document, type **Printer problems solved by yourname**.

Save the document to the desktop as **Printer Works**.

Try printing the "Printer Works" document.
Did the document print?

Students start by troubleshooting the computer for problems. Answer the following questions after each problem is solved. The instructor may inform you of the number of troubleshooting problems to complete.

Problem 1

What problem did you find?

What steps did you take to determine the problem?

What is causing the problem?

List the steps taken to fix the problem.

Problem 2

What problem did you find?

What steps did you take to determine the problem?

What is causing the problem?

List the steps taken to fix the problem.

Problem 3

What problem did you find?

What steps did you take to determine the problem?

What is causing the problem?

List the steps taken to fix the problem.

Problem 4

What problem did you find?

What steps did you take to determine the problem?

What is causing the problem?

List the steps taken to fix the problem.

Problem 5

What problem did you find?

What steps did you take to determine the problem?

What is causing the problem?

List the steps taken to fix the problem.

Problem 6

What problem did you find?

What steps did you take to determine the problem?

What is causing the problem?

List the steps taken to fix the problem.

12.5.1.7 Lab - Troubleshooting Printer Problems in Windows Vista

Introduction

In this lab, the instructor will introduce various printer problems. The student will diagnose the causes and solve the problems.

Recommended Equipment

The following equipment is required for this exercise:

- A computer running Windows Vista
- A printer connected to the computer

Scenario

You must solve printer problems for a customer. You may need to troubleshoot both the printer and computer. Make sure you document and solve the problems, and then document the solutions.

There are several possible errors. Solve one problem at a time until you can successfully print a document from Notepad.

Step 1

Log on to the computer with the Administrator account.

Click **Start > Start Search >** type **Notepad >** press **Enter**.

In the Notepad document, type **Printer problems solved by yourname**.

Save the document to the desktop as **Printer Works**.

Try printing the "Printer Works" document.
Did the document print?

Students start by troubleshooting the computer for problems. Answer the following questions after each problem is solved. The instructor may inform you of the number of troubleshooting problems to complete.

Problem 1

What problem did you find?

What steps did you take to determine the problem?

What is causing the problem?

List the steps taken to fix the problem.

Problem 2

What problem did you find?

What steps did you take to determine the problem?

What is causing the problem?

List the steps taken to fix the problem.

Problem 3

What problem did you find?

What steps did you take to determine the problem?

What is causing the problem?

List the steps taken to fix the problem.

Problem 4

What problem did you find?

What steps did you take to determine the problem?

What is causing the problem?

List the steps taken to fix the problem.

Problem 5

What problem did you find?

What steps did you take to determine the problem?

What is causing the problem?

List the steps taken to fix the problem.

Problem 6

What problem did you find?

What steps did you take to determine the problem?

What is causing the problem?

List the steps taken to fix the problem.

12.5.1.8 Lab - Troubleshooting Printer Problems in Windows XP

Introduction

In this lab, the instructor will introduce various printer problems. The student will diagnose the causes and solve the problems.

Recommended Equipment

The following equipment is required for this exercise:

- A computer running Windows XP
- A printer connected to the computer

Scenario

You must solve printer problems for a customer. You may need to troubleshoot both the printer and computer. Make sure you document and solve the problems, and then document the solutions.

There are several possible errors. Solve one problem at a time until you can successfully print a document from Notepad.

Step 1

Log on to the computer with the Administrator account.

Click **Start > Run >** type **Notepad >** click **OK**.

In the Notepad document, type **Printer problems solved by yourname**.

Save the document to the desktop as **Printer Works**.

Try printing the "Printer Works" document.
Did the document print?

Students start by troubleshooting the computer for problems. Answer the following questions after each problem is solved. The instructor may inform you of the number of troubleshooting problems to complete.

Problem 1

What problem did you find?

What steps did you take to determine the problem?

What is causing the problem?

List the steps taken to fix the problem.

Problem 2

What problem did you find?

What steps did you take to determine the problem?

What is causing the problem?

List the steps taken to fix the problem.

Problem 3

What problem did you find?

What steps did you take to determine the problem?

What is causing the problem?

List the steps taken to fix the problem.

Problem 4

What problem did you find?

What steps did you take to determine the problem?

What is causing the problem?

List the steps taken to fix the problem.

Problem 5

What problem did you find?

What steps did you take to determine the problem?

What is causing the problem?

List the steps taken to fix the problem.

Problem 6

What problem did you find?

What steps did you take to determine the problem?

What is causing the problem?

List the steps taken to fix the problem.

12.6.1.4 Lab - Fix a Security Problem

In this lab, you will gather data from the customer, and then instruct the customer on how to correct a security issue that is preventing connection to the wireless network.

Recommended Equipment

- A computer running Windows 7

- Linksys E2500 wireless router

- Ethernet patch cable

Scenario

The computer will not connect to the Internet.

Step 1

Open a command line and use command-line tools to determine the IP address, subnet mask, and default gateway of the computer.

Step 2

Use command-line tools to attempt to fix the network connection problem.

Step 3

Verify the settings in the wireless router configuration screens.

Step 4

What steps did you perform to fix the network?

12.6.1.5 Lab - Remote Technician - Fix a Security Problem

(Student Technician Sheet)

Gather data from the customer to begin the troubleshooting process. Document the customer's problem in the work order below.

Company Name: Smith Lumber Supply
Contact: James Smith
Company Address: 1234 S. Main Street
Company Phone: 801-555.1212

Work Order

Generating a New Ticket

Category _Security_   Closure Code_____   Status _Open_

Type_____   Escalated_____   Pending_____

Item_____   Pending Until Date_____

Business Impacting?   X Yes   O No

Summary____Customer cannot use laptop wireless connection at work_____

Case ID#_____   Connection Type___Wireless_____

Priority_____   Environment_____

User Platform_____Windows 7_____

Problem Description: Customer's wireless connection does not work in any_____

location at the work place. The customer can use wireless connection at home_____

and other places._____

Problem Solution:_____

_____

_____

_____

_____

_____

(Student Customer Sheet)

Use the contact information and problem description below to report the following information to your lab partner who will be acting as a level-two technician. Your lab partner will guide you through the process of troubleshooting and fixing your wireless connection remotely. You must perform the tasks your lab partner recommends.

Contact Information

Company Name: <u>Smith Lumber Supply</u>

Contact: James Smith

Company Address: 1234 S. Main Street

Company Phone:801-555-1212

Category: Security

Problem Description

You are unable to use your laptop's wireless connection while at work. The wireless connection works fine at home and the coffee shop downstairs, but for some reason, it will not connect to the wireless anywhere in the office. Since you are unable to access the wireless connection, you have been using the Ethernet cable connection instead. The cable connection is working fine.

(NOTE: Once you have given the problem description, use the Additional Information to answer any follow-up questions your lab partner may ask.)

Additional Information

- Windows 7.

- XP Wireless Client.

- Wireless client can see the wireless network.

- My wireless connection worked yesterday at work.

- I can connect using an Ethernet cable.

- My wireless account is in good standing.

- Wireless connection works for other employees.

- I have not made any changes to my wireless security settings.

- A new wireless router was installed on the network yesterday.

12.6.1.6 Lab - Troubleshooting Access Security in Windows 7

Introduction

In this lab, the instructor will introduce various access security problems. The student will diagnose the causes and solve the problems.

Recommended Equipment

The following equipment is required for this exercise:

- One computer running Windows 7 on an NTFS partition

Scenario

Company XYZ has hired Devon to manage the training department. Shawna was also hired as a temporary employee to replace Brooks, who is no longer working for the company. You must solve access security problems for the training department. You might need to access the computers as each user and the administrator. Make sure you document and solve the problems, and then document the solutions.

There are several possible errors. Solve one problem at a time until there are no security breaches and access problems. Use the following tables when solving problems. The user account information is listed in Table 1. Use only the groups shown in Table 2; they are set up with the proper permissions. The instructor will provide the administrator's account information.

Table 1: Accounts

User Name	Password	Group for User
Brooks	Cisco2001	Guests
Shawna	Cisco2010	Guests
Devon	Cisco2100	Academy Student
Administrator user name:	Administrator password:	Administrators

Table 2: Groups

Groups	Group Permissions
Academy Student	Read & Execute, List Folder Contents, Read, Write
Guests	Read & Execute, List Folder Contents, Read
Administrators	Full Control

Note: There is a file, with a message, in the C:\CiscoCCNA\ Exploration folder.

Step 1

Log on to the computer as Brooks and, then try saving text to the both files.

Can Brooks log on to the computer?

Can Brooks access both files?

If you answered "yes" to either question then there is a security breach in the system.

Can Shawna log on to the computer?

Can Shawna only read both files?

If you answered "no" to either question then there is an access problem in the system.

Can Devon log on to the computer?

Can Devon save text to both files?

If you answered "no" to either question then there is an access problem in the system.

Did you encounter any security breaches or access problems?

Log on to the computer with the Administrator account.

Students start by troubleshooting the computer for problems. Answer the following questions after each problem is solved. The instructor may inform you of the number of troubleshooting problems to complete.

Did you encounter any security breaches or access problems?

If there were no security breaches and no access problems, you have successfully solved all security problems.

If there was a security breach or an access problem, continue troubleshooting the problem.

Problem 1

What problem did you find?

What steps did you take to determine the problem?

What is causing the problem?

List the steps taken to fix the problem.

Problem 2

What problem did you find?

What steps did you take to determine the problem?

What is causing the problem?

List the steps taken to fix the problem.

Problem 3

What problem did you find?

What steps did you take to determine the problem?

What is causing the problem?

List the steps taken to fix the problem.

Problem 4

What problem did you find?

What steps did you take to determine the problem?

What is causing the problem?

List the steps taken to fix the problem.

Problem 5

What problem did you find?

What steps did you take to determine the problem?

What is causing the problem?

List the steps taken to fix the problem.

12.6.1.7 Lab - Troubleshooting Access Security in Windows Vista

Introduction

In this lab, the instructor will introduce various access security problems. The student will diagnose the causes and solve the problems.

Recommended Equipment

The following equipment is required for this exercise:

- One computer running Windows Vista on an NTFS partition

Scenario

Company XYZ has hired Nathan to manage the training department. Natashia was also hired as a temporary employee to replace Ben, who is no longer working for the company. You must solve access security problems for the training department. You might need to access the computers as each user and the administrator. Make sure you document and solve the problems, and then document the solutions.

There are several possible errors. Solve one problem at a time until there are no security breaches and access problems. Use the following tables when solving problems. The user account information is listed in Table 1. Use only the groups shown in Table 2; they are set up with the proper permissions. The instructor will provide the administrator's account information.

Table 1: Accounts

User Name	Password	Group for User
Ben	Cisco2001	Guests
Natashia	Cisco2010	Guests
Nathan	Cisco2100	Academy Student
Administrator user name:	Administrator password:	Administrators

Table 2: Groups

Groups	Group Permissions
Academy Student	Read & Execute, List Folder Contents, Read, Write
Guests	Read & Execute, List Folder Contents, Read
Administrators	Full Control

Note: There is a file, with a message, in the C:\CiscoCCNA\ Exploration folder.

Step 1

Log on to the computer as Brooks and, then try saving text to the both files.

Can Ben log on to the computer?

Can Ben access both files?

If you answered "yes" to either question then there is a security breach in the system.

Can Natashia log on to the computer?

Can Natashia only read both files?

If you answered "no" to either question then there is an access problem in the system.

Can Nathan log on to the computer?

Can Nathan save text to both files?

If you answered "no" to either question then there is an access problem in the system.

Did you encounter any security breaches or access problems?

Log on to the computer with the Administrator account.

Students start by troubleshooting the computer for problems. Answer the following questions after each problem is solved. The instructor may inform you of the number of troubleshooting problems to complete.

Did you encounter any security breaches or access problems?

If there were no security breaches and no access problems, you have successfully solved all security problems.

If there was a security breach or an access problem, continue troubleshooting the problem.

Problem 1

What problem did you find?

What steps did you take to determine the problem?

What is causing the problem?

List the steps taken to fix the problem.

Problem 2

What problem did you find?

What steps did you take to determine the problem?

What is causing the problem?

List the steps taken to fix the problem.

Problem 3

What problem did you find?

What steps did you take to determine the problem?

What is causing the problem?

List the steps taken to fix the problem.

Problem 4

What problem did you find?

What steps did you take to determine the problem?

What is causing the problem?

List the steps taken to fix the problem.

Problem 5

What problem did you find?

What steps did you take to determine the problem?

What is causing the problem?

List the steps taken to fix the problem.

12.6.1.8 Lab - Troubleshooting Access Security in Windows XP

Introduction

In this lab, the instructor will introduce various access security problems. The student will diagnose the causes and solve the problems.

Recommended Equipment

The following equipment is required for this exercise:

- One computer running Windows XP on an NTFS partition

Scenario

Company XYZ has hired Nathan to manage the training department. Natashia was also hired as a temporary employee to replace Ben, who is no longer working for the company. You must solve access security problems for the training department. You might need to access the computers as each user and the administrator. Make sure you document and solve the problems, and then document the solutions.

There are several possible errors. Solve one problem at a time until there are no security breaches and access problems. Use the following tables when solving problems. The user account information is listed in Table 1. Use only the groups shown in Table 2, they are set up with the proper permissions. The instructor will provide the administrator's account information.

Table 1: Accounts

User Name	Password	Group for User
Ben	Cisco2001	Guests
Natashia	Cisco2010	Guests
Nathan	Cisco2100	Academy Student
Administrator user name: _____	Administrator password: _____	Administrators

Table 2: Groups

Groups	Group Permissions
Academy Student	Read & Execute, List Folder Contents, Read, Write
Guests	Read & Execute, List Folder Contents, Read
Administrators	Full Control

Note: There is a file, with a message, in the C:\CiscoCCNA\ Exploration folder.

Step 1

Log on to the computer as Brooks and, then try saving text to the both files.

Can Ben log on to the computer?

Can Ben access both files?

If you answered "yes" to either question then there is a security breach in the system.

Can Natashia log on to the computer?

Can Natashia only read both files?

If you answered "no" to either question then there is an access problem in the system.

Can Nathan log on to the computer?

Can Nathan save text to both files?

If you answered "no" to either question then there is an access problem in the system.

Did you encounter any security breaches or access problems?

Log on to the computer with the Administrator account.

Students start by troubleshooting the computer for problems. Answer the following questions after each problem is solved. The instructor may inform you of the number of troubleshooting problems to complete.

Did you encounter any security breaches or access problems?

If there were no security breaches and no access problems, you have successfully solved all security problems.

If there was a security breach or an access problem, continue troubleshooting the problem.

Problem 1

What problem did you find?

What steps did you take to determine the problem?

What is causing the problem?

List the steps taken to fix the problem.

Problem 2

What problem did you find?

What steps did you take to determine the problem?

What is causing the problem?

List the steps taken to fix the problem.

Problem 3

What problem did you find?

What steps did you take to determine the problem?

What is causing the problem?

List the steps taken to fix the problem.

Problem 4

What problem did you find?

What steps did you take to determine the problem?

What is causing the problem?

List the steps taken to fix the problem.

Problem 5

What problem did you find?

What steps did you take to determine the problem?

What is causing the problem?

List the steps taken to fix the problem.